The Fashion History Reader

History is uncomfortable with fashion and fashion frequently denies its own history. Why? This path-breaking analysis presents the views of over seventy leading academics of all cultures and spans the twelfth to the twentieth centuries.

The Fashion History Reader is an innovative work that provides a broad introduction to the complex literature in the fields of fashion studies, and dress and fashion history. Twenty-three chapters and over forty shorter 'snapshot' texts cover a wide range of topics and approaches within the history of fashion, ranging from object-based studies to theory-driven analyses. Themes also move in and across time, providing a chronology to enable student learning.

A comprehensive introduction by the editors contextualises the debates for students, synthesising past history and bringing them up to date through a discussion of globalisation. Also, each section includes a brief, accessible introduction by the editors, placing each chapter within the wider, thematic treatment of fashion and its history. There are also highly detailed further reading sections which encourage students to enhance their learning independently.

The contributors are Patricia Allerston, Rebecca Arnold, Djurdja Bartlett, Linzy A. Brekke, Christopher Breward, Stella Bruzzi, Alex M. Cain, Michael Carter, Hazel Clark, Diana Crane, Hilary Davidson, Rebecca Earle, Caroline Evans, Suraiya Faroqhi, Marc de Ferrière le Vayer, Antonia Finnane, Elizabeth Fischer, Will Fisher, Giovanni Luigi Fontana, Carole Collier Frick, Susan C. Frye, Sally Gray, Hannah Greig, Negley Harte, Maria Hayward, Sarah-Grace Heller, Ken'ichiro Hirano, Katrina Honeyman, Clair Hughes, Alan Hunt, D. J. Huppatz, Jennifer M. Jones, Miles Lambert, Ulrich Lehmann, Beverly Lemire, Janine Christina Maegraith, Margaret Maynard, Peter McNeil, Patricia Mears, Lesley Ellis Miller, Sanda Miller, Maria Giuseppina Muzzarelli, Llewellyn Negrin, Alistair O'Neill, Alexandra Palmer, Eugenia Paulicelli, Daniel L. Purdy, Annika Rabo, Aileen Ribeiro, Catherine Richardson, Giorgio Riello, Christine Ruane, Simona Segre Reinach, Toby Slade, Valerie Steele, John Styles, Emma Tarlo, Alice Taylor, Lou Taylor, Karen Tranberg Hansen, Nancy J. Troy,

Olga Vainshtein, Gregory Votolato, Louise Wallenberg, Evelyn Welch, Elizabeth Wilson and Verity Wilson.

Giorgio Riello is Associate Professor in Global History and Culture at the University of Warwick. He has written extensively on early modern textiles, dress and fashion, and material culture in Europe and Asia. He is the author of *A Foot in the Past: Consumers, Producers and Footwear in the Long Eighteenth Century* (2006) and has co-edited four volumes including (with Peter McNeil), *Shoes: A History from Sandals to Sneakers* (2006). Giorgio is currently writing a monograph entitled *Global Cotton: How an Asian Fabric Changed the World Economy*.

Peter McNeil is Professor of Design History at the University of Technology Sydney and Professor of Fashion Studies at Stockholm University. His anthology *Shoes: A History from Sandals to Sneakers* (with co-editor Dr Giorgio Riello) has been acclaimed by *The Observer* as 'an exceptionally beautiful and wide-ranging history of footwear'. His recent publications include *Fashion: Critical and Primary Sources from the Renaissance to Today* (4 volumes) and the co-edited *The Men's Fashion Reader* and *Fashion in Fiction*.

The Fashion History Reader

Global perspectives

Edited by

Giorgio Riello and Peter McNeil

LONDON AND NEW YORK

First published 2010
by Routledge
2 Park Square, Milton Park, Abingdon, Oxon OX14 4RN

Simultaneously published in the USA and Canada
by Routledge
270 Madison Ave, New York, NY 10016

Routledge is an imprint of the Taylor & Francis Group, an informa business

Typeset in Perpetua and Bell Gothic by The Running Head Limited, Cambridge,
www.therunninghead.com
Printed and bound in Great Britain by MPG Books Limited, Bodmin, Cornwall

British Library Cataloguing in Publication Data
A catalogue record for this book is available from the British Library

Library of Congress Cataloging in Publication Data
The fashion history reader: global perspectives/edited by Giorgio Riello and Peter McNeil.
p. cm.
Includes index.
1. Fashion—History. I. Riello, Giorgio. II. McNeil, Peter, 1966–
GT511.F36 2010
391—dc22

2009046604

ISBN10: 0–415–49323–4 (hbk)
ISBN10: 0–415–49324–2 (pbk)

ISBN13: 978–0–415–49323–9 (hbk)
ISBN13: 978–0–415–49324–6 (pbk)

Contents

Figures

The images below and the snapshot illustrations have been reproduced with kind permission. While every effort has been made to trace copyright holders and obtain permission, this has not been possible in all cases. Any omissions brought to our attention will be remedied in future editions.

Snapshot illustrations

Acknowledgements

We gratefully acknowledge permission to reproduce the essays below. While every effort has been made to trace copyright holders and obtain permission, this has not been possible in all cases. Any omissions brought to our attention will be remedied in future editions.

Chapter 1 Sarah-Grace Heller (2007) *Fashion in Medieval France*, Cambridge: Cambridge University Press, pp. 46–60. Courtesy of Boydell & Brewer Ltd.

Chapter 2 Alan Hunt (1996) *Governance of the Consuming Passions. A History of Sumptuary Laws*, Basingstoke: Macmillan, pp. 22–41. Reproduced with permission of Palgrave Macmillan.

Chapter 3 Reduced edition of Will Fisher (2006) *Materializing Gender in Early Modern English Literature and Culture*, Cambridge: Cambridge University Press, pp. 59–82 and 184–87. © Will Fisher 2006, published by Cambridge University Press. Reproduced with permission.

Chapter 4 Revised and reduced edition of Patricia Allerston (2000) 'Clothing and Early Modern Venetian Society', *Continuity and Change*, 15, 3, pp. 367–90. © Cambridge University Press, reproduced with permission.

Chapter 5 Maria Hayward (2002) '"The Sign of Some Degree"? The Financial, Social and Sartorial Significance of Male Headwear at the Courts of Henry VIII and Edward VI', *Costume*, 26, pp. 1–17. www.maney.co.uk/journals/cos and www.ingentaconnect.com/content/maney/cos. Reproduced with kind permission of Maney Publishing.

Chapter 6 Revised and reduced edition of Eugenia Paulicelli (2008) 'Mapping the World: The Political Geography of Dress in Cesare Vecellio's Costume Books', *The Italianist*, 28, pp. 24–53. www.maney.co.uk/journals/ita and www.ingentaconnect.com/content/maney/ita. Reproduced with kind permission of Maney Publishing.

Chapter 7 Jennifer M. Jones (2004) *Sexing La Mode: Gender, Fashion and Commercial Culture in Old Regime France*, Oxford and New York: Berg, pp. 19–25. © Berg Publishers, an imprint of A & C Black Publishers.

Chapter 8 John Styles (2003) 'Custom or Consumption? Plebeian Fashion in Eighteenth-century England', in M. Berg and E. Eger (eds), *Luxury in the Eighteenth Century: Debates, Desires and Delectable Goods*, Basingstoke: Palgrave, pp. 103–18. Reproduced with permission of Palgrave Macmillan

Chapter 9 Beverly Lemire (2003) 'Fashioning Cottons: Asian Trade, Domestic Industry and Consumer Demand, 1660–1780', in David Jenkins (ed.), *The Cambridge History of Western Textiles*, Cambridge: Cambridge University Press, vol. 1, pp. 493–512. © Cambridge University Press 2003, reproduced with permission.

Chapter 10 Aileen Ribeiro (1991) 'Fashion in the Eighteenth Century: Some Anglo-French Comparisons', *Textile History*, 22, 2, pp. 329–45. www.maney.co.uk/journals/tex and www.ingentaconnect.com/content/maney/tex. Reproduced with kind permission of Maney Publishing.

Chapter 11 Daniel L. Purdy (1998) *The Tyranny of Elegance: Consumer Cosmopolitanism in the Era of Goethe*, Baltimore: The Johns Hopkins University Press, pp. 1–21. © 1998 The Johns Hopkins University Press. Reprinted with permission of The Johns Hopkins University Press.

Chapter 12 Valerie Steele (1985) *Fashion and Eroticism: The Ideals of Feminine Beauty from the Victorian Era to the Jazz Age*, New York: Oxford University Press, 1985, pp. 121–44. Reproduced with kind permission of Valerie Steele.

Chapter 13 © Christopher Breward.

Chapter 14 © Ulrich Lehmann.

Chapter 15 Revised and reduced edition of Diana Crane (1999) 'Clothing Behaviour as Non-verbal Resistance: Marginal Women and Alternative Dress in the Nineteenth Century', *Fashion Theory*, 3, 2, pp. 241–68. © Berg Publishers, an imprint of A & C Black Publishers.

Chapter 16 Antonia Finnane (2007) *Changing Clothes in China: Fashion, History, Nation*, New York: Columbia University Press, pp. 43–56. © 2007 Columbia University Press. Reprinted with permission of the publisher.

Chapter 17 Emma Tarlo (1996) *Clothing Matters: Dress and Identity in India*, London: Hurst & Co., pp. 33–42. Reproduced with kind permission of C. Hurst & Co. (Publishers) Ltd.

Chapter 18 Hirano Ken'ichiro (1993) 'The Westernisation of Clothes and the State in Meiji Japan', in Hirano Ken'ichiro (ed.), *The State and Cultural Transformation: Perspectives from East Asia*, Tokyo: United Nations University, pp. 121–31. Reproduced with the permission of United Nations University.

Chapter 19 Verity Wilson (2002) 'Western Modes and Asian Clothing: Reflections on Borrowing Other People's Dress', *Costume*, 36, pp. 139–56. www.maney.co.uk/journals/cos and www.ingentaconnect.com/content/maney/cos. Reproduced with kind permission of Maney Publishing.

Chapter 20 Nancy J. Troy (2007) 'Introduction: Poiret's Modernism and the Logic of Fashion', in Harold Koda and Andrew Bolton (eds), *Poiret*, New Haven: Yale University Press and New York: The Metropolitan Museum of Art, pp. 17–24. © The Metropolitan Museum of Art. Reproduced with permission.

Chapter 21 Gregory Votolato (1998) *American Design in the Twentieth Century*, Manchester: Manchester University Press, pp. 237–50. Reprinted with permission of Manchester University Press, Manchester, UK.

Chapter 22 Llewellyn Negrin (1999) 'The Self as Image: A Critical Appraisal of Postmodern Theories of Fashion', *Theory, Culture and Society*, 16, 3, pp. 99–118. © 1999, Theory, Culture and Society Ltd. Reprinted with permission of Sage.

Chapter 23 © Simona Segre Reinach.

Contributors

Patricia Allerston is Head of Education at the National Galleries of Scotland in Edinburgh, Scotland.

Rebecca Arnold is Lecturer in Dress and Textiles at the Courtauld Institute of Art, London.

Djurdja Bartlett is Research Fellow at London College of Fashion, University of the Arts London.

Linzy A. Brekke is Assistant Professor of History at Stonehill College, Massachusetts, USA.

Christopher Breward is Head of Research at the Victoria and Albert Museum, London.

Stella Bruzzi is Professor of Film and Television Studies and Chair of the Faculty of Arts, University of Warwick, UK.

Alex M. Cain lives in the UK and is an independent scholar and editor of *Mallarmé on Fashion* (2004).

Michael Carter is Emeritus Fellow at the Department of Art History, University of Sydney, Australia.

Hazel Clark is Dean of the School of Art and Design History and Theory at Parsons The New School for Design in New York.

Diana Crane is Professor Emerita of Sociology at the University of Pennsylvania, USA.

Hilary Davidson is Curator of Fashion and Decorative Arts at the Museum of London.

Rebecca Earle is Reader at the Department of History, University of Warwick, UK.

Caroline Evans is Professor of Fashion at Central Saint Martins, University of the Arts London.

Suraiya Faroqhi is a Professor of History at Istanbul Bilgi University after retiring from Ludwig-Maximilians Universität, Munich, Germany.

Marc de Ferrière le Vayer is Professor of Economic History at the Department of History, Université François Rabelais, Tours, France.

Antonia Finnane is Professor at the School of Historical Studies of the University of Melbourne, Australia.

Elizabeth Fischer is Head of the Jewellery Design Department at the Haute école d'art et de design in Geneva, Switzerland.

Will Fisher is Associate Professor at the Department of English, Lehman College, City University of New York.

Giovanni Luigi Fontana is Professor of Economic History and Head of the Department of History, University of Padua, Italy.

Carole Collier Frick is Associate Professor at the Department of Historical Studies, Southern Illinois University at Edwardsville, USA.

Susan C. Frye is Professor of English, University of Wyoming, USA.

Sally Gray is an Australian Research Council Post-doctoral Fellow at the University of New South Wales, Sydney, Australia.

Hannah Greig is Lecturer at the Department of History, University of York, UK.

Negley Harte is Honorary Fellow at the Department of History, University College London.

Maria Hayward is Reader in History at the School of Humanities, University of Southampton, UK.

Sarah-Grace Heller is Associate Professor at the Department of French and Italian at the Ohio State University, USA.

Ken'ichiro Hirano is Professor Emeritus of International Relations, University of Tokyo and Waseda University, Japan.

Katrina Honeyman is Professor of Economic and Social History at the University of Leeds, UK.

Clair Hughes is an independent scholar, living in France, and author of two books on the role of dress in literature.

Alan Hunt is Chancellor's Professor in the Sociology/Anthropology and Law departments at Carleton University, Canada.

D. J. Huppatz is Coordinator for Interior Design at Swinburne University of Technology in Melbourne, Australia.

Jennifer M. Jones is an Associate Professor of History at the Department of History, Rutgers University, USA.

Miles Lambert is Senior Manager at the Gallery of Costume, Platt Hall in Manchester, UK.

Ulrich Lehmann is Professor at the University for the Creative Arts at Canterbury, UK.

Beverly Lemire is Henry Marshall Tory Chair at the Department of History and Classics, University of Alberta, Canada.

Janine Christina Maegraith is Research Associate at the Faculty of Economics of the University of Cambridge, UK.

Margaret Maynard is Honorary Research Consultant at the University of Queensland, Australia.

Peter McNeil is Professor of Design History at the University of Technology, Sydney, Australia, and Professor of Fashion Studies at the University of Stockholm, Sweden.

Patricia Mears is Deputy Director of the Museum at the Fashion Institute of Technology, New York.

Lesley Ellis Miller is Senior Curator at the Department of Furniture, Textiles and Fashion, Victoria and Albert Museum, London.

Sanda Miller is Senior Lecturer in Media and Visual Arts at Southampton Solent University, UK.

Maria Giuseppina Muzzarelli is Professor of Medieval History, University of Bologna, Italy.

Llewellyn Negrin is Senior Lecturer and Head of Art and Design Theory at the Tasmanian School of Art, University of Tasmania, Australia.

Alistair O'Neill is Research Fellow at Central St Martin's, University of the Arts London.

Alexandra Palmer is Senior Curator in Textiles and Costume at the Royal Ontario Museum in Toronto, Canada.

Eugenia Paulicelli is Professor in the Italian Program in the Department of European Languages and Literature at Queens College, CUNY, New York.

Daniel L. Purdy is Associate Professor at the Department of German and Slavic Languages and Literatures at Pennsylvania State University, USA.

Annika Rabo works at the Department of Social Anthropology and the Centre for Research in International Migration and Ethnic Relations, University of Stockholm, Sweden.

Aileen Ribeiro is Professor of History of Art at the Courtauld Institute of Art in London.

Catherine Richardson is Senior Lecturer at the Department of English, University of Kent at Canterbury, UK.

Giorgio Riello is Associate Professor at the Department of History, University of Warwick, UK.

Christine Ruane is Professor at the Department of History, University of Tulsa, Oklahoma, USA.

Simona Segre Reinach is a cultural anthropologist and fashion consultant, and teaches Fashion Studies at IULM in Milan, and IUAV in Venice, Italy.

Toby Slade is an Assistant Professor at the University of Tokyo.

Valerie Steele is Director of the Museum at the Fashion Institute of Technology, New York and is the editor of the journal *Fashion Theory*.

John Styles is Research Professor in History, School of Humanities, University of Hertfordshire, UK.

Emma Tarlo is Reader at the Department of Anthropology of Goldsmiths, University of London.

Alice Taylor is a SSHRC Postdoctoral Fellow in Atlantic World History at the University of Toronto, Canada.

Lou Taylor is Professor of Dress and Textile History, University of Brighton, UK.

Karen Tranberg Hansen is Professor at the Department of Anthropology, Northwestern University, USA.

Nancy J. Troy is Professor of Art History at the University of Southern California, USA.

Olga Vainshtein is a Senior Researcher in Cultural Studies at the Russian State University for the Humanities, Moscow.

Gregory Votolato teaches at the Faculty of Creativity and Culture of Buckinghamshire New University, UK.

Louise Wallenberg is Director of the Centre for Fashion Studies, Stockholm University, Sweden.

Evelyn Welch is Professor of Renaissance Studies at Queen Mary, University of London.

Elizabeth Wilson is an author and journalist and Fellow at London College of Fashion, University of the Arts London.

Verity Wilson is the Editor of the journal *Costume* and was for 25 years Curator in the Far Eastern Department at the Victoria and Albert Museum, London.

Preface

The Fashion History Reader is an innovative work that provides a broad introduction to the complex literature in the fields of costume, dress and fashion history. It is a comprehensive resource for those who wish to further their engagement with fashion as a contemporary phenomenon. This book connects a diverse range of approaches and incorporates non-Western literature within better-known studies on Europe and North America. It identifies the history of fashion as a meeting point between the long-standing historical investigation of 'dress' and 'costume' and the more recent development of those sociological and anthropological-inspired studies that have come to be called 'fashion theory'.

One of our aims has been to emphasise the methodological richness of the field by drawing on a vast array of places and times and by bringing together and putting into contact different ways of investigating fashion in its historical forms. Empirical methods are useful only when applied in systematic connection with theoretical developments in the field, and when empirical evidence stimulates fundamental theories. Needless to say that theoretical considerations can drive new approaches in empirical methodology and methods.

The Fashion History Reader is composed of significant essays that have influenced scholarship in the history of dress and fashion over the last generation. Twenty-three chapters and forty-four shorter pieces ('snapshots') cover a variety of topics and approaches within the history of fashion, ranging from object-based studies to theory-driven analyses, and are authored by leading academics, curators and fashion specialists. The new 'snapshots' function in this text as 'talking points' for discussion and debate. We hope that this book will be of use to undergraduate and postgraduate students of fashion and dress history, as well as researchers and museum professionals working in the field. *The Fashion History Reader* presents readers with the tools to understand significant fashion trends and phenomena, present and past, as well as the shifts in the scholarship of dress that enable new perspectives and questions to be posed.

As with all academic enterprises, during the long gestation of this work we have accumulated a series of debts to colleagues and friends. We would like to thank in the first instance all of the authors who accepted to have their work reprinted in this volume and worked with us in revising and updating their texts. Our thanks extend also to the conspicuous number of colleagues who have written new texts for this book, often making available the most current research and thus providing cutting-edge methodological and historical scholarship.

This book has been completed thanks to the continuing support of the University of Stockholm, the University of Technology Sydney and the University of Warwick. We would like to thank in particular Richard Butler, Andrew Littlejohns, Masafumi Monden and Marco Pecorari for their assistance. Several of our colleagues have advised us on what *their* students needed from a reader. We are very grateful to them all and we would like to thank in particular Michael Carter, Caroline Evans, Ulrich Lehmann, Colleen Kriger, Sanda Miller, Alexandra Palmer, Aileen Ribeiro, Valerie Steele and John Styles.

Finally, as with our previous collaborations, this book is the result of globalisation of scholarship and scholars. Contributors from more than a dozen countries in four different continents have participated in this project. The editors, based in England and Italy, and Australia and Sweden, have met around the world and kept in constant communication via email. Texts were sent electronically from one country to another, generating thousands of emails and the occasional scribbled page sent from remote provincial airports and Bangkok hotel lobbies.

This book would have not been possible without the friendship between the editors and most of the contributors. One forgives anything of a friend, even if this is one's co-editor. This is why this volume is dedicated to Friendship.

GR and PM, July 2009

Introduction

The Fashion History Reader: global perspectives

Giorgio Riello and Peter McNeil

Scholars have paid a great deal of attention to the changing role and nature of fashion, both conceptually and practically. They have underlined how present-day societies find their identity and formulate their understanding of change not simply by referring to technological progress, economic growth or cultural transformation in society, but also through the medium of fashion. Today few individuals would deny the powerful role of fashion in everyday life. The media presents us with an array of images from the real to the fantastic. Large multinational corporations and powerful fashion houses shape the discourse of fashion, influence public opinion and set in place global productive and distributive structures. Fashion is thus a specific vision of change that is shaped by practices, economic systems and actors. Fashion is also heavily contested, opposed and criticised. It retains in the public mind strong connections with vanity, frivolity, waste and folly. It can be conveniently blamed for everything from psychological illness, the ratings of Miss World, nastiness on *Project Runway* and the death of baby animals. 'There is something about fashion that can make people very nervous' remarks *Vogue* editor Anna Wintour in the 2009 film *The September Issue*.

Fashion and time

How much are these definitions of fashion the fruit of the present? The idea of a *History of Fashion Reader* derives from the editors' conviction that fashion (as a concept and a material manifestation) is the result of a historical process: *fashion as a flux in time*.[1] If one accepts this premise, it becomes paramount to understand how people in different times interpreted the importance, value and significance of fashion. Fashion in this case is a process that extends over time and takes on different characteristics. It often negates what had been present just a moment before in a continuous search for the new, the different and the unexpected. Fashion is therefore not just the 'now', the 'wow' or the 'hottest new thing', but

Figure 0.1 Installation shot of the Madame Grès Sphinx of Fashion exhibition, held in 2007 at the Museum of the Fashion Institute of Technology, New York.

also how the 'now' and the 'latest' have come into being and are part of wider processes that go backwards sequentially in time and will also continue in the future. Such an understanding goes against a certain commonsensical view prevalent in the industry itself: thus Anna Wintour justifies her ruthless behaviour in the recent film as a fashion editor by stating that 'Fashion's not about looking back. It's always looking forward' (September issue, *Film*, 2009). This is why, despite what is sometimes misunderstood about fashion's link to what the editors call the problem of the 'eternal present' in contemporary society (see introduction to Part 6), most of the characteristics of today's fashion have a long history. Think, for example, of its contested nature: from medieval sumptuary laws, to mercantilist bans and the more recent regulations of dress in private organisations: laws set limits on what and who should engage with fashion. But the study of history also shows how 'similarities' across time do not explain 'concepts': phenomena should be always contextualised within their own specific time and place. Sumptuary laws, for example, emerged from a historically specific context and are quite different from today's dress codes imposed by bouncers at a smart nightclub or casino. The editors identify as an ongoing challenge for this field a tendency to collapse time when analysing fashion, in order to make it either attractive to the public, or to respond to simple notions of the universality of the human subject and emotions. This is sometimes the case also with artefacts and practices such as food, furniture or sex, but the lived and quotidian dimension of fashion makes it more susceptible to this cultural amnesia.

Historical processes are not formed just by continuities and evolutions. They are often the result of profound transformations that might be political, social or economic. Today we live in societies that preserve some of the features of the world our grandparents and great-grandparents inhabited; yet our lives are profoundly different from theirs. Fashion can be used as a lens to consider change – sometimes dramatic – as it embodies and materialises the 'interruptions' and 'discontinuities' of history. Actually, fashion seems to often be at the fore-front of change, preceding wider socio-cultural transformations. Think about how the modifications of women's fashion in the early twentieth century that gave women more physical freedom preceded women's political franchise; or how the pervasiveness of casualwear since the 1930s was not just a prop in people's changing lives, but a way to structure social change itself.

Fashion is therefore both a passive receiver of historical transformation and an active shaper of change. It is also a phenomenon that should be studied per se, rather than in conjunction with other forms of historical change. The fact that people over the ages spent a great deal of time, effort, and above all very large amounts of their money, to shape their appearances is something that should not be dismissed simply as trivial. Appearance is an integral part of culture, as underlined by Breward, Perrot, Roche and others. It structures itself not just through people's acquisitive actions, their thoughts and aspirations, but also through material things. These things might be a gown, a hat, a bow-tie, a jewel or a 1920s' billboard advertising a new brand of lipstick. Fashion is constructed in time through material artefacts as well as behaviours and meanings. This is something distinctive of fashion whose historical understanding and integration remains heavily reliant on materiality, be this the presence of costumes in museum collections or the many reproductions and images accompanying the essays in this volume.

Finally, there is a further way in which fashion and history interact. Fashion, defined by change in time, becomes a historical process that defines time itself. This was something noted by Werner Sombart a century ago when he observed how fashion could be seen as a tool for men and women to shape their own time against the 'natural' or 'godly' time of seasons, life-cycles and lifespans. The frenzy, the fad, the transient became, according to Sombart, material manifestations of how time could be contracted or dilated, sometimes even suspended, but surely shaped by the human hand. Even the novelty of holidays and railway travel, the early sociologists explained, broke up time and created new fashion cycles within the fixity of a 'year'. Fashion complicates notions of time as a linear or cumulative phenomenon. It presents us instead with cyclical notions of time (the seasonal catwalks, or the retro phenomena) or with major turning points (Dior's New Look; the invention of prêt-à-porter). In the contemporary fashion designs of Vivienne Westwood and John Galliano, history is as much a catalogue of past times, as it is a unique laboratory for contemporary design direction. Designers, fashion communicators, journalists and fashionistas engage with history in order to better understand what fashion means in the present day.

Fashion and space

While it is obvious that history is interested in time, it might come as a surprise to some that history also has a keen interest in space. The more one looks at the vast expanses of time from the Middle Ages to the early twenty-first century, the more one realises that fashion has been incorrectly contextualised within a rather narrow tradition in which Europe, and Western Europe in particular, has the lion's share. Even the philosopher Gilles Lipovetsky, whose scholarship has profoundly influenced the study of fashion in all its possible dimensions, presents an emphatic argument that fashion 'took hold in the Modern West and nowhere else'.[2] He follows a string of celebrated scholars who have seen fashion quintessentially as the fruit of capitalism first, and modernity later.[3] Although historians and fashion scholars disagree on when exactly fashion emerged (and indeed disagree also on what fashion might entail), they all implicitly or explicitly accept that until recent times fashion was one of the privileges of the affluent West (of the Europeans firstly and later the neo-Europeans of America, Australia, South Africa, etc.).

This type of premise is convenient and is supported by strong historical narratives backed up by good and solid research – something that this *Reader* does not wish to conceal. The editors work from the conviction that one cannot simply ignore all scholarship that has gone before in order to miraculously concoct a politically correct new history of fashion. This we detect in certain outputs in the field that ignore the dimension of history and dismiss a century of investigation as ignorant. This situation, however, presents us with two serious issues conveyed under the accusatory label of 'Eurocentrism' of which we have been very aware from the beginning of this project. The first is the challenge we face today in redefining the meaning of fashion to include fashion consumers, producers and mediators well beyond the geographical boundaries of Western Europe, North America and perhaps those outposts frequently forgotten in the northern hemisphere, of South Africa, Australia, and parts of South America, the latter two being in the post-war period significant markets for French couture. The emerging economies of India and China present challenges not just in terms of labour de-localisation, reduction of costs of production or competition in mass markets. The strengthening economic and cultural roles of parts of Asia, but also metropolitan areas in Latin America and Africa, are leading to a truly global understanding of fashion.[4] This is a challenge that is as much true for the scholars and students of fashion as it is for the producers: fashion for the global consumer is born out of shared sensibilities, reciprocal tastes and understandings, and an assessment of culturally specific factors. It becomes imperative to know the main features of sartorial traditions that are the outcome of practices that have received little if any attention at all within fashion studies.

This leads us to a second point, one with more historical importance. If we wish to understand fashion beyond Europe, we must refrain from thinking that this has suddenly emerged in the last few decades as the result of globalisation and the growth of new middle classes. Recent innovative research underlines how places as disparate as Ming China, Tokugawa and Meiji Japan, Moghul India or Colonial Latin America and Australia, engaged and produced their own fashions both in conjunction, competition, collaboration *and* independently from Europe.[5] The fact that these historical traditions of fashion are not as well known or advertised as the European one should not diminish their value (see introduction to Part 5). Braudel famously wrote that 'Europe invented historians and then made good use of them'.[6] And historians have done for Europe a very thorough job of studying fashion in the past, something that is just commencing in other parts of the world, and being undertaken in academic disciplines as different as literature and business.

The problem of the abundance of research, and the 'conceptual cornucopia' on fashion in Europe vis-à-vis its relative scarcity in other parts of the world is also evident in this *Reader*. The editors do not hide from the difficulty of engaging with a 'global history of fashion' when there is little scholarship beyond Europe in comparative terms. We have done our best to convey research-in-process through the concise snapshots and through the associated bibliographies that accompany each section's introduction. Yet, our attempt can be still seen as partially unsuccessful and likely to be heavily criticised. The problem we face is that the history of fashion already comes packaged with strong 'stories' or 'narratives' and even its set areas of debate – these might be the consumer revolution of the 'long' eighteenth century; the birth of couture in the last third of the nineteenth century; or the importance of subcultural style in the mid- to late twentieth century. Such narratives form the basic ways in which histories of fashion are written and taught at both humanities departments and design colleges, and are underpinned by chronologies, facts and a cast of characters straight from European history.

The section on the early modern period, for instance, might contain a chapter on the clothing at the Ming court, yet it would be difficult to understand how this relates to the dress of the Italian court. There are two risks that could be noted here: the first is to be led into easy and attractive juxtapositions (different global courts at the same time, for instance; nice comparative imagery in double-projected Powerpoints); the second is to incorporate the non-European as a separate or residual category ('fashion was there too! – you are all wrong!'). Between the two positions, this *Reader* has preferred the latter as the lesser evil. Section 5 deals entirely with the academic 'problem' of fashion outside Euramerica.

While a global dimension is evident when dealing with the twentieth-century parts, the notion of the 'global' is only tangentially present in other sections. The 'global perspectives' provided by this *Reader* and announced in its subtitle are not a random selection of places to 'back up' the role of Europe as the core and historical centre of fashion. Rather we have attempted to provide a flavour of the variety of geographical, as well as chronological con-texts in which fashion and notions of fashionability emerged. These might be found in the most unlikely of places such as colonial Latin America (in our imagination a land of silver mines and little more; yet one of the most thriving consumer cultures in the early modern period globally), or on the African catwalks of the early years of the twenty-first century. We highlight these two cases as we wish to avoid the idea that 'global perspectives' are synony-mous with 'globalisation', the integration of cultures, economies and polities that social sci-entists see as emerging in the last thirty years. There is a serious need to warn new as well as experienced scholars not to fall into the easy trap of using the global to create 'participatory narratives' in which China or India – much more so than Latin America or Africa – deserve a place in the history of fashion in the light of their recent socio-economic achievements, their 'convergence' with the rich West, and their successful engagement with fashion as consumers and producers.

Fashion, dress and costume, and the role of history

One of the criteria guiding the construction of this *Reader* has been the importance of pro-viding chronologies and geographies that are as broad as possible. This was done in order to ground the understanding of present-day fashion within long-standing processes of change and continuity and to provide a geographical dimension that is commensurate with that of fashion in a 'globalised' present. The broad remit of this *Reader* is, however, also to be found in its subject matter: fashion and the complex relations that such a phenomenon has with dress, costume and clothing.[7]

The words 'fashion', 'dress', 'clothing' and 'costume' are often used interchangeably. How-ever, they have rather different meanings within discipline-specific contexts and suggest dif-ferent things to different scholars. Until the 1990s it was *dress* not *fashion* that was at the centre of historical attention. Negley Harte, a prominent economic historian, presents the intellectual and historiographical contexts explaining this state of affairs in the opening part of this *Reader*. Until recently, what had been central was not the study of fashion as a con-cept, but the study of the material forms (dress and costume) through which fashion itself was materialised. Such studies were generally not carried out by professional historians but were the remit of the everyday job of museum curators whose task was to preserve, as well as study and understand garments in their extensive collections.[8] They borrowed from history to provide a 'contextual' background for garments and textiles, often positioning them in terms of notions of evolution and displaying them in low-lux level spaces (generally called 'galleries of costume' and generating a reverential aspect owing to the low light levels) in sequential progression of time. This the public expected and to a certain degree still demands of their museums; it is an expectation that curators such as the London-based Judith Clarke have disrupted in recent years.[9]

What we have just described is to a certain degree a generalisation, but it captures the centrality of the artefact within fashion studies, and the fact that 'fashion' and 'fashionability' were very useful concepts not to understand so much people's behaviour, but to understand the value (intrinsic monetary value as well as that within museum settings) of historic artefacts. Thus a Chanel gown was not necessarily collected, displayed or included in a written text as an example of how couture influenced the elite as well as the less affluent consumers in their aesthetic choices, but as the 'best example' of one of the 'best' couturiers. We are not implying that this approach has little value. We believe quite the opposite. Judgements still need to be made, quality has not disappeared with postmodernism, and not everything and everyone can be equivalent, or a book such as ours is not even worth contemplating. Major works and exhibitions on fashion still adopt revised formulations of this approach and respond to the need to understand clothing, as Aileen Ribeiro puts it, 'through a complex and overlapping series of assessments and interpretations with the object, what is actually worn, firmly and constantly in mind'.[10]

The idea that garments, and artefacts in general, could challenge the interpretations of history, is something that has slowly emerged over time and has not yet found total acceptance among historians. From the 1970s historians started being interested in dress, costume, and later fashion, and sometimes even visited museums and their storage in order to make arguments and create theses. Curators, too, became increasingly well informed about history, not just its contents but also its making, weaknesses and continuous reinterpretations. Fernand Braudel, who was always well ahead of his time and extremely observant, noticed that: 'The history of costume is less anecdotal than would appear', explaining how 'it touches on every issue – raw materials, production processes, manufacturing costs, cultural stability, fashion and social hierarchy'.[11] He opened the doors for historians to include dress and costumes along with politics, religion and economics among the subject worthy of historical investigation. This led to a narrowing of what Lou Taylor calls 'the great divide' between academia and museums.[12] Today history-based and object-based research endeavours are not seen as alternatives or opposites. It is not uncommon for fashion scholars to move from academia to museums and vice versa, and projects bringing together these two types of institutions are no longer rare.[13]

It should be noted, however, that such collaborations lag a great deal behind the study of fine art, anthropology and archaeology, and that this adversely affects both the status and the academic rigour of the whole field. Very few amateurs are put in charge of Baroque paintings or Bauhaus tea-services in modern society; yet this situation persists with fashion, which remains poorly funded and associated with the skills of under-paid women. The bulk of the volunteers working in a museum are generally in the costume department, and for 'volunteer' we could substitute unpaid labour. A great deal of the world 'stock' of historical and significant contemporary fashion also remains in private hands, including designers themselves, who treat it as a personal reference tool for collections and publicity.

These caveats notwithstanding, one can say that this convergence of methodologies and interests has created the need for the adoption of a new label: that of 'fashion' rather than dress and costumes.[14] Braudel included fashion among historians' interests but saw it as an attribute of the materiality of costume or dress. Today this view would not be widely accepted. Partially this is the result of profound changes within intellectual and popular culture. Since the 1960s a wave of feminist scholars have contributed an enormous amount to the understanding of how people shaped their identities and contested that identity. Dress is central to such a shaping of personal and collective identities, for what one wears tells other people who this person is or might wish to be.[15] 'Fashioning' – in the sense of giving shape to something material but that is often, as in the case of identities, conceptual – becomes an appropriate gerund for a concept called 'fashion'.

Both 'fashioning' and 'fashion' have become key areas of interest within the field of cultural studies since its inception in the 1960s and 1970s. Cultural studies scholars have pushed the debate beyond traditional ideas of class by considering the importance of groups, families and subcultures, and the role of the individual in society. Fashion is again a central topic for research. This is especially evident when we consider the study of consumption in people's lives. The anthropologist Mary Douglas (1921–2007) but also the French cultural theorist Jean Baudrillard (1929–2007) have given historians and fashion experts a series of conceptual tools to understand the role of fashion in people's lives, not just in the present but also historically. Their contribution, for instance, has been fundamental for the formulation of a so-called 'consumer revolution' for the eighteenth century (see Part 3).

Postmodernism, both in academia and design practice (for instance architecture), has also provided a new intellectual background for the understanding of fashion. By highlighting the linguistic and discursive nature of reality it has further complicated the relationship between material object (dress, costume or clothing) and fashion. At the same time this has allowed fashion to become a topic of study for disciplines as different as sociology, anthropology, ethnography, museum studies, cultural studies, media and film studies, philosophy, design studies, business studies, literary studies and, of course, history and art history. Several of the contributors in this *Fashion History Reader* are not historians or curators. They come instead from all the above mentioned fields and, while preserving their disciplinary identity, belong to a field that we now call 'Fashion Studies'.

It would be incorrect to see Fashion Studies as simply the sum of the parts. It is a dynamic interdisciplinary field of research in which the study of the past (not necessarily that studied by historians) is still central for the reasons exposed above. It is also a field that over the last two decades has striven to create a shared vocabulary and a communal view of the subject, something that has profoundly enriched historians and curators working on the more historical side of fashion. Theory might be seen at face value as the 'superglue' of Fashion Studies (and indeed this might be suggested by the fact that *Fashion Theory* is also the most prominent journal in the field) but both the objects of fashion and the historical understanding of fashion are integral to the research agenda of Fashion Studies. This might be seen as a positive feature of the methodological richness of Fashion Studies; yet at the same time it poses a challenge to the student working in this new field as few have both practical hands-on knowledge of materiality as well as a grasp of both history and theoretical practices. Indeed, it might be argued that this skill set is exactly what the students of fashion studies must aim to acquire, or they risk being irrelevant to the staff in the local museum or the head of department of the philosophy school.

Why a *History of Fashion Reader*?

This volume is not necessarily conceived to be a tool for historians interested in learning about fashion; rather it aims to provide all those who are interested in fashion with a tool to understand this complex phenomenon across time. The French critic and historian Jacques Barzun (b. 1907) gave a paper in 1954 which expressly addressed these matters.[16] In 'Cultural History: a Synthesis' Barzun outlined the shift from 'state-ridden' histories to those privileging underlying economic theory during the course of the nineteenth century.[17] He rather brilliantly argued that the devastation of the First World War, which was in effect an 'industrial effort', led to the growing understanding of struggle, interests and ideology. As intellectuals sought refuge in Paris bars or Capri beaches, they reflected on cultural differences, Freud's unconscious mind and the intangible but very real 'influence of habits, assumptions, and beliefs'.[18] Within this framework, 'cultural history' replaced the old-fashioned idea of 'manners and morals' with specialist graduate studies being created in which 'culture' came to mean something different to a historian than an anthropologist.

Barzun provided us in 1954 with a wonderful warning that in studying a field such as fashion, one must have an ability to see the whole field in order to produce meaningful comparisons: 'cultural life is both intricate and emotionally complex. One must be steeped in the trivia of a period, one must be a virtual intimate of its principal figures, to pass judgement on who knew what, who influenced whom, how far an idea was strange or commonplace, or so fundamental and obvious as to pass unnoticed . . . The cultural historian lives imaginatively in his own culture and also in that he has made his own by study . . . Just as in biography we take for granted the subject's daily routine of hair-combing and tooth-brushing, so in history we take for granted the great dull uniformities of vegetative behavior'.[19] These comments have real pertinence for the study of fashion for, in order to know if a woman is participating in fashion at a particular moment, in say 1934, requires enormous contextual information before one can even begin to speculate as to motives, strategies and identities, let alone assessing a relationship to place, occupation, cosmopolitanism or provincialism.

Barzun's analysis provides the editors with an intellectual excuse and a practical reason to present a work that helps students, scholars and the public in the difficult work of 'contextualisation' of fashion in society and of society in fashion. This is done by following an old-fashioned device in history, that of thematic and chronological divisions. The *Reader* is thus divided into six parts, surveying some of the key themes in the history of fashion. Themes also move in and across time, providing a 'disguised' chronology with Parts 1–3 covering the long period from the twelfth to the eighteenth centuries; Parts 4 and 5 considering the period from the nineteenth century to the contemporary (with particular attention given to extra-European countries); and Part 6 surveying the last century especially by emphasising the global setting and current globalised nature of fashion.

Part 1 asks when, where and why fashion first appeared. It asks if the concept of fashion can be really used in a medieval context and what it might have meant to be a 'fashionable' person in a society still characterised by strong social hierarchies and low purchasing power for the masses. This part introduces readers to the period before the end of the sixteenth century and the early expression of fashion as distinct from dress and livery, that is, something handed or gifted to another. Three texts have been selected. Sarah-Grace Heller critically analyses the paradigm of the 'birth of fashion' in Europe; Alan Hunt provides a broad overview of the meaning and relevance of sumptuary laws in medieval Europe and finally Will Fisher concentrates on the construction of identity through the analysis of the specific case of men's codpieces in the Renaissance. Shorter texts by Renaissance specialists discuss respectively the influence of Asian textiles in the creation of fashion in Europe (Giorgio Riello); the role of specific social groups in navigating their religious difference through dress (Maria Giuseppina Muzzarelli); and the importance of fashionable objects in a wider participation in fashion culture (Evelyn Welch).

Part 2 moves in time to consider the period between the sixteenth and the beginning of the eighteenth century, what in history is defined as the 'early modern' period. It asks if fashion was still the preserve of the elite in this period and how society at large reflected upon dress. Patricia Allerston introduces the relationship between dress and social structure in sixteenth- and seventeenth-century Venice, questioning the value of simple emulation in explaining fashion's expansion to the lower strata of society. As with the piece by Will Fisher in Part 1, Maria Hayward considers the complexity of court attire through a specific case study, that of headwear, thus showing the methodological richness of object-based research. Eugenia Paulicelli brings us back to Venice and focuses on 'fashion on the page' by considering Vecellio's famous costume book *Habiti antichi et moderni*. Her analysis shows the extent to which fashion and fashionability were constructed within a 'world' that was as much geographic as cultural. Finally, Jennifer M. Jones develops the analysis of the inter-relationship of court and fashion by introducing us to late seventeenth-century fashion at the court of Louis XIV. These key texts, considering both popular and elite fashion, are accompanied by shorter pieces dedicated to specific themes: the relationship between women's work and fashion mediated through the medium of embroidery (Susan Frye); the importance of costume and the stage in Elizabethan sartorial display (Catherine Richardson); the meaning of fashionability within the Renaissance court (Carole Collier Frick);the ways in which inventories help us to retrieve information on early modern dress (Janine Maegraith); and the influential and sombre fashions of the Spanish court during the Golden Age of Spain (Hilary Davidson).

Part 3 concentrates on the eighteenth century and questions the idea that it was during this century that something approaching present-day fashion emerged. If so, what were its components? How did bourgeois acquisition relate to it? What was the function of retailers such as the luxury purveyor who 'made' nothing directly himself, the *marchand de mode*? And how did the non-elite afford fashion? Four essays survey a vast array of topics related to the so-called 'consumer revolution' of the eighteenth century and its implications for fashion. John Styles considers how fashion might be the result of complex family and individual choices concerning expenditure over lifetime, rather than a simple whimsy as some fashion literature suggests. Beverly Lemire draws on Styles's considerations by examining a diverse range of fashionable textiles that transformed the appearance of plebeian consumers in the eighteenth century and focusing on cottons in particular. Aileen Ribeiro contextualises these consumer changes by rebutting the idea of a unified European fashion and pointing instead to distinct national traditions of France and England as European paradigmatic examples of fashion alternatives. Finally Daniel L. Purdy, by drawing on the case of the German states, considers the creation of new forms of 'representation' of fashion based on reading and viewing of written and visual materials. Again, shorter texts provide readers with focused cases and reflections: the importance of material artefacts in costume museums (Miles Lambert); how design and innovation was conveyed through the appearance of silks (Lesley Miller); the importance of prestige and fashionablity among the eighteenth-century London *beau monde* (Hannah Greig); fashion as represented and imagined in the large number of satirical prints produced in this period (Peter McNeil); and the negotiation of fashion by citizens in early Republican America (Linzy Brekke).

Part 4 considers instead how nineteenth-century fashion acquired a symbolic value that exceeded its economic and traditional attributes. Massive social change, development of ready-made fashions, the rise of popular journalism and print culture changed attitudes towards fashion in the nineteenth century. Why and how did society in this period reflect on the nature of fashion? Why was reform advocated? Was fashion proposed for mass markets? Rather than considering these questions by referring to fashion as a series of progressive style changes, Valerie Steele examines how fashion became closely related to new concepts of personality, self-definition and identity. Christopher Breward develops Steele's argument by disputing the idea that men 'renounced' fashion in the nineteenth century (as had been advocated by the psychologist J. C. Flügel) and by considering the complexity of fashion within the modern metropolis. The importance of the city as a space where fashion is formed and develops is further considered in a essay by Ulrich Lehmann, in which he argues that 'modern' fashion cannot exist without the city. Lehmann persuasively argues that the nineteenth-century metropolis fuelled a new language that still characterises fashion today. Finally Diana Crane returns to the issue of fashion and gender and argues for an interconnection between the emancipation of women and the profound changes in their sartorial life at the end of the nineteenth century. These essays are accompanied by shorter essays on fashion's place in the nineteenth-century novel (Clair Hughes); the ways in which industrialisation changed fashion and the lives of workers (Katrina Honeyman); the place of jewellery in the nineteenth-century fashion imagination (Elizabeth Fischer); the figure of the 'dandy' as a quintessential man of fashion (Olga Vainshtein), fashionability and political life in the French Second Empire (Alex Cain); and finally how birth and death dominated many sartorial choices of Victorian consumers (Lou Taylor).

Part 5 does not move in time but rather shifts spatially, taking the reader mostly outside the confines of Europe. It asks if fashion was a tool of power in the processes of European colonialism in the nineteenth century and if so, in what ways it was used to convey European superiority. Colonial and non-colonial experiences are considered to elucidate some of the key questions concerning the European nature of fashion, the ways in which European fashion was 'exported' and how non-European fashions existed independently from Europe. This section gives particular importance to the political and cultural value of fashion in the nineteenth and early twentieth centuries. Antonia Finnane introduces the meaning of fashion in late imperial China and puts in place a picture of a vestimentary system that was only later challenged by Western fashion. Emma Tarlo considers how the control of appearances was used as a tool of colonial domination in nineteenth-century India. By contrast, Ken'ichiro Hirano presents the case of Japan, where the free and widespread adoption of Western fashion was seen as integral to the 'modernisation' programme supported by the Meiji regime. Fashion in this case was used as a tool to assert modernity and equality, rather than to emphasise difference and economic underdevelopment as in the case of India. Finally, Verity Wilson attempts a mediation between different concepts ('exoticism' vs. 'modernity' for instance) by proposing a comparative exercise that puts the 'East' and the 'West' on the same conceptual plane. Shorter pieces consider specific cases such as dress reform in Peter the Great's Russia (Christine Ruane); the relationship between clothing and ethnicity in colonial Latin America (Rebecca Earle); notions of respectability in nineteenth-century Australian colonial fashion (Margaret Maynard); how fashion was used in Abolitionist campaigns fighting the slave trade (Alice Taylor); and changes in the Ottoman clothing rules in the nineteenth and twentieth centuries (Suraiya Faroqhi). These are complemented by more contemporary studies such as fashion in Africa (Karen Tranberg Hansen); the current emergence and attention paid to the concept of contemporary Islamic Fashion (Annika Rabo); and a reinterpretation of the meaning of orientalism in the light of present-day global fashion products (Hazel Clark).

The final part of the *Reader* is dedicated to the twentieth century and in particular to historical perspectives that help to understand more recent times. What Gilles Lipovetsky has defined as the 'century of fashion' (1860–1960) saw epochal changes in the very notion of fashion. The intricacy of fashion within the twentieth century is examined by a range of experts who consider the 'aura' of fashion in the 'modern' age, the rise of ready-to-wear clothing and the cult of expected obsolescence, the persistence of the notion of an exclusive and iconic aspirational couture, and fashion created in new forms and in new materials for the masses. This is done through the re-publication of a selection of key pieces as well as the inclusion of a number of snapshots that attempt to guide students through the complexity of twentieth-century fashion. As by the twentieth century the notion of the fashion designer and the extension of branding practices had became so extensive, twentieth-century fashion is a most difficult period to characterise in a simple manner. Nancy Troy presents the classic theme of high fashion through the case of French impresario Paul Poiret and reveals the extent to which 'the rules' of fashion, fashionability and the fashion business in the first third of the century were heavily influenced by concepts originally formulated within the tiny slice of total production called 'couture'. Her analysis is complemented by shorter pieces on 'couture' as an institution within the history of fashion where consumers had more say than we might imagine (Alexandra Palmer); the origins of the fashion show with its mesmerising and modernist aspects (Caroline Evans); the re-evaluation of the work of the couturier Madame Grès (Patricia Mears); and the complex association between fashion, craft, couture and art (Sanda Miller).

In this final part of the book particular attention is given to the role of the media and of lifestyles in the definition of twentieth-century fashion. How was fashion to remain powerful when it was sold through copies? What happened to fashion when it was represented through new media such as film and television? Did fashion become part of mass democracy and self-determination in the post-Second World War period? These are topics considered in Gregory Votolato's essay on American casualwear and are further developed through shorter texts on the relationship between modernity, the modern woman and fashion design (Rebecca Arnold); fashion, consumers and the silver screen (Louise Wallenberg); fashion in twentieth-century totalitarian regimes (Djurdja Bartlett); and fashion vs. costumes in cinema (Stella Bruzzi).

Llewellyn Negrin reflects on the ways in which postmodernism in the last thirty years has challenged our understanding of fashion, including its historical importance. She surveys the now vast literature on the body and asks in what ways this scholarship has challenged the position that the industry and advertising hold in constructing both identity and the body. Several themes of the history of fashion converge in this essay. She points to the very important shift in the 1980s writing about fashion conducted by Hollander, Evans, Wilson and Steele in which fashion was argued to be potentially a tool of self-fashioning or at least agency and play. This argument, Negrin suggests, which was always more nuanced by the original scholars mentioned, has tended to create a rather utopic vision for fashion in which we all can be anyone at any time and throw our identities on or off with regular abandon. Negrin is particularly critical of the possible impact and effect of the ideas of Jean Baudrillard, who in holding up the postmodern condition of artifice, plays straight to the hands of advertising and media practices which have no interest in real lived lives. Women, she argues, are the ones with most to lose, as they continue to be judged by their styling and their looks. Negrin's essay is accompanied by analysis of fashion as influenced within 1970s and 1980s club culture

(Sally Gray); the importance of historicism and a specific moment of revival in 1980s fashion (Alistair O'Neill); the relationship between fashion and adornment in an intellectual framework (Michael Carter); and the ethical role of fashion and its futures (Elizabeth Wilson).

The *Reader* concludes by investigating how the present is reshaping the past both by changing established national and international equilibria in fashion and by restructuring fashion through the use of the past as both catalogue and marker of difference. Simona Segre Reinach shows in a newly commissioned essay how Italian fashion is affirming its strength and even superiority over Chinese consumers and producers by drawing on a mythologised past made up of artisanal figures and Renaissance metaphors that are suitably 'globalised' and generalised to make them suitable for a non-European context. The global scenario of fashion, she argues, is not the simple result of globalisation but is profoundly influenced by the long history of fashion and its practices. This is further underlined through shorter texts on the evolution of the Made-in-Italy (Giovanni Luigi Fontana); the mind-set and consumption practices of contemporary Japanese youth consumers (Toby Slade); the transformation of couture into luxury brands that border on a new porno chic (Marc de Ferrière le Vayer); and the creation of new fashion branding strategies through the inter-relationship of fashion imagery, retail spaces and publicity (D. J. Huppatz).

Conclusion

In producing this *Reader* the editors have faced the challenge of working outside narrow historical, methodological and stylistic interests and preferences. Most university courses and texts are taught and constructed either thematically – generally with a preference towards twentieth-century material – or by geographic and historical truncation. This makes sense, as history too is generally taught through location and time. But does this also work for fashion? In engaging with cultures and modes of scholarly writing beyond our immediate experience, we hope that students and scholars alike embrace not just the trend to describe a contemporary global fashion, so dear to the media, but a global history of fashion reaching far in time and space.

Notes

1 The same idea is shared by other works by Peter McNeil (ed.) (2009) *Fashion: Critical and Primary Sources*, Oxford and New York: Berg, 4 vols; Peter McNeil and Vicki Karaminas (eds) (2009) *The Men's Fashion Reader*, Oxford and New York: Berg.

2 G. Lipovetsky (1994) *The Empire of Fashion: Dressing Modern Democracy*, trans. by C. Porter, Princeton: Princeton University Press, p. 15.

3 See for instance F. Braudel (1973) *Capitalism and Material Life, 1400–1800*, trans. by M. Kochen, London: Fontana.

4 E. Paulicelli and H. Clark (eds) (2008) *The Fabric of Cultures: Fashion, Identity, Globalization*, New York: Routledge.

5 See B. Lemire, and G. Riello (2008) 'East and West: Textiles and Fashion in Eurasia in the Early Modern Period', *Journal of Social History*, 41, 4, pp. 887–916; C. M. Belfanti (2008) 'Was Fashion a European Invention?', *Journal of Global History*, 3, 3, pp. 419–43.

6 F. Braudel (1979) *Civilization and Capitalism, 15th–18th Century: Vol. 2. The Wheels of Commerce*, London: Collins, p. 134.

7 On the etymologies of fashion and clothing, see M. Barnard (2002) *Fashion as Communication*, London: Routledge, pp. 8–26.

8 Negley Harte recently observed how until the 1980s 'Historians were defeated by clothes. Archaeologists fussed about the surviving evidences of their absence; art historians were interested only in the portrayed upper classes; social historians were torn between thinking clothes were either too trivial to bother with or too complex to master, and economic historians could not count them and therefore paid no attention. Clothes were dismissed from academic history.' N. Harte (2009) 'Review of John Styles, *Dress of the People*', *Costume*, 43, p. 176.

9 J. Clark (2004) *Spectres: When Fashion Turns Back*, London: V & A Publications.

10 A. Ribeiro (1998) 'Re-fashioning Art: Some Visual Approaches to the Study of the History of Dress', *Fashion Theory*, 2, 4, p. 320.

11 F. Braudel (1979) *Civilization and Capitalism, 15th–18th Century: Vol. 1. The Structure of Everyday Life*, London: Collins, p. 311.

12 See L. Taylor (2002) *The Study of Dress History*, Manchester: Manchester University Press, esp. pp. 64–90.

13 For a useful overview see C. Richardson (2004) 'Introduction', in C. Richardson (ed.), *Clothing Culture, 1350–1650*, Aldershot: Ashgate, pp. 1–25.

14 Harte believes that the label 'fashion' is more understandable than 'costume', and in a review in the journal *Costume* comments that 'No reader of this journal should be affronted; the Costume Society carries a name suggestive at best of the 1950s and at worst of the theatre', N. Harte (2009) 'Review of John Styles, *Dress of the People*', *Costume*, 43, p. 176.

15 On this methodology see the magisterial E. Wilson (1985 [2nd ed. 2003]) *Adorned in Dreams: Fashion and Modernity*, London: Virago.

16 J. Barzun (1956) 'Cultural History: A Synthesis', paper delivered before the European History Section of the American Historical Association, 1954, in F. Stern (ed.), *The Varieties of History: From Voltaire to the Present*, Cleveland and New York: Meridian Books, pp. 387–402.

17 Ibid., p. 388.

18 Ibid., p. 389.

19 Ibid., pp. 394–7.

Bibliography and further reading

General works and overviews in the history of fashion

Ash, J., and Wilson, E. (eds) (1992) *Chic Thrills: A Fashion Reader*, London: Pandora.

Breward, C. (1995) *The Culture of Fashion: A New History of Fashionable Dress*, Manchester: Manchester University Press.

Breward, C. (2003) *Fashion*, Oxford: Oxford University Press.

Crane, D. (2001) *Fashion and Its Social Agendas: Class, Gender and Identity in Clothing*, Chicago: Chicago University Press.

Hollander, A. (1993) *Seeing through Clothes*, Berkeley: University of California Press.

Hollander, A. (2004) *Sex and Suits: The Evolution of Modern Dress*, New York: Knopf.

Laver, J. (2002) *Costume and Fashion: A Concise History*, London: Thames and Hudson (rev. edition by A. de la Haye).

McNeil, P. (ed.) (2009) *Fashion: Critical and Primary Sources*, 4 vols, Oxford and New York: Berg.

Ribeiro, A. (2004) *Dress and Morality*, 1st edition 1986, Oxford and New York: Berg.

Welters, L., and Lillethun, A. (eds) (2007) *The Fashion Reader*, Oxford: Berg.

Wilson, E. (1985) *Adorned in Dreams: Fashion and Modernity*, 2nd edition, 2003, London: Virago.

Methodological texts in the history of fashion

Cumming, V. (2004) *Understanding Fashion History*, London: Batsford.
Fashion Theory, special issue (1998) 2, 4.
Taylor, L. (2002) *The Study of Dress History*, Manchester: Manchester University Press.
Taylor, L. (2004) *Establishing Dress History*, Manchester: Manchester University Press.

Primary and contextual sources

Carter, M. (2003) (ed.) *Fashion Classics from Carlyle to Barthes*, Oxford and New York: Berg.
Johnson, K. K. P., Torntore, S. J., and Eicher, J. B. (eds) (2003) *Fashion Foundations: Early Writings on Fashion and Dress*, Oxford and New York: Berg.
McDowell, C. (1995) *The Literary Companion to Fashion*, London: Pimlico.
Purdy, D. L. (2004) (ed.) *The Rise of Fashion: A Reader*, Minneapolis: University of Minnesota Press.

Visual sources in the history of fashion

Ashelford, J. (1996) *The Art of Dress: Clothes and Society 1500–1914*, London: National Trust.
Boucher, F. (orig. edition 1967) *20,000 Years of Fashion: The History of Costume and Adornment*, New York: various editions.
Crill, R. (2004) *Dress in Detail: From around the World*, London: V & A Publications.
Crill, R., Wearden, J., and Wilson, V. (2009) *World Dress Fashion in Detail*, London: V & A Publications.
Hart, A., and North, S. (1997) *Historical Fashion in Detail: The 17th and 18th Centuries*, London: V & A Publications.
Johnston, L. (2005) *Nineteenth-century Fashion in Detail*, London: V & A Publications.
Peacock, J. (1996) *Men's Fashion: The Complete Sourcebook*, London: Thames & Hudson.
Rieff Anawalt, P. (2007) *The Worldwide History of Dress*, London: Thames & Hudson.
Rodini, E., and Weaver, E. B. (2002) *A Well-Fashioned Image: Clothing and Costume in European Art, 1500–1800*, exhibition catalogue, Chicago: The David and Alfred Smart Museum of Art, University of Chicago.
Rothstein, N. (1997) *Four Hundred Years of Fashion*, London: V & A Publications.
Squire, G. (1974) *Dress, Art and Society, 1560–1970*, London: Studio Vista.
Wilcox, C., and Mendes, V. (1998) *Modern Fashion in Detail*, London: V & A Publications.

Introductions to fashion studies

Barnard, M. (2002) *Fashion as Communication*, London: Routledge.
Barnard, M. (ed.) (2007) *Fashion Theory*, London: Routledge.
Craig, J. (2008) *Fashion: The Key Concepts*, Oxford and New York: Berg.
Entwistle, J. (2000) *The Fashioned Body: Fashion, Dress and Modern Social Theory*, Cambridge: Polity.
Kawamura, Y. (2004) *Fashion-ology: An Introduction to Fashion Studies*, Oxford and New York: Berg.
McNeil, P., and Karaminas, V. (eds) (2009) *The Men's Fashion Reader*, Oxford and New York: Berg.
Welters, L., and Lillethun, A. (eds) (2007) *The Fashion Reader*, Oxford and New York: Berg.

The study of fashion and dress

Negley Harte

It was in the eighteenth century that a strong antiquarian tradition of writing about dress emerged – look, for example, at Joseph Strutt's *Complete View of the Manners, Customs, Arms, Habits, etc., of the Inhabitants of England . . .* (London, 1775), continued in a second volume in 1799, or at M. A. Racinet, *Le Costume Historique* (Paris, 1888), in six volumes, Max von Boehn's *Die Mode: Menschen und Moden* (Munich, 1905–13) in eight volumes, or at Alice Morse Earle's *Two Centuries of Costume in America, 1620–1820* (New York, 1903), in only two volumes.

In the twentieth century this tradition came to be augmented by a growing number of specialist writings on the history of dress that had an increasingly popular appeal largely derived from adding a good dash of Freudian psychology to the simmering casserole. The leading examples of this new approach to the history of dress can be found in the work of Dr (Dr med., that is, as they would say in Germany) C. W. Cunnington. His *Feminine Attitudes in the Nineteenth Century* (1935), and the even more suggestively entitled *Why Women Wear Clothes* (1941) are thoughtful (and wonderfully dated) contributions, and the five *Handbooks* he and his wife produced at regular intervals in the 1950s dealing with what they called *costume* in England in the Middle Ages and the sixteenth, seventeenth, eighteenth and nineteenth centuries remain very helpful guides.

Meanwhile, history as an academic discipline was transformed. In Germany from the 1820s and in Britain from the 1860s, history became an academic discipline, with its published sources, its professors, textbooks, journals, degrees, examinations, students and its identity. It was increasingly political, constitutional, ecclesiastical, diplomatic. The history of clothing was thought too trivial to figure. In the early twentieth century, economic history went on to emerge as a discipline. This economic history was much concerned with textile production, with wool and the wool trade, with cotton and factories, and every aspect of *supply*; it pretty well ignored *demand*, evidently the trivial side of economics. What was done with the wool and the cotton and the silk and the flax that went into the production process was simply ignored. The uses to which the measurable production was put were unquantifiably too various to merit attention, and in any case only frivolous. Clothes – as distinct from cloth – got no attention from economic history.

The situation began to change in the 1960s. The change, in the English case, can be dated from the creation of the first academic post in the history of dress established at the University of London's prestigious Courtauld Institute of Art in 1965. Stella Mary Newton was appointed. She began to organise an MA course in the history of dress, and this course and its students were to be of great influence. And in 1966 the Costume Society was founded in the UK. It attracted a wide membership and its journal

Costume was also to be an important influence. In the United States the Costume Society of America was founded in 1973 and its official journal *Dress* was launched in 1975.

The world of history as an academic subject continued to pay no attention. The history of dress, focusing on fashion and on dress as shown in portraits, a nice little field of its own, did not appear to offer the consumption link to the history of production. A new development came when economic and social historians eventually deigned to begin to look at the consumption of textiles in terms of the complex mix that made them into clothes. One of the first historians in the field was Françoise Piponnier; her *Costume et vie sociale: la cour d'Anjou, XIVe–XVe siècle* (1970) marks the beginning of a new approach.

Questions are clearly specified; quantification is undertaken as appropriate; sources are specifically identified; clothes are not treated as trivial byways but as legitimate objects of historical inquiry. Clothes are part of our endeavour to understand the past. Two important books show how the history of clothing has been brought into the historical mainstream: Daniel Roche's *La Culture des apparances* (1989), translated into English as *The Culture of Clothing; Dress and Fashion in the 'Ancien Régime'* (1994), and John Styles's *The Dress of the People: Everyday Fashion in Eigtheenth-century England* (2007).

It is important that the history of clothing should not be left to subsidiary studies, or left in a ghetto of its own. Much of interest has been published, for example in *Fashion Theory: The Journal of Dress, Body and Culture*, a new journal begun in 1997. But it would be a retrograde step if this was read only by an inward-looking coterie of fashion specialists.

Let me give two examples of important questions that must be asked by historians, and which cannot be answered – probably not even asked – by a ghettoised separate history of fashion. What was the connection between the new high average age of first marriage in the fourteenth century in Western Europe and the new spread of fashion in the same period? The emergence of the 'western European marriage pattern', with people not getting married to partners of their choosing until they were in their late 20s, created a different world from that obtaining earlier in Europe and still continuing in the Asian civilisations. Surely it cannot be coincidence that it was this world that saw the emergence of fashion in the new sense?

And the second question. Did changes in domestic heating arrangements in the sixteenth century lead to lighter clothes being worn, made out of lighter textiles? The sixteenth century saw rising coal consumption, falling prices for window glass, the rise of a type of draft-excluders known as tapestries. The domestic environment became warmer, and silk replaced fur as the status symbol and the demand increased for various sorts of new draperies. And this too can surely not be a coincidence.

The resurgence of interest in the history of clothes must not be allowed to sink back into a separate little field of its own. The field can build on its rich traditions, the antiquarian strand, the psychology strand, the art history strand, the social history strand. It must take its place among the big issues in history. Clothes, after all, are the most conspicuous of all articles of consumption, as well as the most revealing and the most interesting.

Bibliography and further reading

Ribeiro, A. (1998) 'Re-fashioning Art: Some Visual Approaches to the Study of the History of Dress', *Fashion Theory*, 2, 4, pp. 315–26.

Roche, D. (1994) *The Culture of Clothing: Dress and Fashion in the 'Ancien Régime'*, ch. 1. 'Clothing or Costume', Cambridge: Cambridge University Press.

Styles, J. (1998) 'Dress in History: Reflections on a Contested Terrain', *Fashion Theory*, 2, 4, pp. 383–90.

Styles, J. (2007) *The Dress of the People: Everyday Fashion in Eighteenth-century England*, London: Yale University Press.

Taylor, L. (2000) *The Study of Dress History*, Manchester: Manchester University Press.

Tozer, J. (2006) 'Cunnington's Interpretation of Dress', *Costume*, 20, pp. 1–17.

PART 1

Fashion's 'Origins'
The Middle Ages and Renaissance

Giorgio Riello and Peter McNeil

The idea that dress has the power 'to express', that is to say that what we wear conveys meaning regarding who we are in terms of gender and class, but also who we are in terms of cultural attributes, education and taste, is something that is relentlessly repeated in nearly all texts on fashion. The semiotic power of clothing, that is to say its capacity to convey messages that go beyond the very materiality of the fabric of which it is made, is a complex subject as it entails the idea that people use material things to create their own personalities and interact with other people. The picture gets even more complicated when you think that is is improbable, although not statistically impossible, to meet someone who is dressed exactly like yourself. The streets of whatever city in Europe, North America, and increasingly elsewhere in the world, are full of people that an inattentive eye would think are dressed more or less in the same way; yet there are profound and subtle differences that mean we could always tell it is not 'us' we see mirrored there.

Fashion stands in a critical but controversial position: while we are all dressed differently, we also seem to follow similar trends. Manufacturers would not do good business if each single individual were unique. While we are asserting the semiotic power of our individual sartorial choice, the engagement with fashion is at the same a shared process that is strictly social. If fashion were an illness – and indeed some have argued it is a psychological problem – then each fashionista would be both a patient and a case in a global pandemic. We draw on this similitude to emphasise how fashion is the result of conscious individual choices often aimed at differentiating ourselves from others. At the same time it is one of the most powerful social processes that bring us all together simultaneously.

Let us step back a few hundred years to the European Middle Ages and in particular the period after year 1000 when records are more abundant. How did the wearing of clothing work at that time? And did fashion exist? These two fairly simple questions that can be easily affirmed for the present are very difficult to explain for the Middle Ages, and as we will see in the rest of this *Reader*, also for most centuries up to the twentieth. The capacity of dress to express individuality is difficult to ascertain in the Middle Ages. Society was hierarchically constructed with an elite at the top (whose power and wealth derived from the ownership of land), a class of clerics, merchants and artisans, and finally a vast number of poor peasants normally living in rather meagre conditions. Birth determined to which of these broad classes one belonged; there was limited social mobility (the capacity to move up the social ladder); and education, taste and personal choices had to conform with one's position in this largely unchangeable social structure. It is not difficult to realise that in such a strict social formation there was little scope to use dress as a tool to communicate anything apart from that which was seen as 'natural': therefore a knight was supposed to wear precious fur to demonstrate his social rank, while the same material would have been seen as totally inappropriate for a merchant, and even more so for a peasant, even if they could afford it. This was the case to such an extent that it was considered perfectly legitimate to establish by law who could wear what, as medieval society was far from being one predicated on equality or on 'equal opportunities'. There was no fashion-affirmative action.

Dress, rather than 'distinguishing' people, was more used to identify them. A prince would have been immediately identifiable in a way in which a prince of a European royal family today would be only if he wore ceremonial robes in the street. Similarly, the doctor, or the merchant, or the servant, or – as considered by Giuseppina Muzzarelli in this *Reader*, the Jew – would have been immediately recognised as belonging to a specific class of people. The idea of the 'livery', a kind of 'uniform' for each social group was of great currency in the Middle Ages, up to the case of the servants of noble and rich families who wore garments whose colours and shapes signified their belonging to a specific household. Fashion, here defined as simply the change of the materiality of clothing over time, was equally difficult. In a similar way in which dress could not convey individuality, so change in dress could hardly signal any purposeful social process. The participatory nature of fashion in today's world was lacking in the Middle Ages.

So far we have presented a rather sober picture of a society whose static nature prevented any playful engagement with clothing, including its most ludic expression called 'fashion'. The fact that clothing was incredibly expensive further complicates the picture, as on average people spent from 20 to 30 per cent of their wealth on textiles and clothing and the textile sector was second only to agriculture. The high cost of fabrics was explained by the fact that they were woven with simple looms and from fibres that were hand-spun, making the emergence of fashion even more improbable. Yet, the period from the twelfth to the fourteenth century saw a recovery of the European economy and a renewed prosperity for many urban centres that had dwindled after the fall of the Roman Empire. This was a period of increasing trade in which cities like the maritime republics of Venice, Genoa and Amalfi, but also the many cities in which yearly fairs were conducted, became flourishing centres of economic, social and intellectual life. Fortunes could be built and knowledge acquired to such an extent to pose a serious challenge to a model of social stasis. Dress for the rich merchant's wife in thirteenth-century Venice was more than simple protection from the damp climate of the city, or a livery of her social condition. It could function as a way to show the economic success of her husband by spending (or one would say investing) a great deal of money on it and by changing outfits more regularly.

A further element conducive to the emergence of fashion was the fact that humanistic ideals spread a consciousness about the 'modernity' of the times. The idea that we are different (and most of us would think better) than the generations before us is based on the principle of progress. Medieval people would have seen time in a more static way: this was true not just for the peasant who cultivated the same field that his father and grandfather had cultivated, but also for the scholar or the ruler whose guiding principles were based on respect for the 'ancient authorities', from the Greek philosophers to the fathers of the Church whose sayings were taken very much like the truth. The literary and philosophical production of the thirteenth and fourteenth centuries (Dante, Boccaccio and Petrarch among the many) constituted a new body of ideas and knowledge that complemented the ancient, and firmly established belief that the present times were different from the past. The twentieth-century sociologist Herbert Blumer (1900–87) explained the emergence of fashion in the Middle Ages as being from the need to be in synchrony with times, the need not to be 'old fashioned'. That his ideas continue to be well used by sociologists of dress indicates how quite unscientific but intuitive understandings of fashion created early last century can be used in this field, something that perturbs those outside the 'discipline'.

Sarah-Grace Heller, in a short and lucid analysis, shows how the birth of fashion is as much a historical as a historians' problem. In 'The Birth of Fashion', she reviews the different positions on the topics by major historians since the early twentieth century. She points out in particular how the French historian Paul Post in the early years of the twentieth century attempted to provide a systematic answer to when, where and how fashion emerged. His analysis, based on visual evidence, pointed to the mid-fourteenth century as the moment in which fashion first appeared, mostly through consideration of the sartorial differentiation of men and women, with the male gender adopting figure-hugging garments that Post thought derived from the padded jerkins that they wore under their armour. Post's hypothesis indicated fashion as a courtly phenomenon affecting mostly males, rather than female taste, something that should be underlined in today's identification of fashion with the female gender. Post developed the ideas of the great French historian of costume Jules Quicherat who observed a radical change in men's attire in the fourteenth century, but underlined how similarly important changes had happened also in the twelfth century, something that modern historians such as Anne Hollander and Jennifer Harris have in turn seen as the 'real' birth of fashion. That the visual evidence of fourteenth-century Franco-Flemish illuminated manuscripts is so alluring and dazzling goes part of the way to understanding the premium placed on the court of Burgundy and its fashions.[1] Heller concludes that the matter of 'when' fashion first appeared remains an elusive issue; she observes that 'The confusion of opinions over dating fashion's birth(s) reveals the vanity of trying to establish a single authoritative moment of incarnation'. While supporting the idea that fashion emerged in a courtly environment, rather than in the streets of dynamic cities as previously suggested by the editors of this *Reader*, or out of the influence of Asian textiles as argued by Giorgio Riello in his 'Fashion, fabrics and the Orient', Heller concludes her piece by suggesting 'multiple births' in which 'fashion seems to stage its own birth again and again . . . Fashion is a phoenix, constantly dying and reincarnating itself'.

'One swallow does not make a summer'. We should not exaggerate the importance of fashion in medieval society. As Negley Harte has warned us, extent and incidence of fashion mean different things. Heller is correct in pointing out that, however we define fashion, it remained a confined phenomenon that did not affect the majority of people, still far too poor and socially excluded to be able to savour any of the pleasure of sartorial consumption. Yet something troublesome was recognised by rulers, legislators and religious leaders who, especially after the mid-twelfth century, started complaining that an increasing number of people dressed 'above their station', that is to say beyond what was acceptable for their social circumstance, and that their behaviour was reproachable as it was against god (as mundane pleasures surpassed the immaterial love for god) and against government, being the material manifestation of insubordination. For us it might appear strange that medieval cities passed a series of laws, called sumptuary laws, that established who could wear what, where and which sort of items of apparel were forbidden. In reality these laws were not just about dress as they regulated also how much one could spend on weddings (including the food to be consumed and the presents exchanged), funerals (for instance how many candles could be burned) and other such ceremonies. Sumptuary laws were therefore not just about what one owned, or what one wore on his or her body, but also about the visibility of rituals. Sumptuary laws did not regulate all types of consumption, but were mostly targeted on what we would call 'sumptuous' or 'conspicuous' (excessive) consumption. What was at stake was not good consumption, the one that allows production to flourish and trade to thrive, but what was considered to be superfluous, or over-indulgent. Here we could expose some of the moralising of our own times, when simplistic understandings of consumption drive a part of the sustainability lobby.

As Alan Hunt shows in a series of quantitative figures included in his essay, between the mid-twelfth and the eighteenth centuries, sumptuary laws were to be found nearly everywhere in Europe, from France to Spain, from England to Germany and in particular in Italy. For Italy alone, there were more than 300 sumptuary laws enacted over the period 1200–1500 (one a year), many of which were for the same city at different times. Hunt warns us against the straighforward idea that sumptuary laws were 'laws against fashion'. Their omnipresence across Europe, but also in countries beyond the old continent such as China and Japan, and also their relative absence or failure in places such as the Netherlands and the North American colonies, make it difficult to determine a direct correlation between sumptuary laws and the occurrence of fashion. Rather, one could observe how they tend to become more common in areas of increasing economic prosperity, first in Southern Europe during the late Middle Ages and the Renaissance and later in France, Germany, and finally England. This might be seen as symptomatic of the conditions that led to the emergence of fashion along with economic growth. Their eventual demise in the seventeenth and eighteenth centuries was the result of a change in the way in which governments controlled production and consumption and an increasing separation between moral and economic discourse.

Moving from the contextual pictures painted by Heller and Hunt, Will Fisher focuses on a specific item of apparel and its importance in the making of the Renaissance man. The codpiece, a phallic-shape garment designed to cover the genitals of Renaissance nobles, can be seen in its various shapes and forms in a vast number of sixteenth- and seventeenth-century portraits (to the great embarassment of prudish museum-goers). Fisher integrates object, historical narrative and literary techniques of analysis to provide a sophisticated reading to show how this rather 'meaningless' accessory was in reality the performativity of male gender. In the same way in which the beard, as Fisher has argued elsewhere, made the man, so the codpiece was not just a symbol of masculinity, but the vestimentary embodiment of being a male. The codpiece belongs to a category of objects that acted as signifiers of gender. Fisher draws on theory and in particular sees clothing as the connecting piece between the body and the discourse that generated what was later 'naturalised' as gender identity.

The codpiece is therefore a 'prosthesis', that is to say a 'multivalent item that slides back and forth between many of the categories that we use to think about subjectivity' (Fisher 2006: 32). A final short piece by Evelyn Welch reminds us that not all objects were necessarily used as deep seats of personal meaning and identity. Using the fan as an example, Welch shows how fashionability too was constructed through the adoption and mundane use of a series of artefacts. Both Fisher and Welch (and later Hayward, Lemire and Verity Wilson) remind us how a serious historical investigation of fashion cannot transcend the materiality of garments. Their integration with archival, printed and representational sources is one of the key methodological tools for the future history of fashion.

Note

1   See P. McNeil (2009) *Fashion Critical Sources*, vol. 1, pp. xxvi–xxix on the historiography of the claims made respectively for Italy and Burgundy by scholars such as Jacob Burckhardt and Johan Huizinga.

Bibliography and further reading

Books and articles

Blanc, O. (2002) 'From Battlefields to Court: The Invention of Fashion in the Fourteenth Century', in D. G. Koslin, and J. E. Snyder (eds), *Encountering Medieval Textiles and Dress: Objects, Texts, Images*, New York and Basingstoke: Palgrave Macmillan, pp. 157–72.

Bridgeman, J. (2000) '"Pagare le pompe": Why Quattrocento Sumptuary Laws Did Not Work', in L. Panizza (ed.), *Women in Italian Renaissance Culture and Society*, Oxford: Legenda, pp. 209–26.

Collier Frick, C. (2002) *Dressing Renaissance Florence: Families, Fortunes, and Fine Clothing*, Baltimore: Johns Hopkins University Press.

de Bellis, D. (2000) 'Attacking Sumptuary Laws in Seicento Venice: Arcangela Tarabotti', in L. Panizza (ed.), *Women in Italian Renaissance Culture and Society*, Oxford: Legenda, pp. 227–41.

Fisher, W. (2001) 'The Renaissance Beard: Masculinity in Early Modern England', *Renaissance Quarterly*, 54, 1, pp. 155–87.

Fisher, W. (2006) *Materializing Gender in Early Modern English Literature and Culture*, Cambridge: Cambridge University Press.

Garber, M. (1991) *Vested Interests: Cross-dressing and Cultural Anxiety*, New York: Routledge, esp. ch. 1.

Harris, J. (1987) 'Thieves, Harlots and Stinking Goats: Fashionable Dress and Aesthetic Attitudes in Romanesque Art', *Costume*, 21, pp. 4–15.

Harte, N. B. (1976) 'State Control of Dress and Social Change in Pre-industrial England', in D. C. Coleman and A. H. John (eds), *Trade, Government and Economy in Pre-industrial England*, London: Weidenfeld and Nicolson, pp. 132–65.

Hughes, M. J. (1975) 'Marco Polo and Medieval Silk', *Textile History*, 6, p. 119–31.

Heller, S.-G. (2002) 'Fashion in French Crusade Literature: Desiring Infidel Textiles', in D. G. Koslin and J. E. Snyder (eds), *Encountering Medieval Textiles and Dress: Objects, Texts, Images*, New York and Basingstoke: Palgrave Macmillan, pp. 103–19.

Heller, S.-G. (2007) *Fashion in Medieval France*, Cambridge: Cambridge University Press.

Hunt, A. (1996) *Governance of the Consuming Passions: A History of Sumptuary Law*, New York: St Martin's Press.

Kovesi Killerby, C. (2002) *Sumptuary Law in Italy, 1200–1500*, Oxford: Oxford University Press.

Kovesi Killerby, C. (1999) '"Heralds of a Well-constructed Mind": Nicolosa Sanuti's Defence of Women and Their Clothes', *Renaissance Studies*, 13, 3, pp. 255–82.

Lemire, B., and Riello, G. (2008) 'East and West: Textiles and Fashion in Eurasia in the Early Modern Period', *Journal of Social History*, 41, 4, pp. 887–916.

Lüttenberg, T. (2005) 'The Cod-piece: A Renaissance Fashion between Sign and Artefact', *Medieval History Journal*, 8, 1, pp. 49–81.

Monnas, L. (2008) *Merchants, Princes and Painters: Silk Fabrics in Italian and Northern Painting 1300–1550*, London: Yale University Press.

Mosher Stuard, S. (2006) *Gilding the Market: Luxury and Fashion in Fourteenth-century Italy*, Philadelphia: University of Pennsylvania Press.

Newton, S. M. (1988) *The Dress of the Venetians 1495–1525*, Aldershot: Scolar Press.

Newton, S. M. (1980) *Fashion in the Age of the Black Prince: A Study of the Years 1340–1365*, Woodbridge: Boydell Press.

Owen Hughes, D. (2002) 'Sumptuary Law and Social Relations in Renaissance Italy', in P. Findlen (ed.), *The Italian Renaissance: The Essential Readings*, Oxford: Blackwell, pp. 124–50.

Paresys, I. (2005) 'The Dressed Body: The Moulding of Identities in Sixteenth-century France', in H. Roodenburg and B. Roeck (eds), *Cultural Exchanges in Early Modern Europe: Vol. 4: Forging European Identities, 1400–1700*, Cambridge: Cambridge University Press, pp. 227–49.

Phillips, K. M. (2007) 'Masculinities and the Medieval English Sumptuary Laws', *Gender and History*, 19, 1, pp. 22–42.

Pipponier, F., and Manne, P. (2000) *Dress in the Middle Ages*, New Haven: Yale University Press.

Ribeiro, A. (2003 [1st edition 1986]) *Dress and Morality*, Oxford: Berg, esp. ch. 3.

Richardson, C. (ed.) (2004) *Clothing Culture, 1350–1650*, Aldershot: Ashgate.

Scott, M. (2007) *Medieval Dress and Fashion*, London: British Library.

Shively, D. H. (1964–5) 'Regulation and Status in Early Tokugawa Japan', *Harvard Journal of Asiatic Studies*, 25, pp. 123–64.

Stallybrass, P., and Jones, A. R. (2001) 'Fetishizing the Glove in Renaissance Europe', *Critical Inquiry*, 28, pp. 114–32.

Staniland, K. (1997) 'Getting There, Got It: Archaeological Textiles and Tailoring in London, 1330–1580', in D. Gaimster and P. Stamper (eds), *The Age of Transition: The Archaeology of English Culture 1400–1600*, Oxford: Oxbow Books, pp. 239–49.

Sutton, A. F. (2005) *The Mercers of London: Trade, Goods and People, 1130–1578*, Aldershot: Ashgate.

Tittler, R. (2006) 'Freemen's Gloves and Civic Authority: The Evidence from Post-Reformation Portraiture', *Costume*, 40, pp. 13–20.

Vincent, J. (1935) *Costume and Conduct in the Laws of Basel, Bern, and Zurich 1370–1800*, Baltimore: Johns Hopkins University Press.

Welch, E. (2005) *Shopping in the Renaissance: Consumer Cultures in Italy 1400–1600*, New Haven: Yale University Press.

Zilfi, M. C. (2004) 'Whose Laws? Gendering the Ottoman Sumptuary Laws', in S. Faroqhi and C. K. Neumann (eds), *Ottoman Costumes: From Textile to Identity*, Istanbul: Eren, pp. 125–42.

Online resources

Elizabethan sumptuary statutes: elizabethan.org/sumptuary/index.html

AHRC Early Modern Dress and Textile Network, at Queen Mary, University of London: www.earlymoderndressandtextiles.ac.uk/

Chapter 1

The birth of fashion

Sarah-Grace Heller

Inde ferunt, totidem qui vivere debeat annos,
corpore de patrio parvum phoenica rinasci . . .
[Then, they say, destined to live for the same number of years,
from the corpse of its father the Phoenix is born, again . . .]
(Ovid, Metamorphoses, XV: 401–2)

CAN WE SPEAK OF A BIRTH OF FASHION? Many scholars have done so, operating under the assumption that, while dress and ornament are universal, fashion is specific to certain times and places. The birth of modern fashion has been discovered in the industrial revolution, in the rise of the department store, and with the advent of cheap print media. Many costume historians have located fashion's birth in the West in the fourteenth- or fifteenth-century courts of Burgundy or Italy, or more generally with the era referred to as 'Early Modernity'. This chapter will survey, and question, some of this dating.

The existence of so many different recorded births of fashion says something important about how fashion functions. Fashion systems constantly reject the immediate past. Every new wave of innovation presents itself, like Ovid's phoenix, as newly born, even while it may be situated along what is really an unbroken (but constantly bending) thread of evolution. Speaking of fashion's birth raises the problems of searching for origins and sources, historically a preoccupation of literary historians, but one critiqued by more recent generations who construe the quest for the origins of medieval texts, themes, and ideas as chimerical.[1] The confusion of opinions over dating fashion's birth(s) reveals the vanity of trying to establish a single authoritative moment of incarnation. Better than trying to fix a single moment for fashion's incarnation is to ask when the cultural value placed on novelty becomes prominent, and when the desire for innovation and the capacity for the production of innovation reach a critical point of becoming a constant and organising presence.

Fashion is born whenever you study it

Partial or limited knowledge of earlier cultures may often contribute to perceiving a birth of fashion. For instance, when the fourth to the fifteenth centuries are popularly viewed as a monolithic cultural wasteland, there is a tendency to assume that there was no fashion in the Middle Ages. This results from perceiving the period uniformly as the Dark Ages: when everyone lived in squalor, wore rough homespun, lived a life of obscure oblivion due to illiteracy, suffered oppression by theological dogma, spurned classical art and literature, and never washed. Such views are not informed by acquaint-ance with the breadth of medieval trade, or the medieval vernacular literary traditions of the twelfth century and onwards that devote attention to splendid attire. Barbara Vinken, for instance, follows Georg Simmel in declaring that fashion is a phenomenon of the modern, emerging in the second half of the nineteenth century as a 'post-feudal phenomenon'.[2] Few medieval or early modern historians would present the feudal and modern periods as contiguous. Moreover, the feudal system was not the only system functioning in the period called, for convenience, the Middle Ages. In short, caution is in order when setting up a culture as the antithesis of a fashion system.

There is a noteworthy tendency to discover a birth of fashion in whatever period a scholar studies. For instance, Grant McCracken argued that the 'first appearance of modern consumption' was a 'dramatic' occurrence, taking place in Elizabeth England.[3] Chandra Mukerji located fashion's birth in the 'hedonistic consumerism' she found in Europe in the fifteenth and sixteenth centuries. She presented medieval dress as stable and stratified up to Philip the Bold's marriage to Margaret of Flanders, which she argued created a large new centre of commerce.[4] This does not account for the centres of commerce thriving much earlier, beginning in the eleventh and twelfth centuries, from the fairs of Champagne to growing cities of northern Europe and the Mediterra-nean. Neil McKendrick, John Brewer, and J. H. Plumb saw the opening event in the birth of fashion as the arrival in England of cheap calico from India in 1690, ushering in a new, intensified tyranny of fashion which characterised the eighteenth century, mani-festing itself in Wedgwood's pottery manufacture, clothing fashions, and the develop-ment of newspaper advertising.[5] Rosalind H. Williams believed seventeenth-century French aristocrats were the first in modern society to experiment with discretionary consumption, but portrayed the Paris expositions of 1889 and 1890 as the first planned environments of mass consumption.[6] Philippe Perrot noticed that a few slow traces of fashion were visible in the twelfth century, although he saw 'extreme inertia' before the Renaissance. Around 1700 he observed courtly competition for 'fashion-setting dominance', but he placed the 'true emergence of modern consumption' in the nine-teenth century.[7] Here are but a few examples. Fashion is often discussed without rigor-ous definition. A comprehensive survey of all the works positing its birth in one form or another would be a monumental task.

Fernand Braudel was a pioneer among historians in the importance he placed on fashion, clothing, commerce, and consumption, recognising that at the heart of the 'great transformation' of the West occurring in the early modern period, there was a 'consumer revolution'. Braudel's attempt to locate a birth of fashion contains a number of contradictions, which are symptomatic of the historiography of fashion's birth. While he held that 'the sovereign authority of fashion was barely enforced in its full rigor before 1700', he recognised the important economic progress made in earlier centuries, although he treats chronology loosely: to support the statement that there was 'no change until the boost in the economy after about 1300', he evoked Orderic Vitalis, without noting that Orderic wrote around 1120–40 concerning changes that took place in the reign of William II of England (1087–1100).[8] Elsewhere, he used European travellers' accounts to substantiate his conclusions that fashion did not exist in India, China, and the Islamic world, a view challenged by scholars of non-European cultures, particularly for the court cultures of China and Japan.[9] Inexact treatments of chronology and foreign cultures in creating 'anti-fashion' scenarios prove to be problematic.

Late medieval Burgundy

The most widely accepted hypothesis dates fashion's emergence to the appearance of a new men's clothing style in mid-fourteenth-century Burgundy. Proposed by Paul Post in the first decade of the twentieth century, based primarily on illuminations and other visual representations, and secondarily on moralist texts, it said that modern male dress first appears in France around 1350 with the revolution produced by the appearance of the short surcoat on young men, in radical opposition to the long robe, which continued to be worn by older and more venerable men. Post examined the evolution in armour, from knee-length coat to the plate armour that appeared in the fourteenth century. Under a coat of mail, men wore long tunics; under plate armour, they wore padded jerkins, closely fitted to the body. Civilian clothes were basically adapted to the forms worn under these different types of armour.[10] As fas as that goes, Post's analysis is methodologically sound and quite useful. His argument that plate armour meant the rediscovery of the long-lost male waistline, however, is open to question. He said that plate armour emerged in a period when the body was being 'differently controlled' because the armour corseted the male form, and that this was 'more in accordance with nature'. There is nothing necessarily natural about corseting, nor does nature provide all men with waistlines. Belts are mentioned for previous periods, if they were not always worn. In any case, his hypothesis that fashion was born with a radical change in the male silhouette, ushering in a period when frequent variation in costume becomes observable in art and artefacts, has made a very significant mark on the historiography of fashion. Although Post himself did not publish a great deal, he was revered as an authority in the 1950s when costume studies were being reorganised in the direction of more rigorous methodology.[11] While his theory was limited to claiming that the modern lines of tailoring for male clothing first appeared between about 1340 and 1370, his conclusions have been generalised to imply more, in part because of the dramatic impact of his use of the term 'the birth of modern fashion' in describing his findings.

The dating of fashion's birth around 1350 based on Post's authority has been adopted by scholars such as Boucher, von Boehn, Flügel, Laver, Brenninkmeyer, Lipovetsky, and others.[12] As the idea has been disseminated, peculiar variations have appeared, especially in popularisations treating the many centuries of the Middle Ages as monolithic. For Michael and Ariane Batterberry, for instance, the world of Eleanor of Aquitaine and the troubadours (twelfth and thirteenth centuries) was amalgamated with the court of Burgundy (flourishing in the fourteenth and fifteenth centuries) as the 'cradle of fashion'.[13]

There are a number of problems with dating Western fashion's birth in the fourteenth century. One lies in the exclusively visual focus, which neglects the signs of the desire for novel consumption in the writing of earlier periods. Moreover, the treatment of fashion based on visual representations and artefacts is obliged to analyse historic costume and textiles with the aid of modern technical vocabulary. Art history and the philology of apparel remain separate because there exist no medieval fashion manuals that juxtapose words and images, an anachronistic expectation motivated by the existence of such fashion manuals today. Romances and other texts supply a vocabulary of colour and style, but it is nearly impossible to know exactly how these terms correspond to extant images. Examining representation is necessary for understanding the mechanics of fashion. Words generally precede visual representation both on the oral level and on the written. It is easiest to make something fashionable by expressing desire or admiration for it aloud. Written expressions require some greater degree of sophistication, but might also reach a wider audience; creating an image expressing fashionability requires greater time, skill, and resources.

Another problem with this dating derives from the uneven chronological distribution of extant sources. There are relatively copious visual records of dress from the fourteenth and fifteenth centuries, when manuscript painting came into vogue.[14] Extant manuscripts from earlier centuries are rarer, and were more rarely illuminated. When they are, figures are often biblical or allegorical, often shown in stylised historical dress rather than in anything that can be reliably considered realistic contemporary dress.[15] Fashions in visual art seem to have evolved at a respectable rate from the appearance of Gothic art at Saint-Denis in 1144 and even before, as Michael Camille suggests when he links the Gothic style and the appearance of modern fashion.[16] It is problematic to conclude, based on comparison of visual evidence, that in thirteenth-century France fashion did not exist and that dress styles did not change, since the development of miniature painting trails the development of vernacular expression and the increases in book production and diffusion. This should hardly be taken to indicate that desire for fashionable consumption was absent. On the contrary, vivid descriptions of dress in literary works probably stimulated the imagination in a way that made a visual translation of the description irrelevant. Whereas romance literature began to develop rapidly in the late eleventh century, miniatures came to be common and well articulated only in the late thirteenth century, once the non-professional reading public had grown sufficiently to create a market for picture books.[17] Illuminated books were objects of fashionable consumption reflecting a complex system already in place, more than vehicles disseminating the desires involved in such a system's initial stages.

Text and image

The modern publishing demand for illustrations to match text has a tendency to promote an inaccurate linking of literary passages from the high Middle Ages and images from the later Middles Ages. While the manuscript tradition clearly shows that many Old French texts of the twelfth and thirteenth centuries were read and copied into later centuries, it should not be ignored that the culture that produced them had its unique set of styles, trends, and social issues.

An example of the problems involved in taking chronological liberties is found in Christopher Breward's *The Culture of Fashion: A New History of Fashionable Dress*. Breward justly critiques traditional costume history for focusing chiefly on physical form, construction, and visual representations of dress, and suggests that attention needs to be turned towards the 'wider implications of what might be termed "the birth of modern fashion" for structures of class and gender within society, or the broader cultural and economic implications of such a "naissance"'.[18] In addressing this 'birth', however he begins by quoting John of Reading's criticism of English court dress around 1340, saying that contemporaries perceived a 'shift in fashionable dress away from the simple, functional style previously popular amongst the European nobility, towards a French-inspired emphasis on contour and cut'.[19] He employs the findings of costume historians who 'have identified the middle years of the fourteenth century as the first period of significant fashion change', but this hypothesis is challenged by his own argument: if the English in 1340 were imitating an already-established French fashion for body-conscious cut, fashion must have existed previously, at least in France. While he carefully considers the problems inherent in extant medieval sources, in discussing England in the 1350s and 1360s he draws heavily on French and Occitan literary and documentary sources from the twelfth and thirteenth centuries.[20] In all, seven of his thirteen primary sources are French. This attests to the importance of the language of fashion in French and Occitan sources from the late twelfth and thirteenth centuries for any discussion of medieval European fashion. His book also demonstrates that to find detailed visual sources for illustrations, one must draw images from the fourteenth century or later. Von Boehn's *Modes and Manners*, like many other books and documentaries, similarly juxtaposes pictures from the fourteenth and fifteenth centuries with texts from the eleventh to the thirteenth. It is a general problem with histories of fashion, which suggests that a shift in methodology is in order. Stella Mary Newton's *Fashion in the Age of the Black Prince: A Study of the Years 1340–1365* stands in contrast as a model of carefully coordinated visual, textual, and documentary sources.[21]

Other scholars have dated fashion's appearance in the fourteenth century based on other kinds of theories and texts. The sociologist Werner Sombart, believing that courts were the basis of the modern capitalist system, saw the birth of the 'modern court', and of consumerism and consumption, in Avignon (as well as in some of the Italian city-states) in the fourteenth century, based on accounts from Petrarch, Pope John XXII, and records of increased prostitution. He believed that women, specifically courtesans, were responsible for the advent of modern consumption and fashion practices. This view displays some of the gender prejudices that construe fashion as an exclusively feminine preoccupation. Sombart discounted the courts of the earlier Middle Ages because their notions of love were not sufficiently 'secularised',[22] a view which suggests that he did not examine French and Occitan vernacular texts, which are often very highly secularised.

Fashion as remodelling the body

A number of scholars have defined fashion as the will to restructure the body through clothing. Anne Hollander's premise in *Seeing through Clothes* is that the silhouette of contemporary fashionable clothing influences the ideal image of the nude body in Western art. The Renaissance nude is upholstered like the stiff brocades and stuffed sleeves of that time; nineteenth-century nudes are corseted without the corset, and so on. She dates fashion's beginnings at 1300 based on the emergence of observable visual fluctuations. The passage is worth quoting:

> The direct reflection of fashion in the image of the nude body can be dem-
> onstrated only during those centuries of Western society when true fashion
> actually existed. If fashion in dress means constant perceptible fluctuations
> of visual design, created out of the combined forms of tailored dress and
> body, then many early civilizations and much of the eastern hemisphere
> have not experienced 'fashion' as we know it. They will have undergone
> changes of surface fashion, such as those in different colors and accessories;
> but basic shapes will have altered only very slowly by a long evolutionary
> process, not dependent on any aesthetic lust for perpetual changes of form.
> The changes in true fashion, ongoing in the West since about 1300, demand
> reshaping of the body-and-clothes unit.[23]

Hollander's dating derives from visual sources, common enough only after about 1300
to observe constant fluctuations in tailoring. Others such as Susan Crane have used
both historical and literary texts to argue that fashion appears in the fourteenth century
with the arrival of 'cutting to fit', due to the arrival of technological advances in cloth
making and body-conscious tailoring, which she interprets as allowing an explosion of
social meaning around clothing.[24]

Similarly defining fashion and its appearance in terms of garment construction, but
refuting the fourteenth-century hypothesis, Jennifer Harris traces the earliest beginnings of Western fashion to the twelfth century. She bases her conclusions on the
increasing complexity of garment construction during the twelfth century and a con-
current acceleration of change in styles of dress and hairdressing:

> Although twelfth-century experiments in garment cutting and construc-
> tion involved manipulating fabric by temporary lacing or stitching instead
> of permanent seams or buttons, they nonetheless called for a great deal
> of ingenuity on the part of the tailor and provided the impetus which led,
> over the next century or so, to cutting-fit and functional buttons. They also
> reflect a sense of change and progress inherent in society at large.[25]

While there is less detailed and realistic visual evidence to support the existence of constant change for the twelfth century than for the fourteenth century, volume and length
were clearly key features of elite dress in this period. Moreover Harris touches on the
importance of psychology and sociology to the arrival of a particular type of production
technology. I would argue that dating fashion's advent to the appearance of any given
type of technology neglects the societal forces that brought about such a development.

The fourteenth-century trend for remodelling the body through cut, corsetry,
décolletage, and padding has been studied as a radical transformation by Odile Blanc.
While her dating corresponds to Post's, like Newton she does not claim any sort of
birth of fashion for this period, although she does discuss the 'invention' of the fashionable body.[26] Blanc is careful to limit inquiry to the range of the information that can be
gleaned from the attitudes and relations between figures in the miniatures of aristocrats'
luxury manuscripts, namely the ways contemporaries conceived their garments and the
relationship they had with the body. Crane is similarly more concerned with how clothing is used to represent the self in this period than with the larger mechanisms of fashion.

The use of tailoring to remodel the body is a remarkable phenomenon, and it is undeniable that 'fashion' can connote the parade of changes in garment silhouette. Tailoring is more a symptom of the type of artifice typical of a fashion system's complex theatricality, however, as fashionable consumption encompasses far more than clothing. The desire to attract attention through altering the body's natural contours should be understood as one desire among many.

Appearance of artistic, literary, and commercial change

While nineteenth-century archivist Jules Quicherat referred to a 'radical change' in men's dress in the fourteenth century, this was not the first such change he had remarked.[27] The first occurred in the period 1090 to 1190, which he called the 'Grand Siècle' of the Middle Ages. By associating the twelfth century with the 'Grand Age' of Louis XIV and the rise of the absolute monarchy, he implied that it was an era when many of the foundations for later times were laid, when many precedents were set, when new modes of living came into force which would set the standard for later times. Of all the periods he discussed, he viewed the twelfth century as a time of new births, particularly in the domains of literature, art, and the industries that were the precursors of those that would differentiate modern times from antiquity.[28] Desire for furs attained a fever pitch, resulting in the formation of more corporations than for most other trades. The growth in silk consumption necessitated the extension of trade. New colours and dyestuffs made variety of colour the law of dress, with any artifice for introducing it anywhere in the costume considered acceptable. Quicherat refers to the twelfth century as 'dedicated to innovations in every matter', as fashion regulated everything from the points on shoes that went in and out of style to men's facial hair trends, calling it the strongest force in all of society.[29]

Eleventh-century Normandy

For a number of costume historians, the first significant signs of Western fashion occur in the late eleventh century, notably as reported by the Anglo-Norman cleric Orderic Vitalis in his *Ecclesiastical History*. A radical change in men's dress took place towards the year 1100, a movement from the short robes of the previous six centuries to long tunics.[30] Art historian Jennifer Harris correspondingly concluded that during the period from the Norman invasion of England (1066) to the Third Crusade to the Holy Land (1189–92), clothing in Western Europe underwent a profound transformation, first among the aristocracy but ultimately extending to the dress of the merchant and labouring classes.[31]

Orderic Vitalis is often mentioned but rarely properly examined. It is worth looking at some of the cultural wording describing the changes he had seen in his day. He mentions the change in manners twice, both with regards to the young men surrounding William II of England (1087–1100). These men wore long pointed shoes with stuffed 'pulley toes', and grew long and luxurious locks like women, and loved to deck themselves in long, over-tight shirts and tunics.[32]

Moreover, they used curling irons, covered their locks with caps, and carefully groomed 'lustful' beards instead of being shaggy, like their forefathers. Further on, Orderic speaks more generally of the era:

> At that time great evils appeared and increased rapidly all over the world.
> Men of knightly rank abandoned the customs of their fathers in the style of
> dress and cut of hair; in a little while townsmen and peasants and all the
> lower ranks followed their example.[33]

These passages are striking for the number of remarks that match the criteria for the
existence of fashion. The chronicler shows anxiety that the reverence for the past was
being overturned in favour of a new style. The new style is not isolated, but spreads
to all social groups, bringing male appearance to a new level of social equilibrium
rather than sharply demarcating one class or another. His feelings that these conditions
appeared and then 'increased rapidly all over the world' suggest that this was not an isolated change in style but a new attitude he sensed emerging to alter the whole demeanour of his society. The presence of his criticism shows an element of fashion itself.

   While a single author's criticism is not enough evidence to prove that these conditions had become constant and institutionalised, Henri Platelle has studied two
waves of vestimentary scandal concerning men from the Loire to the Rhine, and in
Norman England.[34] In chronicles and church councils from the first part of the century, first Raoul Glaber (1002), then Guillaume de Volpiano (1017), and Siegfried de
Gorze (1043) anathematise the unbridled luxury of clothing and arms, immodest short
tunics, and indecent haircuts and shaved faces which first arrived from Aquitaine, and
were quickly adopted by French and Burgundian knights. Orderic Vitalis can be placed
among a second group of clerics at the end of the eleventh century who were shocked
by the long trailing robes, short beards, and curled hair of the new generations. Platelle analyses these scandals in term of violation of codes of appearance understood by
the clerics to correspond to God-given social orders. When knights could be confused
with priests and penitents, or men with women, this excited insecurity. This interpretation coincides to some degree with Vinken's contention that before 'modern fashion',
there were only dress codes intended to convey class information at a glance, which
were constantly violated and so required the invention of new codes. Ironically, given
that Vinken considers fashion 'post-feudal', the repeated complaints of male effeminacy
coincide with her rather eccentric definition of fashion as transvestism, which is to say a
phenomenon manipulating gender codes more than class codes.[35]

   The difficulty with identifying fashion in the eleventh century is the relative pau-
city of surviving evidence. For every subsequent century the extant traces multiply,
often exponentially. However, with the arrival of the twelfth century, there is enough
information coming from multiple sources to begin to argue more conclusively for fashion's continuous, systematic presence.[36]

   The first widespread trend Mane and Piponnier label 'fashion' was the new
eleventh-century configuration in men's clothing. The first chronological 'fashions' they
speak of are those described at Charlemagne's court, but they emphasise that the chronicler's description of rich styles are 'probably simply poetic license', that miniatures
from the period are highly stylised, and that it was only queens who adorned themselves
with ribbons, fancy girdles, and pointed shoes.[37] The appearance of the long *bliaut* and
chainse[38] in the eleventh century contrasts with Carolingian styles in that they eventually spread beyond the court to become common dress for all men. According to the
second criterion of a fashion system, the trends of the Carolingian courts could not be
described as the result of a fashion system because they did not produce constant cycles

of change-seeking, but were eclipsed for a few centuries. Since the eleventh-century style spread and became generalised, it better meets certain criteria for fashion.

Emergence of a cyclical economy

Economic historians rarely discuss the nature of fashion, but some have had recourse to the term to describe certain changes in the European economy in the high Middle Ages. It is generally agreed that a period of urban growth began in the late eleventh and twelfth centuries, following agricultural expansion and increased production that permitted the nourishment of a larger population. Over the course of the 'long thirteenth century' (for Peter Spufford this would comprehend the years 1160–1330, for Gérard Sivéry 1180–1315, corresponding roughly to Quicherat's 'période brillante du Moyen Age', 1190–1340) the cloth trade was the key factor leading to urban growth, increased long-distance commerce, and craft specialisation, producing a new economic system.[39] David Abulafia dates the birth of the European fashion industry to the late twelfth century, when not only do Western merchants begin importing more Eastern products such as dyes, alum, luxury cloth and spices, but they manage to create demand at Muslim princely courts for Western products such as woollens, silver, arms and timber.[40] Sivéry observes that in certain areas of Europe – certainly not everywhere – there was a movement from a traditional economy, where price and crisis cycles depend on catastrophic factors such as weather and war, to a cyclical economy, in which prices fluctuate according to supply and demand.[41] Jacques Heers observes that to make a profit, the Genoese merchants working in the French markets (whose records are among the earliest such extant) had to become adept at judging tastes and anticipating desires: they calculatingly limited novel types of fabric or risked a drop in prices when a flooded market rendered a colour or texture artificially ordinary.[42] Sivéry similarly asks whether records indicating price fluctuations according to city of origins and colour should be attributed to improvements in dye technology. That was surely true to some degree, but cannot be the only explanation: both authors observe that fashion and demand for novelty must have had a role in the equation.[43] From an economic point of view, inexplicable fluctuations in prices and periods of non-catastrophic cyclical booms and depression signal fashion's presence in a culture. It is the only system that can explain such otherwise irrational phenomena.

Multiple births

Many scholars, some probably inadvertently, assign multiple births to fashion. Von Boehn dated fashion's birth variously to the crusades, to the emergence of town life, and also at around 1350, applauding Post's work.[44] Anne Hollander gave the approximate date of 1300 at one point (as quoted above), but elsewhere dated the change earlier, saying, 'Sometime in the thirteenth century, the aesthetic impulse toward significant distortion and creative tailoring . . . arose in European dress and established what has become the modern concept of fashion'.[45] While Gilles Lipovetsky works from the assumption that fashion has a beginning which can located in history, he also wavered in his dating, at times accepting the Post hypothesis, elsewhere acknowledging that for a radical change to occur, a fashion-orientated network of already highly specialised crafts and artisans had to be in place, such as clearly existed from at least the thirteenth century, when innovations in weaving, dyeing, garment construction, commerce, and banking permitted increases in bourgeois fortunes which led them to imitate the nobles. When he said that the emergence of fashion is inseparable from the Cultural Revolution and the emergence of courtly values in the twelfth century, he also suggested that fashion was already a growing system before the 'great change' of 1350.[46]

What becomes clear from the disagreements over dating is that fashionability is in the eye of the beholder. An observer from outside the stylish culture of this period might look at long, ample garments and think that they look clerical, or biblical, just as a young person might look at a photograph from their parents' teenage years and not be able to distinguish the fashionable from the unfashionable people. They might see nothing obscene enough to have aroused the ire of contemporary moralists. The specialist who knows the dress of 1350 well might, like contemporaries in 1350, scorn previous dress as lacking fashion; but this would only serve to demonstrate the principle of rejection of the past that is fundamental to the fashion-seeking eye. The 'absent beholder' creates problems as well. Neglecting close examination of the evidence of previous periods can lead to the assumption that fashion was absent, following that other cliché, 'out of sight, out of mind'. The medieval periods deserve to be recognised more often than they are as part of the continuum of developments forming modern culture.

Ultimately, this book does not hope to solve the problem of whether fashion has an identifiable birth or even the problem of whether fashion is exclusively Western. There is evidence that there are cultures and micro-cultures where fashion does not exist as a major and defining social force, although some desire for social competition and self-expression in personal display may be present in a more marginal or marginalised form.[47] Balzac said that there could be no 'élégance' in the busy life of the type of working person he called 'l'homme-instrument', because there is no freedom of time or thought to study the individual expression that is fashion.[48] There may be some truth in this, although a rigorous measurable definition of 'la vie occupée' would prove no doubt elusive, including some members of many different cultures and excluding others.

Rather than prove that fashion was born in a particular time and place, this book hopes to show that it existed in developing stages in thirteenth-century France. It appears that it began sufficiently affecting the cultures in this area sometime in the eleventh century that significant traces of it can be found. Conception, birth? This study cannot locate a single, indisputably clear moment for either one. Nor can it say how long a gestation period there may have been. Should fashion be understood anthropomorphically? Should we understand that it had an infancy, an age when it was not capable of independent action? The conclusion to which we must return is that fashion seems to stage its own birth again and again, because a fundamental characteristic of fashion is declaring the past invalid in favour of a new, improved present. Fashion is a phoenix, constantly dying and reincarnating itself. It annihilates everything immediately previous as completely devoid of relevance and appeal, yet its general forms remain recognisable. The beholder must be wary not to fall prey to this trick of denying the past in favour of a present introducing itself with great passion as the only imaginable reality. A fashion system was initiated in some of the growing towns and courts of France in at least the twelfth century, so that, by the thirteenth century, full-blown fashionable values were in evidence. Fashion would stage many more would-be births in the centuries that followed, always gaining momentum with new technologies and greater populations affected. The radical change in male dress that was staged by the young men of the wealthy fourteenth-century Burgundian court could only have happened because a fashion system was already in place, just as with the adoption of the new poetry. From *pourpoint* to poetic form, fashionable objects change, always multiplying, always seeming newly invented; but the desire to consume them and invent them has been steadily present in the West for at least eight centuries.

Notes

1 Zumthor, *Essai de poétique médiévale*, p. 21, criticises medieval studies as excessively swollen with 'the literature of origins'; the very title of Dragonetti's *Le mirage des sources: l'art du faux dans le roman medieval* suggests that origins are chimerical; David Hult likewise questions the possibility of finding them in 'Vers la société de l'écriture: le *Roman de la Rose*', p. 158.

2 Vinken, 'Transvesty – Travesty', p. 33. Rimmel, 'Die Mode'.

3 McCracken, *Culture and Consumption*.

4 Mukerji, *From Graven Images*, pp. 170–80.

5 McKendrick, Brewer and Plumb, *The Birth of a Consumer Society*.

6 Williams, *Dream Worlds*, p. 57.

7 Perrot, *Les Dessus et les dessous de la bourgeoisie*, pp. 31–46.

8 Braudel, *Capitalism*, p. 231.

9 Adshead, *Material Culture in Europe and China*; Newton, 'Couture and Society'; Steele and Major, *China Chic*.

10 Post, 'Die französisch-niederländische Männertracht'; *idem*, 'La naissance du costume masculin moderne'.

11 See the proceedings of the 1er Congrès international d'histoire du costume (Venice, 31 August–7 September 1952), Introduction to Post's contribution: 'Il y a 40 ans l'auteur, par sa thèse de doctorat, a élevé l'étude du costume au niveau de la recherche sérieuse dans le domaine des arts', p. 28.

12 Boucher, *20,000 Years of Fashion*, p. 192; Brenninkmeyer, *The Sociology of Fashion*, pp. 126–9; Flügel, *The Psychology of Clothes*, p. 160; Boehn, *Modes and Manners*, p. 215; Laver, *Costume and Fashion*, p. 62. Hunt refers to it without clearly adopting it, *Governance of the Consuming Passions*, pp. 44, 157. Revisiting the issue, Piponnier, 'Une révolution dans le costume masculin au XIVe siècle'.

13 'Together with the courts of Burgundy, Provence and Languedoc, this sunny realm [Aquitaine] would become the cradle of fashion': Batterberry and Batterberry, *Fashion*, p. 86. Certain elements of medieval history are handled clumsily in this account. Another example is the reference to outrageous fashions seen under 'Philip the Fair of Burgundy (1285–1314)', on p. 87, confusing the king of France (reigned 1285–1314) and Philippe le Beau of the Low Countries (reigned 1482–1506), or possibly Philippe le Bon, Duke of Burgudy (1419–67).

14 This was a fashion imported to France from England in the mid-thirteenth century, according to Bourin-Derruau, *Temps d'équilibres, temps de ruptures*, p. 36.

15 Mane and Piponnier, *Dress in the Middle Ages*, pp. 5–6. Georges Duby mentions the astonishment of the schoolmaster at Angers at the 'idols' he saw on a trip to early eleventh-century Aquitaine, demonstrating contemporary discomfort at figurative art, *Liber miraculorum sancte Fidis*, 1.13, quoted in Duby and Mandrou, *Histoire de la civilisation française*, p. 132.

16 'Gothic was the first historical style totally to permeate the world of things. Not just found in architecture, its pointed arches and tracery patterns appeared in everything from spoons to shoes. It is also the first truly international style, spreading throughout Europe. Gothic artists were in this sense the first to create what we would call today "fashion"'. Camille, *Gothic Art: Glorious Visions*, pp. 12–14.

17 Saenger, 'Lire aux derniers siècles du Moyen Age', p. 165.

18 Breward, *The Culture of Fashion*, p. 9

19 Breward, *The Culture of Fashion*, p. 8

20 Including the *Romance of the Rose* (c. 1225–30), troubadour Marcabru (mid-twelfth century), Huon de Bourdeaux (second half of the thirteenth century), and Étienne Boileau's *Livre des Mestiers* (c. 1268). Breward, *The Culture of Fashion*, pp. 9–13, 22–34.

21 Newton, *Fashion in the Age of the Black Prince*.

22 Sombart, *Luxury and Capiatalism*, pp. 2, 43, 64–6.

23 Hollander, *Seeing through Clothes*, p. 90.

24 Crane, *The Performance of the Self*, p. 13.

25 Harris, 'Estroit vestu et menu cosu', p. 99. See also *idem*, 'Thieves, Harlots and Stinking Goats', and *idem*, *Textiles, 5,000 Years*.

26 Blanc, *Parades et parures*, pp. 26–32, 73, 96.

27 As noted in Piponnier, 'Une révolution dans le costume masculin au XIVe siècle', pp. 225–6.

28 Quicherat, *Histoire du costume en France*, pp. 151. See also Evans, *Dress in Medieval France*, p. 4.

29 Quicherat, *Histoire du costume en France*, pp. 152–67.

30 Quicherat, *Histoire du costume en France*, p. 146.

31 Harris, 'Estroit vestu et menu cosu', p. 89.

32 'longos crines ueluti mulieres nutriebant, et summopere comebant, prolixisque nimiumque strictis camisiis indui tunicisque gaudebant'. Chidnall, *The Ecclesiastical History of Orderic Vitalis*, book VIII, ch. 10: vol. 4, pp. 186–9.

33 'Eo tempore multa malicia in terris orta est, et uehementer augmentata est. Militares uiri mores paternos in uestitu et capillorum tonsura derelinquerunt, quos Paulo post burgenses et rustici et pene totum uulgus imitati sunt.' Chidnall, *The Ecclesiastical History of Orderic Vitalis*, book VIII, ch. 22: vol. 4, pp. 268–9.

34 Platelle, 'Le problème du scandale', pp. 1071–96.

35 Vinken, 'Transvesty – Travesty'.

36 The Batterberrys conclude that fashion was on the verge of beginning in the twelfth century based on their readings of Saint Bernard's writings, 'Fashion in the modern sense of continuously revised modes of dress . . . was suddenly gathering steam. Little more pressure would be needed to set the mechanism of changing styles into motion'. This claim on its own is weak, drawing almost exclusively on the perspective of a single person (and an ardent preacher and moralist at that), but worth retaining as a complement to other evidence, Batterberry and Batterberry, *Fashion: The Mirror of History*, p. 85.

37 Mane and Piponnier, *Dress in the Middle Ages*, p. 78.

38 A *bliaut* is a fitted outer tunic and a *chainse* a chemise worn under the *bliaut*.

39 Quicherat, *Histoire du costume en France*, p. 178; Sivéry, *L'économie du Royaume de France*, p. 13; Peter Spufford, 'Le rôle de la monnaie dans la révolution commerciale du XIIIe siècle', pp. 355–95; idem, *Power and Profit*, p. 60.

40 David Abulafia, 'The Role of Trade in Muslim–Christian Contact during the Middle Ages', pp. 8–10.

41 Sivéry, *L'économie du Royaume de France*, pp. 52–4, 101.

42 Jacques Heers, 'La mode et les marchés des draps de laine', p. 1094.

43 Sivéry, *L'économie du Royaume de France*, p. 157.

44 Boehn, *Modes and Manners*, vol. 1, pp. 166–257, esp. 186–7. Also positing city life as essential to fashion, Wilson, *Adorned in Dreams*, pp. 134–54.

45 Hollander, *Seeing through Clothes*, p. 17.

46 Lipovetsky, *L'empire de l'éphémère*, pp. 25, 32–3, 45, 59, 72, 76.

47 For example the Amish or the Mennonites, who have historically scrupulously and consciously avoided fashion, or impoverished subcultures of nations where consumption is not made an option due to lack of resources, leisure time and/or social interaction. With the invention of telecommunications, few places in the world are isolated enough to be completely removed from the influence of what has become almost a global fashion system.

48 Balzac, 'Traité de le vie élégante', pp. 211–57.

Bibliography

Abulafia, David, 'The Role of Trade in Muslim–Christian Contact during the Middle Ages', in *The Arab Influence in Medieval Europe*, ed. Dionisius A. Agius and Richard Hitchcock (Reading: Ithaca Press, 1994), pp. 1–24.

Adshead, Samuel, *Material Culture in Europe and China, 1400–1800: The Rise of Consumerism* (New York: St Martin's Press, 1997).

Balzac, Honoré de, 'Traité de le vie élégante', in *La Comédie Humaine*, vol. 12 (Paris: Bibliothèque de la Pléiade, 1981), pp. 211–57.

Batterberry, Michael, and Ariane Batterberry, *Fashion: The Mirror of History*, 2nd edition (New York: Greenwich House, 1982).

Blanc, Odile, *Parades et parures: l'invention du corps de mode à la fin du Moyen Age* (Paris: NRF, 1997).

Boehn, Max von, *Modes and Manners*, trans. Joan Joshua, vol. 1: *From the Decline of the Ancient World to the Renaissance* (Philadelphia: J. B. Lippincott, 1932).

Boucher, François, *20,000 Years of Fashion: The History of Costume and Personal Adornment*, rev. English edition (New York: Abrams, 1987).

Bourin-Derruau, Monique, *Temps d'équilibres, temps de ruptures: XIIIe siècle, Nouvelle histoire de la France médiévale* (Paris: Seuil, 1990).

Braudel, Fernand, *Capitalism and Material Life, 1400–1800*, trans. Mirian Kochan (London: Weidenfeld and Nicolson, 1973).

Brenninkmeyer, Ingrid, *The Sociology of Fashion* (Paris and Cologne: Librarie du Recueil Sirey and Westdeutscher Verlag, 1963).

Breward, Christopher, *The Culture of Fashion: A New History of Fashionable Dress* (Manchester: Manchester University Press, 1995).

Camille, Michael, *Gothic Art: Glorious Visions* (New York: Abrams, 1996).

Chidnall, Marjorie, ed., *The Ecclesiastical History of Orderic Vitalis*, 6 vols (Oxford: Clarendon Press, 1969–80).

Crane, Susan, *The Performance of the Self: Ritual, Clothing, and Identity during the Hundred Years War* (Philadelphia: University of Pennsylvania Press, 2002).

Dragonetti, Roger, *Le mirage des sources: l'art du faux dans le roman médiéval* (Paris: Seuil, 1987).

Duby, Georges, and Robert Mandrou, *Histoire de la civilisation française*, vol. 1: *Moyen Age–XVIe siècle*, 11th edition (Paris: Armand Colin, 1998).

Evans, Joan, *Dress in Medieval France* (Oxford: Clarendon Press, 1952).

Flügel, John-Carl, *The Psychology of Clothes* (London: Hogarth, 1930).

Harris, Jennifer, 'Thieves, Harlots and Stinking Goats: Fashionable Dress and Aesthetic Attitudes in Romanesque Art', *Costume*, 21 (1987), pp. 4–15.

Harris, Jennifer, ed., *Textiles, 5,000 Years: An International History and Illustrated Survey* (New York: Abrams, 1993).

Harris, Jennifer, '"Estroit vestu et menu cosu": Evidence for the Construction of Twelfth-Century Dress', in *Medieval Art: Recent Perspectives. A Memorial Tribute to C. R. Dodwell* (Manchester: Manchester University Press, 1998), pp. 89–113.

Heers, Jacques, 'La mode et les marchés des draps de laine: Gênes et la montagne à la fin du Moyen Âge', *Annales: Économies, Sociétés, Civilisations*, 26, 5 (1971), pp. 1093–117.

Hollander, Anne, *Seeing through Clothes* (New York: Viking, 1978).

Hult, David, 'Vers la société de l'écriture: le *Roman de la Rose*', *Poétique*, 50 (1982), pp. 155–72.

Hunt, Alan, *Governance of the Consuming Passions: A History of Sumptuary Law* (New York: St Martin's Press, 1996).

Laver, James, *Costume and Fashion: A Concise History*, 2nd edition (London: Thames & Hudson, 1995).

Lipovetsky, Gilles, *L'empire de l'éphémère* (Paris: Gallimard, 1987).

McCracken, Grant, *Culture and Consumption: New Approaches to the Symbolic Character of Consumer Goods and Activities* (Bloomington: Indiana University Press, 1988).

McKendrick, Neil, John Brewer, and J. H. Plumb, *The Birth of a Consumer Society: The Commercialization of Eighteenth-Century England* (Bloomington: Indiana University Press, 1982).

Mane, Perrine, and Françoise Piponnier, *Dress in the Middle Ages*, trans. Caroline Beamish (New Haven, CT: Yale University Press, 1997).

Mukerji, Chandra, *From Graven Images: Patterns of Modern Materialism* (New York: Columbia University Press, 1983).

Newton, Stella Mary, 'Couture and Society', *Times Literary Supplement* (1976).

Newton, Stella Mary, *Fashion in the Age of the Black Prince: A Study of the Years 1340–1365* (Woodbridge: Boydell, 1980).

Perrot, Philippe, *Les Dessus et les dessous de la bourgeoisie* (Paris: Arthème Fayard, 1981).

Piponnier, Françoise, 'Une révolution dans le costume masculin au XIVe siècle', in *Le Vêtement: histoire, archéologie et symbolique vestimentaires au Moyen Age*, ed. Michel Pastoreau (Paris: Léopard d'or, 1989), pp. 225–41.

Platelle, Hanri, 'Le problème du scandale: les nouvelles modes masculines aux XIe et XIIe siècles', *Revue Belge de philologie et d'histoire*, 53, 4 (1975), pp. 1071–96.

Post, Paul, 'Die französisch-niederländische Männertracht einschliesslich der Ritterrüstung im Zeitalter der Spätgotik, 1350–1475. Ein Rekonstrucktionsversuch auf Gründ der zeitgenössichen Darstellungen' (Halle a. d. Saale, dissertation, 1910).

Post, Paul, 'La naissance du costume masculin moderne au XIVe siècle', in *Actes du 1er Congrès International d'histoire du costume, Venise, 31 août–7 septembre, 1952* (Venice, 1952), pp. 28–41.

Quicherat, Jules, *Histoire du costume en France depuis les temps les plus reculés jusqu'à la fin du XVIIIe siècle* (Paris: Hachette, 1877).

Saenger, Paul, 'Lire aux derniers siècles du Moyen Age', in *Histoire de la lecture dans le monde occidental*, ed. Guglielmo Cavallo and Roger Chartier (Paris: Seuil, 1997).

Simmel, Georg, 'Die Mode', in *Philosophische Kultur: Über das Abenteuer; die Geschlechter un die Krise der Moderne. Gesammelte Essai* (Leipzig: A. Kroner, 1919), pp. 38–63.

Sivéry, Gérard, *L'économie du Royaume de France au siècle de Saint Louis (vers 1180–vers 1315)* (Lille: Presses Universitaires de Lille, 1984).

Sombart, Werner, *Luxury and Capitalism*, trans. W. R. Dittmar (Ann Arbor: University of Michigan Press, 1967).

Spufford, Peter, 'Le rôle de la monnaie dans la révolution commerciale du XIIIe siècle', in *Études d'histoire monétaire*, ed. John Day (Lille: Presses Universitaires de Lille, 1984), pp. 355–95.

Spufford, Peter, *Power and Profit: The Merchant in Medieval Europe* (New York: Thames & Hudson, 1998).

Steele, Valerie, and John S. Major, *China Chic: East Meets West* (New Haven: Yale University Press, 1999).

Vinken, Barbara, 'Transvesty – Travesty: Fashion and Gender', *Fashion Theory*, 3, 1 (1999), pp. 33–49.

Williams, Rosalind H. *Dream Worlds: Mass Consumption in Late Nineteenth Century France* (Berkeley: University of California Press, 1982).

Wilson, Elizabeth, *Adorned in Dreams: Fashion and Modernity* (London: Virago, 1985).

Zumthor, Paul, *Essai de poétique médiévale* (Paris: Seuil, 1972).

Fashion, fabrics and the Orient

Giorgio Riello

Snapshot 2.1 Replica of medieval silk damask produced by the Manifattura bevilacqua, Venice, Italy, using eighteenth-century hand-looms. This textile is now used for furnishing, but before 1600 large motifs were used both for dress and furnishing.

Today we think of fashion in terms of change, multifarious alteration of shapes and colours coupled with shifting consumer behaviours and corporate communication strategies. The world of fashion until the age of industrialisation and commercial capitalism (that occurred in the nineteenth century) was dominated instead by textiles. The type of fabric that one wore conveyed with a certain degree of immediacy the social status of its wearer. In the same way in which society was hierarchical, with princes, nobles and rulers at its top, followed by professionals, merchants, shopkeepers, artisans, peasants and, at the very bottom, vagrants; so textiles were available in a variety that ranged from the expensive silk damasks and velvets for the very rich, to the more sturdy woollens of the citizens, to the rough linens made of flax and, more often, hemp. The medieval and early modern society was one in which fashion was a function of luxury, a point underlined by Werner Sombart, and wealth and splendour were communicated mostly through the use of expensive, sometimes flashy textiles.

The analysis of paintings from the period 1300–1600 shows how the upper ranks of society made use of a variety of silks. These were not just extremely expensive but often imported from the Middle East or from as far as China. The Venetian Marco Polo ventured in the late thirteenth century through what is appropriately called the Silk Road all the way to China following the trade routes that brought silks to Europe. Crusaders and Mediterranean merchants from the twelfth century brought back to Europe not just Middle Eastern silks, but also a keen taste for such commodities that quickly spread at court and in urban society.

Some dress historians have argued that this passion for Asian silks should be considered as one of the major stimuli in the birth of fashion in medieval Europe. This hypothesis might be far fetched, but it points out how silks reformed 'the look' of the European elites and sumptuary laws show how their appeal allured also the wider strata of society. The discovery of how to breed silkworms in fourteenth-century Italy and the spread of silk weaving especially in southern Europe contributed to the success of silks and to a further increase of patterns, shades and shine.

Silks might have indeed contributed a great deal to the development and spread of fashionability in medieval Europe, but their impact must have been overall rather modest: they remained expensive and the majority of the population could afford only the occasional trimming or accessory rather than one of the splendid silk gowns or silk embroidered men's coats to be seen in museums of costume. Cottons were however different. As for silks, cotton textiles, especially those brightly printed and painted, originated in Asia, in particular in India. Until 1500 few cotton textiles were available to European consumers, but in the course of the following two centuries chintzes, calicoes and other flowered cottons came to add colour, decoration and one can dare to say, fashion, to European dress.

They were imported in large quantities by the so-called European East India companies, trading corporations that were given a monopoly from their respective states to trade with Asia. The cottons that they brought back to Europe were cheap enough to be within the reach of most consumers and were beautiful enough to resemble the intricate woven patterns of silks. Gone were the times in which only the rich could aspire to show colour and complex floral decorations on their silken garments; cottons allowed also the lady's maid or the artisan's apprentice to show off bodices, gowns and waistcoats with an enormous range of patterns, motifs and colours. As for silks, cotton textiles too came to be produced in Europe from the end of the seventeenth century, eventually leading to the cotton revolution that is often called 'the Industrial Revolution'.

Bibliography and further reading

Lemire, B. (1991) *Fashion's Favourite: The Cotton Trade and the Consumer in Britain, 1660–1800*, Oxford: Oxford University Press.

Lemire, B., and Riello, G. (2008) 'East and West: Textiles and Fashion in Eurasia in the Early Modern Period', *Journal of Social History*, 41, 3, pp. 887–916.

Molà, L. (2000) *The Silk Industry of Renaissance Venice*, Baltimore: Johns Hopkins University Press.

Riello, G., and Parthasarathi, P. (eds) (2009) *The Spinning World: A Global History of Cotton Textiles, 1200–1850*, Oxford: Oxford University Press.

Chapter 2

A short history of sumptuary laws

Alan Hunt

Sumptuary laws under feudalism

SUMPTUARY LAWS HAVE GENERALLY BEEN VIEWED as attempts to consolidate and reinforce the formalised hierarchy of social relations characteristic of feudal societies. The evidence is contradictory. I will assume for present purposes that the generic term feudalism can be employed to describe both European and the two Asian feudalisms of China and Japan.[1] During the supremacy of European feudalism, while sumptuary laws were periodically enacted, their presence was occasional and episodic. It is only with the decline of feudalism that the emergence of the 'bastard feudalism' that succeeds the monetisation of land rents, and the long rise of merchant capitalism, gives rise to what may be regarded as the high period of sumptuary law (Bellamy 1989). [. . .].

In both China and Japan it was only with the subordination of localised militaristic forms of feudalism by centralised and bureaucratised systems of governments associated with formalised social hierarchies that sumptuary law came to the fore. In schematic terms in China it was with the consolidation of the mandarin bureaucracies over local warlordism from the Wei dynasty of AD 220–250 that a strictly defined system of personal status was translated into the legal form of sumptuary codes that were firmly in place by the T'ang period, AD 618–906. While the details underwent bewildering changes, the basic mechanism whereby custom, law, religion and politics operated to provide the meticulous definition of all aspects of the life-styles of the fundamental social categories persisted down to the very brink of the struggles around modernisation. In Japan it was under the centralised Tokugawa system between 1600 and 1868 that sumptuary law found its highest level of development. In both the cases of China and Japan, with the passage of time the key target of sumptuary regulation became the merchant classes whose irresistible rise was eating away at the very possibility of a stable system of social closure required by the bureaucratic regimes.

In China the system of sumptuary laws was an expression of the politico-ideological systematisation of norms of personal status (Ch'ü 1961). The *wei payi* system, from its formal articulation during the Wei period, distinguished between *jian min* (good people) who were worthy of consideration and the great majority *liang min* (mean people) who were excluded; this basic conceptualisation was to remain intact through all the subsequent dynasties. In its major institutionalisation in the T'ang, eight primary groups amongst the privileged, stretching from the Emperor's household to the mandarin officials, were identified and made subject to hierarchically defined regulation of life-styles. These regulations were both extensive and intensive. In addition to the extensive coverage of virtually every aspect of life-style, these regulations were distinguished from any others encountered in this study in that they also included rules imposing class exogamy. Some idea of the tyranny of detail is exemplified in two features shared by feudal sumptuary laws in China and in Europe concerning the status attached to falconry. Chinese law specified the species of raptors allowed to each social category. Lower officials and commoners were prohibited from taming 'grey falcons' (probably peregrine falcons), but were allowed to tame 'eagles'; in Europe, England and France both had a similar hierarchy of birds of prey although it was never fully encapsulated in legislation. Similarly furs in both Asia and Europe were also subject to hierarchical ordering. An eleventh-century Chinese edict allowed only nobles to wear the fine black sables and ermine, while commoners were permitted only ordinary sable, sheep and moleskins (Wittfogel and Chia-shêng 1949); late medieval English laws employed a similar hierarchical ordering of furs.

While the high period of sumptuary law in Japan was in the Tokugawa period between 1600 and 1868 there is evidence of sumptuary regimes under militaristic feudalism.[2] A hierarchical dress code of AD 681 was reputedly modelled on Chinese Tang law (Hearn 1904). In the main, the sumptuary codes of the feudal period were concerned with regulation within the feudal hierarchy and took little or no interest in merchants and other commoners. Shively identifies the first appearance of concern with frugality in both housing and dress in 1261; he suggests it may reflect a concern with the solvency of vassals (Shively 1964–5). The first comprehensive set of prohibitions affecting the dress and life-style of town dwellers, *chonin*, was introduced in 1649; its contents have a now familiar ring with prohibitions on finer silks and on the use of gold lacquer and gold or silver leaf in interiors or on household articles and saddles. Another comprehensive sumptuary code in 1661 required 'simplicity' in house and pleasure boat construction, and limited conspicuous display at weddings and funerals, and imposed strict limits on the number of dishes whilst entertaining.

Periodic sumptuary legislation followed with marked regularity and was increasingly directed against the *chonin*, a category that became synonymous with the merchant class; this shift was sparked not only by their growing affluence but also by the fact that previously specialised techniques in the production and handling of silk became more widespread and thus opened up wider availability. This provides an illustration of a more general interconnection between technical change and its impact on patterns of consumption. In the twentieth century we have become familiar with the rapidity with which today's innovative and expensive item of conspicuous consumption becomes tomorrow's mass commodity. Study of the shifting relationship between consumption and its regulation needs to attend to the impact of changing production techniques and other factors affecting availability and price. There are two processes here:

not only does an expanding range of commodities become available through technical innovation and expansion of trade, but at the same time novelty and distinctiveness in and of themselves come to play an increasingly significant role in opening up trade and commerce. The case of Japan is a useful one from which to insist that this process is not one confined to high modernity, but has been an increasingly significant dynamic from the earliest stages of the development of trade.

This dynamic also helps toward an understanding of the material basis of the conflict between the nobility and the merchants. The increased availability of commodities provided the aristocracies with an ever-wider range of opportunities for self-indulgence and conspicuous consumption. But in so doing it also produced a shift in the balance of economic forces with the dwindling riches of the 'old' classes and the increasing disposable resources of the merchants. Wolfgang Haug's argument that luxury commodities are associated with powerful sensual stimuli can also be applied to the symbolic and erotic significance of sumptuousness in dress in pre-modern societies, and nowhere more so than in Japan (Haug 1986).

When economic change disrupts a 'static' system of social relations, emulation becomes an increasingly available strategy by which people lower in the social hierarchy attempt to realise their aspirations towards higher status by modifying their behaviour, their dress and the kinds of goods they purchase. At the same time it becomes even more significant for the economically weakened nobility to resist these changes that express themselves in the frequently voiced anxiety about the difficulty of distinguishing between different categories of persons. In Japan it was the regulation of silk, its varieties and forms that was a primary site at which the struggle between the declining samurai and the rising merchant was fought out. As this tension sharpened it is noticeable that by the eighteenth century sumptuary laws had become more detailed and more frequently sought to inhibit any innovation in consumption. By the end of the century sumptuary discourses become more closely linked to the discourses of governmental economy, frugality and protectionism; sumptuary laws became integrated in the new field of economic government. The Meiji Restoration after 1867 formally abolished sumptuary laws.

In medieval Europe the presence of sumptuary regulation is at first uncertain and irregular. The first traces are found in Charlemagne's extension of the range of governmental action to secure the general conditions of feudal relations. In this context sumptuary features emerge from what was primarily a system of labour regulation. That an edict was necessary specifying that peasants were required to work on the land for six days each week indicates a recognition that feudal relations could not be relied upon to reproduce themselves at the local level. A related anxiety, this time of a security nature, is suggested by the fact that peasants were prohibited from carrying a sword; here, as in Japan, the monopoly of arms was both a practical and a symbolic preoccupation. Symbolism comes to the fore in the provision that peasants were required to walk to church on Sunday carrying a cattle prod; this suggests a concern that peasants should know their place and should be provided with regular reminders of it. It was in this context that the requirement that the clothing of peasants be restricted to a single colour, either black or grey, came about (Bonawitz 1964).

From the early ninth century there is evidence of periodic attempts to link dress to rank, and in the eleventh century to impose restrictions on the colours that were permitted to the peasantry. More regular sumptuary regulation begins to appear by the end of the twelfth century (1157 Genoa, 1188 in France) and becomes more frequent in the thirteenth century (1234 Aragon, 1249 Siena, 1250 Florence, 1256 Castille). There were significant bursts of activity in the final quarter of the century (1276 Bologna, 1277 Padua, 1297 Venice, 1304 Zurich). In the thirteenth century sumptuary enactments came from both church and state: in 1274 Pope Gregory X issued an edict banning 'immoderate ornamentation' throughout Christendom and in 1279 a Papal legate issued regulations on women's apparel in Lombardy. Thereafter sumptuary law became increasing secular, even though there was much reinforcement from the Church of the moral rationale of such restrictions through the critique of luxury. By the second half of the fourteenth century sumptuary laws are present in significant numbers over most of Europe (in 1363 England had its first significant sumptuary enactment). By the middle of the fifteenth century Scotland and the German cities and principalities had established sumptuary legislation.

Some patterns are detectable in this early phase of European sumptuary law. They are far from easy to summarise because they are cross-cutting, laid one atop the other across a complex panorama of economic and political regimes. All that I plan to do at this stage is to list (with occasional illustration and comment) some of the more evident shifts that traversed the multiple projects of sumptuary regulation in medieval Europe.

Continuity with ancient societies is evident in the widely imposed restrictions on conspicuous consumption in connection with funerals and weddings and, to a lesser degree, other public celebrations of private rites of passage (births, christenings, betrothals, etc.). The regulation of dress is also present from the beginning, but it becomes increasingly important; it comes to be the typical target of medieval sumptuary law, to such an extent that the term sumptuary law itself, both in its historical usage and my own, becomes almost synonymous with the regulation of dress, ornamentation and personal appearance.

Dress regulation took two distinctive forms, the first being the imposition of expenditure limits (either on whole outfits or on the price per piece of cloth, or on individual items). The second form was to reserve particularly significant types of cloth or style of dress for designated categories; this was done either by granting a privilege to a social category (e.g. only nobles may wear ermine) or by negative prohibition (e.g. no female servant may wear her robes with a train). While the form is not always closely linked to the substance of law a general inference can be drawn from these two types of dress rule: reserved privileges tend to be associated with the internal regulation of a social hierarchy where the concern is to limit or to channel competition that occurs within the dominant classes. The negative prohibition tends to be associated with the imposition of an imagined social order on real or imagined disruptions or challenges from below; typical of this category are rules that relate to merchants, commoners, apprentices, servants and prostitutes.

There was a complex articulation alongside hierarchical considerations in the use of sumptuary dress provisions to regulate gender relations. In its simplest form a sumptuary dress code provides a codification of the dress restrictions for males and for females in each designated social category. This type is epitomised by the summaries or 'breviats' circulated with Elizabethan sumptuary proclamations. There were significant shifts as to which sex was targeted for regulation [. . .]. Many ordinances were gender neutral, while others differentially imposed restraints – sometimes it was men who were targeted and at other times it was women; those statutes that target women frequently employed strongly misogynistic attitudes and language. For present purposes, it is sufficient to comment that, on balance, medieval sumptuary law was directed against men more often than it was against women. It was women who came to be the object of sumptuary regulation in the early modern period. However, there is abundant evidence to show that, throughout, enforcement was directed more rigorously against women than it was against men.

Sumptuary law in the early modern period

As European feudalism waned and was replaced by bastard feudalisms in many key areas, and especially in Renaissance Italy, mercantile capital achieved economic power and even political power in some cases. If Europe stood on the brink of modernity then it did so with sumptuary regulation at its most active and extensive. This should be sufficient to dispel the tendency to equate sumptuary projects with the kind of social hierarchy conceived of as typically feudal or pre-modern. Sumptuary laws straddle the often imperceptible but fundamental divide between the pre-modern and the modern. (Figures 2.1 and 2.2 provides an overview of the quantity and periodisation of sumptuary legislation.)

The economic historian N. G. Harte has been one of the more perceptive recent commentators on sumptuary law. He resolves the periodisation of sumptuary law by suggesting that it was an 'identifying characteristic' of the pre-industrial period (Harte 1976: 134). I have no quarrel with this; in virtually all cases the typical dress codes of the late medieval/early modern period had disappeared by the advent of the Industrial Revolution. What Harte's periodisation does not grapple with is a more interesting and difficult question about the place of sumptuary law in the early modern period in which commercial capital had come to the fore, a period that spanned the sixteenth to the eighteenth centuries. During this period there was a great volume of sumptuary law and its characteristic was conspicuous consumption in matters of dress and ornamentation. I will add the thesis that dress codes become more, rather than less, preoccupied with the preservation of hierarchy.

	1100–99	1200–99	1300–99	1400–99	1500–99	1600–99	1700–99
France	1	4	5	6	13	19	1
England	1	0	5	4	20	1	—
Italian cities*	2	7	16	24	12	17	1
Florence	—	1	13	10	7	21	—
Venice	—	1	8	11	17	28	2
Spain	—	7	7	2	16	4	2
Switzerland			3	0	3	3	2
Germany				3	7	7	2
Scotland				7	12	12	1
North America						9	1

*Except Florence and Venice

Figure 2.1 A quantification of sumptuary laws.

My purpose here is to review and illustrate the major trends that manifest themselves in the transition to modernity. I will argue that there was significant continuity; sumptuary regulation that had been born in the heart of feudalism came to expand its range and its volume; it increased rather than decreased with the decline of feudalism. Sumptuary projects became a standard feature of governmental activity in the early modern period and only declined when capitalism had triumphed and the modern state, but not yet the modern representative state, had come into being. (Figures 2.3 to 2.9 provide an illustration of the volume of sumptuary legislation in Europe.)

With the passage from feudalism to early modernity four major trends affecting sumptuary law are observable. First is the gradual disappearance of funeral and wedding regulations. The second is that dress becomes the central target and dress codes become more comprehensive and increasingly codified in form.[3] The third feature is that the legislation becomes more focused upon preservation of the external symbols of class hierarchy. As dress becomes the major regulatory object, attempts at alimentary regulation, whether in the form of general expenditure limits or the reserving of privileged items for the upper classes, decline.[4]

The fourth significant trend involves the shift that takes place against the background of an incipient economic debate, one which flowers again with the rise of classical political economy in the eighteenth century, as to whether expenditure on perishable luxuries, such as food, is economically more beneficial than indulgence in more durable luxuries – clothes, precious metals, jewels.[5] As the restraints on food disappear it becomes harder to sustain the logic that sumptuary laws are motivated by a general concern to restrain extravagance since there is no reason why extravagance on food is less damaging to the nation than extravagance on dress. The fact that by the late Middle Ages dress codes had become the paradigmatic case of sumptuary restriction requires some explanation that goes beyond the critique of extravagance and luxury that had provided the standard and oft repeated legitimation for such sumptuary ordering in previous centuries.

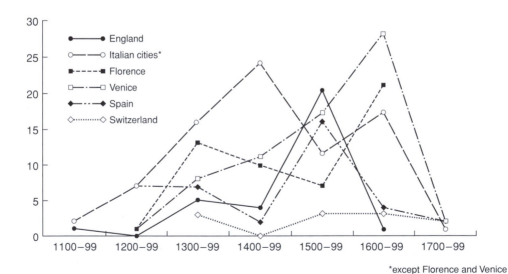

*except Florence and Venice

Figure 2.2 European sumptuary law.

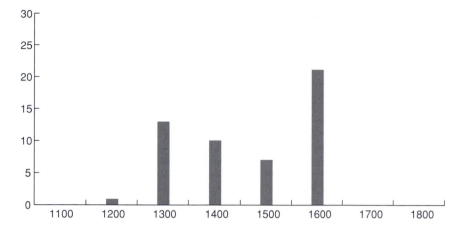

Figure 2.3 Florence: the volume of sumptuary law.

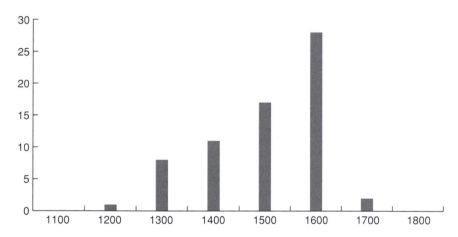

Figure 2.4 Venice: the volume of sumptuary law.

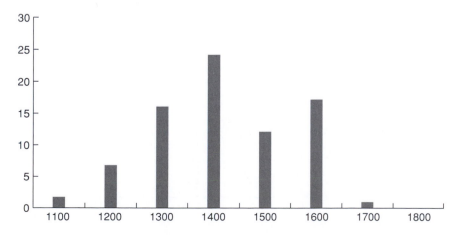

Figure 2.5 Italian cities (excluding Florence and Venice): the volume of sumptuary law.

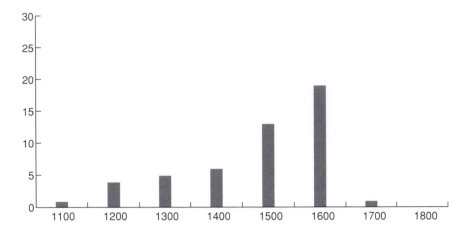

Figure 2.6 France: the volume of sumptuary law.

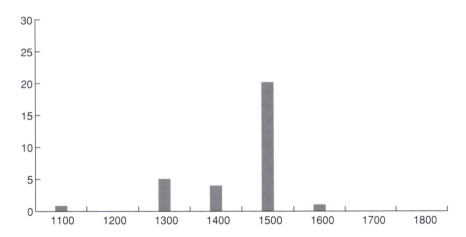

Figure 2.7 England: the volume of sumptuary law.

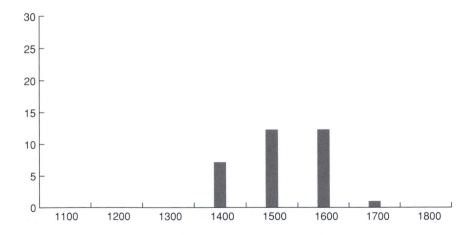

Figure 2.8 Scotland: the volume of sumptuary law.

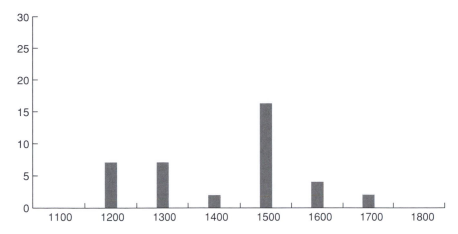

Figure 2.9 Spain: the volume of sumptuary law.

The legitimatory motives that were invoked in the legislative preambles reveal a number of 'shifts' in medieval sumptuary law. In the early phases sumptuary laws which appealed to the associated phenomena of 'dearth' and 'ruin' gradually gave way before two other loosely connected considerations. The first being that 'extravagance and luxury' became the central discursive features. What is at stake here is a shift away from 'dearth' or 'ruin' concerned with actual or imagined shortage of the means of sustenance, whereas the discourses of extravagance and luxury imply that economic resources are being diverted from more useful or profitable investment. The other strand was the emergence of a conception of a 'national economy'.

The fourth trend in the trajectory of sumptuary law saw a marked turn toward protectionist discourses and preoccupations. This shift was articulated in terms of a sequence of concerns which, while not strictly sequential, go through a number of distinguishable stages. An initial bullionist concern with the outflow of gold and silver was succeeded by considerations about the balance of trade focused on the relationship between imports and exports, and finally became expressed within increasingly protectionist discourses in which the projects became those of advancing some particular domestic trade or industry. An illustrative case of the latter approach was the case of Siena where in 1433 citizens were restricted to a single pair of silk sleeves. In 1438 the commune officially sponsored a local silk industry, but it was not until 1460 that sumptuary restrictions on locally produced silk garments were lifted when, as it were, legal ideology caught up with economic exigency (Hughes 1983: 78). A more extensive version of this distinctive admixture and supersession was the official sponsorship of luxury industries in France in the second half of the seventeenth century and the elaboration of protectionism into a national economic policy during the course of which the discourses of luxury waned rapidly in the face of 'national interest' such that imports, especially English ones, become the evil to be combated. [. . .]

These trends are of course far from universal. The case of Scotland may be cited to illustrate some interesting variations on the trajectory of sumptuary regulation. Sumptuary impositions started a little later than in England – 1424 rather than 1363 – but they lasted significantly longer, with full-blown sumptuary enactments as late as 1691. Scottish sumptuary laws started out with the imposition of what was in essence a two-class hierarchic model that sought to ensure an enduring distinction between the nobility and the urban burghers. These regulations provide rare instances of attempts to prescribe positive dress regulations. The major statute of 1429 required that all men with an income above £20 a year should be well horsed and equipped 'as a gentleman ought to be'; some of these requirements were specific requiring a fur hat, 'doublat hab-ergone' [sleeveless armoured jacket] and the provision of stipulated weaponry (APS[6] 18: 8–10).

The discourses within which Scottish laws were located made much more of the invocation of fears of death and poverty and this may well have reflected relative eco-nomic backwardness. These concerns link up with the fact that Scotland only turned to alimentary regulation after standard dress codes had been attempted. Not until 1551 was a statute passed linking the number of dishes allowed to each social rank (earls not more than 8 dishes, lords 6, barons 4, burghers 3), with hospitality rules stipulat-ing that the number of dishes should be determined by the rank of the chief guest (APS II: 488, c. 22).[7] From this point through until 1629 alimentary regulation was the pri-mary form of sumptuary order. In 1581 the quality of provisions that could be supplied to horses was prescribed; they were denied 'hard meat' (oats and hay) in summer (APS III: 225, c. 29; APS 452, c. 40 (1587)). It was not until 1672 that the main focus swung back onto extravagance in dress, and by now this was squarely located within a pro-tectionist discourse. Again, very much at odds with the chronology of the sumptuary regimes elsewhere in Europe, Scotland did not 'discover' the need to regulate funer-als, weddings and other ritual occasions for extravagance until the very final phase of its sumptuary initiatives, in 1681 an *Act Restraining the Exorbitant Expense of Marriages, Bap-tisms and Burials* was passed (APS VIII: 350. c. 80). It had all the traditional features of this 'early' form of sumptuary enactment, limiting the number of guests on hierarchi-cal principles (Shaw 1979: 92). I attach some significance to the inclusion of a prohi-bition on the carrying of 'pencels [pennants], banners, and other honours' at burials (J.C. 1891: 297), and suggest that such public events were feared by the English author-ities as potential opportunities for the expression of nationalist sentiments and the assertion of the prestige of the clans. This, in turn, supports my reflections about the political role of the archaic restrictions on funerals in Athens that also reappear in thir-teenth- and fourteenth- century Italy as components of struggles against the vestiges of clan power. There are sufficient differences between the patterns of Scottish sumptuary history and those in England and elsewhere in Europe that they would repay the atten-tion of those with an expertise in Scottish history that I do not pretend to possess.

Sumptuary laws were found in virtually every type of political system in medieval and early modern Europe; they were as prevalent in highly centralised nation-states already well on the way to absolutism as they were in the relatively democratic cities and communes. A few broad generalisations are possible. The paradigm cases of pro-tracted state unification, France and Spain, that went on to become highly centralised absolutist states had sumptuary laws by the late twelfth or early thirteenth centuries, and there was a more or less continuous history down until the eighteenth century. The fragmented city-states of Italy and Germany exhibit a mass of sumptuary legisla-tion for much the same period as France and Spain. There was surprisingly little differ-ence between both the temporal span and the general characteristics of the sumptuary law of such divergent cases as England, the great Italian cities like Venice and Florence, and the intensely Protestant Swiss towns. There seems to have been little difference in either the volume or the character of sumptuary regimes in Protestant or Catholic societies.

The city-state of Venice epitomises the long duration of sumptuary legislation through its rise to mercantile and political power and in its decline. The history of Venetian sumptuary law stretches from the end of the thirteenth century until the end of the eighteenth (Newett 1907; Longworth 1974). Early legislation in 1299 imposed limitations on weddings, feasts and funerals (Newett 1907; Davis 1962: 44; Hale 1973). From 1323 and 1334 regulatory attention shifted to excess in women's dress and to reinforcing ceremonial dress on patrician males (Brucker 1971: 318). From this period the communal treasury records are full of fines for sumptuary violations (Becker 1967: 228). After the plague of 1347–8 the Senate issued sumptuary laws forbidding dark-blue or green raiment to encourage general happiness (Newett 1907: 249). In the fifteenth century a long struggle over dowries and their implications commenced; limits were placed on the size of dowries and wedding costs aimed at discouraging the practice of sending younger daughters into convents (Brucker 1971: 318). In 1472 enforcement officials, *Provveditori sopra le Pompe* [supervisors of luxury], were appointed to enforce the sumptuary ordinances. As the rate of changes in fashion increased legislation became more complex, striving for comprehensive restrictions on the latest fashions. In 1511 the Senate went so far as to order that 'all new fashions are banned' (Okey 1907: 281).

When in 1512, during the political crisis of the League of Cambrai, as Venice's enemies gathered for the attack, the Senate debated dress materials, the size and design of sleeves, fringes and ornaments, belts and headdresses, shoes and slippers, home furnishings and bed-linen (Hughes 1983: 71). In the sixteenth century there was an increasing focus on the hierarchical ordering of appearance and also a more pronounced 'social purity' dimension; it was ordered that men's shirts must cover the entire upper body and be closed at the neck, while women's necklines as usual attracted the legislator's attention (Newton 1988). There was also an expansion of the range of targets with a series of ordinances limiting expenditure on interior decoration; the painting and upholstery of gondolas also attracted attention (Gilbert 1973: 279–80). Sumptuary energy did not slacken in the seventeenth century.[8] Legislative activity persisted into the eighteenth century; the last edict I have record of was from 1781 which continued to complain of the wasteful living of citizens, the destruction of fortunes and the loss of government revenue (Davis 1962: 45).

In Switzerland sumptuary laws spanned nearly 530 years from the very beginning of the fourteenth century until the end of the eighteenth century. John Vincent's study remains the primary source (Vincent 1935); his project was organised around the tradition of costume history, and he used the content of sumptuary prohibition to identify changes in contemporary fashion. What distinguishes his work, and goes way beyond his concern with the empirical history of fashion, is the careful attention he paid to evidence of enforcement in which context I will have cause to return to consider the material he collected. In the meantime some general patterns in Swiss sumptuary law can be identified. In the fourteenth century the focus was, as elsewhere, on the regulation of expenditure on weddings and funerals. Later the same century there is a shift of attention to dress organised around a mix of economic and moral considerations, with typical concern with female décolletage, while requiring that men's coats should be sufficiently long to cover 'his shame' (Vincent 1897: 360). Significantly during the height of the

Calvinist ascendancy, although there was vigilant enforcement of sumptuary law, there was no new legislative activity. The mix of moral and economic considerations in the attempt to hold fashion at bay persisted through the sixteenth and seventeenth centuries. Legislation made attendance at church compulsory and prohibited rival activities such as leaving the town during church services. Legislation also prescribed child-rearing patterns: children had to be off the streets after the 'bed bell' (Vincent 1897: 365). A distinctively Swiss extension to the range of sumptuary targets was provided by tight restrictions on sleigh riding; women were banned from riding in sleighs except when accompanied by their fathers or husbands. Sleigh-riding presumably provided opportunities for public display, youthful exuberance and courting (Vincent 1897: 367–8).

It seems evident that there are grounds for stressing the generality of European sumptuary law, a generality that transcends differences in political organisation, economic system and dominant religious ideology.

Sumptuary law in North America

North America is a significant case because the sumptuary regimes that were initiated in most, but not all, of the New World colonies were initiated at a time when the sumptuary impulse in Europe, and in particular in England, was showing signs of flagging. Given the close association with England it is significant that England had repealed its last dress legislation around the time the colonists set sail.[9] There was considerable variation between different settlements. The Massachusetts Bay colony has left the fullest record of its sumptuary provisions (Shurtleff 1968), but no such laws existed in Plymouth colony (Demos 1970). From very early days of settlement nearly all colonies had rules concerning non-attendance at Sunday worship, that subsequently acquired the label 'blue laws' and came to have a persisting significance into the twentieth century (Dilloff 1980). The first instance encountered was from Vermont in 1610 where non-attendance could attract the death penalty; more pragmatically in Virginia after 1623 fines for non-attendance could be paid in tobacco (Laband and Heinbuch 1987: 30).

In 1619 the first representative assembly held in Massachusetts approved an enactment 'Against Idleness, Gaming, Drunkenness and Excess in Apparel' (Miller 1928: 94). Much sumptuary energy was directed against the interconnected evils of luxury, fashion and dressing above one's rank (Warwick et al. 1965). When in 1638 the Boston court recognised 'the great disorder general through the country in costliness of apparel, and following new fashions' they required the elders to impose sumptuary restrictions, but expressed concern that some of the elders' wives were themselves party to the general disorder of apparel (Flaherty 1972: 185). The hierarchic sumptuary legislation rules did not become concretised until 1651 (Foster 1971: 28). They prohibited particular luxury items such as gold or silver lace, gold or silver buttons, silk hoods or scarves, and 'great boots' to those with an annual income of less than £200.[10] Selectmen were entitled to assess those who dressed above their rank as if they were worth £200 or more and then to tax them accordingly in an interesting example of deploying a fiscal trap against dressing beyond one's means. The boundaries of sumptuary order become very blurred; included alongside sumptuary provisions in Massachusetts in 1639 was a prohibition against the practice of drinking the health of one's companions on the grounds that it is 'a mere useless ceremony'.

The general moral tone is exemplified by a Connecticut law that required that 'no person, Householder or other, shall spend their time idly, or unprofitably' (Flaherty 1972: 180–1); there is no record of what was deemed to constitute 'idleness' but it seems be have borne a meaning close to 'not gainfully employed' or 'vagrant'. By the middle of the eighteenth century the standard dress rules had been repealed or fallen into disuse; but as late as 1750 the Massachusetts General Court prohibited all theatrical entertainment (Weeden 1890: 289). The inclination to control the recreational and cultural consumption of its citizens has never been far below the surface of American life and surfaced powerfully in the twentieth century with Prohibition. These potentialities linger, and are manifest again in the current pornography censorship movement [. . .].

On gaps and linkages in the sumptuary records

It should be noted that there are some countries for which I have turned up relatively little evidence of the presence of sumptuary laws. It is very likely that this reflects the inadequacy of my coverage and, in particular, the limited availability of works in English. For example, I have only encountered passing references to Portuguese sumptuary law (Hanson 1981; Marques 1971). The most interesting case is that of the Netherlands. Here we have a major player in the growth of mercantile capitalism in Europe and it does seem to be the case that the Dutch had relatively little sumptuary law and what they did have was significantly late. The only two substantial pieces of sumptuary legislation date from the second half of the seventeenth century by which time a comparable country such as England had long ceased to have active sumptuary laws. More significant perhaps is that the sumptuary laws that were passed, in 1655 and 1672 respectively, were instances of 'early' sumptuary law being concerned with expenditure on wedding celebrations and alimentary restrictions against 'unnecessary and sumptuous banquets' (Schama 1987: 182).

The existence of gaps in the record is in part evidence of the limitations of this study, but also indicates that there was considerable variation in the density of sumptuary regulation. To pursue this aspect further would require specialist local and regional knowledge of the social and political locations in which these 'gaps' in the generality of European sumptuary law occur.

Another important source of variation in the sumptuary relates to the complex interconnections between sumptuary and other forms of governmental action. There are numerous instances where a single legislative provision seeks to regulate different types of activity. An English statute in 1388 illustrates this general issue of linkages between different governmental projects. It required rural and urban labourers to desist from 'all playing at Tennis or Football and other Games called Coits, Dice, Casting of the Stone and other such importune Games' on Sundays and Holydays (12 Rich. II, c. 6; SR 2: 57[11]), but required them to practise archery. Alongside the quasi-sumptuary dimensions of social order and anti-gambling there was an obvious attempt to direct recreation into a militarily useful direction [. . .]. To establish linkages between projects is more difficult when they are not part of the same legislative initiatives. For example, the late medieval/early modern period in which sumptuary laws abounded was also a period in which there were important upheavals in the regulation of labour that produced a mass of vagrancy legislation. Another potentially significant linkage between sumptuary law and other projects is with the general field of moral regulation, in particular of prostitution, public health and sanitation regulation. In general it will be argued that an understanding of sumptuary law during its most active period requires attention to the linkages between different regulatory and governmental projects.

The most important linkage that affects the later history of sumptuary law is the connection between restraints on consumption and protectionist economic policies. For example, the question arises as to whether we should regard a French law prohibiting the import of English wool as a sumptuary law or as a very typical instance of economic protectionism. There is, of course, no solution to be found in the realm of definitions. Rather what is involved is a process whereby a series of shifts occur that have the result of disrupting one set of discursive linkages (e.g. that between moralising luxury and restricting consumption) and establishing another (e.g. that between 'national interest' and restraints on consumption). What is important to note is that the different discursive elements were present from the beginning; what changes is their respective 'weight' and the combinatory repertoires. One way of viewing the general demise of sumptuary law is to see it as a process in which a 'gap', in the form of a discursive separation, occurs between moral regulation and economic regulation. It was at the interface between these traditions that the distinctive phenomenon of sumptuary law existed. As the gap widens, sumptuary law diminishes, if not disappears, while moral and economic regulation march on as central arenas of governmental activity down to the present.

Notes

1   For present purposes I define feudalism in the following terms: a system of closed hierarchical relations in which the direct producers are tied to the land, first by military force and later by religious-political authority, in such a way that the extraction of surplus is secured by the linkage between social hierarchy and the distribution of privileges over land.

2   The sources primarily relied upon concerning Japanese sumptuary law are Hall (1906, 1908, 1989, 1979), Hearn (1904), McClain (1982), Shively (1955, 1964–5) and Wigmore (1969).

3   It is interesting to note that the first English statute in 1363 dealt systematically with differential alimentary rules for a set of social class and occupational categories.

4   Alimentary regulation was to persist until the end of the seventeenth century in Scotland (Shaw 1979) and into the eighteenth century in Portugal (Marques 1981).

5   I class clothing as 'durable' luxury because, given the high cost relative to income of most clothing subject to sumptuary rules, it was made to last, as is evidenced by the fact that clothes not infrequently formed a major part of both medieval and early modern inventories and bequests (Braunstein 1988; Thrupp 1948).

6   Acts of Parliament of Scotland; hereafter APS.

7   Other alimentary legislation followed in 1581, 1584, 1621, and 1629.

8   There is a collection of 32 sumptuary edicts of remarkable detail covering the period 1650–82 in the British Library (Venice, n.d.); others report that Venice passed more than 80 sumptuary laws during the seventeenth century (Burke 1987: 144).

9   There were also sumptuary rules imposed in the French settlements in 'New France' that is now Quebec. The law imposed on the settlers was French domestic sumptuary law, and

since I have little evidence beyond its existence I will focus attention on the New England colonies.

10   In 1676, Connecticut copied the 1651 Massachusetts law; earlier Connecticut laws gave town constables the general power to restrain 'all such as they judge to exceed their conditions and ranks' (Foster 1971: 29).

11   Statutes of the Realm.

Bibliography

Becker, Marvin (1967) *Florence in Transition, Vol. I: The Decline of the Commune*, Baltimore: Johns Hopkins University Press.

Bellamy, John (1989) *Bastard Feudalism and the Law*, London: Routledge.

Bonawitz, Achim (1964) 'Helmbrecht's Violation of "Karles Reht"', *Monatshefte*, 56, pp. 177–82.

Braunstein, Philippe (1988) 'Towards Intimacy: The Fourteenth and Fifteenth Centuries' in Georges Duby (ed.) *A History of Private Life, Vol. II: Revelations of the Medieval World*, Cambridge, MA: Harvard University Press, pp. 535–630.

Brucker, Gene (ed.) (1971) *The Society of Renaissance Florence: A Documentary Study*, New York: Harper & Row.

Burke, Peter (1987) 'Conspicuous Consumption in Seventeenth-Century Italy', in *The Historical Anthropology of Early Modern Italy: Essay on Perception and Communication*, Cambridge: Cambridge University Press, pp. 132–49.

Ch'ü, T'ung-Tsu (1961) *Law and Society in Traditional China*, Paris: Mouton.

Davis, James (1962) *The Decline of the Venetian Nobility as a Ruling Class*, Baltimore: Johns Hopkins University Press.

Dilloff, Neil (1980) 'Never on Sunday: The Blue Laws Controversy', *Maryland Law Review*, 39, 4, pp. 679–714.

Flaherty, David (1972) *Privacy in Colonial New England*, Charlottesville: University Press of Virginia.

Foster, Stephen (1971) *Their Solitary Way: The Puritan Social Ethic in the First Century of Settlement in New England*, New Haven: Yale University Press.

Gilbert, Felix (1973) 'Venice in the Crisis of the League of Cambrai', in John R. Hale (ed.), *Renaissance Venice*, London: Faber.

Hale, John (ed.) (1973) *Renaissance Venice*, London: Faber.

Hall, John (1906) 'Japanese Feudal Law. I: The Institutes of Judicature', *Transactions of the Asiatic Society of Japan*, 34, 1, pp. 17–44.

Hall, John (1908) 'Japanese Feudal Law. II: The Ashikaga Code (Kemmu Shikmoku AD 1336)', *Transactions of the Asiatic Society of Japan*, 36, 2, pp. 1–23.

Hall, John (1909) 'Japanese Feudal Law. III: The Tokugawa Legislation', *Transactions of the Asiatic Society of Japan*, 36, 4, pp. 683–804.

Hall, John (1979) *Japanese Feudal Law* [1906], Washington, DC: University Publications of America.

Hanson, Carl (1981) *Economy and Society in Baroque Portugal, 1668–1703*, Minneapolis: University of Minnesota Press.

Harte, N. B. (1976) 'State Control of Dress and Social Change in Pre-Industrial England', in D. C. Coleman and A. H. John (eds), *Trade, Government and Economy in Pre-Industrial England*, London: Weidenfeld and Nicolson, pp. 132–65.

Haug, W. F. (1986) *Critique of Commodity Aesthetics: Appearance, Sexuality and Advertising in Capitalist Society*, Minneapolis: University of Minnesota Press.

Hearn, Lafcadio (1904) *Japan: An Attempt at an Interpretation*, New York: Macmillan.

Hughes, Diane (1983) 'Sumptuary Laws and Social Relations in Renaissance Italy', in John Bossy (ed.), *Disputes and Settlements: Law and Human Relations in the West*, Cambridge: Cambridge University Press.

J.C. (1891) 'The Sumptuary Laws of Scotland', *Journal of Jurisprudence*, 35, pp. 290–7.

Laband, David N., and Heinbuch, Deborah H. (1987) *Blue Laws: The History, Economics, and Politics of Sunday-Closing Laws*, Lexington, MA: Lexington Books, 1987.

Longworth, Philip (1974) *The Rise and Fall of Venice*, London: Constable.

Marques, A. H. de Oliveira (1981) *Daily Life in Portugal in the Late Middle Ages*, Madison: University of Wisconsin Press.

McClain, James (1982) *Kanazawa: A Seventeenth Century Japanese Castle Town*, New Haven: Yale University Press.

Miller, Sylvia (1928) 'Old English Laws Regulating Dress', *Journal of Home Economics*, 20, 89–94.

Newett, M. Margaret (1907) 'The Sumptuary Laws of Venice in the Fourteenth and Fifteenth Centuries', in T. F. Tout and J. Tait (eds), *Historical Essays*, Manchester: Manchester University Press, pp. 245–78.

Newton, Stella Mary (1988) *The Dress of the Venetians 1495–1525*, Aldershot: Scolar Press.

Okey, T. (1907) *The Old Venetian Palaces and the Old Venetian Folk*, London: J. M. Dent.

Schama, Simon (1987) *Embarassment of Riches: An Interpretation of Dutch Culture in the Golden Age*, New York: Knopf.

Shaw, Frances (1979) 'Sumptuary Legislation in Scotland', *Juridical Review*, 24, pp. 81–115.

Shively, Donald (1964–5) 'Sumptuary Regulation and Status in Early Tokugawa Japan', *Harvard Journal of Asiatic Studies*, 25, pp. 123–64.

Shively, Donald (1955) 'Bakufu versus Kabuki', *Harvard Journal of Asiatic Studies*, 18, pp. 326–56.

Shurtleff, Nathaniel (ed.) (1968) *The Records of the Governor and Company of the Massachusetts Bay Company* [1853] (5 vols), New York: American Medieval Society Press.

Thrupp, Sylvia (1948) *The Merchant Class in Medieval London, 1300–1500*, Chicago: University of Chicago Press.

Vincent, John (1897) 'European Blue Laws', *Annual Report of the American Historical Association*, 355–73.

Vincent, John (1935) *Costume and Conduct in the Laws of Basel, Bern, and Zurich 1370–1800*, Baltimore: Johns Hopkins University Press.

Weeden, William (1890) *Economic and Social History of New England 1620–1789* (2 vols), Boston: Houghton Mifflin.

Wigmore, John (1969) *Law and Justice in Tokugawa Japan*, Toyko: University of Toyko Press.

Wittfogel, Karl A., and Fêng Chia-shêng (1949) *History of Chinese Society, Liao*, Philadelphia: American Philosophical Society.

The 'fashion other'
Jews in the late Middle Ages

Maria Giuseppina Muzzarelli

Historians agree that from the thirteenth century it was considered necessary to make the identity of a person to a specific social category visible: the clothing of both individuals and groups became legible, especially in the urban spaces of the rising European cities. In many cases it was established by law that most of the population had to conform to precise clothing specifications that allowed people of different social strata but also of different moral standing and religious affiliation to be distinguished immediately. It is not surprising that a society as deeply hierarchical and profoundly segmented as the medieval one used the exterior and visible signifiers of clothing to impose order and classify its population. A second principle dominated this endeavour: what we would call an 'equitable logic' that assumes the use of specific signs by people with different birth, social standing and wealth. What was proposed was far from any 'logic of equality' as it aimed to reinforce separation and distinction across society.

Clothing rules were written by moralists – often men of the cloth – and legislators whose aim was to maintain and consolidate their power by governing what we might call 'appearances'. There are two main historical sources that allow us to understand the pervasive nature of this complex attempt to create harmony between appearance and social circumstances: firstly the tracts and moral preaching of religious men and secondly the so-called sumptuary laws enacted by governments to control what people wore. The picture that emerges shows how 'otherness' was not uncommon in the medieval world. However exclusion was often partial, discontinuous and intermittent. The many thousands of Jews who populated the cities of medieval Europe are a good example of this.

Jews were present in all cities in central and northern Italy from the thirteenth century onwards. They were often given the right to exercise the pawnbroking business as Christians were forbidden to engage in any activities charging interest rates. During the Middle Ages and the early modern period this activity secured high profits. Jews were therefore an integral part of the economy of a city and, even if they were banned from becoming members of one of the many guilds that controlled the productive, financial and trading economies, they could freely enter two key professions: that of medicine and that of money-lending. This explains why it is incorrect to think of Jews as marginal. The 'otherness' of the Jew was a form of distinction from the Christian citizens, but did not necessarily means a subaltern position. Their faith meant specific liturgical and alimentary practices that were key to Jewish identity and at the same time used by Christians to underline difference and separation.

Clothing too acted as a way to distinguish the Jew. The fourth Lateran Council held in 1215 established that Jews had to wear a specific sign in order to be recognised in public. This rule was not regularly applied and remained during the following

Snapshot 3.1   The Betrothed, miniature in the Miscellany of Hamburg, Padua 1477, cod. 132 (previously hebr. 337), f. 75v. Hamburg, Staats- und Universitätsbibliothek. A circle can be seen on the man's breast which shows that he is a Jew.

centuries a possible legal tool for those public administrations who wanted to 'mark' the difference between Jews and Christians. Once applied, its repeal could be linked to the payment of substantial amounts of money from the Jewish community. These signs include a yellow 'O' symbol to be worn by all Jewish men on their chest. In central Europe it was not uncommon for Jews to wear a yellow pointed hat. Jewish women were required to wear yellow veils or ribbons of the same colour. The symbolism of yellow – the colour of exclusion as Michel Pastoureau has pointed out – was less than clear. In a city like Bologna, in northern Italy, yellow was imposed as a distinctive mark for common prostitutes thus creating an embarrassing association between respectable Jewish ladies and prostitutes. This is why in this city Jewish women had to be invariably accompanied by a man wearing a yellow 'O' symbol in order to avoid confusion. What is certain is that the legislators who created this overlap of symbols did not do it unknowingly.

The compulsory nature of the wearing of a distinctive sign for Jews was confirmed in 1555 with the Papal edict *Cum nimis absurdum* that also imposed that all Jews should live within a distinct area of the city, enclosed and accessible only through two gates. The sixteenth century was perhaps the pinnacle of an obsession to separate, distinguish and divide, and this extended to sartorial choice. The overall aim was not necessarily to exclude: everyone had a place within the social hierarchy but what was forbidden was the aspiration to achieve someone else's place, especially if this was done through the tools of clothing and appearances.

Bibliography and further reading

Muzzarelli, M. G. (2000) 'Il vestito degli ebrei', *Zakhor*, 4, pp. 161–8.

Pastoureau, M. (2001) *The Devil's Cloth: A History of Stripes*, New York: Washington Square Press.

Sansy, D. (2001) 'Marquer la différence: l'imposition de la rouelle aux XIIIe et XIVe siècles', *Médiévales*, 41, pp. 15–36.

Toaff, A. (1996) 'La vita materiale', in C. Vivanti (ed.), *Storia d'Italia: Annali* 11, I, *Gli ebrei in Italia*, Turin: Einaudi, pp. 245–8.

Chapter 3

Codpieces and masculinity in early modern England

Will Fisher

O NE OF THE MOST STRIKING ELEMENTS of early modern dress was
the codpiece. The *Oxford English Dictionary* describes this accessory as 'a bagged
appendage to the front of the close-fitting hose or breeches worn . . . [in England] from
the 15th to the [beginning of the] 17th century'. Codpieces were first introduced,
according to fashion historians, as a means of concealing the genital area in masculine apparel. Earlier, this task had been performed by knee-length surcoats, but when
shorter doublets were adopted at the beginning of the fifteenth century, the genital area
was left at least partially exposed, and the codpiece was created as a way of dealing with
this problem.[1]

The definition from the *OED* provides a good overview of what the codpiece was. It
is, however, a bit misleading in that it gives the impression of a simple, uniform object.
The truth is that codpieces came in a variety of shapes and styles. One common style
was, as the *OED* implies, a 'bagged appendage'. This particular type of codpiece was essentially a triangular flap or gusset that was attached to the front of the hose or breeches
(Figure 3.1). The bottom corner of the triangle was sewn to the inseam of the garment
and the top two corners were attached near the hips with either buttons or laces called
'codpiece points'. One writer from the late seventeenth century describes this style of
codpiece in his account of 'the Suits that [were] generally worn heretofore in *England*':
he says the codpiece 'came up with two wings fastened to either side with points'. The
writer notes, moreover, that this 'large and ample Codpiss supplied the want of Pockets'
for when the points were 'unknit', they 'made way to the Linnen bags tyed to the inside
between the Shirt and Codpiss, these Bags held every thing they carried about them'.[2]

But if the codpiece was sometimes a 'bagged appendage', it also took other forms as
well. The most common of these was an ornate (sometimes even jewel-encrusted) phallic sheath that protruded conspicuously from the front of the outfit.[3] This second type

Figure 3.1 Albrecht Dürer, *The Standard Bearer* (1498) wearing a scrotal codpiece. British Museum, Department of Prints and Drawings, E, 4.157. © The Trustees of the British Museum.

of codpiece was constructed out of layers of woven cloth with inner padding and stays (Figure 3.2). According to the fashion historian Aileen Ribeiro, the 'modest codpiece of the late fifteenth century . . . assumed the shape of a permanent erection'.[4]

   This essay sets out to analyse the gendered work performed by the codpiece, but it will not offer a semiotic analysis of this accessory. Instead, I hope to provide a more materialist account, considering the way in which the codpiece quite literally helped

Figure 3.2 Agnolo Bronzino, *Portrait of Guidobaldo della Rovere* (1532), wearing a phallic codpiece. Photo © Scala, Florence – courtesy of the Ministero per i Beni e le Attività Culturali.

to fashion manhood. Indeed, I will argue that when this artefact was incorporated into the physical portrait in the fifteenth century, it helped to remake the male body, and by extension, the ideologies of gender circulating at the time.

Anne Hollander's *Seeing through Clothes* provides the theoretical framework for this essay insofar as it demonstrates the extent to which clothing can shape perceptions of the human body. Hollander's art-historical study begins by looking at nudes from many different time periods and noting the drastic variations in the corporeal form of the women depicted therein. She then argues that the stylised form of the body presented in each painting corresponds roughly to the form of the garments popular at the time. So, for example, she observes that the bodies of women in paintings by Tintoretto or Bronzino have small, flattened breasts and cylindrical torsos, and simultaneously notes that this corresponds to the shape of dresses from the period. Hollander thus convincingly concludes that it is as if the nude bodies in these paintings are quite literally 'shaped' by the 'absent' clothing, and as a result, it is as if we are 'seeing through' the invisible clothes when we look at them.[5]

Following Hollander, I want to suggest that the codpiece shaped the vision of the body (and specifically the male genitalia) in early modern England. But I also want to add another dimension to Hollander's analysis by insisting that there are important gendered aspects to this process that need to be considered. Thus, I don't simply want to contend that the codpiece formed ideas about the body in general, but rather that it formed ideas about *the male body*. Moreover, I hope to show how these ideas related to the early modern ideologies of masculinity.

Texts from early modern England that discuss the codpiece tend to perform two types of cultural work with regard to this object, and with regard to gendered ideologies of the era. First, many of them work to figure the accessory as an integral element of masculinity. For example, a character in Henry Medwall's *Fulgens and Lucrece* claims that 'a new man of fascyon now a day' must have a 'codpiece before almost as large, and therein restith the greatest charge'.[6] Medwall's play – the earliest existent secular drama – was first staged at the end of the fifteenth century when codpieces were just coming into fashion. This may help to explain why the character claims that the codpiece is necessary for the '*new* man of fascyon'.

Dramatic texts from later in the period also contain similar pronouncements about the codpiece's role in constituting masculine identity. In the play *Wiley Beguiled* (1606), for instance, the character – William Cricket – provides a catalogue of his masculine features, pointing out that he has 'a fine beard, [a] comely corps, And a Carowsing Codpeece'. He is so proud of these attributes that he challenges 'All England if it can / [to] Show mee such a man / . . . As William Cricket is'.[7] There are two primary things I want to note about these statements. First, I simply want to point out the centrality of the 'Carowsing codpiece' as a guarantor of masculinity. But in addition, it is worth noting that this part is listed alongside more corporeal features such as the 'fine beard' and the 'comely corps'. While modern readers might be tempted to place more emphasis on the body than on dress, these items seem to carry equal weight here. Given this emphasis placed on the codpiece, it is hardly surprising to find that later in the play, Cricket 'swear[s] . . . by the round, sound, and profound contents . . . Of this costly Codpeece', claiming that it makes him 'a good proper man as yee see' (48).

Another seventeenth-century text that attempts to establish the codpiece as a constitutive component of masculinity is an epigram by Richard Niccols. He writes:

'Tis strange to see a Mermaide, you will say,
Yet not so strange, as that I saw to day, . . .
One part of this was man or I mistooke,

> The other woman, for I pray (sirs) looke,
> The head is mans, I iudge by hat and haire,
> And by the band and doublet it doth weare,
> The bodie should be mans, what doth it need?
> Had it a codpiece, 'twere a man indeed.[8]

In this passage, Niccols describes an ambiguously gendered figure who is reminiscent of those portrayed in the *Hic Mulier* and *Haec Vir* pamphlets. Although the individual that Niccols depicts already has a number of masculine attributes such as the 'hat', 'haire', 'band' and 'doublet', Niccols implies that without the *pièce de resistance*, the 'bodie' remains feminine, and hence the whole is a 'monstrous' amalgam of contraries. With the codpiece, however, the scales would be tipped and the individual would become definitively masculine. Thus, for my purposes, the crucial thing to note is that even though the codpiece does not act alone, it seems to have the power to constitute the gendered identity of this individual – to help to make him/her into 'a man indeed'.

Like Medwell and Niccols, the satirist John Marston suggests that the codpiece establishes the masculinity of the person who wears it. Indeed, the normally satirical Marston is at first surprisingly restrained in front of this artefact. He states that he will

> . . . never raile at those
> That weare a codpis, thereby to disclose
> What sexe they are, since strumpets breeches vse,
> And all men's eyes save Linceus can abuse.[9]

In these lines, Marston suggests that the codpiece has the ability to 'disclose' the 'sexe' of its wearer. Although he acknowledges that 'strumpets' might 'use' breeches to 'abuse' men's eyes, he implies that they could not do the same with the codpiece. In this sense, Marston's description is quite similar to that of Niccols: both writers intimate that even when other gendered items (whether they be 'breeches', or 'hats' and 'hair') fail to secure masculinity, the codpiece nevertheless serves as an incontrovertible anchor.

Finally, Shakespeare's *Two Gentlemen of Verona* shares much in common with these other texts. It too stages the codpiece as a necessary element of masculine attire and identity. But there is also a crucial difference in Shakespeare's play: in it, the item is worn by a *female* character. When Julia decides to dress herself as a man, Lucetta first tells her that she must wear a pair of 'breeches'. She then adds that she 'must needs have them with a codpiece' because 'A round hose . . . now's not worth a pin, Unless you have a codpiece to stick pins on' (2.7.49–56).[10] The codpiece thus occupies a central place in this scene. It seems to carry even more cultural weight than the breeches/hose alone. Lucetta states that, without the codpiece, the hose alone are 'not worth a pin' (with the obvious phallic pun). Also, it is worth saying that in the exchange Lucetta gradually works her way up to suggesting that Julia don a codpiece, with the implication being that her recommendations are becoming more and more outrageous.

Julia, for her part, is reluctant to appropriate this accessory. She responds to Lucetta's suggestion that she wear a codpiece by insisting 'Out, out, that would be ill-favored' (2.7.54). This scene therefore seems to be structured by a logic similar to that found in Marston's text: it indicates that even though women might 'use' breeches to deceive 'men's eyes', they would not use the codpiece. In this case, however, Julia *does* eventually adopt the codpiece, and consequently Shakespeare, unlike Marston, ends up foregrounding the transferability of the item. Whereas Marston draws a distinction between the breeches and the codpiece, Shakespeare's play emphasises that both objects can be appropriated. This point will, I hope, help us to recognise the cultural work performed by the other texts that I have been discussing. Those texts forge a connection between the codpiece and masculinity, and when they are viewed in relation to Shakespeare's play, it becomes evident that this connection was not something 'natural' or unremarkable, but rather something they laboured to establish.

But early modern texts do not simply characterise the codpiece as a crucial attribute of masculinity, they also work to conflate this part with the male genitalia. Indeed, these two interventions are related to one another. This is evident if we return to the play *Wiley Beguiled*. As I noted earlier, at one point in the play, the character William Cricket declares that his 'carrowsing codpiece' is one of the things that establishes his masculinity. Later, he 'swear[s] . . . by the round, sound, and profound contents . . . Of this costly Codpeece' and insists that this makes him 'a good and proper man'. In these passages, Cricket seems to elide the difference between his 'carrowsing codpiece' with its 'round, sound, and profound contents' and to imply that the two are virtually identical. This conflation is reiterated in a different form later in the play when Cricket 'sweare[s] by the blood of [his] codpiece'. This remarkable oath seems to confer a measure of corporeality onto the codpiece.

This is not to say that the codpiece was always melded with the male genitalia. As we saw earlier, one of the characters in Medwall's *Fulgens and Lucrece* distinguishes between the item and its corporeal contents when he indicates that the 'new' man's 'greatest charge' still rests 'within' his codpiece. Nevertheless, there are many texts that do actively conflate the two. For example, at the beginning of the seventeenth century (after the codpiece had already gone out of fashion), the playwright Barten Holyday writes nostalgically of 'that Cod-piece-ago, when the innocency of men did not blush to shew all that Nature gaue them'.[11] In this passage, Holyday implies that the codpiece 'shew[ed]' the genitals, much as Marston implied that it 'disclosed' the 'sex' of the wearer. Holyday suggests, moreover, that this was done with an almost prelapsarian innocence. Indeed, he somewhat paradoxically insists on the 'Naturalness' of the fashion, claiming that the men that wore this accessory 'did no more, then, that [*sic*] nature taught them'.

Other seventeenth-century writers, like John Bulwer, had a less nostalgic view of the accessory and the era in which it was worn. Bulwer describes the 'Breeches' of the previous century as being 'filthy and Apish' and claims that they 'openly shew'd our secret parts, with the vaine and unprofitable modell of a member which we may not so much name with modesty'.[12] Although Bulwer's *evaluation* of the codpiece is thus radically different from Holyday's, his description of the item is remarkably similar: just as Holiday says that the codpiece 'shew[s] all that Nature' gave men, Bulwer says that it 'shew[s]' men's 'secret parts'. For Bulwer, however, this is an index of the item's unnaturalness rather than its naturalness. In fact, he subtly emphasises the indecency of the codpiece by using the term 'secret parts' to refer to the genitalia – thus indicating that they ought to be hidden from public view rather than 'openly' displayed.

Bulwer's condemnation of the codpiece seems to echo the polemical literature from sixteenth-century Germany. Andreas Musculus's *Hosen Teuffel*, for instance, was a book-length invective against youthly fashions that reserved some of its sharpest criticism for the codpiece.[13] Musculus's text, and others like it, have been perceptively analysed by Lyndal Roper in *Oedipus and the Devil*. Roper maintains that 'moralists like Musculus . . . condemned the codpiece not because it paraded the phallus, but because it was a form of nudity. It displayed the penis to . . . lascivious eyes'.[14] These German denunciations clearly resemble Bulwer's diatribe: whereas the German writers claim that the codpiece 'displayed the penis' and that it 'was a form of nudity', Bulwer asserts that it 'openly shew'd our secret parts'. It is worth saying, however, that in the process of articulating their objections to this item, these writers ironically perform some of the same cultural work as those writers with a more favourable opinion of the codpiece like Holyday and Medwall: they all effectively fuse the codpiece and the male genitalia. Consequently, I would argue that even though moralists like Bulwer and Musculus condemn the wearing of this accessory, they also unwittingly construct it as a masculine feature.

*   *   *

It should, I hope, be clear by now that the codpiece was an article of clothing that helped to make early modern individuals 'men in body by attire'. What we have seen here, moreover, are some of the steps through which this fashioning was achieved: first, attaching the accessory to male bodies, then, conflating it with the male genitalia, and also insisting that it made the individuals into 'men indeed'. But if many early modern writers maintained that the codpiece 'showed' all that 'Nature' gave men, and that it could establish the masculinity of its wearer, these cultural fantasies have too often been taken at face value by modern historians.[15] Leo Steinberg, for example, discusses the vogue for codpieces in his *Sexuality of Christ in Renaissance Art and Modern Oblivion*.[16] He contends that this accessory was meant to indicate 'a permanent state of erection' and that it was therefore a 'token of [sexual] prowess'.[17] Moreover, Steinberg maintains that the codpiece was also an 'instrument of power' and that the 'conceit of the phallus as a manifestation of power' (90) was 'constant' throughout Renaissance culture. While it may seem pretty straightforward to say that the codpiece was a priapic stand-in for the penis beneath it, this description does not achieve enough metacritical distance on the accessory, and therefore does not adequately acknowledge the problem of representation it posed. In reality, of course, the codpiece did not 'show' anything; on the contrary, its purpose, as we have seen, was to conceal. Nor for that matter did this elaborately decorated cultural artefact have any transparent connection with nature.

Marjorie Garber is much more attentive to the ambiguous status of this accessory. In *Vested Interest*, she emphasises the detachability of the codpiece and insists that the item bears no necessary relationship to the body beneath. In fact, she goes so far as to assert that the codpiece is a 'sign of gender undecidability'. As she puts it, the object 'confounds the question of gender, since it can signify yes or no, full or empty, lack or lack of lack'.[18] If Garber provides a much needed corrective to critics like Steinberg who assume the accessory to be transparently related to the body, I would argue that her emphasis on the indeterminacy of this item, while true, is also ultimately somewhat problematic in that it fails to adequately acknowledge the cultural work that the object itself performed.

What I therefore hope to do in this essay is to find a theoretical middle ground between Steinberg and Garber. Instead of seeing the codpiece either as a simple indication of what nature gave men, or, conversely, as an empty cipher, we ought to see it as an item through which male bodies and masculinity were culturally constructed. Put differently, we might say that although early modern writers like Bulwer claim that the codpiece was simply a 'model of' the male genitalia, it was in reality as much a model *for* the genitalia as a model *of* them.

But if this was the case, then we need to be especially attentive to the codpiece's material manifestations. In particular, it is important that the codpiece was not always phallic, and did not always, as Steinberg maintains, imply a 'permanent state of erection'. The codpiece came in a range of styles and many of them were distinctly non-phallic. Indeed, the very name 'codpiece' implies that there is a link between this accessory and the scrotum/testicles rather than the phallus. The word 'cod' was, of course, a slang term for the 'scrotum' and the plural form 'cods' almost always referred to the testicles. One seventeenth-century anatomist described the testicles as being 'seated externally in Men in their *Cod* or Covering'.[19] Another said they 'hang . . . without the Abdomen . . . in the cod'.[20] Thus, even though early modern writers often conflate the codpiece with the male genitals, it is not always entirely clear exactly what is being conflated. For example, when the character in the play *Wiley Beguiled* speaks of the 'round, sound, and profound' contents of his codpiece, he could be referring to either the phallus or the testicles (or, for that matter, both or neither of these).

What I am trying to suggest here is that these two forms of the codpiece worked to fashion slightly different versions of the male genitals, and by extension, slightly different versions of masculinity. Recent research has suggested that in the early modern period, the concept of manhood underwent a significant shift. According to Jean Howard and Phyllis Rackin's *Engendering a Nation*, 'a man's identity' had, prior to the Renaissance, been 'defined on the basis of patrilineal inheritance' and linked with his ability to reproduce himself, but over time, an 'emergent culture' of 'performative masculinity' developed in which masculine identity was secured through the sexual 'conquest' of women.[21] So if the older model of masculinity emphasised reproduction as a key to establishing a masculine identity, the newer 'performative' one emphasised sexuality and especially phallic penetration. Howard and Rackin suggest that the dark underside of this emergent ideal can be glimpsed in changing ideas about rape. They insist that in older texts 'where the logic of patrilineal feudal succession is privileged, rape is [not usually] associated with military conquest or valorised as the "natural" instinct of men. Instead, it serves to separate "low" from their betters' (198). By contrast, in texts which exemplify the new 'performative masculinity' rape sometimes serves as a 'model of masculine dominance' and even a 'gatekeeper for the gendered hierarchy' (196).

Gary Taylor's work on castration corroborates many of the assertions made be Howard and Rackin. In *Castration: An Abbreviated History of Western Manhood*, Taylor points out that although the term castration originally referred to the surgical process of removing the testicles, it increasingly came to be associated with the amputation of the penis as is typified by the term's use within Freudian psychoanalysis.[22] These changing ideas about castration are, for Taylor, indicative of a larger shift in the notions of manhood that had its roots in the Renaissance. Taylor labels the earlier ideology of masculinity 'the regime of the scrotum' to the newer one 'the regime of the penis'. Rebecca Ann Bach similarly refers to the older model of masculinity as 'testicular' and says that it 'values breeding for itself and not for the sexual act'.[23]

If both of these 'regimes' of masculinity were operative in early modern England and stood in tension with one another, the gradual displacement of the former by the latter is suggested by the changing accounts of the testicles in anatomy books from the period. According to the anatomical tradition, the 'coddes' were considered to be a 'principal part' of the body, along with organs like the heart, the liver, and the brain. In fact, Galen claims that the testicles are not simply *one* of the principal parts, they are *the* principal part, edging out even the heart. As he puts it, '*The Heart is indeede the author of living; but the Testicles are they which adde a betternesse or farther degree of perfection to the life*, because if they be taken away, the jollity and courage of the Creature is extinguished'.[24]

During the sixteenth and seventeenth centuries, however, the traditional centrality of the testicles began to wane. Nicholas Udall's 1553 translation of Thomas Gemini's *Compendiosa Totius Anatomie Delineatio* still claimed that the testicles are one of the principal parts: they are, as he puts it, 'a priyncipal membre, for withoute it is no generation'.[25] Similarly in 1586, Thomas Vicary asserted that 'The Coddes . . . is called a principal member'.[26] However, as early as 1615, Helkiah Crooke acknowledged that there were 'adversaries who would thrust them out of this ranke of dignity'. According to Crooke, these 'adversaries' insisted that 'the testicles do not give life at all' and therefore 'there is no necessity of them, for *Eunuches* live without them'. Crooke did not agree with these writers: he admits that the testicles 'are not necessary for conservation of the life of the *individuum* or singular man', but nevertheless claims that they are 'an absolute necessity' for 'the propagation of the whole species, or of mankinde'. As he puts it, 'they are principall parts in respect of mankinde, not in respect to this or that particular man'.[27]

By the mid-seventeenth century, the 'adversaries' seem to have been gaining ascendancy. In 1668, Nicholas Culpepper no longer felt compelled to include the testicles in his list of principal parts: Culpepper writes that 'The *Principal* [parts] are the Liver, Heart, [and the] Brain'. He acknowledges that 'Others add the Testicles', but claims that this is 'without any need, because they make nothing to the Conservation of the Individual'.[28] Interestingly, the rubric of 'principal parts' was completely abandoned by anatomists in the eighteenth century. This may have been done for scientific reasons – as the profession became increasingly empirical, perhaps anatomists decided that the category itself was not scientifically necessary or useful. Nonetheless, the timing of this decision seems also significant. It may be that the designation was dropped instead of establishing a new pantheon of principal parts that excluded the testicles. But whatever the rationale behind this decision, the crucial thing is that, in the aggregate, these anatomical texts suggest that there was a gradual erosion of the cultural centrality of the testicles over the course of the early modern period.

The codpiece helped to materialise both of the competing 'regimes' of masculinity. While some forms of this accessory worked to construct the male genitalia as distinctly phallic, others worked to construct them as scrotal/testicular. The tension between these two models becomes apparent if we look at the writing about the codpiece of one of the most important masculine icons from the period – Henry VIII. Apparently, during the seventeenth century, one of Henry's codpieces was put on public display in the Tower of London. It remained there until the middle of the eighteenth century, when it was finally removed as an 'offence to decency'. The letters of a French visitor, César de Saussure, provide a detailed description of the layout of the display in the Tower. First, he says that there was a large hall 'containing statues and figures of a score or so of ancient English Kings', and 'near the entrance of the hall is the figure of Henry VIII' who is 'represented standing in his royal robes'. According to de Saussure, there was also some sort of mechanical contrivance in place to reveal the King's codpiece. He states that 'If you press a spot on the floor with your feet, you will see something surprising with regard to this figure, but I will not say more and leave you to guess what it is'.[29]

This mechanised display codes the king's codpiece as obscene – that is to say, something that cannot be staged in public. A similar strategy is used to deal with the codpiece by Thomas Boreman in his account of the 'curious figure of king Henry the eighth' in *Curiosities in the Tower*. At the end of his description, Boreman writes 'I have now told my young readers all the fine things that I know of in this pompous place, excepting one,

> And that's a secret
> Which king Harry has to show;
> And so it must remain,
> Till they to men and women grow.[30]

Boreman's decision to relegate the codpiece to the status of the 'open secret' was undoubtedly a consequence of the fact that his book was written primarily for children, but it nevertheless replicates, on a verbal level, the strategy used for exhibiting the item itself.

John Dunton and Ned Ward provide more 'adult' accounts of the Tower display. Dunton, in his *Voyage Round the World* (1691), declares that 'the most remarkable thing I saw [in the Tower] was *Old Hary's Cod-piece*'. He writes it was 'such a sizeable one that I shall never more wonder there belong'd *so many Wives to't*'.[31] This quip clearly associates Henry's codpiece with his virility. It also imagines that virility to be sexual rather than reproductive. Indeed, the very size of the codpiece is taken as an index of Henry's gargantuan sexual appetite. Moreover, that appetite is figured, not in terms of the number of children Henry sired, but in terms of the number of women he married (and by extension, had sexual relations with). In the end, Dunton's comment implies that Henry needed these multiple partners to satisfy his 'sizable' sexual desire.

Similar assumptions about Old Harry and his codpiece underlie Ned Ward's account of his visit to the Tower of London published in 1699 in *London Spy*. Ward mentions that he saw 'the *Codpiece* of that Great Prince who never spar'd a *Woman* in his *Lust*'.[32] In this formulation, Henry's codpiece is again associated with his 'lust'. In this case, however, that 'lust' is not only directed at his six wives (and crudely quantified by them); instead, it is directed at any and all women. Strangely, Ward then goes on to explain that the codpiece was 'Lin'd with Red' and that it 'hung gaping like a *Maiden-Head* at full Stretch, just Consenting to be Ravish'd' (321). If earlier, the codpiece seemed to stand in for Henry's phallus as an index of his 'lust', here it is figured as a vaginal receptacle for the phallus itself. It is as if Ward first viewed the codpiece from the outside, and then viewed it from the inside. Consequently, the codpiece emerges as what Freud would eventually label a 'bisexual' artefact: that is to say, an artefact that can be associated with either 'the male or female genitalia according to context'.[33] For my purposes, the thing to note about this latter description is that it still clearly links Henry's masculinity with sexual penetration by comparing the codpiece to a 'maidenhead' that he could 'ravish'. In fact, this metaphorical comparison associates Henry not just with sexual penetration in general, but more specifically with the penetration of virgins. This is an extreme form of penetrative sexuality insofar as it involves the rupture of the hymen/maidenhead.

Finally, it must be said that Ward seems to evoke the spectre of rape in his text, both in the comparison of Henry's codpiece to a maidenhead that he could 'ravish' and in the comment that Henry 'never spared a woman his lust'. He papers over the unseemly implications of this by representing the codpiece/maidenhead in typically sexist form as a 'consenting' participant in the 'rape'. According to Ward, the codpiece/maidenhead is 'just consenting to be ravished'. Nevertheless, it might seem odd that Ward would risk referring to rape at all in the context of the monarch's masculinity and sexuality. This can perhaps be explained by returning to the observation made by Howard and Rackin: namely, that within the emergent regime of performative masculinity, rape is not only a demonised practice but also a 'model for masculine dominance'. The point, then, is not that Ward is suggesting that Henry is a rapist, but rather that in describing Henry's penetrative masculinity, Ward consistently evokes this act.

Although all of these seventeenth-century accounts of Henry's codpiece in the tower of London thus imagined the King's masculinity in distinctly penetrative terms, it should be noted that the older reproductive model had not completely disappeared. This is made clear by a story that Ward repeats about the codpiece. He says that, according to his guide, 'in [Henry's codpiece], to this Day, remains this Vertue, That if any Married Woman, tho' she has for many Years been Barren, but sticks a *Pin* in this *Member-Case*, the next time she uses proper means, let her but think of her *Tower Pin-Cushion* and she needs not fear *Conception*'.[34]

Henry's codpiece thus seems to have served as a kind of fertility talisman. There are, however, a number of odd elements about this practice. First, it is strange that the object became a fertility symbol in the first place, given Henry's well-known reproductive tribulations. But in addition, it is interesting that the codpiece came to serve as a reproductive aid for women rather than men. And finally, it is worth noting that this scenario inverts traditional gender roles insofar as it is the women who stick phallic 'pins' into the vaginal 'pin-cushion'.

The practice of sticking pins into Henry's codpiece is also mentioned in a seventeenth-century ballad from the Pepys' collection entitled 'The Maids New All-a-mode Pincushing'. One of the verses states that 'People in the tower / stick forty in an hour / Upon an old Pincushing there . . . For Codpiece does never cry, forbear, forbear, forbear'.[35] These verses do not mention the fact that the practice of sticking pins into the codpiece was considered a fertility rite. Instead, the act is sexualised through an extended allusion to prostitution and sticking 'pins' into this 'pincushion'.

If, in this ballad, the codpiece is returned to a sexual and, more specifically, penetrative economy, the fact that it was sometimes used as a fertility symbol means that the cultural work it performed was somewhat uneven or contradictory. Indeed, it would appear that both of the ideologies of masculinity circulating at the time were in one way or another articulated through this object. The representations of Henry VIII's codpieces from his own lifetime also illustrate this point. Most of them, no matter what their form, seem to have been used to construct a more 'testicular masculinity'. For example, the well-known Holbein mural at Whitehall portrays Henry with a somewhat phallic codpiece, but at the same time, the portrait emphasises genealogical concerns. Indeed, Louis Montrose argues that 'The prominence and ample proportions of the king's codpiece . . . are especially appropriate to the dynastic theme of this particular painting, which commemorates the birth of Prince Edward, thus guaranteeing (so it seemed) the continuity of the Tudors in the male line'.[36] This same theme and trope are repeated in a portrait of Henry's son. This image of Edward VI mirrors the painting of his father in many of its compositional elements, from the hat down to the codpiece and dagger. The art historian Karen Hearn notes that 'the positioning of [Edward's] left hand draws attention to his codpiece'. She claims, moreover, that this gesture is meant to assure 'the viewer of the future continuance of the dynasty'.[37] Thus, both of these paintings (and the codpieces in them) construct masculinity in largely reproductive terms, but when we consider these paintings alongside the later representations of Henry's codpiece, it is clear that the accessory was figured as both penetrative and reproductive.[38]

* * *

So far, I've been analysing the cultural construction of masculinity in early modern England and the role that the codpiece(s) played in this process. But I now want to return to something that I mentioned at the beginning of this essay: namely the fact that the codpiece disappeared from general usage sometime around the turn of the seventeenth century. Signs of its decline began to appear as early as 1594. Thomas Nashe describes a man wearing a 'codpiece' in *The Unfortunate Traveler* and notes parenthetically that 'they were then in fashion'.[39] The implication, of course, is that they no longer are. In 1600, another writer insisted that the 'codpeece breech' was 'cleane out of fashion'.[40] And finally, in 1628, Robert Hayman celebrated the demise of this fashion in a poem entitled 'Two Filthy Fashions'. He writes

> Of all fond fashions, that were worne by Men,
> These two (I hope) will ne'r be worne againe:
> Great Codpist Doublets, and great Codpist britch,
> At seuerall times worne both by meane and rich:
> These two had beene, had they beene worne together,
> Like two Fooles, pointing, mocking each the other.[41]

As Hayman's verses begin to suggest, the codpiece was not only out of fashion, but also increasingly disarticulated from masculine identity. In Hayman's poem, the codpiece is no longer a guarantor of masculinity or an indication of what 'nature' has given men; rather, it is a ridiculous 'fool'.

We might therefore say that the codpiece eventually became a failed means of establishing masculinity. But how did this transformation occur? First of all, we need to recognise that this was not simply a whimsy of fashion. Instead, it was a change that had to be culturally enacted or produced. That is to say, the link between the codpiece and masculinity had to be actively disarticulated. This disarticulation was, moreover, an 'uneven development'.[42] Despite the overall trend, there were early texts that distanced the codpiece from masculinity in one way or another (such as Shakespeare's *Two Gentlemen of Verona*), and there were later ones that continued the productive investment in it long after it had gone out of fashion (such as the discussions of Henry VIII's codpiece).

In the remainder of the essay, I will be analysing some of the seventeenth-century writing that helped to divorce the codpiece from masculine identity. I should begin by saying that some of the texts that I discussed earlier are actually somewhat more complicated then they might at first appear. The best example of this is the verses by Marston. As I noted earlier, Marston says:

> . . . I'll never raile at those
> That weare a codpis, thereby to disclose
> What sexe they are, since strumpets breeches vse,
> And all men's eyes save Linceus can abuse.

If these lines seem to suggest that the codpiece is a necessary means of securing masculine identity, their meaning is radically altered by the lines that follow. Marston goes on to say

> Nay, steed [instead] of shadow, lay the substance out,
> Or els faire Briscus I shall stand in doubt
> What sex thou art, since such Hermaphrodites
> Such Protean shadowes so delude our sights.[43]

Here Marston essentially reverses himself and advises men who wear codpieces (emblematised in the foppish figure of 'faire Briscus'[44]) to 'lay the substance out'. In doing so, he implicitly acknowledges that the codpiece is not any different from the 'breeches' he mentioned earlier – both of these things could be used to 'abuse' or 'delude our sights'. Moreover, Marston, like Haymen, ultimately suggests that the codpiece is ridiculous. He does this, in part, though the humorous pun on 'steed'. The two possible readings of the line are thus: 'Nay, *instead* of shadow, lay the substance out' and 'Nay, *steed* of shadow, lay the substance out'. In the second, Marston addresses men who wear codpieces directly, referring to them as 'steed[s] of shadow'. This moniker implies that they are trying to turn themselves into 'steeds', or 'stud horses',[45] by means of the 'shadow[y]' codpiece. When seen from this perspective, the 'nay' at the beginning of the sentence also takes on a humorous equine resonance. But Marston does not simply ridicule the codpiece-wearing men by comparing them to horses, he also does so comparing them to the 'strumpets' who use 'breeches': all of these people are, he implies, trying to become something they are not. Indeed, in an ironic reversal, Marston suggests that the foppish men who wear codpieces are actually feminine. Therefore, unless they 'lay the substance out' he will still 'stand in doubt' of 'what sex' they are.

For my purposes, the important thing to notice about Marston's text is that he at first ventriloquises the discourses on the codpiece that I analysed at the beginning of this essay in claiming that the item 'discloses' the 'sex' of the wearer, and then later turns and undermines them when he says that it is only the genital 'substance' and not its 'shadow' that can 'remove' his 'doubts' about 'what sex' these individuals are. Marston thus questions the codpiece's role as a constituent element of masculinity, in part, by producing a disjunction between the object ('shadow') and the genitals ('substance').

The discussion of the codpiece in *The Minte of Deformities* (1600) – written by 'C.G, Gent'. – does some of the same cultural work as Marston's verses. C.G. writes:

> A codpeece breech . . .
> is used of all: oh spightfull forgerie.
> When God fayre fashion'd partes, vnfashioning,
> they both deforme those gratious parts, & him.[46]

These fascinating lines portray the codpiece, first and foremost, as a 'forgerie' of the 'partes' God created. This description implicitly counters the claim put forward by writers like Holyday that the codpiece was a transparent manifestation of those parts. Indeed, we might say that C.G. drives a conceptual wedge between the codpiece and the genitals in much the same way as Marston had, though obviously to less humorous effect.

Even though C.G. condemns the use of the codpiece, he tacitly acknowledges the power that this item had to constitute or 'fashion' the body. He says that 'God . . . fashion'd partes', and that by wearing the codpiece, men 'unfashion' or 'deforme' them. The assumption the author makes about clothing's ability to 'deforme' the body might be compared to the theoretical point made by Anne Hollander in *Seeing through Clothes*: whereas Hollander maintains that clothes can shape the body, C.G. gives this idea negative spin, saying that they 'deforme' or 'unfashion' it. If C.G. thus recognises the constitutive power of the codpiece, it is hardly surprising to find that he also endeavours to distance the object from the male body. He does this in both a literal way (by insinuating that it should not be worn) and in a more figurative one (by labelling it a 'forgery'). He was not alone in this. Other seventeenth-century writers also challenged the seemingly transparent connection between the codpiece and the male 'parts'. They did so, not only by referring to the codpiece a 'forgerie', but also by revealing the contents of the codpiece to be almost anything but the male genitals. In other words, if, in earlier texts, characters like William Cricket boast about the 'contents' of their codpieces and claim that this is what makes them 'good and proper' men, in later ones, the 'round, sound and profound contents' of the codpiece are revealed to be an object like an orange. This is precisely the object that Panurge is said to carry in his codpiece in a mid-seventeenth-century translation of Rabelais' *Pantraguel*.[47] In other seventeenth-century texts, codpieces are said to hold things such as ballads, bottles, napkins, pistols, hair, and even a looking glass. And in Thomas Middleton's *Your Five Gallants* (1608), several of the characters joke about a 'great codpiece with nothing in't'.[48]

These descriptions of people revealing the contents of their codpieces are almost invariably humorous. Nevertheless, the fashion-historian Max von Boehn 'explains' these representations by noting that the codpiece 'served as a pocket in which a gentleman kept his handkerchief, purse, and even oranges'. He also points out, moreover, that gentlemen would often pull these items 'out before the ladies' eyes and hand to them'.[49] The 'joke' involved in this gesture is quite similar to the humour that arose from revealing the contents of the codpiece in the texts I mentioned above. Both follow the typical pattern described by Freud in *Jokes and Their Relation to the Unconscious*: first, anxiety is created by the potential exposure of the genitals, and then it is dispelled by revealing the alternate object.[50] But if the humour involved in all of these 'revelations' is predicated upon the assumed connection between the codpiece and the male genitalia, I want to stress that the social practices and the texts that describe them would ultimately have worked to disarticulate that connection insofar as they suggested that it was not the male genitals that were actually contained in the codpiece.

Another way in which seventeenth-century writers worked to dissociate the codpiece from the male body and from masculinity was by highlighting the transferability of the accessory. If, as we have already seen, Marston recognises the possibility that women might 'use' the codpiece to 'abuse men's eyes', there are a number of other instances in drama and poetry from the period where this is precisely what happens. I have already discussed Julia's decision to don a codpiece in Shakespeare's *Two Gentlemen of Verona*, but perhaps the most well-known codpiece-wearing woman from the period was Moll Frith. In Middleton and Dekker's play *The Roaring Girl* (1611), they coin the term 'codpiece daughter' to refer to Moll and other women like her.[51] Another such 'codpiece daughter' is Constantina in Lording Barry's play *Ram Alley*, published the same year as *The Roaring Girl*. Finally, Francis Kynaston's narrative poem *Leoline and Sydanis* (1642) describes the Princess Sydanis:

Who without scruple instantly put on
The cloathes Prince Leoline on's wedding day
Had worne, and drest her selfe without delay:
Nor were the Breech, or Codpiece to her view
Unpleasing . . .

The contrast between the descriptions of Julia and the Princess Sydanis is, I believe, striking and is undoubtedly a function of the fact that the first appeared in the sixteenth century and the latter in the mid-seventeenth. Although both of these characters are the heroines of their respective stories, they behave very differently with regard to appropriating the codpiece. Whereas Julia is uncertain about using the item and has to be convinced by Lucetta, Sydanis adopts the item 'without scruple' or hesitation. Kynaston reiterates this point later, saying that she 'drest her selfe without delay'. Moreover, whereas Julia initially states that it would be 'illfavored' for her to wear the codpiece, the Princess has no such misgivings. In fact, she supposedly does not find the item 'unpleasing'. The contrast between these two stories indicates that the item had, in the intervening years, lost some of its cultural power, and it was therefore no longer quite as transgressive for a woman to appropriate the object.

A scene from Middleton and Dekker's *The Honest Whore, Part I* indicates that, by 1604, the codpiece had already been substantially disarticulated from masculinity. In it, a servant refuses admission to a messenger because he fears that he might be a woman: he states 'I would not enter his man, tho' he had haires at his mouth, for feare he should be a woman, for some women have beardes, mary they are halfe witches. Slid you are a sweete youth to weare a codpeece, and haue no pinnes to sticke upon't'.[52] This passage demonstrates, on the one hand, the continued cultural centrality of the beard and codpiece simply by virtue of the fact that the servant looks to these items to evaluate the masculinity of the messenger. But, on the other hand, the servant also clearly questions the reliability of those very items. He does so primarily by drawing attention to their transferability. First, he observes that although the messenger has 'haires at his mouth', 'some women have beardes'.[53] And he questions the codpiece's role as a guarantor of masculinity even more forcefully. He says that the messenger is 'a sweet youth' to 'wear a codpiece, and have no pinnes to stick upon't'. On the surface, this comment simply means that the messenger is a somewhat naive or unsophisticated gallant in that s/he does not have pins to stick in his codpiece (as was the custom).[54] But it also has other resonances that undermine the masculinity of the figure. Most obviously, the servant seems to be questioning whether the messenger has a 'pin' (in a phallic sense), but this quip may also have a more sexual significance as well. Apparently, bestowing a pin on someone was slang for having intercourse with them. A servant in *Misogonus* says that 'As for my pinnes, ile bestowe them of Jone when we sit by ye fier and rost a crabb. [S]he and I have good sporte when we are all alone'.[55] When seen from this perspective, the servant would be indicating that the messenger is unmasculine, not only because s/he does not have a pin/penis, but also because s/he does not have sexual experience.

Other writers from the period pushed this idea a step further and suggested that if the codpiece was detachable/transferable, then patriarchal power itself must be open to appropriation. For example, in the play *Apius and Virginia* (1575), the character 'Haphasard' describes several potential scenes of the-world-turned-upside-down. He warns not only that 'wives' might 'wear the Codpeece, and maydens coy strange', but also that 'maides would be masters by the guise of this country'.[56] In this formulation, the idea of women wearing the codpiece goes hand in hand with them being masters. Indeed, it is 'by the guise of this country' that women seem to become 'masters'. If this fantasmatic description was meant primarily as a warning against women's appropriation of the codpiece, it was also potentially subversive in that it acknowledged the transferability of both the codpiece and patriarchal power.

At first glance, William Gamage's 'On the feminine Supremacie', written in 1613, seems quite similar to *Apius and Virginia*. Gamage writes

> I often heard, but never read till now,
> That Women-kinde the Codpeeces did weare;
> But in those Iles, the men to women bow . . .
> I should therefore the woman iudge to be
> The vessell strongst, but Paule denies it me.[57]

In this poem, as in *Apius and Virginia*, the transferability of the codpiece is foregrounded and is again taken as a correlative of the transferability of patriarchal power: Gamage says that he has heard that 'Women-kind' wear 'the Codpeeces', and that in the 'Isles' where this happens, the men 'bow' to women. It might thus seem as if Gamage is warning against English women appropriating the codpiece and thereby inverting gendered relations, much as in *Apius and Virginia*. I believe, however, that Gamage is actually questioning the use of the codpiece altogether, rather than playing with its potential appropriation. Even though Gamage initially highlights the transferability of both the codpiece and patriarchal power, he later makes an effort to (re)secure the latter, but he does so without the former. This is a crucial point of departure from the scenario described in *Apius and Virginia*, and one which might be related to the fact that Gamage's text appears after the codpiece had gone out of fashion. Whatever the reason, Gamage says that while he might be tempted to generalise based on the social arrangements of this fantasmatic 'Isle' and judge women to be 'the vessell strongst', 'Paul denies' him this possibility. With this all-important qualification, Gamage attempts to guarantee the legitimacy and stability of the patriarchal order in the British 'Isles' by grounding it in biblical authority – and specifically in Paul's pronouncements about gender relations in Corinthians. We should note, however, that Gamage conspicuously avoids rehabilitating the codpiece. In the end, his comments (re)assert the gendered hierarchy while also disarticulating the codpiece from it. As a result, he implies that materialising masculinity through this part threatens to destabilise patriarchal gendered relations on account of its transferability.

* * *

By now, it should be clear that one of the primary strategies used to disarticulate the codpiece from masculine identity in the seventeenth century was emphasising its prosthetic nature. It is important to recognise, however, that despite the prevalence of this strategy in texts from the period, it does not follow that detachable/transferable parts were *necessarily* less essential than other parts in early modern England. Thus, instead of seeing the codpiece's prosthetic nature as an indication of the item's inevitable dispensability or superfluidity, I would propose seeing it as a chance to witness the process of construction at work. That is to say, the various manipulations of the codpiece are particularly evident because the item itself is prosthetic, and we are therefore able to see it being attached, detached, or transferred. This is true at both an individual and a cultural level. But if we remember that these manipulations are also acts of intervention with regard to the dominant ideologies of the time – since these ideologies are constantly reiterating themselves (or failing to do so) through the item – then the item's prosthetic nature might be seen as an indication of its participation in the ongoing process of ideological construction, and an indication of the 'instability' of the ideology itself.

I now want to turn to what might seem a paradox regarding the codpiece, and that is that even though both forms of this accessory eventually disappeared around the beginning of seventeenth century, the emergent ideology of masculinity did not disappear along with them. This emergent ideology is what Phyllis Rackin and Jean Howard call 'performative masculinity' or what Gary Taylor calls 'the regime of the penis', and it was becoming dominant around the turn of the century. And, if, as I've suggested, the phallic codpieces helped to instantiate this ideology, then why did they disappear along with their more scrotal counterparts?

Although my answer to this question must remain somewhat speculative, I believe that it has something to do with the emergent ideology of masculinity itself. I have tried to suggest in the course of this essay that the various changes and developments regarding the codpiece need to be studied in relation to the ideologies of gender. The texts that I have been studying provide some indication of the rationale for the renunciation of the codpiece, and the fact that the newly emergent ideology of masculinity began to be materialised through the penis itself, as opposed to the codpiece.[58] John Marston, for instance, claims that it is only the 'substance' and not the 'shadow' which can really remove doubts about 'what sex' an individual is. Similarly, the messenger in Middleton and Dekker's *The Honest Whore* suggests that the messenger is not a man if he has only a codpiece without a 'pin' to put in it. We might therefore say that the cultural investment in the penis arises out of, and in conjunction with, the decline of the codpiece. It may, moreover, also have been at least partially an attempt to disavow transferability and detachability of masculinity and masculine/patriarchal power.

Notes

1   This essay first appeared in my book *Materializing Gender in Early Modern English Literature and Culture* (Cambridge: Cambridge University Press, 2006). The book focuses on the gendered work performed by a series of detachable parts: in addition to this chapter on codpieces, it contains chapters on beards, hair, and handkerchiefs. For general information about the history of the codpiece, see Grace Q. Vicary, 'Visual Art as Social Data: The Renaissance Codpiece', *Cultural Anthropology* (1989): 3–25; Jeffrey C. Persels' article 'Bragueta Humanística, or Humanism's Codpiece', *Sixteenth Century Journal*, 28 (1997): 79–99; and W. L. McAtee, *On Codpieces* (n.p., Chapel Hill, 1954). There are also many studies in fashion history that include information about codpieces. See, for example, Michael Batterberry, and Ariane Batterberry, *Mirror, Mirror: A Social History of Fashion* (New York: Holt, Rinehart & Winston, 1977), François Boucher, *20,000 Years of Fashion: The History of Costume and Personal Adornment*, 2nd edition (New York: Harry N. Abrams, 1987), C. W. Cunnington, P. Cunnington, and C. Beard, *A Dictionary of English Costume* (Philadelphia: Doufour, 1960), and Milla Davenport, *The Book of Costume* (New York: Crown, 1976).

2   *Englands Vanity: or the Voice of God against the Monstrous Sin of Pride, in Dress and Apparel* (London, 1683), 123. This is an almost verbatim repetition of a description from a much earlier source. See *The Treasurie of Auncient and Moderne Times* (London, 1613), p. 371.

3   Vicary analyses representations of codpieces by approximately forty different Renaissance artists and maintains that 'The crucial fact learned from studying visual art data is that between 1400 and 1600 there was more than one kind of codpiece. Codpiece number one was, as we have seen, a soft, triangular flap attached to the hose with laces made of the same material as the hose . . . Next came stiffened, padded, protruding codpieces worn as additions matching either the clothes or the clothing. The first were worn generally in the 15th century, the others in the 16th century'. See Vicary, 'Visual Art as Social Data', p. 8.

4   Aileen Ribeiro, *Dress and Morality* (New York: Holmes & Meier Publishers, 1986), p. 62.

5   Anne Hollander, *Seeing through Clothes* (New York: Viking Press, 1978).

6   Henry Medwall, *The Plays of Henry Medwall*, ed. Alan H. Nelson (Totowa, NJ: Rowman and Littlefield Inc., 1980), p. 49.

7   Anon., *Wiley Beguiled* (London, 1606), p. 48.

8   Richard Niccols, *The Furies with Vertues Encomium* (London, 1614), Epigram VII.

9   These lines appear in 'Satire 2: Quidam sunt, et non videntur' from *The Metamorphosis of Pigmalions Image and Certaine Satyres* (London, 1598), p. 46.

10 Throughout this essay, I will be using *The Norton Shakespeare*, ed. Stephen Greenblatt (New York: W. W. Norton & Co., 1997).

11 M. Jean Carmel Cavanaugh, *Techonogamia by Barten Holyday, A Critical Edition* (Washington, DC: The Catholic University of America Press, 1942), 1.4.460–3.

12 Bulwer, *Anthropometamorphosis*, p. 539.

13 Andreas Musculus, *Hosen Teuffel* (Frankfurt, 1555).

14 Lyndal Roper, *Oedipus and the Devil: Witchcraft, Sexuality and Religion in Early Modern Europe* (London: Routledge, 1994), p. 117.

15 See, for example, Batterberry and Batterberry, *Mirror, Mirror*; Pearl Binder, *The Peacock's Tail* (London: Harrap, 1954); and James Laver, *The Concise History of Costume and Fashion* (New York: Scribners, 1969).

16 Leo Steinberg, *The Sexuality of Christ in Renaissance Art and Modern Oblivion* (New York: Pantheon/October, 1983), p. 90.

17 Steinberg, *The Sexuality of Christ*, pp. 183 and 190.

18 Marjorie Garber, *Vested Interest: Cross-Dressing and Cultural Anxiety* (New York: Routledge, 1992), p. 122.

19 Published by Nich. Culpeper Gent. And, Abdiah Cole, Doctor of Physick, *Bartholinus Anatomy; Made from the Precepts of His Father* (London, 1668), p. 55.

20 Thomas Gibson, *The Anatomy of Humane Bodies Epitomized* (London, 1688), p. 110.

21 Jean Howard and Phyllis Rackin, *Engendering a Nation: A Feminist Account of Shakespeare's English Histories* (New York: Routledge, 1997), p. 187.

22 Gary Taylor, *Castration: An Abbreviated History of Western Manhood* (New York: Routledge, 2000).

23 Rebecca Anne Bach, 'Tennis Balls: *Henry V* and Testicular Masculinity; or, According to the *OED*, Shakespeare doesn't have any balls', *Renaissance Drama*, 30 (1999–2001), p. 5. Bach sees the shift that I have been discussing taking place at a slightly later historical moment, near the end of the seventeenth century.

24 Quoted in Helkiah Crooke, *Microcosmographia* (London, 1615), p. 45.

25 Quoted in Bach, 'Tennis Balls', p. 6.

26 Thomas Vicary, *The Englisheman's Treasure, or Treasor for Englishmen* (London, 1586), p. 58.

27 Crooke, *Microcosmographia*, p. 243.

28 Culpepper, *Bartholinus Anatomy*, p. 2.

29 *A Foreign View of England in the Reigns of George I and George II: The Letters of Monsieur César de Saussure to his family*, trans. and ed. Madame Van Muyden (London: John Murray, 1902), pp. 87–8.

30 Thomas Boreman, *Curiosities in the Tower of London* (London: Thomas Boreman, 1741), pp. 2: 55 and 60.

31   John Dunton, *Voyage Round the World* (London 1691), p. 134.

32   Ned Ward, *The London Spy Compleat in Eighteen Parts*, with an introduction by Ralph Straus (London: Casanova Society, 1924), p. 321.

33   From Freud's *On Dreams. The Freud Reader*, ed. Peter Gay (New York: W. W. Norton & Company, Inc., 1995), p. 171.

34   Ward, *London Spy*, p. 321.

35   *A Collection of Ballads originally formed by John Selden* (London, *c*. 1575–1703), 3, p. 178.

36   Louis Montrose, 'The Elizabethan Subject and the Spenserian Text', in *Literary Theory/Renaissance Texts*, ed. Patricia Parker and David Quint (Baltimore: Johns Hopkins University Press, 1986), pp. 313–14.

37   *Dynasties: Painting in Tudor and Jacobean England, 1530–1630*, ed. Karen Hearn (New York: Rizzoli, 1996), p. 49.

38   A detailed analysis of the various representations of Henry VIII (in his own lifetime and afterward) and their relationship to the ideologies of masculinity lies outside the purview of this essay. While there is an obvious biographical 'explanation' for the changing perceptions of Henry and his codpiece, it would be a mistake to divorce the biography from a discussion of the historical shifts in the ideologies of masculinity. Indeed, the two were mutually constitutive.

39   Thomas Nash, *The Unfortunate Traveller*, ed. Philip Henderson, illustrated by Haydn Mackey (London: The Verona Society, 1930), p. 20.

40   C.G., *The Minte of Deformities* (London, 1600), p. 4. One of the characters in Samuel Rowlands's *The Knave of Harts* (1612) is said to be 'as stale as Breech with Cod-piece fashion'.

41   Robert Hayman, *Quodlibets, Lately Come over from New Britaniola* (London, 1628), p. 3.

42   Mary Poovey, *Uneven Developments: The Ideological Work of Gender in Mid-Victorian England* (Chicago: University of Chicago Press, 1988).

43   Marston, *The Metamorphosis of Pigmalions Image*, pp. 46–7.

44   According to the *OED*, a 'brisk' was 'a gallant' or 'fop'.

45   *OED*.

46   C.G., *The Minte of Deformities*, Bv.

47   François Rabelais, *Gargantua and Pantraguel, Book 1 English* (London, 1653).

48   Thomas Middleton, *Your Five Gallants* (London, 1608), D3v.

49   Max von Boehn, *Modes and Manners: Sixteenth Century*, translated by J. Joshua (London: Harrap, 1932), p. 128.

50   Sigmund Freud, *Jokes and Their Relation to the Unconscious*, translated by James Strachey (New York: Norton, 1963).

51   Thomas Middleton and Thomas Dekker, *The Roaring Girl*, ed. Paul A. Mulholland (Manchester: Manchester University Press, 1987), 2.2.93.

52   Thomas Middleton and Thomas Dekker, *The Honest Whore*, Part I (London, 1604), 1.10, G3v.

53   He also then makes a common misogynistic rhetorical manoeuvre of virtually excluding these women from humanity in general, saying 'mary they are halfe witches'.

54   As I noted earlier, this practice is mentioned in *Two Gentlemen of Verona*. It is also described in Webster's *The White Devil* (London, 1622).

55   See the entry for 'pin' in Gordon Williams' *A Dictionary of Sexual Language and Imagery in Shakespearean and Stuart Literature* (London: The Athlone Press, 1994), 1032.

56   R.B., *Apius and Virginia* (London, 1575), BIVv.

57   William Gamage, *Linsi-Woolsi* (London, 1613), D4v.

58   Gamage's verses make it clear that masculinity was not simply secured by 'natural' corporeal features, but also by biblical authority.

Objects of fashion in the Renaissance

Evelyn Welch

In her many portraits, Elizabeth I of England is often portrayed holding a range of objects, one of which is almost always a fan. Sometimes, as in the Ditchley portrait of Queen Elizabeth I, these are the rare, imported folding fans which had only been recently imported from Ceylon via Portugal and Spain. In other cases she is seen holding elaborate ostrich feather fans. But fans were not exclusive to royalty. A snapshot survey of other late sixteenth- and early seventeenth-century portraits shows a similar preference for fans in the hands of women across England, Italy, Spain, France, Holland and Scandinavia. Is this simply a pictorial convention? After all, as artists moved over to three-quarter or full-sized portraits, they had to put something in the hands of their sitters; other popular objects include books, handkerchiefs, gloves and jewellery.

Gauging when and why an object becomes fashionable is problematic in the Renaissance and early modern period, and economic, social and theories of artistic agency can be deployed as explanations. But studying early fashion is rendered problematic by the fact that while reasonably large numbers of items such as fans survive for the late seventeenth and eighteenth centuries, few remain from the earlier period. There are two late sixteenth-century examples in the Royal Collection in England and in the Fashion Museum in Bath (made from mica), but these are very rare. Capturing historical fashion often involves matching up documentary, visual and material records. But what do we do when one of these categories is missing?

In the case of Renaissance fashion objects such as fans, we need to look more closely at the materials from which these were made, a strategy that allows us to find items often misfiled or in unusual places. While the expensive prototypes have proved fragile, the cheaper paper versions, designed to be used and disposed of, have been more durable. There are numerous cut-out paper fans that survive in print collections across Europe, many designed with pictorial games, descriptions of military or festive events or the lyrics and even the music for popular songs. Here fashion is not exclusively in the hands of milliners, tailors or mercers or even in the control of the elite. Instead, artists, printers, street-hawkers and the men and women attending popular festivals were all involved in designing, marketing and selecting an item more usually associated with the court. Sometimes there were deliberate overlaps between these social groups. A surviving example of a paper fan designed to give the same impact as one made in feathers has the Medici crest at the centre. Likewise, we know that in the early seventeenth century, the Grand Duke of Tuscany ordered 500 copies of a fan showing a water-battle for the women who were attending – a form of 'souvenir' for viewers who were not allowed to get too close to the actual event (Snapshot 4.2).

What can we learn from this case? Firstly, the fan is an object that crosses multiple boundaries and we need to ask whether the ways in which it is used and understood in England at the court of Elizabeth I differed from its meanings in Japan or Ceylon or

Snapshot 4.1 Engraving for a fan, Italian, *c.* 1589–95. © Civica Raccolta delle Stampe Achille
Bertarelli, Milan. All rights reserved.

Snapshot 4.2 Engraving for a fan (second state), *c.* 1589–95. © Civica Raccolta delle Stampe Achille Bertarelli, Milan.

those we impose today. How does this differ in turn when it is used, not by an English Queen but by a London or Venetian butcher's bride? Does the object define its owner or is the inter-connection more subtle? Above all, this is one of many cases now being explored which suggest that goods once dismissed as frivolous, feminine and a source of vanity need to be re-inscribed into our histories of the Renaissance.

Bibliography and further reading

Arnold, J. (1988) *Queen Elizabeth's Wardrobe Unlock'd*, Leeds: Maney.

Welch, E. (2005) *Shopping in the Renaissance: Consumer Cultures in Italy, 1400–1600*, New Haven: Yale University Press.

Welch, E. (2009) 'Art on the Edge: Hair and Hands in Renaissance Italy', *Renaissance Studies*, 23, pp. 241–68.

(1990) *Ventagli italiani: Moda, costume, arte*, Venice: Marsilio.

PART 2

Fashion and Social Order
The early modern world

Peter McNeil and Giorgio Riello

The influential scholar Daniel Roche wrote of seventeenth-century clothing that it 'was at the centre of debates about wealth and poverty, excess and necessity, superfluity and sufficiency, luxury and adequacy' (Roche 1994: 5). Fashion also mattered a great deal to the cultural mind-set of early modern society as its meanings contained a paradoxical flip-side. Fashion in the early modern period might, Roche argues, be seen as a very dignified aspect of the notion of civility, restraint, manners and codes of conduct, or clothes might become 'weapons' in a game of swiftly moving and seductive appearances (ibid.: 5–6). So clothes and grooming were described in conduct books and instruction manuals as something that had to be carefully managed depending on social needs and settings. Many of these detailed directives were written for young men, the most famous of the texts being Castiglione's *The Book of the Courtier*, whose form came from a classical model by Cicero and which was widely copied and modified for the following three centuries, forming the basis of the 'etiquette' manual.

If we read the fashions of Renaissance Europe through the lens of modern values and outlooks, we obscure the expectations and priorities of subjects very different from us indeed. One of the first obstacles to be overcome is the modernist distaste for excessive detail and ornamentation, which is seen today as either superfluous, corrupt or folly. We also have to break down the twentieth-century division of tastes and objects into very separate categories. Modern-day viewers think that a dress must be very different from a book in its inspiration, production and meaning. Yet to a Renaissance viewer it was precisely the inter-relationships and contrasts between things, patterns and materials that created meaning. Thus Juliet Fleming, in writing on graffiti and the writing arts of early modern Europe, points out that the page was not necessarily the most obvious place for 'writing' – but that this 'writing' might be found in embroidered clothes, jewels, linens for table and painted grotesques on walls (Fleming 2001). Some garments were even embroidered with sacred or profane texts in pearls.

Boundaries were not so important; the edge of a page or the hem of an embroidered dress flowed on to ancillary objects and spaces, picking up and underlining emblematic themes in objects as diverse as furniture, fresco or tapestry, architecture and civic spaces. Medieval art, Fleming argues, was not organised for the perception of the subject looking at it – the 'I' of Cartesian thought and Absolutist aesthetics – but meaning was generated through structure and relationships. As Susan Frye presents in her short essay for this *Reader*, women stitched allegiances, messages and debates through the embroideries they created for objects from pocket books to book covers that were linked through both motifs and intentions.

Pattern, texture and colour were read quite differently in a system of correspondences. A paradoxical mind-set that prioritised a system of social order within a rapidly evolving society could state that both magnificence and modesty were 'virtues', in a way that seems incompatible today. Of course, depending on who you were and what position you occupied, consumer virtues were different. This notion, derived from classical notions of decorum or *bienséance*, continued to influence European life until the relative fixity of the *ancien régime* was replaced by the bourgeois value system of earning, acquiring and systematically negotiating deliberate fashion choices that sent out messages about a family's relationship to thrift, respectability or prodigality.

Early modern Europeans were not simply 'snobs' in any sense of the word. They revelled in the connections and contrasts between the social orders, the occupations, the seasons, the humours of the body. Classical decoration was set against the so-called 'grotesques' that both were anti-classical and emphasised decoration; all of this visual imagery was also available for clothing. The nobility was not, as some think, immune from the stench of the street and the crush of the people. They enjoyed the contrast between the high and the low, the elevated and the vulgar, and as Evelyn Welch shows in her perceptive reading of that accessory the fan, the ordinary people looked back and participated in the public entertainments of the elites too. In 1685 Bérain designed costumes for a masque at Versailles based on the 'Cries of Paris' with figures dressed as coarse and colourful street sellers. The richly dressed audience gazed back at the purveyors who made their appearances possible through a complex network of craft skill and entrepreneurial activity.

Patricia Allerston, in 'Clothing and early modern Venetian society', argues that clothing was 'paramount'. Just as Renaissance citizens were taught that they should be able to read the occupations and wealth of a distant city by reading the faces of its houses, so they were fascinated by the diverse dress traditions that extended across Europe and beyond. Clothing began to be included in collections of curiosities as early as the Renaissance, a portent of the later interest that anthropologists would take in the decorative coverings of strange people they encountered on their travels. In her detailed case study of Venice, Allerston argues that artisans and shopkeepers had access to varied and complex wardrobes as early as the sixteenth century, yet lived side by side with the poor who had nothing. She points to the limits of documentary evidence such as probate inventories, the topic of a specific snapshot in this section by Janine Maegraith. Inventories show how much people had, but *not* how they acquired it, leaving many questions unanswered in the supply side of the equation. Clothing was valuable and formed a chain of credit, providing even guarantees against loans and functioning as pledges, rental income and goods for hire. Allerston's study demolishes the simple notion of clothing emulation that has dominated simplistic understandings in writing about fashion. Clothing could be rented, frequently was, and appearances upheld for set purposes and strategies. The classes were far from spatially separate and dressing well was 'good for business'.

Eugenia Paulicelli, in an innovative analysis of Cesare Vecellio's illustrated text *Degli*

Habiti antichi et moderni di diverse parti del mondo (1590 and 1598), crafts a new picture of this important encyclopaedic study of dress. Vecellio, she argues, maps the diversity of dress and customs of the world that the Renaissance conquerors were at that moment 'discovering'. Fashion in his schema is something that changes so quickly that it can never be a finished project. In emphasising the relationship between word and image, modes and memory, place and identity, Vecellio went beyond both the conduct and travel book in creating a new type of product made possible by the innovations in print technology that in turn drive and generate new fashions. Vecellio, Paulicelli argues, highlights a consciousness of national dress that is simultaneously developed through *inter*-national contexts, products and markets. In a wide-ranging analysis, she argues that this period was crucial for the future of fashion, being the time when the fundamental gendered forms of men's and women's garments were consolidated. In concluding that the very structure and framing of Vecellio's printed book created the sense of an unfinished project, Paulicelli points to the dynamic nature of both writing and print culture in creating modern subjectivities.

It is probably true that fashion's relationship with different parts, zones or 'cartographies' of the body, as the French intellectual Georges Vigarello puts it, shifts dramatically over time. The notion of the erogenous zones proposed by James Laver to understand the rise and fall of the twentieth-century woman's bust and hips might not be so absurd after all (Laver 1950). Maria Hayward, in a carefully researched essay on the social and sartorial significance of male headwear at the courts of Henry VIII and Edward VI, argues that the hat was the central focus of male fashion in creating notions of standing, age and affluence. Just as the neck is both a real and an imaginary fragility which both men and women manage every day, so the head is a special zone and, in a period before men wore wigs, must have been doubly important. In explaining the range, types and complex construction of sixteenth-century male hats, Hayward complicates what we mean by dress and accessory. Hats were garnished and fastened with a range of badges, pins, aiglets and enamels, stored in special cases and on a par in terms of value with other jewellery. Hats were essential for the non-noble and professions, and despite being less valuable, used the skilful craft of cutting and shaping to create proud effects. Hayward's essay is exemplary in working in an area with few surviving artefact sources and in its mobilisation of archive and image to re-imagine the power of a fashion item.

More recent speculations on dress and gender have transferred ideas elaborated in the history of sexuality. Thomas Laqueur's influential notion of the continuum of sexuality which privileged masculine traits until the development of separate spheres is employed by Jennifer M. Jones, who reads the gendered address of one of the first fashion periodicals, the *Mercure Galant*, issued from 1672. In her 'Clothing the Courtier' she exposes the contradictions inherent in the notion of fashion that perplexed rational thinkers, moralists and economic theorists throughout the seventeenth century. Was *la mode* a mask that deceived, in which female treachery was central, or was fashion a symbol of royal authority, homogenisation and civilisation? Jones concludes that this printed medium issued news to the people of the town about the luxuries worn at court and speculated on the relationship of fashion to age, physique, rank and even the weather. In publishing twice a year, in spring/summer and autumn/winter, the journal set up a model for fashion practice which persists today, even while the seventeenth-century journal editors complained that sometimes the seasons simply refused to match the proposed fashions. This focus on the seasons surely relates to very ancient ideas about birth and renewal, which would seem germane for fashion's definition. Furthermore, the *Mercure Galant* introduced a self-reflexive attitude towards fashion that 'eschew[ed] explicit explanations'. Fashion was not something that needed to be explained in a rational manner, but something to be recounted and unmasked, in a deliberately enigmatic way. In this way, we see fashion becoming embedded in written cultures and popular thought whose ironies can be exploited several centuries later by the brilliant poet-journalists Baudelaire, Mallarmé and Oscar Wilde.

The early-modern mind blended elements from the natural and supernatural world in order to create contrasts that carried powerful meaning. As Umberto Eco has so vividly shown in his *Art and Beauty in the Middle Ages* (1986), this was not a puritanical age, but rather one in which a sense of beauty was keenly felt, even more so by those religious sects such as the ascetics who absented themselves from fashion. We might conclude this introduction with a few lines from Dante's *Divine Comedy*, in which the mechanical arts are merged with nature and raw materials to create one overwhelming perfume. The point to note here is that to an early modern Christian, only Eden is pure and celestial; all other things and spaces, no matter how beautiful or carefully wrought, carry within them the notion of the Fall:

> Think of fine silver, gold, cochineal, white lead,
> Indian wood, glowing and deeply clear,
> fresh emerald the instant it is split –
> the brilliant colours of the grass and flowers
> within that dale would outshine all of these,
> as nature naturally surpasses art.
>
> But nature had not only painted there:
> the sweetness of a thousand odours fused
> in one unknown, unrecognisable.
>
> Canto VII/70–81, Dante, *Divine Comedy* (Purgatory)

Bibliography and further reading

Books and articles

Arnold, J. (1975) 'Decorative Features: Pinking, Snipping and Slashing c. 1600', *Costume*, 9, pp. 22–6.

Bastl, B. (2000) 'Clothing the Living and the Dead: Memory, Social Identity and Aristocratic Habit in the Early Modern Habsburg Empire', *Fashion Theory*, 5, 4, pp. 357–88.

Benhamou, R. (1989) 'The Restraint of Excessive Apparel: England 1337–1604', *Dress*, 15, pp. 27–37.

Bremmer, J., and Roodenburg, H. (eds) (1991) *A Cultural History of Gesture*, Ithaca: Cornell University Press.

Bryson, A. (1990) 'The Rhetoric of Status: Gesture, Demeanour and the Image of the Gentleman in Sixteenth- and Seventeenth-century England', in L. Gent and N. Llewellyn (eds), *Renaissance Bodies: The Human Figure in English Culture c. 1540–1660*, London: Reaktion Books, pp. 136–53.

Carlano, M., and Salmon, L. (eds) (1985) *French Textiles from the Middle Ages through the Second Empire*, Hartford, CT: Wadsworth Atheneum.

Clarke, G., and Crossley, P. (eds) (2000) *Architecture and Language: Constructing Identity in European Architecture, 1000–1600*, Cambridge: Cambridge University Press.

Collier Frick, C. (2002) *Dressing Renaissance Florence: Families, Fortunes, and Fine Clothing*, Baltimore: Johns Hopkins University Press.

Currie, E. (2000) 'Prescribing Literature: Dress, Politics and Gender in Sixteenth-century Italian Conduct Literature', *Fashion Theory*, 4, 2, pp. 157–77.

Eco, E. (1986) *Art and Beauty in the Middle Ages*, New Haven and London: Yale University Press, 1986, pp. 4–16: 'The Medieval Aesthetic Sensibility'.

Ffoulkes, C. (1988 [orig. edition 1912]) *The Armourer and His Craft, from the XIth to the XVIth Century*, New York: Dover.

Fisher, W. (2006) *Materializing Gender in Early Modern English Literature and Culture*, Cambridge: Cambridge University Press.

Fleming, J. (2001) *Graffiti and the Writing Arts of Early Modern England*, London: Reaktion Books.

Foucault, M. (1984) 'The Means of Correct Training' [from *Discipline and Punish*], in P. Rabinow (ed.), *The Foucault Reader*, London: Penguin, pp. 188–205.

Frye, S. (1999) 'Sewing Connections: Elizabeth Tudor, Mary Stuart, Elizabeth Talbot, and Seventeenth-century Anonymous Needleworkers', in S. Frye and K. Robertson (eds), *Maids and Mistresses, Cousins and Queens: Women's Alliances in Early Modern England*, New York and Oxford: Oxford University Press, pp. 165–82.

Geuter, G. (2000) 'Reconstructing the Context of Seventeenth-century English Figurative Embroideries', in M. Donald and L. Hurcombe (eds), *Gender and Material Culture in Historical Perspective*, Basingstoke: Macmillan, 2000, pp. 97–111.

Harte, N. B. (1976) 'State Control of Dress and Social Change in Pre-industrial England', in D. C. Coleman and A. H. John (eds), *Trade, Government and Economy in Pre-industrial England: Essays in Honour of F. J. Fisher*, London: Weidenfeld and Nicolson, pp. 132–65.

Harte, N. B. (1991) 'The Economics of Clothing in the Late Seventeenth Century', *Textile History*, 22, 2, pp. 277–96.

Hayward, M. (1996) 'Luxury or Magnificence? Dress at the Court of Henry VIII', *Costume*, 30, pp. 37–46.

Hayward, M. (2007) *Dress at the Court of King Henry VIII*, Leeds: Maney.

Howard, Jean E. (1988) 'Crossdressing, the Theatre, and Gender Struggle in Early Modern England', *Shakespeare Quarterly*, 39, 4, pp. 418–40.

Huizinga, J. (1996 [original edition 1919]) *The Autumn of the Middle Ages*, Chicago: University of Chicago Press.

Jones, A. R. (2006) 'Habits, Holdings, Heterologies: Populations in Print in a 1562 Costume Book', *Yale French Studies*, 110, pp. 92–121.

Jones, A. R., and Stallybrass, P. (2000) *Renaissance Clothing and the Materials of Memory*, Cambridge: Cambridge University Press.

Laver, J. (1950) *The Changing Shape of Things: Dress*, London: John Murray.

Levy Peck, L. (2005) *Consuming Splendor: Society and Culture in Seventeenth-century England*, Cambridge: Cambridge University Press.

Mentges, G. (2002) 'Fashion, Time and the Consumption of a Renaissance Man in Germany: The Costume Book of Matthaus Schwarz of Augsburg, 1496–1564', *Gender and History*, 14, 3, pp. 382–402.

Newton, S. M. (1988) *The Dress of the Venetians 1495–1525*, Aldershot: Scolar Press.

Orgel, S. (1996) *Impersonations: The Performance of Gender in Shakespeare's England*, Cambridge: Cambridge University Press.

Pastoureau, M. (2001) *The Devil's Cloth: A History of Stripes and Striped Fabric*, trans. Jody Gladding, New York: Columbia University Press.

Ribeiro, A. (2003 [1st edition 1986]) *Dress and Morality*, Oxford: Berg, esp. pp. 74–94.

Ribeiro, A. (2005) *Fashion and Fiction: Dress in Art and Literature in Stuart England*, New Haven: Yale University Press.

Roche, D. (1994) *The Culture of Clothing: Dress and Fashion in the 'Ancien Régime'*, Cambridge: Cambridge University Press.

Rosenthal, M. F. (2006) 'Cutting a Good Figure: The Fashions of Venetian Courtesans in the Illustrated Albums of Early Modern Travellers', in M. Feldman and B. Gordon (eds), *The Courtesan's Arts: Cross-cultural Perspectives*, Oxford: Oxford University Press, pp. 52–74.

Saunders, A. S. (2006) 'Provision of Apparel for the Poor of London, 1630–1680', *Costume*, 40, pp. 21–7.

Schick, L. M. (2004) 'The Place of Dress in Pre-modern Costume Albums', in S. Faroqhi and C. K. Neumann (eds), *Ottoman Costumes: From Textile to Identity*, Istanbul: Eren, pp. 93–102.

Scott, K. (1995) *The Rococo Interior: Decoration and Social Spaces in Early Eighteenth-century Paris*, New Haven and London: Yale University Press.

Sekules, V. (2001) 'Spinning Yarns: Clean Linen and Domestic Values in Late Medieval French Culture', in A. L. McClanan and K. Rosoff Encarnacion (eds), *The Material Culture of Sex, Procreation and Marriage in Premodern Europe*, Baskingstoke: Palgrave Macmillan, pp. 79–91.

Sleigh-Johnson, N. (2003) 'Aspects of the Tailoring Trade in the City of London in the Late Sixteenth and Earlier Seventeenth Centuries', *Costume*, 37, pp. 24–32.

Sleigh-Johnson, N. (2007) 'The Merchant Taylors' Company of London under Elizabeth I: Tailors' Guild or Company of Merchants?', *Costume*, 41, pp. 45–52.

Spufford, M. (1984) *The Great Reclothing of Rural England: Petty Chapmen and their Wares in the Seventeenth Century*, London: Hambledon Press.

Stallybrass, P. (1996) 'Worn Worlds: Clothes and Identity on the Renaissance Stage', in M. De Grazia, M. Quilligan and P. Stallybrass (eds), *Subject and Object in Renaissance Culture*, Cambridge: Cambridge University Press, pp. 289–320.

Stannek, A. (2003) '*Vestis Virum Facit*: Fashion, Identity, and Ethnography on the Seventeenth-century Grand Tour', *Journal of Early Modern History*, 7, 3–4, pp. 332–44.

Styles, J. (2001) 'Innovation and Design in Tudor and Stuart Britain', *History Today*, 51, 12, pp. 44–51.

Sutton, A. F. (1991) 'Order and Fashion in Clothes: The King, His Household and the City of London at the End of the Fifteenth Century', *Textile History*, 22, 2, pp. 253–76.

Swain, M. (1990) *Embroidered Stuart Pictures*, Princes Risborough, UK: Shire, 1990.

Vigarello, G. (1988) *Concepts of Cleanliness: Changing Attitudes in France since the Middle Ages*, Cambridge: Cambridge University Press.

Vigarello, G. (1989) 'The Upward Training of the Body from the Age of Chivalry to Courtly Civility', in M. Feher et al. (eds), *Fragments for a History of the Human Body*, part 2, New York: Zone, 1989, pp. 148–99.

Vincent, S. (2003) *Dressing the Elite: Clothes in Early Modern England*, Oxford: Berg.

Vincent, S. (2009) *The Anatomy of Fashion: Dressing the Body from the Renaissance to Today*, Oxford and New York: Berg.

Wilson, B. (2005) 'Costume and the Boundaries of Bodies', in *The World in Venice: Print, the City, and Early Modern Identity*, Toronto: University of Toronto Press, pp. 70–132.

Printed resources

Arnold, J. (1985) *Patterns of Fashion 3: The Cut and Construction of Clothes for Men and Women c. 1560–1620*, London: Macmillan.

Arnold, J. (ed.) (1980) '*Lost from Her Majesties Back'*: Items of Clothing and Jewels Lost or Given Away by Queen Elizabeth I between 1561–1585*, Costume Society Extra Series, London: Costume Society.

Arnold, J. (ed.) (1988) *Queen Elizabeth's Wardrobe Unlock'd: the Inventories of the Wardrobe of Robes Prepared in July 1600*, Leeds: Maney.

Arnold, J. (2008) *Patterns of Fashion 4: The Cut and Construction of Linen Shirts, Smocks, Neckwear, Headwear and Accessories for Men and Women c. 1540–1660*, ed. J. Tiramani, London: Macmillan.

Castiglione, B. (2002 [1528]) *The Book of the Courtier: The Singleton Translation: An Authoritative Text Criticism*, ed. Daniel Javitch, New York and London: W. W. Norton & Co.

Cumming, V. (1984) *The Visual History of Costume: The Seventeenth Century*, London: Batsford.

Cunnington, C. W., and Cunnington, P. E. (1972) *Handbook of English Costume in the Seventeenth Century*, London: Faber & Faber.

Della Casa, G. (2001) *Galateo: A Renaissance Treatise on Manners*, ed. Konrad Eisenbichler and Kenneth R. Bartlett, Toronto: Centre for Reformation and Renaissance Studies.

Deserps, F. (2001) *A Collection of the Various Styles of Clothing Which Are Presently Worn in Countries of Europe, Asia, Africa, and the Savage Islands, All Realistically Depicted*, Minneapolis: James Ford Bell Library.

Evelyn, M. (1977 [1690]) *Mundus Muliebris, or The Ladies Dressing-Room Unlock'd*, Costume Society Reprint, London: Costume Society.

Lens, B. (1970) *The Exact Dress of the Head*, facsimile of 1725–6 sketchbook, London: V & A Publications.

Rosenthal, M. F., and Jones, A. R. (eds) (2008) *The Clothing of the Renaissance World: Europe, Asia, Africa, The Americas*, London: Thames & Hudson.

Vecellio, C. (1977) *Vecellio's Renaissance Costume Book: All 500 Woodcut Illustrations from the Famous Sixteenth-century Compendium of World Costume (1598)*, New York: Dover Publications.

Weiditz, C. (ed.) (1994) *Authentic Everyday Dress of the Renaissance: All 154 Plates from the 'Trachtenbuch'*, London: Dover Publications.

Online resources

The Royal Danish Collections at Rosenborg Castle: www.dragt.dk/samling/rosenborg/index.eng.html

AHRC early modern dress and textile network, at Queen Mary, University of London: www.earlymoderndressandtextiles.ac.uk/

Chapter 4

Clothing and early modern Venetian society

Patricia Allerston

C LOTHING WAS PARAMOUNT in early modern Europe. It accounted for a significant proportion of household expenditure at many different levels of society, and attracted much comment. Just as contemporaries described, often in minute detail, the garments worn by their compatriots, so foreign visitors to cities and courts devoted considerable attention to the appearance of the people they encountered. Such close observation was motivated by a serious purpose since clothing was thought to offer a kind of window on individuals and societies alike. The instructive qualities attributed to clothing may help to explain why so many costume books were printed during the late sixteenth and seventeenth centuries; they also shed light on the inclusion of exotic garments in the collections of curiosities which similarly characterise the period.[1]

A Milanese cleric, Pietro Casola, who visited Venice en route to the Holy Land in 1494, surveyed the Venetian inhabitants with as much care as he described their religious sites and artefacts. One of the many insightful remarks which he made about his encounter with Venetian society was that 'those [women] who are able as well as those who are not dress very sumptuously'.[2] Casola sought an explanation for this paradoxical state of affairs. Similarly, this essay tries to make sense of the rather contradictory images of early modern Venetians which can be formed from a study of their clothing.

Clothing consumption

Academic study of clothing as a means of understanding society was advocated by *fin-de-siècle* pioneers of sociology, such as Georg Simmel (1858–1918) and Thorstein Veblen (1857–1929).[3] In the late nineteenth century, clothing had featured in the popular histories of private life, and prompted some specialised studies, but it was more commonly the subject of historical anecdotes.[4] Almost a century passed before clothes were to be appreciated more generally by the historians of their societies. Fernand Braudel was one of the first scholars of international repute to broach the subject, including clothing in the major study of the latter part of his career, *Civilisation matérielle, economie et capitalisme, XVe–XVIIIe siècle*. Volume 1 of this trilogy, first published in 1967 and later retitled *Les structures du quotidien: le possible et l'impossible*, was concerned, unusually, with consumption.[5] It presented this phenomenon as the most fundamental and least sophisticated of three different types of economic activity, the other two being distribution and production. Accordingly, and again most unusually, Braudel centred his discussion on the mundane necessities of life, such as food, clothing, housing and furniture.

The originality of Braudel's approach lay not in its analysis of material culture, but in the place it claimed for that subject within the mainstream of economic and social history.[6] The increasing number of studies of material goods undertaken since the late 1960s attests to the increasing acceptance of the topic, as does its inclusion in more general historical works.[7] Many of the specialised studies of the last few decades are based, in contrast to the rather unrigorous examination of visual and anecdotal sources favoured by Braudel, on the systematic analysis of probate inventories and similar types of evidence. They have explored different sets of problems as well as methodologies, partly reflecting contemporary historians' committed engagement with a broad range of academic disciplines.[8] Whereas many have stressed the importance of social status, the perceived limitations of the determinist approaches to social analysis adopted by the previous generation of historians, including Braudel, also encouraged the pursuit of other objectives.[9] Of the various sorts of objects studied, clothing has been investigated from a particularly wide variety of angles. Although relatively few quantitative studies of clothing were undertaken in the 1980s, within the past 25 years it has been explored as an indicator of value systems, signs, attitudes and identities, as well as being examined for what it says about economic wealth and social status.[10]

In spite of the recent explosion in historical studies, consumption is a subject which remains poorly understood. Just as periodisation has been an issue, so explanations of early modern consumer behaviour have also provoked considerable debate.[11] For Braudel, writing in the late 1960s, variations in consumption were explained simply, in terms of structural inequalities within society: since most people were limited in what they could consume, superfluity was afforded only to the privileged few. Thus the clothing worn in early modern Europe, like the other artefacts used, simply reflected the gulf which existed between the social orders.[12] The display of luxuries was considered by Braudel to be part of a constant 'drama' enacted between those social orders – what he called the *comédie sociale*.[13] In the 1980s, a vigorous debate on consumer behaviour was provoked among British historians of consumerism, by the publication of an influential study by Neil McKendrick, John Brewer and J. H. Plumb, *The Birth of a Consumer Society: The Commercialization of Eighteenth-century England*.[14] This focused on the assumption that the lower social orders would, if they were given the opportunity, copy the consumption patterns of privileged groups within society rather than establish their own. Social emulation of this nature was a topic of discussion in the eighteenth century, and it has proved to be an enduring concept in studies of early modern consumer behaviour.[15] The problems it presents have engaged continental as well as British scholars. For Giovanni Levi, an historian of Venice with close links to the Ecole des hautes études en sciences sociales in Paris, the recurrent reference to social emulation denotes the reductive manner in which consumption has consistently been analysed.[16]

Levi's criticisms reflect the awareness of the complexity of late medieval and early modern social structures which has informed recent historical thinking in a number of fields. Calls have been made for more sophisticated conceptualisations of society which would allow for the complicated realities (*vécus*) of social life in the past.[17] Micro-analysis offered Levi a means of highlighting the intricate nature of consumer behaviour within early modern Venetian society: by focusing on two families within the same social group, he was able to demonstrate that different patterns of consumption were followed by siblings.[18] This essay is also concerned with the complications inherent in early modern Venetian consumption, but it approaches the topic from a very different angle.

In a valuable addition to the literature, Cissie Fairchilds argued that much had still to be learnt about the goods consumed before definite conclusions could be drawn about consumer behaviour. This discussion considers one of the two topics identified by Fairchilds, a subject also championed by Braudel some 30 years ago: the distribution of material artefacts.[19] More particularly, it explores the supply of clothing in the dynamic and densely populated setting of Venice in the sixteenth and early seventeenth centuries. In so doing it demonstrates the great variety of means by which clothing could be acquired in a highly developed urban centre, and indicates the broad spectrum of the city's inhabitants who, as a result, could participate in the clothing market in some means or form. An examination of the demand for clothing from the point of view of supply sheds light on the association of relatively expensive items of dress with members of the Venetian populace, such as Casola's well-dressed women of slender means. It also, like Levi's micro-analytical approach, exposes the limitations of a simple explanation of consumer behaviour within such a sophisticated early modern setting. First, some information on the structures of Venetian society as well as on the general place of clothing within that society is required. Having introduced this framework, the various means by which clothing could be acquired in early modern Venice can then be discussed. The range and nature of these supply mechanisms indicate that clothing served a variety of uses in the city. This essay therefore concludes by highlighting a number of possible explanations for consumer behaviour in Venice.

Venetians and their clothing

Venetian society in the sixteenth and seventeenth centuries has been variously characterised. Contemporary commentators, such as the eulogist Francesco Sansovino, created an ideal image, elaborating on the myth of an harmonious constitution. The Venetians whom Sansovino represented had always endeavoured to play down their social differences in the interests of general stability.[20] Thus, in the words of a fictional contemporary, 'everyone is contented with his position and existence, and does not attempt to advance any further by disturbing the universal peace'.[21] Social restraint has little place in the view of Venetian society presented by the goldsmith-poet Alessandro Caravia in 1541. Criticising the great religious confraternities of the city, he noted that 'now everyone takes a pride in pursuing caprices and selfish ambition . . .'.[22] Modern historians have tended to side with Caravia instead of Sansovino, and have depicted a stratified and unashamedly hierarchical social structure, dominated by a closed patrician caste. According to such interpretations, apart from a small, secondary group with particular economic and bureaucratic privileges known as the *cittadini*, the vast majority of Venetians had no role in government and thus had little chance of gaining social status.[23] For many, this legally defined social structure, like that of many other Italian centres, was becoming increasingly hierarchical during the early modern period.[24] Indeed, a provocative argument has been made that an important Venetian social group – the poor – became completely marginalised over the course of the sixteenth century.[25]

Interest in the composition of the patriciate, as well as in lower social groups, has given nuances to this rigidly hierarchical model of early modern Venetian society. It has highlighted the existence of great variations in wealth among the patriciate, and it has also focused attention on the diverse 80 per cent or so of Venetians – made up mainly of artisans, labourers and their families – who were excluded from political life.[26] Thanks to its port, its manufacturing industries, its many shops and warehouses, as well as the administrative, religious and social services which it provided, Venice was a bustling and cosmopolitan centre in the sixteenth and early seventeenth centuries. For much of the period, the city was a magnet for successive waves of incomers – both rich and poor alike – from the Italian mainland and much further afield.[27] Early modern Venetian society thus encompassed a fluctuating and potentially volatile mix of immigrants, extremes of wealth and poverty and large communities of workers dependent on international trade. Peter Burke suggested that material goods such as clothing played an increasingly important role as 'indicators of status' in dynamic urban contexts such as this. In 1981, for example, he argued that larger populations created 'opportunities which some would-be social climbers were quick to seize and exploit'.[28] The legally defined social structures of Venice placed formidable obstacles in the way of such opportunism. To be able to assess whether clothing consumption was dynamic in other respects, the general place it held within Venetian society should also be explored.

By the sixteenth century, Venice already had a well-established reputation as a centre of clothing consumption. The rich apparel of the city's female inhabitants had been one of its distinctive features highlighted in the mid-thirteenth century by the chronicler Martino da Canal.[29] In 1494, Casola described the sumptuous appearance of Venetian men as well as women, although like many commentators he dwelt upon the latter. 'Above all else', he concluded, 'Venetian women of all conditions take great pleasure in being seen and looked at in public . . . '.[30] Casola's other remarks suggest that this was a specific reference to the city's many courtesans. Nearly a century later, the urbane traveller Michel de Montaigne was more impressed by the expensive outlay on sumptuous clothes and other material goods by such women than by their much-famed beauty.[31] A more enthusiastic commentator, Thomas Coryate, described one of these 'sumptuous' courtesans, in the early 1600s, as being 'decked like the Queene and Goddesse of love' herself, in precious jewels, damask edged with gold, a red petticoat and stockings of rose-pink silk.[32]

The comments of Casola, Montaigne and Coryate suggest that this type of clothing was extremely expensive. The high cost of fine-quality garments in general can be demonstrated by an episode in the life of the Venetian artist Lorenzo Lotto. Impecunious and typically shoddily dressed, when Lotto moved in with a wealthier cousin (a lawyer) in 1540, he borrowed 120 ducats. Just over a third of this substantial sum of money was spent on clothing.[33] Among the various items which Lotto acquired at this time were a woollen cloak and a lined woollen tunic, costing about 8.5 ducats and 5.5 ducats respectively.[34] This represented a considerable outlay for a master craftsman such as Lotto. On the basis of average builders' wages calculated for 1546, they translate into just under 43 days' wages for the cloak, and 28.7 days' wages for the tunic.[35] In these terms, the total sum Lotto spent on clothing during the 27 months he lived with his wealthier cousin was the equivalent of 202 days' work.[36] Far from being an opportunity to 'seize and exploit' as described by Burke, social mobility – even within the same social order – could thus represent a considerable financial undertaking. It was perhaps partly for this reason that the time Lotto spent in his cousin's house was the cause of some considerable apprehension to him.[37]

The high cost of clothing in Venice imposed constraints upon the city's patricians, as well as its *popolani*. Spare capital was not a given of patrician life in the early modern period and the requirement to acquire the expensive garments deemed suitable for official duties as well as for public social occasions could prove a heavy burden.[38] In the financially difficult post-war year of 1530, for example, the Venetian government awarded 100 ducats apiece to the four patricians appointed to accompany a special envoy to Rome. This was to make the red-velvet, fur-lined cloaks which were customary for such purposes.[39] Concerning a similar ambassadorial trip to Rome in 1585, the future doge Leonardo Donà recorded his redeployment of existing garments as well as his new acquisitions (a tactic also deployed by Lotto when moving in with his cousin in the 1540s).[40] In 1611 Donà noted that for 37 years he had 'avoided spending on my desires, subjecting them to reason and abstaining from all kinds of personal pleasures'.[41] The family tax return which he submitted in 1582 indicates why such caution was necessary. The total annual income which he and his two brothers declared – some 985 ducats – was a respectable sum for that time, but it would soon have been consumed by expensive outlays on clothing.[42]

Donà's careful approach to his possessions was not particularly unusual. Before entering a hermitage in 1511, the Venetian patrician Vincenzo Querini paid singular attention to the fate of his worldly goods. Rather than making an appropriately charitable (or noble) gesture by giving away two expensive velvet garments, he sought to sell them.[43] It was for such careful management of their resources – Querini's clothes had cost him 110 ducats – that James Cushman Davis considered Venetian patricians to be 'a conservative force' in the distribution of wealth.[44] The contemporary views of such activities are, however, ambiguous. Whereas Venetian patricians were expected to set such examples of restraint in their consumer behaviour, they were also criticised for doing so. In this respect Leonardo Donà is an appropriate example for he was accused by his enemies of miserliness.[45]

Part of the myth of social harmony propounded by Francesco Sansovino in the late sixteenth century concerned the choice of clothing favoured by Venetians. It was to avoid the problems arising from inequality that, according to Sansovino, they wore 'quasi-religious clothes, demonstrative of peace and love'.[46] This was a reference to the toga, a long, simple gown which had been worn by male Venetians in the upper reaches of society since the Middle Ages.[47] For many of the visitors to Venice who commented on the toga, this dignified form of dress shed light on the upright character of the Republic's leaders.[48] The ideal of restraint in patrician appearances which the garment denoted was reinforced by sumptuary regulations, a large number of which were issued in sixteenth- and seventeenth-century Venice. Much has been written on Italian sumptuary legislation and an extensive discussion of the Venetian clothing

regulations is included in an article on the material culture of Venetian élites by Patricia Fortini Brown.[49] These regulations were intended to govern ostentatious displays of
wealth by private individuals, yet it is still far from clear exactly why they were introduced or how effective they proved to be. The sheer volume of sumptuary laws issued
in Venice during the period suggests that they failed to prevent ostentation.[50] Although
the remaining Venetian documentation is extensive, it is formulaic and contains few
details of enforcement. As such it is more useful for what it says about corporate patrician ideals than about specific social realities.[51] For example, a sumptuary decree of
1549 which forbade the use of gold cloth by patrician brides illustrates the belief that
such cloth should demonstrate the magnificence of the state rather than that of a family
or individual; as such it was meant to be worn solely by the doge on designated public
occasions.[52]

Sansovino noted an increasing predilection for ostentatious display when discussing
the clothes worn in Venice in the 1580s, and this was also a regular cause of complaint
among Venetian sumptuary regulators.[53] The cultivation of magnificence fits in with
humanist ideas about virtuous noble behaviour, and the diffusion of such ideas among
urban patricians may help to explain the criticisms of Leonardo Donà's parsimony.[54]
Such indications of an increasing demand for worldly goods among the Venetian patriciate are by no means conclusive and they are contradicted by James Cushman Davis's
study of the Donà family.[55] However they have been cited as proof of the intensifying
élitism on the part of the ruling group which was mentioned above. In the 1980s, Peter
Burke argued that the 'conspicuous consumption' of luxury goods offered a means by
which Venetian patricians, like their counterparts in other Italian cities, could accentu-
ate their social superiority and form an increasingly aristocratic identity. He described
this process as 'the aristocratic social drama' – a phrase strongly reminiscent of Braudel's *comédie sociale*.[56] Burke noted the need for systematic studies of household inventories to ascertain how much was actually spent on luxury goods in Italy. Such research
on Venetian probate inventories has been undertaken but, reflecting the shift towards
the lower reaches of the social spectrum which has characterised the city's social history in recent years, it has so far focused more on artisans and shopkeepers than on the
social élite.[57] In the absence of detailed studies it is difficult to draw firm conclusions
about developments within patrician consumer behaviour.

The picture which emerges of popular consumption in sixteenth- and seventeenth-
century Venice, on the other hand, is quite distinct and rather perplexing. It shows
that certain members of the populace owned a considerable amount of clothing. In his
study of the Venetian community of dockyard workers in the seventeenth century, the
American historian Robert Davis noted with surprise that many of these workers lived
and died 'in the midst of personal worlds filled with material goods'.[58] These personal
worlds included a good many clothes. In 1633, for example, an oarmaker called Alvise
left his widow six trunks of goods containing 43 shirts along with numerous other items
of clothing;[59] 43 shirts is a lot judged even by modern standards. The Venetian authorities clothed poor people leaving the city's pesthouses during a plague epidemic in 1557,
and considered one shirt to be sufficient for them.[60] In seventeenth-century Venice
these basic garments varied enormously in quality, but even the most abject items had a
certain monetary value. In spite of being worn and dirty, for example, the three shirts
bought at a petty debtors' auction in 1601 cost Master Anzolo, a broker, 10 lire – the
contemporary equivalent of nearly four days' work for a master craftsman.[61]

The contents of such household inventories underline the need for subtler approaches to working-people's material lives.[62] Just as they undermine the monolithic interpretation of popular consumption made by Braudel in 1967, so they also invite us to question the static character which he attributed to such dress.[63] Interestingly, they also suggest that Burke's compelling notion of 'conspicuous consumption' in early modern society might not necessarily have been restricted to the social élite. Applying quantitative analysis to the household inventories of relatively affluent Venetian artisans and shopkeepers, Fritz Schmidt concluded that they acquired increasing quantities of possessions, including clothes, from the late sixteenth century onwards.[64] This does not mean that Venice witnessed a 'consumer revolution' in the early modern period. There are too many problems associated with the evidence consulted by Schmidt to interpret his findings in this way. Moreover, a great many other sources demonstrate the abject poverty in which many Venetian *popolani* continued to live.[65] In keeping with the qualitative analysis of household inventories undertaken by other Venetian researchers, Schmidt's research does show, however, that in the late sixteenth and early seventeenth centuries the wealthier members of the Venetian populace possessed surprisingly large amounts of clothes. This may support Burke's dynamic interpretation of clothing in early modern urban contexts, but it does not prove his assertion about the opportunistic consumer behaviour of social-climbing city-dwellers: probate inventories do not reveal how (or when) these clothes were acquired, nor do they explain why such articles were possessed.[66] Information about the first of these topics can help to shed light on the second, and that is the purpose of the following section.

The supply of clothing

Clothing, like other household goods, was acquired in a great many ways in developed urban centres such as early modern Venice.[67] These included shop-centred trading practices. They also embraced a broad range of alternative distributive mechanisms, since clothing served as an item of exchange in its own right. It is only by appreciating the structural complexity of such markets for material goods that consumer behaviour can ever hope to be understood, since non-commercial exchanges were as much a part of early modern urban life as financial transactions. In 1644, an urban trader was reported as saying that 'money and friendship smother justice and giving a pair of silk hose to a captain of the watch shuts everyone up . . .'.[68] While this is probably an apocryphal story, it gives a good idea of the different historical reality which we are exploring – the use of clothes as 'pay-offs' was not unknown within the Venetian judicial system.[69] The role of commercial traders, like the corporative bodies which regulated them, should not, however, be under-estimated. Tailors had a very long history in Venice; their earliest surviving guild statutes – *the* earliest surviving guild statutes of Venice – predate the chronicle of Martino da Canal.[70] Tailors crop up regularly in studies of the city during the sixteenth and seventeenth centuries and records which date from this period show that they represented a source of clothing for members of the Venetian populace, as well as for those of the patrician élite.[71] Data gathered by Richard Rapp in his study of seventeenth-century Venetian manufacturing indicate that the number of guild-registered tailors in the city at that time was relatively high in comparison with other clothing trades.[72] Much else about the trade, however, such as the involvement of unregistered tailors and seamstresses, which would give an idea of the real extent of the trade, is difficult to ascertain. The tailors' guild records are uneven, and no detailed investigation has yet been made of early modern Venetian tailors like that of Carole Frick and Lizzy Currie's studies of their Florentine counterparts.[73]

Fabric to make clothing could be acquired from numerous sources. In this respect, drapers and mercers, whom Rapp's figures indicate to have been as numerous as tailors in seventeenth-century Venice, represent merely the tip of the iceberg.[74] Mercers, who dealt in a wide range of clothing accoutrements as well as cloth, were distributed throughout the city, although they are best known for their famous streets of shops linking Piazza San Marco to Rialto (the *Mercerie*).[75] The supply of cheaper types of new cloth such as the coarse woollen fabrics *griso* and *schiavina* came officially within the remit of the city's second-hand dealers.

As Daniel Roche has shown for eighteenth-century Paris and Beverly Lemire for English cities of the same period, second-hand dealers played an important role in centres of clothing consumption.[76] Venice was no exception. In the sixteenth and early seventeenth centuries, the city supported a dynamic and elaborate second-hand trade which supplied items of clothing of many different qualities and in a great variety of ways, to a broad spectrum of the Venetian population. Clothes could be bought new and second-hand from the workshops of guild-registered dealers, in the Ghetto, at market stalls, from pedlars passing through the city's streets, as well as in taverns.[77] They could also be bought directly from public auctions, which probably proved a cheaper alternative, unless they were rigged by unscrupulous dealers.[78] To cite an intriguing example, in May 1602 a Franciscan friar bought a yellow bodice and skirt at one of the city's many public debt sales.[79] Vincenzo Querini's attempts to sell his valuable black and scarlet velvet clothes in 1511 indicate that sumptuous cloth was expensive second-hand as well as new. Yet, if buying was out of the question, clothes could also be hired on short-term rental agreements. In 1557, the year of the plague epidemic when a single shirt was thought sufficient for Venetian paupers, the great many poor women who were hiring items of clothing which they could ill afford – including married women, widows, young maids and servants (also very young, indentured serving girls) – was noted with concern by the city's civil justice authorities. These clothes included shirts, caps, hose, shoes, skirts, scarves, hoods, veils and aprons, as well as various types of jewellery.[80] Since servants were usually given clothes as part of their work contracts, we can assume that they, at least, were renting such goods in addition to their basic, working garb.[81] The rental agreements which caused such concern in 1557 appear to have lasted several months, but they could also cover very short terms. To visit the Ghetto briefly in 1629, Felice Magalotti, a Jewish convert to Christianity, replaced his black hat with a red one of the kind worn by the Jews, which had been rented from a Jewish hatmaker.[82]

The alternative means of clothing acquisition which co-existed with these commercial practices were more diffuse. Like the informal aspects of the commercial sector, many of these alternative mechanisms of distribution have only recently started to be understood. The charitable practice of clothing the poor, for example, was demonstrated by the Venetian government during the plague of 1557 and was perhaps also the reason for the Franciscan friar entering the clothing market in 1602. This charitable mechanism was particularly advocated by Jesuit sponsors of religious confraternities and we would expect it to be prevalent in Venice, since it was a staunchly Catholic city noted for its religious brotherhoods as well as for its treatment of the poor, and responsive to the Tridentine decrees.[83] This is an aspect of early modern clothing supply which also requires further investigation. Given the changing attitudes associated with charitable provision in the sixteenth and seventeenth centuries and the high costs of new and used clothing – as well as the established practice of bequeathing luxury fabrics for liturgical uses – it is unlikely that many sumptuous garments were passed on directly in this way.[84]

Documentary references are rare, but borrowing clothes also appears to have been a relatively common practice in the early modern period. In 1531 the scurrilous writer Pietro Aretino boasted that he had lent shirts and hats to his friends during Carnival.[85] A century later in 1616, the patrician Giovanni Battista Barbo was obliged to take a man to court for failing to return a cloak which he had been lent but had not returned.[86] Clothes changed hands as gifts (the shirts and hats lent by Aretino had arrived in this way) – unlike charitable donations, this is a form of exchange which has started to attract historical attention.[87] Garments were also acquired in lieu of wages. Servants often acquired clothing in this way, and as well as their working garb they were also given ornate dress for important household occasions such as weddings, births and funerals. The government authorities' attempt to stop this practice in a sumptuary law of 1562 indicates that these 'special-issue' clothes could be quite elaborate.[88] When accused of excessive ostentation on the birth of his child in 1605, the wool merchant Vincenzo Zuccato denied that the elderly women (his relatives) who worked in his household had been wearing anything other than their normal widow's weeds and aprons.[89] Contractual obligations drawn up for domestic employees in 1595 stipulated that menservants could not own such clothes unless they had worked for six months since receiving them (female retainers were required to work for a year), and this confirms that they were valuable items of clothing.[90] Clothing theft, often involving such household servants, represented another typical means by which valuable clothes changed hands and passed between social groups. This was an old problem in Venice. Just as Aretino lost several finely worked shirts to a trusted servant in 1537, so, in 1592, the patrician Sebastian Morosini lost two tunics lined with silk – 'one like new' and the other 'used' – like Aretino, in the middle of the night.[91]

The pawnbroking activities of the Jews have attracted much attention from historians, unlike many of the alternative clothing-exchange mechanisms mentioned hitherto. However, the general importance of credit in early modern societies has only recently begun to receive the notice which it deserves.[92] This is another common reason why clothes changed hands in Venice as elsewhere – they were given as guarantees against loans, payments and debts, to artisans, retailers and innkeepers among others. When renting his red hat to visit the Ghetto in 1629, for example, the neophyte Felice Magalotti left his own black hat as security against the hired item; it was this which proved his undoing.[93] In April 1622, a certain Domenico Mezzalengua was sequestered *in casa* – apparently an inn – for failing to pay his bills. The innkeeper seized Domenico's two cloaks as security and threatened to sell them to cover a debt of 12 ducats. On the cloaks' retrieval one of them was immediately seized by another creditor.[94] Unscrupulous creditors made additional capital out of the clothes deposited against loans, by illegally renting them out. A garment left as a pledge in 1582 was rented out in this manner and ruined, causing the two patrician debtors to press charges against the moneylender concerned.[95] This is a good example since it sheds light on various facets of the clothing market. For a start, it indicates the broad scope of the rental trade in clothes which incorporated illicit as well as licit transactions. It also shows that people outwith the clothing trades could supply items of dress. In the same way that the moneylender in this case, a Jew, was not one of the official bankers of the Ghetto, so he does not appear to have been one of the city's officially recognised Jewish second-hand dealers. The pledge fraud he perpetrated coincided with the city's annual Ascensiontide festivities (the *Sensa*), and this also indicates the sorts of festive occasions for which expensive rented clothes might be required by those who could not otherwise afford them.

Knowledge of the bewildering variety of means by which clothing changed hands in early modern Venice helps to explain how Venetians might come to own a significant number of these items. It also suggests why relatively expensive items of dress were associated with members of lower social groups, since the acquisition of such goods did not necessarily require large outlays of cash. Casola reported, for example, that the poor but sumptuously dressed women who intrigued him on his visit to Venice in the 1490s had hired their splendid outfits.[96] An understanding of supply mechanisms, as Cissie Fairchilds has suggested, can also shed light on the reasons why Venetians might wish to own quantities of clothing. In so doing it highlights the problems posed by a hierarchical notion of social emulation as the sole explanation for popular consumer behaviour.

Accounting for popular consumption

The idea that the lower social orders would, if given the opportunity, copy the consumption practices of privileged groups within society can explain some but not all of the consumer practices noted above. It might be argued, for example, that the female servants who rented expensive clothes in the mid-sixteenth century did so because they wished to resemble their mistresses. This is the image of Venetian maidservants which is often conjured up in the comedies of the eighteenth-century playwright Carlo Goldoni.[97] Such emulation does make sense within the Venetian context of legally defined social orders; conspicuous consumption on the 'noble model' might be seen as offering a form of compensation for the political exclusion of lower social groups.[98] However, a hierarchical paradigm of social emulation does not satisfactorily explain why the likes of seventeenth-century dockyard workers lived and died 'in the midst of personal worlds filled with material goods'. There were a few noble palaces in the neighbourhood where most of them lived and worked, and with which they apparently identified. According to Robert Davis, the *arsenalotti* (as they were known) formed a reasonably self-contained community which was more likely to measure itself against the city's community of fishermen – the *Nicolotti* – rather than against the nobility.[99]

The economic security afforded by material goods in uncertain times has been suggested as an alternative reason for the consumer behaviour of such Venetians. This is how Robert Davis explained the hoards of possessions cited in dockyard-workers' inventories and it also fits in with sixteenth-century humanist depictions of 'plebeian parsimony'.[100] It is a forceful argument. We have seen that the Venetians had access to a number of facilities which allowed garments to be pawned and sold easily in times of adversity. The possession of clothing as a form of social insurance might also help to explain why Venetian artisans and shopkeepers were, as Schmidt's statistics indicate, acquiring more belongings as the city entered a difficult period of economic readjust-ments.[101] Another utilitarian motivation can be suggested for the consumer behaviour of these better-off *popolani:* that dressing well was good for business. Mention was made in the opening paragraph of this essay of the contemporary belief in clothing as a kind of window on individuals and societies. Since both international and domestic trade in the early modern period was based on trust, reputation and credit, an appearance of suc-cess could help to foster and maintain confidence. This extended to merchants' fam-ilies and may help to explain the ostentatious display of wealth reported to have been made by Vincenzo Zuccato on the birth of his child in 1605.[102] The instructive quali-ties attributed to clothing shed light on all types of Venetian workers. The importance of clothes to the 'honest courtesans' of Venice, for example, was noted by Montaigne in the 1580s and these women were regularly criticised for ostentation by the city's sump-tuary authorities. Pasquetta, a well-known courtesan who was denounced to the offi-cials in 1639, was seen being rowed down the Grand Canal – perhaps the most public thoroughfare of Venice – in very elaborate attire. She also flaunted these garments when appearing to answer this accusation, presumably assured that the French ambassador would intervene favourably on her behalf.[103] The considerable number of descriptions of such women by visitors to Venice suggests that their clothing served as a successful advertisement. Equally, dressing sumptuously allowed these women to advertise their success. It was perhaps to simulate an appearance of such success that prostitutes further down the professional scale were typical clients of clothes-hirers.[104]

Though plausible, these functional explanations of consumption do not cover all aspects of the consumer activities related above. The civil justice authorities' concerns about debt spirals involving poor women who were hiring clothes in 1557 indicate, for example, that not all popular consumers of expensive items of dress were intent solely on furthering their economic interests; a parallel might be drawn here with the modern use of credit cards.[105] The hierarchical paradigm of social emulation could well explain some individuals' behaviour, yet reference can also be made to numerous other factors, many of which were shared by various social groups.

Most Venetians, the non-patrician as well as the city's social élite, were, for ex-ample, open to similar commercial and social stimuli. They shared access to the famous shopping streets and squares of Venice, such as the *Mercerie* where luxury fabrics and trimmings were displayed for all to see.[106] Most sectors of society also participated in the city's festive occasions such as the above-mentioned *Sensa* and Carnival, both of which required additional adornment.[107] The chaotic, dynamic and densely populated nature of Venice can be seen as another powerful stimulus affecting all social groups. Patricians are credited with trying to distinguish themselves as a separate social group within this complicated urban context and, if they did, it is unlikely that they monop-olised this activity. As well as serving the kind of individualistic functions within the lower reaches of Venetian society highlighted by Peter Burke, clothes can also be seen as useful tools of collective identification. In this respect, the involvement of young women and indentured serving girls in the rental market is intriguing and may reflect the existence of an early modern form of 'youth culture'. Young Venetians, both male and female, were usually hard up for cash and yet appear to have been avid consum-ers of dress. Just as Goldoni's fictional maidservants surreptitiously borrowed clothes to 'dress up' at Carnival, and Momolo, his apprentice baker, took himself off to rent a Carnival outfit, in the early 1650s Antonio, a real-life apprentice apothecary, stole property belonging to his employer to become a consumer. By making 'certain acquisitions', however, he gave himself away.[108] A desire to consume among the young cut across social as well as gender divisions: in the 1570s the Venetian government was twice obliged to forbid traders from providing jewels, moveable goods and other assorted items on credit to patrician youths, to prevent the erosion of patrimonies.[109]

These are just a few of many possible interpretations of the consumer practices revealed by a study of clothing supply. An understanding of the many means by which clothing was distributed in sixteenth- and seventeenth-century Venice does not permit us to draw definite conclusions about consumer behaviour. It does, however, allow us to see cases for which a hierarchical notion of social emulation is not a convincing or sufficient explanation. It also opens up a great many other possibilities. Just as functional reasons can be suggested for the acquisition of items of clothing by popular consumers, so the city's commercial and festive structures can be seen as powerful social stimuli affecting all societal groups. The dynamic, unsettled and exciting nature of life in a major urban centre such as Venice was for immigrants one of its compelling attractions. This is likely to have acted as an additional impetus to consumption. Given these various explanations, to highlight a single reason for early modern consumer behaviour seems arbitrary as well as reductive, for it denies the possibility that early modern Venetians of many social groups could, like modern consumers, derive a variety of benefits as well as enjoyment from their stock of clothes. Findings such as these point to the preliminary conclusion that, in Venice at least, consumption was not the unsophisticated activity described by Fernand Braudel in his pioneering study of material culture, but a remarkably complicated phenomenon.

Acknowledgements

This essay is an expanded version of a paper given at the Second European Social Science History Conference held in Amsterdam in 1998. I am grateful to Marco Belfanti for inviting me to join his session on 'Fashion and social inequality'.

Notes

1   On expenditure on clothing in early modern Italy, see P. Burke, 'Conspicuous Consumption in Seventeenth-century Italy', in *The Historical Anthropology of Early Modern Italy: Essays on Perception and Communication* (Cambridge, 1987), p. 142; and P. Malanima, *Il lusso dei contadini: consumi e industrie nelle campagne toscane del sei e settecento* (Bologna, 1990), p. 41. For French comparisons, see D. Roche, *Histoire des choses banales: naissance de la consommation XVII–XIX siècle* (Paris, 1997), p. 222. On interest in clothes, costume engravings and collections of curiosities, see G. C. D. Griffo, 'Cronache di moda illustri: Marin Sanudo e le vesti veneziani tra quattro e cinquecento', in D. L. Bemporad, ed., *Il costume nell'età del rinascimento* (Florence, 1988), pp. 259–71; O. Blanc, 'Images du monde et portraits d'habits: les recueils de costume à la renaissance', *Bulletin du Bibliophile*, 2 (1995), pp. 221–61; and K. Pomian, *Collectors and Curiosities: Paris and Venice, 1500–1800*, trans. E. Wiles-Portier (Cambridge, 1990), pp. 48, 69.

2   P. Casola, *Viaggio di Pietro Casola a Gerusalemme* (Milan, 1855), p. 15.

3   See D. Frisby and M. Featherstone, eds, *Simmel on Culture: Selected Writings* (London, 1997), pp. 187–217; T. Veblen, 'The Economic Theory of Women's Dress', *Popular Science Monthly*, 46 (1894), pp. 198–205.

4   R. Barthes, 'Histoire et sociologie du vêtement: quelques observations méthodologiques', *Annales HSS*, 12 (1957), p. 430. Venetian examples are P. G. Molmenti, *La storia di Venezia nella vita privata dalle origini alla caduta della repubblica*, 3 vols (Trieste, 1973, facsimile of 1927 edition), vol. I, pp. 363–98, vol. II, pp. 263–3 12, vol. III, pp. 157–90; and G. M. Urbani de Gheltof, *Di una singolare calzatura già usata dalle donne veneziane* (Venice, 1882).

5   Revised second edition, Paris, 1979. On this work, see P. Burke, *The French Historical Revolution: The Annales School 1929–89* (Cambridge, 1990), pp. 44–53.

6   Burke, *French Historical Revolution*, pp. 46–7. See also P. Burke, '"Material Civilisation" in the work of Fernand Braudel', *Itinerario*, 5 (1981), p. 39.

7   See, for example, E. Cameron, ed., *Early Modern Europe: An Oxford History* (Oxford, 1999), pp. 233–64; P. Musgrave, *The Early Modern European Economy* (Basingstoke and London, 1999), pp. 59–85.

8   See C. Fairchilds, 'Consumption in Early Modern Europe: A Review Article', *Comparative Studies in Society and History*, 35 (1993), pp. 850–1. Influential works include M. Foucault, *Les mots et les choses: une archéologie des sciences humaines* (Paris, 1966); R. Barthes, *Système de la mode* (Paris, 1967); and M. Douglas and B. Isherwood, *The World of Goods: Toward an Anthropology of Consumption* (New York, 1979).

9   On such limitations, see R. F. E. Weissman, 'Reconstructing Renaissance Sociology: The "Chicago School" and the Study of Renaissance Society', in R. C. Trexler, ed., *Persons in Groups: Social Behaviour as Identity Formation in Medieval and Renaissance Europe* (Binghampton, NY, 1985), p. 41; on reaction to Braudel and his Annales contemporaries, see Burke, *French Historical Revolution*, pp. 65–91.

10 On identity formation see D. O. Hughes, 'Earrings for Circumcision: Distinction and Purification in the Italian Renaissance City', in Trexler, ed., *Persons in Groups*, pp. 155–77; and R. Jütte and N. Bulst, eds, 'Zwischen Sein und Schein: Kleidung und Identität in der ständischen Gesellschaft', *Saeculum*, 44 (1993). On social symbolism, see D. Roche, *La culture des apparences: une histoire du vêtement XVIIe–XVIIIe siècle* (Paris, 1989); also R. Jütte, *Poverty and Deviance in Early Modern Europe* (Cambridge, 1994), pp. 78–82. Other works include A. G. Cavagna and G. Butazzi, eds, *Le trame della moda* (Rome, 1995); J. Bottin and N. Pellegrin, eds, *Echanges et cultures textiles dans l'Europe pré-industrielle*, special issue of *La Revue du Nord*, Collection histoire, no. 12 (Lille, 1996); B. Lemire, 'The Theft of Clothes and Popular Consumerism in Early Modern England', *Journal of Social History*, 24 (1990), pp. 255–76, and *Dress, Culture and Commerce; The English Clothing Trade before the Factory, 1660–1800* (London and Basingstoke, 1997).

11 P. N. Stearns, 'Stages of Consumerism: Recent Work on the Issues of Periodization', *The Journal of Modern History*, 69 (1997), pp. 102–17.

12 Braudel, *Les structures du quotidien*, pp. 153–6, 271–9.

13 Ibid., p. 154.

14 Bloomington, 1982. On the debate, see Fairchilds, 'Consumption', p. 852; and L. Weatherill, 'Consumer Behaviour and Social Status in England, 1660–1750', *Continuity and Change*, 1 (1986), pp. 191–216.

15 See, for example, J. Brewer, *The Pleasures of the Imagination: English Culture in the Eighteenth Century* (London, 1997), p. 72.

16 G. Levi, 'Comportements, ressources, procès: avant la "révolution" de la consommation', in J. Revel, ed., *Jeux d'échelles: la micro-analyse à l'expérience* (Paris, 1996), pp. 187–207.

17 See G. Rosser, 'Crafts, Guilds and the Negotiation of Work in the Medieval Town', *Past and Present*, 154 (1997), pp. 3–31; Weissman, 'Reconstructing Renaissance Sociology', pp. 44–5; and Weatherill, 'Consumer Behaviour', p. 211.

18   Levi, 'Comportements, ressources', pp. 202–6. Micro-situational analysis was also advocated by Weissman, in 'Reconstructing Renaissance Sociology', p. 40.

19   The other topic was how goods were made; see Fairchilds, 'Consumption', p. 858.

20   F. Sansovino, *Venetia città nobilissima et singolare* (revised edition by G. Martinioni, Venice, 1663), p. 399. This topic is discussed in P. Hills, *Venetian Colour: Marble, Mosaic, Painting and Glass 1250–1550* (New Haven and London, 1999), p. 173, and in P. Fortini Brown, 'Behind the Walls: The Material Culture of Venetian Élites', in J. Martin and D. Romano, eds, *Venice Reconsidered: The History and Civilization of an Italian City-state, 1297–1797* (Baltimore and London, 2000), pp. 295–338.

21   Antonio Milledonne, *Ragionamento di doi gentil' huomini l'uno romano, l'altro venetiano* (Venice, 1581), cited in B. Pullan, '"Three Orders of Inhabitants": Social Hierarchies in the Republic of Venice', in J. Denton, ed., *Orders and Hierarchies in Late Medieval and Renaissance Europe* (Manchester, 1999), p. 153.

22   Cited in D. Chambers and B. Pullan, eds, *Venice: A Documentary History, 1450–1630* (Oxford, 1992), p. 216.

23   See G. Trebbi, 'La società veneziana', in G. Cozzi and P. Prodi, eds, *Storia di Venezia dalle origini alla caduta della serenissima*, 8 vols (Rome, 1992–8), vol. VI: *Dal rinascimento al barocco* (1994), pp. 129–238; and Pullan, 'Three Orders of Inhabitants', pp. 157–62. On *cittadini*, see A. Zannini, *Burocrazia e burocrati a Venezia in età moderna: i cittadini originari (sec. XVI–XVIII)* (Venice, 1993).

24   On this literature, see D. Romano, *Housecraft and Statecraft: Domestic Service in Renaissance Venice, 1400–1600* (Baltimore and London, 1996), pp. 227–35.

25   M. A. Laughran, 'The Body, Public Health and Social Control in Sixteenth-century Venice' (unpublished DPhil thesis, University of Connecticut, 1998).

26   On this shift, see N. Davidson, 'In Dialogue with the Past: Research on Venice from the 60s to the 90s', *Bulletin of the Society for Renaissance Studies*, 15 (1997), p. 19. Examples are A. F. Cowan, 'Rich and Poor among the Patriciate in Early Modern Venice', *Studi Veneziani* n. ser. 6 (1982); B. Pullan, 'The Occupations and Investments of the Venetian Nobility in the Middle and Late Sixteenth Century', in J. R. Hale, ed., *Renaissance Venice* (London, 1973), pp. 379–408; R. Mackenney, *Tradesmen and Traders: The World of the Guilds in Venice and Europe, c. 1250–c. 1650* (Totowa, NJ, 1987); R. C. Davis, *Shipbuilders of the Venetian Arsenal: Workers and Workplace in the Preindustrial City* (Baltimore and London, 1991); J. Martin, *Venice's Hidden Enemies: Italian Heretics in a Renaissance City* (Berkeley, 1993); and D. Romano, *Housecraft and Statecraft*.

27   The population of Venice in 1509 was *c.* 110,000. By 1563 it was *c.* 175,000. Devastated by plague, it recovered to *c.* 155,000 by 1593. It levelled out after another serious plague epidemic in the 1630s, to *c.* 120,000–130,000. See G. Beloch, 'La popolazione di Venezia nei secoli XVI e XVII', *Nuovo Archivio Veneto*, 3 (1902), pp. 40–4; D. Beltrami, *Storia della popolazione di Venezia dalla fine del secolo XVI alla caduta della repubblica* (Padua, 1954), p. 59 and Table 2.

28   See Burke, 'Material Civilisation', p. 41; and on the social élite, Burke, 'Conspicuous Consumption'.

29   Cited in A. Pertusi, 'Maistre Martino da Canal interprete cortese delle crociate e dell' ambiente veneziano del secolo XIII', in V. Branca, ed., *Storia della civiltà veneziana*, 3 vols (Florence, 1979), vol. 1, p. 287.

30   Casola, *Viaggio*, p. 15.

31   M. de Montaigne, *Journal de voyage de Michel de Montaigne*, ed. F. Rigolot (Paris, 1992), p. 69.

32   T. Coryate, *Coryats crudities*, 1611 (facsimile edition, London, 1978), pp. 265–7. On such prostitutes, see C. Santore, 'Julia Lombardo "somtuosa meretrize": A Portrait by Property', *Renaissance Quarterly*, 41 (1988), pp. 44–83.

33   See M. Muraro, 'I conti in tasca a Lorenzo Lotto', *Notizie da Palazzo Albani*, 13 (1984),

pp. 157–8, and n. 25. On this period, see L. Lotto, *Il 'Libro di spese diverse' con aggiunta di lettere e d'altri documenti*, ed. P. Zampetti (Venice, 1969), pp. 1–16, 21, 232–44.

34   Lotto, *Libro di spese*, p. 233. These costings were worked out on a basis of one Venetian ducat equalling six lire, or 124 soldi; see Chambers and Pullan, eds, *Venice*, p. 461.

35   The wages used for these calculations are from B. Pullan, 'Wage-earners and the Venetian Economy, 1550–1630', *Economic History Review*, 2nd ser. 16 (1964), pp. 425–6; a journeyman of 1545 would have had to work for 59 days and 39.4 days respectively.

36   A journeyman builder of 1545 would have had to work for 277.7 days. The total sum borrowed was the equivalent of 601.21 working days of a master builder, and 826.66 working days of a journeyman.

37   Lotto, *Libro di spese*, p. 215.

38   See J. C. Davis, *The Decline of the Venetian Nobility as a Ruling Class* (Baltimore, 1962), pp. 28–9; Pullan, 'Occupations and Investments'; and Pullan, 'Three Orders of Inhabitants', p. 158.

39   Archivio di Stato, Venice (hereafter ASV), Senato, Terra, reg. 25, fo. 226v [modern pagination], 5 January 1529 *more veneto* (hereafter *mv*).

40   A. Cutolo, 'Un diario inedito del doge Leonardo Donà', *Nuova Antologia* (1953), pp. 275–8. On Donà and his ambassadorial responsibilities, see J. C. Davis, *A Venetian Family and Its Fortune 1500–1900: The Donà and the Conservation of Their Wealth* (Philadelphia, 1975), p. 37. For Lotto refurbishing his old clothes, see Lotto, *Libro di spese*, pp. 232–3.

41   Cited in Davis, *Venetian Family*, p. 42.

42   Davis, *Venetian Family*, pp. xi, 23

43   S. D. Bowd, 'How to Be a Renaissance Hermit', *Bulletin of the Society for Renaissance Studies*, 16 (1998), pp. 11–13. For an example of the noble practice of making gifts, see P. Allerston, 'L'abito come articolo di scambio nella societa' dell' età moderna: alcune implicazioni', in Cavagna and Butazzi, eds, *Le trame della moda*, p. 111.

44   Davis, *Venetian Family*, p. xi.

45   On Donà's thriftiness and consequent unpopularity, see Burke, 'Conspicuous Consumption', pp. 143–4.

46   Sansovino, *Venetia città nobilissima*, p. 399.

47   See S. M. Newton, *The Dress of the Venetians, 1495–1525* (Aldershot, 1988). For a contemporary depiction, see C. Vecellio, *Habiti antichi et moderni di tutto il mondo* (first published 1590; second edition, Venice, 1598), fos. 81v, 83v.

48   For examples, see Casola, *Viaggio*, p. 14, and Chambers and Pullan, eds, *Venice*, p. 258.

49   See C. Kovesi Killerby, *Sumptuary Law in Italy 1200–1500* (Oxford, 2002); and M. G. Muzzarelli, ed., *La legislazione suntuaria secoli XIII–XVI: Emilia-Romagna* (Rome, 2002). On Venice, see G. Bistort, *Il magistrato alle pompe nella republica* [sic] *di Venezia: studio storico* (Bologna, 1969); P. Mometto, '"Vizi privati, pubbliche virtù": aspetti e problemi della questione del lusso nella repubblica di Venezia (sec. XVI)', in L. Berlinguer and F. Colao, eds, *Crimine, giustizia e società veneta in età moderna* (Milan, 1989), pp. 237–70; and Fortini Brown, 'Behind the Walls'.

50   Bistort, *Magistrato alle pompe*, pp. 113–49; on bending rules, see ASV, *Provveditori e Soprapprovveditori alle Pompe* (hereafter Pompe), *busta* 1, fo. 161r, 10 February 1649 *mv*.

51   A permanent magistracy was founded in 1515. Its archive is ASV, Pompe. See especially *busta* 1 (Capitolari 1562–1673) and *busta* 6 (miscellaneous material including some denunciations).

52   See ASV, Senato, Terra, reg. 36, fo. 74v, 5 January 1548 *mv* [regulation]. On this decree, see P. Allerston, 'Wedding Finery in Sixteenth-century Venice', in T. Dean and K. J. P. Lowe, eds, *Marriage in Italy, 1300–1650* (Cambridge, 1998), pp. 30–1; and M. Sanudo, *I diarii*, ed. R. Fulin et al. (Venice, 1879–1903), vol. 13, coll. 143, 10 October 1511 [doge wearing gold cloth].

53   Sansovino, *Venetia città nobilissima*, p. 400; ASV, Senato, Terra, *filza* 24, 9 January 1556 *mv*; ASV, Pompe, *busta* 1, Capitolare primo, fo. 53v, 21 January 1599 *mv*, fo. 121r, 19 December 1631; ASV, Pompe, *busta* 2, Capitolare secondo, fos. 19v–21v, 3 September 1644.

54   See, for example, P. Paruta, *Della perfettione della vita politica* (Venice, 1579), pp. 185–6. For Contarini's criticism of 'plebeian parsimony', see Pullan, 'Three Orders of Inhabitants', p. 157.

55   Davis, *Venetian Family*.

56   Burke, 'Conspicuous Consumption', pp. 132–49 (quote p. 140).

57   P. Pavanini, 'Abitazioni popolari e borghesi nella Venezia cinquecentesca', *Studi Veneziani*, new ser. 5 (1981), pp. 63–126; I. Palumbo-Fossati, 'L'interno della casa dell'artigiano e dell'artista nella Venezia del cinquecento', *Studi Veneziani*, new ser. 8 (1984), pp. 109–53; and Santore, 'Julia Lombardo'.

58   Davis, *Shipbuilders of the Venetian Arsenal*, p. 100.

59   Ibid., p. 100.

60   ASV, Provveditori e Sopraprovveditori alla Sanità (hereafter Sanità), reg. 730, Notatorio 7, fo. 171v, 23 August 1557; fo. 181v, 20 October 1557.

61   ASV, Signori di Notte al Civil (hereafter SNC), *busta* 271, Vendite, reg. 1, fo. 3r, 7 April 1601. The wage rates are from Pullan, 'Wage-earners', p. 426.

62   For similar findings elsewhere, see Roche, *The People of Paris*, pp. 160–94 and H. Medick, 'Une culture de la considération: les vêtements et leurs couleurs à Laichingen entre 1750 et 1820', *Annales HSS*, 50 (1995), 770–1. Compare to Jütte, *Poverty and Deviance*, pp. 78–82.

63   See Braudel, *Les structures du quotidien*, pp. 273–5.

64   F. Schmidt, 'Zur Genese kapitalistischer Konsumformen im Venedig der Frühen Neuzeit', in J. Reulecke, ed., *Stadtgeschichte als Zivilisationsgeschichte: Beiträge zum Wandel städtischer Wirtschafts-, Lebens- und Wahrnehmungsweisen* (Essen, 1990), pp. 23–40.

65   Nicolò Massa's harrowing mid-sixteenth-century description of the living conditions of the poor is included in Laughran, 'The Body, Public Health', p. 125. See also the description in Chambers and Pullan, eds, *Venice*, pp. 181–2.

66   See P. Allerston, 'Reconstructing the second-hand clothes trade in sixteenth- and seventeenth-century Venice', *Costume*, 33 (1999), p. 50; and D. Roche, *The People of Paris: An Essay in Popular Culture in the 18th Century* (Leamington Spa, Hamburg and New York, 1987), p. 162. On the lack of inventories for the very poor and for transients, see ibid., p. 165, and Jütte, *Poverty and Deviance*, p. 78.

67   This section develops upon Allerston, 'Wedding Finery', pp. 25–40; 'L'abito come articolo di scambio'; and Allerston, 'The Market in Second-hand Clothes and Furnishings in Venice, *c.* 1500–*c.* 1650' (unpublished DPhil thesis, European University Institute, Florence, 1996). Roche discussed such supply mechanisms as a distinctively Parisian phenomenon, see *The People of Paris*, p. 186. Other research shows that it was a general feature of developed urban centres, see references cited in Allerston, 'Reconstructing', p. 46.

68   ASV, Sant'Uffizio, *busta* 101, processo Stefano Valetta, strazzaruol, denuncia Francesca della Fonte, 17 March 1644.

69   See, for example, ASV, SNC, reg. 3, Capitolare, fo. 145r, 29 March 1555.

70   G. Monticolo, ed., *I capitolari delle arti veneziane sottoposte alla giustizia e poi alla giustizia vecchia dalle origini al MCCCXXX*, 3 vols in 4 parts (Rome, 1896–1914), vol. I (1896), pp. 9–21, 1218 *mv*; B. Cecchetti, 'Le industrie in Venezia nel secolo XIII', *Archivio Veneto*, 4 (1872), pp. 231–2.

71   See Martin, *Venice's Hidden Enemies*, p. 151. For Lotto's use of tailors, see Lotto, *Libro di spese*, pp. 233.

72   R. T. Rapp, *Industry and Economic Decline in Seventeenth-century Venice* (Cambridge, MA, 1970), pp. 58–62.

73   Angela Groppi, 'Une ressource légale pour une pratique illégale: les juifs et les femmes
     contre la corporation des tailleurs dans la Rome pontificale (XVIIe–XVIIIe siècles)',
     paper given at the Third European Social Science History Conference, Amsterdam, 14
     April 2000. On Venetian tailors, see the catalogue section, and G. Butazzi, 'Le scandalose
     licenze de sartori e sartore', in *I mestieri della moda a Venezia dal XIII al XVIII secolo* (Venice,
     1988), pp. 63–9, 233–72; further insights can be had from T. Garzoni, *La piazza universale
     di tutte le professioni del mondo*, 2 vols (Turin, 1996), vol. II, pp. 1308–12. On Florence, see
     C. Collier Frick, *Dressing Renaissance Florence: Families, Fortunes and Fine Clothing* (Baltimore,
     2002); and E. Currie, 'Diversity and Design in the Florentine Tailoring Trade, 1550–
     1620', in M. O'Malley and E. Welch, eds, *The Material Renaissance* (Manchester, 2007),
     pp. 154–73.

74   See note 72 above.

75   Mercers are discussed in Mackenney, *Tradesmen and Traders*, pp. 90–111.

76   Roche, *La culture des apparences*, pp. 313–45; B. Lemire: 'Consumerism in Preindustrial
     and Early industrial England: The Trade in Secondhand Clothes', *Journal of British Stud-
     ies*, 27 (1988), pp. 1–24; 'Peddling Fashion; Salesmen, Pawnbrokers, Taylors, Thieves
     and the Second-hand Clothes Trade in England, *c.* 1700–1800', *Textile History*, 22 (1991),
     pp. 67–82; and *Dress, Culture and Commerce*.

77   These outlets are discussed in Allerston, 'The Market'. Aspects of the Venetian second-
     hand market are also discussed in Allerston, 'L'abito come articolo di scambio', P. Aller-
     ston, 'Le marché d'occasion à Venise aux XVIe–XVIIe siècles', in Bottin and Pellegrin,
     eds, *Echanges et cultures textiles*, pp. 15–29, and Allerston, 'Wedding Finery' and
     'Reconstructing'.

78   On illicit agreements between traders at auctions, see ASV, Senato, Terra, *filza*, p. 141, 31
     January 1596 *mv*, report by the Sopraconsoli dei Mercanti.

79   ASV, SNC, *busta* 271, fo. 50v, 18 May 1602 (costing 2 ducats, about five days' wages for a
     master craftsman, this was not a particularly expensive item). On such auctions as well as
     the following means of distribution, see Allerston, 'The Market'.

80   ASV, SNC, *busta* 1 bis, Capitolare A, fo. 139, 20 December 1557.

81   On clothes and servants' wages, see Romano, *Housecraft and Statecraft*, pp. 138, 142–3; and
     Allerston, 'The Market', pp. 68–9.

82   ASV, Sant'Uffizio, Processi, *busta* 87, Felice Magalotti, 4 September 1629. On hats in the
     Ghetto, see B. Ravid, 'From Yellow to Red: On the Distinguishing Head-Covering of the
     Jews of Venice', *Jewish History*, 6 (1992), pp. 179–210.

83   On the charitable practice of clothing the poor, see Jütte, *Poverty and Deviance*, pp. 81–2.
     On such practices in Italy, see C. F. Black, *Italian Confraternities in the Sixteenth Century*
     (Cambridge, 1989), pp. 3, 71, 178. The classic study of Venetian poor relief is B. Pullan,
     Rich and Poor in Renaissance Venice: The Social Institutions of a Catholic State, to 1620 (Oxford,
     1971); see also B. Pullan: 'The Old Catholicism, the New Catholicism, and the Poor', in
     G. Politi, M. Rosa and F. della Paruta, eds, *Timore e carità: i poveri nell' Italia moderna* (Cre-
     mona, 1982), pp. 13–25; and 'The Relief of Prisoners in Sixteenth-century Venice', *Studi
     Veneziani*, 10 (1968), pp. 221–9.

84   On bequests of fine clothes to religious institutions, see Allerston, 'Reconstructing',
     pp. 47, 51–2.

85   P. Aretino, *Il primo libro delle lettere*, ed. F. Nicolini (Bari, 1913), p. 30 (7 January 1531).

86   ASV, SNC, *busta* 1, Capitolare B, fo. 74r, 28 November 1616.

87   Gifts were, for example, a focus of a session at the Third European Social Science History
     conference, Amsterdam, 15 April 2000: 'Gender and Material Culture II: Men, Women
     and the Art of the Gift', chaired by Hester Dibbits.

88   ASV, Pompe, *busta* 1, fo. 3r, 8 October 1562; see also Romano, *Housecraft and Statecraft*,
     pp. 205.

89   ASV, Pompe, *busta* 6, Denuncie, 18 January 1604 *mv*; on this document see P. Allerston, 'Contrary to the Truth and Also to the Semblance of Reality'? Entering a Venetian "Lying-in" Chamber (1605)', in M. Ajmar-Wollheim, F. Dennis and A. Matchette, eds, *Approaching the Italian Renaissance Interior: Sources, Methodologies, Debates* (Malden, MA, Oxford and Carlton, Victoria, 2007), pp. 7–17. On the cost of putting a large household 'into mourning weeds' in Venice in 1619, see L. P. Smith, ed., *The Life and Letters of Sir Henry Wotton*, 2 vols (Oxford, 1907), vol. II, pp. 166–7.

90   ASV, Censori, *busta* 1, Capitolare 2, fo. 59, 16 September 1595.

91   Aretino, *Primo libro*, pp. 123, 12 March 1537; ASV, Ufficiali al Cattaver, *busta* 244, reg. 5, fo. 46v, 10 July 1592.

92   See L. Fontaine, G. Delille, P. Spufford etc., in 'Les réseaux de crédit en Europe, XVIe–XVIIIe siècles', *Annales HSS*, 49 (1994), pp. 1335–1442; and the important work by C. Muldrew, *The Economy of Obligation: The Culture of Credit and Social Relations in Early Modern England* (New York, 1998).

93   ASV, Sant'Uffizio, Processi, *busta* 87, Felice Magalotti, 4 September 1629.

94   Archivio delle Istituzioni di Ricovero e di Educazione, Venice, Ospedale dei Derelitti, *busta* 156, Sebastiano Migliori, fasc. 2, fos. 12–14v, 24–28 April 1622.

95   ASV, SNC, *busta* 1, Capitolare B, 19 January 1581 *mv*.

96   Casola, *Viaggio*, p. 15.

97   *Le Massere* (1755), for example, has maidservants borrowing a mistress's clothes to dress up at Carnival; see Act I, scene 9; Act II, scene 6; Act IV, scene 7; Act V, scene 8.

98   See Allerston, 'L'abito come articolo di scambio', pp. 122–3.

99   See R. C. Davis, *The War of the Fists: Popular Culture and Public Violence in Late Renaissance Venice* (New York, 1994), as well as his *Shipbuilders of the Venetian Arsenal*.

100 See Pullan, 'Three Orders of Inhabitants', p. 157.

101 On these economic problems, see 'L'economia', in *Storia di Venezia*, vol. VI, ed. Cozzi and Prodi, 692–701; and U. Tucci, 'Vita economica a Venezia nel primo seicento', in *Galileo Galilei e la cultura veneziana* (Venice, 1995), pp. 123–35.

102 ASV, Pompe, *busta* 6, Denuncie, 18 January 1604 *mv*.

103 ASV, Pompe, *busta* 6, Denuncie, 27 August 1639. Initially condemned to a closed prison for six months and fined 150 ducats, Pasquetta was let off after the ambassador's intervention.

104 See ASV, SNC, *busta* 1, Capitolare A, fo. 129, 31 July 1533; ASV, Sanità, *busta* 729, Notatorio, 6, fo. 7, 27 July 1542; fo. 205v, 30 August 1550; Allerston, 'Reconstructing', p. 52. On the economic problems facing prostitutes, see M. F. Rosenthal, *The Honest Courtesan: Veronica Franco, Citizen and Writer in Sixteenth-century Venice* (Chicago, 1992), p. 132.

105 ASV, SNC, *busta* 1 bis, Capitolare A, fo. 139, 20 December 1557.

106 See Mackenney, *Tradesmen and Traders*, p. 107.

107 On participation in the *Sensa*, see Vecellio, *Habiti antichi*, fos. 128v–9r; G. Gallicciolli, *Delle memorie venete antichi profane ed ecclesiastiche*, 8 vols (Venice, 1795), vol. 1, 284–9; G. R. Michiel, *Origine delle feste veneziane*, 6 vols (Milan, 1829), vol. 1, 142–95; L. Padoan Urban, 'La festa della sensa nelle arti e nell'iconografia', *Studi Veneziani*, 10 (1968), pp. 330–3. On artisans' use of costumes in Carnival, see J. Martin, 'Popular Culture and the Shaping of Popular Heresy in Renaissance Venice', in S. Haliczer, ed., *Inquisition and Society in Early Modern Europe* (London and Sydney, 1987), pp. 120–1.

108 See Goldoni, *Le Massere*, Act I, scene 9; Act II, scene 6; Act IV, scene 7; Act V, scene 8; and also Act I, scene 8. On Antonio see ASV, Sant'Uffizio, Processi, *busta* 108 (Isaac Levi), 4 February 1659 *mv*.

109 ASV, Maggior Consiglio, *Libro d'Oro Vecchio*, no. 14, fos. 8–9, 1572 and 1577.

Embroidery, women and fashion in the early modern period

Susan C. Frye

Snapshot 5.1 Jacket, *c.* 1610 (linen, embroidered with coloured silks, silver and silver-gilt thread). This fine early seventeenth-century woman's jacket is significant because it is shown being worn in the *Portrait of Margaret Layton* (V & A E.214-1994), attributed to Marcus Gheeraerts the Younger (1561–1636), Victoria and Albert Museum, T-228-1994.

In sixteenth-century England, embroiderers tended to fall into two groups: professional embroiderers, most often men, who produced expensive objects and clothing, and well-born women who learned complex needlework skills as part of a courtly education. In spite of the importance of male embroiderers, sewing was considered the most womanly of activities. Even basic sewing was practised by royalty and aristocrats. The young Elizabeth Tudor, the future Queen Elizabeth I, sewed some shirts for her brother Edward when she was six years old. Later, she used her own embroidered designs to cover handwritten translations that she gave her father, King Henry VIII, and her step-mother, Katherine Parr.

After Elizabeth I became queen in 1558, the lists of New Year's gifts presented to her included embroidered sleeves, petticoats, sheets, and purses by her ladies-in-waiting, and by England's aristocratic women, as well as professionally embroidered work. Such lists reveal how the ceremonial clothing of this time was made up of pieces that were sewn or pinned together on each person's body – sleeves were attached to the bodice, for example, and the bodice to the skirts. During this period of time, embroidery – especially professional embroidery – included pearls and diamonds, emeralds and rubies, sewn into patterns with thread wound with gold and silver. These gifts to the queen also make clear how important clothing was to Elizabeth's exalted social position. Her clothing, whether worn everyday at court, at public events, or pictured in her portraits, visualised her semi-divinity as anointed monarch. In the Phoenix portrait of Elizabeth I, dated 1575–6, she is wearing a linen ruff, jewelled collar, and blackwork smock. Her slashed sleeves and bodice are worked with gold satin stitched knots and leaves, among which appear pearls, rubies, and black diamond rosettes. On her chest, just above her hand, a Phoenix, embroidered into her bodice and yet free-standing, simultaneously dies and gives birth to its heir. The phoenix emblem, appropriated from Mary, the mother of Jesus, suggests the queen's unique connection to god through her virginity.

As the seventeenth century began, many more women of the gentry and middling classes were learning complex needlework skills in order to increase their households' wealth or 'store'. By the 1630s, books and pictures were more widely available, as women began to afford to buy pattern books, which contained a variety of needlework designs to cut out and copy. Also, women began to go to print shops to have pictures drawn onto cloth to be embroidered. From the 1630s on, the row sampler also began to be common, as girls embroidered rows of different stitches, often with an alphabet, a picture or short verse. As they imitated the rooms and clothing of the upper classes, but also created their own genres and traditions, increasing numbers of needleworkers embroidered bed hangings, cushions, book covers, gloves, petticoats, and bodices at a time when such activity was highly prized.

The embroidered bodice now at the Victoria and Albert Museum, is the same one that Marcus Gheeraerts, the most famous portrait painter of his day, painted as part of a portrait of Margaret Layton, who was the wife of a Yeoman of the Jewel House at the Tower of London (Snapshot 5.1). The bodice, which was domestically embroidered about 1610, was completed using a variety of stitches. The vine design, with leaves, flowers, and two birds perched in its tracery on the upper chest, evokes the fashion for threaded fertility designs in early modern spot samplers, row samplers, and apparel produced within the household. Embroidered vines often featured oak leaves and acorns, peascods and leaves, and the strawberries referred to in Shakespeare's description of Othello's handerchief.

Bibliography and further reading

Arnold, J. (1988) *Elizabeth's Wardrobe Unlock'd*, Leeds: W. S. Maney & Son.
Frye, S. (1999) 'Sewing Connections: Elizabeth Tudor, Mary Stuart, Elizabeth Talbot, and Seventeenth-century Anonymous Needleworker' in S. Frye and K. Robertson (eds),

Maids and Mistresses, Cousins and Queens: Women's Alliances in Early Modern England, New York: Oxford University Press, pp. 165–82.

Frye, S. (forthcoming) *Women's Textualities in Early Modern England: Writing, Portraiture, and Needlework*.

Jones, A. R., and Stallybrass, P. (2000) *Renaissance Clothing and the Materials of Memory*, Cambridge: Cambridge University Press.

Swain, M. (1980) *Figures on Fabric: Embroidery Design Sources and Their Application*, London: Adam & Charles Black.

Chapter 5

Male headwear at the courts of Henry VIII and Edward VI

Maria Hayward

The Monmouth cap, the sailors thrum,
And that wherein the tradesman come,
The physic, lawe, the cap divine,
The same that crowns the muses nine,
The cap that fools do countenance,
The goodly cap of maintenance,
And any cap, where're it bee,
Is still the sign of some degree.[1]

AS THE ELIZABETHAN *Ballard of the Caps* illustrates, the hat in its various forms was an essential accessory for all but the poorest men in sixteenth-century England. This was because the hat, more than any other garment, was integrally linked with social standing, age and affluence. In order to explore this point further, this essay will focus on a cross-section of male headwear worn at the courts of Henry VIII and Edward VI. Here members of the social elite, both secular and ecclesiastical, mixed with the staff of the royal household and suppliers to the court. Headwear will be considered in a range of specific contexts: as a record of materials and makers, as a mark of individuality or corporate identity, and as a sign of authority or dependence. Much of the evidence relates to the monarch and the opulence of royal headwear. This raises several particular questions: what headwear did the King wear for public and private dress, who cared for his hats and were the King's hats thought of more as jewellery than as dress?

This essay works within the constraints imposed by patchy evidence, an almost complete lack of surviving artefacts and questions over terminology. A fairly limited vocabulary was used to describe headwear in sixteenth-century documents and it is necessary to observe it. The 1582 *Book of Rates* provides a good insight from the government's point of view into the terminology and the values associated with imported headwear.[2] The *Book of Rates* has entries for caps, hats and night-caps, but not bonnets.[3] Yet bonnets were more common than caps, hats and night-caps, in inventories and Great Wardrobe warrants recording court headwear between 1509 and 1553. So the term bonnet is used here as a generic term because it does not feature regularly in the royal sources of this period.

A record of materials, construction and makers

The small size of men's hats in the sixteenth century made them ideal vehicles for display. Hats were often made of expensive materials, as Philip Stubbes noted in his *Anatomy of Abuses*:

> Some are of silk, some of velvet, some of taffeta, some of sarcenet, some of wool . . . he is of no account or estimation amongst men, if he have not a velvet or taffeta hat and that must be pinked and cunningly carved of the best fashion.[4]

Black silk was used to make the majority of Henry VIII's caps and a lighter-weight silk fabric such as sarsenet or taffeta was used as a lining. The caps were pieced, with a separate crown, pleated to fit into the brim. The brim could be a continuous band, a full brim slashed in one or more places, or with the front cut away. A bonnet made from black silk velvet and of similar style to those worn by Henry VIII and members of his court was excavated from the tomb of Don Garcia de Medici, who died in 1562.[5] While bonnets for the leading members of society were made from silk velvet, those made for their social inferiors echoed the shape but not the materials. A flat cap dating from 1560–70 and found in Finsbury, London, has a slashed brim, the edge of which is tabbed, but the cap was knitted rather than made from woven fabric.[6]

Felt, made from either fur or wool, was the alternative to silk for making bonnets. The most common type of fur felt used for men's hats in the late Middle Ages was made from beaver pelts, which produced a lightweight, soft, strong, flexible material. During the fourteenth and fifteenth centuries the best quality beaver fur felts were made in the Low Countries. Indeed, Chaucer's merchant wore 'upon his head a Flaundrish beaver hat'.[7] Fur felts of this type were more expensive than wool felts. Felts hats could be made from a single piece of felt that was shaped, probably over a wooden block, with the aid of heat, moisture and manipulation. Alternatively, the crown was shaped by cutting and seaming the fabric. This technique was used to form the crowns of two sixteenth-century thrummed felt hats (i.e. with a wool pile) in the collection of the National Museum of Ireland.[8]

Linen was sometimes used to make night-caps, such as that worn by Henry Fitzroy, Duke of Richmond.[9] These caps were made from four to six sections of fabrics, with or without a brim. Two seventeenth-century examples can be seen in the collection of the Museum of Costume and Textiles in Nottingham. They are embroidered with polychrome silk and metal thread.[10] However, most of the night-caps ordered for

Henry VIII were made from silk satin, suggesting that they were intended as informal dress, as in the case of 'a night cappe of crymsen satten allover embrawdered' (9568).[11] The more ornate examples were used during the day as in the case of a 'night cappe garnished with stone' that Henry VIII wore in combination with a bonnet that 'was so ryche of Juels that few men could value them'.[12]

Wool was sometimes used for night-caps that were intended for sleeping in, such as a night-cap made from scarlet and purchased for Henry VIII for 4s.[13] This cap would certainly have fitted with contemporary thinking on a healthy lifestyle. Andrew Boorde advised readers in his *First Boke of the Introduction of Knowledge* published in 1547 'Let your nyght cap be of scarlet . . . and in your beed not to hote nor to cold, but in temper-ence'.[14] Wool was also used for hats intended for daywear by the middling and lower ranks of society.[15] The price of these hats was linked to the type and quality of the fleece used. So caps made from the finest grade of Leeminster wool cost 3s 4d, while the lower grades were priced at 2s 6d, 20d and 12d.[16]

The different types of headwear described above required different quantities of fabric. The 1538 Michaelmas Great Wardrobe account for Prince Edward's clothes reveals that Christopher Milliner received half a yard of velvet for each bonnet, three-eighths of a yard of satin for each-night cap and three-quarters of a yard of black velvet for a hat.[17] There was a marked gulf between the value of the materials and the price paid to the craftsman for making them up into the finished article. Christopher was paid 2s 8d each for making two white satin night-caps for Prince Edward, 3s 4d each for the four velvet bonnets, 6s each for four night-caps and 10s for one hat of black velvet.[18]

Decoration

Most men's hats of this period were black and Henry VIII's were no exception (Figure 5.1). This preference for black has been associated with the arrival of Catherine of Aragon and her entourage in 1501 and the influence of court fashion.[19] While this may have been a consideration, other factors also played a part. Dyeing fabric black in the sixteenth century was an expensive, labour-intensive process, often requiring skilled over-dyeing, and consequently it conveyed a direct statement about the wealth of the wearer. Black also provided a very good background to offset feathers and gold orna-ments, often embellished with enamel and jewels, embroidery in polychrome or metal wrapped threads, metal thread lace, fringes, tassels and short decorative lengths of chain, used to decorate many bonnets (Figure 5.2).[20] However, hats could be made in a range of colours, and evidence from visual sources indicates that red was a popu-lar choice, for example the red bonnet worn by Prince Edward in the Holbein portrait *c.* 1538, Holbein's sketch of James Butler, ninth Earl of Wiltshire and Ormond, drawn wearing a red bonnet, and the picture of an unknown man *c.* 1548 dressed all in red.[21]

Aglets and buttons were by far the most common form of decoration found on Henry VIII's caps and they were often used in combination. Many were plain gold, while others were embellished with enamel or gem stones, with pearls being the most popular. The overall impression is of a wealth ornament that reflected the wearer's wealth and status. Indeed, the jewels removed from a group of Henry VIII's bonnets were set in the new crown made for Edward VI's coronation in February 1547, for bonnets worn at his meeting with the French Ambassador in 1550 (e.g. 3273) and a new circlet for Mary I.[22]

Colour	Number of occurrences	
Black	60	(85.7%)
Unspecified	3	(4.3%)
Crimson	2	(2.9%)
Green	2	(2.9%)
Orange	1	(1.4%)
Purple	1	(1.4%)
Yellow	1	(1.4%)
Total	**70**	**(100%)**

Figure 5.1 The colour of Henry VIII's caps recorded in the 1547–50 inventory.

Type of decoration	Number of occurrences	Quantity
Agate, pieces of	1	1
Aglets	43	Single – 2
		Double – 632
Balases	2	9
Branches	1	1
Brooches	29	29
Buttons	60	Unspecified – 1,263
		Long – 51
Cameos	1	1
Chains	6	Number not given
Chains, double	2	27
Colettes	6	Numbers not given
Diamonds	12	46*
Embroidery	1	1
Emeralds	2	13
Feathers	1	1
Gaudies	4	Numbers not given
Jacinth, pieces	1	1
No decoration	4	—
Pearls	14	572*
Rubies	10	52
Sapphires	1	1
Troches	2	23*

*The actual figure is higher than this because several of the entries mention a type of decoration but do not specify the quantity.

Figure 5.2 Types of decoration found on Henry VIII's caps recorded in the 1547–50 inventory.

The inventory entries give no indication of how the decoration was attached and it is quite possible that some of the ornament was hooked into the fabric of the cap rather then stitched on or laced through the material. Changes in the Treasure Act (1996) have resulted in the opportunity to study a small group of silver-gilt ornaments that may be cap hooks. Hooked ornament would be quick to apply, easy to move from one hat to another and could be used to pin the brim to the crown of the hat.[23] A range of hat ornaments can be seen in the top left corner of Holbein's sketch of William Parr, first Marquis of Northampton (Figure 5.3).

Most bonnets had a narrow brim sometimes called a 'turf', as in the case of 'a black vellat Cappe with a Turfe with xj Buttons with peerle and xij pair of aglattes of golde' (3333). As the example given below demonstrates, the turf was the main area for decoration, and on bonnets that were 'double turfed', the decorative potential was even greater:

> the over turffe of the Cappe garnshed with buttons golde enameled with bourchers knottes of golde and peerle with Aglattes of golde enameled blacke and settes of peerles hauing three peerles and two Beades in everie sette and the vnder turff garneshed with Bourchers knottes of goldes and peerle (3259).

Sometimes the brim was not stiffened and it would be held upright with ties and aglets. Alternatively, stiffening materials could be inserted into the brim. The roll of the cap of maintenance worn by Richard III at his coronation was stiffened with the pith of rushes.[24] Other stiffening materials might include heavyweight fabrics like buckram, paper or parchment.[25] Equally bonnets made from heavier materials, such as felt, could be given an interlining to help support the crown, as in the case of the bonnet dating from 1568 found in Uppsala Cathedral.[26]

Judging by portraits alone, feathers appear to have been a very popular form of ornament, especially for French bonnets.[27] Examples owned by Henry VIII included 'oon rounde white feather for a Cappe' (17285) and 'oon faier Herons feather trimmed at the stalke with veanice golde and peerle' (17259).[28] Most commonly they were black or white but dyed plumes which could be parti-coloured: 'one white and purple one purple and yellowe and one redd and yellowe' (11712). However, in 1547 only one of Henry VIII's caps was trimmed with a feather. The most likely explanation is that when the hat was not being worn, the feathers were removed and stored separately because these feathers were expensive. Christopher Milliner was paid 2s for a simple white feather to trim a black velvet bonnet. Indeed feathers could very lucrative for the men who traded in them. Thomas Brown, capper, received £130 5s 6d for caps and feathers from Edward VI's privy purse.[29] The large-scale use of feathers is indicated by three sets of matching feathered top-knots for men and horses of blue, red and yellow feathers bought by the Lord Great Master, possibly for Edward VI's coronation in 1547 (11751–6).

Subtle changes in the style, decoration and construction of hats did occur during Henry VIII's reign but they are not always easy to distinguish. The New Year's gift roll for 1539 is one of the three complete surviving Henrician gift rolls and it highlights an interesting and seemingly short-lived court fashion for thrummed hats.[30] In that year the King received six hats, one bonnet, one night-cap and a cap: five of the six hats were thrummed with silk, such as the 'crimson hat thrommed with a band of pirled gold

Figure 5.3 Drawing of William Parr, 1st Marquis of Northampton, 1541–2, by Hans Holbein (1497/8–1543). The Royal Collection © 2009, Her Majesty Queen Elizabeth II.

Figure 5.4 Linen night-cap attributed to Sir Thomas More. Reproduced with permission of the North West Museums Service and Stonyhurst College.

and four tarsols' from Edmund Harman, the King's barber. Eight years later, none of the King's hats recorded in the 1547–50 inventory was described as being decorated in this way, indicating that this style was now out of vogue. A slight variant on this theme appears on a felt bonnet with a wool pile. The tufts were arranged in rows, creating a very distinctive effect.[31]

Hat-makers and suppliers: tailors, cappers, milliners and haberdashers

Male headwear of this period was generally defined by its low profile and soft construction. As their construction was relatively simple, the production of headwear was not restricted to one group of craftsmen. The warrants sent to the Great Wardrobe for bonnets, caps, riding caps and night-caps reveal that tailors often made these items from woven fabrics. On 28 June 1535 John Malt, the King's tailor, was required to make one green velvet hat, three velvet caps of yellow, orange and green and a cap for Henry VIII, along with the hood for William Somer, the King's fool.[32]

Cappers could work with woven textile or non-woven materials such as knitting or felt. In May 1514 according to the *King's Book of Payments* money was paid to Bartholemew, the King's capper, for bonnets and to other unspecified individuals for kersey and other cloth for the King's cordwainer.[33] It is not clear from this reference what materials Bartholemew was working with, but there is a suggestion that he was working with wool. Several months later on 20 October 1514 Lawrence Englefield, clerk of the check for the Yeomen of the Guard, received eighteen hats for the Guard from Bart Whale, the King's capper.[34] Wool caps, possibly with a fulled surface, would be more water resistant than silk and so more practical for the King's guard. Other cappers made knitted caps from English wool, as in the case of Tomas Capper who leased a house in Monroe Street, Monmouth, in 1523.[35]

The tailors and cappers serving the King were likely to be English but one other small group of individuals involved in hat-making was probably not. Henry VIII's privy purse accounts for 1528–32 record that he dealt regularly with Christopher Carcano. Christopher was described as the King's milliner and he was very probably the Christopher Miller mentioned in the 1547–50 inventory who had sold two knitted sets of doublet and hose to Henry VIII.[36] By the eighteenth century milliners made women's hats, while hatters produced male headwear. However, prior to this the term milliner is believed to have indicated the origin of the craftsman rather than his craft.[37] Thus, in the early sixteenth century milliners were usually individuals from Milan, who frequently traded in fancy goods, which might include hats. Thomas Smith linked many of these goods with the haberdashers' trade in his work the *Discourse of the Commonweal of this Realm of England*, first published in 1549. Haberdashers sold 'White paper, looking glasses, pins, pouches, hats, caps, brooches, silk and silver buttons, laces, perfumed gloves . . . the list descends from luxuries to frivolities'.[38]

The evidence suggests that Christopher Carcano's hat-making skills brought him a royal appointment, while a side-line in fancy goods provided a valuable supplement to his income.[39] Christopher received £18 14s 11d for making hats and supplying feathers, tassels and aglets to decorate headwear in a single warrant to provide clothing for Prince Edward dated 21 July 1539.[40] Christopher was not the only milliner serving the King and the two bills submitted by Mark Milliner indicate a similar pattern of goods and expertise. The bills itemised a number of caps and night-caps, amongst a profusion of gloves, buttons, aglets and hunting equipment.[41] The items were delivered to Edmund Harmen, groom of the privy chamber and the King's barber.

This diversity of hat-makers continued into Elizabeth I's reign. Shortly after her accession Richard Hammond was named as the Queen's capper, a position that he held until 1583.[42] His successor William Cookesbury was also periodically called by this title. However, Hammond was also referred to as 'oure Myllener' and 'our haberdasher'. This suggests that by the latter part of the sixteenth century milliners were distinguished more by their crafts skills than their nationality and that the terminology used to describe the different spheres of the hat-making was blurring.

Individuality and corporate identity

Men's hats of the type worn in the first half of the sixteenth century, rather like the shoes of the period, would gradually mould to fit the wearer. The angle they were worn at was also personal: from flat on the head as in the portrait of George Brooke, ninth Baron Cobham, to the jaunty angle favoured by Sir Thomas Wyatt. The ornamentation could express an individual's learning, religious views or their marital status. Holbein painted Sir Henry Guildford wearing a hat badge illustrating the instruments of the 'Typus Geometriae', which Dürer had included in his engraving *Melencolia*.[43] Guildford's knowledge of such a work could have come through his correspondence with Erasmus, who had visited England in 1499. Erasmus was a friend of Holbein, who in turn benefited from the patronage of Guildford.

The influence of classical learning spread further: the cap badge in Sir Richard Southwell's portrait has been interpreted as representing Lucretia, worked in agate and set in gold.[44] Lucretia was a popular and slightly salacious classical subject – Henry VIII himself owned a number of paintings of her rape.[45] One of Henry's cap was ornamented with a brooch 'hauinge therin an Antique womans hedde with a Saphere and a Ballace on hir breste' (3258), while another had 'a Brouche of golde having in it a moores hedde of Jacincte' (3435). In a portrait of 1536 attributed to Joos van Cleve, Henry VIII wears a black velvet bonnet with an enamelled badge of the Virgin.[46] Although this year saw the act for the dissolution of the lesser monasteries, Henry VIII remained conservative in his own religious beliefs.

Service to the crown could be shown in a variety of ways, not just in the more familiar livery collar, such as that worn by Sir Thomas More. Holbein's sketch of William Parr, Marquis of Northampton, includes rough indications of a medallion and hat badge that may have been the insignia of the Gentlemen Pensioners (Figure 5.3).[47]

Turning in another direction, different messages were conveyed in Holbein's portrait of Simon George. The finished portrait, unlike the preparatory sketch, shows George's bonnet heavily ornamented with enamelled violets, a medallion of a saint, small gold ornaments shaped like crossed fishes and vases and a feather.[48] The sitter's pose (holding a carnation), in combination with his fine clothes and the presence of violets on his hats (symbolic of faithfulness), have been seen to suggest that this was a marriage portrait: the eligible bachelor converted into a loyal husband.

Three main groups of professional men served Henry VIII as members of his household, the court circle and royal government: clerics, doctors and lawyers. One notable feature of their headwear, as depicted in portrait and drawings, is that these groups did not generally favour the fashionable Milan bonnet but a style of cap or bonnet that resembled those worn by Henry VII in the later years of his reign. In both the Sittow portrait and the bust by Torrigiano, Henry VII was depicted wearing a close-fitting black hat probably made from blocked felt. The cap had an upturned brim, cut away at the front. This basic style could be modified with ties under the chin, ear flaps and ribbons to hold the brim upright and was not embellished.

The headwear worn by the English clergy between 1509 and 1547 combined continuity with change. Holbein sketched William Warham, Archbishop of Canterbury, and John Fisher, Bishop of Rochster, wearing close-fitting felt hats. In both cases the caps extended down over the men's ears, had shaped crowns and no brim. Ridges running from ear to ear and front to back were formed in the crown, either by blocking the felt or by stitching. Richard Fox and Thomas Wolsey were also painted wearing similar bonnets, although Wolsey's, of course, was scarlet. Although the clergy continued to wear small fitted caps of this type throughout this period, other types of headwear that were synonymous with ecclesiastical authority disappeared. One type of hat to make a brief appearance was the cardinal's hat. Wolsey made special arrangements for the delivery of his cardinal's hat in 1515 and the representation of this hat can be seen in the terracotta plaque of Wolsey's arms at Hampton Court.[49] Equally the bishop's mitre, of the type seen in the background of Warham's portrait, was to disappear.[50] This mitre, along with the processional cross, was symbolic of Warham's ecclesiastical authority as primate of the English church. In contrast, Warham's successor Thomas Cranmer, relied on his simple white surplice and the works of St Paul and St Augustine to indicate his religious calling.[51]

Doctors and apothecaries had a choice of headwear. Firstly there was the close-fitting, dark-coloured cap of the type depicted by Holbein in his portrait of Doctor Butts, royal surgeon and in the group painting *Henry VIII and the Barber Surgeons*.[52] Butts was portrayed wearing a bonnet with no brim at the front but a brim running round the back of the bonnet from to ear to ear. This partial brim was held in place by two ribbons, tied in a knot in the middle of the crown. The bonnet extended down over Butt's ears and there were ribbon ties to secure it under his chin. Secondly there was the coif of the type recovered from the wreck of the *Mary Rose* from the surgeon's cabin.[53] It was cut from a single piece of silk velvet and the shaping was achieved by a series of small darts, the stitching of which was covered with narrow ribbon. The lining consisted of a similarly shaped piece of silk tabby.[54]

The legal profession also favoured the felt cap. Sir Thomas More, a lawyer by training, wore a rich robe in his formal portrait with a black felt cap similar in style to that worn by Dr Butts. What he might have worn in private is another matter and possibly is answered by a linen night-cap as before attributed to More at Stonyhurst College, Lancashire (Figure 5.4).[55] Thomas Cromwell and Sir Thomas Elyot wore a similar cap but they were not worn exclusively, as indicated by the portrait of Sir Richard Southwell. Southwell wore a fashionable bonnet.

Looking beyond these professional bodies other informal groupings could be found in, and on the periphery of, the court. The styles favoured by the 'intellectuals' who visited Henry's court are hard to pin down, partly because of the lack of images and partly because they did not form a cohesive group. Holbein's portraits of Erasmus date from nearly two decades after he met the young Prince Henry in 1499. But they present him wearing the shaped felt hat favoured by clerics and lawyers. In contrast, Nicolaus Kratzer, the King's astronomer, Nicholas Bourbon, a French poet who visited England in 1533, and Sir Thomas Wyatt, poet and diplomat, wore the more fashionable bonnet. An unknown man with a lute, possibly a musician emplyed at court, wore a flat bonnet rather like a beret, with a small continuous brim. Coming almost full circle, Sir Thomas Eliot, who published *The Boke Named the Governour* in 1531, wore a cap with the brim cut away at the front, similar to that worn by Sir John More. This style was part way between the type of cap both men could have worn to denote their legal training and the more fashionable full-brimmed bonnets.

Interestingly, Holbein's portraits of the German Hanse merchants working in London reveal that they generally favoured an unadorned black Milan bonnet rather than the more old-fashioned felt cap. These caps, as worn, for example by Derich Born,

Hillebrandt Wedigh and Derich Tybis, were usually placed flat on the head rather than at the jaunty angles favoured at court.[56] This also true of the portrait of Sir Thomas Gresham painted by a member of the Flemish School in 1544.[57] However it is clear that their understated but expensive and fashionable black headwear and dress were intended to convey messages of wealth and worldliness tempered with financial prudence.

Authority and dependence

Two types of headwear associated primarily, but not solely, with the monarch, acted as a symbol of royal authority and the leading role of the nobility. The first was the cap of maintenance, which could be worn with a crown, as on Holbein's frontispiece for the 1535 Coverdale Bible, or alone.[58] When the King processed to open the new session of parliament in 1512, Edward Stafford, third Duke of Buckingham, preceded him carrying the cap of maintenance.[59] The details of Henry's cap of maintenance in the 1547–50 inventory are vague: 'a Capp of purple vellat lined with blacke satten' (I).[60] Far more illuminating is the entry describing the four caps and one hat of maintenance made for Edward VI's coronation in 1547. Three of the caps were made from purple velvet and lined with crimson satin. Crimson satin was also used for the fourth cap and the hat. Each cap was decorated with 'a great rose of gold raised' and forty pearls, while 'a greate bawle of damaske golde' was set on the hat. In addition 6 oz of gold lace and gold tassels weighing 4 oz were provided. The total cost was £15 18s 4d and the satin was provided by the Great Wardrobe.[61]

The King's other ceremonial robes, for the chivalrous orders of the Garter (14178), St Michael (14182) and the Toison d'Or (14180), had hoods rather than caps. The robes and hoods were all similar, distinguished by subtle nuances of colour, fabric and decoration, for example, the hood for the Garter robes was made of crimson velvet lined with white damask. Although the hood had passed out fashionable use, the traditional style was retained with these robes, so lending them an air of historical *gravitas*.

Some men appointed to offices outside the royal household could receive gifts of a cap and sword of maintenance as a symbol of their loyalty to the monarch. One such example is the Waterford cap of maintenance, a cap of red silk velvet embroidered with Tudor roses in gold thread on the crown and around the brim.[62] Henry VIII presented the cap to the city of Waterford and its Mayor, William Wise in 1536, 'to be borne at times thought fit before our mayor'.[63] A second cap dating from 1580 has survived in York. The Mayor's Esquire of the Sword wore the cap as he carried the sword and mace before the Mayor of York.[64] Just as the monarch gave gifts of this type, he could also receive them. In such cases the subtle niceties of relationship between donor and recipient are harder to discern. In January 1497 Henry VII's chamber accounts contain a reference to the provision of a case costing £1 2s for a sword and cap of maintenance. This sword and cap were a gift from Pope Alexander VII in recognition of Henry's support for the papacy.[65]

The wearing or doffing of a hat could be used to express the niceties of rank. According to an Italian observer at Henry VII's court: 'In addition to their civil speeches, they have the incredible courtesy of remaining with their heads uncovered, with an admirable grace, whilst they talk to each other'. This habit was still in vogue in 1599 when Thomas Platter observed that 'the nobles . . . they greet each other with bared head and a bow, sometimes gentle gripping each other on the outside of the knee'.[66] The wearing of a hat could also indicate less laudable characteristics. In Castiglione's *The Book of the Courtier*, Federico described a mutual acquaintance to signor Gaspare as 'a conceited and frivolous man . . . walking with that head tossing and wriggling about and smiling invitations to all and sundry to doff their caps to him'.[67] He had previously noted that 'I would like our courtier always to appear neat and refined . . . and not exaggerate one feature . . . as do some who . . . concentrate on their . . . bonnets and their coifs'.[68] According to Castiglione a man's hat could be the defining point of his personality and his outfit or it could act as an expression of vanity and extravagance. In terms of size, the bonnet was a small but highly illuminating accessory that was socially important and financially significant.

A man's hat could also be used to reflect deference. The Eltham Ordinances of 1526 required men to doff their cap to the cloth and chair of estate on the presence chamber, which represented the King's authority in his absence. Wearing a hat that was a part of the King's livery was a further act of deference. Henry VIII gave livery to selected members of his household, some of whom received headwear in addition to clothing.

Certain groups, such as the footmen, members of the hunts and the King's henchmen, were provided with headwear twice yearly as part of their livery. All these groups served the King in public and often their duties required them to be outside. Milan bonnets were given as livery to only certain members of the royal household – to footmen (6*s*).[69] Others received bonnets of an unspecified but cheaper type – for example, the sergeants of the buckhounds (5*s*), the yeomen prickers of the buckhounds (3*s* 8*d*) and the children of the leash (3*s* 4*d*).[70] Men of higher social standing received their outer garments but were expected to provide their own bonnets or caps. This would allow them to bring an element of individuality to their dress.

Further items, in the form of gifts, could be given to individuals. For example William Toke, page of the laundry, received a gown, a jacket, a doublet and a bonnet at the time of his marriage.[71] Although Toke received a bonnet, Will Somer, the King's jester, usually wore a hood. In June 1535 Henry ordered two coats 'of grene clothe with a hoode to the same' to be made for Will. In addition, Will received a 'coote and cappe of grene clothe fringed with red crule'.[72] By the sixteenth century, hoods were mainly worn by people of low social standing. This would accord with Will's position within the household hierarchy and the idiosyncratic post of royal fool. Hoods were also prepared annually by the staff of the Great Wardrobe, along with gowns and shoes, so that they could be given away for the King's Maundy. On 12 March 1532 forty-two gowns and hoods of russet cloth were ordered.[73] Here the hood acted as an indicator of the venerability of the Maundy observations and visibly identified the recipients of the King's bounty.

Henry VIII's headwear

Henry VIII's had a weakness for hats, a weakness he indulged via regular warrants to the Great Wardrobe and impromptu purchases using the privy purse. Henry VIII was usually portrayed wearing a bonnet of the Milan type, with a low crown and a turned-up brim that was often slit at the sides or a French bonnet, usually worn with a feather.[74] Both styles were fashionable during Henry's reign and in 1542 Hall wrote in his Chonicle of 'Myllaine bonettes of crymosyn sattin drawen through with cloth of golde'.[75] The nobility generally followed the King's sartorial lead. Sir Henry Guildford was also painted by Holbein wearing a Milan bonnet but with one difference.[76] Ribbon ties were attached to the brim at the sides and tied with a knot at the top of the crown. A further variant can be seen in the 'riding cappe of blake satten garnisshed with roses white enameled' that Lady Fitzwilliam gave Henry in 1534 as a New Year's gift.[77]

Although rarely alone, once Henry VIII entered the privy lodging he was free from public scrutiny. Here he could continue to wear his formal bonnet or replace it with a caul, coif or night-cap. Cauls were often quite fancy ('wrought of gold and Silke' (2609)) or plain ('blacke Silke' (2610)) and they could be worn alone or under a bonnet. Holbein recorded the latter in his portrait of Sir Nicholas Carew, c. 1528.[78] Although Carew was painted in armour, he wore a pleated caul of cloth of gold under a Milan bonnet, rather than his helmet that would have obscured his face. Coifs were generally simpler in construction than cauls and made of cheaper materials. When Henry VIII bathed in his bath house at the new palace of Westminster (Whitehall) he wore one of 'fyve Coiffes of Hollaunde' (11521).[79]

Only one painting of Henry VIII actually depicts him in his night attire: the post-humous, anonymous picture *Edward VI and the Pope: A Protestant Allegory*.[80] The painted details of Henry's night-cap worked with gold thread are rather sketchy and a better sense of these caps can be gained from a miniature of Henry Fitzroy (d. 1536), painted in *c.* 1534–5 and attributed to Lucas Horenbout. The duke wears a white linen night-shirt and night-cap, the latter embroidered with black work.[81] The informality of the image suggests that it was taken during one of the duke's periods of illness. In both instances, although the subjects were represented as though dressed for bed, they are actually on display and so are depicted in a fancy night-cap, just as women lying-in after childbirth received visitors in their finery.

The social and financial value of the bonnet is admirably demonstrated by George Boleyn's choice of New Year's gift for the King in 1534. George Boleyn, the Queen's brother, presented Henry VIII with 'a bonnet of blake veluet with iij paire of buttons viij paire of Aglettes xvj other buttons enamiled white and a broche of golde'.[82] To set this gift in context, in 1534 six of the nineteen men ranked as lords gave gifts of plate, four selected hats, one a book, one a wood knife, one a garter, one a hawk's lure and one opted for food. This clearly indicates that hats were acceptable gifts. In part this was a reflection of the King's fondness for them and in part it acknowledges the quantity of precious metal used to decorate them.

During the King's lifetime, responsibility for Henry VIII's caps rested with the groom of the stool and the officers of the privy chamber rather than the officers of the wardrobe of the robes, who cared for the rest of the King's clothes. On 18 January 1526, Henry Norris received a selection of objects from Sir William Compton, his predecessor as groom of the stool. After a list of jewel, including nine carcanets or collars, two 'toisons' of gold for the Order of the Golden Fleece and a garter of gold with nine diamonds and a pearl, there were nineteen decorated bonnets, three hats and a night-cap.[83] This was very similar to the situation in Scotland.[84] Henry Kemp of Thomastoun, keeper of the King's jewels, cared for James V's bonnets. After Henry's death his caps and bonnets were stored in the jewels house, reflecting the financial value of the ornaments.

When not being worn, the King's bonnets and caps were provided with special protective storage cases. Cases of this type would help to keep the bonnets clean, reduce the risk of the casual theft of the expensive ornament and help prevent these small dress accessories getting squashed by heavier items of clothing at the King's removal from one property to another. Some of the cap cases were quite basic in construction, for example 'three Cappecases of blacke leather for the kinges Cappes'. Others were more luxurious, such as 'A Case coverid with grene vellut garnished with fringes of golde and silver havinge within the same diuerse Romes to laie Cappes in' (16025).

Conclusion

Small and relatively expensive, male headwear at the Tudor court was as significant to its makers as it was to its wearers. The financial value of the raw materials, in combination with the surface decoration on bonnets and mitres, for example, meant that these objects could be considered on a par with jewellery. While the hats made for the nobility were predominantly a vehicle for jewelled decoration, those made for the professional groups and members of the household relied primarily on cut and materials to convey the correct social nuance.

Henry VIII used his headwear, starting with the crown and working down through fashionable, heavily jewelled bonnets, to demonstrate his place at the top of the social order. He had two caps decorated with buttons 'of Esses of golde' (3328, 3331) – his ministers wore chains of 'SS' around their necks, as a sign of his authority over them. In turn, his courtiers and household expressed a range of complex and subtle messages about their social standing, profession and intellectual inclinations. Age was harder to determine. Childhood was hardly acknowledged, with young boys wearing miniature versions of adult styles.[85] Old age was generally acknowledged by wearing hats that verged more towards comfort than style.[86] Henry VIII was the exception to this rule, as he continued to wear a fashionable bonnet throughout his life. While a man's hat was a defining element in his ensemble, it should not be seen as more than that. Henry was reputed to have said that 'If I thought my cap knew my council I would cast it into the fire and burn it'.[87] And there was little chance of that.

Acknowledgements

I would like to thank Nell Hoare, Director of the Textile Conservation Centre, University of Southampton, for permission to publish this essay. Grateful thanks go to Dinah Eastop, director of the AHRB Research Centre for Textile Conservation and Textile Studies for her valuable comments on earlier drafts of this essay. I would also like to thank Jan Graffius, curator at Stonyhurst College, for showing me the hats attributed to Sir Thomas More, Jane Mathews for discussing hat-making with me and Karen Parker for a copy of a Winchester capper's inventory. Finally, I would like to acknowledge the help of Rachel Phelan, Ròisìn Miles, Cliodna Devitt, Sian Cooksey and Eleanor Palmer.

References

Brewer. J. S., Gairdner, J., and Brodie, R. H. (eds), *Letters and Papers, Foreign and Domestic of the Reign of Henry VIII, 1509–1547*, 21 volumes and addenda (London, 1862–1932) has been abbreviated as *LP*.

Starkey, D. R. (ed.), *The Inventory of King Henry VIII* (London, 1998). The reference numbers given to the entries in this edition are given, when appropriate, in round brackets in the text.

Notes

1   Quoted in G. Clinch, *English Costume from Prehistoric Times to the End of Eighteenth Century* (Wakefield, 1909, 1975), p. 90.

2   T. S. William (ed.), *A Tudor Book of Rates* (Manchester, 1962), pp. 14, 32, 42.

3   Duty was assigned to caps with single crowns, pressed or 'prest' caps, double turfed caps called 'cocked' caps; hats of satin and velvet; hats of silk, French making; hats called Spanish or Portuguese felts, hats called Spanish or Venetian, hats of worsted short thrummed, or thrummed wool or worsted, night-caps of linen, of satin, of knit silk, of velvet and of wool.

4   Quoted in J. Arnold, *Patterns of Fashion: The Cut and Construction of Clothes for Men and Women c. 1560–1620* (London, 1985), p. 31.

5   The crown of the black velvet bonnet made for Don Garcia de Medici was shaped with 'thirty-nine evenly spaced dart tucks', Arnold, *Patterns of Fashion: c. 1560–1620*, p. 55.

6   Museum of London, A6340. Illustrated in K. Baclawski, *The Guide to Historic Costume* (London, 1995), p. 59. An act relating to cappers prescribes the materials and cost of cheaper, woollen caps; see K. Buckland, 'The Monmouth Cap', *Costume*, 13 (1979), pp. 23–37.

7   G. Chaucer, *The Canterbury Tales*, ed. D. Wright (London, 1965, 1982), p. 8.

8   See M. Dunlevy, *Dress in Ireland* (London, 1989), p. 62. With thanks to Ròisìn Miles.

9   In the Royal Collection. Fitzroy does not appear to have shared his father's passion for hats. An inventory taken of his goods in 1526 recorded two black velvet bonnets and two hats, one green and one white, see 'Inventory of the Goods of Henry Fitzroy, Duke of Richmond', *Camden Miscellany*, 3 (1855), pp. 3–4.

10   The caps are illustrated in F. Clark, *Hats*, The Costume Accessories Series (London, 1982, 1983), p. 68. There is a similar example in the collection of the Victoria and Albert Museum.

11   Also 'a night Cappe of blacke veluet partely embrawdered' (9568). [Throughout, numbers in parentheses refer to Starkey (ed.), *The Inventory of King Henry VIII*]

12   E. Hall, *The Union of the Two Noble and Illustre Families of Lancaster and York* (London, 1809), p. 255.

13   The relatively high cost reflects the price of the dyes used to produce scarlet.

14   C. W. Cunnington and P. Cunnington, *Handbook of English Costume in the Sixteenth Century* (London, 1954), p. 17.

15   Edward IV's wardrobe account from 1480 suggests that he wore hats made from wool or was providing them for members of his household, Hats ranged in price from 8*d.* to 12*d.*, while bonnets cost from 2*s.* 6*d.* to 3*s.* See N. H. Nicholas (ed.), *Privy Purse Expenses of Elizabeth of York, Wardrobe Accounts of Edward the Fourth, with a Memoir of Elizabeth of York and Notes* (London, 1830), p. 119.

16   3 Henry VIII, *c.* 15, Statutes of the Realm, I, pp. 33–4.

17   J. L. Nevinson, 'Prince Edward's Clothing', *Costume*, 2 (1968), p. 6. The level of import

duty charged on these fabrics indicates their relative value. The rates for velvet ranged from 15*s*. to 25*s*. per yard and from 2*s*. to 26*s*. 8*d*. per yard for satin: see Willan, *Book of Rates*.

18   Nevinson, 'Edward's Clothing', p. 6.

19   The emphasis in early sixteenth-century Spanish dress was on black, russet and crimson, velvets and other heavy fabrics and the use of fur. These features were offset with white shirts, pale feathers and jewellery; see C. Breward, *The Culture of Fashion: A New History of Fashionable Dress* (Manchester, 1995), pp. 42–5.

20   Lettice Worship, the King's silk woman, supplied 'three pecies of cappe reabande' for the King's use in 1535; see 'Wardrobe Account of Henry VIII', *Archaeologia*, 9 (1789), p. 250. The 1582 *Books of Rates* recorded duty of 26*s*. 8*d*. per dozen pieces (length unspecified) of cap ribbon; Willan, *Book of Rates*, p. 14.

21   Both the painting and the drawing are in the Royal Collection.

22   Society of Antiquaries MS 129, f. 205v; BL. Add. MS 46, 384, f. 192r.

23   See D. Gaimster, M. Hayward, D. Mitchell and K. Parker, 'Tudor Silver-gilt Dress Books: A New Class of Treasure Find in England', *The Antiquaries Journal*, 82 (2002).

24   A. Sutton, 'The Coronation Robes of Richard III and Anne Neville', *Costume*, 13 (1979), p. 14.

25   Similar stiffening materials were used for clothing. For example, the collar of a fragmentary seventeenth-century child's doublet found in Abingdon, Oxford, was stiffened with a piece of card.

26   In this case, the interlining was a second piece of felt; see Arnold, *Patterns of Fashion: c. 1560–1620*, p. 93.

27   The probate inventory of William Heycrofte (died 1552), a capper, mercer and Alderman of Winchester, reveals that this pattern was echoed further down the social order. His inventory included eighteen ostrich feathers priced at 3*s* and two white feathers at 8*d* (HRO 1552B/101). I am very grateful to Karen Parker for this reference.

28   In a portrait of *c*. 1546 attributed to William Scrots, Prince Edward wears a black bonnet trimmed with a jewelled plume (National Gallery, London).

29   The National Archives, Kew, London (henceforth PRO), E101/426/8, m.2r.

30   While there are limited references to thrummed silk hats, thrums were a more important decorative feature of woollen hats.

31   Arnold, *Patterns of Fashion c. 1560–1620*, p. 31.

32   'Wardrobe Account of Henry VIII', *Archaeologia*, 9 (1789), pp. 247, 249.

33   *LP*, I, ii, p. 1464.

34   *LP*, I, ii, p. 3373.

35   Buckland, 'Monmouth Cap', p. 23.

36   Starkey (ed.), *Inventory of King Henry VIII* (14230, 14255, 14231, 14256).

37   See P. Clabburn, 'A Provincial Milliner's Shop in 1785', *Costume*, 2 (1977), p. 101.

38   Quoted by J. Thirsk, *Economic Policy and Projects: The Development of a Consumer Society in Early Modern England* (Oxford, 1978), pp. 14–16. Quoted by Breward, *Culture of Fashion*, p. 56. Haberdashers in Henry VIII's reign also dealt in more mundane materials. For example, Robert Dobbes, haberdasher of London, sold 710 ells of Normandy white canvas and thirty-eight bolts of poldavis (a coarse canvas) to the crown for £60 8*s*. 6*d*., BL Stowe MS 146, f. 70r.

39   In February 1544 Carcano imported a variety of luxury items under licence: one marten skin with the head and claws of gold, the head garnished with three emeralds, two diamonds, three rubies, a carcanet of gold garnished with four great table diamonds, four great rock rubies, eight pearls and a pearl pendant as well as a gold chain, two crosses and two rings, *LP*, XIX, i, p. 88.

40   PRO, E315/456, ff. 32r–33v.

41   *LP*, XXI, ii, 769.III.3.

42   J. Arnold, *Queen Elizabeth's Wardrobe Unlock'd* (Leeds, 1988), pp. 200–6.

43   J. Roberts, *Holbein and the Court of Henry VIII, Drawings and Miniatures from the Royal Library, Windsor Castle* (Edinburgh, 1993), p. 36.

44   Roberts, *Holbein*, p. 64.

45   For example, 'a Table with a picture of Lucressia Romana beinge all naked havinge like a Sipres aboute her' (10625).

46   In the Royal Collection.

47   J. Ashelford, *A Visual History of Costume: The Sixteenth Century* (London, 1985), p. 43; Roberts, *Holbein*, p. 72. Also see a miniature of *An Unknown Man* by Holbein (Yale Center for British Art, New Haven) that Strong considers similar to Holbein's sketch of Parr; see Strong, no. 36, p. 51.

48   Ashelford, *Sixteenth Century*, p. 43. The painting of an unknown Italian nobleman by Moretto of 1526 shows the sitter wearing a large medallion of St Christopher at the centre-front of the brim.

49   'It shall be necessary that I have the habit and hat of a cardinal . . . send me two or three hoods of such fashion and colours as cardinal's wear', *LP*, II, ii, p. 894.

50   A mitre of this type was recorded in the 1547–50 inventory: 'Item a Mytor garneshed with siluer and gilte and sett with counterfeit stones and glasses standing in Collettes of siluer and full sett with small seede peerle the two pendauntes or Labells sett Likewise with small seede peerles . . . hanging at thendes of the said Labelles tenne Bells of siluer' (2022).

51   See K. Hearn (ed.), *Dynasties: Paintings in Tudor and Jacobean England 1530–1630* (London, 1995), p. 49.

52   In the Isabella Stuart Gardiner Museum in Boston, USA, along with its couplet of Mrs Butts.

53   The *Mary Rose* Trust (MR81 A4706).

54   This style was not restricted to medical men, as is indicated by Holbein's drawing of Sir John Russell, later Earl of Bedford (*c.* 1486–1555), although Russell's coif lacks the ribbon trim.

55   Stonyhurst College owns two hats attributed to Sir Thomas More (1447–1535). The first is a felt hat (possibly rabbit felt) and the second is a linen night-cap embroidered with metal thread. When the pieces were conserved by Jean Glover, doubts were raised over the dating of both pieces.

56   In the Royal Collection, Windsor Castle, the Staatliche Museum, Berlin and the Kunsthistoriches Museum, Vienna, respectively.

57   At the Mercers' Company, London.

58   SA MS 129, f. 7r–v (I): there are two other references to this crown in jewel house inventories from earlier in Henry VIII's reign: 'Henry VIII's Jewel Book', pp. 158–9 and PRO, E36/85, ff. 4v–5r, For the slight discrepancies in the crown's weight in the three inventories, see A. J. Collins (ed.), *Jewels and Plate of Queen Elizabeth I* (1955), no I, pp. 264–6.

59   Trinity College, Cambridge.

60   In 1483 a cap of estate made from half a yard of velvet, furred with sixteen ermine backs and 150 powderings was made for Richard III. A bonnet was also supplied, made from three-quarters of a yard of purple silk velvet decorated with a gold tassel; see Sutton, 'Coronation Robes', p. 14.

61   PRO, LC 2/3. I, p. 29

62   This cap has been conserved in the studios of Cliodna Devitt and I am most grateful to Cliodna for discussing the cap with me.

63   E. McEncaney (ed.), *A History of Waterford and Its Mayors from the Twelfth to the Twentieth Centuries* (Waterford, 1995), pp. 104–13. With thanks to Rachel Phelan for this reference.

64   S. Landi, 'The York Cap of Maintenance', *The Conservator*, 10 (1986), p. 25.

65   BL Add. MS 7099, f. 37 printed in S. Bentley (ed.), *Excerpta Historica* (London, 1831), p. 111.

66   From Platter's *Travels in England* quoted in Cunnington and Cunnington, *Handbook of English Costume*, p. 131.

67   B. Castiglione, *The Book of the Courtier* (Harmondsworth, 1967, 1976), p. 137.

68   Castiglione, *Courtier*, p. 136.

69   PRO, E101/420/I, no. 75.

70   PRO, E101/420/I, no. 78 and E/101/418/5, no. 12.

71   PRO, E101/420/I, no. 29.

72   'Wardrobe Account of Henry VIII', *Archaeologia*, 9 (1789), p. 249. An illustration in Henry VIII's psalter depicts Will wearing a coat with a hood: BL, Royal MS 2A, f. 16r.

73   PRO, E101/420/I, no. 26.

74   C. W. Cunnington, P. Cunnington and C. Beard, *A Dictionary of English Costume* (London, 1960).

75   Cunnington et al., *Dictionary of English Costume*, p. 135.

76   In the Royal Collection.

77   PRO, E101/421/13, m. 2.

78   In the collection of the Duke of Buccleuch and Queensberry.

79   Associated entries relate to the other linen items used by the King when bathing.

80   In the National Portrait Gallery, London.

81   In the Royal Collection.

82   PRO, E101/421/13, m.2. A much shorter gift roll recording the presents given to Prince Edward in 1539 included one bonnet; BL Cotton MS 89, f. 41v.

83   BL Rot. Reg. 14. B. XLIII, unfoliated.

84   See R. K. Marshall, '"To be the Kingis Grace ane Dowblett": The Costume of James V, King of Scots', *Costume*, 28 (1994), p. 17.

85   The miniatures of Henry and Charles Brandon, the sons of the first Duke of Suffolk, provide a good example, Henry (the elder brother, painted aged five) wore a black bonnet at a slight angle and trimmed with a white feather. Charles's bonnet was plain and worn flat on his head indicating that he was younger (three). In the Royal Collection.

86   George Neville, Lord Abergavenny (*c.* 1460–1535), was drawn by Holbein in June 1535. This image, drawn shortly before the sitter's death, depicts Neville wearing a close-fitting black cap, possibly of blocked felt. The simplicity and warmth of the cap are offset by a jewelled brooch with three pendant pearls. In the Royal Collection.

87   Quoted in E. W. Ives, *Anne Boleyn* (Oxford, 1986), p. 75.

The stage, costume and fashion

Catherine Richardson

Performances at the theatres of early modern London are famous because the plays written by Shakespeare and his contemporaries are considered among the finest in the English language. What is less familiar is the fact that the main attraction of these plays may well have been the costumes in which their actors were dressed, and their connections to metropolitan fashion at the time. It has been calculated that the costumes at the Rose Theatre were worth at least as much as the theatre building itself; a company of actors restaging an old play paid 50 shillings to have the text updated, but nearly four times as much for costumes in which to perform it. This was a theatre which drew audiences through its use of spectacle, and clothing was the main focus of its show. Actors wore clothes made of cloth of gold and silver, of velvet and satin, embellished with gold and silver lace.

Such clothing on the bodies of lowly actors drew scorn and fury from moralists, because everyday dress in early modern England was governed by sumptuary legislation which controlled who could wear which kinds of fabric and decoration, dependent upon their income and social status. This led to a rather static concept of fashion in which the raw materials which made up garments had a lasting and intrinsic relationship to rank. However, for the elite in society and especially in London, a fashion system was beginning to develop which drew upon continental styles of dress which altered with increasing frequency.

Evidence for the sourcing of costumes is piecemeal and anecdotal, but it appears that actual pieces of elite clothing found their way onto the stage, hence the presence of incredibly costly gold lace in players' wardrobes. The Swiss traveller Thomas Platter stated that

> it is the English usage for eminent lords or Knights at their decease to bequeath and leave almost the best of their clothes to their serving men, which it is unseemly for the latter to wear, so that they offer them for sale for a small sum to the actors.
>
> (Platter 1937)

Because of the sumptuary legislation, scholars have argued that plays also offered an outlet for the unredeemed pledges of pawnbrokers. There is some evidence that the rich robes of the pre-Reformation church were hired out, as were the costumes of the Office of the Revels which organised court entertainment.

But these sources had to be supplemented, making costume a fragmentary affair. Performances were put together from the second-hand clothing of elevated owners, dress which counterfeited elite fashion in its use of cheaper alternatives such as copper lace, and some garments specific to peculiar roles. For plays in Classical settings, in exotic Eastern lands, or in the distant British past of Robin Hood or Cymbeline, costumes which bore no relation to contemporary dress may have been used, at least in proportions determined by the company's finances. For the majority of plays, however, there was no distinction between theatrical costume and metropolitan clothing – audiences came to see a display of material finery, and it was one which used or at least

Snapshot 6.1 Drawing of a scene from William Shakespeare's *Titus Andronicus* (c. 1595), Longleat House Portland Papers, vol. 1, f. 159v. Reproduced by permission of the Marquess of Bath, Longleat House, Warminster, Wiltshire, Great Britain.

imitated the fashions which could be seen on the streets of London and in the court. If this was an illusion, constricted by the precarious economics of playing, then it worked within the confines of theatre's own magic: what is seen on stage is always interpreted by audiences in relation to the narrative within which it is situated; actors become kings, fur becomes ermine and copper-lace becomes gold in relation to the story in which an audience invests their imagination.

Bibliography and further reading

Jones, A. R., and Stallybrass, P. (2000) *Renaissance Clothing and the Materials of Memory*, Cambridge: Cambridge University Press.

MacIntyre, J. (1992) *Costumes and Scripts in the Elizabethan Theatres*, Edmonton: University of Alberta Press.

Platter, Thomas (1937) *Thomas Platter's Travels in England, 1599*, trans. Clare Williams, London: Jonathan Cape, p. 167.

Richardson, C. (ed.) *Clothing Culture 1350–1650*, Aldershot: Ashgate.

The courtier and fashion

Carole Collier Frick

The fashion worn by courtiers at sixteenth- and seventeenth-century European courts was calculated to demonstrate the virtues of military men (courage, bravery, eloquence) while not being actively engaged in military pursuits. In spite of Machiavelli's admonishments to the Italian city-states that their defensive forces should be composed of citizen-soldiers, soldiery in the first decades of the sixteenth century became increasingly professionalised and dominated by mercenary German *Landsknechte*, Swiss pikesmen, and *condottieri* of international origin in the Italic wars. The medieval paradigm of military activities being the pursuit of men of noble rank became unrealistic owing to the engorgement of lands under the control of Charles V, Holy Roman Emperor and King of Spain after 1519, and his subsequent need to rely upon troops that could be hired to fight the changing challenges to his new hegemony.

Many nobles were therefore newly relegated to the domestic realm where they adapted the latest styles of military armour to garments that merely mimicked its lines. This resulted in the *capi maschili* (men's clothing) which had echoes of the armour, but was softer and more elegant; domesticated velvet and brocade replacing leather and metal. Flamboyant fashion elements that originated with the new mercenary military included decorative diagonal slashing; the peascod shape of the breastplate or cuirass; the sleeveless tabard vest (originally of leather); frog closures on doublets (originally braided decorations); trimmings of chevrons and stripes; prominent padded and decorated codpieces (*braghette*); square-toed soled shoes (*calzatura a punta quadrata*); berets (*berrette*) for headwear; and short cloaks (*cappe*) worn casually over one shoulder.

The challenge for the courtier was to present himself as virile, active and loyal to his overlord while at the same time demonstrating a calmly civilised and refined masculinity as he jockeyed for a position of social importance within a newly constructed international ambit dominated by political forces outside his control. Styles became reactive rather than proactive. The strictures of local sumptuary legislation also attempted to control ornamentation and colour by rank to stabilise social order and new laws were continually passed Europe-wide.

The silhouette for men at court changed regularly over time, ensembles becoming larger and more ornate. The traditional upper-body doublet called the *farsetto* disappeared in the 1540s, being replaced by the *giubbone*, which was longer and stiffer, and could be collared, collarless, or open down the middle as can be seen in Moroni's *Portrait of the Cavalier in Red*, 1560 (Snapshot 7.1). The *giubbone* was itself replaced by the longer and more ornate *giustacuore*, cinched in at the waist. This style lasted, with subtle regional differences, until the 1690s. The round white ruched or pleated collar (*gorgiere* or *lattuga*) made its appearance in the 1550s, and, like the *giustacuore*, took many regional shapes. The Spanish court wore the ruffs more severely tight than in Italy; and in the north, these starched collars were often flatter and larger in diameter. For the

Snapshot 7.1 Giovanni Battista Moroni (*c.* 1525–78), *Portrait of the Cavalier in Red*, or *Portrait of Gian Gerolamo Grumelli*, Italian statesman and noble, 1560 (oil on canvas, 216 × 123 cm). Collection of Count Antonio Moroni, Bergamo, Italy/The Bridgeman Art Library.

lower body, at the beginning of the sixteenth century, courtiers were wearing lined and soled hose which then morphed into close-cut breeches or slim trunk hose, complete with prominent codpiece. Codpieces became necessary for modesty at the fork of the hose as the doublets of the Renaissance became shorter and then shorter again, and continued to be worn and conspicuously displayed throughout the sixteenth and into the seventeenth century. Over time, the style in breeches expanded, and the voluminous paned pantaloons called 'pumpkin breeches' became fashionable at the beginning of the seventeenth century as well. Along with the clothes, the masculine display of hair changed also: hair was cut shorter, and previously shaven men now sported close-cut goatees and moustaches, with a sword, commander's staff (*bastone del commando*) and large hunting dog often included in formal portraits. Court ensembles were eventually influenced by the reforming dicta of the Reformation and Counter Reformation which attempted to reign in sartorial excess with varying degrees of success.

Bibliography and further reading

Arnold, J. (1988) 'Preliminary Investigation into the Medici Graves Clothes', in *Il costume nell'età del Rinascimento*, Florence: Edifir, pp. 149–57.

Butazzi, G. (1995) 'Il modello spagnolo nella moda europea', in A. G. Cavagna and G. Butazzi (eds), *Le Trame della moda*, Rome: Bulzoni, pp. 80–94.

Frick, C. C. (2007) 'Painting Personal Identity: The Costuming of Nobildonne, Heroines, and Kings', in *Italian Women Artists from Renaissance to Baroque*, Rome: Skira, pp. 63–74.

Chapter 6

Mapping the world
Dress in Cesare Vecellio's costume books[1]

Eugenia Paulicelli

CESARE VECELLIO PUBLISHED HIS COSTUME BOOKS in two editions, the first, *Degli Habiti antichi e moderni di diverse parti del mondo*, in Italian in 1590, then an expanded bilingual version in 1598.[2] Vecellio, a relative of the Venetian painter Titian, aimed in his work at giving an encyclopaedic approach to dress. In attempting a visual and discursive cartography of the whole world as it was then known, through dress, the author also gives his readers a picture of the class and gender relationships that are manifested in a diversified geography of taste, politics of style and production of fashion and textiles. Fashion and the discovery of the new world had a great deal in common, says Vecellio, as each new discovery brought to the fore new clothes, styles and tastes in dress. Vecellio's ambition, in fact, is to map the diversity of dress, ornaments and customs of the world that was then, as he tells us, being discovered before his very eyes. Fashion, Vecellio tells us, changes fast, according to individual desires and for capricious reasons, and it is on account of this that his project is, and can only be, an unfinished and provisional one.

Vecellio's encyclopaedic approach to dress (he both produced the images and later wrote the text) and the way he sought to represent a codification of taste and behaviour link his work to both the genre of conduct literature – books that gave advice on how to behave, perform, talk and dress in public, epitomised by Castiglione's *Il libro del cortegiano* (1528) – which boomed in sixteenth-century Italy, and to the moral geography emerging with the creations of maps and atlases. Vecellio's books are multifaceted and can be appreciated from at least three standpoints that cannot be isolated from one another, but which are linked in a relational way. In fact, insofar as they have a moralising intent, his texts can be likened to books on conduct and behaviour; insofar as they foreground the interaction between word and image they exploit the modes of the art of memory; and lastly, insofar as they establish a connection between dress, place and identity, they can be compared to travel books, such as that written in 1567 by Nicolas de Nicolay d'Arfeuilles, *Les Quatres premieres livres des navigations et peregrinations orientales, Navigazioni orientali.* Nicolay's book, which numbered several editions in Latin, French, German, and Italian, contains several sketches of foreign costumes and types, and represented a source and an inspiration for Vecellio and others for the reproduction of foreign dress.[3]

Just as fashion and the New World cannot be kept far apart, neither can the New World and the publishing industry. Suffice to say that access to information about the newly discovered territories and peoples became available to a larger European audience only through the nascent publishing industry that produced diaries, travel reportages, maps, and so on, that represented in word and image the new discoveries.[4] A process of *longue durée* of institutionalisation of norms, taste, and discipline, as Foucault put it, was made possible by the development of the print industry, which brought about the spread of fashion beyond the relatively limited space of the court as an institution of modernity and led to its sedimentation in the folds of Western culture.[5]

Among these publications were costume books, a successful European genre in the sixteenth century. These contributed to an understanding of the social, political and aesthetic dynamics of cultural production of the time and its material culture. Despite Vecellio's curiosity toward other cultures and geographical spaces, it is clear that his depictions of the 'other' are set against a European model in which Italy and Venice play a major role. Such mechanisms are recurrent in other costume books, as in the case of François Desprez's *Recueil d'habits* (1562–7), studied by Isabelle Paresys, where the representation of the 'other' forces Europeans to ponder their own aesthetic and cultural identity.[6] Indeed, the sequence of fashion plates in the different sections of Vecellio's books is an attempt to define a sense of a 'national character' for the peoples with whom he deals in his text, such as the Turks, the Germans, and the French.[7]

It was through printing that the world was translated into images, bringing the faraway and the unknown closer to Europeans and therefore closer to knowledge of the 'other' via linguistic and visual representation.[8] In this way the dressed and adorned, often foreign, bodies represented in costume books fulfilled both the desire and the need of Europeans to locate the features of their own culture and identity. Foreign bodies in Vecellio's 1598 text, especially those in the Florida sections, are represented in their almost total nakedness, this being the symbol *par excellence* of the savage body that was to be clothed and 'civilised' by the Western colonisers. Brought into contact with otherness through the medium of print, Europeans came to develop a more clearly defined picture of their own culture, seen always in term of superiority.[9] As has been noted by David Harvey: 'Geographical knowledge became a valued commodity in a society that was becoming more and more profit-conscious. The accumulation of wealth, power, and capital became linked to personalised knowledge of and individual command over, space'.[10]

My aim, in this essay, is to offer an overview of Vecellio's *Habiti*, considering it in the context of cultural production concerning fashion and dress. Parallel to a growing expansion of fashion goods and cosmetic products, Vecellio's age witnessed a massive and diversified cultural production in which the dressed body and social appearance were embedded, via the discourse on them, in a 'civilising' process. Beauty and grace, as Castiglione wrote in his *Cortegiano*, are not God-given qualities but can be acquired through the exercise of 'honest dissimulation', whether via the rhetoric of language or the rhetoric of dress, that becomes part and parcel of political and aesthetic performance. Fashion, then, becomes a discourse, a process of codification and idealisation of body features, behaviour, manners, and style, and so takes on all the features of an institution of modernity. Vecellio's text is crucial for an understanding of the subtle mechanisms underlying fashion and its links to the interplay between individualism and uniformity, identified by Simmel as being at the core of fashion. The complexity of Vecellio's *Habiti* can best be gauged in the light of recent scholarship in the fields of fashion and dress studies.[11] In fact, this may well be one of the reasons why Vecellio's books have received the critical attention they deserve only in the last few years.[12] Furthermore, Vecellio's *Habiti* allows us to see how an interdisciplinary approach to the study of dress is key in order to understand the formation of a geography of taste and the process of codification of manners and cultural/political hegemonies. Vecellio's work is not merely a catalogue illustrating the variety of styles in Italy and around the world. Rather, it is a text that helps us to trace the process of definition and inscription of identity (personal and of given countries) in the fabric and folds of dress.

In sixteenth-century Italy, cultural production on conduct flourished both before and after the Council of Trent (1545–63) and gave special attention to dress and social appearance as a gauge that defined territorial and national boundaries as well as moral and aesthetic codes. The presence and the success of a genre such as conduct literature confirm one important characteristic of fashion: its institutional and normative side. But they also offer eloquent and ample testimony to the anxiety that accompanied, as it always accompanies, the blurring of the boundaries of gender, identity, appearance, and moral codes that characterised early modernity. As Ribeiro has pointed out, it was in the Renaissance that the Church's power over all aspects of morality, including clothing, started to crumble. Coincidentally, it was also in this period that the shape of the male and female body began to be exposed through the cut and construction of dress.[13]

In addition, it was at this time that a national aspect of fashion emerged.[14] Dress, for Vecellio, is an object that has a social and political life that is acquired through the various stages of production and consumption within the growing exchanges of domestic and international markets. Vecellio was writing at a time in which 'fashion capitalism', to borrow Jane Schneider's definition, was being shaped via communication and trade.[15] Consumers' demands were formed and spread as a result of the expansion of markets and the availability of goods like luxury textiles, paintings, the spices and food from the East, and the newly discovered American continent. If 'print capitalism', as Anderson has noted, fuelled the process of imagining nations, fashion capitalism, as illustrated in costume books, in the circulation of types, and the development of local industries, engendered a culture of fashion linked to particular places and nations.[16] One can, in fact, trace the creation of a 'national' style and image that continuously interacted with foreign or global images. It is not by chance that Vecellio's treatment of the *diversità* ('diversity') and *varietà di habiti* ('variety of costumes'), is accompanied by a parallel mechanism of uniformity of dress and style. Turning to his text, we often see headings that stress local dress phenomena, such as: 'Clothing of Venice and other places in Italy' (1598, pp. 96, 148); 'Clothing of Modern Merchants of Italy'; 'Dress of the Duchessess from Parma or other noble ladies from all of Italy' 'who use a lot of jewellery, gold buttons, pearls, chains and farthingales to keep their gowns ample. This style of dress is also used almost all over Italy' (1598, p. 169). [. . .]

Still, in order to understand the complexity of Vecellio's work we cannot see it solely as an illustration of different types of dress and style. Rather, what I would suggest as a general interpretative framework is that Vecellio's treatment of dress can be better understood if we link his project, first, to the creation of a language of the dressed body in social and political spaces, similar to what Castiglione did in his *Cortegiano*; and second, to the creation of the meanings of dress linked to nations and cultures (European and otherwise), via 'cartographic writing' and its implications for the art of memory.[17] More precisely, Vecellio's approach to the *cosa de gli habiti*, as he called it, establishes connections between dress, culture and power that make explicit the links between, on the one hand, what we might call the fabric of cloth and the fabric of society; and, on the other, between the codification of dress and politics both in local and in the then-emergent global contexts. At the heart of Vecellio's texts lies a moral geography that seeks to preserve and bolster the European sense of superiority that was shared by his immediate Christian readers. Indeed, the Christian nature of Europe is stressed as early as the second chapter of Vecellio's text, when he writes:

> The world, then, was divided into three principal parts by ancient cosmographers, though they did not divide these parts equally: one of these is called Europe, the second Africa, and the third Asia. We read that Europe and Asia took their names from two women so named. Europa, in our days consists of all the part of the world in which the faith of Jesus Christ is known and also some parts of Turkey.
>
> (1590, chapter II)

The organising principle according to which he lists cities, places, and clothing in a relational way makes his overall intent clear. Although the text offers its readers a survey of clothing from all over the globe as it was then known, it is also careful to view that emerging world from the standpoint of the world as it was then known to Vecellio, namely Italy, Venice, and Rome. Vecellio, of course, was not alone in this. But what makes his texts different is how they feature text and image as mnemotechniques that sought to render their message in as powerful and memorable a way as possible. Differently from other Italian and European costume books, which had little or no text, Vecellio's books feature both verbal and visual language. [. . .]

Vecellio's interpretation of the costumes, cultures, and peoples of the lesser-known geographical spaces such as Africa, Asia and America is multi-layered, achieved through the juxtaposition of image and text interacting on the same page. In fact, one of the most distinguishing and original features of Vecellio's work is its richness and the variety of its repertoire of images, which was much broader than an earlier illustrated costume book by Ferdinando Bertelli (*Omnium fere gentium nostrae aetatis habitus*; Venice, 1563), illustrated by Enea Vico.[18] What really makes Vecellio's *Habiti* stand out and create an *unicum* in its own genre is the verbal commentary he provides and the rhetorical strategies he adopts to organise his discourse on the images he collects and selects. Indeed, as Jeannine Guérin Dalle Mese has noted, the commentary broadens the scope of his work.

Vecellio is highly aware of the mechanism according to which the image impacts on memory, while the verbal text pins down meanings. The images, in fact, inserted within pre-ordered spaces that as *loci* are organised by the author within a persuasive and meaningful trajectory, draw on the personal and emotional power of the dressed figures. This procedure is also a great illustration of fashion's *double face* that links it not only to exteriority and social space, but also to the inner space of emotions and personal memories, and to senses like touch. But let us see how Vecellio makes us travel the world through dress and see in his 'dedication' and the section addressed 'to the reader' how the *diversità degli habiti*, which is their distinctive trait, is a result of individual choices, and cultural differences, as well as of ever-changing political and moral regulations and codes. [. . .]

The whole question of change underlies Vecellio's work from the start, in all the parts, including what Genette would call the paratext. After the note to the readers, one finds a '*Tavola delle cose più notabili contenute nel presente libro*', followed by thirteen short chapters in which he discusses the ideological motivations for his choices, something that will be taken up again in the descriptions of individual plates. What emerges from this threshold is a spatial dimension of the book itself, which is built like a palace. As the readers enter his gallery of images and memory and the symbolic courtyard, the author, aiming at clarifying his project, lists the material and detailed items the readers will find in the book. As we have seen already, in the first chapter of this section he reiterates how the notion of change is key for understanding 'that thing about clothing' while also expanding on the concept and its links to history, making references to how cities and civilisations have been shaped and reshaped over time. Interestingly enough, he does not mention Rome among the 'fallen cities'. The sack of Rome in 1527 was not so distant and certainly did not offer any reason to be proud of the Roman past.[19] Vecellio will say in the sections dedicated to Venice: 'Venice is similar to the greatness of Rome, but at the same time it surpasses it because differently from Rome it was never sacked' (1590, p. 39). Vecellio, then, chose the Roman past to be taken as a foundational stage in his process of imagining nations and inscribing their narratives. In the spatial organisation of the book, in fact, it is Rome that opens his treatment of *habiti*. Within this context, he positions Italy's destiny and transformations from the glorious past of the Romans till the present when Venice, among all Italian cities, takes centre stage.

For Vecellio, then, when writing of Italy, variety is the order of the day. In chapter VII of his treatise, for example, he lists the 'different peoples who live in Italy', concluding that such diversity is mainly due to the fact that Italy had been on several occasions 'prey to foreigners and the site of fate; and for these reasons it should not be a surprise if here one can see much more variety in clothing styles than in any other nations or regions'. In order to corroborate his point, Vecellio refers to the artist Baldo Antonio Penna who, charged with the task of drawing costumes from several provinces, found himself in a difficult position when it came to drawing Italian clothing. In fact, Vecellio anecdotally reports that Penna chose to represent the Italian as a naked man, carrying on his shoulder a piece of cloth ('a cloth of wool on his shoulder'). When asked why he chose this kind of unusual representation for Italians, Penna replied that he had not been able to find any one single dress that epitomised them, whom he describes as being, and wanting to be, different, capricious, and changeable in their style of dress. Out of this kind of individualism a sort of 'national character' emerges, and it is on his shoulders that Vecellio drapes a piece of cloth so that the naked 'national character' himself can choose the tailor to cut his dress according to his own taste and will.[20]

Of course, this is just one more tirade about the individualism of Italians. But it is also more than that: in fact, it acts as a justification of Vecellio's need, as well as that of many of his contemporaries, to give a semblance of order to the chaos they saw in the emerging and ever-changing world and so establish a paradigmatic structure of codes, moral, aesthetic and political, with which to rein that chaos in. It is in this context that dress and fashion play a crucial role. It is not by chance, for instance, that, for the sake of order and in an attempt to establish a point of 'origin' for 'Italian dress', as well as for the 'splendour of the Italian past', the next chapter in Vecellio's treatise is about Rome, *caput mundi*, and the fact that it represents the 'seat of Christianity'. Rome has of course played a crucial role in the foundational myths of the Italian nation. But, more importantly, it has been central to a Eurocentric vision of the world where Christianity is seen as a superior form of religion and civilisation.[21] Interestingly enough, the section on Rome in the 1598 edition of the *Habiti* starts with the image of the '*sommo Pontefice*' (the Pope) luxuriously dressed (Figure 6.1), while the 1590 edition opens with an illustration of a Roman patrician. In addition, striking similarities can be noted between the representation of the Pope and that of the Doge that opens the section on Venice

Figure 6.1 The Pope, from Cesare Vecellio, *Habiti antichi, et moderni di tutto il mondo* (1598).

(Figure 6.2). Here the Doge, in Vecellio's description, is a quintessential combination of religious and political power. In his section on Rome, Vecellio emphasises the city's republican past, that made it appear as the 'natural' predecessor of the Venetian republic.

But as well as the territorial and 'national' boundaries, what played a massive role in the definition of fashion were moral and religious boundaries. As is testified by the condemnation of luxury and extravagant styles of dress and ornaments on the part of preachers and by way of the emanation of sumptuary laws, a phenomenon that lasted for about five hundred years, tensions pertaining to the definition and boundaries of the self both in private and in public were present during this time. When a style of dress did not conform to the laws, local legislators punished the transgressors (mostly women

Figure 6.2 'Principe o Doge' [The Doge of Venice], from Cesare Vecellio, *Habiti antichi, et moderni di tutto il mondo* (1598).

or cross-dressers) with fines and the *bollatura delle vesti* (marking of clothing). Despite the strict legislation on dress and luxury, the desire to cross social and class boundaries was, for the wealthy middle classes, always strong. The economic transformations taking place at this time had given rise to a social mobility that meant that the wealthy middle classes were now able to afford to buy and wear princely attire. Such a craze for luxury items and cloth was only the most outward sign of the development of a capitalist economy and a wealthy bourgeoisie, the new aspiring ruling class, who now challenged the primacy of the aristocracy. Within this process of transformation, fashion emerged as one of the economic and cultural forces that determined, through its new industrial base, changes in the identities of several Italian cities. Economic, social, and cultural transformations thus engendered two opposite and yet complementary forces that competed on the terrain of social life, appearances, morality, and decorum. On the one hand, the gradual and steady growth in availability of luxury goods like textiles and jewels, which catered to the tastes of an urban entrepreneurial middle class; on the other, the moralists and state legislators who tried via the sumptuary laws and sermons to control the social body, class mobility, the desire for luxury goods, and the concomitant changes in dress, class, and gender codes. These laws, however, never completely succeeded in creating the order they aimed to establish or maintain. Not only were they not always observed literally, they were also at times creatively interpreted by women in such a way that new styles were invented. This was the case of Nicolosa Sanuti (1420?–1505) who wrote a letter in response to the Bologna sumptuary legislation in which she affirms that female dress and ornamentation do not diminish her virtue, but illustrate it.[22]

Dress was akin to the passport of an identity that was regulated by strict moral codes accepted by both Church and State officials.[23] The growing scholarship on these laws, as well as accounts of how medieval preachers condemned the display of luxury and desire, illustrate well the tensions within social classes and gender relations that resulted from the formation of a proto-capitalist, cloth-producing society, an area in which Italy was at the time one of the most important European exporters. In many Italian cities, thanks to the variety of fashions that were produced and which represented a variegated geography of taste, there existed a flourishing textile and fashion industry.[24]

It is not by chance, then, that Vecellio's books, reflecting their author's intuition about what was to become known as the 'Italian style', aim to map and so to some extent control the cultural diversity and sense of aesthetic and beauty in various Italian northern, central, and southern cities. Vecellio, in fact, noted how the nation was, at a local level, diversified and shaped by the tastes of the elitist society ruling the territory. He writes that: 'Le nuove maniere di vestire quasi per la maggior parte sono in ogni tempo uscite, tanto di maschi, quanto di femmine, da' Principi' (1598, p. 51). In addition, the many differences in habits and aesthetic modes were dictated by geographical differences, the local economy, and political alliances that had been realised by marriage through which families merged their cultural preferences and tastes. [. . .]

Symbolic and geographic space in *Habiti*

There is another feature of Vecellio's text that I would like to bring to the fore. The book itself is symbolically a space conceived of as a portable museum that readers enter.

In alphabetical order in the 'Table of the most notable things contained in this current book of clothing', Vecellio's cataloguing spans the 'a' of *acconciature* (hair styles) to the 'z' of *zazzere* (hair cuts), not forgetting spices such as *zafferano* (saffron) or luxurious fur, *zibellino*, or coats, *zimarre*. It is in the process of reading a section or a single costume plate that readers also visit a different geographical space, a city, a house, a harem, or a country. Thus, the sections and the chapters are virtual spaces explored by readers through the costume plate that opens the door to a familiar or unfamiliar geographical place. Old civilisations and cities, through their modes of dress – as in the case of the Romans – become for Vecellio important memory devices that enable him to bring back to life almost forgotten cultures.[25] As mentioned earlier, the use of images and words and the way he employs the multifaceted category of space have a great deal to do with how the techniques of the art of memory establish a mental path that leads to an identification of places.[26] Therefore, Vecellio's rhetorical and visual organisation of his material is akin to a mental process in which, as in other treatises, he wishes to instruct readers and develop their awareness of the significance of dress and appearance, creating in their minds a sort of mental cartography with which to locate information about his subject matter. In this way the role of both the physical and mental image, as in memory and thought, becomes a sort of foundation on which to base his discourse.

Fabric is to dress what words are to language, and in treating clothing Vecellio starts from its material foundation: cloth. He lists the different kinds of cloth such as cotton and silk, as well as listing the variety of colours available. In this description of the materiality of fabric and colours, Vecellio entices his readers into almost sensing the process of the cloth's making. He has an entry in the table of contents on the 'variety of fabric and materials used for making clothes in ancient times', listing 'wool', and 'silk', and concluding with 'feathers', by which he means the mode of dress of Native American Indians. In addition, he makes specific reference to 'brocade' as well as to different kinds of headgear (22 entries on 'caps', increasing to 51 in the 1598 edition, 13 on 'hats' and 3 on 'hoods').[27]

The book, in fact, can be consulted through the list of items or through geographical places and cities. Among the Italian cities, however, it is Venice that takes pride of place in Vecellio's treatment of dress.[28] Venice, it is clear, is his true love, his still point in a turning world: 'Famous city and so illustrious that after Rome she deservedly in Europe held the primacy and is named Queen of the Sea and immaculate and intact virgin for never having been attacked or sacked' (1590, p. 39). This text appears side by side with an etching of Piazza San Marco overlooking the sea, the heart of Venetian splendour and international trade. But including one picture of Piazza San Marco was evidently not enough for Vecellio (Figure 6.3). [. . .]

In the description of male Venetian attire, Vecellio offers very precise information regarding men's public roles. In fact, he specifies that 'The clothing seen here belongs to the leaders of the Council of Ten, of whom there are three in number, who change every month and are elected by lot. This is an office of tremendous, indeed the greatest, power. These men sometimes wear a red overgarment' (Rosenthal and Jones, 1598, pp. 81, 105–57). He then goes on to describe the male 'citizens', 'merchants and shop keepers' who wear shorter dress and a 'high, fully rounded cap' (Rosenthal and Jones, 1598, pp. 116–68). The illustrations of Venetian patrician and upper-class male attire (sixteen woodcut illustrations) are more numerous than any other description of male dress in the entire text.

Figure 6.3 'Terza perspectiva della Piazza San Marco' [Third perspective of Saint Mark's Square in Venice], from Cesare Vecellio, *Habiti antichi, et moderni di tutto il mondo* (1598).

On account of its location, the 'Serenissima' had enjoyed privileged links to the Eastern countries that brought to the city trade and travellers, but also wars.[29] Vecellio goes to great lengths to illustrate exotic costumes from Turkey, Africa, and America. Among the 'exotic' lands, Turkey attracts Vecellio's special attention and admiration on account of the refined taste and strengths of its army and of its many trade relations with the Serenissima. His attention is no surprise given the important role the Ottoman Empire had vis-à-vis Italian and European trade and imperialist interests. One of the links between East and West bears on women when seen in public. Vecellio tells us that Muslim, Christian and Jewish women wear a veil to cover their face and protect it from the external male gaze (Figures 6.4 and 6.5).[30] We can also note some elements

Figure 6.4 'Donzelle' [Young women], from Cesare Vecellio, *Habiti antichi, et moderni di tutto il mondo* (1598).

Figure 6.5 'Turca di mediocre condizione' [Turkish woman of inferior social position], from Cesare Vecellio, *Habiti antichi, et moderni di tutto il mondo* (1598).

of interaction between Turkey and Venice in the female use of the 'pianelle', the two styles being very similar indeed. He depicts Turkish costumes in a similar way to how he structures the space of representation in Venice. In both cases, he distinguishes the domestic sphere from the list of several public spaces (Figure 6.6). The space that is almost impossible to represent for Western eyes is the *seraglio* and the harem, the site of romanticisation of the mysterious Eastern eroticism for Western narrative accounts and painting, a space forbidden to foreign eyes and which has no equivalent in the West.

Figure 6.6 'Donna turca in casa' [Turkish woman at home]. From Cesare Vecellio, *Habiti antichi, et moderni di tutto il mondo* (1598).

'Since so many wives or concubines are chosen to serve only the Turkish lord, they are considered worthy of equal treatment in the way they live and dress. So only one style of attire will be shown here, as representative of what all these women wear' (Rosenthal and Jones, 1598, pp. 394–446).

But in treating European dress, Vecellio spars with two of the major powers: namely, France and Spain and notes the differences in taste between the two cultures.[31] He mentions, for example, how common it is among Spanish noblemen to 'pierce their ears and attach gold earrings with jewellery of a certain value, a [style] that was once detested by the French, but now adopted not only by French women but also French men' (1598, p. 266). The initial differing taste of wearing gold rings for men and women becomes a fashion dictated this time by Spain, one of the hegemonic political and colonial powers. Emphasising other differences in the style of war, language, and what we might call today national character, Vecellio meticulously catalogues his information in the different sections of the book, all the time following the same method and approach. He offers a background of the city or country to which the costume plate belongs. Geography is linked to the political and economic history of a given place. After this, Vecellio follows another hierarchical criterion by defining and representing dress according to class and social status. As already mentioned, the variety of individual types and dress was quite broad and included nobles, merchants' wives, women of modest means, courtesans, peasants, and royals, as in the case of the Sultan of the Ottoman Empire. Within these categories and the similar typology followed in the majority of cases, Vecellio identifies other kinds of geographical, cultural, and political variants that determined the changes in the choice of dress and ornaments as well as in social appearance. By way of example, we can see how Vecellio comments on the differences in the attire of Roman noble women and Roman merchants' wives. In the iconographic representation of Roman noble women the use of gloves and fans is emphasised as if to underline a sense of decorous elegance when they are seen in public. With this kind of demeanour, Vecellio contrasts the pompous elegance displayed by the merchants' wives:

> Women citizens, or wives of merchants, dress very sumptously and grandly, wearing gowns with low-cut bodices that expose their breasts, adorned with many strands of heavy gold necklaces, from which jewels also hang. Their overgarments are of damasco [damask, a self-patterned reversible fabric made of silk and linen] or beautifully patterned broccatello [a heavy fabric combining linen and silk], floor-length, encircled with borders of gold brocade.
>
> (Rosenthal and Jones, 1590, pp. 32/84)

Here, Vecellio stresses that noblewomen dress more modestly than wealthy commoners. Continuing his analysis within the Roman territory, Vecellio describes 'Roman women of artisan and plebeian rank', and, before going into the details of their clothing, the author contextualises his commentary saying that just as 'nature' offers a great diversity in its fruit and plants so does the existing diversity of dress:

> In the same way that nature creates wide variety among flowers, grass, trees, and fruits, assigning a particular virtue more to one than another, so wise human judgment in cities and other well-ordered places has established certain forms and kinds of clothing, as different in cost as they are in color and shape. We see that the clothing illustrated here is different from that of noble and rich women. These wives of artisans wear garments of colored cloth, floor-length, with low-necked bodices, horizontally trimmed in silk and belted with a gold chain.
>
> (Rosenthal and Jones, 1590, pp. 34/86)

Vecellio concludes his treatment of Roman female dress with the description of two types of courtesan belonging to different time periods, one living during Pope Pius V's pontificate, the other in the modern age. The latter, according to Vecellio, could easily be confused with noblewomen because of their fine and elegant attire. The courtesan during the time of Pope Pius V, who was in office from 1566 to 1572, does not show her face and is very modestly dressed when seen in public. Known for his Dominican training and monastic austerity, Pius V even excommunicated Queen Elizabeth I. Besides being a defender of Catholicism and the inspiration for the edicts of the Council of Trent, one year before his death, the Pope faced the famous battle of Lepanto (7 October 1571) fought by the Venetians and Genoese against the Ottoman Empire's navy, considered a constant threat to the Italian peninsula and an obstacle to the Italian desire to control and expand its territories in the Mediterranean. In presenting the two courtesans from different time periods Vecellio draws attention to the moral and cultural differences in dress codes and policies, as well as to the fact that Venice remained free from any kind of foreign subjugation:

> Modern Roman courtesans dress in such fine style that few people can tell them apart from the noblewomen of that city. They wear sottane of satin or ormesino, floor-length, over which they wear zimarre of velvet, decorated from top to bottom with gold buttons, with low necklines that expose their entire breast and neck, adorned with beautiful pearls. [. . .] They make their hair blonde by artificial means, and they curl it and tie it up with silk ribbons inside a gold net, prettily ornamented with jewels and pearls.
> (Rosenthal and Jones, 1590, pp. 36/88)

From this description, it is possible to gauge some of the common trends in luxury attire characterising fashion in sixteenth-century Italy: namely, the use of 'zimarre of velvet', *zimarre di velluto*, one of the most expensive fabrics, decorated with gold buttons with emphasis given to the cleavage that is embellished by wearing necklaces of white pearls. To this image of seductive feminine elegance we learn that dying hair blonde was a very common trend followed by the majority of wealthy or noble women who believed, as the painters and the poets did, that blonde was the colour of ideal beauty (Figure 6.7). Giovanni Battista della Porta, in his 1558 treatise *Magia Naturalis*, offers several recipes on how to beautify and modify one's physical appearance, including how to dye the hair blonde, how to eliminate pimples, or even how to restore lost virginity in order to regain social acceptance and hopefully re-enter the marriage market. The manipulation of appearance though dress is touched upon in Vecellio's text several times, although always in relation to women, which of course is another example of his moral and ideological approach to fashion: 'Hence sometimes courtesans and marriageable women appear similar to the married ones, they even wear rings like married women and it is for these reasons that if people are not alert they can be deceived' (1598, p. 106).

Vecellio's references to courtesans, *meretrici*, and prostitutes are also diversified according to geography and local history although they share some common features. Namely, they represent a threat to morality and a source of confusion of status, as in the aforementioned examples, or of gender, as in the example he describes from Venice. In particular, this is the case of the 'prostitutes in public places' where, he affirms, there is no uniformity in the way they dress because this clearly depends on their good fortune

Figure 6.7 Venetian woman bleaching her hair in the sun on a rooftop gallery, from Cesare Vecellio, *Habiti antichi, et moderni di tutto il mondo* (1598).

in being wealthier than others. Vecellio notes another important trait of these prostitutes, namely, the fact that they adopt 'men's clothing':[32] 'They wear a doublet of silk or linen or some other fabric, more or less rich depending on what they can afford', adding that 'Next to their skin they wear a man's shirt, made with as much delicacy and elegance as they can afford. [. . .] Many wear *braghesse* like men, made of *ormesino*' (Rosenthal and Jones, 1598, pp. 114, 98–9).

This form of cross-dressing was, on the one hand, used by the *meretrici* as a sign of both their diversity and freedom to transgress gender boundaries in dress, while on the other it served to attract men who were actually pursuing sexual encounters with same-sex partners. The cases of Roman prostitutes, whose number abounded in centres like Venice, have been recently studied. Cross-dressing and disguise were considered particularly dangerous by the law-makers, because more than anything else they bore the signs of confusion of sex and status and therefore erased the social, sexual, and class boundaries established by the state and the church.[33]

Vecellio's text lists a series of social categories in descending order from top to bottom. In the penultimate category he places courtesans and prostitutes; in the bottom one, peasants, as in this example from Rome:

> The majority of the peasant women of the Roman territories, in the villages and hill towns of Rome, and in all the places subject to Roman lords and barons, wear a dress of turquoise or green cloth, ending above their feet, with a border of velvet, and with low-cut bodices that leave their necks bare; adorning these bodices with silver brooches, they lace them across a wide opening. [. . .] And as brides, their custom is to wear sleeves of red satin.
>
> (Rosenthal and Jones, 1590, p. 37)

La cosa degli habiti has, for Vecellio, a political concern. It is indicative of the changes in tastes and styles of dress that are in a constant dialogue with external forces and create hegemonies both domestically and internationally, as still is the case today. Through the lens of the iconographic reproduction of dress and the text accompanying it, Vecellio's book opens a window onto the complexity of Italian and European Renaissance culture. Illustrating how fashion is linked to both individual and collective history, as noted by Guérin Dalle Mese, Vecellio's *Habiti* can be considered a precursor to modern ethnographic research that, at the beginning of the twentieth century, was theorised by Bogatyrĕv and furthered by Lévi-Strauss. For both of them clothing was a system of signs through which different societies and cultures organised themselves and were able to communicate.[34]

In concluding, I would like to emphasise that Vecellio's treatise on the history of global dress is not only a wonderful illustration of his aesthetic and anthropological interests in human habits, but also a rich visual source for the documentation of dress as an object in its own right.[35] Vecellio links dress to the industry and the production of fashion in various geographical places and observes the clothing practices and uses in given social and political contexts. If dressing courtly society, as we have noted, became one of the main concerns addressed by the literature on the topic, Vecellio's work furthers the notion of space in all its dimensions: geographical, public, and personal.

Yet, side by side with Vecellio's meticulous catalogue of the state of the world of dress and costume is something that is characteristic of much of the conduct literature of the time: namely, an anxiety to control the ever-changing, potentially ungraspable world. At a time of shifting horizons, Vecellio's is a search for a sense of balance, measure, and order that will contain the shifting sands of the early modern world. His text reflects the curiosity to know about other geographical areas with their costumes and cultures lived side-by-side with a sense of unease and anxiety about not being able to control the much bigger social and geographical space that was gradually opening up before his eyes. Of no little importance was the fact that at this time Italy was almost entirely dominated by foreign powers, which were transforming themselves into strong national kingdoms and empires. Vecellio is quick to note, in fact, that Italy was a politically unstable entity, whose very instability and domination by foreign powers had led to a variety of *habiti* as noted at the beginning of this essay (Vecellio, 1590, *Discorso*). Castiglione in his *Cortegiano* had already noted something similar seventy-five years earlier:

> But I do not know by what fate it happens that Italy does not have, as she used to have, a manner of dress recognised to be Italian: for, although the introduction of these new fashions makes the former ones seen very crude, *still the older were perhaps a sign of our freedom, even as the new ones have proved to be an augury of servitude, which I think is now most evidently fulfilled.* And as it is recorded that when Darius had the Persian sword he wore at his side made over into the Macedonian style, the year before he fought with Alexander, this was interpreted by the soothsayers to mean that the people into whose fashion Darius had transformed his Persian sword would come to rule over Persia. Just so our having changed our Italian dress for that of foreigners strikes me as meaning that all those for whose dress we have exchanged our own are going to conquer us: *which has proved to be all true, for by now there is no nation that has not made us its prey. So that little more is left to prey upon, and yet they do not leave off preying.*
>
> (II, XXVI, p. 121, emphasis mine)

There is no doubt that Italy offered a great range and variety of styles in dress and ornaments, although some common features were shared from north to south. If, on the one hand, this led to a lack of a 'national costume', when compared to other cultures, such as in Asia, which Vecellio notes to be more stable in its features, on the other, it leads one to reflect on some of the reasons why the history of Italian fashion has not been characterised by a single style.

The originality and modernity of Vecellio's *Habiti* lie in his approach to dress and the way in which he connects the notions of 'Italian dress' to other aesthetic traditions and cultures and makes them interact in his gallery of memory. We must not forget, however, that his *Habiti* are, as for any kind of narration, inscribed in a rhetorical and ideological structure. In other words, we would always do well to bear in mind that they are translations. Vecellio stresses the fact that fashion always changes, as do the concepts of both national and transnational identity, as we might say today. Indeed, *la cosa de gli habiti* and our being in the world are both caught by Vecellio in their process of transformation. His is an attempt to find a way of cataloguing modes of dress and being, but this is a task that by his very own definition can never be completely fulfilled. If, as Anderson has noted, 'print capitalism' shaped and spread the initial ideas and desire for nations, image/visual capitalism and the discourse around them made possible the circulation of types that could be 'recognised' by the viewers as 'national types and costumes' and as such reproduced and consumed. This is why the importance of the genre of costume books cannot be underestimated. They can be a useful source not only for costume historians but also to further our understanding of the links between fashion and the construction of national and transnational identities, which are issues that are now at the core of contemporary study on fashion. Vecellio is aware, however, that his treatment is inevitably partial, no matter how great his anxiety to map the entirety of the world through dress. Yet, in Vecellio's *Habiti*, a tenuous gleam appears in the tensional relationship between transience, the not yet known, and the need to build a theatre of memory of things seen or mediated through other texts. In this way culture already looks like a complex web of different languages, modes of dress, manners and religions. Vecellio has put forward a labyrinth of economies and passions that recount the intricate and yet discernible boundaries of a geography of identity. His aim 'to be true to the world' remains both his desire and his unfinished project in the midst of the unpredictability of chance.

Notes

1   This chapter has been edited and reduced by the author. The original quotations in Italian have been here translated into English by Eugenia Paulicelli or where indicated are from the recent translation of M. F. Rosenthal and A. R. Jones (eds) (2008) *The Clothing of the Renaissance World: Europe, Asia, Africa, The Americas* (London: Thames & Hudson). 1590 and 1598 refer to the years of publication of the two editions of Vecellio's book.

2   In order to gain a more accurate and complete perspective of Vecellio's creation of a discourse on dress it is well to consult both editions of his *Habiti* since the first contained a longer text or commentary. In the first edition, the verbal commentary is longer than in the second edition, where it is reduced to allow space for the Latin translation. In addition, the 1598 edition has several plates from the *nuovo mondo*.

3   Cosmographies, written in Latin, French, German, and Italian, were a very successful genre throughout the Cinquecento. They were usually illustrated and created an interest in ethnographic studies about foreign people and lands. See J. Guérin Dalle Mese, *L'occhio di Cesare Vecellio. Abiti e Costumi esotici nel 500* (Alessandria, Edizioni dell'Orso, 1998). In her introduction she offers an overview of these publications. See also B. Wilson, *The World in Venice. Print, the City, and Early Modern Identity* (Toronto, University of Toronto Press, 2005).

4   As has been noted by B. Anderson: 'Nothing served to "assemble" related vernaculars more than capitalism, which, within the limits imposed by grammars and syntaxes, created mechanically-reproduced print-languages, capable of dissemination through the market [. . .] These print-languages laid the basis for national consciousness in these distinct ways. First and foremost, they created unified fields of exchange and communication below Latin and above the spoken vernaculars' ('Imagined Communities', in *Nationalism*, ed. J. Hutchinson and A. D. Smith (Oxford, Oxford University Press, 1994), pp. 89–95 (p. 94). As a consequence, print capitalism, while stabilising language, also went a long way toward establishing a hegemonic language and with it 'a new form of imagined community', which in turn, created the conditions for the formation of the modern nation.

5   W. Sombart, *Luxury and Capitalism* (Ann Arbor, University of Michigan Press, 1967); *The Social Life of Things: Commodities in Cultural Perspective*, ed. A. Appudurai (Cambridge, Cambridge University Press, 1986), especially 'Introduction: Commodities and the Politics of Value', pp. 3–64. Appadurai stresses that Sombart's 'emphasis on demand, in his key observations about the politics of fashion, in his placement of economic drives in the context of transformations of sexuality, and in his dialectical view of the relationship between

luxury and necessity anticipates recent semiotic approaches to economic behaviour, such as those of Baudrillard, Bourdieu, Kristeva and others' (p. 37).

6   I. Paresys, 'Images de l'Autre vêtu à la Renaissance: le recueil d'habits de François Desprez (1562–7)', *Journal de la Renaissance*, 4 (2006), pp. 15–56. I wish to thank G. Mentges for mentioning the work of Paresys and the author herself for sending me proofs of her article. See also G. Mentges, 'Fashion, Time and the Consumption of a Renaissance Man in Germany: The Costume Book of Matthäus Schwarz of Augsburg, 1496–1564', *Gender and History*, 4, 3 (November 2002), special issue on 'Material Strategies. Dress and Gender in Historical Perspective', ed. B. Burman and C. Turbin, pp. 382–402.

7   Something similar is described by Paresys: 'Chaque figure décrit donc l'Autre dans la singularité d'habits qui permettent au lecteur de le percevoir comme proche ou différent, en marquant son identité sexuelle, son appartenance sociale, et surtout son identité géographique. Cette singularité s'avère, en outre, paradigmatique. D. Defert relève justement le processus d'exemplarité de la figure qui, d'individu, devient le *specimen* représentatif d'une nation' (pp. 17–18).

8   See Sloterdijk, pp. 93–7.

9   For the relationship between Vecellio and de Bry and for her focus on the representation of the 'other' in Vecellio's *Habiti*, see Dalle Mese, p. 218. See G. Butazzi, 'Tra mode occidentali e 'costumi' medio orientali: confronti e riflessioni dai repertori cinquecenteschi alle trasformazioni vestimentarie tra XVII e XVIII secolo', in *Il vestito dell'altro. Semiotica, arti, costume*, ed. G. Franci and M. G. Muzzarelli (Milan, Lupetti, 2005), pp. 251–70.

10   D. Harvey, 'The Time and Space of the Enlightenment Project', in *The Condition of Postmodernity* (Cambridge and Oxford, Blackwell, 1990), pp. 240–59. The first part of the chapter deals with the Renaissance and the drastic changes that occurred in the notions of time and space owing to geographical explorations and a new theory of perspective that was first elaborated by L. B. Alberti.

11   G. Simmel, 'Fashion', *American Journal of Sociology*, 62, vi, pp. 541–58 (first published in *Die Zeit* in 1895).

12   Dalle Mese organised a conference on Vecellio's work as an engraver, painter and writer. The conference resulted in the publication of the volume *Il vestito e la sua immagine: atti del convegno in omaggio a Cesare Vecellio nel quarto centenario della morte, Belluno 20–22 settembre 2001* (Provincia di Belluno Editore, 2002). I would like to thank the Amministrazione Provinciale di Belluno for sending me a copy of the book.

13   A. Ribeiro, *Dress and Morality* (Oxford and New York, Berg, 2003).

14   *Clothing Cultures, 1350–1650*, ed. C. Richardson (Aldershot, Ashgate, 2004). See 'The Fabric of Nations', and U. Ilg, 'The Cultural Significance of Costume Books in Sixteenth-century Europe' (pp. 29–47).

15   J. Schneider, 'The Anthropology of Cloth', *Annual Review of Anthropology*, 16 (1987), pp. 409–48.

16   This principle is at work in the nineteenth century, a period in which nationalism and the struggles for independence marked historical events in Europe and in Latin America. The pertinence of these events for costume books has been explored in a recent exhibition held in New York: *Reproducing Nations: Types and Costumes in Asia and Latin America, ca. 1800–1860* (New York, Americas Society, 2006). In particular see N. Majluf, 'Pattern-book of Nations: Images of Types and Costumes in Asia and Latin America, ca. 1800–1860', pp. 15–56.

17   'Cartographic writing' is T. Conley's definition. The implications between the art of memory and moral geography constitute the core of G. Mangani's study *Cartografia morale: geografia, persuasione, identità* (Modena, Panini, 2006). Mangani's book both confirmed and enriched my reading of Vecellio's work.

18   E. Vico was a well known artist and engraver who worked for Cosimo de' Medici, and

lived in Venice for fifteen years, dying in Ferrara at the court of Alfonso II d'Este (*c.* 1567) after publishing other books that came out in France, Germany, and Flanders. *Costumi di Spagna e d'Italia* (1563), a second book was published, also in 1563, by F. Bertelli, *Omnium fere gentium nostrae aetatis habitus numquam ante hoc aediti, Ferdinando Bertelli aenaeis typis excudebat* (Venice, 1563). See also J. Bridgeman, '"A guisa di fiume . . ." I "ritratti" di Cesare Vecellio e la storia del vestire', in Dalle Mese, *Il vestito e la sua immagine*, pp. 81–95; Butazzi, 'Repertori di Costumi e Stampe di Moda tra i secoli XVI XVIII', in Varese and Butazzi, pp. 2–25; and R. Colas, *Bibliographie générale du costume et de la mode* (Paris, René Colas, 1933), 2 vols.

19   On the meanings of Rome or the Roman Empire as a 'universal history' to which non-Italian kings and emperors, such as Charles V and even Napoleon, linked their name and their political and religious power, see S. Settis, *Futuro del classico* (Turin, Einaudi, 2004). On the notions of the term 'classico' and its uses in different historical epochs, see Settis, when the author stresses that '*lo sforzo di legittimare il presente scegliendosi nel passato i modelli "giusti"*' (p. 80) has been recurrent in Western cultural history since Petrarch.

20   Vecellio is not alone in representing the 'national costume' as a naked man. In B. Grassi, *Dei veri ritratti degli habiti di tutte le parti del mondo* (Rome, 1585), the author depicts a naked man holding a bundle of cloths and a pair of scissors to mean that he has nothing that can be defined as 'national' and is ready to take ideas from foreign styles. As R. Levi Pisetzky has pointed out, the same kind of reproach and iconography can be found in France and in England in the second half of the Cinquecento (R. Levi Pisetzky, *Storia del costume in Italia*, reprinted in *Enciclopedia della moda* (Rome, Treccani, 2005), p. 499). This confirms the emergence of fashion as an economic force and an institution parallel to the emergence of a sense of 'nation' which will materialise in the subsequent epoch. Fashion, however stands out as one of the most powerful mechanisms to convey and fabricate national, trans-national, and global identities.

21   Sloterdijk describes the role of Rome in the context of his philosophical history of globalisation thus: 'Roma assurse al rango di città eterna non soltanto in nome delle sue autoctone divinità di successo Giove, Marte, Virtù e Vittoria, ma perché fu in grado di trasformarsi in una seconda Gerusalemme e, in limiti più ristretti, in una seconda Atene. Grazie alla propria forte capacità di assimilazione e di traduzione Roma si è eretta a capitale della prima ecumene e a fulcro metafisico della vecchia Europa. Molto tempo prima delle università e delle accademie moderne, la Roma aeterna si presenta come sede terrana dell'evidenza: dopo Atene e Gerusalemme, intende essere la città in cui si mostra ciò che è; ed esige che ogni viaggio a Roma diventi un pellegrinaggio alla volta dell'evidenza (e del mistero)' (pp. 163–4).

22   C. Kovesi Killerby, '"Heralds of a Well Instructed Mind": Nicolosa Sanuti's Defense of Women and their Clothes', *Renaissance Studies*, 13 (1999), pp. 255–82, and *Sumptuary Laws in Italy, 1200–1500* (Oxford, Clarendon Press, 2002). Note also Tullia D'Aragona who was denounced in Siena (1544) for refusing to wear the *velo giallo*, a recognisable sign for courtesans, and later excused after a written petition. See S. Bongi, 'Il velo giallo di Tullia d'Aragona', *Rivista critica della letteratura italiana*, 3, 3 (1886), pp. 85–95. Later writers such as the author of *Moderata Fonte in Merito delle donne* (1600) will stress the fact that clothing and make-up do not undermine female intellect. Arcangela Tarabotti wrote *Antisatira d'Arcangela Tarabotti in risposta alla satira Menippea contro il lusso donnesco di Francesco Buoninsegni* (Venice, 1644) in response to Buoninsegni's satire 'Contro il lusso donnesco' in order to mock the vanity of women. On sumptuary laws and women, see D. Owen Hughes, 'Regulating Women's Fashion', in *A History of Women in the West: vol. 2, Silences of the Middle Ages*, ed. C. Klapisch-Zuber (Cambridge, MA, Belknap Press, 1992), pp. 136–58.

23   See G. Muzzarelli, *Gli inganni delle apparenze disciplina di vesti e ornamenti alla fine del medioevo*

(Turin, Paravia, 1996); 'Le leggi suntuarie', in *Moda e società dal Medioevo al XX secolo, Annali Einaudi*, ed. C. M. Belfanti and F. Giusberti (Turin, Einaudi, 2003), pp. 185–220; *Guardaroba medievale: vesti e società dal XIII al XVI secolo* (Bologna, Il Mulino, 1999); and *Belle vesti dure leggi* (Bologna, Costa, 2003).

24 See S. Mosher Stuard, *Gilding the Market: Luxury and Fashion in Fourteenth-century Italy* (Philadelphia, University of Pennsylvania Press, 2006); L. Molà, *The Silk Industry of Renaissance Venice* (Baltimore, Johns Hopkins University Press, 2000); E. Welch, *Shopping in the Renaissance* (New Haven, Yale University Press, 2005).

25 See Jones and Stallybrass, *Renaissance Clothing and the Material of Memory*.

26 There is of course a long bibliography on the art of memory. In the context of the present essay, my aim is to point at the cultural and some structural links between costume books and their use of physical and symbolic spaces to build memory and meaning. Let me mention the studies by F. Yates, *The Art of Memory* (Chicago: Chicago University Press, 1966); M. Carruthers, *The Book of Memory* (Cambridge: Cambridge University Press, 1990) and *The Craft of Thought* (Cambridge: Cambridge University Press, 1998); P. Rossi, *Logic and the Art of Memory* (Chicago: Chicago University Press, 2000); and L. Bolzoni, *The Gallery of Memory* (Toronto: Toronto University Press, 2001).

27 C. Collier Frick, 'Gendered Space in Renaissance Florence: Theorizing Public and Private in the Rag Trade', *Fashion Theory*, 9, 2 (June 2005), pp. 125–46, special issue, edited by S. White, dedicated to dress and gender. See also by Collier Frick, 'Cappelli e copricapo nella Firenze rinascimentale: l'emergere sartoriale dell'identità sociale', in *Moda e Moderno*, ed. E. Paulicelli (Rome: Meltemi, 2006), pp. 103–28.

28 See T. E. Timmons, '*Habiti antichi e moderni di tutto il mondo* and the "Myth of Venice"', *Athanor*, 15 (1997), pp. 28–33.

29 For the trade and political relationship between Venice and other Italian cities such as Florence and the Ottoman Empire, see I. Halil and D. Quataert, *An Economic and Social History of the Ottoman Empire, 1300–1914* (Cambridge, Cambridge University Press, 1994).

30 Butazzi points out the similarity in the use of the veil between Eastern and Western women in 'Tra mode occidentali e 'costumi' medio orientali: confronti e riflessioni dai repertori cinquecenteschi alle trasformazioni vestimentarie tra XVII e XVIII secolo', in Franci and Muzzarelli, *Il vestito dell'altro: semiotica, arti, costume*.

31 See Dalle Mese, 'Cesare Vecellio e le belle Europee', in *Il vestito e la sua immagine*, pp. 55–80.

32 Levi Pisetzky reports the diffusion of *braghesse* for women, the so-called *calzoni alla galeotta* which were inspired by the *moda del turco* and were to become the forerunner of underwear. Bernardino Prosperi in his correspondence with Isabella D'Este calls them *I calzoni che non si veggono*, which were also the object of sumptuary legislation in Ferrara where men were given the liberty (*facoltà*) to ascertain if women were invading their wardrobe: '*sino a cazzar la mano sotto alle gonne per sentir se avevano i calzoni*' (Levi Pisetzky, p. 62).

33 See T. Storey, 'Clothing Courtesans: Fabrics, Signals, and Experiences', in Richardson, *Clothing Cultures, 1350–1650*, pp. 95–107.

34 See *Cloth and the Human Experience*, ed. J. Schneider and A. Wiener (Washington, DC, and London: Smithsonian Institute Press, 1989).

35 I am thinking here of a new development in anthropological research outlined by K. Tranberg Hansen, 'Anthropological Perspectives on Clothing, Fashion, and Culture', *Annual Review of Anthropology*, 33 (October 2004), pp. 369–92.

Fashion in the archive

Janine Christina Maegraith

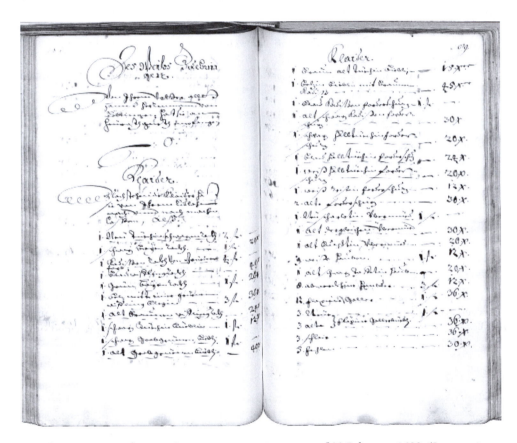

Snapshot 8.1 Extract from an Auingen marriage inventory of 20 February 1682 ('Inventarium Wass Hanss Hürning und Barbara, Hanss Herrenmann von Böttingen ehliche Tochter, sein Hirrnings Eheweib, einander in die Ehe zuegebracht.'), Stadtarchiv Münsingen B au 1, fol. 88v–89r. The extract shows the beginning of the bride's inventory with a part of her clothing list. Reproduced with the kind permission of the Stadtarchiv Münsingen.

A considerable amount of archival documents exists which allow insights into the history of fashion – examples include account books, pattern-books and shop inventories. Some documents might come as a surprise, such as medical surveys. The medical survey of the principality of Ochsenhausen in Upper Swabia, for example, written by the local physician in 1805, describes in detail the regional fashions of the mostly rural population, and adds his aesthetic and medical opinions. The women's clothing he dismisses as bulky and ugly: 'The greatest beauty of their attire they put into numerous broad silk ribbons of all colours, and such a girl in her Sunday attire looks more like a chapman's shop than a human figure' (Joseph von Schirt, quoted in Diemer 2006: 106). This statement highlights the collision between the rural Swabian perception of beauty and urban and medical views. But the Ochsenhausen physician also provides a revealing sidelight on fashion in a particular region and time.

To gain insight into changes in fashion over time, one particular type of archival document comes to mind: inventories, lists of belongings to be found in a household ranging from furniture, to precious objects, to everyday commodities, including people's clothing. Inventories, as in the case of the southwest German territory of Württemberg, were drawn up at both marriage and death for most adults in both villages and towns. They list the entire possessions of the persons in question and were drawn up to assist in the legal regulation of property divisions in order to avoid inheritance conflicts. Inventories survive across Europe in large quantities (sometimes millions) from the Renaissance to the nineteenth century, although their presence is linked to the different regulations of states and principalities. In Württemberg, marriage inventories usually record brides' and grooms' possessions separately, and death inventories usually itemise women's and men's clothing in separate lists. This remarkable quality of documentation makes it possible to distinguish the attire of both women and men at various ages and life-cycle stages over a long period.

An ongoing research project which analyses the inventories of two Württemberg communities, Wildberg in the Black Forest and Auingen on the Swabian Jura, is providing initial glimpses into changes in attire and fashion. For the first half of the seventeenth century clothing is not yet recorded in a consistent way in the Wildberg inventories. Sometimes the clothes were valued so little that they were only recorded as an unspecified group or were left out completely. But a more consistent situation emerged around 1660, when almost all marriage inventories started providing detailed catalogues of the clothing of both bride and groom, and death inventories provided similar clothing lists for the deceased person and his or her widow or widower.

These lists of clothing developed into highly detailed catalogues of every single garment, starting with the main items such as skirts, trousers, shirts, and jackets, and going on to list different kinds of bonnets, veils, shawls and handkerchiefs, ribbons, socks and shoes. We often encounter garments which may remain a mystery, since they are depicted in no surviving illustrations. The inventories describe the quantity and value of garments, and often also the material, colour, and quality. The Württemberg inventories therefore provide an exceptional opportunity to explore changes in attire and fashion over time within a specific society.

Such lists can also provide insight into changes in clothing as a representation of a person's identity, especially the individual's social status. In Württemberg until the late eighteenth century, sumptuary ordinances sought to control the range of clothing, ornaments and colours that could be worn by each social stratum. But inventories show increasing numbers of accessories in many different colours and material and a rising quantity and value of clothing, illustrating how people nonetheless strove to represent their identities using attire and fashion. An important indicator for changes in fashion in this case is the bonnet which appears in numerous varieties. One might compare the eighteenth century, when French culture had a huge influence in Württemberg, with the seventeenth century, which had a distinct Spanish influence, in these relatively provincial areas in the Black Forest and the Swabian Jura. Inventories are thus archival documents that open up vast possibilities for researching the history of fashion.

Bibliography and further reading

Arkell, T., Evans, N., and Goose, N. (eds) (2000) *When Death Do Us Part: Understanding and Interpreting the Probate Records of Early Modern England*, Oxford: Leopard's Head.

Diemer, K. (ed.) (2006) *Medizinische Topographie des Fürstentums Ochsenhausen. Joseph von Schirt. Bearbeitet von Eberhard Silvers, Karl Werner Steim und Hans Joachim Winckelmann*, Freiburg.

The ESRC project 'Human Well-Being and the "Industrious Revolution": Consumption, Gender and Social Capital in a German Developing Economy, 1600–1900'. <www.econ.cam.ac.uk/Ogilvie_ESRC/index.html> (accessed 6 May 2009).

Mannheims, H. (1991) *Wie wird ein Inventar erstellt? Rechtskommentare als Quelle der volkskundlichen Forschung*, Münster, Coppenrath.

van der Woude, A., and Schuurman, A. (eds) (1980) *Probate Inventories: A New Source for the Historical Study of Wealth, Material Culture, and Agricultural Development*, Wageningen: H & S Publishers.

Weatherill, L. (1996) *Consumer Behaviour and Material Culture in Britain, 1660–1760*, 2nd edition, London: Routledge.

Chapter 7

Clothing the courtier

Jennifer M. Jones

THE FIRST OBLIGATION OF ANY MAN OR WOMAN upon arriving at French court was literally to be made over through clothing into a proper French courtier. In 1671, when Philippe d'Orléans (1640–1701), the king's brother, married the German princess Elisabeth Charlotte, special French clothes, including a white wedding gown, had to be made for Elisabeth Charlotte in order to transform her into a properly French member of the royal court. In her study of Elisabeth Charlotte's correspondence, Elborg Forster relates that during the princess's journey to France, her chaperone, the Princess Palatine, made a shocking discovery: the bride had only six shifts and six nightgowns. This, she informed the Palatine *chargé d'affaires* in France, must be remedied immediately, lest it become known through the bride's chambermaids or other French attendants, and Madame be made the laughing stock of the French court. Three to four thousand *livres*, she said in her urgent message, would purchase everything needed.[1]

The proper costume was not only necessary to 'make' a French aristocrat, but to 'mark' one as well. Thirty years later, in 1698, when her own daughter left the French court to marry the Duke of Lorraine, Elisabeth Charlotte wrote proudly to her aunt Sophie, 'I don't think the Duke of Lorraine will consider my daughter ill-provided for; she has twenty thousand crowns' worth of linen, and great quantities of laces and embroidery. It is all very handsome and fills four huge chests'.[2] Before leaving France, Elisabeth Charlotte's and Monsieur's daughter's trousseau was publicly displayed in Monsieur's gallery so that visitors could admire the fifteen lavishly embroidered dresses, two of which were so heavily decorated with gold that Elisabeth Charlotte worried her daughter would be unable to wear them.[3] Monsieur clearly delighted in the splendour of his daughter's trousseau as much as did her mother. At the court of Louis XIV there was no better way for a nobleman to show off than to display his daughter's trousseau. Clothing was, under Louis's regime, first and foremost a marker of privilege and social hierarchy.

Court costume and absolutist court culture came of age together during the reign of Louis XIV. In the early years of Louis's reign the court was small and itinerant; several hundred courtiers moved with the king and the royal family as they periodically travelled from the Louvre in Paris to royal chateaux at Fontainebleau, Marly, Saint-Germain, or Compiègne, to the Orléans family estate at Saint Cloud, or to the hunting lodge at Versailles. As Louis extended his control over the French aristocracy and the French state, the number of courtiers and bureaucrats at court increased considerably. By the time the court took up permanent residence at Versailles in 1682 it is estimated that more than 15,000 men and women lived and worked there. In addition to the royal family, the princes of the blood, the dukes and peers, foreign princes such as the dukes of Lorraine, Savoy, Mantua and Rohan, the highest military officers and great officers of the state, and hundreds of ordinary courtiers, artists, valets, lackeys, ladies-in-waiting, Swiss and French guards, and other servants also made their home at Versailles.

In the first decade of Louis's personal rule (1661–70) there was no official court costume: the fashions worn at court were merely sumptuous variations of the elite dress of the mid-seventeenth century. In the 1660s the dominant style for men was full petticoat breeches or 'Rhinegraves', a kilt-like culotte skirt ornamented with vast quantities of ruffles, lace and coloured ribbons. Petticoat breeches extended anywhere from mid-thigh to mid-calf and were worn with canons, tubes of white linen with lace ruffles and bows tied around the knees. On top men wore a short doublet (similar to a modern bolero jacket) with sleeves extending to the elbow. The doublet was often left unbuttoned, revealing a full-cut silk or linen shirt beneath and ruffled sleeves. The large lace collar of the shirt was tied in front, creating the tie-like rabat. Some men wore a longer jacket (cassock) similar to the leather military cassocks of the early seventeenth century. By the 1660s men had begun to wear wigs instead of long hair and wore hats with a low crown and a wide brim edged with plumes and ribbons. Men's shoes had high heels (with red heels for all noblemen) and square toes. Boots, commonly worn in the earlier seventeenth century, were now reserved exclusively for riding and hunting.

Until the second half of the seventeenth century the main form of elite female dress was a two-piece dress ensemble that comprised a skirt and a boned bodice. The skirt (*jupe de dessus* or *manteau*) fell to the floor and ended in a train, the length of which signified the woman's social station. An underskirt (*robe du dessous*), often of taffeta, was worn beneath the skirt. This was worn without hoops, but over full petticoats. The skirt could be split and drawn back on each side of the hips better to reveal the underskirt beneath. The top part of the dress, the bodice (*le corsage*), was either sleeveless or had short sleeves that ended before the elbow in rows of lace. The bodice had a low, oval neckline and lace or muslin draped around the neckline formed a bow in the middle. A blouse (*la chemise*) often peeked out from under the dress at the neckline and sleeve. On formal occasions women's natural hair was loosely curled at the back and tightly curled around the face. At home and on informal occasions, women wore small lace caps. Outdoors and while riding and travelling, women wore broad hats similar to men's. Loose hoods, kerchiefs, and hooded cloaks were worn at night and in bad weather. At court women wore heavy make-up, including foundation, rouge, and beauty patches.

Bows, ribbons, and lace were the most important ornaments for both men and women. An elegantly dressed person, whether male or female, often used as much as

300 yards of ribbon on all parts of dress, including the hair. By the 1670s and 1680s trimmings became even more ornate; *falbalas* (in English, furbelows) referred to any decorations of court costume ranging from flounces, tassels, fringe and lace, to braid and heavy embroidery. Between 1685 and 1690 greater amounts of gold and silver brocade were used to decorate costly satins and velvets for both men and women. Although both men and women in the 1650s and 1660s had favoured bold colours such as yellow and shades of red, ranging from cherry to scarlet to flame (*couleur de feu*), after 1670, these gave way to darker, more subdued colours, stripes and floral prints.

A classic work of fashion history aptly describes the transformation of fashion during Louis's reign: 'The long personal reign of Louis XIV opened with men dressed as beribboned birds of plumage and closed with them having the look of heavily upholstered furniture, whereas women started the reign as youthful maidens and ended it as forbidding matrons'.[4] During the decade of the 1670s, the pious Madame de Maintenon, governess to Louis's illegitimate children, and later his second wife, ushered in a more solemn style of court dress. In the 1670s as court costume became more formal, elite women began to experiment with wearing a new, one-piece dress called the mantua (*mantos*) for less formal occasions in town and at court. The mantua was a simpler and more comfortable style of casual dress (*déshabillés*) than the formal two-piece skirt and bodice. Mantuas wrapped in front like a dressing gown or kimono and were fastened by a sash. Often the sides of the dress were drawn up to display the underskirt beneath. In contrast to formal court attire, mantuas were not rigidly boned and required only a small corset underneath to shape the silhouette. Some women used a stomacher to conceal the front of the corset and some wore aprons. The new printed calicoes (*indiennes*) introduced during the 1680s and 1690s were suited to these lighter garments, especially for summer wear. Although originally worn only at home, by the final third of the seventeenth century the mantua became popular among elite women in Paris and was worn for a variety of informal occasions. As Clare Crowston argues in her important re-evaluation of the birth of the mantua, it opened up 'a new conceptual and visual terrain in which women could experiment with self-presentation in ways that challenged traditional social hierarchies'.[5] [. . .]

During Louis's reign significant changes transformed men's as well as women's fashions. In the 1670s, men at the French court inaugurated arguably the most important change in the history of French fashion since the fourteenth century, donning the precursor of the modern three-piece suit. The adoption of the new style of male suit had as much to do with nationality as gender and was sparked by international emulation and national rivalry between the French, British and Spanish over styles of male dress. French and Spanish sartorial rivalry had proceeded hand-in-hand with French and Spanish-Hapsburg rivalry for power since at least the early seventeenth century. In an attempt to counteract French stylistic dominance at court, in 1623 the Spanish monarch Philip IV banned the French styles of huge lace collars, long hair, and slashed and embroidered clothes and imposed a more restrained male style consisting of plain doublets, narrow knee breeches, and a plain white linen collar stiffened with shellac.[6]

The English staged their own rebellion against French fashion in the 1660s. The poet Samuel Butler's *Satire upon our Ridiculous Imitation of the French* (1663) lamented English men's and women's slavish imitation of French styles, while John Evelyn protested against the tyranny of French fashions directly to King Charles II in his 1661 treatise *Tyrannus, or the Mode*: 'Would the great Persons of England but owne their

Nation, and assert themselves as they ought to do, by making choice of some Virile, and comely Fashion, which should incline to neither extreme, and be constant to it, 'twould prove of infinite more reputation to us, than now there is'.[7] Heeding the growing complaints that French fashions imperilled both English virility and the English economy, Charles II decided in 1665 that he and his Queen would forgo French lace and silk and wear only English textiles (with the exception of imported linen and calico). By 1666 Charles II had employed two English tailors, John Allen and William Watts, to devise a more virile, anti-French and anti-Catholic style. The narrow breeches worn in Spain replaced French petticoat breeches; and, for the sake of 'Protestant' modesty, the doublet or undervest and the outer coat were both lengthened to the knee to cover the breeches.[8]

Although he railed against the effrontery of the English for banishing French fashions from their court, as early as 1667 Louis XIV donned the new English style of long vest and overcoat. In France this long jacket extending to the knees was called the *justaucorps* or habit, and was worn with a vest or sleeveless doublet (*veste*). The jacket was left open to reveal the doublet and shirt, which now sported a knotted tie (*cravate*). Louis and his courtiers persisted in wearing petticoat breeches, however, until around 1678. During these years the Brandenburg greatcoat, adapted from the coats worn by Prussian soldiers, became the forerunner of the male overcoat of the next three centuries. The new 'modesty' of men's fashions was more than offset, however, by increasingly ornate fabrics and wigs, which grew larger throughout the 1680s until they reached the waist in front and back and rose high on the head. Male courtiers continued to wear rouge and make-up and, by the end of the 1690s, sported powdered wigs.

As art and costume historian Anne Hollander has argued in her important study *Sex and Suits: The Evolution of Modern Dress*, the new male three-piece suit, with its slim, sober line that unified the body, was an important harbinger of sartorial modernity. Although the aesthetic foreshadowed by the late-seventeenth-century suit would not emerge fully in Europe until the neoclassical movement in the arts in the latter eighteenth century, by the late seventeenth century men's fashion already stood at the aesthetic forefront. 'Male dress', Hollander argues, 'was always essentially more advanced than female throughout fashion history, and tended to lead the way, to set the standard, to make the esthetic propositions to which female fashion responded.'[9]

Although Hollander's claim regarding the more 'advanced nature' of men's clothing and her contention that the adoption of the three-piece suit marked the beginning of the divergence between the 'aesthetic logic' of men's and women's dress are intriguing, they leave unanswered the question of how precisely fashion was 'sexed' as feminine in the wake of the adoption of the male suit: if we accept Hollander's conclusions, why was the aesthetic of feminine dress culturally constructed as 'traditional' as opposed to 'modern'? [. . .] We can best understand the 'sexing of la mode' not by essentialising the logic of masculine and feminine aesthetics, but by examining the social practices and cultural discourses that gendered modern aesthetics. In addition, we should consider that the one-piece mantua adopted by French women in the 1670s shared many of 'modern' aesthetic qualities of the three-piece suit. Despite the novelty of the three-piece suit and its important legacy by the nineteenth century in driving a sartorial wedge between men's and women's fashions, we also need to be attentive to the continuing overlap between men's and women's fashions and textiles well into the late eighteenth century. From the point of view of the seventeenth and eighteenth centuries, the growing distinction between fixed costume and changeable fashion, between ceremonial dress and 'undress', and between court dress and town dress were as important as the incipient distinction between the aesthetic form of men's suits and women's dresses.[10]

Whether dressed in the restrained English suit or extravagant petticoat breeches, protean *la mode* remained a troubling and uncertain marker of rank and privilege in a society of orders: people might dress above their station; fashions might flagrantly sidestep the privileged absolutist gaze and contradict the king's taste; or vogues for imported fashions and fabrics might hamper the development of the French economy. Throughout the early decades of his reign Louis searched for a way to create an aristocratic sartorial culture that would better serve both his ceremonial politics and his mercantilist economy. In the early 1660s Louis envisioned creating an official court dress that could be bestowed as a reward for those who chose to take up residence at Versailles. An official ordinance of 29 December 1664 granted fifty privileged male courtiers the right to wear the *justaucorps à brevet* (warrant coats), specially tailored blue coats lined with scarlet and embroidered with gold and silver thread. The *justaucorps à brevet* entitled the wearer to a variety of privileges: those who wore the coat were permitted to follow the king on his excursions to Saint-Germain or Versailles without an invitation, and the coat could on certain occasions be substituted for mourning wear at court. Although the duc de Saint-Simon, who lived at court after 1691, claimed that he never saw Louis XIV or his brother wear the *justaucorps à brevet*, the privilege to wear the coat was still so coveted in the 1690s that when the possessor of a coat died it would be quickly transferred to another aristocrat.[11] Men who were not permitted to wear the *justaucorps à brevet* were expected to wear a suit of velvet or better quality fabric while at court. The imposition of the *justaucorps à brevet* was inspired by the desire to use royal authority both to underscore court hierarchy and to consolidate bonds among the aristocracy: court costume worked both to distinguish and to unite.

A similar desire both to create *esprit* and to perpetuate *différence* stood behind the codification of military uniform which took place under Louis (known as the 'king of reviews').[12] As part of their effort to organise the French army between the 1660s and 1690s, Louis XIV's great military bureaucrats, Le Tellier and Louvois, helped him devise a more consistent French military uniform which, following the lines of men's contemporary civilian fashions, included an ample broadcloth jacket, a double-breasted vest and knee breeches. By the end of Louis's reign, uniformed soldiers had become perfect iconic embodiments of the success of royal authority and the rigorous discipline of the absolutist gaze; yet well into the eighteenth century, there was still much debate within the army over the best means for provisioning soldiers with uniforms. Although Louis imposed military uniforms, the centralisation and bureaucratisation of provisioning were far from complete by his death in 1715. The economic reality of clothing a professional army of 100,000 men that swelled to 400,000 in times of war was often at odds with the absolutist goal of uniformity. It was difficult to impose the absolutist vision of perfectly uniformed soldiers on a reality of muddy, frayed jackets, stubborn corporals bent on subverting royal ordinances, and the desire of some regiments to distinguish themselves from others.

If Louis found it difficult to impose order on his soldiers' dress, the clothing of aristocratic women at court proved even more difficult to control. Louis had been willing to tolerate the sartorial idiosyncrasies of his cousin, La Grande Mademoiselle, of his mistresses, and of his sister-in-law, who often wore her hunting jacket to solemn court occasions. But, after 1670, when women began to wear the new style of casual dress, the mantua, at court, Louis decided to take action by creating the *grand habit* and declaring it mandatory for all formal occasions. As the Duc de Saint-Simon complained,

> Whether pregnant, ill, less than six weeks after a delivery, and whatever the ferocity of the weather, they had to be in the *grand habit*, dressed and laced into their corsets, to go to Flanders, or farther still, to dance, to stay up, attend festivities, eat, be gay and good company, change locations, without appearing afraid, nor incommoded by heat, cold, air, dust, and all that precisely on the days and the times directed without disturbing arrangements for so much as a minute.[13]

By the end of the seventeenth century, the *grand habit* was the norm in courts across Europe. Even the Hapsburgs and the English, who had rebelled against French men's court fashions, readily embraced this fashion for women.

Notes

1   *A Woman's Life in the Court of the Sun King: Letters of Liselotte von der Pfalz, 1652–1722*, trans. and ed. by Elborg Forster (Baltimore: Johns Hopkins University Press, 1984): p. 6.
2   *Letters from Liselotte*, trans. and ed. Maria Kroll (London: Victor Gollancz, 1970): p. 83.
3   Kroll, *Letters from Liselotte*, p. 83.
4   Douglas Russell, *Costume History and Style* (Englewood Cliffs, NJ: Prentice-Hall, 1983), p. 269.
5   Clare Crowston, *Fabricating Women: The Seamstresses of Old Regime France, 1675–1791* (Durham, NC: Duke University Press, 2001), p. 41.
6   See Diana De Marly, *Louis XIV and Versailles* (London: Batsford, 1987), pp. 21–5.
7   John Evelyn, *Tyrannus, or the Mode* (1661), p. 5.
8   On the development of the three-piece suit in England, see David Kuchta, '"Graceful, Virile, and Useful": The Origins of the Three-Piece Suit', *Dress* 17 (1990), pp. 118–26.
9   Anne Hollander, *Sex and Suits: The Evolution of Modern Dress* (New York: Alfred Knopf, 1994), p. 6.
10 On these distinctions, see Daniel Roche, *The Culture of Clothing: Dress and Fashion in the 'Ancien Régime'*, trans. Jean Birrell (Cambridge: Cambridge University Press, 1994), chapter 2.
11 De Marly, *Louis XIV and Versailles*, pp. 62–3. See Marquis de Sourches, *Mémoires sur le regne de Louis XIV*, ed. le Comte de Cosnac and E. Pontal, 13 vols (Paris: Hachette, 1883). See vol. 2, February 1688 and vol. 3, 22 September 1691.
12 Roche, *The Culture of Clothing*, pp. 227, 244.
13 Louis de Rouvroy, Duc de Saint-Simon, *Mémoires*, ed. Yves Coirault (Paris: Gallimard, 1984), vol. 3, p. 112.

Fashion in the Spanish court

Hilary Davidson

The pervasive influence of Spanish dress across late sixteenth-century European fashion can be attributed to two reasons: power and style. The Spanish monarch was the most powerful secular figure in the world. In 1556, Felipe II of the Habsburg dynasty ascended to rule, for half a century, a global empire encompassing the Iberian peninsula, the Low Countries, Italian territories, and extensive New World colonies generating astonishing wealth. Spain's political and fashion powers waxed and waned in tandem from this time.

The defining elements of court dress during this Golden Age are rigid geometry of line, understated luxury, and a material proclamation of the Counter-Reformation spirit. Restrained ornamentation and pattern allowed an exceptional precision of cut and construction to take centre stage. Spanish tailors had achieved remarkable arts of subtle shaping, making their skills – or imitations of them – in demand across Europe in the century when tailoring first dominated fashion. Court painters established portraiture conventions that constructed strong visual identities and crystallised a dignified, imposing iconography of the extended royal family's dress. The formal clothing depicted by artists appeared to shape the body underneath with a controlled sensuality, flamboyant denial, and subdued yet majestic wealth. The style was as compelling as it was contradictory, a powerful elegance exerting an attraction beyond flattery or display of political affiliations.

During the religious upheavals of the sixteenth century, Europe polarised around Catholic and Protestant faiths. Spain established itself as the beacon of 'true' Catholicism under the personality of the deeply religious Felipe II. His austere personal tastes encouraged imitation of both his devotion and his dress. Clad habitually in unadorned black, as was Felipe's inimitable and equally devout sister Juana of Portugal, the colour soon became the hallmark of court dress. Although in the rebellious Low Countries black signified fervent Protestant beliefs, it is the enduring colour to define sober 'Spanishness' in contrast to riotous English and French fashions. Colour in court dress is limited to white, reds, pinks, yellows, occasionally green, all turned inwards to garments worn in private or below the outer layer. Even the patterns and decoration of textiles are small scale and mostly geometric, applied in regular parallel rows to further emphasise clothing's crisp linear shapes. Highest-quality, deceptively plain satins, damasks and velvets formed a discreet vehicle for demonstrating appropriate status and its corresponding expenditure, whatever the wearer's spiritual humility. Ostentation was concentrated into magnificent gold and gemstone ornamentation.

Certain items of Spanish clothing became the key stylistic markers through which fashion influence can be traced. Women's farthingales (*verdugados*), a hooped conical skirt giving shape to the gown, were known elsewhere as the 'Spanish' farthingale. The garment's bell-shape epitomises the sixteenth-century European female silhouette.

Snapshot 9.1 Infanta Isabella Clara Eugenia, by Sofonisba Anguissola, 1599, Museo del Prado, Madrid. © Museo Nacional del Prado, Spain.

In contrast with wider trends for décolletage necklines, in Spain the stiffened 'high' bodice (*cuerpo alto*) encased women's torsos from chin to increasingly pointed waistline. Long, pointed sleeves, or semi-circular ones slit horizontally at the elbow were distinctly Spanish, as was a ground-length mantle. For men, the tailored doublet (*jubón*) with round peascod belly enhanced the physique while numerous varieties of short round cloaks afforded opportunities for elegant display. Both sexes' passion for white linen neck and wrist ruffs formed a stark contrast to their sombre clothing. The overall effect suppressed and covered the wearers' shape to embody pious ideals of unworldly modesty.

Throughout the unstable reigns of Felipe III and IV, court dress evolved into distorted and exaggerated versions of the earlier styles. From the 1620s, the shift began from widespread imitation to the ridiculing of styles that looked increasingly archaic as the century progressed. The farthingale became the broad *guardainfante* exemplified by Velasquez's royal portraits. Like ruffs, it continued to be worn in Spanish territories long after disappearing everywhere else. By Felipe IV's death in 1665, Spanish court dress was a fashion 'backwater'.

Bibliography and further reading

Bernis, C. (1990) 'La moda en la España de Felipe II' in *Alonso Sánchez Coello y el Retrato en la Corte de Felipe II*, Madrid: Museo del Prado.

de Alcega, J. (1978 [orig. edition 1580 and 1589]) *Libro de Geometria, Pratica y Traça*, Madrid; facsimile edition *Tailor's Pattern Book*, Bedford: Ruth Bean Publishers.

Reade, B. (1951) *The Dominance of Spain 1550–1660*, London: George G. Harrap and Company Ltd.

PART 3

The Fashion Revolution
The 'long' eighteenth century

Giorgio Riello and Peter McNeil

The so-called 'long' eighteenth century, the period spanning from the end of the seventeenth to the beginning of the nineteenth century, has in recent decades been seen as pivotal to the history of fashion. This was not the case just a generation ago. Research tended to concentrate either on the court and elite dress of the period ranging from the Renaissance to the reign of Louis XIV (1643–1715) (characterised by conspicuous consumption and the emergence of a 'civilised' society of manners and etiquette) or on the bourgeois ascendancy of the nineteenth and twentieth centuries (accompanied instead by mass production and large-scale distribution as in the case of department and chain stores). The eighteenth century sat as a 'difficult' period, sandwiched between two areas of research considered of much higher importance in the history of fashion and not seeming to connect to theories and notions of modernity expressed in the writings of, say, Walter Benjamin and Georg Simmel, whose work revolved around nineteenth-century cultural patterns.

From the late 1970s to the early 1990s, however, a series of influential studies emphasised the importance of the eighteenth century as the moment when European societies acquired the political, economic and social features that still characterise them today. This was, after all, the period of the industrial revolution, and of major political upheavals including the American revolution, the French revolution and the short but profoundly important Napoleonic period, establishing a great swathe of civil law. But historians claimed that the importance of the eighteenth century in structuring the world we live in went well beyond economic and political revolutions and included profound changes in the way people lived, in particular in the way in which they consumed things. Historians such as Neil McKendrick and John Brewer proposed the idea of a 'Consumer Revolution' for the eighteenth century to match the more traditional concepts of the Industrial and French revolutions, which had so preoccupied the study of eighteenth-century history.

What is a consumer revolution? McKendrick and Brewer's original concept, extended and expanded in a number of studies in the following two decades, observed how consumption at all levels of society increased substantially in the eighteenth century. The favourite area of study has been England, although other areas of Europe such as France, Spain and The Netherlands, experienced similar dynamics of change. The majority of people started consuming not just 'necessities' but also small luxuries, 'niceties' as they are called by historian Joan Thirsk, items consumed out of personal satisfaction. Indeed it has been argued that women young and old, and also men, started working longer hours in order to afford new trimmings, or pocket watches. The 'consumer revolution' was accompanied by an 'industrious revolution': an intensification of labour in order to afford an 'accumulation' of objects.

It is in the eighteenth century that 'the consumer' appears for the first time as a social character. People were no longer just citizens, tax-payers or identified by their occupation or social status: what they consumed came to communicate their identity. The very expression 'to shop' came into common parlance only in the mid-eighteenth century. As the readings included in this part underline, it was not just a matter of consuming more. The consumer revolution and the creation of the 'modern consumer' heavily relied on the provision of new and cheaper goods, on the appearance of more complex forms of distribution and retailing, and on new forms of communication including early advertising, marketing and long-distance selling. Cissie Fairchilds underlines, for instance, how cheap copies of expensive and fashionable goods such as parasols or snuff-boxes (what she calls 'populuxe goods') became part of the consuming habits of Parisians in the second half of the eighteenth century. Several new products, ranging from medicines to new textiles and furnishings, were sold by a variety of shops that displayed them in increasingly alluring ways. Shops, as Claire Walsh underlines, increased in number and were frequented by consumers of all social classes. Some of them, such as Wedgwood's showroom in the Mall in London, were places of luxurious display and attracted hundreds of people every day. Maxine Berg reminds us that such shops used complex marketing techniques and forms of advertising such as tradecards (large advertisements to be given to customers), newspapers, and catalogues through which consumers from far away could buy 'fashionable' goods.

In this context fashion flourished. Consumers were no longer content with using the same old things until they fell apart, but increasingly aimed at 'the latest fashion' or something 'fashionable'. The new, the novel and the exotic were increasingly affordable not just for the rich or the aristocrat, but also the merchant's wife, the middling-class girl and even the relatively poor apprentice or maid. The idea of fashion as the aspiration to something new, in replacement of what one already owns, emerges in this period. The role of fashion was already central in McKendrick's original formulation of a consumer revolution. He claimed that fashion acted as the dynamic force that linked people at different levels of the social hierarchy. Fashion was generated by the aesthetic choice and taste of the elite and 'filtered' down the social hierarchy through a process of aping: the maid imitated her mistress, or the shopkeeper's wife her husband's wealthier customers. Fashion did not propagate randomly through society but it percolated from the top to the bottom.

This model was borrowed from the American sociologist Thorstein Veblen who wrote on similar mechanisms of taste formation and consumer choice for late nineteenth-century American society. It is also an explanation that has been criticised by historians who observed how it did not distinguish enough between different types of consumer goods and gave little importance to the meaning that such objects might have had for consumers. Lorna Weatherill provided the most comprehensive critique of McKendrick's inner workings, suggesting a consumer revolution in which what people consumed went well beyond fashionable goods and included a variety of objects, some of which had a highly personal or familial value. Weatherill's contribution is particularly important as she reminds us that fashion should never be decontextualised from the wider web of actions, choices, consumer behaviours and relationships in which individuals are enmeshed.

The divergent views on consumption and fashion expressed by McKendrick and Weatherill are significant in understanding how the poorer parts of eighteenth-century society engaged with fashion. John Styles agrees with McKendrick that an increasing number of plebeian consumers engaged in consumption of stylish clothing, but this was not done by imitating their social superior. In his 'Custom or consumption?', Styles contrasts the optimistic view of a commercialised society generated by a consumer revolution against the interpretation of the famous English social historian E. P. Thompson who saw instead 'custom' as the driving force in people's lives in the eighteenth century. Styles explains the power of local custom through the story of James Gee, who arrived in Walsall from Dublin in search of work in the 1760s. But his smart Dublin cocked hat was out of place in Walsall and he soon had to conform to 'the custom of the place'. But Styles warns us against seeing custom as the opposite of free market and consumption. Consumption was influenced by custom and vice versa. Through the micro-case of the eighteenth-century Latham family, Styles observes how engagement with fashionable items could only happen at specific times in one's life. The life-cycle of the family overlaps with that of fashion expenditure and both are in turn supported by the household cash-flow. Fashion is therefore not a force to be found everywhere in eighteenth-century society in equal intensity, but strongly depends on specific – sometimes local or even familial – conditions.

The textile and fashion scholar Beverly Lemire, in her 'Fashioning cottons', moves away from the understanding of the ways in which a consumer revolution impacted on people's lives and their fashionable consumption, to consider instead the wider changes brought about by new commodities. Lemire expands the original formulation of a European (or English) consumer revolution by analysing the importance of Asian textiles, in particular brightly coloured and appealing chintzes and calicoes imported into Europe in the seventeenth and eighteenth centuries. The transformation of the consuming habits of rich and poor alike was dominated by the availability of new commodities ranging from Chinese porcelain, to Japanese lacquer to Indian cottons. Cottons were imported in large quantities by the European companies trading with Asia, most notably the English and Dutch East Indian Companies, and before them the Portuguese Carreira da India. Lemire shows how the softness and resistant qualities as well as their brightness of colour and the capacity to be washed helped the spread of the use of cottons: by the late seventeenth century they were used in imitations of more expensive textiles and allowed even poor people to look 'smart' but also to change outfits more often than before. Lemire charts the success of cotton textiles in England by drawing on a variety of historical sources including inventories of people's belongings, pawnbrokers' accounts showing the different types of textiles pawned, artefacts, diaries, prints and tradecards. Her rich analysis shows the importance of cottons in changing people's sartorial engagement and expenditure. But Lemire's essay reminds us how personal choices are also mediated by the political, social and economic contexts. Imported cottons were deemed to drain the resources of Europe who had to pay for them in silver. Opposition was also expressed by the producers of woollens and silks who thought cottons to be competitors in the national market. Such opposition to imported Asian textiles escalated to an outright ban on their import and consumption in the early eighteenth century. The consumption

of locally produced (printed in England, but also France and Spain) copies of cotton textiles was encouraged instead, leading to the establishment of the first nucleus of a European
cotton industry that from the end of the eighteenth century became central to the process of
industrialisation of the continent.

The issue of the geographies of fashion is further explored by Aileen Ribeiro in her essay
on 'Anglo-French comparisons'. In the eighteenth century, France and England – and especially their respective metropolises, Paris and London – assumed a key role in a new 'fashion
system' increasingly dominated by national traditions and the economic, business and communication models developed in each of these nations. Yet, the English and the French models
of fashion were different, at times seen in opposition. While France followed an over-ornate
aesthetic clearly influenced by the world of the Court in Versailles, England refused self-
conscious richness and embraced a more sober notion of elegance that was ironically often
very expensive. Ribeiro challenges this easy separation by noting how the two nations developed their own distinctive fashion by looking across the Channel. Anglophilia and francoph-
obia were essential in shaping the attitudes to fashion not just in France and England but in
all of Europe. Ribeiro uses art historical and literary methodologies and analyses images and
texts related in particular to the position of French fashion in Europe.

The final chapter, 'Fashion journals' from Daniel Purdy's book *The Tyranny of Elegance*,
considers again the role of London and Parisian fashion, but this time from the perspective
on those 'minor' centres of European fashion such as the German states that were influenced
by the fashions of distant metropolises. Purdy asks what was the influence of high fashion in
the creation of a 'modern' consumer in eighteenth-century Germany. He considers in particular the role of fashion journals, most notably *Journal des Luxus und der Moden*, to show how
fashion – as printed text and image – instilled desires among consumers. But journals acted
also as a means to reassure consumers about the rational behaviour of their choices, showing
again as we have seen in Styles, a tension between a world of illusions and acquisition generated by the allure of fashion and the same fashion as seen as part of the everyday experience
of citizens, family members and economic agents.

The four chapters included in this section raise the issue of a new position for the consumer in society. Fashion became in the eighteenth century a matter of discussion, choice and
identification. It even assumed national characters and stereotypes as shown by Ribeiro. The
expansion of the 'language of fashion' to include new materials and artefacts, but also visual
and textual representations used in journals, advertisement and marketing devices shows the
basis on which present-day fashions still rest.

Bibliography and further reading

Books and articles

Berg, M. (2005) *Luxury and Pleasure in the Eighteenth Century*, Oxford: Oxford University Press.
Berg, M., and Clifford, H. (1998) 'Commerce and the Commodity: Graphic Display and Selling New
    Consumer Goods in Eighteenth-century England', in M. North and D. Ormrod (eds), *Art Mar-
    kets in Europe, 1400–1800*, Aldershot: Ashgate, pp. 187–200.
Buck, A. (1978) *Dress in Eighteenth-century England*, London: Batsford.
Chrisman-Campbell, K. (2004) 'French Connections: Georgiana, Duchess of Devonshire, and the
    Anglo-French Fashion Exchange', *Dress*, 31, pp. 3–14.

Chrisman-Campbell, K. (2007) 'From Baroque Elegance to the French Revolution, 1700–1790', in L. Welters and A. Lillethun (eds), *The Fashion Reader*, Oxford: Berg, pp. 6–19.

Crowston, C. H. (2001) *Fabricating Women: The Seamstresses of Old Regime France, 1675–1791*, Durham, NC: Duke University Press.

Delpierre, M. (1997) *Dress in France in the Eighteenth Century*, New Haven: Yale University Press.

Fairchilds, C. (1993) 'The Production and Marketing of Populuxe Goods in Eighteenth-century Paris', in J. Brewer and R. Porter (eds), *Consumption and the World of Goods*, London and New York: Routledge, pp. 228–48.

Fine, B., and Leopold, E. (1990) 'Consumerism and the Industrial Revolution', *Social History*, 4, pp. 151–79.

Ginsburg, M. (1972) 'The Tailoring and Dressmaking Trades 1700–1850', *Costume*, 6, pp. 64–9.

Greig, H. (2006) 'Leading the Fashion: The Material Culture of London's *Beau Monde*', in J. Styles and A. Vickery (eds), *Gender, Taste, and Material Culture in Britain and North America, 1700–1830*, New Haven and London: Yale University Press, pp. 293–314.

Harte, N. B. (1991) 'The Economics of Clothing in the Late Seventeenth Century', *Textile History*, 22, 2, pp. 277–96.

Jones, E. L. (1973) 'The Fashion Manipulators: Consumer Tastes and British Industries, 1660–1800', in L. P. Cain and P. J. Uselding (eds), *Business Enterprise and Economic Change: Essays in Honour of F. Williamson*, Kent, OH: Kent State University Press, pp. 198–226.

King, S. (2002) 'Reclothing the English Poor, 1750–1840', *Textile History*, 33, 1, pp. 37–47.

Lemire, B. (1991) *Fashion's Favourite: Cotton Trade and the Consumer in Britain, 1660–1800*, Oxford: Oxford University Press and Pasold Research Fund.

Lemire, B. (1991) 'Peddling Fashion: Salesmen, Pawnbrokers, Tailors, Thieves and the Second-hand Clothes Trade in England *c*. 1700–1800', *Textile History*, 22, 1, pp. 67–82.

Lemire, B. (1997) *Dress, Culture and Commerce: The English Clothing Trade before the Factory, 1660–1800*, Basingstoke: Macmillan.

Lemire, B. (2003) 'Domesticating the Exotic: Floral Culture and the East India Calico Trade with England, *c*. 1600–1800', *Textile: A Journal of Cloth and Culture*, 1, 1, pp. 65–85.

McKendrick, N., Brewer, J., and Plumb, J. H. (1982) *The Birth of a Consumer Society: The Commercialisation of Eighteenth Century England*, London: Europa.

McNeil, P. (2004) 'The Appearance of Enlightenment: Refashioning the Elites', in M. Fitzpatrick et al. (eds), *The Enlightenment World*, London and New York: Routledge, pp. 381–401.

McNeil, P., and Riello, G. (2005) 'The Art and Science of Walking: Gender, Space and the Fashionable Body in the Long Eighteenth Century', *Fashion Theory*, 9, 2, pp. 175–204.

Munns, J., and Richards, P. (eds) (1999) *The Clothes that Wear Us: Essays on Dressing and Transgressing in Eighteenth-century Culture*, London: University of Delaware Press.

North, S. (2008) 'The Physical Manifestation of an Abstraction: A Pair of 1750s' Waistcoat Shapes', *Textile History*, 39, 1, pp. 92–104.

Parmal, P. A. (1991) 'Fashion and the Growing Importance of the *Marchande de Modes* in Mid-eighteenth-century France', *Costume*, 31, pp. 68–77.

Ribeiro, A. (1984 [2nd edition 2002]) *Dress in Eighteenth-century Europe, 1715–1789*, London: Batsford.

Ribeiro, A. (1988) *Fashion in the French Revolution*, London: Batsford.

Roche, D. (1994) *The Culture of Clothing: Dress and Fashion in the 'Ancien Régime'*, Cambridge: Cambridge University Press.

Sanderson, E. (1997) 'Nearly New: The Second-hand Clothing Trade in Eighteenth Century Edinburgh', *Costume*, 21, pp. 38–48.

Sargentson, C. (1996) *Merchants and Luxury Markets: The Marchands Merciers of Eighteenth-century Paris*, London: V & A Publications.

Spufford, M. (2000) 'The Cost of Apparel in Seventeenth-century England and the Accuracy of Gregory King', *Economic History Review*, 53, 4, pp. 677–705.

Spufford, M. (2003) 'Fabric for Seventeenth-century Children and Adolescents' Clothes', *Textile History*, 34, 1, pp. 47–63.

Styles, J. (2002) 'Involuntary Consumers? Servants and Their Clothes in Eighteenth-century England', *Textile History*, 33, 1, pp. 9–21.

Styles, J. (2007) *The Dress of the People: Everyday Fashion in Eighteenth-century England*, New Haven and London: Yale University Press.

Thatcher Ulrich, L. (2001) *The Age of Homespun: Objects and Stories in the Creation of an American Myth*, New York: Knopf.

Walsh, C. (1995) 'Shop Design and the Display of Goods in Eighteenth-century London', *Journal of Design History*, 8, 3, pp. 157–76.

Weatherill, L. (1988 [2nd edition 1996]) *Consumer Behaviour and Material Culture in Britain, 1660–1760*, London: Routledge.

Printed resources

Arnold, J. (1972) *Patterns of Fashion 1: Englishwomen's Dresses and Their Construction, c. 1660–1860*, London and New York: Macmillan/Drama Book.

Cunnington, C. W., and Cunnington, P. E. (1972) *Handbook of English Costume in the Eighteenth Century*, London: Faber & Faber.

Donald, D. (2002) *Followers of Fashion: Graphic Satires from the Georgian Period: Prints from the British Museum*, London: British Museum.

Koda, H. (ed.) (2006) *Dangerous Liaisons: Fashion and Furniture in the Eighteenth Century*, New Haven, Yale University Press.

Lens, B. (1970) *The Exact Dress of the Head*, facsimile of 1725–6 sketchbook, London: V & A Publications.

Shesgreen, S. (2002) *Images of the Outcast: The Urban Poor in the Cries of London*, New Brunswick: Rutgers University Press.

Rothstein, N. (ed.) (1987) *A Lady of Fashion: Barbara Johnson's Album of Styles and Fabrics*, London: Victoria and Albert Museum.

Weatherill, L. (ed.) (1990) *The Account Book of Richard Latham, 1724–1767*, Oxford: Oxford University Press.

Online resources

Collage image, Guildhall Library, Corporation of London: collage.cityoflondon.gov.uk/collage/app

Collection of tradecards at the John Johnson Collection of Printed Ephemera, Bodleian Library, Oxford: www.bodley.ox.ac.uk/johnson/johnson.htm

Lewis Walpole Library digital collection: lwlimages.library.yale.edu/walpoleweb/

The proceedings of the Old Bailey, London's central criminal court, 1673 to 1913, online: www.oldbaileyonline.org/

Chapter 8

Custom or consumption?

Plebeian fashion in eighteenth-century England

John Styles

BREAD, CHEESE, BUTTER, MEAT AND POTATOES: the '5 principel Things that poor Peple want to bye', asserted an anonymous threatening letter received at Lewes in Sussex during the famine year of 1800.[1] Although the precise composition of the plebeian diet varied from region to region, there is little doubt that in good years, as in bad, basic foodstuffs represented the largest single item in the budgets of plebeian families in eighteenth-century England. But should we assume that because basic foodstuffs were the principal things that plebeian men and women wanted to buy, they were the only things that they wanted, or, for that matter, were able to buy? Did they aspire to purchase, or succeed in purchasing, commodities that we might usefully describe as luxuries?

There is currently a tendency among historians whose sympathies lie with 'those whom the consumer society consumed' to deny that labouring people were much affected by those changes in consumption that have been identified as comprising an eighteenth-century consumer revolution, and then mainly to their disadvantage.[2] For Edward Thompson, throughout the eighteenth century 'capitalist process and non-economic customary behaviour are in active and conscious conflict, as in resistance to new patterns of consumption'. It was only in the aftermath of the Industrial Revolution and its accompanying demographic revolution, well into the nineteenth century, that, according to Thompson, the 'needs' of working people were remodelled, the threshold of their material expectations raised, traditional cultural satisfactions devalued and the authority of customary expectations destroyed.[3] For Robert Malcolmson, the 'expanding culture of consumerism . . . was almost entirely inaccessible to the great majority of the nation's population'.[4] In a more technical vein, Adrian Randall and Andrew Charlesworth worry that 'the boundary line between the consuming classes and the poor may have been set rather higher than some of the more optimistic accounts of market penetration might presume'.[5]

Like almost all the opinions expressed by historians on the subject of plebeian consumption in the eighteenth century, these views are not grounded in substantial empirical work. Rather, their proponents assert a number of powerful objections to those meliorist interpretations of eighteenth-century England that have presented it as a socially inclusive 'consumer society', in which the labouring poor enjoyed increased access to what are defined as luxuries or conveniences, as opposed to necessities. They offer three main objections. First, a straightforward denial of Neil McKendrick's influential claim (itself based purely on the views of polite commentators) that his eighteenth-century consumer society extended to many among the labouring poor; that 'the expansion of the market [for fashionable clothing], revealed in the literary evidence, occurred first among the domestic-servant class, then among the industrial workers, and finally among the agricultural workers'.[6] Second, a reassertion of the pessimistic view of the effects of early factory industrialisation on working-class living standards. Third, an insistence that any increase in the threshold of material expectations among plebeian men and women was incompatible with the continuation of their traditional customary satisfactions and defences.

This chapter intervenes in the argument between pessimists and optimists by considering the ways plebeian women and men spent on clothes in eighteenth-century England. Clothing is crucial to this argument because it was the element of plebeian expenditure most likely to embrace fashionable display. The capacity of fashionable display to provoke emulation has been a central element in efforts to define and explain plebeian luxury, whether by eighteenth-century commentators, or by modern historians. The chapter argues that McKendrick and other optimists have been right to insist on the capacity of large numbers of young adult plebeians to indulge in the pleasures of stylish clothing, although the evidence they use is of questionable value. The chapter goes on to argue, however, that such behaviour did not necessarily require these young plebeian consumers to give up the commitment to custom that Edward Thompson saw as the principal defence of working people against the rigours of the free market.

*   *   *

Custom and consumption were often allies, not enemies. Plebeian custom embraced the market as often as it resisted it. The customary assumptions and practices that ordered many aspects of plebeian life in early modern England were symbiotically entwined with the development of the early modern market economy. Often they flourished precisely because they provided opportunities and legitimising excuses to participate in attractive forms of commercialised consumption. As Hans Medick has argued, '[Edward] Thompson's work lacks an analysis of those quieter, but equally "communal" characteristic manifestations of the everyday life of the plebeian lower orders, which developed – to a considerable extent in harmony with the growth of capitalistic markets – in consumption, fashions and especially in drinking culture'.[7]

Even Medick, however, puts too much stress on the elements of resistance and picaresque 'irrationality' in everyday plebeian consumption, so concerned is he to distinguish plebeian life from the stereotype of an emerging, rational 'bourgeois' culture. Such cultural stereotypes, too often derived uncritically from eighteenth- and nineteenth-century models, can be profoundly misleading in the study of eighteenth-century consumption. This is true at every social level.

Thus the stereotype of the ultra-fashionable, gambling, spendthrift aristocrat, itself assiduously cultivated and disseminated in the late eighteenth century by the circle around

Georgiana, Duchess of Devonshire, and the Prince of Wales, entirely ignores those prudent and pious nobles whose sympathies lay with George III. Equally, the stereotype of the rational, calculating, self-denying bourgeois fails to comprehend the often ruinous expenditure on personal and commercial display incurred by many eighteenth-century businessmen.[8] In the same way, the stereotypical view of eighteenth-century plebeian culture, which presents it as collectivist, anti-individualistic, immune to economically rational calculation and overwhelmingly short-term in its time horizons, ignores the obvious variations of plebeian experience which grew out of differences of gender, age, location, and employment. Even among single adult working men, who were perhaps the group in the plebeian population most likely to fall into unpredictable, picaresque lives, patterns of consumption varied considerably.

At one extreme was Johnny Chapman, the pitman employed by the father of the wood engraver, Thomas Bewick, on the banks of the Tyne in the 1750s and 1760s. Bewick describes him, not unsympathetically, in the *Memoir* he wrote towards the end of his life, as dressing in rags, living on the most meagre of diets and spending all his spare cash on periodic drinking binges in Newcastle.[9] At the other extreme were working men like the teenage William Hutton, in 1739 an impoverished apprentice stocking weaver at Nottingham, who spent two long years 'with a little over work and a little credit, to raise a genteel suit of clothes' and who goes on in his autobiography to plot the failures and successes of his late teens and early twenties in terms of his ability to accumulate clothes that were stylish by the standards of his peers.[10]

Not that we should conceptualise patterns of consumption among single plebeian men as a single spectrum bounded by these two extremes. There were working men hungry to acquire petty, fashionable luxuries like watches or laced hats, who subsequently discarded them with little concern for accumulation – many deep-sea sailors appear to have behaved in this way while on shore. There were also working communities which enforced limits on sartorial display. The buckle-maker James Gee, who arrived in Walsall from Dublin looking for work in the 1760s wearing a cocked hat that was smart by Dublin standards, was reluctantly obliged to conform to what he called 'the custom of the place' and wear a round hat with a brim that flapped down over the face.[11] Nor were these variations simple reflections of occupational or residential stability. It was the improvident pitman Johnny Chapman who enjoyed settled residence and employment, and the calculating, accumulating apprentice William Hutton who took to the road in search of material self-advancement.

What follows is an exploration of the clothing practices of some important sections of the young adult population between the 1740s and the 1790s. It indicates that the material aspirations of plebeian English women, in particular, were higher and more dynamic than the pessimists contend.[12] It also suggests how, at some stages in their lives, they might have enjoyed the means to fulfil those aspirations. But let me begin in the harsh final decade of the eighteenth century, with some of the most impoverished groups in English society – the labouring families whose budgets were recorded and analysed by the Reverend David Davies in his *Case of the Labourers in Husbandry* of 1795 and by Frederick Morton Eden in his *State of the Poor* of 1797. Both these men collected detailed information on income and expenditure for large numbers of labouring families spread across Britain, including information on clothing. The picture that emerges is a dreary one of shabby clothes made from coarse materials that were worn for too long. Things do not appear to have been so bad that adults were obliged to wear all the clothes they owned at once; most of the budgets allow for a change of undergarments, stockings and, in some of the more fortunate cases, outer garments and even footwear. Usually adults (although sometimes not their children) appear to have possessed all the basic elements that constituted a decent eighteenth-century English wardrobe, in contrast to some of their Scottish equivalents. But for a number of the families it was only with extraordinary difficulty that these minimal standards were sustained.

This bleak picture of the clothing of the labouring poor is in marked contrast to the generally positive impression of their dress offered by foreign commentators such as the Swede Kalm, the Frenchman Grosley and the German Moritz between the 1740s and the 1780s.[13] The immediately obvious reason for these inconsistencies is chronological. The researches of both Davies and Eden were prompted by concerns about deterioration in the economic position of the labouring poor in the 1780s and 1790s, as registered in the rising cost of poor relief. There is little doubt that the progressive rise in the cost of basic foodstuffs in the second half of the eighteenth century, which does not seem to have been matched by a corresponding improvement in wages in the south at least, meant that Davies's southern agricultural labourers were under considerable financial pressure when their budgets were drawn up at the end of the 1780s. Eden's budgets for labouring families were compiled in the war years between 1794 and 1796, the majority of them in the immediate aftermath of the devastatingly bad harvest of 1795. Many of his families faced a ruinous combination of unprecedentedly high food prices, falling industrial wages and reduced opportunities for industrial work.

There remains, however, another crucial consideration – the family life-cycle. Almost all of Davies's and Eden's budgets are for families, mainly families with large numbers of young dependent children. This was the first of the two stages in the life-cycle of the family when the balance between income and expenditure was at its most precarious (the second being old age).[14] As Davies pointed out, mothers with very young children were restricted in the amount of paid work they could undertake, even if it was available. Although children might secure some money income from the age of five or six, their earnings at that early age were very small. This, however, was a limited stage in the life of most parents. Between leaving home and marriage, the majority of labouring people spent a long period during which many of them earned and, at least as far as clothing is concerned, consumed independently. Usually this involved one of the various forms of live-in service or apprenticeship, with adult wages sometimes achieved for men by the age of nineteen.[15] Typically the majority of late eighteenth-century labouring children left home in their mid-teens, but the average age of first marriage was nearly 26 for men and over 24 for women.[16] Earlier in the century, the period between leaving home and marriage was longer still, because both sexes tended to marry later.

Savings and stocks of clothing accumulated in the financially independent years before marriage might see a couple through the first few years of childbearing, but the need to support several infant children and a nursing mother who could earn little must have progressively impoverished many labouring families. Nevertheless, the heavy initial financial burden of young children began to reduce (assuming both parents remained alive) by the time the parents turned 40, as childbearing ended and children grew older. At this stage, older children and wives who did not have to look after infants could provide an increasing contribution to family income (assuming paid work was available for them). At the same time, some of the older children began to leave home (at least semi-permanently), reducing claims on family resources. It is the fact that most of the families in the Eden-Davies budgets were at or near the first trough in the family poverty cycle that accounts for some of the worst deficiencies in their clothing.

The pressure that infant children placed on family resources was not, of course, just a problem for labouring families. Detailed, long-term family accounts do not survive for eighteenth-century labouring families. It is possible, however, to observe the effects of the family life-cycle on clothing expenditure in the accounts of at least one plebeian family, the Lathams of Scarisbrick in west Lancashire, between the 1720s and the 1760s.[17] The Lathams are the poorest family for whom long-term, detailed financial records survive from the period. Nevertheless, they enjoyed many economic advantages not available to the Eden-Davies families. They farmed a smallholding of approximately 20 acres on fertile land suitable for mixed agriculture in an economically expanding region; they had access to grazing and turbary rights on newly reclaimed common land; they lived in an area where industrial outwork for women was increasingly plentiful.

Families like the Lathams are usually identified by historians as part of that extensive middling sort that was such an important feature of the eighteenth-century English social hierarchy. There is good reason to admit them to that category's broad and ill-defined embrace, but we should not forget that the Lathams were far removed from its upper echelons and were in no sense wealthy in the contemporary sense of the word. Unlike most yeoman farmers, they did not employ permanent domestic or farm servants. Indeed, it could accurately have been said of them, just as it was of petty landholders in nearby Cumberland in the 1760s, that 'they work like slaves; they cannot afford to keep a man servant, but husband, wife, sons and daughters all turn out to work in the fields'.[18]

As landholders, the Lathams had a significant economic advantage over the Eden-Davies labourers, but they did not inhabit an alien world of goods. They bought only a very narrow selection of the small domestic luxuries that spread among the middling sort during the first half of the eighteenth century and seem to have become increasingly common among the labouring poor during the second half of the century. Their purchases included books, newspapers, tobacco pipes, and knives and forks, but excluded crockery and tea wares. In terms of access to material possessions, therefore, the Lathams lived a life which was probably no better than, and in some respects may have been inferior to, that of the hard-pressed agricultural labourers at the end of the eighteenth century.[19] Nevertheless, the Lathams were not a typical plebeian family. Their children were disproportionately female and most of them continued to live at home until they were relatively old. Between their marriage in 1723 and the birth of their youngest child in 1741 Richard and Nany Latham produced seven children who survived at least into young adulthood, of whom six were daughters.

The Latham account book covers the 43 years of their married life from 1724 until Richard Latham's death in 1767, including a period after the children had left home. Neither the amount nor the proportion of expenditure devoted to clothes remained constant. Richard and Nany Latham's married life, and their spending on clothes, fell into three distinct periods. During the first 18 years between 1724 and 1741, when their children were young and increasingly numerous, clothes expenditure was limited. The second period between 1742 and 1754, when the children were older and earning more, but still largely resident at home, saw spending on clothes rise dramatically, both in absolute terms and as a proportion of total expenditure. In the third period, after the children left home in the mid-1750s, clothes spending fell back. The focus of this chapter is on the first and second periods.

The experience of the Lathams in the first 18 years of married life was one of intense pressure on the family's budget that bore many similarities to the Eden-Davies labouring families. The early years of marriage and childbearing imposed heavy financial demands and placed considerable restrictions on family earnings. If a money value is ascribed to the cloth the Lathams made at home and is added to the rest of their clothes spending, their average annual expenditure on clothing in these years, at just over 50 shillings, was not very different from Davies's most pessimistic calculation for his Berkshire labouring families. Like several of the Davies labourers, Richard Latham appears to have owned at least two sets of outer garments during this period, but he can have renewed them only very intermittently. Nany Latham appears more abstemious than the labourers' wives in doing without new gowns, but like the adults in the labouring families, both the adult Lathams appear to have been able to acquire footwear and undergarments annually. If anything, Richard and Nany Latham spent less on themselves and more on their children than Davies's labourers. The cost of most of what the adult Lathams bought was low and they purchased virtually no petty clothing luxuries like lace, silk hats, patterned gown fabrics or fine linen aprons.

The second period, the 13 years from 1742 to 1754, witnessed a transformation in the family's spending on clothes. Their annual expenditure on clothing was on average three times higher than in the first period, a leap in expenditure that was funded principally by the Latham daughters' earnings as outwork spinners for the Lancashire cotton industry. The principal beneficiaries were those who made it possible – the older children. We can observe the change in the family's circumstances by examining purchases of two different types of clothing – gowns and accessories.

Before 1742, no adult gown lengths of cloth were purchased for Nany Latham or any of her daughters. Thereafter, as each of the daughters reached her mid-teens, gowns began to be bought. Between 1742, when Betty, the eldest daughter, was 16, and 1749, when she was 23 and had already been in service, she acquired four gowns on the family account. Two of these were relatively cheap, with fabric costing 7s 6d and 12s 4d respectively. They were probably working gowns made from a plain worsted cloth such as camblet at less than 16½d a yard. The other two gowns were much more stylish and expensive, made from patterned cloths. Although the word is not used in the accounts, these were almost certainly her 'best' gowns. When she was 16 Betty acquired 11½ yards of blue flowered damask, costing over 20 shillings, which at 20½d a yard was probably a mixed worsted-silk fabric. Her plain, workaday gowns used only 9 yards of fabric or less, but a gown made from a flowered fabric required a longer (and more costly) length to allow the pattern to repeat harmoniously across the surface of the garment when cut out and assembled. Later, when she was 23, she acquired a printed gown costing 20 shillings, the fabric for which was probably either linen or cotton.[20] A similar pattern emerges for the next daughter, Sara, who acquired four cheap, workaday gowns, costing well under 14 shillings, and two expensive, stylish gowns, one of flowered damask and the other of a printed cotton or linen fabric. Gowns were likewise bought for the four younger sisters once they reached their mid-teens.

The change in the Lathams' clothes purchases after 1742 can also be observed in accessories and footwear. The increase in the number of accessories bought is easily illustrated by hats and handkerchiefs, which between 1742 and 1754 were bought much more frequently than before. In these 13 years, handkerchiefs were purchased in sufficient numbers to provide approximately one every 18 months for each member of the family, compared with approximately one every two years previously.[21] With hats, the contrast is even more marked. The family bought 30 during these 13 years, whereas only eight had been acquired in the previous 18. But it is the increase in the range and the quality of the accessories purchased that is most striking. Neither Nany Latham nor any of her daughters acquired any petty clothing luxuries before 1742. But thereafter, just as with gowns, when the daughters reached their mid-teens, they each began to acquire relatively costly and decorative accessories, such as shag hats, probably made from silk and costing between 5 and 8 shillings, silk handkerchiefs and expensive white aprons made from fine fabrics like cambric. It is only in this period, moreover, that there are entries in the account book for borders for caps and aprons, and for costly bone lace.

For the Lathams, clothing was a luxury in the technical sense used by economists. As the family's income grew as a consequence of the daughters' industriousness, so did both the amount and the proportion of family spending devoted to clothes. Appropriately, this new spending was led by the unmarried daughters themselves, whose purchases also embraced luxury in a sense more familiar to eighteenth-century social commentators, in that they purchased stylish accessories and garments in addition to practical, workaday items of clothing. Yet it is important to stress that the increase in family spending required to make all these new luxury purchases was small, no more than an extra 1s 8d a week, considerably less than the estimated weekly earnings of just one regularly employed outwork cotton spinner in the period. Relatively small shifts in family income could produce dramatic transformations in material culture.

The Latham daughters were unusual in that they stayed at home into their late teens and early twenties. Was theirs a typical pattern of expenditure and acquisition among young plebeian women? The evidence of female domestic servants' expenditure on clothing suggests that it was. Service of one kind or another was the experience of vast numbers, perhaps a majority, of adolescents and young adults in early modern England. A status as much as an occupation, service could involve a variety of different kinds of work, but for women domestic service predominated. Vast numbers of young women entered domestic service. Patrick Colquhoun's 1806 estimate of 910,000 domestic servants in England and Wales, of whom 800,000 were women, in a total population of approximately nine million, may have been exaggerated, but it is suggestive both of the enormous numbers involved and the sex ratio.[22] A large majority of these women were drawn from the plebeian classes and were under 25 years of age; in general female domestic servants were expected to be young and unmarried.

Female servants (unlike their male equivalents) were not usually provided with clothing under the terms of their contract of employment. They received payment in kind in the form of accommodation, food, heat, light and washing, and in addition a small money wage. How did they spend it? The records of Robert Heaton throw some light on this matter.[23] He was a medium-sized manufacturer of worsted cloth and small landowner who lived high in the Yorkshire Pennines at Ponden near Howarth in the second half of the eighteenth century. For most of the period from 1768 to 1793 he had two female servants. Turnover was high: only three of them stayed with him for more than three years. This was normal. Where Heaton was unusual was in keeping detailed accounts of how his servants spent their meagre wages, probably so that he could settle with them for purchases made on his credit from local retailers. With only one exception, all Heaton's female servants devoted the bulk of what they spent out of their wages to the purchase of clothing. Moreover, a majority spent more than they earned and they did so by borrowing from Heaton.

Like the Latham daughters, their purchases represented a combination of the stylish and the mundane. The most extreme was Alice Hutchinson, hired by Heaton in 1781 at an annual wage of 78 shillings. In her first year of service she actually laid out almost 102 shillings – a 31 per cent overspend. All but 10 shillings of this went on clothes. She made 28 separate clothing purchases in that year, including expensive, indeed fashionable, items like a muslin neckcloth for 3s 6d, a silk hat for 6s 10½d with a paper hat box worth 2 shillings, and a new linen gown for 20s 6d, as well as shoes, clogs, pattens, other handkerchiefs, a petticoat, a shift, yarn for stockings and various kinds of cloth, including a length of callimanco for 7 shillings, which was probably used to make her a gown for everyday use. She went on to serve for another two years, continuing in debt to Heaton but none the less making yet more expensive clothes purchases, including another gown for 21 shillings, lace worth 12 shillings, a cloak, neckcloths in silk and muslin, and another hat and hatbox. Alice Hutchinson may have been extreme in the number of clothing items she bought, but the items she bought were not uncharacteristic, either of her fellow servants in the Heaton household, or of servants elsewhere whose purchases are recorded in the servants' books kept by drapers and other shopkeepers.[24]

Female servants' money wages may have been small, but like the industrial earnings of the Latham daughters, they were sufficient to provide a range of petty clothing luxuries. Like the Lathams, most of what they bought was new; they appear to have made hardly any purchases on the second-hand market. Of course, their little luxuries did not match either for price or quality the more expensive purchases of the daughters of the local gentry and a great gulf separated them from the clothes bought by those among the nobility who aspired to lead metropolitan high fashion. Nevertheless, the prices these young plebeian women paid for their more expensive gowns, for example, overlapped with the lower end of the range of prices paid for gowns by provincial women from lesser gentry, professional and mercantile families. In so far as the stilted descriptions of the account books allow us to establish, the young plebeian women's more expensive purchases reflected, albeit in a muted, limited manner, the broad trends of high fashion (see Figure 8.1).

It is not easy from the terse descriptions and figures of an account book to reconstruct the terms in which Robert Heaton's servants or the daughters of the Latham family understood their activities as consumers of clothing, particularly as purchasers of their more expensive and stylish items, those clothes which are repeatedly identified in plebeian and elite sources alike by the adjective 'best'. Yet both daughters and servants probably shared many of the concerns of the 16-year-old William Hutton while apprenticed to a stocking weaver at Nottingham in 1739.

> I was arriving at that age when the two sexes begin to look at each other, consequently wish to please; and a powerful mode to win is that of dress. This is a passport to the heart, a key to unlock the passions, and guide them in our favour. My resources were cut off; my sun was eclipsed. Youth is the time to dress; the time in which it is not only excusable, but laudable. I envied every new coat; I had the wish to earn one, but not the power.[25]

Figure 8.1 Henry Singleton, *The Ale-House Door*, 1790, printed engraving, private collection. Two working people are shown outside a country ale house. Their clothing incorporates a number of the fashions of the 1780s, notably the huge buttons on the man's coat, and the woman's cap, shoes, and cuffs extending over her elbows.

It took Hutton two years, but he did manage to acquire a best suit, and also a best wig and a best hat. 'The girls eyed me with some attention; nay, I eyed myself as much as any of them.'[26] For young adult plebeians, then, stylish or 'genteel' clothes could be a sign of sexual maturity, an emblem of material self-advancement, a means of sexual attraction, a currency in sexual competition and a source of self-regarding pleasure. There were also economic considerations. The romantic success that Hutton believed to flow from stylish clothes could eventually lead to marriage, without which plebeian women especially found it very hard to survive economically. A stock of clothes built up while single could see the owner through the impoverished early years of married life. Being well dressed was one of the criteria that might secure a privileged service in a more wealthy household.[27]

It was not just in sexual encounters or when seeking employment that clothing aroused feelings of respect and shame. Plebeian men and women felt a profound obligation to maintain a decent, respectable appearance before their peers in a variety of settings. Cheshire clergy in the 1778 visitation returns attributed low church attendance among the lower rank to their false shame or pride in not having decent clothes.[28] Sig-nificantly, parish vestries hardly ever provided paupers with clothing in the materials or at the prices that distinguished the 'best' clothes bought by the Latham daughters, Robert Heaton's servants, or the young William Hutton, although they might require paupers to wear 'decent' clothing on Sundays, sometimes of a slightly better quality than that to be worn on 'common days'.[29] The significance of these distinctions is con-firmed by the fact that the 'best' clothes acquired by the young plebeian adults dis-cussed here, particularly the accessories, were precisely those that bore the brunt of internal discipline among Quakers, who were required to avoid 'the world's customs and fashions in apparrel'.[30]

Yet to locate plebeian consumption of clothing in relation to the historical debates outlined at the start of this chapter, we need to look beyond the personal satisfactions and rewards stylish clothing might afford to those who could acquire it. We need to consider the circumstances in which those satisfactions and rewards were typically enjoyed. The visual distinctions between 'best' clothes and 'work' clothes were rooted in a fashion system that was an integral component of eighteenth-century commercial expansion. Nevertheless, the occasions when 'best' clothes were worn were shaped by a festive calendar that found its legitimacy in emphatically customary usage and some-times had to be defended against attack by local elites.[31] It was above all on special days like Sundays, Christmas, Easter and Whitsuntide, at fairs and at hirings, at parish feasts and at harvest home that plebeian men and women, especially young men and women, were able to observe and be observed in their finery.

Towards the beginning of the century, Henry Bourne noted in his *Antiquitates Vulgares* (1725) that it was at wakes that the people 'deck themselves in their gaudiest clothes, and have open doors and splendid entertainments, for the reception and treat-ing of their relations and friends, who visit them on that occasion, from each neighbour-ing town'. Sixty years later, young women continued to come to fairs like the one at Turton in Lancashire 'deck'd in the gayest fashion of the year'.[32] Indeed, wakes and fairs were occasions for the exhibition of plebeian consumer luxuries of all kinds. The radical weaver Samuel Bamford recalled that at Middleton wake in Lancashire in the late eight-eenth century, it was the custom for the women of each household to make a display of their 'silver watches, trays, spoons, sugar-tongs, tea-pots, snuffers, or other fitting art-icles of ornament and value . . . and in proportion as it was happily designed and fitly put together or otherwise, was their praise or disparagement meted out by the public'.[33]

Fairs, moreover, were not simply events where best clothes were worn, but also places where they could be acquired. Retailers of cloth and clothing of every kind set up their stalls in large numbers at fairs, taking advantage of the crowds and provid-ing them with an unusually wide choice of merchandise. Clothing also featured promi-nently among the prizes offered to the winners of the sporting contests that proliferated at fairs and other recreations. At Boughton Green fair in Northamptonshire in 1721, prizes included two hats worth a guinea each and six pairs of buckskin gloves, each worth 5 shillings.[34] The significance these customary festivities held for plebeian con-sumers of clothing can, once again, be registered in the attitude of the Quakers, who discouraged attachment to worldly show and were consistently hostile to attendance at fairs. Dorothy Garbutt was disciplined by the Thirsk Monthly Meeting in the North Riding of Yorkshire in 1797 for having two sorts of dress, one to attend meetings, the other for fairs and markets.[35]

The unfortunate Dorothy Garbutt was one of a large number of young plebeian men and women who, as this chapter has argued, enjoyed disposable incomes sufficient to acquire petty luxuries, especially clothes. Their choices as consumers of clothing suggest a set of material expectations profoundly influenced by the operation of the fashion system in the commercial marketplace. Yet these material expectations found fulfilment in modes of self-representation rooted in the customary calendar which ordered so many of the key life decisions – courtship, marriage, employment – of young plebeian adults. In the sphere of clothing at least, custom and consumption were not incompatible.

Notes

1   R. Wells, *Wretched Faces: Famine in Wartime England, 1793–1801* (Gloucester, 1988), p. 13.

2   E. P. Thompson, quoted on the dust jacket of P. Linebaugh, *The London Hanged* (London, 1993).

3   E. P. Thompson, *Customs in Common* (London, 1991), pp. 12 and 14.

4   R. W. Malcolmson, *Life and Labour in England, 1700–1780* (London, 1981), p. 149.

5   A. Randall and A. Charlesworth, eds, *Markets, Market Culture and Popular Protest in Eighteenth-Century Britain and Ireland* (Liverpool, 1996), p. 8.

6   N. McKendrick, 'The Commercialisation of Fashion', in N. McKendrick, J. Brewer and J. H. Plumb, *The Birth of a Consumer Society* (London, 1982), p. 60.

7   Hans Medick, 'Plebeian Culture in the Transition to Capitalism', in R. Samuel and G. Stedman Jones (eds), *Culture, Ideology and Politics* (London, 1982), p. 89.

8   Julian Hoppit, *Risk and Failure in English Business* (Cambridge, 1987), pp. 71–2 and 168–9; also Daniel Defoe, *The Complete English Tradesman*, vol. 1 (London, 1745), chapters 10 and 22.

9   Iain Bain, ed., *A Memoir of Thomas Bewick Written by Himself* (Oxford, 1979), pp. 28–9.

10 William Hutton, *The Life of William Hutton* (London, 1817), *passim*. A similar use of clothing as a measure of personal advancement can be found in the autobiography of Francis Place; see Mary Thale (ed.), *The Autobiography of Francis Place* (Cambridge, 1972), *passim*.

11 Walsall Local History Centre, 'The Life and Times of James Gee of Walsall, 1746–1827', unpaginated typescript, chapter 4.

12 The most comprehensive statement of the pessimist position with regard to clothing is to be found in John Rule, *The Labouring Classes in Early Industrial England, 1750–1850* (London, 1986), pp. 66–71, which covers a slightly later period than that addressed here. Based mainly on the evidence of contemporary commentators, it notes that little is known about actual plebeian consumption patterns.

13 P. Kalm, *Account of His Visit to England . . . in 1748* (London, 1892); M. Grosley, *A Tour to London* (London, 1772); K. P. Moritz, *Travels Chiefly on Foot, through Several Parts of England in 1782* (London, 1795).

14 See Keith Snell, *Annals of the Labouring Poor: Social Change and Agrarian England, 1660–1900* (Cambridge, 1985), pp. 358–9.

15 Snell, *Annals of the Labouring Poor*, p. 333.

16 E. A. Wrigley and R. S. Schofield, *The Population History of England, 1541–1871* (Cambridge, 1981), p. 424.

17 The following discussion is, unless otherwise indicated, based on L. Weatherill, *The Account Book of Richard Latham* (London, 1990), a transcription which does contain inaccuracies; see the review by S. Harrop and P. Perrins in *Transactions of the Historic Society of Lancashire and Cheshire*, 141 (1991), pp. 234–6. In using the accounts for this chapter,

inconsistencies within the printed text have been corrected, but it has not been possible to check the whole of the printed text against the original manuscript. As most of the inaccuracies are minor, it is unlikely that they have a substantial effect on the conclusions. I would like to thank Andy Gritt of the University of Central Lancashire for additional information on the Latham family.

18 *Gentleman's Magazine* (1766), p. 582.

19 For a pessimistic assessment of the material circumstances of agricultural labourers at the end of the eighteenth century, see I. Dyck, *William Cobbett and Rural Popular Culture* (Cambridge, 1992), chapter 5, and J. M. Neeson, 'An Eighteenth-Century Peasantry', in J. Rule and R. Malcolmson (eds), *Protest and Survival* (London, 1993), pp. 51–8. For a more optimistic assessment of their access to material possessions, see P. King, 'Pauper Inventories and the Material Lives of the Poor in the Eighteenth and Early Nineteenth Centuries', in Tim Hitchcock, Peter King and Pamela Sharpe (eds), *Chronicling Poverty: The Voices and Strategies of the English Poor, 1640–1840* (London, 1997).

20 Shopkeepers' inventories for the period 1720 to 1750 often include cloth described as printed linen and printed cotton. Occasionally printed flannel and printed linsey woolsey also occur.

21 Based on the average cost of the Lathams' purchases of handkerchiefs where prices are itemised between 1742 and 1754, the total sum spent on handkerchiefs, and the number of family members alive and resident in each year.

22 P. Colquhoun, *A Treatise on Indigence* (London, 1806), p. 253.

23 West Yorkshire County Record Office (Bradford), B149, Heaton of Ponden mss, account book of Robert Heaton, 1764–92. For an extended analysis of this source, see John Styles, 'Involuntary Consumers? Servants and Their Clothes in Eighteenth-Century England', *Textile History*, 33 (2002), pp. 9–21.

24 Hampshire Record Office, 96M82 PZ25, account book of Mary Medhurst and Thomas North, drapers, 1762–81; University of London Library, mss 625/3, R. Flowers, grocer and draper at Westoning, Bedfordshire, servants' book. It is not possible to reconstruct individual servant's clothes purchases as a whole from these books, because they must almost always have bought clothing from more than one supplier.

25 Hutton, *The Life of William Hutton*, pp. 96–7.

26 Hutton, *The Life of William Hutton*, p. 101.

27 Greater London Record Office, MJ/SP, Middlesex Sessions Papers, January 1699, pp. 146–7. Margaret Edwards, confessing to the theft of table linen, a spoon and two silver buckles, said she 'intended to dispose of the same to buy herself clothes to put herself into a service'.

28 J. Howard Hudson, *Cheshire, 1660–1780: Restoration to Industrial Revolution* (Chester, 1978), p. 47.

29 Essex Record Office, DIP 30118: Witham overseers miscellanea/1: Agreement between the Parish of Witham and John Darby for running the workhouse, 1790, and 17: Orders for regulating the workhouse, 1726.

30 Brotherton Library, University of Leeds, Special Collections, Quaker Records, SE 2: Minutes of Settle women's monthly meeting, 1701–38, meeting of 7/3/1735.

31 For attempts to suppress fairs, see R. W. Malcolmson, *Popular Recreations in English Society, 1700–1850* (Cambridge, 1973), *passim*.

32 Malcolmson, *Popular Recreations*, pp. 53 and 86.

33 Samuel Bamford, *The Autobiography of Samuel Bamford, vol. 1, Early Days* (London, 1967), pp. 149–50.

34 Malcolmson, *Popular Recreations*, p. 57.

35 Jean E. Mortimer, *Quakers in Gildersome* (Leeds, 1990), p. 16.

Fashion in the museum
The material culture of artefacts

Miles Lambert

Snapshot 10.1 Girl's embroidered jacket, 1610–20. Gallery of Costume, Platt Hall –
Manchester City Galleries, 2001-131.

Surviving garments 'make real' the most unknown consumers of the past. They allow
researchers to address issues of utility and ornament, but also the meaning and sentiment
embodied by clothing and its role in defining personal and social identity. Apart from
contemporary fashion entering the museum, surviving clothes have generally been worn;

any item that has survived 200 years or longer has probably endured a fashionable life of use and re-use, and even a later existence of survival and even misuse. Such worn garments are never generic artefacts. They retain a 'footprint' of the wearer as their unique 'memory': they reveal signs of use, and they often show cut and construction choices made for specific consumers. Where unworn clothing is donated to a museum directly from the manufacturer, as in the case of a designer giving an example of work, little sign of wear will be manifest, and this, crucially, omits a wearer. Most donated garments arrive at the museum showing variable signs of soiling and wear, and unless of symbolic or commemorative significance, this is usually ameliorated by a textile conservator, who also keeps a detailed record of the treatment. The conservator may have power of veto on some problematic donations on grounds of poor condition, as dirt, staining and poor alteration can only lessen the life of an outfit. The curator records what evidence is available about all new accessions, including any provenance of wearer's details and memories, while also seeking to research further the context of the item.

West European garments survive in increasing quantities from the seventeenth century onwards, and their survival often surprises visitors to museums, but their natural fibres were spun and woven to last. Clothes could be restyled and remodelled for decades for a number of different wearers and it was not uncommon to buy them second-hand. This explains why those garments that have reached us provide information not just on their production, marketing and retailing, but also on wearing, rewearing, alteration and transfer from owner to owner. Garments may help to make concrete a range of research questions or issues. The historical practice of gifting, for instance, can be studied by analysing love-tokens such as garters, which in the seventeenth and eighteenth centuries were sometimes woven with a loving message. In 1721, James Huson presented such a pair of garters to his beloved, 'Betty Porter of Henstridge, this and the giver is yours for ever and so pray God bless us both to gethre, I am your humble servant James Huson 1721' (Sotheby's).

Museum collections include considerable quantities of clothing that have been altered or remade. In the collection at the Gallery of Costume in Manchester in the United Kingdom, there are over ninety women's dresses from the period from 1700 to 1800, most of which have gone through alterations, and many can be reconnected to specific individuals. The striking Spitalfields-woven floral silks from the 1730s and 1740s were particularly valued and popular, and have thus often been remodelled a generation later in the 1760s or 1770s. Manchester's dress collection also contains at least six highly fashionable dresses whose style and cut date them between 1830 and 1840, but which have re-used silk brocades from a century earlier. Fine embroidery could be reworked into a new garment by selecting areas that had not worn through or become stained. So, an early linen jacket of about 1610, decorated with coiling-coloured silk embroidery and sequins, recently acquired by the Gallery of Costume in Manchester, had been carefully cut down, remade, and recycled for an adolescent girl from an adult woman's garment (Snapshot 10.1). In 'shrinking' in size, the garment 'expanded' in use and in memories.

Bibliography and further reading

Arnold, J. (1973) *A Handbook of Costume*, London: Macmillan.

Baumgarten, L. (2002) *What Clothes Reveal: the Language of Clothing in Colonial and Federal America*, New Haven: Colonial Williamsburg Foundation and Yale University Press.

Buck, A. (1979) *Dress in Eighteenth-century England*, London: B. T. Batsford.

Sotheby's 'Costumes, Textiles, Louis Vuitton Luggage and Fabric Swatch Books' sale, 9 October 1997, lot 107, 'A love token garter or ribbon, circa 1721'.

Chapter 9

Fashioning cottons

Asian trade, domestic industry and consumer demand, 1660–1780

Beverly Lemire

T HE INDIGENOUS EUROPEAN STAPLES of linen, wool, silk and leather persisted as the basic constituents of attire through the seventeenth and eighteenth centuries. But a counterpoint to this traditionalism came with the introduction of East Indian cottons; cottons rapidly became part of the vernacular of daily dress over this same period. The trade in Oriental textiles transformed the context in which all other textiles were made and sold. East Indian fabrics challenged the products of European manufacture, displaying properties which appealed to common and to cultivated consumers. Ultimately, these textiles became a model to which European manufacturers subscribed, capturing the interest and responding to the sensibilities of Europeans. The characteristics of the textile products – cost, composition, colour and design – accounted for their rapid adoption. However, these characteristics alone did not guarantee their success. Chaudhuri noted two decades ago that 'cultural values' also played a part in the craze for calicoes which distinguished the seventeenth and eighteenth centuries (Chaudhuri 1978: 224). This chapter will consider, in sequence, the characteristics of East India textiles, their effect on patterns of dress and fashion and the products which followed their example, feeding the popular passion for cottons over the eighteenth century.

'New fancyes' and the calico craze

Cotton textiles were known, and in some regions well known, long before Asian products flooded European markets in the late seventeenth century. European-made cotton fabrics were brought to markets, initially from Italy, but although the tradition of manufacture had spread from Italy to southern Germany by the fourteenth century, in that period, as later, 'linen remained the basic fibre in mixed cloth where it was combined with wool, cotton and even silk' (Mazzaoui 1981: 138). Southern and south-central Europe were the sites of a vibrant production and trade in mixed cotton goods, like fustians. Maureen Mazzaoui contends that 'until the late sixteenth century, the Italian and Swabian monopoly over the export trade [in cotton fabrics] proved a formidable obstacle to the growth of rival industries' (Mazzaoui 1981: 158). However, internal and external forces ultimately constrained these regions and their textile trades. Wadsworth and Mann identified what they called 'a shift' in the economic centre of gravity to the more dynamic regions of the north-west, the thriving trading regions along the Atlantic (Wadsworth and Mann 1931: 23). European fustians continued as staples, as perennial constituents of dress and furnishings. Moreover, the skills needed to produce these goods spread throughout Europe. However, while the production of this category of fabric represented an important element of the new textile industries, the most radical innovations sprang from external influences. European patterns of dress and domestic textiles were refashioned through the commercial, cultural and economic exchanges with Asia. Asian textiles redefined standard fabrics and reformulated consumer demand. Thereafter, Asian patterns and Asian cotton defined the ideal, ultimately sparking the emulative talents of European producers.

Sixteenth-century trade between India and the Iberian Peninsula introduced Iberian royalty and nobility to the distinctive floral patterns of printed and embroidered Asian textiles. In the seventeenth century, at the time of intensive contact with European trading companies, the Indian sub-continent was the largest producer of cotton textiles in the world. The scale of manufacturing was matched by the diversity of qualities, colours and patterns of the goods. In the early seventeenth century, Dutch and English traders auctioned novelties like painted quilts and these sold for a surprising profit. Individual items were soon followed by bales of textiles whose colours and designs were modified for the Western buyer at the direction of European merchants. Producers from many regions of the Indian sub-continent readily adapted their products for long-distance customers; the commercial appetite of the European traders seemed limitless (Irwin and Brett 1970: 1–4; Chaudhuri 1978b: 7; S. Chaudhuri 1997: 9–10). Between 1664 and 1678, the value of the English East India Company textile imports averaged between 60 and 70 per cent of their trade. Approximately one quarter of a million pieces of cloth were shipped to England in 1664; more than one million pieces were imported in 1684, comprising 84 per cent of the English trade with India. The Dutch East India Company was also responsive to the demand for textiles. Cottons and silks reached a value of 55 per cent of Dutch imports by about 1700 (Chaudhuri 1978a: 96–7, 282). Chintzes were soon the acknowledged 'ware of Gentlewomen in Holland' and were worn too by many others throughout northwestern Europe (Irwin and Schwartz 1966: 17).

East Indian textiles possessed distinctive features. First and foremost, the cottons were all washable and the dyes were generally colour-fast; these two factors alone represented a huge advantage over many fabrics of European manufacture. But this was not the only advantage enjoyed by Asian fabrics. These imports came in a diverse assortment of qualities and prices. Thus this miscellany of materials attracted consumers with pounds or pennies to spend. A guide book, written in 1696 for pedlars and shopkeepers in the textile trade, recorded information on over sixty textiles widely available at the end of the century. Over half the fabrics in this guide were of East Indian origin and the author's descriptions suggest the breadth of the market for these goods. For example, an 'ordinary sort' of muslin, called bettilies, was commonly used for head cloths and cravats, while the cheap dyed and flower-printed dungarees found regular sales among the 'ordinary People'; serunge, a chintz printed with 'very pretty Flowers', was bought by more affluent shoppers (F. J. 1696: 2, 7, 14; Lemire 1991: 12–21).

Calicoes and chintzes were among the new colonial consumer products which redefined material expectations and standards of comfort. In order to comprehend this impact, one must appreciate how widely these products were distributed and the breadth of the market they acquired. The leaders of trading companies, like Sir Josiah Child, long-time head of the English East India Company, worked assiduously to find buyers for their products where none previously existed. For example, it was not self-evident that cotton could be worn in northern climates. Child recognised that he and his associates had to work hard to 'introduce the using of Callicoe . . . in all these Northern parts of the world' (Chaudhuri 1978a: 287). One way to promote these goods was to produce commonly used ready-made articles of East Indian fabrics. The English East India Company arranged for the manufacture in India of vast quantities of goods, like shirts and shifts, which were then offered to European buyers. The promotion of high- to low-quality garments brought new types of utilitarian products to the attention of potential customers. The careful presentation of plain, painted and printed wares, at varying prices, offered novelty and comfort, and, for the merchants, the 'Possibility some of these things may gain that repute here as may give us cause of greater enlargement in them hereafter' (Irwin and Schwartz 1966: 36–7).

How effective were these bids to cultivate new markets? One fragmentary notation confirms the breadth of sales claimed by the 1696 guide book. The ledger of a south London haberdasher and pawnbroker hints at the degree to which these products permeated the market, even among the labouring classes. This shopkeeper resided in one of the poorer parishes of south London and he numbered among his customers a cross-section of skilled and unskilled men and women, working and trading in these environs. In 1669, against the name of his customer, Mary Taner, he listed a 'remnt of callico', which she had pawned (PRO, C 108/34). The 'meaner sort' readily adopted these bright washable fabrics into their daily dress, according to correspondents of the East India Company (Irwin and Schwartz 1966: 17).

The introduction of Asian fabrics into stylish wardrobes was tentative at first. In the mid-seventeenth century, painted cotton robes were initially worn by the fashionable only before retiring or on rising. However, the general movement of European fashions away from stiff, restrictive garb assisted the diffusion of Indian fabrics through the elite and middling ranks. Contemporaries remarked on the extent to which Indian materials became a part of normal attire. Decorative muslin aprons joined chintz petticoats and painted gowns as articles of display; they in turn were followed by calico head-dresses, hoods, sleeves and pockets for women, and shirts, cuffs, night shirts, robes, neckcloths and handkerchiefs for men (Cary 1696: 4–5).

Consumer choice: product competition

Retailers of East India products broached every channel of trade, domestic and colonial. Distribution began with the seasonal quarterly auctions by the principal East India trading companies in Amsterdam and London. These auctions were the first steps in a distribution network linking shopkeepers, great and small, with armies of pedlars

(Chaudhuri 1978a: 131–4). The characteristics of this trade are exemplified in the 1674 probate inventory of a London merchant tailor, Richard Read, seen in Figure 9.1.

The value of Read's 'East India commodities' was almost equal to the value of all the other textiles in his shop; moreover, the East India goods competed directly with the hollands, dimities and ossenbrigs of European make. East India merchandise pervaded the retail sector. In warehouses and shops there was a host of Oriental fabrics and ready-made items: Indian taffeta, 'bengale stuffe', pieces of 'Dungeree' and 'plaine bengall' (CLRO, Court of Orphans Inventories, 301 and 1885). In 1714, the London merchan tailor, Richard Cock, held over £1,000 in East India textiles in a London warehouse, as well as stock, such as cottons called 'mullmulls', in the hands of Mr James Ellwick of Amsterdam (CLRO, Court of Orphans Inventory, 3013). In the 1670s, specialist shops like that of the 'Indian Gown Maker', Edward Gunn, offered London shoppers a profusion of plain and fancy robes for men and women (GLRO, AM/Pi (I) 1673/33). The London merchant, William Taylor, died in 1692 with over £340 worth of stock in his shop, including a wide range of men's and women's accessories made from assorted cotton fabrics. Women could choose from muslin coifs, head cloths of striped or 'ordinary' muslin, quilted calico caps and calico hoods; men could pick out neckcloths from a choice of 'sea', flowered or mazareen muslin. Prices ranged from a few pence for a calico cap to over a shilling for more elaborate head cloths (CLRO, Court of Orphans Inventory, 2197). Consumers could buy East Indian cottons by the yard or ell, but also in ready-made forms, a fact that enhanced the sale of these commodities.

Outside the metropolis, shopkeepers of various sorts supplied muslin and calico to their customers. Legions of pedlars linked the urban retail outlets with rural buyers. For example, in 1669, a chapman in Cheshunt, Hertfordshire, numbered a dozen calico hoods among his stock priced at 5d each (PRO, PROB 4, 5058). Margaret Spufford affirmed the breadth of commercial activity among English pedlars during the seventeenth century. Their network moved copious quantities of merchandise from city tradesmen to towns, villages and rural communities. Spufford notes that in the late seventeenth century 'cottons, muslin, dimity and calico, were an important minor line' in the chapmen's stock-in-trade (Spufford 1984: 90). And, indeed, there is ample evidence of cheap striped and plain muslins and calico in the inventories of pedlars and shopkeepers in the provinces. The recent work of Laurence Fontaine on European pedlars charts an equally vigorous pedlar network throughout the north-west of continental Europe, one which grew on a somewhat later time frame than in England. However, in terms of the functioning of the trade Fontaine asserts that: 'The "Scotch Draper's"

Item	Value
A parcel of Lawns & cambricks & ossenbrigs	£328.08.05
A parcel of East India commodities	£619.02.10
A parcel of bag Cloth hollands & German Linen	£306.16.00
A parcel of canvas & dimities & other goods	£62.19.05
Summa	£1,317.06.08

Figure 9.1 Shop goods of Richard Read, merchant tailor, 1674. Source: CLRO, Court of Orphans Inventory, 122.

campaign was no different from that undertaken by the pedlar from the Auvergne or from the Dauphine' (Fontaine 1996: 88). Fed from urban stores, peripatetic traders conveyed cheap and attractive items to the hands of a wide assortment of buyers. Trade was cultivated among the wealthy, as well as among folks with only pennies to spare. Moreover, customers displayed an allegiance to these novel commodities.

Price was an important factor in the success of East Indian items. This, combined with aggressive marketing, opened areas of sale where none previously existed. Thus, during the 1680s, commercial patterns arose which foreshadowed those of the English cotton trade in the next century. For a time, in some markets, linen was overshadowed by calico. In the 1680s, in a bid to squeeze out illegal interlopers in their trade, the English East India Company flooded the market with textiles, reducing prices as well. Evidence of the significance of this manoeuvre survives in the records of the Hudson's Bay Company. Its accounts show that, for a time, aggressive marketing enabled cheap cottons to challenge European-made linens. From 1678 to 1689, the Hudson's Bay Company made steady purchases of quantities of calico shirts, along with linen shirts. There are nine years in which full records survive of these orders. Over this interval, the cheapest calico shirts were more frequently lower in price than the cheapest linen shirt. Calico shirts were more costly than the cheapest linen shirt during one year only. Cotton shirts cost less than linen in five out of the nine years of orders and could be bought for the same price as linen shirts on three occasions. As a consequence, the Hudson's Bay Company bought hundreds of calico shirts for shipment to trading stations in the North American sub-arctic (Hudson's Bay Company Archives, A 15/1–4). This pattern of substitution reflects the commercial strength of cotton, even when directed at an unlikely market. The price differential and aggressive selling had an even greater impact when directed at local customers, where knowledge of regional fashions and cultures could be put to good effect.

Floral fashions and the restructuring of textile demand

The European trading companies were very sensitive to the question of cost and struggled to keep prices low over the late seventeenth century. Their intermittent success accounts, in part, for the tremendous impact of these commodities in European markets. But there was another equally powerful factor which excited desire for East Indian textiles; that factor was rooted in a Western cultural response to flowers. Contemporaries recognised that the most distinctive visual feature of East Indian textiles was the vibrant 'Oriental' floral and arboreal designs applied to light textile surfaces. It was these motifs, perhaps more than the feel and weight of the fabrics, which intrigued the earliest buyers. Indeed, it was these motifs that were discussed at length by the opponents of East Indian textiles. 'On a sudden', wrote a critic of the imports, 'we saw all our women, rich and poor, cloath'd in Callico, printed and painted: the gayer and more tawdry the better' (N.A. 1727). As a fibre, cotton accepts dye better than does linen; moreover, Indian painting and dye techniques were far superior to those then current in Europe. The strength and vividness of the colours were outstanding. The visual impact was tremendous. As one expert noted in 1696: 'those [fabrics] that come from the Indies ready dyed blue, are much the better, they never lose the colour in washing as English-dyed cloth; you may know the English-dye from the Indian by the colours, for the Indian-dye is much evener dyed than the English, for the English hath brown and dark spots in it' (F.J. 1696: 27). A process of material transformation was under way by 1700, as more and more people wore or aspired to wear garments embellished with vivid blooms, trailing vines and botanic fancies.

Daniel Roche traced the composition and colour of the wardrobes of Parisians of several social ranks across the eighteenth century. Overall, the aristocracy displayed the most vibrant attire, as one might expect; among this group silks and cottons were in general use early in the eighteenth century. The bourgeoisie embraced the wearing of painted muslins and 'indiennes' (Figure 9.2). The patterned Indian garments stood out against a general backdrop of earth tones, solid greys, blacks and browns worn by most of the population that changed only slowly. But from their introduction, Indian fabrics became a less expensive alternative to the costly flowered brocades and brilliant damasks (Roche 1994: 126–33). Roche suggests that the most dramatic change in the composition of dress could be seen later in the eighteenth century. In this instance, the transformations in clothing and soft furnishings did not take place as soon in France as in England (Fairchilds 1993: 229). In England, as in Western Europe generally, one finds ample evidence of a passion for Indian painted fabrics among the affluent, for example in the 1684 inventory of a Surrey merchant, Peter Pruby. In his bedrooms and 'Closett' were listed 'Callicoe hangings about the Roome', 'a suite of painted Callicoe Curtains and Valences with white inside', plus 'two peeces of new Callicoe' and 'foure yards of fine painted Callicoe' for later use. Expensive fabrics were also decorated with floral prints and these found buyers among the middling and even lower social ranks. Indeed, it was the breadth of demand for these highly decorative fabrics which most concerned critics of luxury and competing manufacturers.

The trade in East Indian textiles brought to Europe a type of decorative material unlike anything previously seen. There was no local equivalent. Costly brocaded silks in floral patterns were certainly available. However, they were the exclusive choice of the elites. Botanic painted and printed fabrics from Asia introduced a type of fluid all-over pattern that did not depend on costly raw materials and high-priced labour. The calicoes, chintzes, muslins and percales, festooned with branches, leaves, repeating blossoms, birds and insects, were radiant expressions of nature which charmed and intrigued. Moreover, these products arrived in Europe when the perception of the natural world was in flux. Associated with this change was a passion for flowers and yearning to control and reorder the natural world. By the early seventeenth century, cut flowers graced the interiors of fashionable city homes, with an associated growth in commercial gardening and flower markets. The same vogue for flowers sparked a rise in floral paintings, which reached its apogee in the Netherlands (Schama 1993: 479). Landscapes, in turn, were modelled into diverse shapes, from the formal symmetric gardens of French and Italian inspiration, to the sculpted naturalised vistas of English estates (Mukerji 1993: 452–7).

Voyages of exploration and colonisation brought flowering plants and shrubs from Asia and the Americas to eager European collectors. Specimens found their way from plant collectors' nurseries to the stylised estates of the nobility, from the formal beds of botanic gardens to the prosaic gardens of humble enthusiasts. The floral fashion captured souls and opened wallets. Fernand Braudel described the 'urbanised countryside', created by an elite with a craze for rural pleasures, in remodelled sylvan settings (Braudel 1981: 281–2). Around 1700, the Earl of Chesterfield's Derbyshire estate was a

Figure 9.2 John Tradescant's botanical discoveries are memorialised in this family portrait, *Portrait of Hester Tradescant and Her Stepson*, which also highlights the striking floral petticoat worn by his wife, E. de Critz. © Ashmolean Museum, University of Oxford.

magnet for travellers like Celia Fiennes, who noted 'that which is most admired . . . by all persons and excite their curiosity to come and see is the Gardens and Waterworks'. This inveterate traveller routinely jotted in her diary the highs and lows of botanic expression in English gardens; the Dean of Winchester's disappointed: 'the Garden is but small . . . in an old fashion'd form, but neatly kept'. It contrasted with the Fellows' garden at New College Oxford, where 'they take much delight in greens of all sorts [like] Myrtle Oringe and Lemons' (Fiennes 1949: 171–2, 37, 47, 90–1). John Evelyn listed the gardens he enjoyed, from the 'Paradise' of the Pitti Palace in Florence to the charm of the more modest English gardens in Norwich, in 'which all the Inhabitans excell in this Citty' (Evelyn 1985: 71, 241). Seventeenth-century Dutch migrants to

England introduced commercial flower growing around Norwich, offering 'pleasurable curiosities' to enthusiasts among the local gentry. At least fifteen commercial nurseries supplied the London market by the 1690s (Thirsk 1978: 46; Thomas 1963: 224). The ephemeral nature of the seasonal blooms stands in contrast to the monumental energies poured into the creation of gardens. In Chandra Mukerji's words, these gardens were 'testifying to the economic reach of the international capitalist trading system . . . gardens were constituted as models of the exercise of power over nature'. The 'culture of collection', as Mukerji terms it, may well have been one of the distinguishing social markers differentiating the aristocracy (Mukerji 1993: 440, 442). But this passion for things floral did not end at their garden walls. The normative patterns of display were also transformed for men and women, as floral motifs were transcribed into printed, embroidered and quilted elements of apparel. Slippers to waistcoats, petticoats to handkerchiefs were ornamented with botanic inventions.

Furthermore, a predilection for flowers was not class-specific. The culture of flowers was entwined in the religious and secular traditions of European society. For example, wreaths, nosegays and decorative flowers were common cultural idioms. Goody notes for the late Middle Ages that: 'The new culture of flowers emerges in the interaction of high and low' (Goody 1993: 164). The same claim could be made for the early modern period. Whether or not the conceptual basis of floral culture was the same for courtiers at Versailles or apprentices in Cheapside, there was a shared attraction across the social classes. Simultaneously, there emerged a wide and deepening market for fabrics embellished with richly naturalistic designs. The passion for flowers provided a medium and a motivation for the developing calico craze. Contemporaries were perhaps accurate in their claims that

> all the mean People, the Maid Servants, and indifferently poor Persons, . . .
> are now cloathed in Callicoe, or printed Linen; moved to it as well for the
> Cheapness, as the Lightness of the Cloth, and the Gaity [sic] of the Colours
> . . . let any one but cast their Eyes among the meaner Sort playing in the
> Street, or of the better Sort at Boarding School.
>
> (*The Just Complaints of the Poor Weavers Truly Represented* 1747, II)

Certainly in 1718 and 1719, ordinary London women made plain their preference for printed calico gowns, to the fury of local weavers. At the height of the campaign to ban flowered cottons, fashionable ladies and the labouring wives clung to their chintz gowns, defying moral and physical coercion.

Prohibition, imitation and English industry

Passionate denunciations inevitably followed the spread of novel colonial wares; the disruptive power of popular luxuries preoccupied commentators. Though coffee, tea, chocolate and sugar brought ancillary employment they also sparked fierce debates about the effect of popular luxury. The success of East Indian textiles unleashed similarly dramatic responses, but with added elements distinct from the question of dress. For these wares charmed generations of consumers at the same time as they challenged local manufacturers and sartorial expectations. Oriental fabrics were imbued with alien and gendered characteristics. They were depicted as effeminate luxuries, corrupting in particular the female populace with their lightness and brightness, while impoverishing deserving artisans. The language of this debate was frequently couched in terms of gender antagonisms with women asserting their right to dress as they pleased and weavers claiming the right to work and constrain the choice of apparel for women, as necessary (Lemire 1991: 38–9). The loud and sometimes violent English campaign against calicoes began in the 1680s and ended finally, in 1721, with a ban on almost all East Indian fabrics. This crusade pitted the interests of the wool trade and silk weavers against those of the East India merchants and consumers. As the fashion for these fabrics swept Europe a number of governments attempted to ban these commodities, forbidding their citizens legal access to these products. In a bid to protect regional industries and to preserve the sumptuary equilibrium, nations invoked legislative prohibitions. Between 1681 and 1716, France produced thirty pieces of legislation against these fabrics; Spain instituted its ban in 1713, while in Prussia, an absolute ban on calicoes, chintzes and other cotton materials was effected in 1721 (Berg 1997: 33–4; Bendewalk and Kasper 1951: 62–3). However, legislative victories could not compel consumer allegiance. In the Netherlands quantities of calicoes continued to be sold and used. Indeed, chintzes and calicoes formed the stuff of everyday regional dress (Irwin and Brett 1970: 30–1). At the national level, the Netherlands acted as a repository for illicit trade with neighbouring countries. One British author applauded the Netherlands for permitting the continued use of Asian textiles:

> Our Neighbours, the *Dutch*, are a wise People, and without doubt, understand all the different Branches of Trade, and their own Interest, as well as any Nation in the World; and though they have many considerable Manufactories of their own, especially of Silk, yet they have not prohibited, or so much as laid any high Duty upon any foreign Manufacture; well knowing, that excessive Duties are great Encouragement to running [smuggling], and that Prohibitions make People more eager for that which is forbid.
>
> (*Weavers Pretences* 1719)

This trade, among other factors, convinced many that consumer preference could not be legislated against. An astute critic of the English ban observed that: 'all those who wear Callicoe or Linen now, wou'd not wear Woollen Stuffs if there was no such thing as Printed Callicoe or Linen, but *Dutch* or *Hambro'* Strip'd and Chequer'd Linens, and other things of that kind' . . . (*Further Examination* 1719: 20).

Almost from the first appearance of East Indian textiles, artisans in Marseille, Amsterdam and London worked to replicate Indian techniques and Indian designs. The process, in Schama's words, 'domesticated . . . exoticism' (Schama 1987: 196). The 1686 diaspora of French Huguenots spread the calico printing trades in which they specialised to Berlin, Bremen, Frankfurt, Neuchatel, Lausanne and Geneva. Migration in the eighteenth century extended the trade from Spain to Moscow. Textile printing provided an avenue whereby Europeans could capitalise on fashion. By the 1670s, plain cotton cloth was being printed in workshops around London and in Essex in the Indian style (Figure 9.3). By 1719, some of the London printing works employed from 100 to 200 men and boys (Chapman and Chassagne 1981: 5–7, 14). Moreover, there was a second area of emulation. Ambitious entrepreneurs proposed, as early as 1691, that

Figure 9.3 Jacob Stampe's seventeenth-century tradecard highlights the transformation of fabric from plain to flowered. © Bodleian Library, University of Oxford, Douce Adds 138, no. 88.

they launch a competitive manufacture of calicoes. Similar proposals were repeated in the 1720s. With little fanfare, generations of local weavers struggled to replicate the Indian fabrics in blends of linen and cotton, with Indian cotton yarn and pure linen. In the textile industry, as in other trades, imitation was the catalyst for innovation (Berg 1998: 76–88).

Innovation was not the preserve of any one region in Europe. From the linen districts of the Lower Rhine to the textile regions of Lowland Scotland, artisans blended imported cotton warps with various sorts of linen weft. Herbert Kisch noted the speed with which cotton warps were introduced by business-minded merchants in the Rhineland, during the late seventeenth century (Kisch 1989: 115–26). In Dutch and Flemish towns the skills in cotton production, known since medieval times, circulated among local communities. Migration brought these arts from the Low Countries to England. Early European-made copies of Asian fabrics found buyers, encouraging experimentation. Ironically, national bans on calicoes, intended to eliminate cottons, actually protected local manufacturers working on calico substitutes. Demand was met increasingly by linen manufacturers and their mixed cotton/linen wares. And it was in the linen trade, most particularly in the English county of Lancashire, where the greatest progress was made in cotton/linen production. Thus, it is this example which will receive the greatest attention here, but Lancashire's successful industrialisation should not obscure the fact that in many other regions of Europe significant advances occurred in the cotton industry (see the list of references for other regional and national studies). The 1696 probate inventory of a London 'outfitter' contains various examples of these goods, probably of English make, including one 'flowered' fustian and another 'coloured'. Both were counterfeits of Indian goods (CLRO, Court of Orphans Inventory, 2262). Over the eighteenth century, regional British industries devised new techniques which enabled them to make better facsimiles of East Indian products. The variety, price and inventive printed designs, characteristic of East Indian textiles, were the models to which manufacturers aspired.

Experimentation persisted and by mid-century a range of cottons, of pure and mixed fibres, were sold to middling and labouring people. The Lancashire cotton/linen industry developed in incremental steps over the first half of the eighteenth century, relying initially on imported Indian thread, but more and more producing cotton weft from imported raw cotton. It continued to be illegal to make, own or use most cottons textiles, according to the Act of 1721. However, in 1734, after a final outburst against the makers of cotton/linen goods by the wool industry, the authorities ceased all official harassment of the nascent English cotton industry. In the 1740 probate inventory of Daniel Silver, a salesmen from Faversham, Kent, one finds several modest examples of these English wares: plain 'white cotton' at 1s a yd, men's and boy's blue and green cotton waistcoats at 2s 6d and 2s each, checked shirts at 2s a piece (Kent Archives Office, PRC/ii/81/238). A later probate inventory from 1750 further illustrates the merchandise provided by this growing industry. This Southampton chapman carried various sorts of cotton accessories: 72 pairs of stockings, 156 pairs of gloves, caps of several sorts and two cotton gowns (Hampshire Record Office, 1750 AD 012/1–2). This and many other examples testify to the successful adaptation of the British cotton/linen industry. These manufacturers were in the fortunate position of having their chief competitors barred from the home market. At the same time there was a seemingly insatiable demand for the closest facsimile to the prohibited textiles. As a contemporary noted, 'the Humour of the People [runs] so much upon wearing painted or printed Callicoes and Linnens' (*Weekly Journal*, 27 June 1719). In 1738, it was claimed that the majority of Manchester linen was in fact mixed with cotton. A fuller record of the state of the English cotton industry survives by chance for the 1750s. Few examples of international industrial espionage are as timely as John Holker's report on the Lancashire textile industry, prepared for the French government. His report reflects the technological challenges faced by that regional industry; it also reveals a product profile modelled on its East Indian precursors.

By mid-century Lancashire offered a diversified range of stock. Some evolved from the traditional European hard-wearing fustians. The advances in fustian manufacture provided a stable foundation for the Lancashire trade. Pure cotton velvets offered a touch of luxury, particularly the flowered velvets, combined with warmth at reasonable price; thickset, diaper, jean, nankin and corduroy promised utilitarian service (Musée des Arts Décoratifs, 54, G.G. 2). However, most of the sixty-seven cotton/linen fabrics, listed in Holker's report, aimed to meet the ongoing trend for light, washable, colourful goods. Checks, chintzes and stripes comprised the bulk of the textiles then made in Lancashire. The plain fabrics afforded a stable medium for the application of prints. The common elements of these three categories of fabrics were colour and pattern; variety was assured in the different weights, finishes and prices (Lemire 1991: 79–86). Even after two and a half centuries, the colours and prints of these samples retain an extraordinary vitality that hints at their impact when first worn. More and more of these fabrics were embellished by British printers, characterised as having 'no great Taste in Painting . . . but a wild kind of Imagination . . . fit to attract the Eye'. This grudging assessment concluded that 'the whole Kingdom is furnished with Commodities of this sort' (Campbell 1747: 115). Holker reported that, in Lancashire, calicoes were produced in such volume that almost every week, 'a thousand rolls [were] being sold and sent to London unbleached' (Musée des Arts Décoratifs, G.G. 2).

Was the 'whole Kingdom' rapt with these printed, painted cloths? So it seems. But the frenzied calico craze of the late seventeenth and early eighteenth centuries, which followed their introduction, had abated by mid-century to a steady infatuation. There was now a more measured expectation that light fabrics, adorned with new prints and motifs, would be part of one's material environment. Moreover, both expectation and demand extended across a broad social spectrum. I undertook an extensive survey of English court records across the eighteenth century, using the Old Bailey Records as a foundation, cross-checking these with legal documents from numerous provinces and regions. This qualitative study indicated who bought and owned the new cottons. I found a pattern of ever-widening ownership among labouring women and working men, artisans and maid servants, home owners and shopkeepers, gentry and aspiring gentry. Seaman, housekeeper, captain, ironmonger, coal-heaver, servant, milkman, stable-keeper, ostler, merchant, gentlewoman, cider-merchant, hairdresser, spinster, shoemaker, apothecary, baker, nurse, ship's captain and 'servant to a milk woman': collectively, these individuals bought, owned and used an ever-wider assortment of cottons, from the 1730s to 1780s (Lemire 1991: 205–19). Thus, one is not surprised to read, in 1765, of the loss by a 'poor Woman' of her much prized 'small running sprigged Purple and White Cotton Gown, washed only once, tied down with red Tape at the Bosom, round plain Cuffs, and the Bottom bound round with broad Tape' (*The Public Advertiser*, 19 February 1765). This is not to suggest that there was a homogeneity of ownership throughout the population. Income, social ranks, occupation and, to a degree, geography, impinged on the capacity of men and women to purchase new consumer goods. However, interest and demand showed a surprising conformity.

French historians are fortunate in having a wealth of personal inventories which enable them to trace consumer choices across the eighteenth century for virtually all ranks. Daniel Roche offers evidence of changing preferences for fabrics and colour. A brief summary of his findings suggests the important place of cottons later in the century, even among the lower social ranks. In the years prior to the Revolution, among all Parisian wage-earners, cottons comprised about 38 per cent of their wardrobes; this figure rose to 40 per cent for domestics (Roche 1994: 138). Roche's data are even more striking for the female sample, thus it is the female sample alone that will be considered in detail. Figure 9.4 summarises his findings. Cotton comprised 57 and 59 per cent of the clothing of Parisian women wage earners and domestic servants respectively, by the 1780s. Clothing for the wealthier bourgeois/rentier class of Parisian women was made up of only 23 per cent cotton, with many more silk and linen garments. Thus,

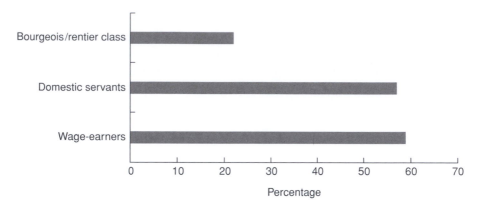

Figure 9.4 Cotton apparel owned by women, Paris, *c*. 1789. Proportion of clothing made of cotton. Source: Roche 1994: 144–7.

cotton textiles assumed a particular importance for the women of the lower social ranks, offering the means to a brighter, more vibrant public appearance. In terms of colour, reds comprised 20 per cent and yellows, blues and greens 26 per cent of female wage-earners' apparel; for domestics, reds comprised 22 per cent and yellows, blues and greens 28 per cent of their wardrobes. This is a startling metamorphosis from the common garb around 1700, predominantly wool in composition and black, grey and brown in colour. Roche confirmed that '[t]here was a correlation between lighter garments and brighter colours' (Roche 1994: 126–7, 144–6). As stated above, the timing of these changes in England and the Netherlands certainly occurred earlier, particularly in the urban commercial regions. Nevertheless, the statistically conclusive findings from Paris are extremely valuable; they depict parallel patterns of change in France that were well established among other populations of wage-earning and labouring people.

A York pawnbroker's ledger offers a mechanism to assess the ownership and use of cotton products, in the 1770s, for equivalent sorts of English people. It has been suggested that the north of England was less closely entwined in the consumer 'revolution' than the south of the country, or at the very least, less well served by retailers (Styles 1994: 139–41). However, in the case of British-made cottons, the north of England was well supplied. Dozens of pedlar firms fixed their home base in proximity to textiles towns like Stockport and Wigan, other firms of Scots pedlars carried Scottish and English fabrics to buyers throughout the north and Midlands. The trade between one Manchester firm and customers in Halifax, Leeds, Wakefield, York and Hull affirmed that this region received steady shipments from the hub of the cotton industry (Lemire 1991: 127, 135–7, 146–60).

The York pawnbroker, George Fettes, began his trade about 1770 and the pledge book covers 1777 to 1779. Two sample periods were assessed: December 1777 and June 1778 (Acc. 38, York City Archives). During these two months all pledges were recorded, along with the name of the borrower, the goods pledged and amount borrowed. These two periods, six months apart, permitted a comparative sampling with seasonal fluctuations taken into account. In the late eighteenth century, as in previous periods, pawning was normally a female occupation. Figures 9.5 and 9.6 present a

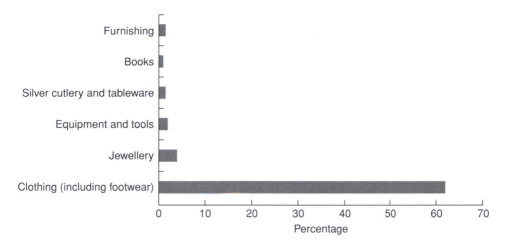

Figure 9.5 Goods pawned with George Fettes, December 1777. Source: Acc. 38, York City Archives.

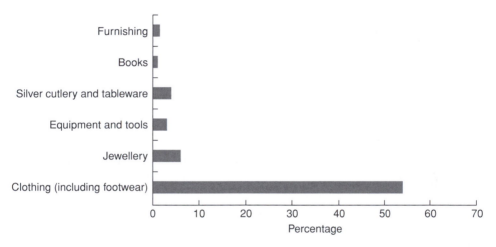

Figure 9.6 Goods pawned with George Fettes, June 1778. Source: Acc. 38, York City Archives.

detailed summary of the categories of goods pledged. In this, as in others pawn books, one finds a disproportionate volume of the most valuable of household property – clothing and textiles (Lemire 1998). Despite the fact that Yorkshire boasted vibrant wool and linen industries, the labouring and artisanal men and women of York also included cottons among their belongings. The pawned goods denote articles already in their possession; these items were not necessarily new. The pawns present a snapshot of commodities in use. However, this sample does not yield a precise picture, since most articles were not identified by fabric. Therefore, this ledger quite possibly under-represents the numbers of cotton goods brought in by customers. For example, by this date check textiles were most probably cotton, or a cotton/linen blend. The fibre composition of these items is stipulated on only two occasions when checks were listed as 'linen check' – no doubt exceptions to the rule. Therefore, all other check goods are

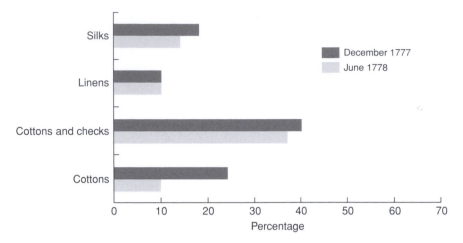

Figure 9.7 Textiles pawned, York 1777–8. Proportion of different textiles, Acc. 38, York City Archives.

counted as cotton, but they are counted separately. Logically, more cotton items were pawned in the December period than in June. Figure 9.7 demonstrates the relative volume of cotton, linens and silks pawned in those two periods. In December 1777, at least 12 per cent of all textiles pawned were cotton; if check wares are included, the number jumps to over 20 per cent. In June 1778, 10 per cent of pawned textiles were cotton and, when checks are added, this figure rises to nearly 18 per cent. Thus, among a largely labouring clientele, in a region distant from the retail dynamics of southern England, cottons comprised a minimum of at least 10 per cent and a maximum of over 20 per cent of textiles pawned in a major provincial centre. In the same December period, fabrics described as silk comprised just 9 per cent of goods pawned, while items specified as linen accounted for about 5 per cent. The June entries show 7 per cent of textiles as silk and about 5 per cent as linen. There may be only a tenuous correlation between the items pawned and the relative quantities of various textiles owned by this population. However, the pledges do reveal the significant integration of cottons into a regional market.

What cottons did these women and men carry from their homes to the pawnshop? The belongings spanned the gamut: coarse cotton stockings and ribbed hose, yards of thickset, velvet and 'Manchester' cotton, women's cotton gowns in great numbers – described as old, dirty, of dark cotton or combining silk and cotton – yards of printed and flowered cotton, petticoats, nankeen and fustian breeches, fustian coats, aprons of muslin – sprigged, striped and plain – handkerchiefs of cotton and fine muslin, a muslin hood, and many dozens of work-a-day check aprons and handkerchiefs. In other words, this cross-section of materials reflected much of the output of the industrialising cotton industry. Over this period there was a steady substitution of cotton textiles for various wool, silk, linen and leathers. That substitution was most marked in the last third of the eighteenth century. Nankeen, corduroy and other sorts of fustian breeches were favoured over leather; while printed cotton gowns were preferable to those made of wool, silk or linen. Production of traditional fustians expanded in quantity and quality over this period, as manufacturers solved various technical problems of production. This evolution in dress accelerated after the 1760s, as price and production innovations brought a greater variety of textiles to the marketplace. As more consumers became familiar with these products they were intrigued by their easy care and by the wide range of fabric weights, patterns and colours. By the late eighteenth century even gentlemen adopted corduroy breeches for athletic endeavours. The new categories of velveteens and corduroys turned a utilitarian staple into a cloth worn by almost all classes. And, on occasion, these fustian fabrics were also flowered, combining the restyled utility fabric with the floral inspired motifs of Asian origin.

Dye techniques were greatly improved by this period (Wadsworth and Mann 1931: 178–821), while printers devised more efficient techniques to produce flowered and sprigged fabrics. Indeed, it is worth noting that the vogue for floral prints was unabated in the late eighteenth century. As the elder Peel explained to a Manchester gathering in 1786, 'three parts out of four of printed goods are consumed by the lower class of people'. These included a majority of floral patterns, of leaves variously disposed, small circles, pippins . . . spots, and flower heads of a daisy or buttercup form, which . . . stared the beholder full in the face' (Chapman and Chassagne 1981: 78). The customers at the York pawnshop owned garments embellished by Peel or his competitors. My earlier studies confirm that the consumer behaviour evident in York was replicated in south Wales, as well as central and southern England. Thus, Mrs Barber, a lighterman's wife living in Surrey, treasured her cotton gowns 'one a hop pattern, the other purple and white'. And Mr Andrews' London servants sorely missed their stolen cotton gowns, 'one a white Ground, with running Sprigs and Flowers, the other a dark Purple, with white Strawberries in Large Diamonds' (*The Gazetteer and New Daily Advertiser*, 16 January 1778; *The Public Advertiser*, 24 January 1766). The fashion for cotton extended from labourers and maid servants, maltsters and joiners, mariners and clerks, through publican and genteel widow, to a clergyman's daughter and other gentle folk. Barbara Johnson, a genteel resident of rural Buckinghamshire, displayed a strong affinity for various light, bright fabrics and botanical prints among her purchases (Rothstein 1987). From the 1760s onwards, her selections included steadily more cottons, such as, in 1780 an English chintz with flowers in two colours, or, in 1792, a dark ground chintz with a leaf pattern in pink and ochre (Lemire 1991: 110–13). Even in the forest hinterland of the new American republic, English chintz formed part of the web of trade. In describing the late eighteenth-century world of Martha Ballard, a midwife in Hallowell Maine, Laurel Thatcher Ulrich, notes that: 'Lumber went down the Kennebec [River] English chintz came up' (Thatcher Ulrich 1990: 90). Similarly, in continental and Scandinavian markets, the genteel and the common favoured the newly made cottons. The taste for light patterned curtains and upholstery, for brighter outerwear and washable innerwear, broke the monopoly of traditional European materials.

Conclusion

In the late twentieth century, running shoes, joggers, light-weight hiking boots and river sandals revolutionised what we wear on our feet, as well as the way footwear is made. Leather shoes and boots, fabric slippers and mules, worn for most of the early twentieth century, would be quite recognisable to our ancestors of centuries ago. The common footwear now striding down pavements and across parks would astonish fore-bears of seventy years' or two hundred years' distance. I mention this to jog our historic imagination to a greater material sensitivity. An equally momentous shift in the physical property of dress occurred during the seventeenth and eighteenth centuries with the diffusion of cotton textiles from rare exotics to daily apparel. The substance of dress was permanently altered; so too was the content and comfort of households. More dramatic still was the visual change. Painted and printed Indian fabrics recast the material idiom of daily life. To the ubiquitous monotony of drab-coloured coats, jackets and gowns were added a constant stream of vivid printed garments. Textiles embellished with stylised floral motifs became a permanent feature of homes and of personal adornment; they became a permanent decorative component of material culture that may be seen in our homes and in our fashions to this day.

East Indian textiles were an archetype of popular consumer merchandise. The products they brought to the market permanently changed the dynamics of textile production and sale. Joan Thirsk identified the importance of this new commercial structure, stating that: 'When we survey the magnificent range of choice available to the customer in seventeenth-century England, we are compelled to think deeply about the economic significance of quality and variety in consumer goods and the influence which different classes exerted upon producers' (Thirsk 1978: 107). Calicoes and chintzes redefined the textile markets of Europe. Among the labouring classes, the middling sort and the elite, East Indian textiles inspired new waves of fashionable demand. This demand was captured in the next instance through the innovations of European manufacturers, most dramatically by the British. That cotton industry thrived by addressing the technical challenges of production, by cultivating new generations of vibrant floral-inspired prints and by assuring a diverse price structure in their products. The East India trade changed both the industrial and the cultural environment of Europe, altering forever Western decor and Western dress, while setting the model to be followed by later industries. Material culture was transformed in the process.

Bibliography

General

Baines, E. (1835) *History of the Cotton Manufacture in Great Britain*, London.

Berg, M., ed. (1991) *Markets and Manufactures in Early Industrial Europe*, London.

Carlano, M. and Slamon, L., eds (1985) *French Textiles from the Middle Ages through the Second Empire*, Wadsworth Atheneum, Hartford, CT.

Cavaciocchi, S., ed. (1993) *La seta in Europa: sec. XIII–XX*, Istituto Internazionale di Storia Economica 'F. Datini', Prato.

Chapman, S. D. (1967) *The Early Factory Masters*, Newton Abbot.

Chapman, S. D. and Chassagne, S. (1981) *European Textile Printers in the Eighteenth Century*, London.

Kerridge, E. (1985) *Textile Manufactures in Early Modern England*, Manchester.

King, D. ed. (1980) *British Textile Design in the Victoria and Albert Museum*, I and II, Tokyo.

King, D. and Levey, S. (1993) *Embroidery in Britain from 1200 to 1750*, Victoria and Albert Museum, London.

Kurrer, W. (1840) *Geschichte der Zeugdruckerei*, Nuremburg.

Lütge, F., ed. (1964) *Die wirtschaftliche Situation in Deutschland and Osterreich um die Wende 18.–19. Jh*, Stuttgart.

Montgomery, F. M. (1970) *Printed Textiles: English and American Cottons and Linens, 1719–1850*, London.

Montgomery, F. M. (1984) *Textiles in America, 1650–1870*, New York and London.

Pollard, S. (1991) 'Regional Markets and National Development', in M. Berg, ed., *Markets and Manufacture in Early Industrial Europe*, London.

Rothstein, N. (1994) *Woven Textile Design in Britain to 1750*, Victoria and Albert Museum, London.

Schwartz, L. (1992) *London in the Age of Industrialisation*, Cambridge.

Torras, J. (1991) 'The Old and the New: Marketing Networks and Textile Growth in Eighteenth-century Spain', in M. Berg, ed., *Markets and Manufacture in Early Industrial Europe*, London.

Primary documents

Manuscripts

Berkshire Record Office, Reading: D/AI 197/64.

Corporation of London Records Office: Court of Orphans Inventories.

Greater London Record Office: AM/PI (I) 1673/33.

Hampshire Record Office, Winchester: 21 M 65 D3/503; 1750 AD 012/1–2.

Hudson's Bay Company Archives, Winnipeg, Canada: Grand Journals, A 15/1–4.

Kent Archives Office, Maidstone: PRC/II/81/238.

Musée des Arts Décoratifs, Paris: G.G. 2.

Public Record Office: C 108/34; PROB 3; PROB 5.

York City Archives: Acc. 38.

Early printed sources

Campbell, R. (1747) *The London Tradesman*, London.

Cary, J. (1696) A *Discourse Conserning the East India Trade*, London.

Defoe, D. (1725) *The London Ladies Dressing-Room: Or, The Shopkeepers Wives Inventory*, London.

Evelyn, J. (1985) *The Diary of John Evelyn*, ed. J. Bowle, Oxford.

F. J. (1696) *The Merchant's Ware-House Laid Open: Or, The Plain Dealing Linnen-Draper*, London.

Fiennes, Celia (1949) *The Journeys of Celia Fiennes*, ed. C. Morris, London.

Further Examination (1719) *A Further Examination of the Weavers Pretences*, London.

The Gazeteer and New Daily Advertiser.

The Just Complaints of the Poor Weavers Truly Represented (1747), in J. Smith, *Chronicon rusticum-commerciale; Or Memoirs of Wool etc.* 2 vols, London, reprinted 1968.

N. A. (1727) A *Brief Deduction of the Original Progress and Immense Increase of Woollen Manufacture*, London.

Pollexfen, J. (1697) A *Discourse of Trade, Coyn and Paper Credit*, London.

The Public Advertiser.

Weavers Pretences (1719) *The Weavers Pretences Examined; Being a Full and Impartial Enquiry*, London.

Weekly Journal.

Secondary documents

Bendewalk, E. and Kasper, K. (1951) *Fairy Fancy on Fabric*, Braunschweig, 2nd edition.

Berg, M. (1994) *The Age of Manufactures, 1700–1820: Industry, Innovation and Work in Britain*, London, 2nd edition.

Berg, M. (1997) Manufacturing the Orient: Asian commodities and European industry, 1500–1800, in *Prodotti e techiche d'Oltremare nelle economie Europee: secc. XIII–XVIII*, 2nd ser., 29, Istituto Internazionale di Storia Economica 'F. Datini', Prato.

Braudel, F. (1981) *The Structures of Everyday Life: Civilization and Capitalism 15th–18th Century*, New York.

Chapman, S. D. (1967) *The Early Factory Masters: The Transition to the Factory System in the Midlands Textile Industry*, Newton Abbot.

Chapman, S. D. (1983) 'David Evans and Co., the Last of the Old London Textile Printers', *Textile History*, 14, 1.

Chapman, S. D. (1985) 'Quantity Versus Quality in the British Industrial Revolution: The Case of Printed Textiles', *Northern History*, 21.

Chapman, S. D. and Chassagne, S. (1981) *European Textile Printers in the Eighteenth Century*, London.

Chassagne, S. (1991) *Le coton et ses patrons: France, 1760–1840*, Paris.

Chassagne, S. (1993) 'L'innovation technique dans l'industrie textile pendant la Revolution', *Histoire, économie et société*.

Chaudhuri, K. N. (1978a) *The Trading World of Asia and the English East India Company, 1660–1760*, Cambridge.

Chaudhuri, K. N. (1978b) 'Some Reflections on the World of Trade of the 17th and 18th Centuries: A Reply', *Journal of European Economic History*.

Chaudhuri, K. N. (1997) 'Indian Cotton Industry and Its Production Organization, *c.* 1600–1750', unpublished conference proceedings, Manchester.

Edwards, M. M. (1967. *The Growth of the British Cotton Trade, 1780–1815*. Manchester.

Evans, J. 1931. *Pattern in Western Europe, 1180–1900*, II, Oxford.

Fairchilds, C. (1993) 'The Production and Marketing of Populuxe Goods in Eighteenth-century Paris', in J. Brewer and R. Porter, eds, *Consumption and the World of Goods*, London.

Fontaine, L. (1996) *History of Pedlars in Europe*, Cambridge.

Goody, J. (1993) *The Culture of Flowers*, Cambridge.

Gullickson, G. (1986) *The Spinners and Weavers of Auffray: Rural Industry and the Sexual Division of Labour in a French Village, 1750–1850*, Cambridge.

Hundert, E. J. (1994) *The Enlightenment Fable: Bernard Mandeville and the Discovery of Society*, Cambridge.

Irwin, J. and Brett, K. (1970) *Origins of Chintz*, London.

Irwin, J. and Schwartz, P. R. (1966) *Studies in Indo-European Textile History*, Ahmedabad.

Kisch, H. (1989) *From Domestic Manufacture to Industrial Revolution: The Case of the Rhineland Textile Districts*, New York.

Lemire, B. (1991) *Fashion's Favourite: The Cotton Trade and the Consumer in Britain, 1660–1800*, Oxford.

Lemire, B. (1998) 'Petty Pawns and Informal Lending: Gender and the Transformation of Small Scale Credit in England, *c.* 1600–1800', in P. K. O'Brien and K. Bruland, eds, *From Family Firms to Corporate Capitalism: Essays in Business and Industrial History in Honour of Peter Mathias*, Oxford.

Mazzaoui, M. (1981) *The Italian Cotton Industry in the Later Middle Ages, 1100–1600*, Cambridge and Madison.

Mukerji, C. (1993) 'Reading and Writing with Nature: A Materialist Approach to French Formal Gardens', in J. Brewer and R. Porter, eds, *Consumption and the World of Goods*, London.

Reddy, W. (1984) *The Rise of Market Culture: The Textile Trade and French Society, 1750–1850*, Cambridge.

Roche, D. (1994) *The Culture of Clothing: Dress and Fashion in the 'Ancien Régime'*, Cambridge.

Rose, M. B., ed. (1996) *The Lancashire Cotton Industry: A History since 1700*, Preston.

Rothstein, N., ed. (1987) *Barbara Johnson's Album of Fashions and Fabrics*, London.

Schama, S. (1987) *The Embarrassment of Riches: An Interpretation of Dutch Culture in the Golden Age*, London.

Schama, S. (1993) 'Perishable Commodities: Dutch Still-life Paintings and the "Empire of Things"', in J. Brewer and R. Porter, eds, *Consumption and the World of Goods*, London.

Schmidt, J.-M. (1982) 'The Origins of the Textile Industry in Alsace: The Beginning of the Manufacture of Printed Cloth at Wesserling (1762–1802)', *Textile History*, 13.

Shteir, A. B. (1996) *Cultivating Women, Cultivating Science: Flora's Daughters and Botany in England, 1760–1860*, Baltimore.

Spufford, M. (1984) *The Great Reclothing of Rural England*, London.

Styles, J. (1994) 'Clothing the North: The Supply of Non-lite Clothing in the Eighteenth-century North of England', *Textile History*, 25.

Thatcher Ulrich, L. (1990) A *Midwife's Tale: The Life of Martha Ballard, Based on Her Diary, 1785–1812*, New York.

Thirsk, J. (1978) *Economic Policy and Projects: The Development of a Consumer Society in Early Modern England*, Oxford.

Thomas, K. (1983) *Man and the Natural World: Changing Attitudes in England, 1500–1800*, Harmondsworth.

Thomas, P. J. (1963) *Mercantilism and the East India Trade*, London, reprinted New York, 1984.

Thomson, J. K. J. (1991) 'State Intervention in the Catalan Calico-printing Industry in the Eighteenth Century', in M. Berg, ed., *Markets and Manufacture in Early Industrial Europe*, London.

Thomson, J. K. J. (1992) *A Distinctive Industrialization: Cotton in Barcelona, 1728–1832*, Cambridge.

Wadsworth, A. P. and Mann, J. de L. (1931. *The Cotton Trade and Industrial Lancashire*. Manchester.

Fashion and silk design

Lesley Ellis Miller

In the first decade of the twenty-first century, the notion of a 'fashion system' is well established. It conjures up regular professional catwalk shows of fashionable dress in a number of cities worldwide, the circulation of those styles to wide audiences via the mass media, and the adoption of some styles by large numbers of consumers, usually via wholesale production and high-street retailing. The 'fashion cognoscenti' recognise instantly creators' hallmark designs and can link them to a particular season. Less familiar – though thoroughly embedded in this system – the fabrics used in these collections are also identifiable by season. Indeed, the very roots of the circulation of dress styles can be traced to a 'textile-fashion system' that emerged in late seventeenth-century France.

Fashion itself was not a French invention and existed long before the seventeenth century. Its organisation via silk design, however, is particularly well-documented from this period onwards in Europe. Moreover, its exploitation became extremely systematic in the sense that a variety of interested parties collaborated consciously in the creation, selection, production and promotion of recognisable seasonal patterns. The mercantilist initiatives of Louis XIV and his first minister Jean-Baptiste Colbert were first to harness fashion in the interests of the French economy. Focusing their attention on certain luxury textiles, notably silks, linens and lace, they sought to make France self-sufficient and to capture overseas markets. They did so by offering financial incentives to manufacturers to encourage development of a wide range of fabrics, improvements in production levels and competitiveness with other European centres.

The nascent fashion press lent force to state policies. At a time when styles of dress changed very gradually, the reports in *Le Mercure Galant* (first fashion issue 1672) emphasised the colours and designs of silks for spring/summer and autumn/winter seasons. In 1731, the Lyonnais manufacturer Barnier posited that the French Court led and legitimised novelties, noting that fashionable fabrics sold for three-quarters of their original value in the seasons after their initial creation. Thirty years later, the Lyonnais Chamber of Commerce debated the pitfalls of their success, as manufacturers battled against design copyists; and by 1787, national copyright legislation forbade such copying, allocating a six-year life span to dress silk patterns and fifteen to furnishings. This extended protection was not long enough for some manufacturers, even though they knew their silks went out of fashion quickly.

From a consumer's point of view, in most cases design was merely a pattern on a fabric, created through a judicious mix of colour, texture and motif. In contrast, in the trade, design was product and process and pattern – in other words, the expression of a concept through a series of drawings, which were then translated via a technical process into a fabric, woven, embroidered, painted, or printed. Design was the outcome of discussion and collaboration between designers, manufacturers and consumers. Designers

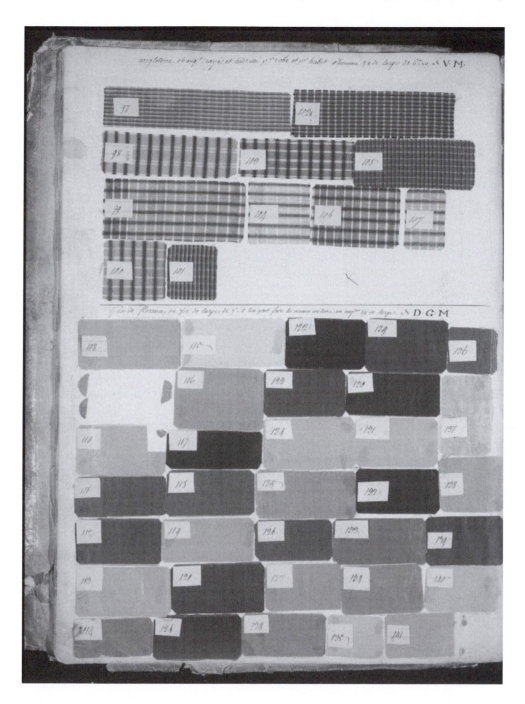

Snapshot 11.1 Travelling salesman's textile swatch book, France, 1763, f. 9 recto. 21.25 × 15.5 × 4 inches (leather bound ledger with paper pages to which silk swatches are stuck with red sealing wax; annotations in ink). This page shows the range of colour combinations available in a simple silk design. The heading reveals the name of the fabric, its width, price per ell and the initials of the manufacturing company that made it. It is one of over 200 different designs on offer for one season from a range of manufacturers. V & A T.373-1972. Acquired with the help of Marks and Spencer Ltd and the Worshipful Company of Weavers. © V & A Images.

kept abreast of current taste in the French capital, and submitted drawings to their manufacturers who selected what they thought would be commercially viable. Manufacturers then commissioned the necessary technical drawing, set up the weaving process and undertook to market and sell the fabrics.

Small variations in motifs gradually modified the dominant aesthetic over a number of seasons or years. Each season compilations of fabric swatches were put together in books to show to prospective retail and private clients outside the city. The downside to this process was that it gave copyists a sneak preview of designs they might reproduce. The scale of design activity was impressive. In Lyon, the city at the vanguard of European design, 200 firms specialising in patterned silks vied with each other, adjusting their output to economic circumstance. The moderately sized firm L. Galy Gallien et compe made as many as 171 designs in a good year (1764–5), and fifty-five in a poor year (1770–1), marketing them in France, Italy, Germany and Spain through a network of agents. In other words, textiles made fashion in dress. Fashionable designs spread through what is now a familiar system of communication.

Bibliography and further reading

Buss, C. (1990) *The Meandering Pattern in Brocaded Silks 1745–1775*, Milan: Ermenegildo Zegna.

Jolly, A. (2002) *Seidengewebe des 18: Jahrhunderts II, Naturalismus*, Riggisberg: Abegg-Stiftung (text in English).

Miller, L. E. (1998) 'Paris–Lyon–Paris: Dialogue in the Design and Distribution of Patterned Silks in the 18th Century', in R. Fox and A. Turner (eds), *Luxury Trades and Consumerism in Ancien Régime Paris: Studies in the History of the Skilled Workforce*, Aldershot: Ashgate, pp. 139–67.

Rothstein, N. (1990) *Silk Designs of the Eighteenth Century in the Collection of the Victoria and Albert Museum, London*, London: Thames and Hudson.

Chapter 10

Fashion in the eighteenth century
Some Anglo-French comparisons

Aileen Ribeiro

'L'HISTOIRE DES MODES n'est pas si frivole qu'on le croit; elle est en partie celle des mœurs.' So wrote Madame de Genlis in her dictionary of etiquette published in 1818, recognising the crucial part played by dress and manners in social history. Dress, more perhaps than any other of the applied arts is closely linked to the society which produces it, a truism particularly apt when applied to the eighteenth century, a period especially characterised by a sophisticated interpretation of status through costume. It is this privilege and wealth, reflected in high fashion and in the often ambivalent relationships between France and England, that will concern this not too serious survey; Anglo-French attitudes were often – indeed usually – a complex mixture of envy, bafflement and dislike.

Madame de Genlis's recollections of court life under Louis XVI were inevitably coloured by the violence of the French Revolution; although her Orleanist allegiance had inclined her towards a republican form of government, she was too much a child of the *ancien régime* not to lament what she considered to be the loss of universally accepted standards in dress and behaviour under the impact of the disintegrating forces both of the Revolution and Romantic individualism.

Uniformity and individualism, conflicting forces in dress and society, were in the eighteenth century linked respectively to the dress of France and England. It was the French who had in the late seventeenth century established the splendours of formal dress, especially the *grand habit*, court dress which was adopted all over Europe[1] and lasted until the Revolution. The English, on the other hand, with a less court-centred society and with greater social mobility, were associated with the introduction of more 'egalitarian' styles and fabrics, some of which derived from working-class traditions. This often resulted in contrasting sartorial aspirations, a point made frequently by visitors to both France and England, such as the Abbé Le Blanc in his *Letters on the English and French Nations*:

> At Paris, the *valets de chambre* and ladies-women are frequently the apes of
> their masters and mistresses in dress. At London 'tis just the reverse: mas-
> ters dress like their valets, and duchesses copy after their chamber-maids.[2]

Journalistic cliché and over-simplification it may have been, but such comments
reflected a belief held widely on both sides of the Channel.

Both sides would also be united in agreeing that France was the dominant fashion influence for most of the eighteenth century, particularly with regard to women's
dress. For at least the first half of the century, the fashionable Englishman too found
Paris a Mecca, although by the 1780s English tailoring and sober English country clothing had come to be widely esteemed all over Europe, even in France.

French pre-eminence in dress and textile production had been firmly established
during the long reign of Louis XIV; it had proved to be an invaluable asset in the cultural propaganda which Versailles exported all over Europe. The English gentleman
may have gone to Italy for culture – and possibly to buy silk velvets in Genoa – but he
went to Paris to order the finest Lyons silks, and to have them made up by a French
tailor. The foppish Bellarmine in Fielding's novel *Joseph Andrews* (1742) was only stating
what was a self-evident truth among his kind – that it was impossible to trust an English
tailor with anything except a greatcoat, a garment which at that time was fairly loose
and shapeless and made of heavy-duty woollen material.

'Everybody dresses with a World of Finery' was Matthew Prior's comment on the
Parisian scene in the early years of the eighteenth century. For men, this finery consisted of a three-piece suit – coat, knee-breeches and waistcoat – of silk (velvet and
woven silks were popular), sometimes trimmed with embroidery and braid; formal
dress also demanded a powdered wig (or hair pomaded and powdered like a wig), and
sword. Women's formal dress for much of the century was an open gown revealing an
elaborate bodice front and decorated skirt. The gown could be tight to the torso and
with an elaborate back drapery (a mantua) or it could take the form of the looser-fitting
sacque dress or *robe à la française*, where the dress fell from the shoulders at the back in
graceful folds.

For those who could not get to Paris – and travel was always more difficult for
women than for men – information on French fashions was gained by dolls, dressed and
sent out at regular intervals from Parisian modistes, to the courts and fashionable dressmakers of Europe. It was particularly irksome for women during times of war to be
deprived of this means of finding out the fashions. The *Spectator* for 12 July 1712 notes
with wry amusement the arrival of one of these 'wooden mademoiselles' at a fashionable mantua-makers in Covent Garden; in the guise of 'Betty Cross-Stich' we read:

> You cannot imagine, worthy Sir, how ridiculously I find we have all been
> trussed up during the War, and how infinitely the French dress excells ours.
> The Mantua has no Leads.[3] in the Sleeves, and I hope we are not lighter than
> the French Ladies so as to want that kind of Ballast; the Petticoat has no
> whalebone, but sits with an air altogether gallant and *dégagée* . . .

Here the *Spectator*, of course, mocks the English servility towards France, expressed
both in the acceptance of the superiority of French fashions, and the somewhat preten-
tious use of French phrases.

Figure 10.1 Taste à-la-mode, 1745, engraving after Louis Philippe Boitard. BM Satires 2774 © The Trustees of the British Museum.

The dress referred to, the mantua, had begun life as an informal gown in the 1670s but by the early eighteenth century it had become increasingly formal, and the original tied-back skirt was now a fairly complex arrangement of drapery. It was then worn over a tightly boned bodice, a style which the English took to, being noted for their fondness for tight, or strait-lacing. 'They seem', said the Baron von Pöllnitz, 'to affect Dressing to their Disadvantage. Their Gowns so close before, with strait Sleeves, which don't reach beyond the Elbow, make them look as if they had no Shoulders or Breasts. And what is worse than all, they have broad flat Rumps to their Gowns, and Hoop-Petticoats, narrow at the Top and monstrously wide at the Bottom. They are always laced, and 'tis as rare to see a Woman here without her Stays on, as it is to see one at Paris in a full Dress'.[4]

This was written in the early 1730s when large conical hooped petticoats (the *Spectator's* 'whalebone') were in fashion, having been introduced some twenty years before by the English; they grew larger and larger until by the mid-1740s they were like huge square tubs, a startling sight to visitors to England from France where they were on the whole by this time restricted to court dress.

While admitting that – apart from the exaggerated hoops – there was a charming simplicity about the everyday dress of Englishwomen as they walked out of doors in their plain morning gowns, white aprons and modest hats worn over linen caps, it had to be said that they did not shine in company. 'They are mightily reserved', says Pöllnitz, 'they have but little Talk, and their chief Conversation is the Flutter of their Fans'.[5]

The situation was very different in France where such gaucherie would have been frowned on; 'Civility is more study'd in France than in the Kingdom of China', was the comment of Matthew Prior, and the French thought that this could best be achieved by bringing the sexes together, and not by segregating them as often happened at social events in England.

French society during the Regency and then the reign of Louis XV was dominated by women who were expected to provide visual and intelligent adornment. This was particularly the case when the presiding genius of taste and fashion was the Marquise de Pompadour throughout the 1740s and 1750s; cultivated (she was an important patron of the arts) and stylish in dress, she has come to be the personification of the rococo in costume with its curving serpentine lines and riotous decoration. The dress most typical of this period is the *robe à la française*, now considerably tightened in at the bodice and with more regulated pleats at the back. It was a style which, by the middle of the century, was also adopted by Englishwomen, initially reluctant to wear the earlier, looser versions which might imply (as some moralists pointed out) a connotation of indecency, a link often made between clothes and the French.[6]

The subject of dress, its actual details and its interpretation, was worthy of discussion by intelligent men and women in France. A Swiss visitor to England and France at the end of the seventeenth century, Béat-Louis de Muralt, devotes in his *Lettres sur les Anglais et les Français* (1725) merely a few lines to the subject of dress in England, but pages on the part played by fashion in French life and values. While he finds that the French love for fashion had its bad side (the rage for novelty, which could be taken sometimes to extremes and even to loss of fortune), he admits that such a vast industry contributed considerably to the economy, a theme which determined the inclusion of fashion in the great *Encyclopédie*.

Like many foreigners he was baffled by the way that the French alone seemed to have the secrets of sartorial refinement, that 'ils semblent être faits pour leurs Habits'.[7] It was undoubtedly true that the French, even wearing sometimes absurd fashions, appeared relaxed and confident, never allowing their clothes to overwhelm them; like the Greeks of old, the French regard the rest of the world as barbarians, and 'les Francais . . . sont les Grecs de nos temps'.[8]

This was the sort of attitude that enraged the Scottish novelist Tobias Smollett, especially as he saw a grain of truth in it. 'The French, with all their absurdities, preserve a certain ascendancy over us, which is very disgraceful to our nation . . . we are slaves to their taylors, mantua-makers, barbers and other tradesmen.'[9]

In his *Travels through France and Italy* (1766) we are spared no details of Smollett's dislike for the French way of life, and in particular the intimacies of the morning toilette, the ritual of formal dressing for the day performed to an appreciative audience composed of both sexes and often attended by the stylish young abbés who feature so much in the *scènes galantes* of the time, and who were often criticised for their somewhat ambivalent role in wealthy and aristocratic households.[10]

At a fine lady's morning toilette, says Smollett (how many did he attend? I wonder, and how welcome was he?) the hairdresser is of crucial importance; he 'regulates the distribution of her patches, and advises where to lay on the paint . . . if he sees a curl, or even a single hair amiss, he produces his comb, his scissars, and pomatum, and sets it to rights with the dexterity of a professed friseur'.[11]

Frenchwomen he found 'plaistered' with cosmetics which they 'daubed on their faces from the chin up to the eyes'. Allowing for his typical hyperbole, it is nevertheless

Figure 10.2 View on the Pont Neuf at Paris, engraving published 1771 after Henry William Bunbury. BM Satires 4763 © The Trustees of the British Museum.

true that, compared to Englishwomen, it was the custom for French ladies of fashion to appear obviously made up with whitened skin and rouge; an artificial, porcelain-like complexion was the aim. Smollett could accept that it was a particular female weakness to be seduced by finery in dress and appearance; a similar trait in men he found particularly disturbing, turning them into 'disagreeable coxcombs' from 'the marquis who glitters in lace and embroidery, to the *garçon barbier* covered with meal, who struts with his hair in a long queue and his hat under his arm'.[12] What he found especially annoying was the importance placed by the French on the correct costume for each and every occasion:

> When an Englishman comes to Paris, he cannot appear until he has undergone a total metamorphosis . . . He must even change his buckles and the form of his ruffles; and though at the risque of his life, suit his cloaths to the mode of the season. For example, though the weather should be never so cold, he must wear his *habit d'été* or *mi-saison*, without presuming to put on a warm dress before the day which fashion has fixed for that purpose.[13]

At a time when masculine English fashions were tending towards greater simplicity (a reflection of the relative informality of even the upper classes outside the court), critics found it tiresome, especially when abroad, to keep up with the ever-changing dictates of Paris. Even when they tried to do so, they were, according to a French visitor, Pierre-Jean Grosley, always just behind the reigning mode:

> A mode begins to be out of date at Paris just when it has been introduced at
> London by some English nobleman. The court and the first-rate nobility im-
> mediately take it up; it is next introduced about St. James's by those that ape
> the manners of the court; and by the time it has reached the city, a contrary
> mode already prevails at Paris where the English, bringing with them the
> obsolete mode, appear like the people of another world.[14]

It is sometimes difficult to know how much credence to give to generalisations like
this; travellers take with them their own inherited prejudices as a form of mental bag-
gage, and it was a deeply held belief that the English, due to their inferiority regarding dress, would be rather risible in their imitations of French styles. By the middle of
the century, the upper-class man, while wearing French formal dress on occasions of
ceremony, would increasingly choose to wear, for everyday, stylish versions of country
clothing, frock suits in sober woollen cloths with the minimum of trimming. It seems
to have been the middle classes, the literate classes who claimed to find evidence of the
all-pervading French influence in dress among the men of fashion. Satires on dress, particularly in the middle of the century – when antipathy to France was exacerbated by
political hostilities[15] – dwell on the baleful influence of the French.

> O France, whose Edicts govern Dress and Meat,
> Thy Victor, Britain, bends beneath thy Feet.
> Strange that pert grasshoppers should lions lead,
> To teach to hop and chirp across the mead . . .

is a typical, patriotic effusion by Soame Jenyns in the 1740s.[16]

Devotion to French tastes in the fashionable world made French tailors, valets,
maids, dancing masters and cooks esteemed commodities; with the sort of snobbery
that lies in most human natures, it was felt that if it was foreign it was bound to be
better then the native product. French valets and maids were, it was felt, better able to
look after dress and suggest how it might be worn to advantage; in addition, they were
particularly skilful at the complicated hair-dressings which fashion dictated in the mid-
eighteenth century. It was a natural consequence that French terms for manners and
appearance entered the English language – 'etiquette' (1750), 'rouge' (1753), 'passé'
(1775) and 'chignon' (1783) are just a few examples.[17]

The undue influence which the French were held to have on honest English manners became the staple fare of farces at the theatre, and in the work of the caricaturists of the time. At the theatre, said Madame du Bocage, 'it gives them high delight to
introduce the character of a ridiculous Frenchman', with an over-refined gentility and
a mincing gait.[18] Caricatures show Frenchmen as foolish coxcombs, emissaries of a government which sent over fashions and fancies with the aim of corrupting the simplicity
of the British. Boitard's *The Imports of Great Britain from France* (1757) shows an array of
French foods (including wines and cheeses) and fashions (chests full of costume accessories and cosmetics), while in the distance there is a swarm of tailors, mantua-makers,
milliners, *valets-de-chambre*, disguised Jesuits, and so on. Four porters struggle under
a chest of 'Birth-Night Cloaths', addressed to a viscount in St James's; the reference
is, of course, to the custom of wearing one's best clothes on the birthdays of the King
and Queen, the implication being that such finery must be French. So much is England

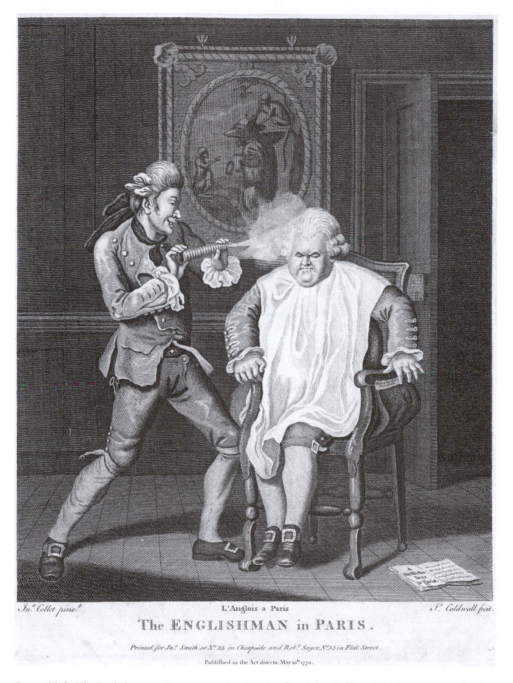

Figure 10.3 The Englishman in Paris, engraving 1770, after John Collett. BM Satires 4478 © The Trustees of the British Museum.

under the sway of all things French that, next to the porters on the left, a 'Lady of Distinction', accompanied by her 'Frenchified well-bred Spouse', offers the tuition of her son to an abbé; in the centre, a fashionable Englishwoman is in raptures over a French

Figure 10.4 The Imports of Great Britain from France, engraving 1757, after L. P. Boitard. Courtesy Library of Congress.

dancer, while the negro page laughs at the strange taste of his mistress. On the same theme, but with a greater lightness of touch, Horace Walpole cautions a friend in 1758:

> You are so thoughtless in your dress, that I cannot help giving you a little warning against your return. Remember, everybody that comes from abroad is sensed to come from France, and whatever they wear at their first appearance immediately grows the fashion. Now if, as is very likely, you should through inadvertance change hats with the master of a Dutch smack, Offley will be upon the watch, will conclude you took your pattern from M. de Bareil, and in a week's time we shall all be equipped like Dutch skippers.[19]

Accustomed to read anti-French diatribes in the popular press, to see the French lampooned on stage and in print, it was no wonder that to many lower-class English people all foreigners were thought to be French, and could be insulted in the streets – a hazard of tourism which French travel guides warned their readers about.

The journalist Louis-Sébastien Mercier in his *Parallèle de Paris et de Londres* (c. 1780) tried to be objective in his survey of Anglo-French attitudes:

> A Paris, on pense qu'un François ne peut traverser une rue de Londres sans être insulté; que chaque Anglois est féroce et mange de la chair toute crue. A Londres, ils croyent que tous les François ont un corps maigre, ventre plat, portent grande bourse, une longue épée, et surtout ne se nourrissent guère que de grenouilles.[20]

Figure 10.5 The Frenchman in London, engraving 1770, after John Collett. BM Satires 4477
© The Trustees of the British Museum.

However far from the truth, images of the rough, oafish Britain and the finicking, ema-ciated frog-eating Frenchman, were further amplified through dress. By the middle of the century it was customary for men of English upper and middle classes to wear on an increasing number of occasions the plain untrimmed cloth suit which had initially been associated with informal country modes. The most popular form of the coat was the frock, with small turned-down collar and small cuffs; instead of the heavy stiff-ened side pleats of the formal coat, there were simple side slits with the minimum of lining. In the early eighteenth century his garment had to be explained to foreigners – 'a close-body'd Coat without Pockets or Plaits and with straight Sleeves', worn by Eng-lish gentlemen upon rising for the day, and for sauntering in the Park.[21] Later in the day, and as formal evening wear, the French *habit à la française*, silk coat and breeches and embroidered waistcoat, would be worn along with a bag wig and sword. In contrast to the situation in France where the nobility had to dance attendance on the monarch at Versailles in order to gain preferment, English upper-class life revolved to a large extent around country activities and looking after the family estates. The English court was, in the words of one visitor, 'the residence of dullness', and did not, unlike that of France, set fashions; in any case, a constitutional monarchy in England meant that there was less money both for the royal family to act as leaders of fashion (although an exception might be made for the Prince of Wales, later George IV, from the 1780s onwards) and for the kind of lavish entertainments which were the rule at absolutist courts.

To an Englishman, sometimes uneasy in the very different social and political sys-tems of France, analogies between dress and politics were quickly made. An English visitor to Paris in 1753 found when in the formal

> full-dressed Coat, with hellish long Skirts, which I had never been used to,
> I thought myself as much deprived of my Liberty, as if I had been in the
> Bastile; and I frequently sighed for my little loose Frock, which I look upon
> as an Emblem of our happy Constitution; for it lays a Man under no uneasy
> Restraint, but leaves it in his Power to do so as he pleases.[22]

A more cynical view was expressed by Soame Jenyns in his poem *The Modern Fine Gentleman* (1746). A young man of fortune, after taking the Grand Tour (where he 'meas-ures St Peter's dome and learns to dance') becomes an MP, and to further his career both inside and outside the House of Commons, he finds dress helps to create the right images:

> Now quite a Frenchman in his garb and air,
> His neck yok'd down with bag and solitaire,
> The liberties of Britain he supports,
> And storms at place-men, ministers and courts.
> Now in cropt greasy hair and leather breeches,
> He loudly bellows out his patriot speeches.[23]

Jenyns points out the paradox here, that although in the popular mind French dress was associated with a despotic political system, it was largely the upper classes (edu-cated and cultivated in French ways) who in government initiated discussion of 'dem-ocracy'; the sort of vulgar, unthinking patriotism which Dr Johnson so deplored as 'the last refuge of a scoundrel' is dressed up in the ostensible egalitarianism of English

Figure 10.6 Englishmen and a Frenchman in Paris, engraving by L. Binet, 1787, for Mercier's *Tableau de Paris*. © The Trustees of the British Museum.

working-class clothing. By the late 1760s and into the 1770s, a fashionable Englishman's wardrobe would be dominated by plain, untrimmed suits in sober colours – shades of brown and blue being the most popular – and made of wool, not silk. Goethe's *succès fou*, the novel *Die Leiden des Jungen Werthers* (1774), helped to popularise this style in Europe generally; Werther, the precursor of the Romantic hero, wears a dark blue coat, buff breeches and waistcoat, and boots – an elegant *tout ensemble* inspired by English country clothing, which the whole of the fashionable masculine world was to adopt by the time of the French Revolution. In spite of the excesses of the macaronies in England with their peacock flamboyance and silken effeminacy (they were imitated, although in a more subdued way, by their counterparts, the *élégants*, in Paris) which was so caricatured in the 1770s, the tide of opinion was moving irrevocably towards a non-aristocratic masculine ideal. Such a man would show by his outward appearance that the world of work was not totally alien to him, and that he was familiar with the new democratic ideals inspired by the great English political writers of the late seventeenth and eighteenth centuries, which were popularised in the works of the French *philosophes*. Writers like Rousseau and Mercier linked freedom in clothing with the liberties of the individual, and while the easy-fitting English frock was not exactly the vague, 'classical'/theatrical costume which republican artists like David designed during the Revolution, it was at least closer in spirit to freedom than the status-conscious, body-distorting silken luxury of French formal wear. The decade of the 1780s is noted for the dominance of English fashion for both men and women. The *Petit Dictionnaire de la Cour et de la Ville* (1788) commented rather sourly that all Paris was taken over by English habits, including dress: 'Habits, voitures, chevaux, bijoux, boissons, spectacles, jardins & morale, tout est à l'angloise. Nous avons pris de ce triste peuple, le vauxhall, le club, les jocqueis, le fracs, le vishk, le punch . . .' and so on.

Looking at the fashion magazines which proliferate in the 1780s, it is notable how many English fashions appear – riding costume for both men and women, caped great-coats for men and 'redingotes' for women, and for children the practical 'skeleton suit' or jacket and trousers buttoned together, and the plain white frock dress. In Paris everything equestrian was all the rage, from racing to riding, and in the parks modelled on the great London pleasure gardens of Ranelagh and Vauxhall, men strolled in frocks and boots, and women in *robes à l'anglaise*, a French interpretation of the close-bodied gown worn throughout the century by Englishwomen.

The deportment of Englishwomen was particularly admired, attributed by some commentators to their love of riding and exercise. 'Riding on horseback is, to the English, what music is to the Italians' was Grosley's comment, adding that the 'good shape' of women was helped by freedom from heavily boned stays in childhood; their clothing he found informal, but of an 'agreeable negligence'.[24]

As well as English styles in dress, English fabrics were all the rage. According to the American Abigail Adams, in Paris in 1784:

> Everything which will bear the name of elegant, is imported from England, and if you will have it, you must pay for it, duties and all . . . The only gauze fit to wear is English, at a crown a yard . . .[25]

Two years later, an Anglo-French commercial treaty allowed for a great increase in imported English fabrics into France, adding to a fashionable market already in existence

FULL DRESS

PARISIAN LADIES in their WINTER DRESS for 1800

Figure 10.7 Parisian Ladies in Their Winter Dress for 1800, by John Cawse.

for fine Indian muslin exported to France by the British East India Company. This muslin was particularly prized during the revolutionary years and under the First Empire, to the annoyance of Napoleon who wished his ladies at court to patronise French fabrics.

With English fashions of all kinds in vogue, it was natural that there should be an increase in French travellers visiting England. For much of the century the traffic had been virtually one way, with the English travelling to Paris as to the fount of good living and elegant manners. There had been a few intrepid travellers, such as Grosley in the 1760s, who, while admiring English institutions, found manners to be sometimes boorish. The English climate with its 'vapours, fogs, rains' he found intolerable, yet – Londoners being 'haughty and ungovernable' – the people 'do not use, or suffer foreigners to use our umbrellas of taffeta or waxed silk'.[26] Although over the next decade or so more men followed the lead of Jonas Hanway and carried umbrellas, they were often laughed at in the streets, and, according to the philanthropist Francis Place, the drivers of hackney carriages used to lash them with their whips as they drove by, shouting 'Frenchman, why don't you get a coach?'.[27]

On the whole, and not surprisingly, French visitors felt as they do today about a visit to England; they liked the shops, especially those in Oxford Street, they liked travelling in the countryside – visits to Windsor, Oxford and Cambridge were popular – they hated the weather, and they felt positively suicidal about the English Sunday.[28]

On the subject of dress, most found, with Grosley, that women were clothed with 'agreeable negligence' but with no innate sense of taste or style, except, as it were, by accident, on informal occasions, such as walking outdoors in pretty straw hats, and white muslin gowns.[29] Some visitors found Englishmen to be dressed with simplicity and a love of cleanliness; others found a negligence not altogether agreeable. 'In the morning you come down in riding-boots and a shabby coat', was the comment made by François de la Rochefoucauld, and even on more formal occasions men wear a 'plain coat with nothing sumptuous about it'.[30] He seems to attribute this negligence in male dress to the custom of segregation of the sexes which was effectively achieved by the masculine preserve of the club, and by the fact that the English of both sexes when young never received instruction on how to behave in society. The link between elegance in dress and grace in manners was dear to the heart of Mercier; while admitting in his great *Tableau de Paris* that English fashions were all the rage, he urged his fellow countrymen to return to their formal dress, with its embroidery, lace and fine silk, to the *chapeau bras* (the formal hat carried under the arm) and to their powdered wigs. This was the costume which for him symbolised all the refinement of French civilisation which he felt was being eroded by tough and slovenly English fashions.[31]

Mercier, however, in the 1780s was not yet the fierce Anglophobe he was to become during the revolutionary years, and he had to admit that the English were superior to his own countrymen in their love of practical and simple clothes for out-of-doors, and their love of clean linen. For travellers to France, while admitting that Paris had all the secrets of an elegant appearance, tended to find a somewhat cavalier attitude to personal cleanliness; the French capital had the best hairdressers and wig-makers in Europe but was renowned for the worst laundresses.

The phrase 'parade and poverty' summed up the situation in Paris for Horace Walpole in 1765; he found a veneer of elegant grandeur over a slightly cracking foundation:

> What strikes me the most upon the whole is the total difference of manners between them and us, from the greatest object to the least . . . It is obvious in every trifle. Servants carry their lady's train, and put her into her coach with their hat on . . . The very footmen are powdered from the break of day, and yet wait behind their master, as I saw the Duc of Praslin's do, with a red pocket-handkerchief about their necks . . .[32]

Twenty years later the mixture of surface pomp and a rotten infrastructure was all the more evident; French society, dressed *à l'anglaise*, was content just to toy with notions of democracy, happy in the knowledge that it was a mere theory and not fact. All this changed with the French Revolution, and the violent events of 1789 startled the world. Many in England remembered with a shudder the Gordon Riots of 1780, and it was a shock that Paris, the centre of the civilised world, should be is such a state. To Mary Berry in 1790, 'the first city in the world in at present much in *déshabille*', something of an understatement. Yet, according to Arthur Young, those in Paris in whose hands lay the destinies of France, were literally 'in *déshabille*', for he found the deputies at the National Assembly in the summer of 1789 'without powder in their hair and some in boots; not above four or five were neatly dressed'.[33]

This was the costume of democracy as perceived by those who now wielded power; had they not seen or read of English MPs rowdying in the Commons dressed in great-coats and boots,[34] and did they not wear such costume themselves – even princes of the blood like the duc d'Orléans, later to be known as Philippe Égalité – to distance themselves from a dying, reactionary court?

It has been stated that philosophers like Rousseau, admirers of the relative freedom of English political institutions, equated plain, simple and cheaper fabrics within the financial reach of greater numbers of people, with equality; expensive silks which required a leisured life-style were identified with an aristocratic regime. Thus with the Revolution came 'egalitarian' clothing – plain cloth suit, plain linen (not lace), boots and one's own hair instead of a wig; women increasingly adopted fabrics such as muslin, linen and printed cottons, and by the early 1790s the Parisian fashion magazines show plates of printed cotton dresses described as 'equality' dresses, or gowns '*à la Républicaine*'.[35] All these trends had first appeared during the 1780s, but the rapid pace of political and social change during the revolution hastened their more widespread adoption, and helped to encourage their more extreme forms during the Directory.

Only the most avid middle-class republican adopted the true working-class baggy trousers and short jacket, the costume of the *sans-culottes*. Mostly, those in power wore, as one would expect, stylish versions of English country clothing, the frock coat, buff breeches or tight-fitting pantaloons, and boots. These styles could be exaggerated, with wit and flair, into the deliberately outrageous dress of the *Incroyables* of the later 1790s, as artistically dishevelled as any late 1970s punk costume; the aim, like that of the macaronies in England in the 1770s, was to shock accepted views – a rare demonstration in France which has always been more restrained and 'classical' in dress than England, and due no doubt to the hysterical reaction to the Terror seen in France after the downfall of Robespierre in the summer of 1794. Women, too, in mockery of Robespierre's Republic of Virtue, adopted extreme forms of dress, a semi-naked, revealing neoclassical costume of clinging white muslin, described by Mercier as '*à la sauvage*'.

While many people in England had at first welcomed the Revolution, attitudes hardened after the demise of the French monarchy, and the imposition of the Terror; the views expressed by Burke in his *Reflections on the Revolution in France* (1790) as a compound of 'alternate contempt and indignation, alternate laughter and tears, alternate scorn and horror', were widespread as events unfolded, and increasing numbers of *émigrés* fled to England. Early in 1793 Paris was closed to the English, and the fashion magazines fell silent.

We would therefore expect, perhaps, that fashions between the two countries might diverge somewhat. Not so much for men, for, as we have seen, the English styles were firmly identified with the republican regime. With women, however, the difference in dress was noticeable, for the English – not having the spur of a revolution which identified the stirring events of Greek and Roman history with those taking place in contemporary France – were not keen in adopting the more extreme neo-classical styles. In spite of the caricaturists' belief that Englishwomen, still under the sway of French modes, were about to throw modesty to the winds, this does not seem to have been the case in reality. In any case even in France the semi-transparent robes were on the whole limited to the more raffish members of the *demi-monde*; when Fanny Burney visited France with her *émigré* husband in 1802, she had to admit that the very immodest dress, with no stays and no petticoat was 'not by any means so notorious nor so common as has been represented'.[36]

If one looks at the fashion plates in France (these re-emerged in the summer of 1797) and those in England in the late 1790s, it is easy to point a contrast between the fine sculptural drapery of French fashions, and the fussier English styles, their outlines broken by decoration and trimming, and with a particular fondness (a recurring English trait) for historic revivals in dress.

This divergence was fully seen when, during the Peace of Amiens (1802–3) Paris opened its doors to the English; a flood of English visitors published their accounts.[37] After so many years at war, and with such a long distrust of the French behind them, it is hardly surprising that they were not, on the whole, disposed to like what they saw, and wished their prejudices to be confirmed. These ranged from the view that the manners and customs of the French had changed for the worse as a result of the Revolution (it was undoubtedly true that the physical appearance of Paris had changed), and that vice and poverty were present in equal measure. They laughed at the colourful new legislative costumes first decreed by the Directory in 1795, and continued under the Consulate, and masculine visitors in particular made great play with the scantiness of female attire, the indecency of the waltz newly imported from Germany, and the general laxity of behaviour – the notion of 'gay Paree' with its opportunities for pleasure took firm root in the Anglo-Saxon heart.

'The more I see of the French people, the more I feel how strong a national distinction, a want of propriety in dress makes between them and the people of England', was Joseph Farington's comment after visiting France in 1802.[38] Throughout the eighteenth century, the relationship between France and England had never been easy; there was no *entente cordiale*, as each country was quick (after sampling only small sections of society) to blame the other for unpopular fashions, and to have existing prejudices underlined. But the contribution which France and England made to the fashion industry through the mutual exchange of ideas between the two countries, not only added to the gaiety of nations, but helped to produce that cultural friction which sparked off new ideas, and which makes a study of this most urbane and intelligent of centuries both interesting and enjoyable.

Notes

1   French court dress, established in the 1670s, consisted of a fiercely boned bodice, a hooped skirt, and a long, detachable train. Although worn all over Europe where French fashions were the reigning mode, it was rarely worn in England except by royal ladies on occasions of exceptional formality, such as royal weddings.

2   J. Le Blanc, *Letters on the English and French Nations*, 2 vols (Dublin, 1747), I, p. 13.

3   Leads were tiny weights (about the size of today's 20p coin) sewn into the short wide sleeves of early eighteenth-century dress to keep them from rising up.

4   C. L. von Pöllnitz, *Travels from Prussia through Germany, Italy, France, Flanders, Holland, England, &c*, 5 vols (London 1745), III, p. 287. I have used the third edition; the first was published in 1734.

5   Ibid., p. 288.

6   See A. Ribeiro, *Dress and Morality* (London, 1986), and the same author's 'Dress and Undress: Costume and Morality in the 18th Century', in *Country Life*, 11 September 1986.

7   B.-L. de Muralt, *Lettres sur les Anglais et les Francais* (Cologne, 1725), p. 160.

8   Ibid., p. 113.

9   T. Smollett, *Travels through France and Italy* (London, 1766), I, p. 95.

10   Abbés, often the younger sons of nobility without any real vocation, attracted the censure of many French and foreign commentators. Among them was L.-S. Mercier whose *Tableau de Paris* of the 1780s is scathing about such 'drones [who] serve neither the church nor the state'.

11   Smollett, op. cit., 1, p. 114.

12   Ibid., I, p. 110. 'Meal' here refers to hair powder, and the 'queue' is a pigtail.

13   Ibid., I, p. 98.

14   P. J. Grosley, *A Tour to London*, trans. T. Nugent (London, 1772), 1, p. 106.

15   France and England were on opposite sides in the War of the Austrian Succession (1740–8) and the Seven Years War (1756–63).

16   S. Jenyns, *A Collection of Poems* (London, 1748), p. 250. This poem, entitled 'Fashion a Satire', is of 1742.

17   See J. J. Hecht, *Continental and Colonial Servants in Eighteenth Century England*, Smith College Studies in History, p. xi. (Northampton, MA, 1954).

18   K. Fiquet du Bocage, *Letters Concerning England, Holland and Italy* (London, 1770), I, p. 16. Although it seems that the English were more civil to foreigners in the streets by the end of the eighteenth century and early nineteenth century, anti-French caricatures proved big business in the print shops. Louis Simond in his *Journal of a Tour and Residence in Great Britain during the Years 1810 and 1811* (Edinburgh, 1817), noted that 'my countrymen never fail to be represented as diminutive starved beings of monkey-mien, strutting about in huge hats, narrow coats and great sabres' (I, p. 27).

19   H. Walpole, *Letters*, ed. P. Toynbee, 16 vols (Oxford, 1903–15), IV, p. 230.

20   L.-S. Mercier, *Parallèle de Paris et de Londres*, ed. C. Bruneteau and B. Cottret (Paris, 1982), p. 61. According to Mercier the French were blamed for the vices which more correctly derived from Italy and Spain. Regarding the anti-French sentiment in England, Mercier attributed its origin to William III in the late seventeenth century.

21   Pöllnitz, op. cit., III, p. 289.

22   *Gray's Inn Journal*, quoted in C. W. and P. Cunnington, *Handbook of English Costume in the Eighteenth Century* (London, 1972), p. 17.

23   Jenyns, op. cit., p. 196.

24   Grosley, op. cit., I, pp. 253, 255.

25   A. Adams, *Letters*, ed. and intr. C. F. Adams (Boston 1848), p. 190.

26   Grosley, op. cit., I, p. 45.

27   Place mss, BM Add. MS 27827, p. 167, quoted in A. Ribeiro, 'Men and Umbrellas in the Eighteenth Century', *Journal of the Royal Society of Arts* (1986).

28   For example, see M. Decremps, *Le parisien à Londres* (Amsterdam, 1789); F. Lacombe, *Observations sur Londre* [sic] (Paris, 1777); J. Marchand (ed.), A *Frenchman in England, 1784, being the Mélanges sur l'Angleterre of François de la Rochefoucauld* (Cambridge, 1933).

29   Madame Roland (later to be a leading figure in the Girondin Party, and guillotined during the Terror) visited England in 1784. She found English women attractive enough in their white muslin gowns (which she notes they wore *à la polonaise*, i.e. with the back drapery puffed up into three swags of material), but 'except in a very small number, there is not to

be found an elegance and taste anything like ours', see *The Works of Jeanne-Marie Phlipon-Roland* (London, 1800), p. 184.

30   Rochefoucauld, op. cit., pp. 28, 57.

31   L.-S. Mercier, *Tableau de Paris*, 8 vols (Amsterdam, 1782–8), VII, pp. 45–6.

32   Walpole, op. cit., VI, p. 309.

33   A. Young, *Travels in France and Italy during the Years 1787, 1788 and 1789*, ed. and intr. T. Okey (London, 1915), p. 325.

34   The German pastor Carl Philipp Moritz visited England in 1782 and was amazed to find MPs at the House of Commons dressed in greatcoats and boots, lounging on the benches eating nuts and oranges, see C. P. Moritz, *Travels in England in 1782*, intr. P. E. Matheson (London, 1924), p. 53.

35   See A. Ribeiro, *Fashion in the French Revolution* (London, 1988).

36   *The Journals and Letters of Fanny Burney*, ed. J. Hemlow (Oxford, 1972–82), v, p. 290. She herself, at the age of fifty, decided that the fashions of 1802 were far too youthful for her, and kept to her stays and petticoats, as a 'Gothic anglaise'.

37   The following are useful, if occasionally highly coloured accounts: F. W. Blagdon, *Paris As It Was and As It Is*, 2 vols (London, 1803); E. J. Eyre, *Observations made at Paris during the Peace* (Bath, 1803); J. D. Paul, *Journal of a Party of Pleasure to Paris* (London, 1802); *An Englishman in Paris 1803: The Journal of Bertie Greatheed*, ed. J. P. T. Bury and J. C. Barry (London, 1953). Not all the reporting, however, was done at first hand, and a number of visitors – without acknowledgement – eked out their own impressions with extracts taken from Mercier's *Le Nouveau Paris* of 1798.

38   *The Farington Diary*, ed. J. Greig, 8 vols (London, 1922–6), II, p. 20.

Fashion, prestige and the eighteenth-century *beau monde*

Hannah Greig

Snapshot 12.1 Scarlet ribbed silk court dress with an estimated 10 lb weight of silver thread embroidery. Made, and presumed to have been worn, in England 1740–5. Victoria and Albert Museum, T.227-1970.

Coronets and inherited countryseats are often taken as the conventional symbols of elite privilege, but in eighteenth-century London fashion held sway. From the 1690s a new phrase – *beau monde* – was coined by English commentators to capture the changing conditions of elite status and categorise what contemporaries regarded as a new, largely metropolitan, and elite 'world of fashion'. Members of the *beau monde* were labelled the 'people of fashion'.

The belief that fashion was a force that denoted the 'rank, state or dignity' of the *beau monde* emerged in response to changing cultural and political conditions. In the late seventeenth century, traditional indicators of elite status (landownership, hospitality and royalism) were undermined by urban growth, constitutional monarchy, parliamentary politics and the burgeoning of a consumer culture. An annual march to the metropolis became the norm for the eighteenth-century elite, responding to a new political timetable and lured by a blossoming social season. For those seeking titled power in the 1700s it was, increasingly, stage-managed performances in the town rather than local paternalism at a country estate that was the determining factor.

Notably, to be 'of the fashion' was regarded by eighteenth-century writers as distinct from being 'fashionable'. The former was applied only to members of the exclusive *beau monde*. The latter suggested a modishness, usually aspirational, of those unable to claim such a privileged social position. Crucially, the form of fashion displayed by the *beau monde* was regarded as both unpurchaseable and inimitable. 'What are they, who are they and what constitutes them people of fashion?' asked the weekly periodical *The World* in 1755. 'People of fashion, it appears, do not earn their designation by birth or fortune, but through a certain *je ne sais quoi* which other people of fashion acknowledge' (*The World*).

'To see and be seen' was the *beau monde*'s mantra, and their self-conscious parades were supported by lavish use of expensive accessories. Gilded, gorgeous, bespangled and opulent, the material goods attributed to the eighteenth-century elite – from embroidered suits and diamond-encrusted snuff boxes to £100 gowns and ostrich feather hair adornments – were purposefully ostentatious. However, while such displays required deep pockets, it was more than wealth that was advertised when these items were displayed. Often these goods were the glue that bound the metropolitan elite together, used both to signal their exclusivity and to communicate internal messages within the 'world of fashion'.

For example, the ready display of diamonds was commonplace to all members of the *beau monde*. While such scintillating shows suggested both wealth and inheritance, the elite also used gems in ways that were less easily replicated by interlopers. Typical of such strategies was the Duchess of Marlborough's decision to give away her own diamond jewellery to all friends sympathetic to the Whig party in 1712, an action driven by political strategy rather than ostentatious whim. When such items were worn by the recipients they were widely recognised as 'Marlborough' jewels, broadcasting networks and allegiances that could never be mimicked by personages wearing newly purchased gems.

In a similar move for exclusivity, both elite men and women active in a metropolitan setting privileged court dress within their wardrobes. Fortunes would be spent on a single item, that might only have been worn once, apparently precisely because it was an item safely removed from a broader consumer marketplace (owing to the closed conditions of court attendance). Furthermore, such garments were used to communicate messages of political participation, with the use of certain colours or certain fabrics (notably imported or home-manufactured) to convey opposition or allegiance to government and the crown. Complicated systems of exchange, borrowing, inheriting and gift giving, using ultra expensive goods that were laced with interpersonal and political connections, created a shared material culture unavailable to the everyday consumer.

Fashion in this regard operated in a somewhat surprising way. The circulation of mass-produced goods did not fuel it. The mass of the population could never attain it. Suppliers, capitalising on a thriving economy and burgeoning marketplace did not dictate it. Fashion can be found to have been the currency that defined elite networks and alliances, and the substance of group identity. It signalled the *beau monde's* exclusivity and distinction. Sensitivity to this alternative interpretation of fashion, deployed at a particular historical moment, not only provides an insight into the ways in which contemporary anxieties about, and perceptions of the fashion process might relate to other forms of historical change. It also draws our attention to distinction engineered by the privileged few, rather than on the modishness and mass consumption available to the many.

Bibliography and further reading

Brewer, J., and Porter, R. (eds) (1993) *Consumption and the World of Goods*, London: Routledge.

Greig, H. (2007) 'Leading the Fashion: The Material Culture of London's *Beau Monde*' in J. Styles and A. Vickery (eds), *Gender, Taste and Material Culture in Britain and North America 1700–1830*, London and New Haven: Yale University Press.

Smith, W. (2002) *Consumption and the Making of Respectability, 1600–1800*, London: Routledge.

Vincent, S. (2004) *Dressing the Elite: Clothes in Early Modern England*, Oxford: Berg.

The World, no. 151 (20 November, 1755), p. 51.

Chapter 11

Fashion journals and the education of enlightened consumers

Daniel L. Purdy

IN NOVEMBER 1785, FRIEDRICH JUSTIN BERTUCH, a young editor at the *Teutscher Merkur*, a leading German literary journal, announced an entirely new enterprise dedicated to the promotion and critique of new fashion and luxury goods.[1] Filled with boastful self-confidence, the novice publisher began with a rhetorical question: why, given the tremendous interest in new reading materials and the concomitant expansion of industry within the German principalities, had no one thought to print a journal solely concerned with *Mode* and *Luxus*? Surely, he reasoned, with so many gifted authors in Germany, someone would have ventured to write directly about the new commodities being produced by Europe's burgeoning manufacturing industries.

The German Enlightenment had produced a class of readers interested in novels, histories, philosophical treatises, scientific manuals, and reports from distant travellers, but Bertuch was aware that the German principalities lagged behind the industrial production of England and France. While eager to cast German aristocratic and upper-class bourgeois society in the light of recent European fashion trends, his *Mode Journal* acknowledged that German cities displayed less luxury than other European capitals. Bertuch explained the absence of luxury according to the precepts of eighteenth-century cameralist thought:

> London, Vienna, Paris, etc., All these cities are as famous for their luxury and fashion inventions as they are for a thousand other wonderful things. They would be just as incapable as we are of sustaining their immense luxury and opulence at the level they do if they did not have what we lack: a large population and a lively circulation of money.[2]

The root problem was, according to Bertuch, a relative weakness in industrial production – a point that the French historian Francois Dreyfus reiterated in his analysis of the eighteenth-century economies of the German states:

Germany around 1790 still had an almost purely agrarian character. The agricultural yields were low, qualitatively mediocre, and highly uncertain. The industrial sector remained very limited. The first efforts at development were confined only to Brandenburg, Saxony, and the northern Rhineland. German production at this time reached only a low level. It amounted to a quarter of Britain's production and barely a third of France's.[3]

Arguing in what might today seem a backward and almost contradictory logic, Bertuch maintained that the underdeveloped state of the German principalities was the very reason for publishing a fashion journal. He expected that his *Mode Journal* would, by instilling in consumers new desires for luxury goods, directly assist in the development of German-based manufacturing. Out of desire would come higher consumer demand, which would in turn produce a number of economic benefits. Implicit in Bertuch's thinking was the assumption that consumer desire was independent of either the ability to purchase commodities or the existence of a domestic market. Written texts, he assumed, were sufficient to inspire a personal inclination for consumer goods, even if those products were not yet widely available in Central Europe. Popular, widespread reading of literary and journalistic writing about fashionable society and its consumer goods was, for Bertuch, a viable mechanism for generating 'home demand'. Once the reading public had been 'educated' to want products, they would find a way to purchase them, preferably at low cost from regional manufacturers.

In tracing the contours and implications of Bertuch's project, I hope to show that eighteenth-century German consumer culture began within the readerly imagination and that an elaborate and self-critical discourse on consumption existed in Germany well before any portion of that diverse Central European region approached industrialisation on the scale of England or France. The one link in Bertuch's argument that, at this point, cannot be demonstrated is his presumption that desire, an imaginary urge inspired by reading, would translate into demand, an economically quantifiable activity.

Without question, Bertuch believed his journal would have far-reaching economic consequences. Only after German speakers had learned to want the material things of an elegant life, he reasoned, would domestic manufacturers be assured of a market for their products. Reading fashion journals, and other tasteful texts, was the avenue toward a consumer *Bildung*, which would in turn propagate commerce. In the long run, Bertuch hoped to reproduce in Germany the industrial developments that were unfolding in England at the end of the century. Written for consumers, the journal would also have a salutary influence on manufacturers, Bertuch insisted, for they too could benefit from the journal's fashion information.

It is the well-known plan and purpose of this journal to make Germany more aware of its own industriousness; to awaken in our rulers, the great, and the wealthy, a warm patriotic support for [this industry]; to give our artists and craftsmen greater trust in their ability to lend taste and artistry to their work while making them familiar with the inventions and beautiful forms of foreigners; and, above all, to protect our purses from being sacked by foreigners.[4]

Educating producers was not Bertuch's primary interest, however; his articles were always directed at the individual user. Only through a revolution in German consumer practices would manufacturing receive the necessary impetus for growth on the scale of England or France.

Bertuch seems to have been correct in linking low manufacturing output with the absence of demand from individual consumers. His diagnosis of German development has been supported by Roman Sandgruber's research on eighteenth-century Austrian consumption. Sandgruber's conclusions about the Austrian textile industry confirmed Bertuch's assertion that weak consumer demand hindered economic development in central Europe at the end of the eighteenth century. Both Austria and Prussia had, through state subsidies, developed significant textile manufacturers, in part to provide a steady, domestic supply of uniforms for their armies. Over the course of the century, the productivity of textile manufacturers had advanced beyond the demands of consumers:

> One cannot ignore that prices had been reduced by advances in productivity to such an extent that they would have allowed a mass market, and yet, on the other hand, that the burning problem for all early factories was the absence of a corresponding market.[5]

Austrian textile producers were, according to Sandgruber, in a position to expand their production significantly; however, they lacked the market demand to support such expansion. Given the uncertainties of distributing products and the imperfect lines of communication between central European marketplaces, it comes as no surprise that demand did not 'automatically' respond to lowered prices and that other, non-economic means of informing potential consumers were necessary to expand the market in manufactured goods. Wilhelm Treue made a similar diagnosis for the textile industry around Berlin. Large-scale textile producers were by 1800 responsible for employing 20 per cent of all skilled workers. The demand that enabled large-scale producers to organise themselves as industrial enterprises was, however, provided primarily by the military and the court. A wider market of middle-class consumers had not yet developed in Berlin/Brandenburg.[6]

Within a few years of its appearance, the *Mode Journal* had become an important voice in the cultural life of the Bildungsbürgertum and had begun to exercise an influence on the traditionally francophile aristocracy. In the years before the French Revolution, the fashion monthly distinguished itself by extending and elaborating upon the discussion of fashion and consumption that had emerged in the Enlightenment critiques of absolutism.[7] The *Mode Journal* redefined the terms of the earlier attacks on courtly luxury by producing its own fashion aesthetic, one that encouraged members of the bourgeoisie to see themselves as 'rational and pragmatic' consumers. Its wide readership, its pre-eminence in Germany as a tastemaker, allowed Friedrich Bertuch to postulate that his journal would have a broad impact on society.

According to this new, critical, bourgeois consumer ethic, the relative backwardness of Germany only heightened the moral imperative that consumer goods should not foster wasteful displays of wealth but, instead, should enhance the mental and physical capabilities of the consumer. Clothes should protect the body while allowing greater physical movement. Household appliances should simplify burdensome household tasks. Decorations should soothe and ease the mind, rather than distract its attention from important tasks. New products should provide technical aids in understanding the natural environment and facilitate meaningful intellectual exchange. They should allow the individual to perform more tasks with greater efficiency. Consumer goods should support the general well-being while advancing the standing of their owners. Ideally, they would assist in the production of wealth and knowledge, producing in the person and the household the same structural transformation that Bertuch imagined a strong consumer market would generate in domestic manufacturing.

Bertuch's larger economic plans depended upon convincing tradition-bound Germans to alter their motives for making purchases. The hope was that, if readers began buying commodities because they were in fashion, then they would be likely to buy more goods more often. The *Mode Journal* presented readers with a range of products they had never seen before, and it provided them with new reasons for wanting to acquire them.[8] At the same time, the journal hoped to shift attention from imported goods already available in German markets to domestically produced goods not yet in existence.

> Our journal, and all our future works about luxury and fashion, shall please and educate our readers, not only through the interesting tableaus we will from time to time deliver but also through the general overview they will receive. Readers will be taught to better evaluate and employ this tremendous ebb and flow. They will thereby hold on to hundreds and thousands of *Livres* that otherwise would leave Germany to buy fashion dolls and useless models.[9]

The purchasing of expensive clothes and household adornments had certainly been customary for provincial Germans before the publication of the *Mode Journal*; however, the occasions that warranted such expenditures were infrequent, and the goods were usually manufactured by local guild artisans committed to their decorative traditions. A wealthy burgher or farmer might have taken the opportunity of his daughter's wedding to spend lavishly. Baptisms, engagements, funerals and religious holidays also were occasions for the purchase of fancy clothes and the presentation of elaborate feasts. The *Mode Journal*, however, sought to move these affluent farmers and burghers beyond their local calendar of consumption.[10]

For the academics and administrators of the Bildungsbürgertum, who were already somewhat removed from rural tradition, the *Mode Journal* offered the opportunity to mark their distinction from agrarian society as well as to display their allegiance to the progressive liberalism associated with many of the *Mode Journal*'s English fashions. By keeping readers informed of changes in foreign styles, the journal dramatically increased the moments in people's lifetimes when they might feel compelled to buy new clothes or redecorate their living quarters. In a sense, the journal sought to alter the temporal rhythm of German consumer habits, a point Georg Lichtenberg acknowledged when, in 1793, he made a pun about a girl barely 'twelve fashions old' (Ein Mädchen, kaum zwölf *Moden* alt).[11]

Bertuch initially proposed three different publications devoted to the continually expanding domain of consumer culture. A monthly pamphlet would keep Germans apprised of the newest foreign styles; an annual pocket-sized *Kalender* would summarise the year's developments in broad terms; and an *Annalen* would be concerned with the comparative history of luxury. These three journals were quickly consolidated into a single entity, *Das Journal des Luxus und der Moden*. Known to virtually all literate Germans simply as the *Mode Journal*, Bertuch's monthly review of contemporary taste and consumer innovations quickly became widely successful. Although scorned by most Enlightenment thinkers as well as by the Weimar literary elite, the *Mode Journal* became a fixture in the many provincial courts throughout Germany.[12] It also served as a valuable resource for Germany's administrative bourgeoisie, who aspired to move in elite circles but lacked the necessary training in elegance. The late Enlightenment philosopher Christian Garve described the awkwardness of the newly elevated burgher as a failure in education:

> Commonly, the affluent burgher learns the etiquette and luxury of the refined world in stages, according to how much his increasing wealth allows him to buy or his accumulated connections allow him to observe. Likewise, he equips himself and his household in stages. However, the traces of his first condition, where he began, almost always remain. The old and the modern, the base and the refined are mixed together far more in his case than with someone who was born and raised in an opulent and fashionable household.[13]

Shut out of the aristocratic travel circuit between European courts, the German Bildungsbürgertum counted on the journal's precise descriptions and coloured prints for knowledge of what passed as elegant in London and Paris. Even the relatively small merchant classes in Frankfurt, Leipzig, Hamburg and the Baltic trading centres were eager to subscribe, even though they already enjoyed direct business contacts with foreign capitals.[14] The *Mode Journal* had declared itself an organ of domestic industrial development, and the prospect of participating within a coherent German consumer culture appealed directly to the interests and inclinations of merchant traders. German enthusiasm for fashion journals was so intense that it quickly became a necessity for any public person. Adolph von Knigge warned German men of the ridicule that accompanied anyone unfamiliar their contents: 'How embarrassed is the man who does not read many journals or the newest fashion publications, when he finds himself in the company of "aesthetic" gentlemen and ladies'.[15] More than Knigge's own *Über den Umgang mit Menschen*, which was the most famous German book on manners, the *Mode Journal* and its smaller German competitors defined how respectable individuals were to act and dress within the public sphere.

For forty-one years, through articles that provided both precise descriptions of tailoring and moral critiques of luxury, the journal's monthly issues instructed Germans on French and English trends. Most important to its success were the three or four hand-coloured lithographs, depicting clothes and furnishings, that accompanied each issue. A 1792 letter to the editor remarked that many young 'Mode-Puppen' hardly even read the articles; they simply imitated the prints.[16] The vividness and detail of these images account for the journal's early success and its continued ability to fend off the many competing publications appearing in its wake.

Monthly reports from Paris and London reported the fabrics, colours, decorative touches, and sewing techniques required to reproduce the clothes at home.[17] Analytical articles organised consumption as a field of knowledge and a means of regulating the body, combining historical ethnography with medical prescriptions. An article might outline the manner in which a given practice, such as the use of cosmetics, had developed in Europe, while emphasising the health risks of facial creams mixed with lead or quicksilver. The warnings were never so sweeping as to forbid the use of cosmetics; rather, the journal inevitably recommended certain powders as acceptable, provided they were applied properly.[18] Critical discussions were generally directed against one particular fashion and in favour of another.

The range of informative and evaluative articles typical of the *Mode Journal*'s first decades is illustrated by the February 1787 issue's table of contents:

1   Musical dice game
2   Historical remarks concerning the application of cosmetics
3   Safe makeup and colouring for actors
4   On children's dress
5   French fashion
6   Furniture – an elegant worktable for ladies and a corner cabinet
7   Letters to the editor

Attached to every issue was an *Intelligenzblatt*, or advertising supplement, listing expensive products manufactured with early industrial techniques: jewellery, clocks, eyeglasses, telescopes, musical instruments, books.

From the start, the journal's articles, its advertisements, and the market for consumer goods were cautiously interconnected. In his own factory, the Landes-Industrie Comptoir, Bertuch sought to reproduce the goods that the journal presented to the public. English products, in particular, were imitated in Bertuch's Weimar enterprise. Just how profitable this venture was remains unclear; for while he alludes in a letter to the duke of Weimar to having employed many local carpenters, glaziers and tin and leather artisans in reproducing English wares, he seems later to have abandoned the manufacturing business once his publishing house expanded.[19]

The journal proceeded cautiously with the manufacturing side of Bertuch's business. Readers were simply informed that they could write to the editors for further information on how to acquire the products depicted. Bertuch made no secret of his desire to foster German manufacturing, so it is unlikely that he feared or was embarrassed by repercussions from England. However, it does seem that other German manufacturers were initially hesitant to advertise their products in the journal out of fear that they would have to provide detailed blueprints and manufacturing specifications. During the first year of publication, Bertuch was obliged to print disclaimers, assuring German craftsmen that their goods could be safely advertised in his pages. The potential conflict between attracting other advertisers and imitating foreign goods might have persuaded Bertuch to abandon manufacturing once his publishing industry flourished.

At almost the same time that Bertuch was preparing to organise consumption into a field of knowledge and economic activity, the first fashion journals appeared in England and France.[20] We know that Bertuch hurried his publication date to prevent the Parisian *Cabinet des Modes*, which had also just appeared in 1785, from developing a readership among Germans.[21] The competition between the *Mode Journal* and the *Cabinet des Modes* continued through the first years. Contemporaries noted similarities between the two journals, and Bertuch was compelled to rebut charges that he copied the Parisian journal.[22] But while he may have drawn 'inspiration' from the *Cabinet des Modes*, the *Mode Journal* differed significantly from the Parisian publication in that Bertuch provided extensive commentary on each fashion, whereas the *Cabinet* reported new styles uncritically.[23]

After the obvious success of the *Mode Journal*, fashion publications appeared throughout northern Germany and Saxony.[24] The first German competitor to establish a wide readership was *Die Zeitung für die elegante Welt*, which appeared three times a week beginning in 1801.[25] In England, *The Lady's Magazine* began in 1801 to include colour prints of contemporary dresses.[26] On the whole, the English magazine did not concentrate on style and consumption, comments on Parisian fashion constituting only a small part of each issue. German fashion journals, on the other hand, focused during the last decades of the century exclusively on fashion and luxury, abandoning this focus only with the emergence of *Die Zeitung für die elegante Welt*, which sought to integrate literature and fashion within a broad Romantic aesthetic.[27]

The two Italian journals that also appeared around the time of the first publication of the *Mode Journal* – the *Giornale delle Dame e delle Mode di Francia* (1786) and the *Giornale delle Mode* (1788) – had only an indirect influence in Germany.[28] While Bertuch promised in his preface to the first edition of the *Mode Journal* to keep German readers abreast of Italian fashions, very little mention was ever made of contemporary Italian fashion in later issues. However, because the *Giornale delle Mode* appeared on a list Bertuch composed of leading European fashion journals, we can assume he had at least a passing knowledge of the Italian fashion scene.[29] Sandgruber claimed that the first Viennese journal devoted exclusively to fashion appeared in 1816 (*Wiener Modezeitung*, renamed in 1817 *Wiener Zeitschrift für Kunst, Literatur und Mode*); however, it seems unlikely that there were no earlier Viennese fashion publications.[30]

Prints were first provided by Bertuch's partner, the Weimar artist Georg Melchior Kraus. Daniel Chodowiecki, the renowned illustrator of bourgeois life in Berlin, had been approached by Bertuch, but he turned down the opportunity, claiming that he was too old to keep up with 'new vanities'.[31] Just how important the prints were to the early success of the journal is demonstrated by the fact that Kraus and Bertuch took equal shares of the journal's profit during the first years. Kraus would produce the master for each print, and then teams of colourists would paint in the figures. In all likelihood, Bertuch relied on his wife's artificial flower factory for the expertise and labour required to colour six thousand to eight thousand prints a month. Fifty young women from the lower *Mittelstand* (middle class) worked on the first floor of Bertuch's house on the Ilm, the largest and most elegant private building in Weimar.[32] Goethe's future common-law wife, Christine Vulpius, was among them. Similar assembly line processes were used in England by the publishers of the *Lady's Magazine*. These prints were intended 'to stimulate demand, to spread new fashions, to encourage imitation of the "taste-makers"'.[33]

Judging by the *Mode Journal*'s addresses to its readers, men were almost as eager as women to read about foreign fashion. And while the journal occasionally alluded to fashion as a feminine activity, it did so far less than the sentimental *Wochenschriften* (weeklies), which were directly aimed at female readers. Not until the first decades of the nineteenth century did fashion journals address men as if they were not regular readers. Unlike later fashion publications, the *Mode Journal* did not make overt appeals to male heads of households to 'tolerate' feminine fashion.[34] Even if the majority of articles and prints in the *Mode Journal* were dedicated to female dress, it was always assumed that male readers would want to be kept abreast of the newest trends. Unquestionably, a significant number of the inventions, mechanical devices, and articles of furniture featured in the journal were intended to appeal to a male readership.

This relative evenhandedness can be detected in other, smaller publications, such as the *Hamburger Journal für Mode und Eleganz*, wherein a great percentage of the prints displayed male and female figures together. The ideal audience for the first German journals included both sexes. In the 1780s, no firm gender ideology separated masculinity from fashion culture. While the English *Ladies Magazine* did imply a female audience, the Parisian *Cabinet des Modes* 'wanted to reach "the two sexes who always and everywhere have sought to adorn themselves in order to please each other" . . . in the last analysis, the target was "good society"'.[35] Bertuch's journal held a similar gender-balanced editorial position; however, unlike the Parisian journal, it appealed to both sexes more out of an ideological commitment to universal Enlightenment reform than an adherence to old-fashioned gallantry.

Without question, the creation and exploitation of a bourgeois fashion culture in Germany was profitable. Christoph Wieland noted in 1802, with some contempt, that fashion journals were among the most lucrative ventures in publishing:

> You can no longer earn a living from journals. The *Zeitung für die elegante Welt* and the *Mode Journal* are virtually the only ones that have a high circulation, because they are based on the public's vanity, frivolity, and lust for anecdotes. What man of feeling and honor would want to live from the vices and follies of his age?[36]

Bertuch did live well. The wealthiest entrepreneur in Weimar, he served as Duke Karl August's treasurer from 1785 until 1796. During the first year of its publication, the *Mode Journal* attracted 1,488 subscriptions and brought Bertuch and Kraus a profit of 1,154 Reichsthaler. (A yearly subscription was a rather expensive 4 Reichsthaler.) Three years later, the journal had 1,765 paying subscriptions, which provided 1,875 Reichsthaler in profit.[37] The short-lived *Mode Kalender*, which Bertuch abandoned after three years, was also extremely well received, selling 2,893 copies in 1787.[38]

These figures can be contrasted with Wieland's *Teutscher Merkur*, which did not sell more than a thousand copies, and G. J. Goschen's 1789 edition of the *Historischer Kalender für Damen*, which had seven thousand subscribers.[39] The actual number of readers for these publications would have been much higher than the subscriptions; the figure Goschen proposed – that each volume sold was circulated to between ten and twenty readers – is still accepted, although some estimates are lower.[40] As letters printed in the journal demonstrate, the multiplier effect was particularly relevant for the expensive *Mode Journal*: one correspondent revealed that her town shared a subscription among sixteen families.[41] A letter from a small-town burgomaster recounted how the leading townswomen would gather with his wife whenever the new *Mode Journal* arrived by mail. He intimated that on rainy days even husbands joined the reading circle.

The *Mode Journal* brought domestic readers monthly accounts of all that was available abroad, presenting London as a consumer utopia, where the material distinctions of rank and wealth were superseded by an abundance of goods. The sheer volume of goods available at low prices gave German visitors the impression that class distinctions were less important in England. The monopoly that the central European nobility maintained over luxury goods and everyday conveniences was, it seemed, overwhelmed in London by the flood of new products. The journal's London correspondent wrote in 1803: 'I have often wondered how in England the class of people who are not really poor, but who cannot be counted as well-to-do, can keep up with ladies' costumes which in Germany only the highest ranks wear, and even then only the richest among them'.[42]

In 1758 the first German fashion journal, a short-lived venture, had declared England the centre of men's fashion.[43] Germans first learned about English designs through the importation of furniture and household appliances.[44] In northern German cities such as Hannover, Hamburg and Altona, which had close connections to the English court or the London trade, it was common to find an English influence in the interiors of bourgeois households. The term *simplicity and solidity* was eventually extended to all English goods, so that clothes were ascribed with the same virtues as cupboards:

> The tasteful simplicity and solidity that England has given all its factory wares is, for us Germans, so exceptionally worthwhile and attractive that the words 'English' and 'product of England' have an irresistible magical allure for us and have become virtual synonyms for perfection and beauty in craftsmanship.[45]

By the end of the century, *Mode Journal*'s readers had become acquainted with a wide assortment of English products. Their enthusiasm for the understated simplicity of Wedgwood china and loose-fitting chemise dresses was so strong that the *Mode Journal* warned that the fervour for English fashion threatened to sweep aside France's long-standing pre-eminence in fashion.

Bertuch himself played an ambivalent role in the German swing toward English commodities. Although he clearly favoured almost everything produced there, he warned that the English 'invasion' of German markets threatened to replace one foreign dependence with another, for while shopkeepers' conveniences displaced noble luxuries, German manufacturers were not in a position to compete with either: 'We do not have to fear only France's magical power. England and the perfected craftsmanship of its factories will inevitably become as dangerous for us if we are not more careful about guarding ourselves against this trap'.[46] This economic concern did not deflect consumer interest, but it did lead the *Mode Journal* occasionally to take a cautious, worried tone as it praised all things English. Bertuch sought to use the example of English commodities and their manufacturers as a model for restructuring local industry; thus, the journal's discussion of English goods took on a prescriptive, rather than a proscriptive, tone. The following letter to the editor summarises the journal's overall position:

> You have warned us often in your journal about the dangers of 'Anglomania', and you have predicted that our wealthy, luxurious, and indolent classes will transfer their thirst for fashion from France to England and, thereby, drown themselves in their own hot thirst. In part, your prophecy seems already to have been fulfilled.[47]

The reader's reference to the journal's 'prophecy' points to its twofold function of criticising fashions while encouraging their adoption simply by informing the public of their existence. As we shall see, this ambiguous role laid Bertuch open to the charge of hypocrisy. Many contemporaries felt that the journal's very existence encouraged precisely the practices it claimed to objurgate.

While the German Bildungsbürgertum developed a zeal for an English lifestyle, Paris continued to function as the acknowledged centre of aristocratic elegance. Its prominence in setting the tone for good taste was perhaps diminished, but certainly not eliminated, by England's emergence. Many English garments became fashionable throughout Europe only after they had first been adopted in Paris. The predominance of French names for English articles of dress (*robe à l'anglaise* and redingote) illustrates the importance of French approval in guiding Continental good taste.[48] For much of the century, the French court's baroque and rococo manners had advised the aesthetic decisions of German aristocrats, who would otherwise have remained isolated within their regional decorative traditions. By praising England, the *Mode Journal* was simply seeking to redefine the German emulation of foreign civilisation. The newfound preference for England was in many ways an attempt to escape the French standard:

> In our day, it is often bemoaned, and with reason, that we Germans are slavish imitators of the French in clothes, manners, and mores and that not only are we daily losing any visible originality or distinctiveness but these imitators are introducing a form of luxury among us that is equally dangerous to our morality, our finances, and our ability to act.[49]

As far as the German reading market was concerned, Bertuch recognised Parisian journals as his primary competitors. His 'bewilderment' that no German publisher had undertaken a fashion journal was quite false, for he acknowledged in his 1785 announcement that the recent appearance in Paris of the *Cabinet des Modes* had spurred his own journalistic efforts. While Bertuch clearly favoured England in matters of taste, he understood that the monthly reports from Paris established his journal's legitimacy as a harbinger of coming trends. Bertuch criticised French designs, he disparaged their decorative character, yet he always included regular accounts of Parisian developments. Indeed, the *Mode Journal* relied on the supposed difference between French and English fashions to generate excitement among readers, a difference that was in many ways a product of the fashion world's own internal discourse. This is not to say that the eighteenth-century contest between England and France was not serious in military, economic and political terms; however, the French–English debate was also a distinction that gave a sense of urgency and importance to differences in dress and interior decor. One dressed in either a French or an English manner; it was unacceptable to mix the two design traditions. The *Mode Journal* invested much of its identity in maintaining this national distinction. Its mission of educating the German public in matters of taste centred in large part on explaining, and thereby preserving, the subtle, and sometimes obvious, differences in the garments and goods produced in the two nations:[50]

> England and France are today the two countries that set the tone in clothing, and in men's clothing, England does so even in France. We Germans have always been imitators of foreign fashions; however, we rarely adopt

them in a pure form. Instead, we usually mix them with an element of our own invention. This produces a kind of hybrid that is neither English, French, nor German; rather, it is a complete crossbreed [*Zwitter*]. The peculiar tastelessness of such practices is obvious. It has the unpleasant result that when a person dressed in this way travels to a large city, he becomes a figure of ridicule because he has a little of everything, but nothing whole, and thereby unmistakably betrays his ignorance.[51]

Historically, the isolation of upper-class Germans from the fashion centres of Europe was remedied by the Grand Tour. While only the wealthy could afford to send their sons on trips to the leading courts of Europe, their journeys had a formative influence on those who never left their homes. A gentleman just returned from a long sojourn abroad could be expected to set the tone within the society of his home.

As the flow of information and people across Europe increased, these fashionable travellers were viewed as an imperfect source of information, for they were often the ones who introduced a mixture of diverse styles. Writing at the end of his life, while living among German communities in Riga, St Petersburg, and Moscow, J. M. R. Lenz confirmed Bertuch's assessment of the stylistic confusion among Germans who copied foreign fashion:

> Dangerous divisions soon developed. One half of the German salons had seen nothing besides England; the other had studied life in Paris. Both camps did battle for their own standard of taste. The one sect introduced among us a type of Anglomania; the other dressed only according to Parisian measure. In the end, the reconciliation of both parties produced the real heresy, whose adherents, like centaurs, set one sort of head on another sort of body without considering whether they fit together. This is how things now stand.[52]

The great advantage of the *Mode Journal* was that it was more reliable than human memory, that it provided regular accounts of foreign styles, and that it formulated a consistent national code of style. The journal's wider information was arranged according to Bertuch's understanding of national differences in dress. Thus, the reader received a much simpler and less contradictory impression of how the residents of Paris and London appeared in public.

By describing fashion culture as a struggle between France and England, the *Mode Journal* placed German society in a simultaneously marginal and privileged position. Removed from the centres of taste, Germans were forced to rely on mediated representations of beauty and consumption. However, this forced isolation had the indirect, but nevertheless important, effect of providing German readers with the opportunity to reflect critically upon foreign trends, and the *Mode Journal* took full advantage of this reflective potential. Only after some time had passed, and a few second thoughts had set in, did foreign styles make their appearance in German households, a lag that allowed the *Mode Journal* to claim a unique vantage point in the European fashion scene. This position required some delicate manoeuvring, for at no point did the journal wish to appear out of fashion or even opposed to it.

Bertuch's persistent use of the term 'German' to describe the economy of the many principalities of Central Europe implied the existence of a coherent market, one in which goods, materials and labour could move unencumbered by political boundaries. Clearly, no such unified system existed in the eighteenth century. German principalities competed against one another as well as against France, England, and Italy. Excise taxes on imported goods were applied at many borders within the Holy Roman Empire. Berlin's textile industry was in large part supported by the strict imposition of excise taxes on imported cloth. Given Prussia's high demand for military uniforms, a large number of textile manufacturers established themselves within its boundaries. Other German states sponsored domestic industries through similar forms of taxation. Porcelain manufacturers, for example, were established in German principalities to supply, without import restrictions, the high demand for china of the princely residences.

In 1819, Friedrich List, the spokesperson for the General German Trade and Manufacture Association, complained that a merchant travelling from Hamburg to Austria had to cross ten countries, pay customs ten times, and learn ten codes of law.[53] Before Napoleon simplified the European map, the situation had been even more complex, so it is not surprising that types of industry and their levels of production varied significantly across the German-speaking regions of Europe.

Added to these legal restraints were technical obstacles. Trade was largely confined to river routes because the network of roads was either in poor condition or incomplete.[54] Bertuch's term 'German' had an ideological rather than a descriptive function. His notion of the 'German nation of consumers and producers' reflected onto Central Europe the coherence and unity Bertuch perceived in England and France.

Despite logistical delays in eighteenth-century communication, by the end of the century bourgeois fashion was becoming an international phenomenon, comparable to the network of courts that had set decorative tastes during the Renaissance and baroque eras. In the *Mode Journal*'s pages, Germany, France and England existed as imaginary sites of production and consumption, which in their relation to one another replicated an idealised international marketplace. Germany played the cautious consumer, while France and England acted as competing manufacturers engaged in aggressive advertising campaigns.

Through the *Mode Journal*'s first decades, this triad was the central organising principle of its fashion reporting. Only occasionally was a dissenting voice heard in its articles and then only from its foreign correspondents, who sometimes sought to demonstrate the lines of influence between the two competing sites of fashion. For example, the English correspondent noted that London and Paris were as likely as any other society to prefer the foreign over the domestic: 'I must confess that here one yearns for the newest French fashions as much as Parisians crave the latest English styles'.[55] The Parisian correspondent also underlined the two-way relationship between fashion centres yet, in keeping with Bertuch's taste, gave preference to English fashion when he wrote:

> If it is true, as the accusation goes, that our women are as infected with *Anglomania* as the majority of our men are, then I must admit that this fever is not particularly harmful, for it produces fewer ridiculous caricatures than the reverse situations would.[56]

These sentiments were largely overlooked by Bertuch when he wrote the *Mode Journal*'s long fashion commentaries. For him, the struggle between English and French consumer manufacturing continued to define *Mode Journal*'s presentation of foreign trends. The influences between these two foreign powers were, for Bertuch, ultimately less important than the fact that the two countries represented a significant drain on the balance of trade of small central and northern European duchies.

Bertuch's reflections on the international character of fashionable tastes always returned to the question of economic development. In the *Mode Journal*'s first issue, Bertuch claimed to seek a middle ground between Physiocratic complaints (that luxury consumption inevitably created an imbalance of trade with more established foreign manufacturers) and the free market position (which saw consumer demand as a motivation for industry on both a personal and market level). The debate over luxury consumption concerned itself with a great deal more than balance of payments and the circulation of money. There was a host of assumptions about economic value, the body's productive forces, sexuality, historiography, cultural ideology and the maintenance of social order:

> Luxury, says the devotee of the Physiocratic system, is the pest of all nations! It wastes a pure yield, turning it into unfruitful expenses; hindering reproduction; enervating the physical strength of the nation; loosening all feeling for morality and honor; ruining the well-being of families; leaving the state with hordes of beggars.
>
> Luxury, says the financier and technologue, is the richest source for the state, the mightiest lever of industry, and the strongest force behind the circulation of money. It erases all traces of barbaric mores; creates the arts, sciences, trade, and commerce; increases the population and the energies of the state while bringing pleasure and happiness to life.[57]

His journal, Bertuch argued, would in the long run help realign the imbalance of trade by fostering home demand for the products of domestic industries. 'It is at least a primary goal of our journal to encourage and lift German industry, to take away the prejudice among our great classes that only foreign products are attractive.'[58]

While there is no indication when Bertuch first read Adam Smith's *The Wealth of Nations*, it did not take long for the journal to align itself with a free market position.[59] The *Mode Journal*'s criticisms of luxury always insisted that limitations on consumer behaviour should be imposed by civil society and the market rather than by the state. As long as an individual's purchases did not exceed his or her financial means, there could be no objection to ostentatious luxury. Bertuch never denied the Physiocratic complaints about the evils of excessive consumption, but he described them as side effects in a liberal economy. Debt spending and bankruptcy were brought on by intemperate personalities. Devastation of family fortunes had to be addressed on the level of personal discipline and moral education.

When the late-Enlightenment moralist Carl Friedrich Bahrdt argued that financial security for the middle classes required abstinence from unnecessary purchases, Bertuch acknowledged the hazards of living beyond one's means but argued that such habits required individualised 'treatment'.[60] 'In his opinions concerning the harmfulness of *abusing luxury*, Doctor Bahrdt seems to agree with our position completely . . . He is in error only with regard to the *causes* that foster such abuse.'[61] A critically informed public, Bertuch insisted, was less likely to fall into insurmountable debt.

Societal restrictions in the form of taxes or sumptuary laws, Bertuch insisted repeatedly, were themselves 'excessive' and (more important) a hindrance to trade. Writing under a pseudonym as an 'enlightened' reader, Bertuch stated that

> luxury is a necessity in the sophisticated world and, given the unequal distribution of resources, a benefit to the state; however, its abuse, with which many a fool and spendthrift has ruined himself, is actually a psychological illness [*Seelenkrankheit*] that cannot be cured by a national costume, nor by clothing ordinances, nor by any other legislation.[62]

In 1790, Bertuch reprinted an actual reader's letter, with the comment that the occasional excess does not justify state intervention in consumer behaviour:

> Vanity, the desire to please, the urge to conquer as well as to imitate are clearly qualities that, as soon as they transgress their appropriate limits, must in the eyes of every reasonable man degrade even the most attractive creation; however, they are at the same time the mothers of so many pleasing, beautiful, useful, and good things that we would be forever impoverished if these goddesses were to lose their influence on our lives.[63]

The answer to personal wastefulness lay, according to the *Mode Journal*, in carefully analysing the value of individual consumer goods. Bertuch developed elaborate criteria for evaluating the specific value of a commodity. Rather than teach restraint, the journal sought to integrate consumption with the demands of economically productive labour. It treated clothing and domestic appliances as instruments that organised the individual, both mentally and bodily, within a capitalist economy.

In defending his journal against critics who argued that it should never have been published at all, Bertuch concentrated primarily on macroeconomic arguments. Throughout his publishing career, Bertuch argued that the net benefit to the operation of consumer demand within a liberal economy outweighed the personal tragedies brought on by bankruptcy. The ripple effect of consumption, its ability to generate employment throughout the economy, meant for Bertuch that the *Mode Journal* could contribute directly to fostering a German manufacturing industry. In the introduction to the first issue, he used the example of coffee to show how the consumption of one product increases demand for others. Coffee drinking increased the production of porcelain cups and metal brewing appliances; it employed shipbuilders and salespeople and lent support to the sugar industry, which had a complex economy of its own.[64] It is hardly coincidental that earlier in the century Bernard Mandeville had used the example of the tea industry to argue, similarly, that consumer habits had a widespread ripple effect on manufacturing.[65]

Bertuch's position was distinct from older, cameralist arguments in favour of luxury, because he presumed that the *Mode Journal* would dramatically expand the types of manufactured goods considered fashionable and thus worth buying at a premium from specialised manufacturers. Previous economic discussions of elite consumption had presumed that the term 'luxury' applied only to the decorative objects found in baroque and rococo palaces. Physiocratic objections would inevitably contrast the labour performed by a handful of highly trained, often foreign, goldsmiths and silversmiths with the potential for employing local workers in factories that produced 'more produc-tive' goods. The Physiocrat Johann August Schlettwein contrasted the small workshops of skilled artisans with regional textiles mills and factories that hired large numbers of semiskilled local workers to make the claim that luxury manufacturers failed to increase local employment:

> All these people that luxury employs in gold and silver factories would find work and sufficient merit if they were employed in the manufacture of linen, textiles, or leather or if they worked in iron and steel factories to help satisfy human necessities by producing a hundred different types of indis-pensable appliances and instruments.[66]

Bertuch's innovation was to help redefine *Luxus* and *Mode* to include precisely those products considered important by Schlettwein. The advertising supplements of the *Mode Journal* were filled with notices from manufacturers of optical devices and meas-uring instruments, from clock makers and publishers – precisely the type of goods that would appeal to an enlightened readership. While the journal devoted considerable space to the 'frivolous' products that Schlettwein derided – hats, shoes, shawls, dresses and men's jackets – there were many articles on new products of industrial manufac-turing, products that had not traditionally belonged to fashion and luxury. At the end of the *Mode Journal*'s first year, Bertuch named some 233 English products available through just a single mail-order catalogue.[67] His intention was not merely to admire the array of goods newly available to the German consumer. Rather, he listed the many wonderful new English products to show how large English imports had become and to provide an inventory of the kinds of merchandise German manufacturers could produce when supported by domestic demand.[68]

Bertuch's optimistic plans were based upon the expectation that, if individu-als were made to recognise that the satisfaction of their desires was dependent upon their own labour, such aspirations could be harnessed toward socially productive ends. Bertuch's free-market defence of consumption linked German consumer demand with economic production. Bertuch postulated this link in two ways: first, consumer demand would provide a market for manufactured goods; second, fashionable products would enhance the consumer's physical and mental productivity.

Notes

1   Known to contemporaries simply as the *Mode Journal*, Bertuch's *Journal des Luxus und der Moden* is available today in three formats. Older German and American libraries have orig-inal copies in their holdings; however, very few collections contain the complete series from 1786 to 1827. (The Lippeheidische Kostümsammlung in Berlin has the largest col-lection of German fashion texts and images.) Citations to original issues appear as *Mode Journal* followed by the month and year of publication. A four-volume abridged edition was published by Müller and Kiepenheuer in Hanau a.M. in 1967 under the Weimar editorship of Werner Schmidt. Citations to the abridged edition appear as *Mode Journal* (abridged) with the volume number. A third source is the collection of passages reprinted with a cat-alogue of fashion prints taken from the journal *Heimliche Verführung*, ed. Christina Kröll

and Jörn Göres (Düsseldorf: Goethe Museum, 1978). Citations to the catalogue appear as *Heimliche Verführung*.

2   *Mode Journal*, January 1971, p. 7. For an overview of German economic theory at the end of the eighteenth century, see Keith Tribe, *Governing Economy: The Reformation of Economic Discourse, 1750–1840* (Cambridge: Cambridge University Press, 1988).

3   Francois-G. Dreyfus, 'Die deutsche Wirtschaft um 1815', in *Deutschland zwischen Revolution und Restauration*, ed. Helmut Berding and Hans-Peter Ullmann (Königstein im Taunus: Athenäum, 1981), pp. 352–3.

4   *Heimliche Verführung*, pp. 53–5.

5   Sandgruber, *Die Anfänge der Konsumgesellschaft*, p. 267.

6   Willhelm Treue, *Wirtschafts- und Technik-Geschichte Preussens* (Berlin: Walter de Gruyter, 1984), p. 179.

7   Norbert Schindler noted that 'a critique of luxury had become for the enlightened heads of the eighteenth century almost an obligatory exercise', see his 'Jenseits des Zwangs? Zur Ökonomie des Kulturellen inner- und außlerhalb der bürgerlichen Gesellschaft', *Zeitschrift für Volkdonide*, 81 (1985), p. 197.

8   German ethnographers long claimed that in the late eighteenth century urban fashions diverged from the traditional costume of society. Eighteenth-century contemporaries had already noted that the separation between urban and rural dress was no longer a function of class (*Stände*) differences alone. This separation of fashionable dress from rural culture acquired political implications during the Romantic period. Wilhelm Heinrich Riehl later involved the distinction between fashion and rural costume in his three-volume treatise, *Die Naturgeschichte des Volks als Grundlage einer deustchen Social-Politik* (Stuttgart, 1854). The third volume sharply attacked urban fashion culture's influence on rural patriarchy. For an abridged English translation, see Riehl, *The Natural History of the German People*, trans. David Diephaus (Lewison, NY: Mellen, 1990).

9   *Mode Journal* (abridged) 1, p. 28.

10   Fashionable clothes, such as cotton print dresses, were already visible among Austrian farmers in the first decades of the nineteenth century; see Sandgruber, *Die Anfänge der Konsumgesellschaft*, p. 288.

11   'Sudelbücher, II/117.5', in Georg Lichtenberg, *Schriften und Briefe* (Frankfurt: Insel, 1983), 1, p. 536.

12   Bringemeier, *Mode und Tracht*, p. 113. Bringemeier based this conclusion on her partial survey of *Adelbibliotheken* (aristocratic libraries).

13   Christian Garve, 'Über die Moden', in *Versuche über verschiedene Gegestände aus der Moral, der Literatur und dem gesellschaftlichen Leben*, reprint (Hildesheim: Olms, 1985 [1792]), p. 241.

14   People in the Hanseatic cities were the first Germans to adopt English dress; see Percy Ernst Schramm, *Neuen Generationen; Dreihundert Jahre deutscher 'Kulturgeschichte' im Lichte der Schicksale einer Hamburger Bürgerfamilie (1648–1948)* (Gottingen: Vandenhoek & Ruprecht, 1964), 1, p. 346.

15   Adolph von Knigge, *Über den Ungang mit Menschen* (Hanover, 1804), 1, pp. 22–3.

16   *Heimliche Verführung*, p. 62.

17   Gisela Jaacks, 'Modechronik, Modekritik, oder Modediktat? Zu Funktion, Thematik und Berichstil früher Modejournale am Beispiel des "Journal des Luxus und der Moden"', *Waffen- und Kostümkunde* 24 (1982), p. 36.

18   For an example, see *Mode Journal* (abridged) 2, pp. 137–9.

19   Ruth Wies, 'Das *Journal des Luxus und der Moden* (1786–1827), Ein Spiegel Kultureller Strömungen der Goethezeit', PhD dissertation, Munich, 1953, p. 35.

20   For a thorough analysis of early French fashion journals, see Annemarie Kleinert, *Die frühen Modejournale in Frankreich: Studien zur Literatur der Mode von den Anfängen bis 1848* (Berlin: Schmidt, 1980). Older works on the subject include Lore Krempel, *Die deutsche*

Modezeitschrift: Ihre Geschichte und Entwicklung nebst einer Bibliographie der deutschen, englischen und französischen Modezeitshriften (Munich: Tageblatt-Haus Coberg, 1935); Elen Riggert, 'Die Zeitschrift "London und Paris" als Quelle englischer Zeitverhaltnisse um die Wende des 18. und 19. Jahrhunderts', PhD dissertation, Göttingen, 1934.

21   *Der Teutsche Merkur*, November 1785, p. 187.

22   The *Cabinet des Modes* was imitated in England (by *The Fashionable Magazine*) and in Milan and Venice; see Roche, *The Culture of Clothing*, p. 487 n. 50.

23   'Only one difference can be found. The Paris periodical does nothing more than report, probably without any critical intention, whereas Bertuch gave his journal from the very start a critical [*räsonierenden*] character and thereby consciously placed it within a certain tradition of intellectual history'; Wies, 'Das *Journal des Luxus und der Moden*', p. 27 (see above, n. 19).

24   An overview of these journals can be found in Joachim Kirchner, *Bibliographie der Zeitschriften des deustchen Sprachgebiets in 1900* (Stuttgart: Hiersemann, 1969), 1, pp. 356–57. According to Wies, 'Das *Journal des Luxus und der Moden*', p. 48 (see above, n. 19), the *Cabinet des Modes* was published in German translation from 1788 to 1808 as the *Pariser Journal der Mode und des Geschmacks* but was not influential, McKendrick, Brewer and Plumb, *The Birth of a Consumer Society*, p. 47, list sixteen English ladies' almanacs dedicated to fashion published in England between 1771 and 1800.

25   *Die Zeitung für die elegantz Welt* focused more broadly on questions of taste in literature and the arts. Fashion was ranked second on the title page (1 July 1808): 'the *Newspaper for the Elegant World* contains according to its plan: 1. General essays intended to correct judgements of art and to ennoble taste as well as essays about all manner of pleasing objects that interest the educated world and that can serve to entertain finer family circles; 2. Reports on the newest fashions and luxuries from foreign and German cities regarding men's and women's clothes, household instruments, interior decorations, furniture, riding equipment . . . Anything that touches on politics or academic scholarship will remain completely excluded from these pages'.

26   C. Willet and Phillis Cunnington, *The History of Underclothes* (New York: Dover, 1992), p. 96. McKendrick, Brewer, and Plumb, *The Birth of a Consumer Society*, p. 47, provided convincing evidence that the *Lady's Magazine* did not colour its prints until 1786.

27   Bertuch's journal tried to keep up with the increasingly literary tone of fashion journals in the early nineteenth century, as the various name changes to the journal suggest. The monthly was founded in 1786 as *Journal der Moden*. Its name was almost immediately changed to *Journal des Luxus und der Moden* and stayed that way until 1812. For one year, the name became *Journal fur Luxus, Mode, und Gegenstände der Kunst*. The order of the title was reversed in 1814 to *Journal für Literatur, Kunst, Luxus und Mode*. In its final year, 1827, the title was changed once more to *Journal für Literatur, Kunst und geselliges Zusammenbleben*. The increasing de-emphasis on the words *Mode* and *Luxus* reflected the increasing self-confidence of German readers in their own fashion judgements as well as the journal's increasingly futile attempt to keep up with its competition. Fashion prints began to disappear from the journal after 1823. The few that did appear accompanied literary references. See Willhelm Feldmann *Friedrich Justin Bertuch, Eis Beitrag zur Geschichte der Goethezeit* (Saarbrücken: Schmidtke, 1902), p. 98.

28   Kleinert, *Die frühen Modejournale*, 126 (see above, n. 20), dated publication of *Giornale delle Dance e delle Mode* between 1789 and 1795.

29   Friedrich Bertuch Nachlaß, Goethe-Schiller Archiv, N.F. 873. Bertuch also listed fashion journals published in Prague, Leipzig, Göttingen and Vienna.

30   Sandgruber, *Die Anfänge der Konsumgesellschaft*, p. 301.

31   Ernst Beutler, 'Georg Melchior Kraus', in *Essays um Goethe*, 5th edition (Bremen: Schünemann, 1957), p. 432.

32   Feldmann, *Friedrich Justin Bertuch*, p. 23 (see above, n. 27).

33   McKendrick, Brewer and Plumb, *The Birth of a Consumer Society*, pp. 47–8.

34   The first issue of the *Allgemeine Moden-Zeitung* in 1820 began with the following gender-specific apology: 'Fathers complain about the changeability of fashion; men bemoan its costliness, and if we were to still these complaints, we would have to demand that the human spirit cease its education and maturation. This would be the death of the spirit, which is, after all, eternal. Thus we ask fathers and men to be a little patient and considerate'.

35   Roche, *The Culture of Clothing*, p. 486.

36   Quoted in Feldmann, *Friedrich Justin Bertuch*, p. 49 (see above, n. 27).

37   Bertuch Nachlaß, N.F. 867/II (see above, n. 29).

38   Ibid., p. 874.

39   W. H. Bruford, *Germany in the Eighteenth Century: The Social Background of the Literary Revival* (Cambridge: Cambridge University Press, 1965), pp. 280–1.

40   Ibid., 281; James Sheehan, *German History: 1770–1866* (Oxford: Clarendon, 1989), p. 157.

41   *Heimlich Verführung*, p. 61.

42   Ibid., p. 48.

43   This journal, which appeared in 1758 in Erfurt, also showed a predilection for English goods. See Dora Lühr, 'Die erste deutsche Modezeitung', *Zeitschrift für deutsche Philologie*, 71, 3, 4 (1953), pp. 329–43; Bringmeier, *Mode und Tracht*, p. 111.

44   Wies, *Das Journal des Luxus und der Moden*, p. 142 (see above, n. 19); Adolf Feulner, *Kunstgeschichte des Möbels* (Frankfurt: Propyläen Verlag, 1980), p. 297.

45   *Mode Journal* (abridged) 1, p. 75.

46   Ibid.

47   *Heimliche Verführung*, p. 51.

48   Bringmeier, *Mode und Tracht*, p. 118.

49   *Mode Journal*, February 1786, p. 72

50   Caroline de la Motte Fouqué, 'Geschichte der Moden, vom Jahre, 1785–1829', *Jahrbuch der Jean-Paul Gesellschaft*, 12 (1977), p. 28, noted that at the end of the eighteenth century neoclassical and English styles were considered interchangeable and were often mixed with traditional costumes, producing an unseemly combination. 'Back then . . . there reigned a strange confusion, in which the craving for English naturalness, or what counted as the same thing – Roman Idealism – was mixed with traditional formalism. This brought highly peculiar caricatures to light'.

51   *Heimlich Verführung*, p. 52.

52   Jakob Michael Reinhold Lenz, *Gesammelte Schriften*, ed. Franz Blei (Munich: Müller, 1910), 4, pp. 382–3.

53   Hubert Kiesewetter, *Industrielle Revolution in Deutschland* (Frankfurt: Suhrkamp, 1989), p. 27.

54   For a concise account of the hindrances to trade movement within German principalities, see Wolfgang Zorn, 'Binnenwirtschaftliche Verflectungen um 1800', in *Die wirtschaftliche Situation in Deutschland und Österreich um die Wende vom 18. zum 19. Jahrhundert*, ed. Friedrich Lütge (Stuttgart: Fischer, 1964), pp. 99–109. For a larger overview of European trade routes from the late Middle Ages to 1815, see Hermann Kellenbenz, 'Landverkehr, Fluß- und Seeschiffahrt im europäischen Handel', *Europa, Raum wirtschaftlicher Begegnung*, 92 (1991), pp. 327–441.

55   *Mode Journal*, January 1786, p. 22.

56   Ibid., July 1786, p. 249.

57   *Mode Journal* (abridged), 1, p. 23.

58   Cited in Bringemeier, *Mode und Tracht*, p. 117.

59   Christian Kraus, the most prominent proponent of free market economic theory, probably

first began working on Adam Smith's writings in 1788. As a professor in Königsberg, Kraus went on to have a significant influence on the education of Prussian officials. See Treue, *Wirtschafts- und Technik-geschichte Preussens*, p. 216 (see above, n. 6).

60   Bahrdt argued that 'the most important thing, particularly for the middle classes, is the avoidance of luxury'. Quoted in Schindler, 'Jenseits des Zwangs?' p. 197 (see above, n. 7). See also Ulrich Hermann, 'Die Kodifizierung bürgerlichen Bewußtseins in der deutschen Spätaufklärung', Carl Friedrich Bahrdt's '"Handbuch der Moral für den Bürgerstand" aus dem Jahre 1789' in *Bürger und Bürgerlichkeit im Zeitalter der Aufklärung*, ed. Rudolf Vierhaus (Heidelberg: Lambert Schneider Verlag, 1981), pp. 321–33.

61   *Mode Journal*, April 1792, p. 184.

62   *Mode Journal* (abridged), 1, p. 71.

63   *Mode Journal*, December 1790, pp. 641–2.

64   *Mode Journal* (abridged), 1, p. 38.

65   For a summary of other versions of this ripple effect argument, see Wolfgang Haug, *Critique of Commodity Aesthetics*, trans. Robert Bock (Minneapolis: University of Minnesota Press, 1986), p. 20.

66   Johann August Schlettwein, *Grundfeste der Staaten oder dis polistiche Okonomic* (Frankfurt: Athenäum, 1971 [1779]), pp. 410–11.

67   See Joyce Appleby, 'Consumption in Early Modern Social Thought', in Brewer and Porter, *Consumption and the World of Goods*. 'Rattling off the name of new condiments, textiles and inventions has served as the incantation for the summoning spirits that presided over the rise of the West' (p. 164). The catalogue Bertuch reprinted in the *Mode Journal* included gold and silver diamond watches, gold and steel watch chains, gold pins, brooches, cuff links, hairpieces decorated with real pearls, elastic sock bands, silver and steel shoe buckles, silver pencil holders, ladies' scissors, travel cases for letter writing, hat pins with jewels, knitting and sewing needles, silver-plated thimbles with inlaid precious stones, tobacco cases, tea brewers, sugar doses, breadbaskets, wine racks, tea services, lacquered coffee tables, cutting knives with mahogany handles, toothbrushes, ladies' hair styling kits, razors, shaving brushes, combs, powder dispensers, bootjacks, crystal writing utensils, miniature globes, compasses, rubber erasers, pistols, powder horns, saddle blankets, ladies' saddles, bridles, hunting horns, men's toolboxes, ladies' sewing kits, mahogany chairs with horsehair upholstery, dining room tables, telescopes, microscopes, perspectives, opera glasses, hearing aids, surgeon's instruments, amputation knives, tourniquets, catheters, dentistry equipment, umbrellas, patent leather gloves, tea, mustard, purses, perfumes, Wedgwood tea services, oval bowls, terrines, dinner plates, dessert plates, salad dishes, red, blue and white cups with or without handles, thermometers, barometers, and a wide variety of scientific equipment. *Mode Journal* (abridged) 1, pp. 76–81.

68   The question of whether domestic demand or foreign and colonial consumption fuelled English manufacturing in the eighteenth century has been central to English historical scholarship. Bertuch seemed to believe that domestic demand in German principalities could hasten the development of a German manufacturing base.

Fashion and the eighteenth-century satirical print

Peter McNeil

As new and cheaper forms of graphic reproduction, and more literate audiences for periodicals and prints arose in eighteenth-century Western Europe, there was a marked increase in the output of satirical printmaking from the 1760s in France, Germany and the Dutch Republic, but notably in England. England's freedom of the press and involvement of the public in political and cultural affairs through coffee house, print and exhibition culture encouraged the production of thousands of satirical broadsheets and individually printed caricatures. Fashion had two principal functions in these prints. In the first half of the century the English political print included dress to indicate class, party-political, geographic, ethnic and national identity. In tandem with theatrical precedents, the shorthand device for a Frenchman was elaborate court-dress and a simpering posture, for a Spaniard a ruff, and a Dutchman round breeches. Nationalist Tories and the English 'John Bull' figure (based on a literary character from John Arbuthnot and popularised further by Jonathan Swift) wore rustic frock coat and boots, in contrast to the rich court dress of Whigs that resembled that of continental court culture. On the continent, graphical fashion satires tended to remain a luxury novelty for the rich. English prints were imported by French dealers and sent as far as St Petersburg. Ambassadorial missions reported on the meaning of their contents to rulers including Louis XVI and international letter-writers such as Horace Walpole frequently referred to them in their correspondence.

In the last third of the century, numerous English print-makers who were also often print-sellers and entrepreneurs greatly increased their output of social caricatures in which fashion formed the principal and not the secondary subject. Caricature prints, sometimes quite obscene, appeared in the expanding number of English periodicals, such as *The London Museum*, *The Oxford Magazine*, *The Town and Country Magazine* and *Bon Ton*. Matthew and Mary Darly, John Dawes, William Humphrey, William Holland, Samuel W. Fores, Carington and John Bowles and John Raphael Smith (1751–1812) exhibited their wares publicly in shop windows and printed single sheet caricatures which were sold in folio sets, reproducing the designs of others such as John Collett, Robert Dighton, Henry W. Bunbury and Thomas Rowlandson (1756–1827). Some were amateurs with elevated posts: Bunbury was groom of the bedchamber to Frederick, Duke of York, second son of George III. It was a leisure pasttime for some aristocrats such as Lady Diana Beauclerk (1734–1808) to design these plates themselves and have them published; several instructional guides were published to teach the skill. Although these plates did not amount to a very large proportion of the output, it added to the excitement generated around these 'caricaturas'. William Holland (1757–1815) published the work of Richard Newton (*c.* 1777–98) whose satires of dress and fashionability were connected to older carnivalesque 'drolls', making extensive use

Snapshot 13.1 M. Darly, *Lady Drudger Going to Ranelagh*, 25 April 1772. 772.4.25.1.1. The print-maker plays on older images of the hag, here in disarray as she prepares her wig to venture to Ranelagh pleasure gardens, referred to by a contemporary French writer as a 'grand rotunda where ones turns endlessly' ['Le Ranelagh est un grande rotonde ou l'on tourne incessament', 'Letters Describing Life in England', Lewis Walpole library, mss vol. 115. Courtesy of the Lewis Walpole Library, Yale University].

of duality, pairing, and vulgar puns. The themes include the speed of new fashionable items, textiles, patterns and bodily silhouettes; the alleged spread of fashionability to the lower orders including the servant class, the concomitant difficulty of reading the social sphere, themes of metropolitan urbanity versus rustic simplicity, the role of the appearance trades such as wig-making and hairdressing in promoting fashion, and alleged relationships between national fashions and character. The disjunction between the applied finery of fashion and the lumpen, deluded or immoral physical body beneath a 'fashion veneer' continued older Judeo-Christian and also classical themes.

The caricature print from 1760 extends the more general cultural association of women with extremes of fashion to that of men, as they scrutinise extensively the airs and dress of the macaroni (c. 1760–80) and later the buck and the dandy (c. 1800–20). In the etched prints of Matthew and Mary Darly, the more low-born the person depicted, the more crude the illustrative style, suggesting a cruder imitation or performance of fashionability (Snapshot 13.1). These differences perpetuate the belief that the orders are inherently either vulgar or superior depending on rank, as well as highlighting the joke contained in the overstepping of sartorial boundaries from class to class. This is not the only meaning, however. It has been argued that caricatures of the over-eating George III worked to humanise the image of the king. As Brian Maidment notes of the early nineteenth-century 'literary dustman' type, in form and technique, such prints might simultaneously highlight the energy and ingenuity of labouring-class subjects at the same time as mocking aspirational behaviour. Caricatures might have *affirmed* certain behaviours and lifestyles. It partly explains the longevity of the caricature print in illustrated periodicals for all classes. Just as the development of caricature demands its opposite, idealised aesthetics, so the convoluted forms, surprising gestures and novel departures of caricature perfectly reflected contemporary notions of the chicanery of fashion.

To crop a print is to completely change its meaning. Eighteenth-century prints were often reproduced in the nineteenth and twentieth century without the context of their original verbal text banners, which were sometimes lengthy. Topics were re-assigned that reflect more nineteenth-century concerns such as 'Caricatures of Women and Matrimony' (in James Parton, 1877). Redrawn caricatures also make them look quite different. This led to different interpretations that were frequently sentimental and nostalgic and generated ideas about either the charm or the boisterous nature of eighteenth-century life. Approaches to the study of caricature reflect shifts in twentieth-century art-historical and sociological analysis. A reflection model used exhaustively by British Museum cataloguer and historian M. Dorothy George analysed caricature prints as representations of real events such as the launch and spread of a new fashion. This approach is reductive in that prints had multiple meanings to different audiences and may have helped create the dynamic of an event (Snapshot 13.2). Whereas the art historian Ernst Gombrich argued that the aim of the print-maker and dealer was to sell the product and not unsettle overly the purchaser, Hogarth historian Ronald Paulson argued that within graphic satire a range of explanations are true and not mutually exclusive. The use of Freudian ideas of the joke have been criticised by some commentators who argue that even humour is historically situated. Like the theatre, which assumed different reading positions from its multiple publics, the power of the caricature print is to function on several levels simultaneously (Snapshot 13.3). Although historian John Brewer notes that there is almost no surviving evidence of how

Drawn & Etch'd by R. Newton   London, Pub. July 1 1794, by R. Newton N.° 20, Walbrook.

A Peep into Brest with a Navel Review!

Snapshot 13.2 A Peep into Brest with a Navel Review!, 794.7.1.1. A rare print not held in the British Library, the caricature puns on the coastal town of Brest and the display of these loose naval followers. The artifice of their fashionable hair-style is matched by the coarseness of their bodily display. As groups of wealthy Englishwomen sometimes endowed naval ships financially, the joke is doubly strong. Courtesy of the Lewis Walpole Library, Yale University.

the common people viewed popular imagery such as the caricature prints, there are many contemporary descriptions of the street and the theatre which emphasise that the fashionable and wealthy were often mocked and abused for their pretension. Fashion caricatures participated in this lively dialogue. It may even be fair to say that such prints intrigued those who were already infatuated with *la mode*.

Snapshot 13.3 Williams, *A Gallic Beauty* (published by J. Johnson, March 1815, 815.3.0.1). This very beautiful image conveys information about fashion clothing but in a heightened manner that veers on caricature. In the Revolutionary and Napoleonic period, dress featured as part of the textual joke in political caricature. Respectful fashion plates and caricatures issued from the same hand of experienced illustrators: Jean-François Bosio (1764–1827) and Philibert Louis Debucourt (1755–1832), who deployed an extremely elegant style and fine colouring as part of the joke. Courtesy of the Lewis Walpole Library, Yale University.

Bibliography and further reading

Donald, D. (1996) *The Age of Caricature: Satirical Prints in the Reign of George III*, New Haven and London: Yale University Press.

Duffy, M. (1986) *The Englishman and the Foreigner: The English Satirical Print 1600–1832*, Cambridge: Chadwyck-Healey.

George, M. D. (1967) *Hogarth to Cruikshank: Social Change in Graphical Satire*, London: Allen Lane/Penguin.

Maidment, B. E. (1996) *Reading Popular Prints, 1790–1870*, Manchester and New York: Manchester University Press.

Paulson, R. (1971) *Hogarth: His Life, Art, and Times*, 2 vols. New Haven and London: Yale University Press.

Ideology and the dangers of fashion in early national America

Linzy A. Brekke

Snapshot 14.1 Third president Thomas Jefferson advocates for the embargo and casts off his clothing 'rather than submit to London or Paris fashion!' Courtesy of the Houghton Library, Harvard University.

When Thomas Dwight, a state senator from Massachusetts, complained in 1796 that 'Fashion, like Robespierre and Marat deals havoc and destruction without ever assigning a reason to any tribunal' (Dwight 1796), he eloquently summarised America's critical attitude towards *la mode* in the early republic. Even as they espoused ideals of equality, early national Americans remained uncomfortably mired in and dependent upon a system of style that upheld fundamentally hierarchical differences – of class, gender, race, ethnicity, age, and region.

That system was primarily European in origin and form, since the United States imported almost all of its finished textiles from abroad and many aspirants to genteel status looked lamentably to England and France for direction. These were cultures which America generally considered effeminate and immoral, ruled by autocratic monarchs (or dangerous mobs). Such associations cemented the impression that fashion served as a dangerous political tool for princes and Jacobins to deprive citizens of both their purses and their free will. The nigh dictatorial force fashion exerted on public life proved especially troubling in a nation dedicated to self-government and the disembodiment of authority. A dizzying array of styles poured forth from metropolitan centres in an accelerating seasonal cycle, frustrating the thriftiness and practicality of farmers and pious Protestants. Valuable garments, worn for mere months, were to be discarded or remade because 'forsooth it is the fashion' seethed one Philadelphia writer.

Anti-fashion discourse and puritanical jeremiads about the dangers of luxury had accompanied almost every new mode in America since the earliest days of colonial settlement, as the presence of unfree labourers and the sheer vastness of the country made stabilising social status a communal imperative. But the imperial crisis with Britain during the 1760s further inflamed fashion's significance, for the imposition of import taxes exposed the economic and cultural domination of British artefacts in daily life. Opposition to imported goods galvanised the independence movement, making a commitment to non-importation/non-consumption central to the ideology of revolution. Patriots after the war could hardly embrace transatlantic consumption and fashion culture without seeming to betray their country. Yet, in the decades following the war, American consumption of European manufactured textiles more than doubled, leading to high rates of personal indebtedness and the flow of precious specie into the pockets of overseas merchants. Many felt the renewal and increase in clothing imports threatened the economic and political viability of the whole nation.

Government officials like George Washington encouraged a conceptual and material transformation of fashion from European luxury to domestic virtue in order to bolster nationalism and encourage domestic manufacturing and consumption. He and others sought to give sartorial expression to America's new political identity by dressing in homespun woollen and cotton clothes, choosing sober colours, and eschewing jewellery and ornamentation. Local communities reinstituted (short-lived) non-consumption pacts, states debated new sumptuary laws, and Congress passed protective tariff legislation to tax goods like silk, lace, gauze, and jewellery beyond the reach of all but the most wealthy consumers. Other concerned politicians like James Madison and Thomas Jefferson felt self-sufficiency in cloth production and a more dramatic curb on imports 'which are destructive of the morals, health, and industry of the people' (Madison 1792) were necessary to achieve true independence and economic growth, ideas that in part inspired Jefferson's Embargo Act of 1807, prohibiting virtually all trade with foreign ports (Snapshot 14.1). Although quickly repealed, the embargo and these other actions revealed Americans' deep ambivalence toward fashion and the ways they sought to reconcile their material life with the political and social imperatives of republicanism.

Bibliography and further reading

Breen, T. H. (2004) *The Marketplace of Revolution: How Consumer Politics Shaped American Independence*, New York: Oxford University Press.

Brekke, L. (2006) '"To Make a Figure": Clothing and the Politics of Male Identity in Eighteenth-century America', in J. Styles and A. Vickery (eds), *Gender, Taste, and Material Culture in Britain and North America*, New Haven and London: Yale University Press, pp. 225–46.

Dwight, T. (1796) 'Thomas Dwight to Hannah Dwight', 31 January 1796, Dwight-Howard Papers, Massachusetts Historical Society, Boston.

Madison, J. (1792) 'Fashion', *National Gazette*, 20 March.

Zakim, M. (2003) *Ready-Made Democracy: A History of Men's Dress in the American Republic, 1760–1860*, Chicago: University of Chicago Press.

PART 4

Between Luxury and Leisure
The nineteenth century

Peter McNeil and Giorgio Riello

> I define the tradition that all ball gowns fulfill as:
> rendering nimble, vaporous and ethereal, by that superior way of
> walking called dance,
> the goddess wrapped in their clouds.
> Stephane Mallarmé, La Dernière Mode (1874)

The nineteenth century was a period of vast transformations and possibilities in terms of a fashion-scape for men and women, from the provincial worker to the patrician industrialist. Yet much of the century's fashion is poorly understood and remains little researched. Enormous changes of style and silhouette swept through the female wardrobe, with most scholarly attention being focused upon those transformations of the second half of the century. This is probably a result of the power of art history in designating impressionist painting practice as central to its scholarship in the past forty years, as well as the attention paid to the greatness of the prose, poetry and journalism of writers such as Baudelaire, the Realists such as Zola and the Symbolists such as Huysmans. Examples of the high level of engagement with the second half of the nineteenth century can be cited in two very different projects. The influential curator Anne Coleman wrote in 1989 her magisterial study *The Opulent Era* based on the significant holdings of the Brooklyn Museum, at around the same time that the paradigm-shifting academic Valerie Steele wrote her *Paris Fashion* (1988), a text which through its mainly literary investigation transformed stereotypes and received wisdom regarding women's relationship to Paris fashion and that object of contempt, the corset. Although their method was very different, they shared a concern to refocus attention on the last third of the nineteenth century as a far from boring or restrictive time for women's fashion, rescuing it from the functionalist critiques into which it fell in the first half of the twentieth century.

The first three to four decades of the nineteenth century were quite extraordinary in terms of the rapid shifts in the definition of female beauty ideals and fashionable clothes, and in the making of those clothes. The period after the Napoleonic Empire, when neo-classical motifs and a straightforward visual programme directed in the service of the power of Napoleon created a fairly understandable iconography and motives for dressing, is not well understood and these editors found it challenging to find good-quality writing on the dress of the years 1820–60, the 'pre-crinoline' era. The dominance of the first two decades of the century has been reinforced by the popularity of Jane Austen and her era, an author who did not dwell so much on clothes as the costume dramas of recent years might suggest.

Fashions of the first half of the nineteenth century were frequently historicising, continued to be complex in formation and trimming, and were made from a wide range of textiles from cotton to silk. The period from 1820 to 1850, in which clothing survivals are ironically less frequent than for the last third of the eighteenth century, was marked by what some contemporary critics saw as the crisis of style. An enormous range of references, from the Romanticism of seventeenth-century Van Dyck dress, to the novelty of the motifs depicted on new printed cottons, make this a complex period. If not stylistically coherent, it is unified by an interest in effects and technologies; from the use of cast-iron in jewels to the growth of the science of pattern making, in which designs for clothes began to be regularly inserted into women's periodicals.

Travel in the late eighteenth century and leisure in the nineteenth century transformed the requirements of clothes. The rise of stage-coach travel encouraged the spread of masculine tailored and collared jackets and the use of durable woollen broadcloth into the female fashionable wardrobe. Late nineteenth-century tailoring also showed a type of *rapprochement* between the genders for amateur riding, in which both sexes wore plainer and tailored coats, women adopting a smaller top hat (Taylor 1999). The nineteenth-century English, great inventors that they were, developed numerous innovative outdoor garments. The Selby 'waterproofer' coat, named after a record ride of Jim Selby in 1888, hung in a complete circle around the man so that water would run off, rather like an umbrella. In such innovations for function, we detect some of the experiments with the human form that the modernists of the early twentieth century would undertake.

Several costume curators have developed tables in order to date garments on the basis of cut. Schlick's algorithm for nineteenth-century ladies' dresses, for examples, posed a checklist of questions such as 'are bodice and skirt separate?', 'are skirt side seams straight grain?' (Pedersen and Loverin 1989). A combination of questions would purportedly bring the assessor or curator to a conclusive date within seven to nine year blocks. The problem with such a system is that the attempt to make the study of surviving costume scientific, ignores the fact that a great deal of surviving clothing was adapted for fancy dress in the Edwardian period, and that a garment might incorporate older components. It also assumes that fashion cadence operates simultaneously in all cities and towns, and forgets the mantra that nineteenth-century Boston matrons would leave their Paris clothes in the closet for one year so that they did not appear too fashionable.

Janet Arnold was among the first to study paper patterns, at a time when they were about to disappear from daily life in the 1960s (Arnold 1972). The first folding full-size paper patterns appeared in *The Lady's Economical Assistant* in 1808 and were for children's dress. Paper patterns were included in French and English magazines from the 1830s. From 1840 home dressmaking increased in popularity and numerous books with diagrams of patterns were also published. French and English magazines provided printed paper sheets of full-sized bodice and sleeve patterns. The large company Butterick Paper Pattern Service of Sterling, Massachusetts, commenced in 1863 and was run by a tailor, Ebenezer Butterick, followed by McCall's Pattern Company (New York) from 1870. Such developments created the possibility that all citizens might be a type of fashion designer or at least have the ability to customise their clothes.

This brief analysis points to the many important changes in dress, but also in the very notion of fashionability that occurred during the nineteenth century. One of the most important forces of change was industrialisation: it not only changed people's lives, creating enormous wealth for the few and the proletarisation of the majority; it substantially altered the ways in which textiles – and to a certain extent garments – were produced. Starting with new and revolutionary machinery for the spinning of cotton in the 1770s (that was applied to other fibres and then wool in particular in the following half-century), the production of textiles was transformed. By the early decades of the nineteenth century, cloth could be produced for a fraction of the price of a generation earlier. Thanks to mechanised and factory production, supply could outpace booming demand both in Europe and in North America. Machines were also used for knitting and lace-making, and weaving with the Jacquard loom using punched cards to produce patterned cloth becoming widespread by the middle of the century (Riello 2010).

These important changes are concisely analysed in a snapshot by Katrina Honeyman in this *Reader*. She notes how this was a partial transformation in which the production of garments remained substantially unmechanised until the 1850s when the sewing machine was invented (Godley 1996). Its fast adoption and global success can be seen as a turning point in the history of fashion: if not a 'democraticisation of fashion', as Lipovetsky argues for the invention and influence of couture, the invention of the sewing machines was truly a 'democraticisation of clothing'. It allowed paper patterns to be transposed into garments cheaply and quickly both by experts as well as neophytes (Burman 1998). The mechanisation of textile and clothing production also caused a cheapening of decoration that many, especially the design reformers, saw as a central part of an incipient decline of taste: wealth and economic development might have been brought about by industrialisation, but choice for consumers was not necessarily seen as either positive or morally acceptable. This concern had major implications later for how nineteenth-century fashion was judged and assessed.

The consequences of the material transformation of clothing are considered in an important essay by Valerie Steele. In her 'Artificial beauty, or the morality of dress and adornment', she confronts the Victorian interest in fashion as a force and a practice that functioned as an aid to correcting flaws. The cheapness of adornment – something abhorred by later modernist thinkers – and the fact that it was now in the reach of the masses, made public opinion unsure of the new aesthetics – especially female – that were taking shape. Many feared the effects of an over-suffused female beauty as something that might trick or deceive. These fears extended well beyond clothing and included all forms of embellishment ranging from cosmetics to jewellery as analysed by Elizabeth Fischer in this *Reader*. Steele provides a detailed account of the contemporary cosmetics debate, in which some saw face painting as wicked and even orgasmic in tone, and in which both moral character and the fibres of the flesh might be damaged by a combination of chemical and moral confusion. Steele's essay makes many links with Clair Hughes on 'Fashion, readers and the novel in the nineteenth century', as comment and even attack on the 'girl of the period' came from the hand of writers such as Mrs Eliza Lynn Linton. Steele points to the nineteenth-century dilemma of accepting and adopting fashions that were set by women of the nether world of the stage and the *demi-monde*. Her essay also indicates many continuities with the eighteenth-century anxiety about fashion, including the figure of the 'man milliner', who profits from his interventions into women's appearance without being a true man himself, owing to his close connection to fashion. Steele provides the best account to date of the seemingly incongruous moral tool-box of nineteenth-century women's fashion, such as the perceived hypocrisy of scanty evening wear. Such dress she argues, is 'a form of conventional dress, legitimised by long custom . . . It was aesthetically tamed eroticism' and a type of *situational* dress. Having been written after Michel Foucault's hugely influential *History of Sexuality*, in which Foucault demolished the idea that Victorianism represented a puritanical age, Steele is able to conclude that 'if we can speak at all of a "Victorian" ideal of femininity, that ideal was, in large part, an erotic one'.

Christopher Breward, in 'Modes of manliness: reflections on recent histories of masculinities and fashion' provides a historiography of the issues and challenges that face the scholar analysing men's dress. He argues for a series of overlapping reasons that came together in order to make it appear that men had either ceased to engage with fashion or did it in such a way that its consequences were socially minimal. He notes the dominance in academic thought of the last thirty years of the notion of the separate spheres for men and women, of the exploration of patriarchal power, and the leitmotifs of those quintessentially female zones, the department store and the bazaar. He also points to the power of collecting and collections in shaping scholarship and naturalising positions: 'Aside from uniform and court dress, everyday clothing for men has tended not to be collected so comprehensively by museums, and equally its survival is rare in comparison to women's items'. In an important analysis that confirms the editors' comments in the introduction that history is a site of both content and theoretical challenge, Breward argues that when contemporary views converge with historical investigation, new models for studying the topic might emerge. Engaging with fashion as a notion of the 'practices of the self' is, to Breward, a means to open up new issues that can be 'brought to bear on questions of gender and its historical construction'. Breward's essay also reminds readers that history is not written by scribes but by subjects with their own priorities, interests and desires in which a personal engagement with scholarship generates new ways of seeing the world.

Ulrich Lehmann, in a newly commissioned essay entitled '*L'Homme des foules*, dandy, *flâneur*: fashion and the metropolis 1850–1940', positions the women and men examined in previous essays within the space of the city. He argues that fashion is a product and a consequence of the city itself: 'Fashion occurs most prominently in a constantly shifting environment, as this provides both the economic conditions and the social impetus for expressing new perceptions of the body, changing one's status, and displaying conspicuous consumption'. Lehmann argues for an expanded sense of the meaning of the term fashion, suggesting that to focus on fashionable clothes alone is erroneous and dangerous: 'Fashion in clothes cannot be singled out in its cultural meaning nor can it be critically analysed or structurally positioned without constant recourse to other fashionable expressions in modern culture'. The tenor of his argument concurs not only with what is known of so-called 'decorative arts' scholarship but also with the system of thought of early twentieth-century intellectuals such as Georg Simmel, who wrote of jewellery that 'Adornment intensifies or enlarges the impression of the personality by operating as a sort of radiation emanating from it . . . an inextricable mixture of physiological and psychic elements' (Simmel 1905b: 207). Lehmann provides the reader with a nuanced and sophisticated reading of the great nineteenth-century debate regarding fashion's central place within aesthetic debate and the realities of the market for forms from paintings to novels: 'The canon of cultural forms has to be subverted and renewed constantly, and the production of new objects and commodities is paramount in introducing such novelties to be reflected in technique, symbolism, and narrative by progressive cultural expressions'. In his summary of the figure of the dandy and his new reading of the *flâneuse*, the woman writer George Sand, Lehmann concludes that: 'The aesthetic perception of the flâneur is subjective and, to the most part, individualist. It might touch on societal ills or political problems like reifying social structures or commodifying human relations but in the end his views are concerned with the corporeal and psychological reaction of himself as subject alone'.

Alex M. Cain's snapshot of 'Fashion and France in the Second Empire' and Olga Vainshtein's essay 'The dandy' can be usefully read as contextual pieces in conjunction with Lehmann's more theoretical essay. Cain argues that Paris provided a type of fashion platform in which the theatre, the streets and the varied commercial diversions of the modern metropolis created a city in which fashion was embedded commercially and physically. Vainshtein, in her perceptive reading of the male figure of fashion, the dandy, points to his novelty and rupture with older models of foppish men from the past, to his very modernity: 'In the contemporary world the dandies mastered the strategy of objectifying the personality, transforming an individual style into marketable goods'.

Diana Crane, trained in sociology, has provided an important theoretical position regarding the study of clothes for several decades. In her important methodological essay 'Clothing behaviour as non-verbal resistance', in which she explores the creation and attribution of symbolic value, she identifies five types of analyses that can be brought to bear on fashion. Crane sets out the analysis of 'material culture as a type of text that expresses symbols and contributes to discourses and to cultural repertoires'. By introducing cross-national studies of the symbolic value expressed in material goods, Crane argues that the adoption of 'marginal dress' was not always undertaken to express rebellion against dominant culture in any straightforward way, rather to 'facilitate certain types of activities, either work or pleasure'.

This position, in which the social outcome is as important as the social force that generated it, can also be seen at work in the scholarship of Lou Taylor, whose object-based studies have been most influential in this field. Through her close reading of objects and public and private written texts, Lou Taylor argues that the clothes required for mourning dress mean much more than their medieval roots in commemoration and honour. Her short text brings us back to clothing and its production and distribution as Taylor argues that in the nineteenth century the provision of mourning dress triggered two important developments: firstly, large-scale mourning warehouses opened by the 1840s and rapidly became department stores; secondly the large-scale manufacture of ready-to-wear mourning clothing from the mid-1860s was influential in the reshaping of the entire clothing sector.

The nineteenth century remains a difficult period for the history of fashion. Characterised as it is by change − in the production, distribution, consumption of clothing, as well as in their cultural and social attributes − the period between the French Revolution and the 'invention of couture' in the 1860s–1880s is still elusive. Victorian notions of renunciation (especially male sobriety and appropriateness) and decadence (especially female whim to be restrained by all means) can hardly be upheld; yet the complexity of this early part of the nineteenth century is still the subject of scrutiny and intense debate. We have also chosen to contextualise the 'modernity' of the later nineteenth century not so much in terms of couture, its protagonists and its influence (see Part 6), but in terms of the people *and* places of fashion. The readings that we included were purposely chosen to provide the reader with a sense of the ways in which nineteenth- and twentieth-century scholarship uses fashion not for fashion's sake, i.e. to know fashion better, but as a tool to illuminate a series of topics that are cultural, social and intellectual and that range from women's request for universal suffrage to the creation of modern sociology. From the nineteenth century, fashions stops being an accessory to history and become one of its driving forces, a topic that we wish to examine in the final part of this *Reader.*

Bibliography and further reading

Books and articles

Aldrich, W. (2000) 'Tailors' Cutting Manuals and the Growing Provision of Popular Clothing 1770–1870', *Textile History*, 31, 2, pp. 163–201.

Anscombe, I. (1984) *A Woman's Touch: Women in Design from 1860 to the Present Day*, London: Virago.

Arnold, J. (1972) *Patterns of Fashion 2: Englishwomen's Dresses and their Construction c. 1860–1940*, 2nd edition, London: Macmillan.

Brekke, L. (2006) '"To Make a Figure": Clothing and the Politics of Male Identity in Eighteenth-century America', in J. Styles and A. Vickery (eds), *Gender, Taste, and Material Culture in Britain and North America*, New Haven and London: Yale University Press, pp. 225–46.

Breward, C. (1994) 'Femininity and Consumption: The Problem of the Late Nineteenth-century Fashion Journal', *Journal of Design History*, 7, 2, pp. 71–89.

Breward, C. (1999a) *The Hidden Consumer: Masculinities, Fashion and City Life, 1860–1914*, Manchester: Manchester University Press.

Breward, C. (1999b) 'Renouncing Consumption: Men, Fashion and Luxury, 1870–1914', in A. de la Haye and E. Wilson (eds), *Defining Dress: Dress as Object, Meaning and Identity*, Manchester: Manchester University Press, pp. 48–61.

Brush Kidwell, C., and V. Steele (1989) *Men and Women: Dressing the Part*, Washington: Smithsonian Institutions.

Burman, B. (ed.) (1998) *The Culture of Sewing: Gender, Consumption and Home Dressmaking*, Oxford: Berg.

Byrde, P. (1992) *Nineteenth Century Fashion*, London: Batsford.

Chapman, S. D. (2004) 'The "Revolution" in the Manufacture of Ready-made Clothing, 1840–1860', *London Journal*, 29, 1, pp. 44–61.

Coleman, A. E. (1989) *The Opulent Era: Fashions of Worth, Doucet and Pingat*, London: Thames and Hudson in association with the Brooklyn Museum.

Cooper, C. (2007) 'The Victorian and Edwardian Eras, 1860–1910', in L. Welters and A. Lillethun (eds), *The Fashion Reader*, Oxford: Berg, pp. 34–45.

Dakers, C. (2005) 'James Morrison (1789–1857), "Napoleon of Shopkeepers", Millionaire Haberdasher, Modern Entrepreneur', in C. Breward and C. Evans (eds), *Fashion and Modernity*, Oxford: Berg, pp. 17–32 and John Styles's 'Response', pp. 33–8.

de Marly, D. (1980 [2nd edition 1991]) *Worth: Father of Haute Couture*, New York: Elm Tree Books.

Fischer, G. (2001) *Pantaloons and Power: Nineteenth-century Dress Reform in the United States*, Kent, OH: Ohio State University Press.

Freegood, E. (2003) '"Fine Fingers": Victorian Handmade Lace and Utopian Consumption', *Victorian Studies*, 45, 4, pp. 625–47.

Fukai, A. (ed) (2002) *Fashion: A History from the Eighteenth to the Twentieth Century, the Collection of the Kyoto Costume Institute*, Cologne: Taschen.

Godley, A. (1996) 'Singer in Britain: The Diffusion of Sewing Machine Technology and Its Impact on the Clothing Industry in the United Kingdom, 1860–1905', *Textile History*, 27, 1, pp. 59–76.

Gundle, S., and Castelli, C. T. (2006) *The Glamour System*, Basingstoke: Palgrave Macmillan, esp. ch. 1.

Harvey, J. (1996) *Men in Black*, London: Reaktion Books.

Honeyman, K. (2000) *Well Suited: A History of the Leeds Clothing Industry, 1850–1990*, Oxford: Oxford University Press.

Hughes, C. (2006) *Dressed in Fiction*, Oxford: Berg.

Kaplan, J. H., and Stowell, S. (1994) *Theatre and Fashion: Oscar Wilde to the Suffragettes*, Cambridge and New York: Cambridge University Press.

Kuchta, D. (1996) 'The Making of the Self-made Man: Class, Clothing and English Masculinity, 1688–1832', in V. De Grazia and E. Furlough (eds), *The Sex of Things: Gender and Consumption in Historical Perspective*, Berkeley and London: University of California Press, pp. 54–78.

Kuchta, D. (2002) *The Three-piece Suit and Modern Masculinity: England, 1550–1850*, Berkeley and London: University of California Press.

Kunzle, D. (2006) *Fashion and Fetishism: Corsets, Tight-lacing and Other Forms of Body-sculpture*, Stroud: The History Press.

Lajer-Burcharth, E. (1999) *Necklines: The Art of Jacques-Louis David after the Terror*, New Haven: Yale University Press.

Lehmann, U. (1999) 'Tigersprung: Fashioning History', *Fashion Theory*, 3, 3, pp. 297–322.

Lehmann, U. (2000) *Tigersprung: Fashion in Modernity*, Cambridge, MA: MIT Press.

Levitt, S. (1986) *Victorians Unbuttoned: Registered Designs for Clothing, their Makers and Wearers, 1839–1900*, London: Allen & Unwin.

Levitt, S. (1996) 'Clothing', in M. B. Rose (ed.), *The Lancashire Cotton Industry: A History since 1700*, Preston: County Books, 1996, pp. 154–86.

Lipovetsky, G. (1994) *The Empire of Fashion: Dressing Modern Democracy*, trans. Catherine Porter, Princeton: Princeton University Press.

McNeil, P. (2000) 'Macaroni Masculinities', *Fashion Theory*, 4, 4, pp. 373–404.

North, S. (2007) 'From Neoclassicism to the Industrial Revolution, 1790–1860', in L. Welters and A. Lillethun (eds), *The Fashion Reader*, Oxford: Berg, pp. 20–33.

Pedersen, E., and Loverin, J. (1989) 'Historic Costume Dating: Further Explorations of Schlick's Algorithm', *Dress*, 15, pp. 38–50.

Perrot, P. (1994) *Fashioning the Bourgeoisie: A History of Clothing in the Nineteenth Century*, Princeton: Princeton University Press.

Rappaport, E. D. (2000) *Shopping for Pleasure: Women in the Making of London's West End*, Princeton: Princeton University Press.

Riello, G. (2010) 'Fabrics of Fashion: The Material Culture of Textiles in European History', in *Berg Encyclopaedia of Dress and Fashion: Western Europe*, gen. ed. Joanne B. Eicher, Oxford: Berg.

Rolley, K. (1990) 'Fashion, Femininity and the Fight for the Vote', *Art History*, 13, 1, pp. 47–71.

Shannon, N. (2006) *The Cut of His Coat: Men, Dress, and Consumer Culture in Britain, 1860–1914*, Athens, OH: Ohio University Press.

Sharpe, P. (1995) '"Cheapness and Economy": Manufacturing and Retailing Ready-Made Clothing in London and Essex 1830–50', *Textile History*, 26, 2, pp. 203–13.

Simmel, Georg ([original ed. 1905] 1967) *The Sociology of Georg Simmel*, trans. Kurt H. Wolff, New York: The Free Press, p. 339.

Steele, V. (1985) *Fashion and Eroticism: The Ideals of Feminine Beauty from the Victorian Era to the Jazz Age*, New York and Oxford: Oxford University Press.

Steele, V. (1988 [2nd edition Berg 1998]) *Paris Fashion: A Cultural History*, New York and Oxford: Oxford University Press.

Steele, V. (1996) *Fetish: Fashion, Sex and Power*, New York: Oxford University Press.

Steele, V. (2001) *The Corset: A Cultural History*, New Haven: Yale University Press.

Taylor, L. (1999) 'Wool Cloth and Gender: The Use of Woollen Cloth in Women's Dress in Britain, 1865–85', in A. de la Haye and E. Wilson (eds), *Defining Dress: Dress as Object, Meaning and Identity*, Manchester: Manchester University Press, pp. 30–47.

Tétart-Vittu, F. (1992) 'The French–English Go-between. "Le modèle de Paris" or the Beginning of the Designer, 1820–1880', *Costume*, 26, pp. 40–5.

Tiesten, L. (2001) *Marianne in the Market: Envisioning Consumer Society in Fin-de-Siècle France*, Berkeley: University of California Press.

Troy, N. J. (2003) *Couture Culture: A Study in Modern Art and Fashion*, Cambridge, MA: MIT Press, esp. ch. 1.

Waugh, N. (1968) *The Cut of Women's Clothes 1600–1930*, London: Faber and Faber.

Wilson, E. (1992) 'The Invisible Flâneur', *New Left Review*, 191, pp. 90–110.

Wilson, E. (1998) 'Bohemian Dress and the Heroism of Everyday Life', *Fashion Theory*, 2, 3, pp. 225–44.

Zakim, M. (2003) *Ready-made Democracy: A History of Men's Dress in the American Republic, 1760–1860*, Chicago: University of Chicago Press.

Printed resources

Baudelaire, C. (1930 [orig. 1863]) *The Painter of Victorian Life: A Study of Constantin Guys*, trans. P. G. Konody, London: The Studio.

Benjamin, W. (1999) *The Arcades Project*, Cambridge, MA, and London: MIT Press.

Carlyle, T. (orig. edition 1838) *Sartor Resartus*, various editions.

Flügel, J. C. (1930) *The Psychology of Clothes*, London: Hogarth Press.

Purdy, D. L. (ed.) (2004) *The Rise of Fashion: A Reader*, Indianapolis: University of Minnesota Press.

Ribeiro, A. (1999) *Ingres in Fashion: Representations of Dress and Appearance in Ingres's Images of Women*, New Haven: Yale University Press.

Ribeiro, A. (2000) *The Gallery of Fashion*, London: National Portrait Gallery.

Simmel, G. (1904) 'Fashion', *International Quarterly*, 10, pp. 130–55.

Simmel, G. (1905a [1997]) 'The Philosophy of Fashion', in D. Frisby and M. Featherstone (eds), *Simmel on Culture: Selected Writings*, London: Sage, pp. 187–206.

Simmel, G. (1905b [1997]) 'Adornment', in D. Frisby and M. Featherstone (eds), *Simmel on Culture: Selected Writings*, London: Sage, pp. 206–11.

Simmel, G. (1950) 'The Metropolis and Mental Life', in K. Wolff (ed.), *The Sociology of Georg Simmel*, New York: Free Press, pp. 409–24.

Veblen, T. (1899) *The Theory of the Leisure Class*, various editions.

Walden, G., and D'Aurevilly, J.-B. (2002) *Who's a Dandy? Dandyism and Beau Brummell*, London: Gibson Square Books.

Zola, É. (1995; several editions) *The Ladies' Paradise*, Oxford: Oxford University Press.

Online resources

Charles Booth online archive at the London School of Economics: booth.lse.ac.uk/static/a/2.html

Heilbrunn timeline of art hstory, The Metropolitan Museum of Art, New York: www.metmuseum.org/toah

Chapter 12

Artificial beauty, or the morality of dress and adornment

Valerie Steele

An approximation of beauty

ONE OF THE GREAT APPEALS OF FASHION has been that it 'divert[s] attention from insoluble problems of beauty and provide[s] a way to buy an approximation of beauty'. As 'A Lady' wrote in 1873, 'Dress has much to do with personal loveliness. It can enhance and set off beauties and conceal defects'.[1] Although Victorian writers emphasised both functions of dress, the greater part of their advice on improving the personal appearance concerned the concealment of physical 'flaws'.

This did not necessarily indicate a negative attitude toward the body. 'Has the race degenerated?' asked Gabriel Prevost.

> Yes and no. It is certain that one could still find these days some individuals having all the characteristics of perfect beauty; but there is no doubt that the enormous majority would present deformed elements and horribly modified proportions.[2]

'If man were under the obligation to be nude, as in Sparta', he wrote, then 'gymnastics and hygiene' would play a crucial role. But modern life exaggerated 'sedentary habits', so that people were too often overly fat or thin. 'Fortunately we have clothing', which, if it cannot 'rectify nature', can at least give 'to each individual the highest degree of beauty that he is capable of acquiring'.

This belief was held not only by interested parties like the corsetiere Madame Roxey Caplin, who thought that ninety-nine women out of a hundred suffered from 'deficiencies' in appearance. Even advocates of the natural beauty of the body, like Mrs Haweis, maintained that 'We are not like the Greeks who made the improvement of the body their dearest study; and, not having reduced our superfluous fat, and cultivated our muscles into perfection, we ought to be careful how we expose them'.[3] Neither men nor women were particularly athletic in the nineteenth century, with the partial exception of the English upper class, whose attachment to rural living gave them more opportunities for sports. In urban centres, these were greatly reduced, so, to some extent, middle-class Victorians were simply being realistic about their far from perfect bodies.

Beyond this, every individual has certain features that are more or less attractive according to the standards of the day, and which may be emphasised or minimised. Charles Blanc's example – that vertical stripes increase the short individual's apparent height – is one that has been repeated to the present day. A very different writer, Mrs Margaret Oliphant, also believed that

> fashion . . . has this one principle of humanity in it, that it is almost always designed to help those who want help, to cover deficiencies of nature, to conceal the evils wrought by time, and to make those look their best to whom no special charms have been given.[4]

If the Victorian ideal of beauty was fairly rigid, nevertheless Victorian clothes concealed physical flaws and signs of age more than modern dress does, and, to that extent, allowed more women to look and feel attractive.

Fashion also served to decorate or 'adorn' women, making even a 'plain' girl look 'ornamental', as well as testifying to her taste and sense of style. Mrs Haweis argued that 'There are some ladies who always look well: they are not necessarily the pretty ones, but they are women gifted with fine natural taste, who instinctively choose right forms, colours, and fabrics'.[5] Fashion journalists repeatedly described articles of clothing as 'beautiful', 'very pretty', and 'charming' – with the clear implication that these qualities would be imparted to the woman who wore them. They sometimes went a step further, and seemed to equate beauty with chic. Dresses were described as 'elegant', 'tasteful', 'fashionable' and, especially, 'stylish'; with the implication that, by dressing fashionably, one not only achieved an approximation of beauty (and freedom from the accidents and defects of physical endowments), but highly valued intangible qualities as well, such as poise, a desirable social status, an artistic temperament, and a refined sensibility.

Writers stressed, however, that it was ultimately less important that clothing should be in the height of fashion than that it should be becoming to the particular individual. Mrs Haweis, for example, advised that 'A head-dress must be – first, becoming – second, beautiful – and third, useful'. The hat should be becoming to the individual in question, since it 'has a powerful effect on the face, in either beautifying it or the reverse'. Its shape, colour, and general style should 'draw the eye' to a woman's good features, while minimising any facial defects. In particular, its colour should 'enhance' her complexion and the colour of her hair. Only later did Mrs Haweis add that the head-dress should be 'a pretty object in itself'. She ignored the issue of its putative usefulness entirely.[6]

Conversely, especially among early Victorian evangelicals, fashion was identified with emotional falsehood. Consider the story, *The History of a Hat*, printed in America's premier fashion journal, *Godey's Lady's Book*:

> It was certainly the prettiest hat in the world – the most elegant, the most graceful, the most coquettish! It was a hat of lilac gauze, with trimmings of straw round the brim, and a bunch of wild poppies and cornflowers

mingled with bows of riband, slightly inclining towards the right, and resting upon the brim!

And it was, also, the frailest and less profound love possible! – a light sentiment of fantasy, with capricious favours and artificial tenderness![7]

It was no accident that a hat was the subject of this moral lesson. Its relative lack of functional character meant that it played an essentially symbolic role.

Artificial ugliness and true beauty

Not everyone was wholeheartedly in favour of the artificial 'improvement of the appearance'. Although some Victorians accepted the idea of possible disparities between being and appearance, others adamantly rejected the idea that beauty could – or should – be the product of a lady's toilette, arguing that while beauty of expression and character should be cultivated, 'false' and 'deceptive' adjuncts to beauty should be avoided. The more conservative believed that to take too great an interest in personal appearance was vain and frivolous and even wicked.

The English novelist Charlotte Mary Yonge, for example, argued that 'All attempts to pretend to beauties that we do not possess are clearly falsehood, and therefore wrong'. *Godey's Lady's Book* repeatedly offered a moral critique of fashion as hypocrisy and vanity, stressing that 'character', 'virtue', and 'transparent sincerity' alone constituted beauty: 'Beauty without virtue is like a painted sepulchre, fair without but full of corruption'. The American advice-writer, John Todd, believed that an attractive exterior concealing a wicked heart was like 'the beautifulness of the serpent, the more hideous in proportion to their power to charm the victim'.[8] It was not merely that a wise person would look at the character, not the surface. Rather, the more conservative and religious writers sometimes regarded feminine physical beauty as a *trick*. Too much beauty was dangerously attractive to the (usually male) spectator. In part as a defence against the fear of seduction, many writers argued that artificial beauty was really ugly.

The anonymous author of 'Artificial Woman-Making' (*c.* 1869) asked rhetorically:

> When will women learn that, with regard to natural objects, there is no such thing as Artificial Beauty; that the two terms mutually exclude one another . . . .? That there is such a thing as Artificial Ugliness, and that it is the invariable result of efforts to create Artificial Beauty.[9]

He (or she) insisted that 'all that can be done to improve [the appearance] is to give . . . perfect health . . . entailing clear skin and bright eyes, and easy, dignified movements; and then add those moral qualities of kindliness, modesty, and self-respect, which shine out through the veil of the body'.

Godey's also advocated only 'moral cosmetics', such as not staying up late or playing cards. The magazine's editors worried that real cosmetics concealed the evidence of true inner emotions that would normally be expressed by blushing or growing pale. Indeed, the emphasis on 'sincerity' and 'honesty' was so strong that some Americans professed to prefer daguerreotypes over painted portraits, on the grounds that their rather harsh 'realism' did not 'flatter' the sitter. To look too good was suspect.

Figure 12.1 Hadol, *Être et Paraître*. Caricature, 1869. Courtesy of the Liddell Hart Collection of Costume at Liverpool John Moores University.

At the opposite end of the spectrum was the outspoken fashion and beauty writer Mrs Haweis, the daughter of an artist and the wife of a clergyman, whose books *The Art of Beauty* (1878) and *The Art of Dress* (1879) were ten years ahead of their time in their open advocacy of artificial beauty aids and dressing to attract attention. She advised her readers to ignore the 'fossilised prejudice' that would stigmatise as 'vanity' any attempts to enhance personal beauty; and even advocated the subtle use of rouge and powder, arguing that 'the culture of beauty need never interfere with that of goodness and usefulness to others'.[10]

The majority took a position somewhere between these extremes, and, while acknowledging the importance of modesty and beauty of character, permitted at least a limited amount of artificial 'improvement' of the physical appearance. Fashion was sometimes presented as the great equaliser that made ordinary-looking or even plain girls look as pretty or prettier than girls who were naturally more beautiful. Not surprisingly, this position was strongly held by fashion journalists.

A writer for the young women's fashion magazine *Sylvia's Home Journal* advised her readers:

> We should all try to be as pretty as we can without resorting to deceptions in the form of cosmetics, hair dyes, and pearl powder. The best way to be really pretty, independently of regular features and good complexions is to have pleasant thoughts constantly in our minds, always to be doing kind and good-natured things, and never to listen to anything unkind or bitter about others. If we do this, the eyes will grow clear and bright, the corners of the lips turn up pleasantly and prettily, and the beauty of countenance be fully developed – a far higher beauty than that of feature. But besides this, we should all wear as becoming dresses as we can get without outrunning our allowance or running into debt.

After this initial (and fairly brief) lecture on correct mental attitudes and their good effects, the author went on to describe girls and women whose appearance was drastically improved by attractive dress: 'I have seen a really beautiful woman quite outshone by one of very inferior claims to good looks, who was well and gracefully dressed, and possessed, besides, those graces of manner which are to the mind as satin and laces are to the body'. Beauty here was a function of both dress and character. As the examples multiplied, however, dress was increasingly emphasised. She described an 'American girl' that she knew – 'a plain girl . . . with an angular figure, and *hardly any hair!*' When the girl 'fixed herself up', though, 'she was really pretty, and all the angularity conjured away from her figure by the charm of a perfectly made dress'.[11]

The concepts of truthfulness, naturalness and appropriateness modified the theoretical legitimacy and desirability of trying to be beautiful. To some extent, the purely decorative qualities of dress escaped censure, because they were perceived as being grafted onto the primary function of dress – the preservation of modesty. Other adjuncts to personal beauty were more controversial. For example, Mrs Yonge thought that a 'virtuous woman' would never wear 'borrowed plaits', but others believed that false hair might be 'excusable', if not fully justifiable, if it concealed a serious deficiency of hair. In fact, the trade in hair was considerable, with the hair often bought from peasant women in Europe who wore traditional head-dresses. Conservatives often maintained that the hair was bought from diseased women and was contaminated – an obvious example of a punitive moralistic threat.[12]

Hair dyes and facial cosmetics often did contain chemicals that were unsafe, but safety was not really the primary issue. The debate about cosmetics and hair dyes was part of a wider controversy about the legitimacy of artifice and the appropriateness of styles of dress and adornment that were overtly erotic.

Opinions varied over time, first permissive, then rigid, then increasingly permissive again. The author of the 1825 book, *The Art of Beauty*, asked, 'Ought people to use paint?' and blithely answered, 'Why not?' Ten years later, a shift in sentiment had begun that seems to have held on for about three decades. 'True' beauty was the product of moral goodness and physical health. 'False' and 'artificial' beauty could destroy them. Doctors, such as the popular author 'Medicus', argued that 'health – bounding saucy health – is the fountain from which all true beauty springs'. While this was to some extent true, as an argument it also served to devalue the erotic aspects of physical beauty. More commonly, writers emphasised moral self-improvement – 'kindliness', 'cheerfulness', and 'a wholesome frame of mind'. According to the authors of one quasi-dress reform text of 1892: 'The use of the intellect has a powerful effect upon the moulding and chiselling of the features, removing the marks of sensuality, and replacing them by the fineness of lofty self-control'.[13]

As late as the twentieth century, Mrs Humphry was telling her young readers that the various 'attitudes of mind', whether good or bad, write themselves 'plainly on the exterior': 'In a measure we make our own faces and mould our own figures'. Thus,

> Lying late in bed in the morning ruins the complexion! . . . Too much novel-reading is fatal to the temper, and bad temper spoils the expression. The novel-reader who neglects duty and exercise is certain to be irritable and disagreeable and these show in the countenance. Nothing, not even ill-health, has such a deleterious effect upon good looks as the sense of duties left undone.

Ultimately, she implied that too single-minded a concern with beauty was 'selfish', and thus self-defeating, as it led to 'discontent', a disagreeable expression, and the use of 'illegitimate' auxiliaries to beauty – with all the bad effects that that entailed.[14]

Yet beauty books gave recipes for facial cosmetics and hair dyes, and they were fairly widely advertised – although often indirectly: '*Beauty* without *paint*. – a natural colour for the cheeks'. Newspapers of the 1860s covered the legal trials of the notorious cosmetician, Madame Rachel, who charged up to 20 guineas for 'enameling' a lady's face with products like her 'Favourite of the Harem's Pearl White'.[15] A little artificial improvement was excusable for mature women, who were more in need of assistance, or less in danger of damaging their 'moral character'.

As well as counterfeiting health and youth, cosmetics seem to simulate the physiological changes that accompany sexual orgasm – the brilliant eye, reddened lips, etc. According to the *Harper's Bazaar* 'Ugly-Girl Papers', 'The painted eye of desire, the burning cheek, and dyed nails, were coeval with the wisdom of Alexandria' – and were certainly 'no cause for divorce'. The Englishwoman Gwen Raverat recalled that such erotic display was popularly associated with 'actresses or certain kinds of women'. When used with discretion, cosmetics apparently were legitimate for married women 'but never young girls'.[16]

Charles Baudelaire's defence of *maquillage* was very much the expression of a minority opinion, the more so since he argued that 'face-painting' should not attempt to imitate Nature or counterfeit health and youth, but rather that it should be *deliberately artificial*, to give the impression of 'a supernatural and excessive life', and to give the wearer a passionate appearance. The very artificiality of fashion was 'a symptom of the taste for the ideal'. Fashion was 'a sublime deformation of Nature, or rather a permanent and repeated attempt at her *reformation*'. These views, of course, were the exact opposite of the widely held belief that Nature was the ultimate source of standards of morality and beauty. In one respect, however, Baudelaire appeared to echo contemporary views of woman's role in life. She had, he argued, 'a kind of duty' to appear 'magical and supernatural . . . the better to conquer hearts'.[17]

The controversy surrounding the cosmetic arts throws into relief some of the issues involved in the related controversy about the morality of dress and the position of the modern woman. In England, some of the most violent attacks on the 'Girl of the Period' came from the pen of Mrs Eliza Lynn Linton, a journalist and novelist, who emphasised the pernicious effects of modern dress on moral character. Specifically, she objected to 'paint and powder'; hair dyes; artificial hair; frizzy and/or loosely flowing hairstyles; small bonnets that did not 'shelter . . . the face'; low décolletage – 'charms that were once reserved are now made the common property of every looker-on'; artificial busts 'of rose-coloured rubber'; tight skirts – 'of those Limbs which it is still forbidden to expose absolutely, the form and contour can at least be put in relief by insisting on the skirts being gored and straightened to the utmost' – in sum, all 'aids' designed 'to give an impression of . . . a more sensuous development of limb, and a greater abundance of flesh than can be either natural or true' (and even artificial ears). 'These fashions', she insisted, 'do not please or attract men'.[18] But that, of course, was precisely the contested issue.

The 'Girl of the Period'

Much of the outcry in the 1860s about the 'Girl of the Period' derived from fears that respectable young women were imitating the dress, manners, and appearance of 'the queens of the demi-monde'. Some people feared that the 'lines of respectability were becoming blurred', and that not only might girls and women be taken for what they were not, but their actual behaviour and character might also degenerate. The girl who wore cosmetics and 'fast' dress might easily lose her modesty and innocence by imitating those whose appearance, it was argued, accurately reflected their corrupt morals. 'She can not be made to see that modesty of appearance and virtue ought to be inseparable, and that no good girl can afford to appear bad.'[19]

What is the significance of Linton's famous attack on the modern girl? Was it true that the modern girl had rejected the old domestic and maternal role of 'friend and companion', 'tender mother', and 'industrious housekeeper', preferring a 'fast' life with 'plenty of fun and luxury'? Did 'the fashionable woman of the period' really live for 'dress, dissipation, and flirting'? Was she 'always' in the midst of 'some love affair, more or less platonic, according to her own temperament or the boldness of the man'?

Mrs Linton's views do not appear to have been entirely representative of public opinion. *The Saturday Review* seemed to have a policy of printing deliberately provocative articles, often focusing on criticism of the modern girl and woman. In 1870, a writer for *The Tomahawk*, a journal of satire, looked back at the 'Girl of the Period':

> People read the article with pleasure. It was very 'dreadful' and 'improper', but pleasant . . . However, everybody more or less agreed that the statements in the article savoured of falsehood. 'Women were certainly bad, and Miss Dash infamous, but then it was a little too strong' . . . 'Girl of the

Period' coats, dresses, shirts appeared, and were successful, even a 'Girl of the Period' Magazine'.[20]

On the other hand, Mrs Linton's article provided ammunition and a handy slogan for writers opposed to current fashions or engaged in the corset controversy, such as the anonymous authors of articles on 'The Waist of the Period', the 'Girl of the Period has taken to tight-lacing again' and 'The Waste of the Period! or A Plate of Fashions for the British Folly'. A cartoon by Howard Del, 'A Modern Work of Art – Building up the Girl of the Period', showed a figure being dressed and decorated by tiny men – with a corset, 'palpitator' (false bosom), 'patent calves', pearl powder and paint, a crinoline, and false hair. The modern girl was attacked as ignorant, vain, pitiable, and unattractive.

These attacks might, to some extent, have reflected a reaction against women's increasing independence. Although Mrs Linton was a complex, intelligent, and independent person, she was very much opposed both to the movement for women's rights and to the fashionable woman. Was fashion, then, a reflection of women's widening sphere? Sixties fashions do seem generally bolder in effect than their immediate predecessors, and some historians have suggested that there was 'almost certainly a connection between this and the nascent efforts towards [women's] social and even political emancipation'.[21] To a limited extent, the criticism of fashion was only the projection of deeper anxieties about changing life-styles (including sexual behaviour).

Yet the invention of aniline dyes permitted the production of bright and even glaring colours, and does not necessarily reflect a greater feminine audacity (although the popular practice of combining what we should consider grossly clashing colours did, perhaps, indicate a desire to attract attention). Similarly, the normal inflationary aspects of competition in dress contributed to the growth of crinoline size.

Many people in the 1860s perceived contemporary fashions as being conspicuously more elaborate and immodest than earlier styles, but one may doubt whether this was entirely true. Even a casual perusal of the earlier literature indicates that this type of moral criticism was always common. An article, 'On Vanity and Love of Dress', from 1843, for example, suggested that vanity was a 'selfish' and 'essentially . . . female passion', and that it was very difficult to keep 'the love of dress . . . within proper bounds, *as the present extravagant mode of dressing will testify*'.[22]

The problem, as a number of Victorians saw it, was that the fashions were set by immoral women. If a woman wanted to look fashionable, she ran the risk of looking immodest. Although women were widely regarded as morally superior to men, they were also regarded, in some sense, as morally feeble; 'proper' and 'modest' dress provided them with a protective shield. Since Paris was the undisputed capital of women's fashion, English (and American and German) writers frequently blamed Parisian dress designers and demi-mondaines for the 'immorality' of contemporary dress. Pernicious fashions were created by 'the Man-Milliner' and launched by 'the demi-monde fashion-mongers of Paris'.[23]

The Queen, for example, printed an article entitled 'What Are the Sources of Beauty in Dress?' by Mrs Harriet Beecher Stowe, in which she violently attacked the '*outré* unnatural fashion [that] comes from the most dissipated foreign circles'. It was 'elaborate', 'complicated' and 'contrary to nature' – and it was not beautiful, because it was not 'appropriate' to the character of the good but foolish girls who copied it. On the other hand, it was

Figure 12.2 'Girl of the Period', cover illustration from *Girl of the Period Miscellany* (1869).

perfectly adapted to the kind of life led by dissipated women, whose life is one revel of excitement, and who, never proposing . . . any intellectual employment or any domestic duty, can afford to spend three or four hours every day under the hands of a waiting maid, in alternately tangling and untangling their hair.

It reflected all too accurately the character and lifestyle of immoral women:

> A certain class of women in Paris . . . make the fashions. . . . They are
> women who live only for the senses. . . . They have no family ties; love,
> in its pure domestic sense, is an impossibility, and their whole intensity of
> existence, therefore, is concentrated on the question of sensuous enjoy-
> ment, and that personal adornment which is necessary to secure it.[24]

Such women, she argued, needed to adorn themselves, however blatantly and deceptively, in order to attract men and hide the ravages caused by a life of dissipation.

Famous courtesans and members of the theatrical profession *were* among the leaders
of fashion, in part because it was especially important for them to look attractive, but
also because they were much less constrained than most women by the fear of looking
immodest or conspicuous. Other women sought to follow fashion closely, but not too
closely. But to lag too far behind the fashion was to risk looking dowdy and unattractive. To attempt to flout the fashion was to look 'eccentric'.

Every new fashion was received with disapproval from at least some quarters.
In 1878, F. T. Vischer, the well-known German philosopher and author of *Mode und
Zynismus*, described contemporary fashion as '*eine Hurenmode*', because it revealed the
contours of the female body. He had been no happier with the previous fashion of crinolines, however, which he condemned as 'impertinent', because they made women
appear larger than men. He also maintained that any fashion that deviated so greatly
from the natural form of the body was immodest, because it was a distortion that
charmed viewers more than the true form would have, and invited curiosity about the
body underneath. He denied that he thought that every woman who wore the crinoline had 'evil thoughts in her little head'. Most were just conforming to the current
fashion.[25]

The anonymous author of the pamphlet 'Who Is to Blame?' blamed men for the
spread of this 'meritricious style' of 'immodest' dress into 'good society'. He (or she)
maintained that girls, 'actuated simply by an innocent desire to please – have followed
the direction of men's gaze, and have copied that which appears to be attractive'. As
Mrs Haweis put it: 'Why don't girls marry? Because the press is great, and girls are
indistinguishable in the crowd. . . . Men, so to speak, pitch upon the girls they can
see'.[26]

To a considerable extent, the attack on the girl of the period reflected the unwelcome perception that fashion emphasised female sexual beauty, and that some young
women were deliberately trying to attract men.

An index of the mind and character

The morality of dress was an important issue to the Victorians, because they perceived
clothing as an 'index of the mind' and 'character' of the wearer. Dress was

> the second self, a dumb self, yet a most eloquent expositor of the person.
> . . . Dress bears the same relation to the body as speech does to the brain;
> and therefore dress may be called the speech of the body.[27]

It was especially true that women were judged on the basis of their appearance. A man's clothing indicated at least his approximate status, but, beyond that, it revealed relatively little about his tastes and character, in large part because men were so constrained in their choice of costume. According to an article in *The Quarterly Review*, 'It is all very well for bachelors to be restricted to a costume which expresses nothing . . . since they can be safely trusted for publishing their characters to the world with that forwardness which is their chief element'. It was very different for women, who were characterised by 'delicacy of mind, and reserve of manner'. For women, dress functioned as 'a sort of symbolical language . . . the study of which it would be madness to neglect, [since] to a proficient in the science, every woman walks about with a placard on which her leading qualities are advertised'.[28]

But which qualities were considered desirable? And which undesirable? How exactly was character expressed by dress? Did everyone 'read' a dress in the same way? Roberts argues that a Victorian woman's dress announced her submissive, masochistic, and narcissistic personality, Kern that it expressed an anti-sexual ideology. Most young women, however, wanted to look both sexually attractive and sufficiently 'modest' to indicate their good character. Their physical beauty was itself supposed to reflect their inner beauty. An article in *Harper's Bazaar* on 'Nice Girls' argued that the expression 'does not necessarily mean a beautiful girl, or an elegant or an accomplished girl, except to the extent that beauty, elegance, and accomplishments are essential to niceness. In a sense, the nice girl always is, and should be, pretty'. Apparently, beauty consisted not only of a 'sweet mouth' and 'kind eyes', but also a perfectly fitting and appropriately decorative dress, gloves, boots, and so on.[29]

Obviously, there were differences of opinion about the degree of sexual display acceptable in dress. According to a writer for *Sylvia's Home Journal*:

> Many persons argue that the love of dress is as harmful to the community as the love of drink; and if they see a girl wearing some garment in a specially becoming manner, they stamp her as vain and coquettish, wasteful of time and thought on a worthless object.[30]

Such a girl might well think that her dress and appearance had been grossly misinterpreted, and that her intention was merely to look 'pleasant and pretty'. Nevertheless, I doubt that these hypothetical disgruntled observers were merely straw men set up by a fashion journalist. It seems probable that many attempts to look attractive and fashionable were perceived negatively by at least some people as 'vain', 'immodest', or 'fast'. According to a writer for *London Society*, 'the dread of being thought *fast*' prevented many Englishwomen from being well dressed. It was difficult to satisfy everyone.[31]

The boundaries of acceptable dress were fairly narrow, and women were constrained in their choice of costume. Manuals of dress constantly cautioned women against appearing 'conspicuous or peculiar'. 'Fashion is an imperious goddess, and exacts unquestioning submission from her devotees. It is useless to denounce her sway or run counter to her behests. No single person can, with impunity, take an independent position.'[32] Even writers for *The Rational Dress Society's Gazette* admitted that

> To affect a singularity in attire is to incur a social martyrdom out of all proportion to the relief obtained . . . It is vain to be comfortable and modestly

attired if one is to be made an object of observation or ridicule to every person high and low whom one may chance to meet.[33]

If rational dress was clearly beyond the pale, it was also true that ordinary fashionable dress – neither ultra-modish nor excessive – could still expose a woman to censure.

According to Theodore Zeldin, nineteenth-century treatises on confession in France emphasised that 'Women's clothes were a constant source of danger'. Yet although fashions could be immodest and an incitement to sin, priests were advised to adopt a relatively tolerant attitude toward the women who wore these styles:

> Married ones who dressed to please their husbands, or girls who dressed in order to win husbands should be given some concessions, but not if they sought to please others apart from their husband, or if their aim was not to get married. Those who leave their arms and shoulders naked or only lightly covered were, if they were following the fashion, not guilty, but those who invented the fashions were guilty of mortal sin.[34]

Presumably, most women wanted to look attractive – but as respectable wives or potential wives, not courtesans. The element of gentility or respectability was part of a woman's sexual arsenal. Both her social position and her own self-perception were related to the aspirations and fantasies that she held and that were part of her cultural milieu. Her clothing proclaimed that she was a sexually attractive woman, but this had a particular meaning within the culture of the time.

It is extremely difficult, of course, to determine the nature of the relationship between the prescribed ideal and the historical reality. The idealisation of female 'purity', the social importance of 'respectability', and the shifting definitions of women's social roles must have set the terms within which 'female sexuality was expressed'. But the rules governing these terms remain somewhat ambiguous. According to the prescriptive ideal of femininity, for example, female sexuality was secondary, and derived from the maternal instinct, but this was not always evident in dress. With regard to modesty and sexual display, the fashion writer, Mrs Merrifield, merely advised her readers that men tended to be more genuinely attracted to modestly dressed women than to those 'who make so profuse a display of their charms'.[35]

Yet there does not seem to have been a clear distinction between the clothing of the 'pure', 'respectable', 'maternal' and 'domestic' middle-class woman and that worn by her sexual counter-ideal. Middle-class girls and women adopted styles that had initially been launched by courtesans, actresses, and aristocratic ladies; while prostitutes dressed professionally as 'ladies'. An analysis of fashion indicates that it was not a question of the denial or domestication of female sexuality, but rather that it was only socially acceptable when it manifested itself in certain forms.

It is possible that sexuality was acceptable to the extent that it was seen as an aspect of *the ideal self*, a concept that incorporates both self-image and social perception, and that is not monolithic like the 'cultural ideal', but rather focuses on the individual person within a particular environment. For example, if fashionable dress helped 'to attract the opposite sex', there was some disagreement about its suitability for unmarried girls, who were, theoretically, supposed to be pre-sexual. (Thus even quite big girls often exposed much of their calves.) Yet in England and America, girls were supposed to attract their own husbands, without, however, overemphasising their sexual charms. In the absence of arranged marriages, 'young ladies' were sometimes even encouraged to wear costumes that were 'as effective and coquettish as possible', or advised to dress as well after marriage as they had before.[36]

Although this distinction between France, on the one hand, and England and America, on the other, should not be overdrawn, nevertheless the French did seem to have dressed their daughters more simply. After their parents had married them off, they could safely and legitimately display their charms. In *The Awkward Age*, Henry James compared the European and the English styles of dressing girls. Little Aggie was clothed according to the former style – in 'an arrangement of dress exactly in the key of her age, her complexion, her emphasised virginity. She might have been prepared for her visit by a cluster of doting nuns'. In *L'Art de la toilette*, Mademoiselle Pauline Mari-ette advised that 'The young girl, like you, my child, renders herself interesting by the qualities of her heart, becomes pleasing by her real and useful talents, touching by her modesty and her virtues'.[37] She stressed that every girl should learn how to make her clothes, because fashion was so important to a *woman*.

Just as society showed a greater tolerance for (and indeed acceptance of) marital sexuality than it did for pre-marital sexuality, so also was the dress of married women permitted to be more erotic and more sumptuous than that of unmarried girls. Simi-larly, many of the rules governing body exposure and sexual display in dress focused on the situation. It was a question less of morals (in the abstract) than of manners. Evening dress was far more revealing than daytime dress, because body exposure was restricted to a circle of one's social equals, who could be expected to understand that this was a form of conventional dress, legitimised by long custom, and not an invitation to 'animal lust'. It was aesthetically tamed eroticism. Fashion historians who have found it ironic or hypocritical that fashions were more revealing in the *evenings* (traditionally the time of sexual activity) have ignored the importance of the social context.

In 1865, one French writer described the dangers to which a woman would be exposed if she flouted the rules governing situational dress:

> Which among you . . . would dare to appear in the street and to walk under the eyes of the people in the costume for a ball . . .? The most auda-cious would not take the liberty, . . . for the jeers of the crowd would im-mediately force her to hide, and the urchins would throw mud and stones at her. Moreover, the police would intervene and probably take her to a safe place, in order to deliver her then to the correctional tribunal, as guilty of an outrage to public morality.[38]

Yet dress that constituted 'an outrage to public morality' when worn on the street was not necessarily even remotely *risqué* when worn at a ball. Custom played a vital role in legitimising sexual display. Evening décolletage was a feature of western women's fash-ion since the fifteenth century. Short skirts, for example, had no such history of accept-ance. Yet rules governing appropriateness could be very strict, even when morality was not an issue: The author of *Etiquette for Women* maintained that 'to wear a morning dress in the evening is to commit an outrage on society itself'.[39]

In general, the French tended more to accept the essential artificiality and eroticism of dress. The Frenchwoman (and especially the Parisienne) was generally acknowledged to be the best-dressed in the world. She was both 'chic' and 'charming'. The English, however, viewed this with some suspicion – could such a woman be truly 'good'? They sometimes argued that the English 'girl' was 'naturally' more beautiful. The French, on the other hand, often implied that natural beauty was only the beginning. A woman learned to *become* beautiful. As she grew older, she would continue to be admired, since she used dress to express her elegance and personal style. The greater acceptance of fashion in France probably stemmed in part from the recognition that the fashion industry was crucial to the economy. But the fact that the industry had developed in France may also indicate a stronger prior interest in fashion.[40]

Nevertheless, in France too the degree of sartorial eroticism and artificiality permissible in any given case varied according to a number of factors, which are not always easy to determine in retrospect. Until recently, for example, most historians have assumed that John Singer Sargent's portrait of 'Madame X' caused a scandal at the 1884 Paris Salon because Mme Virginie Gautreau is shown wearing a very low-cut black dress. In fact, as Trevor Fairbrother has demonstrated, the original painting was 'far more shocking than the work we now know. It had a fallen shoulder strap (long since adjusted by Sargent), emphasising the brazen aspect of an apparently insolent personality'. Mme Gautreau's black satin evening dress was indeed somewhat daring, particularly since it had no sleeves but only diamond-studded shoulder straps; but the heart-shaped décolleté bodice was not unusually low, and even the straps would have been acceptable – had one strap not slipped completely off her shoulder. As Albert Woolf wrote in *Le Figaro*, 'One more struggle and the lady will be free'.[41]

What 'gave more offence than the perilously décolleté costume', however, was 'the paint and powder with which Mr Sargent plastered the face of this Parisienne belle'. Even after Sargent had repainted the shoulder strap, critics continued to complain about the sitter's bluish-white complexion, which indicated a heavy use of 'pearl-powder'. Apparently, Mme Gautreau did wear cosmetics: while painting his *Portrait of a Great Beauty*, Sargent had described her as one of those 'people who are "fardées" to the extent of being a uniform lavender or blotting paper colour'. And when Mme Gautreau and her mother 'tearfully' begged Sargent to withdraw the picture, he argued that 'He had painted her exactly as she was dressed, that nothing could be said of the canvas worse than had been said in print of her appearance *dans le monde*'. Ultimately it was her notorious reputation as a 'professional beauty' that permitted 'her extraordinary personal displays [which] would have been scandalous on a less sensational woman'. It was her reputation (rather than her clothes as such) that caused a scandal when set on canvas.[42]

The best and most becoming dress

'C. T.', the author of *How to Dress Well*, stressed that 'No man is caught by the mere display of fine clothes. A pretty face, or a good figure, may captivate, but fine clothes never. Though it be said that fine feathers make fine birds, yet no man will be caught by a trimming or a flounce'. Beauty did captivate, however, and dress did potentially improve the appearance.

> To what end then should attention be given to dress? . . . Because *it is one of beauty's accessories*; because as dress of some kind is absolutely necessary and

indispensable, it is better that *people of all classes should dress well* rather than ill. . . . When we may, *why should we not choose the best and the most becoming?* Why are we to mortify ourselves and annoy our friends by choosing something because it is especially hideous? No law, human or divine, enjoins us to disfigure ourselves.[43]

But what kind of clothing was 'best and most becoming' for specific people when dress communicated so much information? Since people judged in large part by appearances, rather than by perhaps unknown realities, it was possible to use dress to create a persona, to appear to be what one wanted to be. As the duplicitous Madame Merle suggested in Henry James's *Portrait of a Lady* (1881), 'What shall we call our "self"? I know a large part of myself is in the clothes I choose to wear . . . Oneself – for other people – is one's expression of oneself'. Isabel Archer disagreed: 'Certainly the clothes which, as you say, I choose to wear don't express me . . . I don't care to be judged by that'. She was, she insisted, more than any external measure might indicate.[44]

Many Victorians apparently found the concept of clothes and the self both distressing and tempting for other reasons as well. The controversy about 'deceptive' aids to beauty reflected this concern, as did the numerous complaints about people who 'dress beyond their means' and 'make-believe that they are richer than they really are'. The problem was not merely one of economic status, however, but even more one of social 'station'. Standards of taste and suitability of dress were closely connected to the class hierarchy of nineteenth-century society. The concept of 'gentility' played a crucial role in a society bounded at one end by a recognisable upper class and at the other by the labouring class, but which contained between these extremes a number of potentially upwardly mobile groups. Originally, gentility was associated with the established landowning class that sought to distinguish itself from the increasingly wealthy members of the industrial and commercial class. The idea of gentility implied that prestige was essentially divorced from economic status, and was associated instead with certain attributes of birth. The concept was then adopted by the middle classes, whose members used it to reinforce their own position in society: a genteel woman was a 'real lady', who knew the rules of etiquette of 'good society'. The distinguishing characteristic of gentle birth was transformed into the quality of being gentle in manners and (acquired) status; it was an assertion of a superior position in society.[45]

The rigid and complex rules governing 'appropriate' dress (and rituals of etiquette in general) were intended to distinguish those of genteel birth from the 'nouveaux riches' and from quasi-fashionably dressed working-class women. The anonymous 'Lady' who wrote *How to Dress on £15 a Year as a Lady* maintained that 'A woman is more or less judged by the style of her dress'.[46] Her readers (among them a number of governesses) might have been in reduced circumstances, but they wanted to be recognised as ladies. Unfortunately for them, so did a great many other people. And, of course, not everyone agreed that a governess was a lady, or that she should dress as one.

At least since the seventeenth century, even moralists had admitted that women in the 'higher circles of society . . . live under a necessity that prescribes propriety . . . and even great splendour of costume'. In light of their 'position' and wealth, 'costly elegance' was in 'good taste'. By the nineteenth century, the obligation of dressing to indicate high social status fell especially on women, since 'men have renounced the gold-laced coats, ruffles, and jewelry of their forefathers'. Indeed, it was widely thought that 'the devotion of much time or care to dress is unmanly' and foppish. On the other hand, 'A married woman has to . . . dress not only to please her husband, but also to reflect credit upon his choice'. 'Even the most devoted domesticity cannot excuse dowdiness'.[47] Veblen, then, was partially correct in his characterisation of women and vicarious consumption.

There were, however, limits to sartorial splendour. Women should dress well, but only the 'nouveaux riches' went in for 'showy' clothes. This aesthetic judgement obviously had class connotations. Even in the age of Louis XIV, there were complaints that wealthy bourgeoises dressed more magnificently than some impoverished aristocrats – and, therefore, if this trend could not be stopped, it would be redefined as unfashionable. Dress that attracted 'observation' was 'bad' and 'vulgar', as such 'gay clothing' would only be admired by 'those who are caught by such outward gew-gaws'. A woman who would wear an 'emerald green' satin dress and a 'bonnet with large scarlet flowers' for a summer fête in the country revealed her 'vulgarity of mind'. Her clothing was too 'dressy' for the occasion and too bright and inharmonious in colour. 'To the educated and refined, glaring tints and discordant combinations are painful and repulsive'. Such 'violent and stunning effects in costume' resulted in 'absurdities', as women 'struggle to compel the eye . . . to make the dress or its wearer say, "Look at me"'.[48]

Those of birth and education learned to discriminate between good taste and 'sham finery', and knew the rules governing suitability in dress 'in regard to time and place, age and social condition'.[49] According to the anonymous author of *Etiquette of Good Society*:

> There is no easier method by which to detect the real lady from the sham one than by noticing her style of dress. Vulgarity is readily distinguished, however costly and fashionable the habiliments may be, by the breach of certain rules of harmony and fitness.

These rules often implicitly reflected distinctions of wealth and status: 'The costume for paying calls when on foot differs from that which should be worn for the same purpose when driving in a carriage'. The former would be plain, so as not to attract unwanted attention from passers-by. A woman wealthy enough to have a carriage was permitted 'much more licence' in her dress – 'handsome silks, with elaborately trimmed and sweeping skirts, feathery bonnets, and lace parasols, which would look quite out of place when walking'.[50]

The rules of dress were sometimes imitated by the 'wrong' people, however. Arthur Munby described in his diary a London prostitute who 'dressed . . . professionally as a "lady" in clothing that was "handsome and good". She was always well but not gaudily dressed'. (Several years later, she bought a coffeehouse with her savings, and dressed 'quietly and well, like a respectable upper servant'.) Other women also dressed to exaggerate their social status, and literature on fashion is filled with diatribes against 'imposture' or 'pretension' in dress. It was 'hateful', 'vulgar' and 'offensive' that 'persons in [a] humble class of life' would 'ape their betters, dressing after them'. 'Can it be said that this is good taste? Assuredly not. It could not well be worse.'[51]

The Victorians were acutely conscious of possible religious objections to fashion, but these tended to be interpreted most rigidly in the case of the least powerful people in society – the poor and, to a lesser extent, the young. According to one vicar, 'the sins and evils which are promoted by an excessive care about dress' included 'worldly-mindedness', pride, extravagance, selfishness, 'grievous waste of time' and immodesty. He argued, though, that good Christians need not, indeed should not, deliberately adopt 'any special plainness or any singular coarseness of dress' (which would have a bad effect on industry), but rather they should dress according to 'their station, and to the wealth of which God has made them the stewards'. The 'Christian woman' would not be the first to adopt a new fashion, 'but when custom has familiarized the strangeness, she will then draw towards it'.[52] Occasionally, even younger, poorer women were told that 'everyone ought to make the best of themselves. There is a great deal in the Bible about dress . . . dress with us ought to be symbolical too . . . of beauty, neatness, and purity . . . only undue vanity is rebuked, . . . dress is not of itself sinful'.[53] But to be fashionable was, perhaps, less commendable.

Attacks on fashion often focused on its pernicious effects on the women of the working class. Dressing well was an obligation for women of position, and dressing neatly and attractively was a virtue for all women; but that working-class girls and women might aspire to fine dress provoked harsh criticism. Louisa Twining, author of an article on 'Dress' in *The Sunday Magazine*, argued that there was a 'close connection between the love of dress and sin'. She described the room in a London prison where the inmates' clothing was kept, and concluded that the prisoners' 'love of . . . tawdry finery . . . had been the first step' to their 'degradation and misery':

> Oh that my sisters of the servant class could see the sight and take warning
> from it! It was impossible to picture . . . those guilty creatures commiting
> such crimes in modest and womanly attire. Such garments and such wearers
> were fitting counterparts of each other.[54]

The theme that love of dress led poor girls to ruin appeared in numerous Christian tracts, such as the anonymous *Dress, Drink, and Debt: A Temperance Tale*, which describes how a girl goes into service, where another housemaid encourages her to stop sending her money to her parents. She learns to despise her simple clothes, and desiring to look 'smart and fine', she buys a 'fine new bonnet trimmed with flowers and a silk dress'.[55] She stops going to church, spends her free time walking with men, and ends by going to prison. Perhaps significantly, there was no hint that her mistress erred in setting a bad example; instead another servant was to blame.

In *Our Domestics and Their Mistresses: A Contribution to 'The Servant Question'*, the young servant was advised that

> *Finery in dress is a beginning of evil* – a first step in a wrong road . . . a love of
> finery . . . arise[s] out of vanity, or a desire to attract attention. Can that
> be right? . . . I am far from thinking that a girl should not think about her
> clothes. Let her think how she can be clean and neat, and how she can save
> her money . . . by making for herself and mending . . . Our clothes are for
> a purpose – for a covering and for warmth. . . . But . . . don't add to these
> necessary and suitable garments gay flowers and bead fringes, or tawdry
> lace. This mode of dressing is a sort of advertisement of a girl's folly, and
> a challenge for the notice (often improper notice) and disrespect of any
> young men who may see her. A quiet dress . . . and a step that shows you
> have somewhere to go, and no time to lose – would not this of itself be a

protection from impertinent notice? Oh why should a girl deprive herself of so needed and so beautiful a shield?[56]

There was probably an element of sincere protectiveness in this type of advice. But it was accompanied by a strong aversion to the idea that women in service should have any form of sexual life, or that they should attempt to blur sartorial class distinctions. It seemed both immoral and presumptuous.

Employers complained that servants wanted 'to dress like ladies and get sweethearts . . . and they take no interest in the work they have engaged to do'. Memoirs indicate that wearing fringes, earrings, stylish hats or decorative dresses could result in instant dismissal. Yet servants resisted the idea that they should be restricted to 'sensible', humble, and modest dress: 'It is complained against as an infringement upon the liberty of the subject. It is very much the fashion for girls to think they may do as they like in this matter; and it cannot be denied that, whatever the station in life, dress is a very strong temptation to most girls'.[57]

Everyone seemed to feel that they were entitled to look as beautiful as they could – and fashionable dress appeared almost essential to that end. In Wilkie Collins' novel, *The Moonstone*, Lady Verinder's house-steward believed that 'to see [Rachel Verinder] walk was enough to convince any man . . . that the graces of her figure (if you will pardon me the expression) were in her flesh and not in her clothes'. But the servant and former thief, Rosanna Spearman, jealously insisted that this reputation for beauty was based largely on fine dress:

> Suppose you put Miss Rachel into a servant's dress, and took her ornaments off . . . It can't be denied that she had a bad figure; she was too thin . . . But it does stir one up to hear Miss Rachel called pretty, when one knows all the time that it's her dress does it, and her confidence in herself.[58]

Even if dress alone did not create the impression of beauty, it played an important part in setting it off.

Furthermore, attractive dress gave its wearer considerable self-confidence, which contributed to an improved appearance. There are innumerable testimonies to its psychological importance: the Edwardian fashion writer, Mrs Pritchard, for example, emphasised that 'Nothing is so conducive to sangfroid as an innate feeling that one is well-dressed'. Or, as the American novelist, Mrs Sherwood, has the character Rose say, 'Clothes have a great deal to do with one's happiness'.[59]

The motives which determine dress

The writers for Victorian women's magazines were fond of debating 'the motives which determine dress'. Did women dress 'for their own satisfaction' or 'to charm the eyes of their masculine admirers' or 'to make other women uncomfortable'? Fashion journalists tended to argue that women dressed to 'be beautiful and fascinate'. Worth, however, was quoted as saying that women dressed 'for the pleasure of making themselves smart, and for the still greater joy of snuffing out the others' – a view that would have seemed cynical to most of his admirers.[60]

If women dressed in part to please men, or to compete with other women, it was nevertheless a tricky business, since men often strongly resisted new fashions. Anthony Trollope's beautiful anti-heroine, Lizzie Eustace, was made to shun all styles that Trollope disapproved of: 'There was no get up of flounces, and padding, and paint, and hair, with a dorsal excrescence [i.e. a crinolette or bustle] appended with the object surely of showing in triumph how much absurd ugliness women can force men to endure'. Lady Linlithgow apparently expressed the author's views when she argued that

> Girls make monsters of themselves, and I'm told the men like it; — going about with unclear, frowsy structures on their head, enough to make a dog sick. How a man can like to kiss a face with a dirty horse's tail all whizzling about it, is what I can't at all understand. I don't think they do like it, but they have to do it.[61]

Yet women continued to wear new styles despite masculine obstinacy or obliviousness.

And despite possibly unwelcome interpretations. Charles Blanc, for example, approved of all the 'coquettish' and erotic aspects of fashion, and he argued that even apparently modest styles were really designed to attract masculine attention: 'To hide, yet to display . . . are the two objects of the bodice; but it must not be forgotten that often what is concealed is just that which is most wished to be displayed'. If a bodice is cut high, it 'seems' to express modesty, while if it is cut low, it 'attracts the attention to the shape of the neck, to the shoulders, to the outline of the bust' – and so on for pages.[62]

Mrs Haweis, who was by no means prudish, quite violently attacked Blanc as a 'fanatic', arguing that he (and the French in general) had 'spoilt and vulgarized the notion of dress as an expression of character' and 'an index of the inner self'.

> It is almost appalling to think of all we may have implied in our dress without knowing it, for so many years. The mind almost quails before a new fashion, lest it should bear some construction contrary to our feelings.

The various forms, colours, and trimmings of fashion might have 'artistic meanings', but she adamantly denied that they had the 'moral significance' that Blanc attributed to them. Rather, she maintained that, in enjoining 'concealment *pour laisser deviner*', Blanc was 'taking the very basest view of the body'.[63]

'The body is so beautiful', she wrote, 'that it is a pity it can be so little seen'. Dress functioned as a means of protection, concealment, and display, but it did not display the female form from any prurient interest. Fashion was 'as direct an outcome of the love of beauty as schools of sculpture and painting' – an ideal that could be interpreted both in terms of sublimated sexuality and image-making. Long before the development of the theory of the shifting erogenous zone, Mrs Haweis explained 'The Restlessness of Fashion' by the conflict between 'the need of being seen and the need of being covered', 'the desire to reveal and the necessity to conceal human Beauty'.[64]

> Although we do not like to confess it, . . . the human animal, by nature not a clothed animal but a naked animal, is ever reverting by bits to its original state. Clothed it must be; and yet it is impelled dimly to be at once clothed and unclothed. Now one bit of the body's beauty is displayed, and the rest

is sacrificed and covered up . . . There is no part of the frame which has not been at some time 'in fashion'. The arm, the bust, the back, the whole outline, has in turn been fully acknowledged.[65]

She admitted that women have 'indeed for many generations refused to confess to legs'. But it was not inconceivable that fashion might emphasise legs eventually; she observed that, although women still resisted 'Turkish' trousers, the styles of the late 1870s clearly indicated the legs.

This description certainly seems to indicate a lack of anxiety about, let alone hatred of, the body. It shows instead a sense of pride and pleasure in the body. Women dressed not only for men or against other women, but also for themselves. Although Mrs Haweis was not a 'typical' Victorian fashion and beauty expert, she seems to have been a well-known and respected one.[66] Ironically, the idea that the Victorians were obsessively prudish developed, in part, precisely because some Victorians were so outspoken in criticising their contemporaries. As the moderate dress reformer, Helen Ecob, maintained, when standards of modesty evolved, 'the prejudice that now exists in the minds of a portion of womankind against such an innovation as liberated legs will vanish'.[67] It seems clear that, although a range of opinion existed on the extent to which fashion should emphasise feminine sexual beauty, if we can speak at all of a 'Victorian' ideal of femininity, that ideal was, in large part, an erotic one.

Notes

1 Theodore Zeldin, *France: 1848–1945*, 2 vols (Oxford: Oxford University Press, 1973, 1977), vol. 2, p. 441; A Lady, *Beauty: What It Is and How to Retain It* (London: Frederick Warne & Co., 1873), p. 92.

2 Gabriel Prevost, *Le Nu, le vêtement, la parure chez l'homme et chez la femme* (Paris: C. Marpon and E. Flammarion, 1883), pp. 3–4, 38.

3 Madame Roxy Caplin, *Health and Beauty, or Corsets and Clothing Constructed in Accordance with the Physiological Laws of the Human Body* (London: Darnton & Co., 1854), pp. 35–6; Mrs Hugh Reginald (Mary Eliza) Haweis, *The Art of Beauty* (London: Chatto & Windus, 1878; reprinted, New York and London: Garland Publishing, Inc., 1978), p. 36.

4 Charles Blanc, *Art in Ornament and Dress* (London: Chapman and Hall, 1877), p. 53; Mrs Margaret Oliphant, *Dress* (London: Macmillan and Co., 1878), p. 4.

5 Arnold James Cooley, *The Toilet and Cosmetic Arts in Ancient and Modern Times* (London: R. Hardwick, 1866, and Philadelphia: Lindsay and Blackiston, 1866; reprinted, New York: Burt Franklin, Research and Source Works Series 511, 1970), p. 160; Haweis, *The Art of Beauty*, pp. 11, 13, 16, 273.

6 Haweis, *The Art of Beauty*, pp. 128–9.

7 *Godey's Lady's Book*, 9 (August 1834), p. 90.

8 Charlotte Mary Yonge, *Womankind* (London: Morley, 1877), pp. 116–17; *Godey's Lady's Book* 7 (December 1833), p. 310; John Todd, *The Young Man: Hints Addressed to the Young Men of the United States* (Northampton, MA, 1850), quoted by Karen Halttunen, *Confident Men and Painted Women: A Study of Middle-Class Culture in America, 1830–1870* (New Haven: Yale University Press, 1982), p. 40.

9 The Sir Basil Liddell Hart 'Scrapbooks', in the Liverpool John Moores University Art Library.

10 *Godey's Lady's Book*, quoted in Halttunen, *Confident Men and Painted Women*, p. 89; Mrs

Hugh Reginald (Mary Eliza) Haweis, *The Art of Dress* (London: Chatto & Windus, 1879; reprinted, New York and London: Garland Publishing Inc., 1978), p. 126; Haweis, *The Art of Beauty*, pp. 195–6, 257, 263.

11   *Sylvia's Home Journal* (January 1878), pp. 6–7.

12   Yonge, *Womankind*, p. 117; *How to Dress or Etiquette of the Toilette* (London: Ward, Lock & Tyler, n.d. [1877]), p. 87.

13   *The Art of Beauty* (London, 1825), quoted by Richard Corson, *Fashions in Make-up from Ancient to Modern Times* (New York: University Books, 1972), p. 295; Gordon Stables, MD, *The Girl's Own Book of Health and Beauty* (London: Jarrold & Sons, 1892), preface, no page numbers; 'Medicus' [Stables], cited by Wendy Forrester, *Great Grandmama's Weekly. A Celebration of the* Girl's Own Paper (Guilford and London: Lutterworth Press, 1980), pp. 50–4; *How to Dress or Etiquette of the Toilette*, p. 50; Frances Mary Steele and Elizabeth Livingston Steele Adams, *Beauty of Form and Grace of Vesture* (London: B. F. Stevens, and Cambridge, MA: Harvard University Press, 1892), pp. 50, 53.

14   Mrs C. E. Humphry, *How to Be Pretty Though Plain* (London: James Bowden, 1899), pp. 10–11; Mrs C. E. Humphry, *Beauty Adorned* (London: T. Fisher Unwin, 1901), pp. 4–5.

15   For information on Madame Rachel, see Richard Corson, *Fashions in Make-up*; Advertisement in *The Queen* (18 February 1871), no page number.

16   *The Ugly-Girl Papers; or Hints for the Toilet* by SDP. Reprinted from *Harper's Bazaar* (New York: Harper & Brothers, 1874), p. 60; Gwen Raverat, *Period Piece: A Cambridge Childhood* (London: Faber & Faber, 1952), pp. 266–7.

17   Charles Baudelaire, 'In Praise of Cosmetics' (1863), in *The Painter of Modern Life and Other Essays*, trans. and ed. by Jonathan Mayne (London: Phaidon Press, 1964), pp. 31–4.

18   [Mrs Elizabeth Lynn Linton], 'Costume and its Morals', *Saturday Review* (13 July 1867), p. 44.

19   [Mrs Elizabeth Lynn Linton], 'The Girl of the Period', *Saturday Review* (14 March 1868), pp. 339–40; Leonore Davidoff, *The Best Circles. Society Etiquette and the Season* (London: Croom Helm, 1973), p. 114; *The Girl of the Period and the Fashionable Woman of the Period*. Reprinted from *Saturday Review* (New York: J. R. Redfield, 1869), especially pp. 17–19.

20   *The Tomahawk: A. Saturday Journal of Satire* (12 March 1870), no page number, in the Sir Basil Liddell Hart 'Scrapbooks'. Other cartoons and articles are also in the Sir Basil Liddell Hart 'Scrapbooks'.

21   W.L. Burn, *The Age of Equipoise. A Study of the Mid-Victorian Generation* (London: George Allen & Unwin, 1964), p. 26.

22   'On Vanity and Love of Dress', *Family Herald* (3 June 1843), p. 60. [Emphasis added.]

23   *Dress, Health and Beauty* (London: Ward, Lock & Co., 1878), pp. 17, 134.

24   Mrs Beecher Stowe, 'What are the Sources of Beauty in Dress?', *The Queen* (12 December 1868), p. 345.

25   F. T. Vischer, cited in Friedrich Wendel, *Weib und Mode: eine Sittengeschichte im Spiegel der Karikatur* (Dresden: Paul Aretz Verlag, 1928), pp. 173–5.

26   'Who Is to Blame? A Few Words on Ladies' Dress, in its Moral and Aesthetic Aspects. Addressed to the "Fast" of Both Sexes', reprinted from *The Journal of Social Science* (London: L. Booth, n.d. [*c.* 1866), pp. 4–5, 7; Haweis, *The Art of Beauty*, p. 263.

27   C. T., *How to Dress Well: A Manual of the Toilet for the Use of Both Sexes* (London: George Routledge & Sons, 1868), pp. 13, 94; Haweis, *The Art of Beauty*, pp. 11, 17.

28   'The Art of Dress', *The Quarterly Review*, 79 (March 1847), pp. 375–6.

29   'Nice Girls', *Harper's Bazaar* (11 April 1868), p. 382. [Emphasis added.]

30   *Sylvia's Home Journal* (January 1878), p. 11.

31   'A Lady's Question: What Shall We Wear?', *London Society* (May 1869), p. 413.

32   Miss Oakey (Mrs Maria Richards Dewing), *Beauty in Dress* (New York: Harper, 1881), p. 145; *The Art of Dressing Well: A Book of Hints*, p. 62.

33 *The Rational Dress Society's Gazette* (October 1888), p. 2.

34 Theodore Zeldin, ed., *Conflicts in French Society. Anticlericalism, Education and Morals in the Nineteenth Century* (London: George Allen & Unwin, 1970), p. 32.

35 Martha Vicinus, 'Introduction', in Vicinus, ed., *A Widening Sphere: Changing Roles of the Victorian Woman* (Bloomington and London: Indiana University Press, 1977), pp. xi, xix; Jeffrey Weeks, *Sex, Politics, and Society: The Regulation of Sexuality since 1800* (London and New York: Longman, 1981), pp. 27, 41; Mrs Merrifield, *Dress as a Fine Art* (London: A. Hall Virtue, 1854, and Boston: Jewitt & Co., 1854), p. 24.

36 C. T., *How to Dress Well*, p. 44; *Etiquette of Good Society*, p. 79.

37 Henry James, *The Awkward Age*, Book Two: *Little Aggie* [first published in 1899] (Harmondsworth, Middlesex: Penguin Books, 1966), p. 87; Mlle Pauline Mariette, *L'Art de la toilette* (Paris: Librairie Centrale, 1866), p. 2.

38 *La Reforme par les dames* (Paris: J.-L. Paulmier, 1865), p. 23, cited by Philippe Perrot, 'Le Jardin des modes', in Jean-Paul Aron, *Misérable et glorieuse. La Femme du XIX siècle* (Paris: Librairie Arthème Fayard, 1980), p. 104. See also Erving Goffman, 'Attitudes and Rationalizations Regarding Body Exposure', in Roach and Eicher, *Dress, Adornment, and the Social Order*, p. 50.

39 'One of the Aristocracy', *Etiquette for Women: A Book of Modern Modes and Manners* (London: C. Arthur Pearson, 1902), p. 14.

40 Louis Octave Uzanne, *The Modern Parisienne* (London: William Heineman, 1912); Sylvaine Marandon, *L'Image de la France dans l'Angleterre victorienne 1848–1900* (Paris; Armand Colin, 1967); Maryléne Delbourg-Delphis, *Le Chic et le Look* (Paris: Hachette, 1981).

41 Trevor Fairbrother, 'The Shock of John Singer Sargent's "Madame Gautreau"', *Arts Magazine*, 55, 5 (January 1981), p. 90; Albert Woolf, quoted in Evan Charteris, *John Sargent* (New York: Scribners, 1927), p. 62.

42 *The Art Amateur* (1889), quoted in Fairbrother, 'The Shock', p. 94; Ralph Curtis, quoted in Charteris, *John Sargent*, pp. 61–2; Fairbrother, p. 91, in the context of an analysis of *Gazette des Beaux-Arts* (1884).

43 C. T., *How to Dress Well*, p. 11. [Emphasis added.]

44 Henry James, *Portrait of a Lady*, chapter 19 [first published in 1881] (Cambridge, MA: The Riverside Press, 1956), pp. 172–3.

45 C. T., *How to Dress Well*, p. 21; W. L. Burn, *The Age of Equipoise*, pp. 253–4.

46 A Lady, *How to Dress on £15 a Year as a Lady* (London: Frederick Warne & Co., 1873), p. 4.

47 'A Lady's Question: What Shall We Wear?', *London Society* (May 1869), p. 410; *The Woman's World* (May 1890), p. 349; *The Art of Dressing Well: A Book of Hints* (London: Lockwood & Co. and Simpkin, Marshall & Co., n.d. [*c.* 1870]), p. 66; C. T., *How to Dress Well*, p. 43; Mrs Aria, 'Dressing as a Duty and an Art', *The Woman's World* (July 1890), p. 476.

48 C. T., *How to Dress Well*, p. 19; Clarke, p. 10; C. T., *How to Dress Well*, p. 14; *The Art of Dressing Well. A Book of Hints*, p. 2; *Sylvia's Home Journal* (February 1878), p. 59.

49 Mrs Aria, 'Dressing as a Duty and an Art', p. 476.

50 *Etiquette of Good Society* (London, Paris, and New York: Cassell, Peter Galpin & Co., n.d. [*c.* 1880]), pp. 77–9.

51 Derek Hudson, *Munby. Man of Two Worlds. The Life and Diaries of Arthur J. Munby 1828–1910* (London: John Murray, 1972), pp. 40–1; C. T., *How to Dress Well*, pp. 22–4.

52 J. Erskine Clarke, *Over-Dress*, Tracts for the Family, no. IX (London: John Morgan, n.d.), pp. 4–9.

53 Rosa Nouchette Carey, 'Aunt Diana', *The Girl's Own Paper* (20 June 1885), p. 595.

54 Louisa Twining, 'Dress', *The Sunday Magazine*, ed. by Thomas Guthrie DD (London: Strahan & Co., 1872), p. 467.

55 *Dress, Drink, and Debt: A Temperance Tale* (London: Society for Promoting Christian Knowledge, n.d. [*c.* 1878]), p. 11.

56   John Forbes Moncrieff, *Our Domestics and Their Mistresses. A Contribution to 'The Servant Question'* (Edinburgh: André Stevenson; and London: Dyer Brothers, n.d. [c. 1895]), p. 55.

57   C. T., *How to Dress Well*, p. 27; Moncrieff, *Our Domestics*, pp. 54, 82.

58   Wilkie Collins, *The Moonstone, Third Narrative and The Loss of the Diamond* [first published in 1868], ed. J. I. M. Stewart (Harmondsworth, Middlesex: Penguin Books, 1966), pp. 363–86.

59   Mrs Eric Pritchard, *The Cult of Chiffon* (London: Grant Richards, 1902), cited in Doris Langley Moore, *The Woman in Fashion*, p. 177. Mrs M. E. W. Sherwood, *A Transplanted Rose* (New York, 1882), cited in Jo Anne Olian, *The House of Worth: The Gilded Age, 1860–1918* (New York: The Museum of the City of New York, 1982), p. 8.

60   *Sylvia's Home Journal* (February 1878), p. 58; *The Queen* (15 November 1879), p. 457; F. Adolphus, *Some Memories of Paris* (Edinburgh and London: William Blackwood and Sons, 1895), p. 189.

61   Anthony Trollope, *The Eustace Diamonds*, chapter 35 [first published in 1873] (Harmondsworth, Middlesex: Penguin Books, 1969), pp. 348, 358.

62   Blanc, *Art in Ornament and Dress*, p. 151.

63   Haweis, *The Art of Beauty*, pp. 18, 20, 21, 22, 23.

64   Haweis, *The Art of Beauty*, pp. 23–4; Haweis, *The Art of Dress*, pp. 13–14.

65   Haweis, *The Art of Dress*, p. 29.

66   Bea Howe, *Arbiter of Fashion* (London: Harvill Press, 1967) [a biography of Mrs Haweis].

67   Helen Gilbert Ecob, *The Well Dressed Woman: A Study in the Practical Application to Dress of the Laws of Health, Art, and Morals* (New York: Fowler and Wells, 1893), p. 261.

Fashion, readers and the novel in the nineteenth century

Clair Hughes

'All is True!' Honoré de Balzac's claim in the prologue to *Père Goriot* (1834) looks contradictory – novels are after all fictions – but the nineteenth-century realist novelist's concern with detail and surface, with dress, for example, was a quest for truths: surfaces communicate with depths. In the new middle-class world of nineteenth-century Europe, whose development paralleled that of the realist novel, dress is the most obvious sign of order, hierarchy and change – key concerns of the novel. It expresses individual taste within social limits; it is a measure of ambition, respect and self-respect. But it also betrays, deceives and seduces – aspects that add to the power of dress for the writer of fiction.

Dress in fiction, however, is rarely described in full: details are foregrounded, while the basic look of an outfit is understood between author and reader. Details figure significantly in the images of character and context that we take away from a novel, as well as contributing to its 'reality effect'. If, as Henry James claimed, Balzac was the master of a novelistic 'reality effect', then, at least as far as dress is concerned, Sir Walter Scott was its forefather. The dress of medieval England in Scott's *Ivanhoe* (1819), for example, is described with an antiquarian minuteness which, at the time, was excitingly novel. The sheer volume of data in *Ivanhoe* convinces us that this is how thirteenth-century Britain looked. Scott uses dress not only to recreate an epoch but also to distinguish rank, moral character and loyalties – and, writing after the Napoleonic wars with France, Scott dresses his Anglo-Saxons more sympathetically than his Normans.

Despite Dickens's reputation as the most important Victorian social realist, dress in his work is emblematic rather than realistic. Clothes are used as quirks to identify character or make us laugh, like Joe Gargery's animated hat in *Great Expectations* (1862). A key image in the novel, however, is Miss Havisham's wedding dress. If Dickens seems to endorse a conventional marriage plot, his novels actually describe unhappy unions. Miss Havisham's dress represents how she was jilted in the past as well as her present prison of hatred, and will ultimately cause her death. Pip, the hero, recognises the traditional wedding dress – 'satins and lace and silks – all of white'; but on looking again: 'everything which ought to be white . . . was faded and yellow'. Dress is a social language, but can also be a writer's own sign-system and Dickens here re-invents the wedding dress, stripping it of all hope.

Scott's accounts of dress have little sense of a wearer's or viewer's perspective. Pip, on the other hand, gives us an emotional perspective. Unsettling aspects of Miss Havisham's dress emerge, part of the mystery at the heart of the novel. Dickens's treatment of clothing here approaches a modernist concern with dress *experienced*.

Modernists did not reject the realist vision but found it inadequate. Henry James, an early modernist, deploys dress sparingly, but acknowledges its powerful if elusive

Snapshot 15.1   Charles Frederick Worth, evening dress, label 'C. Worth, 50939'.

nature. In James's novel, *The Ambassadors* (1902), Lambert Strether is sent to Paris to extract Chad Newsome from his relationship with Marie de Vionnet, and return him to puritan New England. Strether becomes confused, for Marie's effect on Chad is beneficial, her appearance and behaviour impeccable. This friendship is surely 'virtuous'. When Strether encounters Marie dressed in 'substances and textures vaguely rich', she seems to him 'a sea nymph waist-high in the summer surge'. Her image is dazzling but also in conformity with current styles (Snapshot 15.1). Strether is enchanted but uneasy. Good women in novels, as Anne Hollander notes, are rarely fashionably dressed. Strether's struggle for moral clarity is frustrated by a truth as nuanced as the dress, where sexuality – what is not seen – swishes like a mermaid's tail beneath a froth of chiffon.

Dress in fiction is then over-determined; no one meaning is final. All might be true, and Strether's vision of Marie reveals as much about himself as about her. As the novelist, Elizabeth Bowen, remarks, no one feels indifferent about dress. 'It is dangerous – it has a flowery head but deep roots in the passions.'

Bibliography and further reading

Bowen, E. (1950) 'Dress', in *Collected Impressions*, New York: Knopf.
Dickens, C. (1996 [orig. edition 1862]) *Great Expectations*, London: Penguin Classics.
Hollander, A. (1993) *Seeing through Clothes*, Berkeley: University of California Press.
James, H. (1984) 'The Lesson of Balzac', *Literary Criticism*, vol. 2, New York: Library of America.
James, H. (1994 [orig. edition 1902]) *The Ambassadors*, New York: W. W. Norton.
Scott, Sir W. (1998 [orig. edition 1819]) *Ivanhoe*, London: Penguin Classics.

Chapter 13

Modes of manliness
Reflections on recent histories of masculinities and fashion

Christopher Breward

IN 1993, WHEN I EMBARKED ON THE DOCTORAL THESIS that would eventually be published as *The Hidden Consumer*,[1] historians interested in issues of manliness and their relationship to fashion seemed to be few and far between, though rich primary sources for the study of men's dress were relatively untapped. My project emerged out of a further frustration with the otherwise highly creative literature on consumer cultures and their relationship to femininities and fashion in the nineteenth century, that in the late 1980s and early 1990s was having such an influence on understandings of Victorian and Edwardian material and visual culture. I argued that three historiographical trends in the field of Victorian Studies had conspired to hide the consuming practices of nineteenth-century men from the attentions of social and cultural historians. Firstly, an emphasis on the discourse of the separate spheres had focused too much on concepts of a decorative and domestic femininity as the site for sartorial expression and responsibility.[2] Secondly, when fashion in the public sphere was discussed, attention had been unduly placed on the extraordinary commodity-fetishism associated with the female-friendly spaces of the department store, itself an atypical institution.[3] And thirdly a burgeoning interest in the social, economic and political manifestations of patriarchy had tended to endorse a renunciatory explanation for the relegation of fashionable taste to the world of women and non-conforming (dandified or effeminate) men.[4]

In costume history the prospects were similarly limited because of that discipline's attention to a narrow conception of the fashion object and its representation, focused as it was on antiquarian sources and approaches alongside surviving garments in public and private collections.[5] Aside from uniform and court dress, everyday clothing for men has tended not to be collected so comprehensively by museums, and equally its survival is rare in comparison to women's items. The lack of space devoted to male attire in the historical record had thus become 'naturalised' as an apparently appropriate reflection of the minimal attention assumed to have been lavished on sartorial matters by

Figure 13.1 'Edgar' 1889 from a family photo album. Victoria and Albert Museum 754-1975.

most nineteenth-century men. The invisibility of Victorian conceptions of male fashionability in the late twentieth century simply seemed to strengthen arguments for fashion as an entirely feminised phenomenon in the nineteenth century. And these were the arguments that provided the basis for fashion histories which, when they did include men, upheld a slow moving rate of style change, functional utility and a well-mannered observance of propriety as the defining, indeed the only features of late-modern patterns of masculine fashionability. As an aside, it was also, uncoincidentally, a similar definition of normative male dressing, that provided Modernist aesthetic theory of the early twentieth century with its anti-fashion, misogynistic rhetoric.[6]

So, in the mid-1990s, when the work of many social and costume historians seemed simply to endorse reductive Victorian conceptions of gender and dress rather than unpack them, the overtly politicised thinking of the cultural studies 'project' seemed to me to offer more creative pathways for discovering hidden behaviours. Work on contemporary masculinities, in particular, illustrated the complex coming-together of institutions, practices, desires, ideologies, beliefs and representations that must be made to cohere in order to sustain even the most commonsensical notions of what men were or are.[7] Gender theorist Ed Cohen put it very well when he claimed in 1993 that 'it comes as little surprise that that recent, highly detailed historiographies [and he was referring here to the work of Mort, Roper and Tosh] provide some of the best "theoretical" insights into the complex dynamics that mark out the somatic terrains mapped by gender and sexuality. Indeed, attempts to account for such assignments of qualitative attributes to bodily signifiers of difference (meaning masculinity and femininity) frequently belie the epistemological distinctions between "theory" and "history" per se, precisely in so far as they ask us to reconsider the "embodied" materiality of these "imaginary" mappings. Hence it is often when discussions of masculinity seem to veer most precipitously towards the "historical" that they most suggestively lead us towards the "theoretical" in ways that provocatively trouble both epistemological distinctions and gendered categories'.[8]

Given that the study of surviving men's clothing itself was not providing me with the answers I craved, provocative discussion of 'the embodied materiality of imaginary mappings' naturally led me to a rich seam of visual and textual representation, a seam I have to admit in which I have always felt most comfortable as a researcher. The traces of male sartorial desire to be found in novels, autobiographies, *cartes de visite* and street photographs, retail catalogues and advertisements, popular songs and theatre programmes all provided me with a sense of the ways in which representations act to give meaning to consumers' relationships with commodities and other consumers, and draw their power from the eroticised motivations associated with the act of fashionable consumption itself. Most importantly these traces all produced what Graham Dawson has described as an 'imagined identity . . . something that has been "made up" in the positive sense of active creation, but has real effects in the world of everyday relationships, which it invests with meaning and makes intelligible in specific ways. It organises a form that a masculine self can assume in the world (its bodily appearance and dress, its conduct and mode of relating) as well as its values and aspirations, its tastes and desires . . . Representations furnish a repertoire of cultural forms that can be drawn upon in the imagining of lived identities. These may be aspired to rather than actually being achieved . . . [and] often figure ideal and desirable masculinities, which men strive after in their efforts to make themselves into the man they want to be. Imagined identities are shot through with wish fulfilling fantasies'.[9]

This relationship between fashionable representation and the formation of identity ('self-fashioning' as scholars of the Renaissance might have it) is suffused with the operation of political, social and sexual power. And in the mid-1990s, other historians of masculinity and dress such as John Harvey and David Kuchta were simultaneously mobilising these connections in relation to the study of the Englishman's suit as the appropriate cipher for the ascendancy of an efficient, professionalised and

Figure 13.2 'Walking in the Zoo', *c.* 1870, music cover by Richard Childs (colour lithograph). Victoria and Albert Museum Enthoven Collection.

patriarchal new public order in the eighteenth and nineteenth centuries: a material projection of the bourgeois desire for self-discipline and the deployment of suppressed lib-
ertinous energy in productive intellectual labour.[10] However, while such readings may
well account for the predominance of black-suited characters in prescriptive literatures
of the time, they appeared less frequently in the material that I was mining. So, my
methods were aligned more closely to the stress on mediation, subjectivity and those
'practices of the self' that the new historicism and cultural studies had brought to bear
on questions of gender and its historical construction. These revealed and mobilised,
rather than simply acknowledged the problems inherent in simple and closed explanations of power and its material manifestations.

Herbert Sussman's work on Victorian masculinities and the poetics of mid-
nineteenth-century industrial and cultural production offered some pointers through
these difficulties, suggesting that

> if women's studies as well as lesbian and gay studies derive their energy and
> purpose from engaging a history of oppression . . . a study of masculini-
> ties examines the history of the oppressors, of the hegemonic discourse,
> of the patriarchy. [The] justifiable anxiety [this gives rise to] . . . must be
> acknowledged and may be addressed in several ways. For one, the empha-
> sis on the constructed rather than the innate, and on the multiple rather
> than the unitary view of the masculine calls attention to the historical con-
> tingency of such formations of manliness and of male power itself, thus
> questioning male dominance and supporting the possibility of altering the
> configuration of what is marked as masculine. Furthermore . . . the prob-
> lem of power and patriarchy calls for a double awareness, a sensitivity both
> to the ways in which these social formations of the masculine created con-
> flict [and] tension in men, while acknowledging that, in spite of the stress,
> men accepted these formations as a form of self-policing crucial to patriar-
> chal domination.[11]

As I completed *The Hidden Consumer* my sense was that most accounts of the appearance of men and their role as consuming subjects (and beyond work on the post-war
era there were not many to chose from at the time) had not grappled with the implications of this 'double awareness', nor fully appreciated the myriad ways in which representations of all kinds informed the formation of gendered identities for men as well as
women. But since then studies in historical and contemporary masculinities and fashion
by among others Laura Ugolini, Paul Jobling, Michael Zakim, Brent Shannon and Will
Fisher have demonstrated the revelatory role dress and its imagery can play in opening
up these issues.[12] Paradoxically, this has also pulled the study of masculinity and consumption back into the orbit of the 'separate spheres' and those theories of political
economy that so frustrated me when I first looked to the historiography of nineteenth-
century social and economic history for guidance, but in a much more positive fashion.
Nancy Cott predicted that this might be the case in 1990 when she concluded that:

> Finding gender the decisive variable, a history of men as gendered sub-
> jects may promise to be truly transformative, making known elements fall
> together – as in a kaleidoscope – in an entirely new pattern. An alternative

reasoning is that acknowledging the gendered nature of men's activities will illuminate all their arenas of life, but emphasise the contingency of gender determination making it one influential variable among others. A third possible justification, stressing method more than narrative, might be to argue that emphasis on the gendered nature of male beings is the best way to bridge the categories of the private and the public . . . The public and the private are more obviously inseparable when we look at men's lives . . . if only because we tend more readily to focus on men's participation in public, while admitting they have private character. If the boundary between private and public does become more elusive when men are studied as gendered subjects that may focus needed attention on it. Demarcation between public and private has been a basic premise of modern life, but without consistent or unanimously shared definitions or boundaries . . . For historians to subject this vexed area to historical scrutiny through the sign system of gender would be a great leap forward.[13]

In the decade since *The Hidden Consumer* was published I have in various ways (like many of my colleagues in the Art and Design School and Museum sectors) continued to act on Cott's exhortation; trying to take her reading of gender as a 'sign system' further and positioning the design, manufacture, exchange and display of fashionable clothing as an essential signifier in its operation. Whether through studies of dandyism and its role in the history of London, the retail ecology of male fashion in the West End of the 1960s, the construction of the image of the cavalier in the 1630s, or an as yet unpublished essay on the sexual identity of male couturiers in the 1950s, the imagery and presentation of masculine fashionability have provided various opportunities to test assumptions about the contingent nature of modish dressing and what it can tell us about wider societal attitudes.[14] In this way I have, I suppose, upheld the now unfashionable view that practices of language, representation and performance have an important, political, role to play in defining and critiquing gendered positions and identities in the past and the present, echoing Kevin Sharpe and Stephen Zwicker's recent argument that 'fashion and role, seemingly vehicles for self-expression, are also the instruments for the social inscribing of the self: social role and persona in the end fabricate personality. The creation of the self, we might discern, is a process of interiorising all the instability and incoherence of society and state'.[15] Such practices also reflect the subjectivity of the historian himself, and if there is a dominant theme in my approach to researching and writing on men's fashion it's a covert acknowledgement of the infinite pleasure and sometimes frustration that the choosing and wearing and viewing of clothes made for men bring to me.[16] I ended the introduction to *The Hidden Consumer* with a quotation from James Eli Adams, who in a review essay titled 'The Banality of Transgression: Recent Works on Masculinity' published in *Victorian Studies* in 1993 endorses:

> An understanding of masculine identity as an intersection of numerous and often-conflicting contexts and axes of meaning . . . And if a particular analysis of masculine identity is inevitably influenced by the critic's own subject position, it is not reducible to that position, which is itself neither fixed nor unitary. To assume otherwise is to embrace a mode of cynicism, which

assumes that the reflection to which we devote so much of our lives has no power to change our minds.[17]

It still seems apposite to end with it today.

Notes

1   C. Breward (1999) *The Hidden Consumer: Masculinities, Fashion and City Life 1860–1914*, Manchester: Manchester University Press.

2   L. Davidoff and C. Hall (1987) *Family Fortunes: Men and Women of the English Middle Class 1780–1850*, London: Hutchinson.

3   E. Abelson (1989) *When Ladies Go A-Thieving: Middle-class Shoplifters in the Victorian Department Store*, Oxford: Oxford University Press; R. Bowlby (1985) *Just Looking: Consumer Culture in Dreiser, Gissing and Zola*, London: Methuen; R. Williams (1982) *Dream Worlds: Mass Consumption in Late Nineteenth-Century France*, Berkeley: University of California Press.

4   A. Mangan and J. Walvin (eds) (1987) *Manliness and Morality: Middle-class Masculinity in Britain and America 1800–1940*, Manchester: Manchester University Press; M. Roper and J. Tosh (eds) (1991) *Manful Assertions: Masculinities in Britain since 1800*, London: Routledge.

5   V. Cumming (2004) *Understanding Fashion History*, London: Batsford.

6   C. Breward and C. Evans (eds) (2005) *Fashion and Modernity*, Oxford: Berg.

7   F. Mort (1996) *Cultures of Consumption*, London: Routledge; S. Nixon (1997) *Hard Looks*, London: University College Press.

8   E. Cohen (1993)'Ma[r]king Men', *Victorian Studies*, 36, 2, pp. 218.

9   G. Dawson (1991) 'The Blond Bedouin' in Roper and Tosh (eds) *Manful Assertions*, pp. 118–19.

10   J. Harvey (1997) *Men in Black*, London: Reaktion; D. Kuchta (2002) *The Three Piece Suit and Modern Masculinity*, Berkeley: University of California Press.

11   H. Sussman (1995) *Victorian Masculinities: Manhood and Masculine Poetics in Early Victorian Literature and Art*, Cambridge: Cambridge University Press, pp. 8–9.

12   L. Ugolini (2007) *Men and Menswear: Sartorial Consumption in Britain 1880–1936*, Aldershot: Ashgate; P. Jobling (2005) *Man Appeal: Advertising, Modernism and Menswear*, Oxford: Berg; M. Zakim (2003) *Ready-made Democracy: A History of Men's Dress in the American Republic, 1760–1860*, Chicago: University of Chicago Press; B. Shannon (2006) *The Cut of His Coat: Men, Dress and Consumer Culture in Britain 1860–1914*, Athens, OH: Ohio University Press; W. Fisher (2006) *Materialising Gender in Early Modern English Literature and Culture*, Cambridge: Cambridge University Press.

13   N. Cott (1990) 'On Men's History and Women's History' in M. Carnes and C. Griffen (eds), *Meanings for Manhood: Constructions of Masculinity in Victorian America*, Chicago: University of Chicago Press, p. 122.

14   C. Breward (2004) *Fashioning London*, Oxford, Berg; C. Breward (2009) 'Fashioning the Modern Self' in K. Hearn (ed.), *Van Dyck and Britain*, London: Tate Publishing.

15   K. Sharpe and S. Zwicker (eds) (1998) *Refiguring Revolutions: Aesthetics and Politics from the English Revolution to the Romantic Revolution*, Berkeley: University of California Press, p. 14.

16   A. Cicolini (2005) *The New English Dandy*, London: Thames & Hudson.

17   J. Eli Adams (1993) 'The Banality of Transgression?' *Victorian Studies*, 36, 2, p. 213.

Fashion, the factory and exploitation

Katrina Honeyman

The rapid expansion of textile production through the eighteenth and nineteenth centuries formed the basis of the industrial revolution in Europe. Although cotton is usually cited as the most important of all the textiles in the technical and organisational transformation in the production process, most textiles including wool, worsted, linen and silk enjoyed growth of output and consumption. Factory production and the intensification of the labour process through the nineteenth century allowed cloth of varying types to become more plentiful and cheaper. Historical analysis of the textile trades has focused on the cloth or material itself to the relative neglect of the production and consumption of garments. Yet it is the growth of the clothing trade that was more significant in the ability of people in all social groups to purchase more clothes and to pay attention to the fashion and style of the garments that they wore. But it should be remembered that until the twentieth century average earnings for most working people were insufficient to satisfy more than basic wardrobe requirements.

A significant feature of the nineteenth-century clothing trade was the development of ready-made garments for men, women and children. It is argued that the production of uniforms for military campaigns, notably the Napoleonic Wars, drove forward the possibilities of mass production. The challenge posed by so-called slop clothing – produced mainly by women – to the quality garments made by male skilled tailors caused tension between these groups and divisions within the sector. The distinction between high-quality made-to-measure garments and less expensive ready-to-wear clothes never subsequently disappeared and became particularly pronounced from the later nineteenth century as the viable sewing machine diffused through the industry.

Although the sewing machine was designed to ease and accelerate the laborious hand stitching which had traditionally dominated the making of all garments whether tailored or not, it soon became identified with unskilled, low paid and mainly female labour. Factory textile workers are often associated with unprecedented levels of exploitation, and certainly they were subject to novel conditions of discipline in the workplace, and long hours of monotonous toil for which they were poorly remunerated. However, it can be argued that the female dressmakers, subjected to sweatshop conditions, were more fully exploited. The seasonality of demand for garments meant that much of the clothing labour force worked excessive hours during the busy parts of the year and were reduced to penury when work was slack. Even those who worked in their own homes, where control over the work process was in principle greater, faced serious exploitation.

The sewing machine was unusual among technologies for its compatibility with a range of different forms of production. Suited to home and workshop production, the sewing machine was also used in the large-scale factories in which ready-made and wholesale bespoke men's tailored outer garments were produced through much of the

Snapshot 16.1 Occupational portrait of a woman working at a sewing machine, c. 1853.
Library of Congress Prints and Photographs Division, Washington, DC, LC-USZC4-3598.

twentieth century. The standard man's suit – a uniform garment with apparently little connection with fashion – became the staple male attire in the first half of the twentieth century. The democratising of menswear was the vision of such multiple tailors as Montague Burton in England. Low labour costs and high turnover allowed the price of a standard man's suit to be kept within reach of many working men; but the wealthier and more discerning male consumer, with a greater sensitivity to fashion, continued to purchase his suits from the individual made-to-measure tailor.

Through the period from the eighteenth century to the present, 'fashion', which ranges from haute couture to mass production, has served as a determinant of social status, and has been increasingly created by a combination of technical ingenuity, creative genius and the sweat of labour.

Bibliography and further reading

Harris, B. (2005) *Famine and Fashion: Needlewomen in the Nineteenth Century*, Aldershot: Ashgate.

Honeyman, K. (2000) *Well Suited: A History of the Leeds Clothing Industry, 1870–1990*, Oxford: Oxford University Press and Pasold Research Fund.

Schmeichen, J. A. (1984) *Sweated Industries and Sweated Labour: The London Clothing Trades, 1860– 1914*, London: Croom Helm.

Jewellery and fashion
in the nineteenth century

Elizabeth Fischer

The major social and industrial shifts of the nineteenth century profoundly influenced the manufacture, materials and market of jewellery. Eclecticism characterised the motifs of jewellery, following the inspiration in other fields of art and design – Greco-Roman, medieval, exotic, naturalistic, sentimental – sparked off by cultural and political events such as archaeological discoveries or military campaigns in foreign countries, commerce with India and renewed diplomatic relations with Japan. The most precious and timeless jewels worn by the aristocracy, as patrimonial symbols of rank, prestige and antiquity of lineage, surrendered to the dictates of fashion. The trappings of the new wealth of businessmen and industrialists increasingly rivalled these prized ornaments, while a growing affluent middle class aspired to new kinds of jewellery.

To meet these various demands, jewellers used cheaper gems and materials, like steel and coloured paste, and devised ingenious technical and aesthetic ways of minimising the amount of precious metal. Industrial processes were developed such as electroplating, which speeded up and cheapened the operation of gilding. The two major centres for machine-made jewellery in Europe were Birmingham in England and Pforzheim in Germany. They flourished in the second half of the century thanks to the easier supply of gold from new sources in California and Australia, the legalisation of the use of 9, 12 and 15 carat gold, and the introduction of steam- and gas-powered machinery. At the exclusive end of the market, a close-knit network of specialised workshops maintained the high standards of hand-made pieces.

Jewellery complemented dress at all times of the day. Its usage was governed by the strict etiquette differentiating informal and formal wear as well as social and civil status. As women's skirts increasingly widened during the course of the century, obliterating the shape of the lower half of the body, jewels adorned every limb from head to waist, underlining the articulations of the upper half of the body. Depending on where emphasis was laid in the shape of bodice and sleeves, the focal point for jewellery changed. However, as the satire in *Punch* emphasises (Snapshot 17.1), as well as elaborately composed hair styles, most parts of the bust were bejewelled; jewels of the same type were worn in number, notably on necklaces, bracelets, armlets and rings.

To quote Roland Barthes, jewels 'modified, harmonised and animated the structure of a set of clothes' (2006). Such is the case for the corseted silhouettes of the nineteenth century, often already lavishly ornamented with lace, ribbons, embroidery, braiding, ruffles, fringes, feathers, artificial or natural flowers. Jewellery imparted movement and sparkle to this ornamental system, with the dangling loops of long necklaces from neck and bosom, the swaying drop earrings long enough to almost rest on the shoulders in the later part of the century, the chink of interlocking bracelets.

Gems mounted on minute springs – *tremblants* – in brooches and head-pieces

Snapshot 17.1 'A Young Lady on the High Classical School of Ornament', from *Punch*, 16 July 1859, p. 30. Jewellery in the archaeological style, in vogue during the second half of the nineteenth century, was directly inspired by archaeological finds and collections such as the Campania antiquities. A visit to the Castellani firm in Rome, which revived not only antique designs but also techniques like Etruscan granulation, was considered essential for any discerning traveller. The caricature aptly emphasises the abundant use of jewellery in nineteenth-century dress. It adorned every limb of the upper part of the female body.

quivered to the wearer's movements. Precious metals, enamels and stones shimmered and glittered in the light of candle or gas flames more than any other ornament or material of female dress. The exceptional refractive index of diamonds was heightened by the 58 facets in the 'brillant cut' refined during the last quarter of the century, still favoured today. It involves a waste of up to 50 per cent of the rough crystal, acceptable once diamonds became more plentiful and less expensive with the 1866 discovery of new mines in South Africa. The developments in interior lighting systems, providing a more constant and strong source of light, may also explain the new emphasis on the stone itself and its optical characteristics rather than its setting, as well as the high favour this colourless gem enjoyed in fashion, gradually supplanting coloured ones.

Men wore discreet stickpins in hat, cravat and shirtfront, as well as waistcoat chains, seals and rings on several fingers, and carried treasured pocket watches. The representation that men dressed only in dark colours and renounced ornament in the nineteenth century must be nuanced. Not to be outdone by women in the use of elaborate ornament, men of the aristocracy and upper echelons of the army paraded at every formal occasion in full military regalia richly adorned with gilt buttons, jewelled orders or medals, and the bejewelled hilts of presentation swords.

Bibliography and further reading

Barthes, R. (2006 [1961]) 'From Gemstones to Jewellery', in A. Stafford and M. Carter (eds), *The Language of Fashion: Roland Barthes*, trans. A. Stafford, Oxford: Berg.

Bennett, D., and Mascetti, D. (1989) *Understanding Jewellery*, Woodbridge: Antique Collector's Club.

Phillips, C. (2008) *Jewels and Jewellery*, 2nd edition, London: V & A Publications.

Scarisbrick, D. (1994) *Jewellery in Britain 1066–1837: A Documentary, Social, Literary and Artistic Survey*, Norwich: Michael Russell.

Chapter 14

L'Homme des foules, dandy, flâneur
Fashion and the metropolis 1850–1940

Ulrich Lehmann

Introduction

FASHION HAS ALWAYS BEEN MADE BY THE CITY. In European languages the etymological root of fashion lies in the word *mode*, although in English it is derived from the Latin *facere* (meaning 'to make'), which might be indicative of Anglo-American pragmatism over Romantic intuition. In *mode*, the two meanings of manner or type – as in 'mode of living' or 'style' – and *modern*, that is contemporary and progressively changing, come together. Fashion occurs most prominently in a constantly shifting environment, as this provides both the economic conditions and the social impetus for expressing new perceptions of the body, changing one's status, and displaying conspicuous consumption.

This does not mean that, throughout history, fashion has not been produced away from the city. Very often forms of dress and body decoration originated in less populated areas, and over time fashion has often adapted from rural and very isolated parts of the world the pragmatic considerations that lead to the development of distinct clothing typologies. But our modern understanding of fashion, as a particular set of cultural parameters, which are subject to constant alteration within capitalist economies and industrialised societies, requires the spatial and conceptual setup of the city.

It is important to remind ourselves that fashion is not limited to clothes alone but defines all forms of the production, distribution, and consumption of objects. Fashion would be inconceivable without the interplay between textiles and furniture, ceramics, or silverware, for instance. At a larger scale, the development of sartorial cover cannot be contemplated without taking into account styles in interior decoration and private as well as public architecture. These connections to other forms of material culture make fashion in modernity – i.e. the period in the industrialised West that begins around the middle of the nineteenth century[1] – such a potent and multi-layered object for inquiry. Fashion in clothes cannot be singled out in its cultural meaning nor can it be critically analysed or structurally positioned without constant recourse to other fashionable expressions in modern culture.

Such spatial proximity and conceptual connection to a vast array of contemporary material objects needs the city as its stage. Historically, no other spatial organisation – not even the extensive court structures of ancient Ethiopia (800 BC), China of the Ming Dynasty (fourteenth to seventeenth centuries), or early eighteenth-century Versailles – allows for the same degree of material manifestation of new norms and morals that require expression in clothes, make-up and hairstyles. In a city the way in which aesthetic ideas are developed from and in opposition to social sanctions, religious morality, or ideological impositions, is marked out by close competition between actors and agencies – which can appear, for example, as people competing for social approval and to vie with each other for subjective self-expression, or through institutions like church or State that prescribe vestments and uniforms for public use and sanction non-conformist choices in dress.

People compete with each other for the most advantageous – which often implies the most contemporary – expression of corporeal perception. Therefore it is paramount for actors in a society to establish, modify, and display the body in order to survive their environment or ascend across social strata, not to fall foul of government decrees while ostentatiously flaunting them, and to attract a potential lover or partner while pertaining precariously to existing gender stereotypes. Such social, political, and sexual negotiations are most difficult, but also most successful, within a socially complex space that comprises various economic and social layers. In short, the close proximity of diverse people living together in one and the same spatial structure poses the greatest challenge and the best opportunity for the progressive development of fashion.[2]

Paris and modernity

In a city the economic conditions for distribution and consumption are most favourably met, even if the production of goods might have been moved away from the centre of towns during progressive industrialisation. An apt and relatively early example for such an economic configuration in the West is the Place Royale in Paris, which was conceived at the very start of the seventeenth century as a fashionable real estate development for an emerging bourgeoisie and originally housed substantial textile works that would produce luxury goods for consumption by precisely the same socio-economic clientele as for the new apartment houses.[3] In this example, the Place Royale – today's Place des Vosges in the Marais quarter of central Paris – shows how fashion is expressed in the production of textiles as much as in the planning and decoration of houses and the staging of public spectacles.

For the purpose of this essay I would like to centre my discussion on the city of Paris. This has a number of reasons that should, however, not detract from the fact that I am thereby succumbing to a Western- and market-centric writing of cultural history that is all too often unacknowledged as critical bias. My excuse, if one can be offered at all, is the relative ease with which the tenets about fashion and the city can be demonstrated within this orthodox perception of the cultural centre. It must be

Figure 14.1 Rue Pont Neuf, Paris, by International View Co., 1901. © 1901 by C. L. Wasson. Reproduced courtesy of Library of Congress. LC-USZ62-96659.

acknowledged, of course, that a case study from outside Europe, for instance the pronounced urbanism of the Mayan Empire in Mesoamerica (250–900 AD), the Dogon culture in West Africa during the twelfth and thirteenth centuries, or the metropolis of Edo, the 'City of the Floating World' in seventeenth- and eighteenth-century Japan, could equally be used as settings for the following observations. Yet the comparative unfamiliarity with some of these historic cultures might necessitate anthropological and geographical discourses that detract from the focus on fashion with a capitalist, industrialised modernity. Also, I am sure that readers are aware that Paris is a very potent ground indeed for such an inquiry as the progressive conception of much of modern fashion in the form of haute couture and its rendition in various contemporary media like journalism, fine art, photography, etc., were here at their most advanced.

The painter of modern life: *l'homme des foules*, dandy, *flâneur*

I would like to turn now to Paris and the advent of modernity, to the coinage of the term *modernité* itself. The concept of modernity, as a cultural phenomenon that is intimately tied to fashion – *la mode* and *la modernité* share the same etymological roots and the latter is developed from the former, as both remain feminine in French – originated in the city of Paris between 1850 and 1860. It was first expressed and analysed in a series of newspaper *feuilletons* by Charles Baudelaire. The fact that a progressive poet chose this journalistic medium to express his ideas is perfectly in keeping with the conceptual relation between fashion and the city. The constant movement in urban space and the economic dynamism of an emerging couture industry demanded flexible and rapid theoretical reaction. Baudelaire not only uses the medium of the newspaper *feuilleton* to postulate his contemporary 'philosophy' for a developing fashion but also invents a fleeting alter ego for his postulates.

This alter ego, or artistic projection, appears at first – confusingly enough – as a real existing artist, Constantin Guys, *Le Peintre de la vie moderne* [*The Painter of Modern Life*], and only later becomes distilled into an ideal actor, *l'homme des foules* (after the eponymous paintings by Guys), the man in and of the crowds. Published in 1863, the *feuilleton* renders the observing artist both ardent observer and philosophical reflection of existing urban fashions:

> [A] convalescent, contemplating with delight the crowd from behind the window of a café, allows his thoughts to mingle with all the thoughts that are active around him . . . He who was on the point of forgetting it all, now remembers, and ardently desires to remember all. Finally, he precipitates himself through this crowd in search of some unknown, by whose physiognomy, caught by a rapid glance, he has been fascinated. Curiosity has become a fatal, irresistible passion![4]

This quote is to be read as imagining a scene as well as a discourse (i.e. both a textual and a metaphysical structure) for the ideal observer, the man of the crowd who not only distances himself through the glass screen from the mundane setting of the street, but also remains inactive while the people bustle around him. Furthermore, he is a convalescent who only remembers at present, which for Baudelaire means that he is physically (and psychologically) primed to take an interest in anything, as he sees with fresh eyes and is not yet jaded by daily urban contact:

> [H]e delights, in a word, in universal life. If some fashion, the cut of some garment, has been slightly transformed; if knotted ribbons or buckles have been dethroned by cockades; if the chignon has come down a peg lower on the nape of the neck; if the waist has been raised and the skirt amplified, believe me his eagle eye has already divined it at an enormous distance.[5]

The fascination with a fleeting and resolutely contemporary world is not only an individual obsession for Monsieur Guys; Baudelaire renders it an aesthetic programme. The fashionable detail becomes the pretext for a new sketch; the latest carriage becomes subject of a painting to be completed within a couple of nights. This allows for the most fundamental analysis in Baudelaire's *Le Peintre de la vie moderne*, the definition of *modernité*. The truly contemporary artist has to seek modernity in order to exist and to distinguish himself, both in aesthetic outlook as well as succeeding in the marketplace. His work has to be ultra-modern to account for the ever-changing modes of thought, patterns of behaviour, and fashions that are present in the metropolis, before the background of cultural and philosophical tenets that constituted ideals to be evoked and quoted from: 'Modernity is the transitory, fugitive, contingent half of art, the other half being the eternal and immutable'.[6]

   This dialectic of the fugitive and the eternal within the construction of art cannot be underestimated as they elevate for the first time the proper meaning and need for fashion, which represents the transitory and ephemeral *per se*. Art can no longer exist in and for itself but requires material culture to negate and substantiate its meaning. The canon of cultural forms has to be subverted and renewed constantly, and the production of new objects and commodities is paramount in introducing such novelties to be reflected in technique, symbolism, and narrative by progressive cultural expressions.

Figure 14.2 Two Ladies and Gentlemen at the Theatre, drawing by Constantin Guys (1805–92). 28 × 22.5 cm. © The Trustees of the British Museum.

Besides the *homme des foules*, Baudelaire introduces another facet into his character of Monsieur Guys that completes the modern artist and activates him from observer to participant in fashion:

> I should like to call him a *dandy*, and I should have some good reasons for it; for the word *dandy* implies a quintessence of character and a subtle comprehension of the whole moral mechanism of the world . . .[7]

Fashion not only provides the subject in modernity and situates the artist in the contemporary marketplace, it renders him, too, victim to the recurring cycles of dress styles, postures, table manners, etc. In order to accommodate and reflect on the dialectic of modernity, the dandy and man of the crowds need to be afforded a counterpart, which, although incorporating their negation, at the same time substantiates their affirmation proper. Therefore Baudelaire introduces the facet of the *flâneur*.

> For the perfect *flâneur*, for the passionate observer, it is an immense pleasure to choose his domicile among the multitude, in undulation and movement, in the fugitive and the infinite. To be away from home, and yet to be always at home; to see the world, to be the centre of the world, and yet to remain hidden from the world – these are some of these independent, passionate, impartial spirits' least pleasures, which can only be clumsily defined by words. The observer is a prince who always preserves his incognito.[8]

Here, the spectator moves from behind the glass screen into the urban street, forcing himself to become part of the crowds, while ensuring never to be one with it. He will always remain at a distance in order to observe and analyse the latest progress, trends, and fashions. The dandy might well emphasise this metaphysical distance structurally and materially by making it his business to constantly stay ahead of the fashion pack and postulate a new aesthetic credo whenever the existing fashion is static. But he, too, partakes directly in the crowd by reflecting the commodity structures that animate it and by requiring the reflection in the window pane (of the urban café or elsewhere) to ensure the correct knot in his tie, which operates as reason for his existence within the hypertrophic capitalist organisation of nineteenth-century European cities. Only the *flâneur* remains in opposition to such demands, by rendering himself inconspicuous and refusing the seasonal change of fashions, although his keen eye is, of course, perfectly aware of new nuances and very capable of describing and analysing them.

La Flâneuse

The language I am using here marks out the composite character of *homme des foules*, *dandy* and *flâneur* as male. This is certainly due to academic conventions in patriarchal cultures, but also alludes to the gender construction in fashion, where the man operates as observer, artist, or even philosopher, while the woman resolutely remains his object, in terms of studying, desiring or abusing her. Can there be female observers of the crowd and fashions? Where are the *flâneuses*?

One historic example immediately comes to mind: a writer at the time of Baudelaire; more famous than he was, more attuned to the marketplace, more revolutionary in practice (although both did fight on the barricades in Paris in 1848), and much more influential in coining a particular fashion in dress than his ostentatious dandyism. I am speaking here of George Sand. Born Aurore Dupin de Franceuil in 1804, she went to Paris to escape provincial life and a failed marriage that had produced two children. Reinventing herself as a writer of Romantic novels meant overcoming male prejudice to literary production. Therefore, similar to her English contemporary Mary Ann Evans, who published under the male moniker 'George Eliot', Franceuil became 'George

Sand' in publication. However, unlike Evans, Sand extended this switch of gender to her social role and, eventually to her style of dress, which became an extremely influential fashion during the latter half of the nineteenth century.[9]

Sand beats the path for the Baudelairean *flâneur* by walking the streets of Paris to find subjects for her modern artistic production. Yet her progress as *la femme des foules*, as woman of the crowds, is impeded by fashion. She recalls in her memoirs *Histoire de ma vie*, the *flâneries* through Paris in 1831, as a 24-year-old:

> I was eager to become deprovincialised and acquainted with all the ideas and arts of my time . . . Except for the most famous works I knew nothing about the contemporary arts. [But] I knew well the impossibilities for a poor woman to indulge in these fancies . . . And yet I saw my young friends from Berry, my childhood companions, living in Paris with as little as I and keeping up with everything of interest to bright young men. Literary and political events, the excitement of the theatre and the museum, clubs, the streets – they saw everything and went everywhere. My legs were as good as theirs, those steady little country legs which had learned to walk on rutted roads, balancing on heavy wooden shoes. But on the Parisian pavement I was like a ship on ice. My thin shoes cracked every second day, my sagging stockings tripped me; I did not know how to lift my skirts. I was dirty, tired, sick with cold, and I saw shoes and clothes, not to mention tiny velvet hats soaked by dripping gutters, ruined with frightening speed.[10]

What is to be read as metaphor for the social disadvantage that a middle-class, educated woman was confronted with – even in artistic circles – is also a very practical dilemma for the female *flâneur*. Her distant spectatorship demands both an inconspicuous and practical outfit to allow the modernist immersion into the transitory while retaining a static position of immutable artistic presence. Sand's solution to the combined pitfalls of cumbersome attire and social disadvantage was as pragmatic as it would be paradigmatic. Remembering the comfort of her childhood which she had spent in boy's clothing, she decided to radically challenge the existing dress code for young bourgeois women in order to have equal access to aesthetic pleasure and, surreptitiously, change her status from passive consumer and representative of conspicuous consumption, to active trendsetter and even stylish subversive:

> I had myself made a 'sentry redingote' of strong grey cloth, with trousers and waistcoat to match. A grey hat and a large woolen cravat completed my outfit . . . I cannot possibly express the pleasure my boots gave me: I would have gladly slept with them on . . . My little iron-tipped heels kept me solid on the sidewalks. I would fly from one end of Paris to the other. Nobody paid attention to me or guessed at my disguise . . . I was unnoticed, unreproached; I was an atom lost in that immense crowd.[11]

The *flâneuse*, like her male counterpart, becomes spectator and investigator of modern mores, yet both still saunter through the city as positivists, as people seduced by progress and in awe of their contemporary times, only very occasionally calling for social change as such. They might criticise the crowds they find and mock extravagant fads and fashions, but they do not judge the commodifying influence of the metropolis on social structures. The aesthetic perception of the *flâneur* is subjective and, to the most part, individualist. It might touch on societal ills or political problems like reifying social structures or commodifying human relations but in the end his views are concerned with the corporeal and psychological reaction of himself as subject alone.

Metropolis and mental life

At the end of the nineteenth century a new discipline emerged from the positivist embrace of progress and belief in scientific methods. In France and Germany theorists like Gabriel Tarde, Émile Durkheim, Ferdinand Tönnies and Georg Simmel ushered in an empirical approach to the analysis of social structures. Emerging from established disciplines like economics, history, or philosophy they started to build a new academic tradition.

Georg Simmel can be regarded as the originator for a sociology of *modernité*, in discussing not only the most contemporary of topics but also rendering this very contemporariness the leitmotif of much of his writing. Simmel is the first sociologist of fashion. In four versions of an essay, which he started in 1895, he investigated the structures and temporal movements of fashion, especially in dress, that would provide the basic structure for much of today's fashion studies. For instance, he postulated the death of fashion at the very moment it becomes socially accepted: when a large number of consumers start to follow a trend, its commercial, and perhaps even metaphysical, impetus shifts the fashion away to another manifestation. This incessant and necessary change subsequently allows him to analyse a particular rhythm to modern life and its social and economic basis, for instance in his investigation of capitalism in *Philosophy of Money* of 1900 (revised edition in 1907).

According to Simmel, the self-styled sophisticated city dweller in turn-of-the-century Berlin, the metropolis constituted the ambiguous space for the production and consumption of fashion. However, his was not only the aesthetic perception of the *flâneur*, he extended it through the scrutiny of an academic researcher. Although his style of writing and frequent excursions into metaphysical musings earned him the unflattering soubriquet of an 'essayist', his quick reaction to new phenomena and his willingness to approach even the most ephemeral of topics made his lectures at the Humboldt University in Berlin widely popular events.

In his essay of 1903 'Die Grossstädte und das Geistesleben' ['The Metropolis and Mental Life'] Simmel developed one of the main themes of his sociological work, the inability of the subject to maintain his position against ever-increasing objectification of his culture. This impotence against reification is particularly apparent in the city and most notable in people succumbing to rapidly changing fads and fashions. Essays like this, although heavily criticised by fellow sociologists like Durkheim, who regarded it as non-empirical, not only had a profound influence on the work of contemporary cultural theories but also gave rise to an international position of sociological research in the form of the Chicago School of Sociology, which from the 1940s onwards would centre on economic dependencies and consumer culture.

Simmel begins 'The Metropolis and Mental Life' by stating:

The psychological basis of the metropolitan type of individuality consists in the *intensification of nervous stimulation* which results from the swift and uninterrupted change of outer and inner stimuli. Man is a differentiating creature. His mind is stimulated by the difference between a momentary impression and the one which preceded it. Lasting impressions, impressions which differ only slightly from one another, impressions which take a regular and habitual course and show regular and habitual contrasts – all these use up, so to speak, less consciousness than does the rapid crowding of changing images, the sharp discontinuity in the grasp of a single glance, and the unexpectedness of onrushing impressions. These are the psychological conditions which the metropolis creates.[12]

The visual impressions that the *flâneur* picks up so eagerly and often renders as an artistic credo are interpreted by Simmel as conflicting and confusing. The subject's reaction to such profusion of sensorial and economic impressions can become pathological. In Simmel's times the fashionable illness of 'neurasthenia' was 'invented', diagnosing the city dweller with a nervous and mostly psychosomatic condition that resulted in migraine and the inability of physical action.

Although far from being a historical, let alone dialectical, materialist Simmel had to acknowledge, similar to his compatriot the economist Max Weber, Karl Marx's emphasis on the exchange value as a universal structuring device as well as the left-Hegelian heritage of defining change through the move from a development of quantitative increments into a qualitative leap, perceived often as a rupture in the socio-cultural fabric. In his essay Simmel exposes the positivist mechanisms in contemporary life that reversed the direction of real change into mere outward alteration of appearances:

Modern mind has become more and more calculating. The calculative exactness of practical life which the money economy has brought about corresponds to the ideal of natural science: to transform the world into an arithmetic problem, to fix every part of the world by mathematical formulas. Only money economy has filled the days of so many people with weighing, calculating, with numerical determinations, with a reduction of qualitative values to quantitative ones. Through the calculative nature of money a new precision, a certainty in the definition of identities and differences, unambiguousness in agreements and arrangements has been brought about in the relations of life-elements – just as externally this precision has been affected by the universal diffusion of pocket watches. However, the conditions of metropolitan life are at once cause and effect of this trait.[13]

The reaction to such conditions is either complete alienation and perfect anonymity in the city – an analogy to Baudelaire's and Sand's *flâneur/flâneuse* who merges with the crowds – or the utmost subjectification – a trait comparable to the dandy who renders individual stylistic preferences, for example in dress, universal postulates to be adhered to by those who aim to be truly elegant; only to be dismissed the moment they become common stylistic currency.

The same factors which have thus coalesced into the exactness and minute precision of the form of life have coalesced into a structure of the highest impersonality; on the other hand, they have promoted a highly personal subjectivity. There is perhaps no psychic phenomenon which has been so unconditionally reserved to the metropolis as has the blasé attitude. The blasé attitude results first from the rapidly changing and closely compressed contrasting stimulations of the nerves. From this, the enhancement of the metropolitan intellectuality, also, seems originally to stem. Therefore, stupid people who are not intellectually alive in the first place usually are not exactly blasé. A life in boundless pursuit of pleasure makes one blasé because it agitates the nerves to their strongest reactivity for such a long time that they finally cease to react at all.[14]

The consumption of fashion appears as an economic necessity in capitalism but also as a recurring psychological stimulus for the jaded perspective of the city dweller. In order to cater for the ever-growing demand for new styles the division of labour within the productive processes has to become all pervasive. Simmel quotes from a historic example:

> Cities are, first of all, seats of the highest economic division of labour. They produce thereby such extreme phenomena as in Paris the remunerative occupation of the *quatorzième*. They are persons who identify themselves by signs on their residences and who are ready at the dinner hour in correct attire, so that they can be quickly called upon if a dinner party should consist of thirteen persons.[15]

Such extreme divisions of labour affect the structure of the commodity, the object proper, as well as the subject's reaction to it. In *The Philosophy of Money*, Simmel rendered the production of fashion a metaphor for both cultural production and social structures in modernity.

> The radical opposition between subject and object has been reconciled in theory by making the object part of the subject's perception. Similarly the opposition between subject and object does not evolve in practice as long as the object is produced by a single subject or for a single subject. Since the division of labour destroys custom production . . . the subjective aura of the product also disappears in relation to the consumer because the commodity is now produced independently of him. It becomes an objective entity which the consumer approaches externally and whose specific existence and quality is autonomous of him. The difference, for instance, between the modern clothing store, geared towards the utmost specialisation and the work of the tailor whom one used to invite into one's home, sharply emphasises the growing objectivity of the economic cosmos, its supra-individual independence in relation to the consuming subject with whom it was originally closely identified . . . It is obvious how much this objectifies the whole character of transaction and how subjectivity is destroyed and transformed into cool reserve and anonymous objectivity once so many intermediate stages

are introduced between the producer and the one who accepts his product that they lose sight of each other.[16]

For Simmel fashion in the modern city must be read as a structural composite of cultural manifestation and rhythm, economic process, psychological primer and metaphysical principle. Such multi-layered significance of fashion accounts for the historical fascination it would exert on a cultural philosopher who had studied at the Humboldt University from 1912–14 when Simmel taught there. This student would become not simply one of the most imaginative analysts of modernity but a dramatic figure himself, whose life was lived on the margins of Parisian culture and Critical Theory alike. His name: Walter Benjamin.

Arcades and the end of the *flâneur*

From 1927 up to his premature death in 1940, Benjamin assembled material for a study of the nineteenth century which was to decipher modernity's political, poetical and philosophical potential from the visual and literary fragments – Baudelaire most prominently among them – he found in the streets and libraries of Paris, a city he proclaimed as the 'capitale du XIXe siècle'. The assemblage of this material he provisionally entitled *Passagenarbeit* [The Arcades Project], after what he considered to be the architectural cradle of modern society. For him, the glass-roofed links between Parisian streets and boulevards maintained in their often dilapidated status the mystique of nineteenth-century life and the remembrance of the dawn of consumerism. Here, fashion is crucial as the manifestation that ties cultural objects to social observation and political critique. In Benjamin's writing the *homme des foules*, *flâneur*, and blasé dandy move from agents and *dramatis personae* to become analytical tools that allow for dissecting the fashionable pre-history of modernity in order to pass judgement on contemporary life and the writing of history as such.

The Arcades Project appears as a poetic assemblage of fragments, fittingly ephemeral in their origins and in their initial reception. Hidden deep in the vaults of the Bibliothèque Nationale in Paris while Benjamin attempted his escape from the advancing German army, they were only published in the 1980s as a series of thematically ordered bundles of manuscripts sheaves, the most extensive of which is marked 'Fashion'. This sheaf is filled with almost one hundred annotated quotes and discursive comments that were to be written up as a central part to the study of the city of Paris across the nineteenth century:

> And nothing else should be told about the arcades; an architecture in which we relive, as in a dream, the existence of our parents and grandparents, similar to the way in which an embryo in his mother relives the genesis of animals. The existence in these spaces, accordingly, passes without accentuation like the dream narrative. The rhythm given to such slumbers is the action of the *flâneur*. 1893 saw in Paris the fashion for tortoises. One can imagine how the *flâneur* adopted their tempo for his sauntering through the arcades rather than for any promenade on the boulevards. Boredom always remains on the outside of unconscious action. Thus it appeared to the great dandies as a mark of distinction.[17]

Such an erratic fragment is typical for Benjamin. In one short paragraph he plays with set pieces from an interpretative vocabulary of nineteenth-century France, from ontogeny conceived as phylogeny to political theory, while historical observation is combined with (literary) references to the *flâneur* and dandy, and an analytical under-current of psychology and sociology is maintained.

Looking closely at Baudelaire's *The Painter of Modern Life* whom he regarded as a central figure for the new perception of the city, Benjamin sees the *flâneur* and his or her atten-tion to fashion not simply as indicative for modernity but as ideological operation. 'The vogue of fashion breaks on the compact crowd of the oppressed',[18] he writes, and: 'Fash-ion puts its fig leaf always on the spot where the revolutionary nakedness of society is to be found. One small shift and . . .'.[19] These reflections respond to the objectifying power of modernity that Simmel had observed. The constant production and consumption of novel commodities mask a social reality that cannot be contained forever in existing ideological structures. Benjamin, aiming to adhere to historical materialism in his later writing, hoped for the eventual liberation of the subject from his alienation. But for a cultural phil-osopher like him this liberation was to occur first within his own discourse, in the writing of history itself. It would remain an intellectual quest rather than a political programme.

Benjamin extracted from the *Arcades Project* in 1939 a further set of fragments, enti-tled 'Über den Begriff der Geschichte' (literally: 'On Defining History' or, as it is offi-cially translated, 'Theses of the Philosophy of History'). In these he lends a particular historiographical potential to fashion that sees the breaking up of any linear progress in culture, society, or politics:

> History is the object of a structure whose site is not homogeneous and empty time but one filled by now-time [*Jetztzeit*]. For Robespierre the Rome of antiquity was thus charged with now-time and blasted from the continuum of history. The French Revolution regarded itself as Rome rein-carnate. It quoted ancient Rome as fashion quotes past attire. Fashion has the scent for the modern wherever it stirs in the thicket of what has been. It is the tiger's leap into the past. Yet this leap occurs in an arena commanded by the ruling class. The very same leap in the open air of history is the dia-lectical one, which Marx has understood as the revolution.[20]

For Benjamin fashion and its stage, the modern metropolis, have reified into a field of social contrast and conflict that cannot be contained. Marx's postulates, formulated already in the decades before Baudelaire penned his *Painter of Modern Life*, are now lived by the *flâneur* whose dependence on fashion, although of great philosophical interest, is now secondary to his involvement in political struggle. He turns from observer to actor and his engagement must be *realpolitikal* in order to be culturally worthwhile. The city and its social structures are no longer a field of fascination but a scene for political edu-cation. This politicised *flâneur* might still be keenly aware of fashion's role but his inter-est turns to its reformation or negation even, as it is unmasked now as the pervasive agent of economic and social alienation. From the contemporary and transitory play-ground that Baudelaire had ascribed to it, the city and its fashion now exist for Benjamin in a space haunted by the ghosts of past revolutions and unfulfilled promise. *La mode*, ingenious and erratic as she is in her quotations, is no longer sovereign but becomes throughout *la modernité* an ambiguous concubine to economic and ideological rule.

Conclusion

The trajectory of the *homme des foules*, dandy, and *flâneur* is not a one-directional descent from positivist observer and commentator to complicit consumer of commodities. Determining such a narrative would mean falling into the trap of teleological argumentation, in which a final condition rounds off progress towards an idea (be it positive or negative). Even in a space as narrowly defined – in terms of its socio-economic parameters and spatial organisation – as Paris in the second half of the nineteenth century any mechanistic interpretation of change in the respective roles of the Man of the Crowd, the streetwalker, or the sophisticated fashion victim must appear as erroneous.

Following the historical method in Hegel, Marx and Benjamin, the change from quantitative growth to qualitative leap, for instance in the commercial success and cultural significance of fashion, must lead to a disavowal of its traditionally understood role as flamboyant object of material culture. Once fashion is exposed within our defined historical period as an ideological operation that fuelled the reification in modernity by objectifying the subject through new styles in clothes, hair, make-up, transport, food, housing, etc., this role has to be reversed. Such reversal occurs in the move away from fashion's superficial appearance (as costume history or social commentator of manners and mores) towards emphasising its structural value for historiography – especially for the historiography of the modern city as fashion's principal stage. For Baudelaire this is postulated by describing fashion as providing a new and decisive rhythm to cultural production and consumption; for Sand a changed dress code erased the spatial restriction on woman's progress through the city; Simmel introduced dialectical thought (perhaps unwittingly) to fashion's negation, as fashion had to die first in order to survive; Benjamin, finally, took Baudelaire and Simmel and radicalised their discourses on art and society into a cultural philosophy in which fashion affects an absolute break within the perception of history as linear: the new fashion always quotes the old in order to invent, and therefore any historiography that emphasises continuation and progress (even in its guise as reaction/counter-reaction) can only produce a false reality. The true understanding of fashion resides in exposing its potential to remove the fig leaf of conspicuous consumption and constantly changing styles in order to expose its own radical character for re-structuring history.

In the city, this dialectic between an appearance that disavows structure and a structure that negates (the significance of) appearances, both in visual character as well as in contents, appears as principal movement. The transitory impressions of the urban crowd display first the primacy of appearance and then quickly shift to reveal its dependence on underlying ideological structures that define its passage, codify its discourse and impose its consumption. *L'homme des foules* who immerses himself in the crowd, the *flâneur* who slowly traverses it, and the dandy who strives to stand out from it, all become willing participants in this dialectic movement, which is defined as much by their own ephemeral roles as it is by the historiographical super-structure of *modernité* that has acted both as their historical space and temporal deconstruction.

Notes

1 For a definition of modernity in relation to the advent of modern fashion, and related discourses on Baudelaire, Simmel, Benjamin, et al., see my book (2001) *Tigersprung: Fashion in Modernity*, Cambridge, MA, and London: MIT Press.

2 As starting points for some of the methodologies that investigate the complex organisation of cities see, for example, the extensive work by sociologist Richard Sennett, in particular the volume by S. A. Thernstrom and R. Sennett (eds) (1969) *Nineteenth-century Cities: Essays in the New Urban History*, New Haven and London: Yale University Press; the collected essays on urban politicised space by structuralist philosopher H. Lefebvre (1996) *Writings on Cities*, Oxford: Basil Blackwell; the literary response to urbanity in R. Lehan (1998) *The City in Literature: An Intellectual and Cultural History*, Berkeley, CA: University of California Press; the anthropologically tinged architecture and art history of J. Rykwert (1976) *The Idea of a Town: The Anthropology of Urban Form in Rome, Italy and the Ancient World*, London: Faber and Faber; the histories of urban architecture and planning in L. Benevolo (1980) *The History of the City*, Cambridge, MA, and London: MIT; W. Braunfels (1988) *Urban Design in Western Europe: Regime and Architecture, 900–1900*, Chicago and London: University of Chicago Press, K. Lynch, *The Image of the City* (1960) Cambridge, MA, and London: MIT; the post-structuralist challenges by the Situationist group, collected in K. Knabb (ed.) (1981) *Situationist International Anthology*, Berkeley, CA: Bureau of Public Secrets; and the classic volume on radical urbanism by M. Tafuri (1979 [1973]) *Architecture and Utopia: Design and Capitalist Development*, Cambridge, MA, and London: MIT Press.

3 In English the most extensive study of the Place Royale is by H. Ballon (1991) *The Paris of Henry IV: Architecture and Urbanism*, Cambridge, MA, and London: MIT Press.

4 C. Baudelaire (1976 [orig. c. 1861]), 'Le Peintre de la vie moderne', in C. Baudelaire, *Œuvres complètes*, Paris: Gallimard, 1976, vol. 2, pp. 690; English trans. by P. G. Konody, in (1930) *The Painter of Victorian Life*, London: The Studio, p. 44.

5 Ibid., pp. 692–3; English trans., ibid., p. 55.

6 Ibid., p. 695; English trans., ibid., p. 67.

7 Ibid., p. 691; English trans., ibid., p. 47 [trans. modified].

8 Ibid., pp. 691–2; English trans., ibid., p. 48.

9 For an English biography of Sand and a critical analysis of her work see, for example, C. Cate (1975) *George Sand: A Biography*, Boston: Houghton Mifflin; P. Thompson (1977) *Sand and the Victorians*, London: Macmillan (on her relation to, among others, George Eliot); D. Dickenson (1988) *George Sand: A Brave Man, the Most Womanly Woman*, Oxford: Berg, 1988, and N. Schor (1993) *George Sand and Idealism*, New York: Columbia University Press.

10 G. Sand (1902 [1854–5]), *Histoire de ma vie*, 4 vols, Paris: Calman-Lévy, vol. 4, p. 80; partial English trans. in J. Barry (ed.) (1979) *George Sand in Her Own Words*, London: Quartet, p. 320.

11 Ibid., p. 81.

12 G. Simmel (1957 [1903]) 'Die Grossstädte und das Geistesleben', in Georg Simmel, *Brücke und Tür*, Stuttgart: Koehler, pp. 227–8; English trans., 'The Metropolis and Mental Life', in Kurt Wolff (ed.) (1950) *The Sociology of Georg Simmel*, New York: Free Press, pp. 409–10.

13 Ibid., p. 230; English trans., ibid., p. 412.

14 Ibid., p. 232; English trans., ibid., pp. 413–14.

15 Ibid., pp. 238–9; English trans., ibid., p. 420.

16 G. Simmel (1989 [2nd edition 1907]) 'Die Philosophie des Geldes', in G. Simmel, *Gesamtausgabe*, Frankfurt a.M.: Suhrkamp, vol. 6, pp. 633–4; English trans. by T. Bottomore and

D. Frisby (1990) *The Philosophy of Money*, London: Routledge, p. 457 [trans. modified by the author].

17   W. Benjamin (1982) 'Das Passagen-Werk', ed. Rolf Tiedemann, in Benjamin, *Gesammelte Schriften*, Frankfurt a.M.: Suhrkamp, vol. 5, part 2, p. 1054; English trans. by H. Eiland and K. McLaughlin (1999) *The Arcades Project*, Cambridge, MA, and London: The Belknap Press and Harvard University Press, p. 881 [trans. modified by the author].

18   Ibid., vol. 5, part 1, p. 460; English trans., ibid., p. 364 [trans. modified].

19   Ibid., vol. 5, part 2, p. 1215; English trans., ibid., p. 909.

20   W. Benjamin (1991) 'Über den Begriff der Geschichte', in W. Benjamin, *Gesammelte Schriften*, Frankfurt a.M.: Suhrkamp, vol. 1, part 2, p. 701; English trans. by H. Zohn (1999) 'Theses on the Philosophy of History', in W. Benjamin, *Illuminations*, London: Pimlico, pp. 252–3 [trans. modified].

The dandy

Olga Vainshtein

The dandy was a fashionable male who achieved social influence by distinctive elegance in dress and sophisticated self-presentation. The dandy appeared as a fashion type from the mid-1790s in England. The nearest ancestors of the dandy were the British beaux and macaronies of the eighteenth century, preferring vibrant colours and sparkling fabrics. In the eighteenth century the fashion leaders mostly came from the aristocracy and were known for their passion for finery and reckless spending habits. With the coming of the industrial revolution and the development of a more democratic society, new 'candidates' with bourgeois backgrounds had more chances for success. The most legendary of the dandies in the Regency period was George Bryan 'Beau' Brummell (1778–1840), originating from a middle-class family. He had the reputation of being 'England's prime minister of taste' and was a celebrity in his day.

George Brummel's exemplary perfection of style was based on the principle of 'conspicuous inconspicuousness': the imperative of dressing elegantly, yet unobtrusively, avoiding undesirable attention and marked ostentation. This was a very important and essentially modern principle of vestimentary behaviour, implying the blurring of class distinctions, since the new tactics erased the aristocratic pretensions to demonstrate wealth and noble origin through lavish clothes. In many ways, Brummell's effortless career anticipated the modern world of social mobility in which deliberate self-fashioning and taste are privileged above birth and wealth.

Brummel preferred clean lines and muted colours, wearing normally a smooth, flawlessly tailored tailcoat with brass buttons, and narrow pantaloons tucked into Hessian boots. For day time, he rejected silks and satins, laces and ruffles. His materials were wool, leather and linen waste: 'Fine linen, plenty of it, and country washing' (Wilson 1929), as the dandy explained. With the help of nearly imperceptible padding, curved seams, discreet darts and steam pressing, the coat was refined into an exquisitely balanced garment that fitted smoothly without wrinkles and buttoned without strain. The fit, the perfection of line and texture transformed the body into a streamlined silhouette, following the Neoclassical-Empire fashions.

By rejecting affectation and effeminacy in dress characteristic of the macaroni, Brummell achieved the universal look, suitable for all classes and occupations. However, since the dandy's aim was to be recognised only by his peers, this recognition had to rely on discreet signs. Thus the expressive details become the leading code in dandified costume. A visual message could be encoded through the careful folds of starched neckcloth, the turn of a collar or cuff, fine gloves or the blackening of the soles of boots. Hence the necessity of optical accessories for scrutinising the subtle details – the dandies' passion for monocles, lorgnettes and quizzing glasses.

The dandy's style can be described in broader terms as aesthetic minimalism: a sign of sartorial understatement in dress, manifesting the priority of functional construction and

"And behold in these times the Dan-dees were"
"arrayed in Garments of divers fashions ... and in "
"fine Linens curiously wrought ... and moreover ... "
"they were gazed upon by the bretheren of the Land "
"in which they dwelt. ... and the people marvelled. "
"Lib. 2 ... ver 6.7.8."

Fashionable reading.
Vide new Church ... Oxford

Snapshot 18.1 *Fashionable reading* (coloured print, early nineteenth century). This caricature depicts the elegant dandy-priest reading from his pulpit. The details of his look – carefully arranged locks, the high collar, wide sleeves, several rings on his fingers, and the quizzing glass – are characteristic for the male fashion of 1816–24. The quasi-biblical quotation from the book mocks the creation of a new sartorial canon; the dandies are presented as people 'arrayed in garments of diverse fashions . . . and in fine linens curiously wrought' (here a reference to the extravagant necktie knots). At the same time it is clear that such appearances still had a shocking effect for the public – and therefore the dandies were 'gazed upon' and the spectators 'marvelled'. The caption proclaiming the 'new church' of the dandies foretells the satire of the new sect of dandies created by Thomas Carlyle in his *Sartor Resartus*. Lewis Walpole Library 818.2.6.1. Courtesy of the Lewis Walpole Library, Yale University.

geometry of the basic form stripped of superfluous embellishment. It can be compared with the dandy's stoical rule of economy of emotions – *nil admirari*, not to be surprised at anything. In the sphere of body politics, minimalism was declared through the imperative of slow gestures and a static facial expression (considered the evidence of self-control and personal dignity), the inhibition that prevented running and fussing. The rhetorical equivalent of minimalism is the genre of aphorism, essentially involving the use of expressive pauses and silence. Minimalism triumphed later in twentieth-century culture: black-and-white photography, constructivism in architecture, cubism in painting.

The dandyism of the Regency period established the models of self-fashioning which became stereotypes of men's behaviour in society during the nineteenth century. They were spread not only through personal communication, but also through the genre of the 'fashionable novel', which flourished in Britain in 1825–30. French culture appropriated the code of British dandyism in the decade 1830–40, transforming it into an intellectual philosophy of life and aesthetics of modern appearance as in Balzac's *Treatise on Elegant Life* (1830); Barbey d'Aurevilly's *On Dandyism and George Brummell* (1845); and Charles Baudelaire's *The Painter of Modern Life* (1863). In these texts the figure of the dandy is conceptualised as a stoic hero of urban modernity, the self-made style-icon. Further development of European literary dandyism is focused around the symbolist novel in England and France, such as *À rebours* [Against Nature] by J. K. Huysmans (1884) and *The Picture of Dorian Grey* by Oscar Wilde (1891), where dandyism becomes the aesthetic manifesto of decadent culture and symbolism. The bohemian dandies reintroduce more flamboyant outfits, trying more evocative and flashy combinations of colour, perfumes and gem-stones.

The dandy's code of behaviour often implied the subversive disregard for the manners of the aristocracy, practical jokes, refined demonstrations of superiority, culminating in the position of intellectual rebellion. The social performative aspects of dandyism included habits of attending all-male social clubs, the art of *flânerie* (strolling in the streets) and ironic conversation in the salons of society. In the contemporary world, the dandies mastered the strategy of objectifying personality, transforming an individual style into marketable goods. One of the last reincarnations of the consumerist dandy was the 'metrosexual'. The dandy style was regularly reinterpreted in contemporary menswear collections, and dandyism became a popular theme on the internet.

Bibliography and further reading

Breward, C. (2004) *Fashioning London: Clothing and the Modern Metropolis*, Oxford: Berg, esp. pp. 21–49.

Moers, E. (1960) *The Dandy*, New York: The Viking Press.

Walden, G. (2002) 'Who is a Dandy?' in J. Barbey d'Aurevilly, *On Dandyism and George Brummell*, trans. George Walden, New York: Gibson Square Books.

Wilson, H. (1929) *Harriette Wilson's Memoirs of Herself and Others: With a Preface by James Laver*, London: P. Davies, p. 40.

Fashion and France in the Second Empire

Alex M. Cain

The period of the Second Empire in France (1852–70) was one of brittle brilliance, a glorious dazzle on the outside but hypocritical and corrupt on the inside; its collapse after the Franco-Prussian War was swift. Napoleon III had originally been elected as Prince-President, but very shortly afterwards had staged a *coup d'état* to become Emperor. Many of his subjects had expected a revival of the glories of his uncle, the great Napoleon I, but the nephew could produce no real glory, only show. His beautiful Empress Eugénie was the icon of his improbably showy court, with its ostentatious court balls and ceremonies based on the imagery of the eighteenth-century court. Empress Eugénie even wore some modified garments from the eighteenth century as well as bringing out of storage some of the remarkable royal furnishings from the *ancien régime*.

The Empress, although interested in this imagery from a past to which she was not connected, also engaged in a new way with a novel and quite revolutionary way to procure clothes. Here there is an interesting connection to Marie-Antoinette and her patronage of the milliner Rose Bertin. The Second Empire needed a catalyst to spark off the latent fireworks, and that was found in the person of a young Englishman who had come to Paris at the age of twenty as a lowly draper, Charles Frederick Worth (1825–95). His place in fashion history is due to the fact that he persuaded women to choose their clothes to suit their own individual personalities. It says much for his persuasive powers that he succeeded in his aims. Most Frenchwomen were conservative, even the Empress at first resisting his styles. But a new social group was emerging in Europe and the United States: the super-rich international set, where women were quite prepared to be a clotheshorse, and husbands were eager to drape their wives with jewellery in an overwhelming demonstration of conspicuous consumption.

At the same time there was an increase in the sale of ready-mades, when a copy, more or less accurate, of these unique items could be turned out at a much reduced price. The introduction of the sewing-machine into many homes facilitated the copying of the elaborate flounces which had previously taken hours of eye-straining work. This meant, of course, that the model gown was no longer unique, so something new must be created. The era of ever-changing fashion had begun. Distinction could also be obtained by the addition of various trimmings – feathers, artificial flowers, beads, lace – the production of which became a leading industry in France, as was that of different cloths – *soies de fantaisie* and the sculpted velvets that many would replicate.

Ladies would request copies of their favourite actress's dresses. At the height of the crinoline craze, when the width of the skirt reached stupendous size (another example of conspicuous consumption), a certain great actress decided to laugh the style out of fashion by appearing on stage in a crinoline of superlative width. Much was her surprise to find that similar monstrosities were to be seen in public places. Real life imitated the

Snapshot 19.1 Ballgown by Jean-Philippe Worth (1853–1924), 1897 (silk, cotton and diamanté). This ballgown was collected by and possibly used as a painting prop by the English artist Sir William Newsam Prior Nicholson (1872–1949). His costume collection, dating from 1770, including five Worth dresses worn at the coronation of Edward VII, was presented to the National Gallery of Victoria by Lady Nicholson and her daughter in 1951. This dress makes its impact through a combination of a large-figured cream woven satin in which lilies harmonise with trimmings of lace and rhinestones. The floral pattern, in which the motif is 82 cm long, has been woven to suggest the narrowing of the waist and the curved shape of the gore panels, which created what contemporaries called the 'lady of fine figure'. Robyn Healy, in conducting detailed research on this garment in the National Gallery of Victoria collection, writes: 'All three ballgowns from the Nicholson collection were made for Lady Florence Phillips in the same year and season. They give us an incredible insight into the extravagance of the wardrobes of the time and the design methods of Worth . . . owing to the death of her husband Lady Phillips could not wear her new dresses for several years and another magnificent Presentation gown (1897) was possible worn at the coronation of Edward VII in 1901. The bodice was slightly altered to accommodate her larger size and the edge of the boned bodice tucked under; this has since been restored to its original shape' (Healy 1993). © National Gallery of Victoria, Melbourne, Australia (gift of Lady Nicholson and her daughter, 1951), 1078D.a-b-D4 and 1078 D-B-D4.

stage as was the case in eighteenth-century London. Much could be said about the feminist attitude to these creations. There are some who claim that the crinoline was one of the most comfortable styles ever created, with the weight of the fabric being taken by the light steel framework, allowing the legs perfectly free movement. However, it has to be admitted that these ungainly skirts, no matter how elegant, were a considerable disadvantage when it came to sitting. Women were dressed so that men could see them performing elegant movements.

During this period there was a plethora of fashion magazines with stylish engravings of dresses and paper patterns for making them at home. One of the most unusual of these, of very short life, was by one of the greatest poets of the day. Stéphane Mallarmé's journal *La Dernière Mode* (1874) covered clothes, accessories, events of the day, current theatre, recipes, advice to correspondents, all together with an original poem and short story by one of the great names of the time. In bringing together dress fashion with lifestyle and even tastes in railway holidays, the journal pointed towards the focus on living a fashionable life that characterised twentieth-century consumption.

Bibliography and further reading

Furbank, P. N., and Cain, A. M. (eds) (2004) *Mallarmé on Fashion: A Translation of the Fashion Magazine* La Dernière Mode, Oxford: Berg.

Healy, R. (1993) *Worth to Dior: 20th Century Fashion from the Collection of the National Gallery of Victoria*, Melbourne: NGV.

Lehmann, U. (2000) *Tigersprung: Fashion in Modernity*, Cambridge, MA: MIT Press.

Simon, M. (1995) *Fashion in Art: The Second Empire and Impressionism*, London: Zwemmer.

Chapter 15

Clothing behaviour as non-verbal resistance

Marginal women and alternative dress in the nineteenth century

Diana Crane

'A woman's dress is a permanent revelation of her most secret thoughts, a language, and a symbol.'

Honoré de Balzac, *Une fille d'Eve*, 1839

THE SUBJECT OF THIS ESSAY IS A PUZZLE: the existence of two distinct styles of dress for women in the second half of the nineteenth century. Fashionable styles originated in Paris and were adopted by women in other parts of Europe and America. Dresses were composed of several separate garments and enormous quantities of fabric and trimmings (Brew 1945: 160–1). These styles were exceptionally restrictive and ornamental, including, at various periods, tightly laced corsets, wide crinolines, tight sleeves, enormous bustles, and long trains. Typically, they impeded even normal activities such as climbing stairs or walking in the streets. Each type of occasion required a specific type of dress. For a costume to be considered elegant, every detail had to be correct (Cunnington and Cunnington 1959: 460, 486).

Coexisting with this style was an alternative style that incorporated items from men's clothing, such as ties, men's hats, suit jackets, waistcoats, and men's shirts, sometimes singly, sometimes in combination with one another, but always associated with items of fashionable female clothing. Trousers were not part of this alternative style, probably because trousers, when worn by women, constituted a greater symbolic challenge to the system than most middle-class women were prepared to make. Women whose behaviour was considered to be in defiance of the social order were sometimes represented as wearing trousers by satirists and cartoonists (Moses 1984: 123–6; Rolley 1990).

Clothing as a form of symbolic communication was enormously important in the nineteenth century as a means of conveying information about the wearer's social role, social standing, and personal character. Upper- and middle-class women devoted enormous amounts of time and money to creating elaborate wardrobes in order to present themselves appropriately to members of their social milieux (Smith 1981). Lacking other forms of power, they used non-verbal symbols as a means of self-expression. Fashionable clothing exemplified the doctrine of separate spheres that was supported by other social institutions. It suited the subordinate and passive social roles women were expected to perform. Industrialisation had removed most middle- and upper-middle-class married women in Europe and America from active participation in the economy. This type of clothing served as an indication that the women who wore it had servants and did not have to perform household tasks or to work outside the home. Effectively denied anything but very limited participation in the public sphere, women were frequently identified in terms of their clothing. Political cartoons, satire, and commentary tended to refer to women as 'petticoats' (Rolley 1990: 48).[1]

The significance of the alternative style is more difficult to assess. It appears frequently in photographs of the period, but is virtually ignored in fashion histories, although some costume historians (for example, Ginsburg 1988 and Ewing 1975) allude to it. While histories of fashionable clothing give the impression of consensus concerning appropriate female apparel, clothing was actually the site for a great deal of debate and controversy. In this essay, I will first provide a more detailed description of the alternative style of dress and will then suggest some tentative explanations concerning its origins and impact.

Components of alternative dress

While the fashionable style originated in France, the English influence on the alternative style was unmistakable, particularly in clothing worn for sports and in the design of the tailored suit jacket, suggesting a receptiveness in English culture to alternative images of women. [. . .]

The alternative style can be understood as a set of signs, borrowed from male clothing, that appeared sometimes singly, sometimes in combination with one another, but always associated with items of female clothing. One of the most frequently worn items of alternative dress was the man's tie. The significance of the tie in the alternative style was related to its function in the male wardrobe. Gibbings (1990: 64) states that in Victorian society: 'The neckwear of each man proclaimed his current position in society . . . and his aspirations'. As nineteenth-century male clothing became increasingly sombre and formulaic, the tie was used to encode information about the wearer's background: 'regimental, club, sporting or educational' (Gibbings 1990: 81). The tie when worn by a woman was in the most general sense an expression of independence; but various alternative life styles were invoked. [. . .]

Photographs of middle- and upper-class women, which became very popular during this period, are useful as an indication of different meanings the tie conveyed. A young woman photographed by an anonymous photographer in 1855 (Gibbings 1990: 67) was wearing four types of neckwear: 'a lace collar, a choker held in place with a butterfly broach, and . . . stylised man's sharp-ended bow tie', in addition to a necklace. Cunnington and Cunnington (1959: 475) mention that cravats and neckties for women 'were conspicuous in 1861'. A photograph of an Englishwoman at the seaside in 1864 shows her wearing a tie with a very full skirt, a jacket whose style was adapted from men's jackets of the period, and a straw sailor's hat. Significantly, a photograph of the University of Wisconsin class of 1876 (which contained almost as many women as men) shows all the young women wearing some version of a necktie (Severa 1995: 357).

Beginning in the 1870s, many young women wore black velvet neck ribbons (Severa 1995: 305, 495). Worn in widths from a quarter to a half inch, the neck ribbon closely resembled the inch-wide black ties worn by men during this period (Severa 1995: 388, 396; Gibbings 1990: 88; Duroselle 1972: 109). At the end of the century, ribbon ties were worn by members of all social classes, including upper-class women, although their presence is barely hinted at in French fashion histories (Delpierre 1990). Middle-class women wore them with business dress, school uniforms (Ewing 1975) and nurses' uniforms (Juin 1994: 168); working-class women wore them with servants' and nursemaids' uniforms (Lister 1972). Ties, in various styles, were frequently a part of costumes for sports, particularly bicycling, which became popular in the last decade of the century (Gibbings 1990: 88, 89; Delpierre 1990: 43). Photographs of women wearing ties increased in frequency in all three countries toward the end of the century. [. . .]

Hats were also potent symbols of masculine identity that were co-opted by women during this period. Top hats were worn with riding habits, beginning in the 1830s right through the century; bowler hats for riding appeared toward the end of the century (Wilcox 1945; Schreier 1989). The use of men's hats by women for other types of activities began in the middle of the century. Sailors' straw hats were first adopted as a fashionable style for children, before becoming fashionable for women in the 1860s (Lambert 1991: 55). According to Brew (1945: 209–10), a popular hat in the seventies was the derby (bowler) 'made almost exactly like those used by men'. Alexandra, then Princess of Wales, was photographed in afternoon dress wearing a round cloth hat with narrow brim, reminiscent of a man's bowler. Felt fedoras identical to those worn by men appeared in the 1880s (Severa 1995: 417). Men's jockey caps, hunting caps, and peaked yachting caps were also worn by women for sports during this period (Wilcox 1945).

In the 1880s the hard straw hat or boater became very fashionable as a man's hat (Wilcox 1945: 254) and was also widely worn by women for the next three decades (Severa 1995: 470, 510). It was so popular with both sexes that it could be described as a 'unisex' accessory (Ginsburg 1988: 94). This very simple hat with its geometrically precise lines provided a stark contrast to the typical hat worn by women during this period, which was often worn with a veil and generally piled high with flowers, ribbon, lace, feathers, stuffed birds, and sometimes reptiles, shellfish, and insects (Brew 1945: 210; Cunnington and Cunnington 1959: 564). Combined with a tie and a suit jacket, the boater expressed the independence of young women in new occupations, such as office workers. Worn with a bow tie and a man's jacket in the costume of a nursemaid, it became a gesture suggesting defiance (Juin 1994: 89).

The suit jacket has been called 'the symbol of the emancipated woman in the nineteenth century' (Chaumette 1995: 9). The simplicity of the woman's suit jacket contrasted with the evolution of fashionable dresses, which became increasingly complicated as the century progressed. [. . .] Waistcoats for women with distinctly masculine connotations appeared in 1846 and were fashionable for about a decade (Byrde

Figure 15.1 Upper-class woman in fashionable dress with friends in 'alternative' dress (England, 1897).

1992: 55). They became fashionable again between 1880 and 1895 as suits began to be widely worn.

The final element in the costume for the independent woman appeared in the United States in the seventies in the form of the shirtwaist, a man's shirt adapted for women, with a stand-up or turn-down collar, often ornamented with a small black tie or bow tie (Brew 1945: 165; Hall 1992: 55). [. . .] The alternative and the dominant styles of clothing provided a notable contrast in photographs (Bradfield 1981: 383; Ginsburg 1988: 94) (Figure 15.1). [. . .]

What is significant is the way in which these items of masculine dress were invariably combined with items of feminine dress, and the lack of social ostracism attached to this mode of dress (Brew 1945: 161).[2] How were these items of masculine clothing understood by the women who adopted them in this fashion? Were these items 'emptied of their original meaning', as Perrot (1981: 343) suggests? The frequency with which women incorporated items from men's clothing into their costumes, the fact that the borrowed items did not lose their masculine connotations, and the way in which this type of clothing behaviour transcended social class lines suggest that these items constituted a symbolic statement concerning their status and the debates concerning women's status that raged throughout the nineteenth century.

Clothing styles and women's roles: France, England, and the United States

French fashion designers responded slowly to changes that were taking place in the life styles of middle- and upper-class women. French clothing styles expressed French conceptions of how bourgeois women should behave. At the turn of the century, the predominant fashionable style in Paris was a statuesque, corseted silhouette suitable for a bosomy matron rather than for a young athletic woman (Steele 1985: 224). In Paris, the fashion icon of the period was the courtesan, whose lavish clothes were virtually a parody of fashionable clothing. By contrast, in the United States in the 1890s, the young, athletic woman in short skirts or gym suit became a popular icon, along with the Gibson girl in shirtwaist, tie, and long skirts.

Although a surprisingly similar ideology of domesticity was shared by middle-class women in France, the United States and Britain (Rendall 1985: 206–7), consensus concerning this ideal of feminine behaviour was much lower in England and the United States compared to France. French women had received an enormous setback from legislation that derived from the French Revolution. A strong feminist movement emerged during the Revolution, but women did not prevail. The Revolution enhanced the rights of men but excluded women. The Civil Code of 1804 enacted under Napoleon's regime incorporated attitudes toward women that represented the legacy of the Revolution (Nye 1993: 54–5). The Code deprived women of virtually all civil rights.

While the ideal French bourgeois matron was a powerful figure in her own home, outside her home she was powerless and had virtually no legal rights over property or children until almost the end of the century (Flamant-Paparatti 1984: 27) and no political rights until the middle of the twentieth century.[3] Her capacities for functioning outside her home were limited by a minimal level of education and by the fact that only a few occupations were open to her, at salary levels that remained approximately 50 per cent of those of men throughout the century (Goulène 1974). Major French intellectuals of the period, such as P. J. Proudhon, Jules Michelet, and Auguste Comte, were passionately committed to the belief that women were inferior to men (physically, morally, and intellectually) and suitable only for marriage (Rendall 1985). What American feminists have referred to as 'the ideology of separate spheres' was taken for granted. Women were expected to devote themselves entirely to their domestic roles (Flamant-Paparatti 1984: 32). Because of an exaggerated concern with safeguarding their 'virtue', young, unmarried, middle-class women in France were not allowed to go out unescorted by female relatives or even to associate with female peers (Moses 1984: 33;

McMillan 1980: 19). Women who remained unmarried, usually because of the lack of a dowry, had very limited resources and endured marginal existences on small incomes or meagre salaries with minimal social contact (Moses 1984; McMillan 1980: 12).

That fashionable styles emanating from Paris were actually injurious to women's physical well-being and therefore not appropriate costumes for child-bearing women seems surprising. One explanation may be found in the fact that maternity was less central to women's activities in France than in other Northern European countries. By the 1860s, France had the lowest fertility levels in Europe. While the population of England and Wales almost doubled between 1851 and 1901, the population of France increased by only 9.5 per cent during the same period (Offen 1984: 651).

In both England and America women, and particularly single women, had greater freedom and many more options outside domestic space. In the middle of the century single women in America were much more independent than their French counterparts. Banner (1984: 78–85) describes the 'bold and provocative' behaviour of young American women in public and the absence of chaperones when young women went out with male friends. Some middle-class English women were not shy and retiring with men, and adopted male pastimes, such as smoking and playing billiards (Crowe 1971: 331–2). Not dependent on dowries in order to marry, American women had more freedom than European women to select their husbands and to engage in activities that interested them.

The surplus of unmarried women in Britain and America influenced the way women were perceived in those countries. In England, this issue became a subject of controversy at mid-century, when it was revealed by the census of 1851. A result of the greater tendency of men than women to emigrate, the surplus of unmarried women increased during the second half of the century, and was more evident in the middle class than in the working class. A similar problem occurred in America in sixteen eastern and southern states, as men rather than women settled in the West (Massey 1994: 350). The absence of men from home and work during the Civil War had a similar effect. Women replaced men in many occupations. The American Civil War has been described as hastening women's emancipation by fifty years (Massey 1994: 339).

The necessity for increasing numbers of middle-class women to work had the effect of changing their images of themselves. Significantly, most of the women in the first organised women's movement in Britain in the 1850s were unmarried (Rendall 1985: 314). At mid-century, the choice of occupations for English middle-class women consisted largely of governess, companion, and seamstress (Vicinus 1985: 3). By the end of the century, middle-class women were working as teachers, nurses, civil servants, saleswomen, and clerks (Holcombe 1973: 197). In the United States, substantial numbers of women physicians and lawyers were practising (Crowe 1978: 138). According to Freeman and Klaus (1984: 394): 'Much of the movement to improve women's education and employment in both countries developed in response to the plight of the impoverished gentlewoman'.

In France, by the end of the century, positions as teachers, clerks and sales personnel were the only middle-class careers open to women (they were not legally permitted to practise law, and encountered enormous prejudice in the medical profession) (Shaffer 1978: 66). Although the proportion of unmarried women who were employed was about the same as in England (52 per cent), a much larger percentage of married women were employed in France (38 per cent compared to 10 per cent) (Holcombe 1973: 217).

However, the negative status accorded to women workers in general is indicated by the fact that their wages relative to those of men remained at the same level throughout the century (Reberioux 1980; Rendall 1985), while the wages of English women workers during the same period increased along with men's wages, but more rapidly and more consistently (Wood 1903: 282–4, 308). French women's wages were deliberately low. French intellectuals, concerned about the declining birth rate, argued that women should not work but should devote themselves to raising families, ignoring the fact that many women lacked husbands to support them. All these factors meant that, in France, women's participation in the labour force did not contribute to their emancipation (Shaffer 1978: 75).

Higher education was an important factor in developing awareness of women's political and social rights and the skills that were necessary to fight for them. Until the middle of the nineteenth century, women in all three countries had little access to education of any sort. Secondary education was not widespread in these countries until after 1870 (Holcombe 1973; Moses 1984). A few colleges were open to American women early in the century, but women's colleges proliferated in the 1870s and 1880s (Graham 1978: 764), including two women's medical colleges and twenty-two nursing schools (Massey 1994: 349). By 1880, one-third of all American college students were women, although college students represented a small proportion of women and of the entire population (Graham 1978: 760). Two colleges for women appeared in England before the middle of the century, but English women's advancement in the university system was slower than that of American women (Holcombe 1973: 26–30). French women were admitted to universities in the 1860s; but again, the numbers of university-educated women remained very small throughout the century. According to Moses (1984: 32), 'For nineteenth century French women, education was mediocre, if it existed at all.' This was true for both middle- and working-class women.

The status and role of women in these three countries were also influenced by their involvement in religious and philanthropic activities that provided English and particularly American women with important skills in running organisations and in communicating with the public. Through women's organisations, American women exerted considerable influence on the practice of social welfare (Ryan 1994: 279). French women remained the most constrained; they had 'limited autonomy and roles in public policy formulation' (Fuchs 1995: 185). The majority of French middle-class women, as seen in their activities in women's organisations, acquiesced to a system that accorded them a very limited and very subordinate position outside their families. Ironically, as the French birth rate declined steadily throughout the century, public policy and public culture increasingly defined the Frenchwoman's role as that of motherhood (Offen 1984). The feminist movement was seen as a potential threat to the welfare of the country because it appeared to turn women away from marriage and maternity.

By the end of the century, in England and America, 'the strong, independent woman' had become 'the New Woman', who was 'visible in education, in athletics, in reform, in the work force' (Banner 1984: 175). In France, significant changes in the legal rights and employment opportunities for middle-class women had only begun in the 1890s; relatively few women had been able to take advantage of them (Silverman 1991: 148).

Given the Victorian ideal of domesticity and motherhood, the role of the middle-class spinster was marginal; but some women, particularly those who were educated and urban, deliberately chose spinsterhood, as a form of revolt and as an escape from the demands and restrictions of middle-class marriage (Freeman and Klaus 1984: 395). Between 1885 and 1910, marriage rates for female college graduates in the United States were distinctly lower than for female college graduates before or after that period. In the 1890s only about half of these college graduates married, in comparison to 90 per cent of all native-born white women (Cookingham 1984: 350–1). In the white female labour force as a whole in this decade, 75 per cent were single (Goldin 1980: 81). Goldin (1980: 88) concluded: 'work in the labour force for women from 1870 to 1920 was the realm of the unmarried'. At the same time, this 'new' spinster was seen as a threat to the institutions of marriage and motherhood. By the 1890s, educated, employed spinsters were viewed as rebels, but also as having distinct advantages in terms of material goods and independence (Freeman and Klaus 1984: 409).

Since middle-class women who worked outside the home represented a set of values in opposition to the Victorian ideal, it is not surprising that, in various ways, their clothing behaviour set them apart from married women. Less controversial than dress reform but more widely adopted, the subtly masculine clothing behaviour of the single employed middle-class woman signified another form of resistance to the dominant culture.

Alternative dress and dress reform

At the centre of much of the debate about women's clothing in the nineteenth century were members of women's movements who attempted to bring about dress reform in the direction of practical, healthy, and comfortable clothing. They deplored the use of corsets and excessively heavy sets of garments. Unlike the alternative style, which was not advocated by any particular group, dress reformers centred their proposals around the adoption of trousers.

Trousers were particularly controversial in the nineteenth century, because a basic premise of nineteenth-century ideology concerning women's roles was the belief in fixed gender identities and enormous differences – physical, psychological, and intellectual – between men and women. The dominant point of view allowed for no ambiguity in terms of sexual identification and no possibility for evolution or change in the prescribed behaviours and attitudes of members of each gender. Throughout the second half of the nineteenth century, dress reforms proposed by women's movements were inconsistent with this point of view and, consequently, were unable to win the support of substantial numbers of women outside these groups.

The first and best-known proposal for dress reform was also the most notorious – the costume proposed by Mrs Amelia Bloomer in the 1850s – because it subverted gender differences. This costume consisted of a short skirt over a pair of full Turkish trousers. Bloomer, a women's activist, and a few of her fellow activists wore the costume because it was 'comfortable, convenient, safe and tidy – with no thought of introducing a fashion' (Russell 1892: 326–7). The salience of the issue of gender differentiation is seen in the fact that the costume attracted an enormous amount of attention and controversy (Fatout 1952: 365). When Bloomer, who published a women's temperance magazine, wrote an article in the magazine in 1851 describing her new costume (Russell 1892), the information in her article was reprinted in a leading New York newspaper and subsequently in newspapers all over the country and abroad. Numerous articles described the costume's appearance in different cities and at various types of social events (Lauer and Lauer 1981: 252). Women who wore the costume attracted huge crowds that were generally male and often hostile. The level of public harassment was so severe that most women stopped wearing the costume in public after a few months. The Bloomer costume was interpreted as a threat to the ideology of separate spheres, on the grounds that it would erase all distinctions between the sexes (Lauer and Lauer 1981: 257). Victorian clothing was a form of social control that contributed to the maintenance of women in dependent, subservient roles.

Owing to the amount of ridicule and censure that the costume engendered, Bloomer and her friends ceased to wear it after a few years. However, adaptations of the Bloomer costume continued to be worn in the private sphere of the home, particularly on the frontier (Foote 1980; Severa 1995: 88, 239). By the 1860s, some women had replaced the Turkish-style trousers with masculine trousers (Severa 1995: 257, 275) (Figure 15.2). Later in the century, dress reform patterns were available and dress reform styles were sold in stores (Banner 1984: 148).

Members of the American women's movement continued throughout the century to lobby for dress reform, forming associations, holding conventions, writing books and articles and seeking to popularise simpler, more healthy styles of dress (Riegel 1963). In 1892 and 1893, dress reformers organised a Symposium on Dress at which they presented three designs that included either a divided skirt or trousers (Sims 1991: 139). These dress reforms were still too radical for many middle-class women, and tended to alienate potential supporters of the women's rights movement, which was the principal interest of these dress reformers (Sims 1991: 141).

Dress reform movements were less evident in England and France. In 1881, a Rational Dress Society was founded in England to promote a knee-length, divided skirt (McCrone 1988: 220–1; Gernsheim 1963: 72). Dress reform was absent in France until 1887, when a society was formed with the goal of eliminating the corset (Déslandres and Muller 1986: 18). From the beginning of the century, pants were forbidden by law in France; special permission from the police was required to wear them (Toussaint Samat 1990: 376). Legislation forbidding women to wear pants was a reaction to the behaviour of French feminists, who had worn trousers with riding habits during the Revolution. Their clothing and their political views were unacceptable to the men who wielded power during the Revolution, who considered dress as 'a statement of freedom and an expression of individuality', but not for women (Ribeiro 1988: 141).

At the end of the century, the French legislative body (the Chamber of Deputies) received several petitions requesting a change in the law. They were refused. The few middle-class women (or women leading a middle-class style of life) who wore pants during the nineteenth century did so from personal preference, and not in order to advance an agenda of dress reform. In various ways, these women, who were often artists, writers, and courtesans, were atypical or marginal.

Sports, alternative dress, and marginal public space

Both in Europe and America, women in the nineteenth century were required to dress according to the dominant fashion on the streets and in other people's homes; but in

Figure 15.2 Dress reformer in reform dress (US, 1866–70).

certain types of public spaces they were able to blur symbolic boundaries by adopting alternative costumes. During the last three decades of the century, there were an increasing number of settings, such as schools, colleges, and resorts, in which women could escape the dominant dress code and discover alternative identities through dress. When American dress reformers wore a skirt over trousers on the street and proposed the costume for general wear, they were widely criticised; but a very similar costume, used in the same period as an exercise uniform in schools, colleges, and sanitoriums, was acceptable, apparently because it was not worn on city streets (Warner

1993: 144–7). Rules governing clothing behaviour in public space were character-ised by subtle differences depending on location, class and gender. For example, trou-sered costumes for women were permitted when swimming in the ocean, but not for promenades on the beach. The introduction of new sports, particularly bicycling, during the second half of the century, produced a redefinition of the way in which sym-bolic boundaries were expressed in public space. In a sense, alternative dress worn in public spaces was a manifestation of more radical changes that were occurring in more secluded spaces.

Until the twentieth century, sports and physical exercise as a leisure activity for women were reserved almost exclusively for the upper and upper middle classes (McCrone 1987: 119, 121; Bulger 1982: 10). What women wore while engaging in these sports depended largely upon the nature of the public spaces in which they were performed. When sports were performed near the home or in social clubs, conform-ity to middle-class standards of feminine dress was generally required. Tennis, croquet, ice skating, and golf were perceived as social rather than sports activities (Bulger 1982: 6). Consequently, in the 1870s, women were expected to dress for these sports as they dressed for other social occasions: long skirts with trains, tight corsets, bustles, and large hats (McCrone 1988: 219, 232). When sports were played in institutions or in the countryside, sports costumes were more likely to include items of masculine clothing.

Riding was one of the earliest sports in which upper-class women engaged. [. . .] Made by tailors rather than dressmakers, the sidesaddle riding habit in 1850 imitated a man's formal suit from the waist up, but incorporated full and long skirts below (Schreier 1989: 107). By the 1880s, most women wore long, straight dark trousers underneath the skirts (Byrde 1992: 164; Albrecht et al. 1988: 59). [. . .] The evolution of riding cos-tume reveals the extent to which upper-class women wore items of masculine clothing, including various forms of trousers, that were considered totally inappropriate in other contexts.

Swimming costume was another area in which upper- and middle-class women were permitted to engage in otherwise inappropriate clothing behaviour. Lencek and Bosker (1989: 27) describe summer resorts as 'fashion laboratories where the well-to-do came to experiment with new styles of dress and behavior'. As early as the 1860s, trousers or bloomers, which were not acceptable in other public places, were adopted for bathing suits for women (Byrde 1992: 170; Cunnington and Cunnington 1959: 474; Brew 1945: 350), for example, trousers worn with a belted jacket (Byrde 1992: 163 illus.). Byrde quotes a magazine of the period saying that young women in this costume resembled 'pretty boys'. In the United States, a knee-length or ankle-length skirt was worn over the trousers. Stockings were optional. By 1909, women's bathing suits had changed very little. Corsets were recommended although the type of corset generally used was much smaller than for landwear (Brew 1945: 364; Lencek and Bosker 1989: 27).

Throughout this period, women were expected to wear their regular clothes – long-sleeved blouses, floor-length skirts, corsets, enormous hats and gloves – on the beach itself and photographs suggest that most of them did (Lencek and Bosker 1989: 26–7; Severa 1995: 415). The sea itself was defined as a liminal space in which normal sartorial (and moral) standards did not apply. The sharp segregation between land and sea was emphasised by the use of wooden huts on wheels at the water's edge in which women changed into bathing suits and from which they entered the sea (Adburgham

1987: 127). Photographs suggest that it was not unusual for young women to show bare legs when wading on the beach or in rivers, in contrast to norms that skirts should cover the ankles in normal circumstances (Severa 1995: 415, 538; Roberts 1984: 162).

Uniforms that young women wore at school or college but not in the street supplied an alternative clothing discourse that was more effective than that of dress reformers, because these clothes were actually worn by hundreds of women. During the middle decades of the century, the opening of American colleges for women coincided with a popular health-exercise movement. The colleges adopted exercise programmes and appropriate costumes that students were required to obtain and probably made for themselves (Warner 1993). One type of costume used in these schools was the gym suit, a knee-length divided skirt, worn with black cotton stockings (Brew 1945: 349). It is significant that these exercise costumes were intended to be worn for exercise only and were not permitted to be worn in public. When there was a possibility that the students could be seen by the public, skirts were required (Warner 1993: 157). However, leading fashion magazines of the period wrote about gym suits and explained how they were made. At the end of the century, a gym suit pattern was available (Warner 1993: 153–4).

School uniforms for athletics also played a role in introducing non-restrictive dress in England (Ewing 1975: 68). Principals of girls' schools were very conscious of their roles as dress reformers. In 1877, a school in Scotland which was 'the model for many future girls' schools in England' introduced a uniform consisting of 'a blue knee-length belted tunic, with knickerbockers or trousers underneath' (Ewing 1975: 71–2), an outfit that anticipated fashionable dresses in the 1920s.

The practice of sports by women in France was more controversial, and confined largely to the middle and upper class (Flamant-Paparatti 1984). A law passed in 1880 required the teaching of gymnastics in public schools for boys, but made it optional for girls' schools. Women were advised in popular magazines that their athletic activities would provoke less criticism if they dressed elegantly and fashionably and did not lose their femininity (Flamant-Paparatti 1984: 182). At the end of the century, women at a training school for teachers in Paris were photographed during their exercise class wearing long, full, black skirts that covered their ankles (Juin 1994: 145 illus.).

The impact of the bicycle on clothing behaviour in the 1890s resulted from the fact that bicycling was a completely new sport, and therefore not identified as a male activity. Bicycling also differed from previous sports in that it was virtually impossible to ride bicycles in the fashionable clothing of the period. The most suitable costumes for bicycling were the divided skirt, which looked like a skirt but was actually a pair of very full knee-length pants, and the knee-length bloomer, or the knickerbocker, as it was called in the 1890s (Figure 15.3). In America, the latter was widely used for about two years (1895–6), as bicycling became increasingly popular, but disappeared rapidly afterward. For the most part, bloomers were worn with skirts. When women wore them without skirts, they were 'jeered and scorned' (Sims 1991; Banner 1984: 149). The solution that was accepted by the end of the decade was shorter skirts. Women had already begun to wear shorter skirts at summer resorts in the 1890s; but the first women who wore ankle-length skirts in the city in the mid-nineties attracted hostile, shrieking crowds (Banner 1984: 149).

In England, a few women wore bloomers; others wore a special type of skirt that could be buttoned around each leg in the form of trousers when on the machine

Figure 15.3 The 'new woman' and her bicycle (colour halftone reproduction of a drawing by F. Opper).

(Gernsheim 1963: 80–1). Outside city parks and in the countryside there was considerable resistance to the use of such costumes, particularly among the working class (Gernsheim 1963: 81; McCrone 1988: 238).

Curiously, in France, where the gym suit was unknown and women had participated relatively little in sports before the advent of the bicycle, the divided skirt for women bicyclists was accepted very rapidly. In 1892, only four years after the invention of a safety bicycle that could be widely used, the Minister of the Interior decreed that the law against women wearing trousers could be lifted for bicycling only (Davray-Piekolek 1990: 46). A French department store sold bicycling costumes with divided skirts or pants concealed by skirts as early as 1893 (Falluel 1990: 85–6). Most women wore skirts over bloomers (Davray-Piekolek 1990: 46; Falluel 1990: 85–6) or wore divided skirts (Déslandres and Muller 1986: 72–3). The level of controversy over the use of these costumes was much less heated than in the United States. The explanation appears to lie in the fact that the sport was adopted largely by a relatively small number of upper-class women (bicycles were too expensive for other women) (Chaumette 1995: 53), and that they practised it in parks, such as the Bois de Boulogne on the edge of Paris (a liminal space) or at the seaside, rather than in city streets (Davray-Piekolek 1990: 46; Delpierre 1990: 43–4).

According to a French costume historian (Monier 1990: 121, 125), the bicycle became 'one of the symbols of emancipation' that definitively changed people's attitudes toward sports clothes for women. She claims (Monier 1990: 127): 'This famous bike in effect still appears as an object that determined the moment when one evokes a modern conception of clothing, pants worn by women, the emancipation and physical freedom of women . . .'

However, in 1911, French designers were still able to provoke controversy by proposing a trouser skirt for regular activities. It attracted very negative reactions when worn at the races (Gernsheim 1963: 92; Steele 1985: 232). Trousers were unacceptable on the street for the average woman.

Alternative dress as symbolic subversion

Victorian culture in the form of literature and women's magazines generally stressed domestic ideology; but clothing was curiously ambivalent. One reason why clothing as opposed to written culture was able to express these tensions has to do with the differences between verbal and non-verbal culture. Non-verbal culture is more susceptible to different interpretations than verbal culture. Those who do not wish to receive a message can refuse to perceive it. Those who send subversive messages by means of non-verbal culture may deny their subversive intentions or, in some cases, not be fully aware of them (Cassell 1974). The alternative style of dress, a style that associated items of masculine clothing with feminine clothing, represented, consciously or unconsciously, a form of resistance to the dominant style of dress. While distinctly different from cross-dressing (wearing costumes composed entirely of items associated with the opposite gender),[4] this style of dressing represented a kind of symbolic inversion of the dominant message of feminine clothing by associating it with masculine clothing. Through a process of symbolic inversion, items associated with masculine costume were given new meanings, specifically, feminine independence, that challenged gender boundaries. Oppositional styles of clothing such as those that emerged in the nineteenth century disrupt existing boundaries and create new boundaries. The dominant style was designed to maintain existing social class boundaries, being relatively inaccessible to the lower middle and working class. It was also very effective at marking gender boundaries. The alternative style, relatively inexpensive and uncomplicated to reproduce, crossed class boundaries.

The alternative style of dress represents an example of a process that precedes and accompanies social change, whereby the meanings of symbols gradually change to correspond with changing definitions of social roles and structures (Cassell 1974). Non-verbal symbols are least stable, and therefore manipulation of these symbols is likely to precede manipulation of verbal symbols. Non-verbal behaviour is a powerful means of conveying social status, particularly because it is often performed on the basis of habit rather than conscious decisions.

The alternative dress style was worn by many women who had no connection with the feminist movement. There are sufficient indications of alienation among middle-class women during the period that the desire to affirm their identity as members of a new social category, the middle-class working woman, cannot have been entirely absent. On the other hand, the level of social control in the form of hostility and ridicule that they encountered in public spaces made a mild form of symbolic inversion, combined with skirts instead of trousers, preferable. [. . .]

After the First World War, the alternative style with its ties, men's hats, men's jackets, and vests was no longer such a dramatic contrast to the dominant style. The dominant feminine ideal of the nineteenth century, the voluptuous matron, had been replaced by the flapper (whom the French called *la garçonne*), an independent yet child-ish young woman with a boyish figure who combined some of the qualities of both the dominant and the alternative female images of the previous century, specifically, the femininity and helplessness of the former and the assertiveness and athleticism of the latter. The alternative style was no longer an oppositional style (Gibbings 1990: 109). Elements of it, particularly the suit-jacket, were now part of the dominant style.

Conclusion

Social theorists from Marx to Foucault tend to emphasise the ways in which dominant discourses concerning, for example, class and sexuality, influence behaviour and atti-tudes. Foucault (1979) argued that Victorian discourse concerning sexuality consti-tuted a 'technology' for exerting power over the individual and the family. What such theories tend to neglect are the ways in which marginal discourses survive and con-tinue to exert an influence alongside hegemonic discourses, which they may eventu-ally modify or displace. Clothing and clothing behaviour in the nineteenth century are valuable sites for examining the relationships between marginal discourses and hegem-onic discourses. In any period, the set of clothing discourses always includes discourses that support conformity toward dominant conceptions of social roles and discourses that express social tensions that are pushing widely accepted conceptions of social roles in new directions. The latter include the perspectives of marginal groups that are seek-ing acceptance for clothing behaviour that is deviant or marginal in terms of dominant conceptions of status or gender roles. In the nineteenth century, fashionable clothing which originated in France reflected the dominance of traditional feminine roles in that country. England and the United States provided more favourable environments for the development of alternative feminine roles and alternative clothing behaviour suitable for those roles.

In the nineteenth century, changes in clothing and physical appearance that were consistent with dominant cultural norms concerning the expression of sexuality and personal identity followed the classic model of fashion change (Simmel 1957 [1904]): they were proposed by fashion designers, popularised by leading entertainers, and adopted first by upper-class women or those aspiring to enter that class. By contrast, changes in clothing and physical appearance that represented modifications of upper- and middle-class norms were likely to begin in 'marginal' or secluded public spaces, or, alternatively, among marginal members of both classes. In the nineteenth century, middle-class women who worked could be characterised as marginal, along with female artists, writers, entertainers, and prostitutes. Both upper- and working-class women took advantage of secluded or marginal public spaces to adopt masculine items of cloth-ing, not to express their rebellion against the dominant culture, but to facilitate certain types of activities, either work or pleasure.

The history of alternative dress in the nineteenth century suggests that marginal discourses concerning gender are not maintained entirely through verbal communica-tion; non-verbal communication involving symbolic inversion performs an important role, affecting people both consciously and unconsciously, and having a high degree of visibility. In the nineteenth century, the alternative dress style, as it added new items to form a complete costume and attracted increasing numbers of women, was an important element in bringing about changes in attitudes that were essential preconditions for structural changes.

Notes

1   For example, a suffragette demonstration was a 'procession of petticoats', a cabinet that supported votes for women was a 'petticoat-elected cabinet' (Rolley 1990: 48).
2   By contrast, Dr Mary Edwards Walker, a physician who became the first female commissioned assistant surgeon in the Union Army, adopted men's trousers and frock coats, but encountered considerable hostility owing to her style of dress. Congress passed a special decree that granted Walker the right to wear trousers (Hall 1992: 238). She also wore a tunic with trousers, reminiscent of the original Bloomer costume (Gernsheim 1963: 11).
3   French women obtained the right to vote in 1944 (Flamant-Papparati 1984: 30), approximately twenty-five years after English and American women, who obtained the vote in 1918 (Kent 1988: 234) and 1920, respectively. American wives obtained control over their wages and property in 1860, English wives in 1882, and French wives in 1907 (Hause and Kenney 1981: 781).
4   After the First World War, a different type of alternative style emerged, which was associated with lesbian subcultures in New York, London, and Paris, but not widely adopted outside these circles (Rolley 1990; Weiss 1995). Instead of combining a few items of masculine dress with feminine dress, this style was much closer to 'cross-dressing'.

References

Adburgham, Alison (1987) *Shops and Shopping, 1800–1914*, London: Barrie and Jenkins.
Albrecht, Juliana et al. (1988) 'Function, Fashion and Convention in American Women's Riding Costume, 1880–1930', *Dress*, 14, pp. 56–67.
Banner, Lois W. (1984) *American Beauty*, Chicago: University of Chicago Press.
Bradfield, Nancy (1981) *Costume in Detail: Women's Dress 1730–1930*, London: Harrap.
Brew, Margaret L. (1945) 'American Clothing Consumption, 1879–1909, unpublished PhD dissertation, Department of Home Economics, University of Chicago.
Bulger, Margery A. (1982) 'American Sportswomen in the 19th Century', *Journal of Popular Culture*, 16: 1–16.
Byrde, Penelope (1992) *Nineteenth Century Fashion*, London: Batsford.
Cassell, Joan (1974) 'Externalities of Change: Deference and Demeanor in Contemporary Feminism', *Human Organization*, 33, pp. 85–94.
Chaumette, Xavier (1995) *Le Costume tailleur: la culture vestimentaire en France au XIXème siècle.* Paris: Esmod Edition.
Cookingham, Mary (1984) 'Bluestockings, Spinsters, and Pedagogues: Women College Graduates, 1865–1910', *Population Studies*, 38, pp. 349–64.
Crowe, Duncan (1971) *The Victorian Woman*, London: Allen and Unwin.
Crowe, Duncan (1978) *The Edwardian Woman*, London: Allen and Unwin.
Cunnington, C. Willett and Cunnington, Phillis (1959) *Handbook of English Costume in the Nineteenth Century*, London: Faber and Faber.
Davray-Piekolek, Renée (1990) 'Les modes triomphantes, 1885–1895', in *Femmes Fin de Siècle 1885–1895*, Paris: Musée de la Mode et du Costume, Palais Galliera, pp. 29–64.

Delpierre, Madeleine (1990) *Le Costume: Restauration, Louis-Philippe, Second Empire, Belle Epoque*, Paris: Flammarion.

Déslandres, Yvonne and Muller, Florence (1986) *Histoire de la mode au XXe siècle*, Paris: Editions Somogy.

Duroselle, J.-B. (1972) *La France et les Français, 1900–1914*, Paris: Editions Richelieu.

Ewing, Elizabeth (1975 *Women in Uniform through the Centuries*, Totowa, NJ: Rowman and Littlefield.

Ewing, Elizabeth (1984) *Everyday Dress: 1650–1900*, London: Batsford.

Falluel, Fabienne (1990) 'Les grands magasins et la confection féminine', in *Femmes Fin de Siècle 1885–1895*, Paris: Musée de la Mode et du Costume, Palais Galliera, pp. 75–117.

Fatout, Paul (1952) 'Amelia Bloomer and Bloomerism'. *The New York Historical Society Quarterly*, 36, pp. 361–73.

Flamant-Paparatti, Danièlle (1984) *Bien-pensantes, cocodettes et basbleus: la femme bourgeoise à travers la presse féminine et familiale (1873–1887)*, Paris: Editions Denoël.

Foote, Shelly (1980) 'Bloomers', *Dress*, 5, pp. 1–12.

Foucault, Michel (1979) *The History of Sexuality*, London: Allen Lane.

Freeman, Ruth and Klaus, Patricia (1984) 'Blessed or Not? The New Spinster in England and the United States in the Late Nineteenth and Early Twentieth Centuries', *Journal of Family History*, 9, pp. 394–414.

Fuchs, Rachel G. (1995) 'France in a Comparative Perspective', in *Gender and the Politics of Social Reform in France, 1870–1914*, ed. Elinor A. Accampo, Baltimore: Johns Hopkins University Press, pp. 157–87.

Gernsheim, Alison (1963) *Fashion and Reality, 1840–1914*, London: Faber and Faber.

Gibbings, Sarah (1990) *The Tie: Trends and Traditions*, Hauppauge, NY: Barron's Educational Series, Inc.

Ginsburg, Madeleine (1988) *Victorian Dress in Photographs*, London: Batsford.

Goldin, Claudia (1980) 'The Work and Wages of Single Women, 1870 to 1920'. *The Journal of Economic History*, 40, pp. 81–8.

Goulène, Pierre (1974) *Evolution des pouvoirs d'achat en France (1830–1972)*, Paris: Bordas.

Graham, Patricia Albjerg (1978) 'Expansion and Exclusion: A History of Women in American Higher Education', *Signs*, 3, pp. 759–73.

Hall, Lee (1992) *Common Threads: A Parade of American Clothing*, New York: Little Brown & Co.

Hause, Steven C. and Kenney, Anne R. (1981) 'The Limits of Suffragist Behavior: Legalism and Militancy in France, 1876–1922', *American Historical Review*, 86, pp. 781–866.

Holcombe, Lee (1973) *Victorian Ladies at Work: Middle-Class Working Women in England and Wales, 1850–1914*, London: Archon Books.

Juin, Hubert (1994) *Le Livre de Paris 1900*, Paris: Éditions Michèle Trinckuel.

Kent, Susan Kingsley (1988) 'The Politics of Sexual Difference: World War I and the Demise of British Feminism', *Journal of British Studies*, 27, pp. 232–53.

Kidwell, Claudia and Christman, Margaret (1974) *Suiting Everyone: The Democratization of Clothing in America*, Washington, DC: Smithsonian Institute Press.

Lambert, Miles (1991) *Fashion in Photographs 1860–1880*, London: Batsford.

Lauer, Jeanette C. and Lauer, Robert H. (1981) *Fashion Power: The Meaning of Fashion in American Society*, Englewood Cliffs, NJ: Prentice-Hall.

Lencek, Lena and Bosker, Gideon (1989) *Making Waves: Swimsuits and the Undressing of America*, San Francisco: Chronicle Books.

Lister, M. (1972) *Costumes of Everyday Life: An Illustrated History of Working Clothes*, London: Barrie and Jenkins.

Massey, Mary Elizabeth (1994) *Women in the Civil War*, Lincoln: University of Nebraska Press.

McCrone, Kathleen E. (1987) 'Play up! Play up! And Play the Game! Sport at the Late Victorian Girls' Public Schools', in *From Fair Sex to Feminism: Sport and the Socialization of Women* in the Industrial and Post-Industrial Eras, ed. J. A. Mangan and Roberta J. Park, London: Frank Cass, pp. 97–129.

McCrone, Kathleen E. (1988) Sport and the Physical Emancipation of English Women, 1870–1914, London: Routledge.

McMillan, James F. (1980) Housewife or Harlot: The Place of Women in French Society 1870–1940, New York: St Martin's Press.

Monier, Véronique (1990) 'Balbec, essai sur l'apparition d'une mode sportive en littérature', in Femmes Fin de Siècle 1885–1895, Paris: Musée de la Mode et du Costume, Palais Galliera, pp. 119–32.

Moses, Claire Goldberg (1984) French Feminism in the Nineteenth Century, Albany: State University of New York Press.

Nye, Robert A. (1993) Masculinity and Male Codes of Honor in Modern France, New York: Oxford University Press.

Offen, Karen (1984) 'Depopulation, Nationalism, and Feminism in Fin-de-siècle France', American Historical Review, 89, pp. 648–76.

Perrot, Philippe (1981) Les Dessus et les dessous de la bourgeoise: une histoire du vêtement aux XIX siècle, Paris: Fayard.

Reberioux, Madeleine (1980) 'L'ouvrière', in Misérable et glorieuse: la femme de XIXe siècle, ed. Jean-Paul Aron, Paris: Fayard, pp. 59–78.

Rendall, Jane (1985) The Origins of Modern Feminism: Women in Britain, France, and the United States, 1780–1860, London: Macmillan.

Ribeiro, Aileen (1988) Fashion in the French Revolution, pp. 59–78. New York: Holmes & Meier.

Riegel, Robert E. (1963) 'Women's Clothes and Women's Rights', American Quarterly, 15, pp. 390–401.

Roberts, Elizabeth (1984) A Woman's Place: An Oral History of Working-Class Women, 1890–1940, Oxford: Basil Blackwell, pp. 59–78.

Rolley, Katrina (1990), 'Fashion, Femininity and the Fight for the Vote', Art History, 13, pp. 47–71.

Russell, Frances E. (1892) 'A Brief Survey of the American Dress Reform Movements of the Past, with Views of Representative Women', Arena, 1892, pp. 325–39.

Ryan, Mary P. (1994) 'Gender and Public Access: Women's Politics in Nineteenth-century America', in Habermas and the Public Sphere, ed. Craig Calhoun, Cambridge, MA: MIT Press, pp. 259–88.

Schreier, Barbara A. (1989) 'Sporting Wear', in Men and Women: Dressing the Part, ed. Claudia Brush Kidwell and Valerie Steele, Washington, DC: Smithsonian Institute Press, pp. 92–123.

Severa, Joan L. (1995) Dressed for the Photographer: Ordinary Americans and Fashion, Kent, OH: Kent State University Press.

Shaffer, John W. (1978) 'Family, Class, and Young Women: Occupational Expectations in Nineteenth Century Paris', Journal of Family History, 3, pp. 62–77.

Silverman, Debora (1991) 'The "New Woman", Feminism, and the Decorative Arts in Fin-de-siècle France', in Eroticism and the Body Politic, ed. Lynn Hunt, Baltimore: Johns Hopkins University Press, pp. 144–63.

Simmel, Georg (1957 [1904]) 'Fashion', American Journal of Sociology, 62 (May), pp. 541–58.

Sims, Sally (1991) 'The Bicycle, the Bloomer, and Dress Reform in the 1890s', in Dress and Popular Culture, ed. Patricia A. Cunningham and Susan Voso Lab, Bowling Green, OH: Bowling Green State University Popular Press, pp. 125–45.

Smith, Bonnie G. (1981) Ladies of the Leisure Class: The Bourgeoises of Northern France in the Nineteenth Century, Princeton, NJ: Princeton University Press.

Steele, Valerie (1985) *Fashion and Eroticism*, New York: Oxford University Press.

Toussaint-Samat, Maguelonne (1990) *Histoire technique et morale du vêtement*, Paris: Bordas.

Vicinus, Martha (1985) *Independent Women: Work and Community for Single Women, 1850–1920*, Chicago: University of Chicago Press.

Warner, Patricia Campbell (1993) 'The Gym Suit: Freedom at Last', in *Dress in American Culture*, ed. Patricia A. Cunningham and Susan Voso Lab, Bowling Green, OH: Bowling Green State University Popular Press, pp. 140–79.

Weiss, Andrea (1995) *Paris Was a Woman: Portraits from the Left Bank*, San Francisco: Harper.

Wilcox, R. Turner (1945) *The Mode in Hats and Headdress*, New York: Charles Scribner's Sons.

Wood, George (1903) Appendix A. 'The Course of Women's Wages during the Nineteenth Century', in *A History of Factory Legislation*, ed. B. L. Hutchins and A. Harrison, Westminster: P. S. King and Son, Orchard House, pp. 257–308.

Fashion, birth and death in the nineteenth century

Lou Taylor

Dress as a form of cultural expression becomes relevant above all, in every culture, at key moments of life – birth, coming of age, marriage and death – when the wealthier and the more powerful wear the grandest garments to publicly mark these occasions.

At christenings in Euro-America from the eighteenth century, it was the newborn baby who became the central focus of sartorial attention, dressed in long white silk or muslin robes with decorative capes and bonnets. Indicators of wealth lay in the delicacy of fine fabric and embroidery on white linen. Mothers often made these robes themselves and many such long-treasured garments survive in museum collections. Guests at the ceremony, of every class, wore their best church-going outdoor dress, which followed the fashions of the day.

Mourning dress was far more complex. It was just one of many forms of coded dress but it was the one that, above all, especially between 1860 and 1914, held families in a stranglehold of social anxiety. Stemming from medieval European Court practice, by the late seventeenth century sumptuary laws restricting the use of black mourning clothes to Royal and Court use were disregarded by the newly wealthy merchant and middling classes. In close replication of the unequal social place of women, the weight of mourning always fell firmly on widows. While men with children were encouraged to remarry, widows were not. After the death of Prince Albert in 1861, Queen Victoria wore black or half-mourning mauve until she died in 1901, setting an example which escalated into a popular cult.

By the mid-nineteenth century the intricate rules for the wearing of mourning dress were published for middle-class consumption in women's magazines and etiquette books. Widows' dress consisted of a First Stage of mourning (black wool and black crape entirely covering garments), to Second Stage (black wool or dull silk with less and more decorative use of crape), to Third or General Mourning (black with no crape), and finally to Half Mourning (use of dull mauve and grey shades with black and white). Mourning periods varied from two and half years for a husband to a few weeks for remote cousins. Styles were always fashionable and had constantly to be replaced. Anxious letters to women's magazines confirm the resultant stresses because errors indicted a lack of *savoir faire*, Christian decency and poverty. To avoid that, impecunious widows even sold their coloured clothes to buy widows' weeds.

Despite its medieval roots, the speedy need for the provision of mourning dress triggered two consumption-related developments now recognised as key moments of mid-nineteenth-century modernity. Firstly, the large-scale mourning warehouses which opened by the 1840s, rapidly became department stores, such as Peter Robinson's in London. The second trigger of modernity was the large-scale manufacture of ready-to-wear mourning clothing, from the mid-1860s. Entire wardrobes were

Chapeau de deuil.
Modèle des *Magasins du Louvre.*

Snapshot 20.1 Widow's outdoor bonnet and veil in dull black silk mourning crape; from Magasins du Louvre, Paris, August 1901, from *La Mode Illustrée, Journal de la Famille,* with thanks to St Peter's House Library, University of Brighton.

provided within a few days — crape-covered capes, indoor widows' bonnets in white, black crape hats for outdoors and delicate underwear with black ribbon. All styles, prices and qualities were offered, including cheap dress for women servants. Stores took care in their press advertisements not to alienate their numerous but less well-off middle-class clientele, while still appealing to their grander clients. As to the mass of poor, who perfectly understood mourning propriety, their focus above all was to avoid the public humiliation of a pauper funeral. Dress was a secondary consideration, often achieved through home dyeing.

The formal practice survives today in establishment society. It waned however in general usage by the late twentieth century, leaving in its wake an ever-widening consumption of fashion through the new stores and ready-to-wear clothing manufacture but also a clear breakdown of nineteenth-century Christian middle-class values.

Bibliography and further reading

Cunnington, P., and Lucas, C. (1972) *Costume of Births, Marriages and Deaths*, London: A. and C. Black.

Morley, J. (1971) *Death, Heaven and the Victorians*, London: Studio Vista.

Taylor, L. (1993) *Mourning Dress, a Costume and Social History*, Allen and Unwin; reprint London: Routledge, 2010.

PART 5

Westernisation and colonialism
The age of empires

Giorgio Riello and Peter McNeil

Fashion, in the age before the mechanical reproduction of objects and images, could only be limited in its reach. Scholars over the last century have discussed, and mostly disagreed, on the extent to which fashion influenced the lives of billions of people across the globe. This *Reader* suggests that fashion, however one might define it, is a phenomenon that goes back in time at least to the Middle Ages, if not earlier, and had substantial importance not just for the rich and famous living in the period before the nineteenth century (monarchs, the court, and rich merchants) but also for the 'common people'. Yet these ideas are mostly applied to the West and in particular to those rich parts of Western Europe, and later North America, South Africa and Australia that enjoyed increasing consumption from the eighteenth century onwards, industrialisation, urbanisation, and in the twentieth century experienced the rise of the affluent middle class and its leisured lifestyle.

Most of the world, including Africa and Asia, as well as great parts of the Americas and Eastern Europe, are sidelined and often totally ignored in histories of fashion. We have mentioned in the Introduction that when the question 'Did the non-European world have fashion before the twentieth century?' was posed, illustrious historians replied negatively. They were not the only ones: the sociologist Georg Simmel, so influential in the study of late nineteenth- and early twentieth-century fashion, proposed a distinction between 'costume' and 'fashion' (Simmel 1904). While 'fashion' characterised advanced societies, 'costume' was to be found among 'traditional' or 'primitive' ones. This was a Eurocentric vision of the world in which the West was characterised by change, a dynamism to which fashion belonged, while other 'civilisations' were living not in the condition of the 'eternal present' (a modern notion of forward-looking but historically unfounded progress; see Introduction to Part 6), but an 'eternal past' (a notion of stability and immutability that led to backwardness). While the 'modern' West embraced change (in line with industrial dynamism, new means of communication and transportation), the rest of the world lived in a state of no-progress as, in the words of Simmel, the

'modes of primitive races are much more stable than ours'. Other voices sounded more cau-
tionary tales: the Czech scholar Petr Bogatyrĕv defines folk costume as 'in many respects the
antithesis of clothing which is subject to fashion changes'. However, in a move which indicates
a nuance lost in many subsequent debates, Bogatyrĕv refuses an opposition of folk dress
versus 'town dress', and notes that 'even folk dress does not remain unchanged, that it does
take on features of current fashion' (Bogatyrĕv 1937: 33).

If fashions were equated with change and costume with stability, the geographic remit
of these two concepts were also different. While fashion modulated constantly, its geographic
remit was vast. Costume was immutable; as for what we call folk dress, it could only characterise very precise places. This explains why Parisian fashion could be followed by ladies living
in early twentieth-century America, or anyone around the world who could afford it, for that
matter. Costume remained instead confined to the local, locking specific communities into
atavistic notions of tradition that could only be dispelled through the magic wand of fashion.
It suggests that those who had fashion, at least according to Simmel and his contemporaries, enjoyed a sort of superiority that was also spatially expansive. Fashion was appropriately
suitable to be carried around the world together with projects of imperial domination that
posed the 'civilised white man' (and to a certain extent also the 'polite white woman') as the
moral and intellectual model for the entire humanity to follow. Needless to say that these 'civilised' beings were dressed from head to toe in European clothing.

The idea that fashion is quintessentially European has been difficult to dispel, at least
historically. Fernand Braudel and other European historians could quote abundantly from
European travellers who experienced first-hand the lack of fashion in places as different as
the courts of Ming China, Mughal India or Ottoman Turkey. The Italian Antonio Menavino,
for instance, who visited Turkey in the 1540s, commented that 'the Turks do not dress like us,
in various fashions (guise), but all generally in one shape of garments'. Yet we find ourselves
questioning what historians call 'the sources'. How reliable is the judgement of an occasional
visitor? How biased might be his comments in describing one of Italy's eternal enemies, the
Ottomans? And what did he actually see there? Frequently their comments derived from sou-
journs at courts and one can only wonder what impression of British fashion and its links to
archaic forms a foreign visitor might gain from taking tea with the Queen, let alone the late
Queen Mother.

The problem of the geographic remit of fashion is neither historical nor about the way in
which history is constructed. It relates instead to the understanding of fashion in the present.
Just switch on your television and you will be bombarded with images of fashionable people
in Tokyo, Beijing or Mumbai, the superluxury of the Russian magnates, the politics of the veil
across Eurasia, the No-Logo (that is in fact a logo) of the exploitation of garment workers in
many part of East and Southeast Asia. In the last decade *the problem of fashion* has become
global. However, when one looks at history one can find little help in explaining the 'world of
fashion'. Both with fashion and design, for instance in the case of China – something considered by Simona Segre Reinach at the end of this volume – there is a tendency to see them
as 'new' and a-historical. Europe is again proposing the idea that, if it is no longer possible
to establish a racial or political superiority, there might be scope for a 'superior experience'
granted to the Old Continent by the long-standing tradition in fashion that European countries – France and Italy in particular – already possess, market and uphold.

This part of the *Reader* provides three areas of contribution to the understanding of
fashion within a global framework, by going back in time to the early modern period and by
focusing on the nineteenth century as a moment of the restructuring of the power relationship

between Europe and other continents. Firstly, it asks in what ways fashion can be found also outside Europe before the age of industrialisation, or as Eric Hobsbawm calls them, the 'Age of Capital' (1848–75) and the 'Age of Empire' (1875–1914). Secondly, it addresses the complex relationship between European and non-European dress and fashion by showing how the 'power' of Europe manifested itself also through the sartorial and the aesthetic dimension. This is the case for the imposition of restrictions on what 'colonisers' and 'colonised' could wear, but also the more suble ways in which the 'exotic', the 'foreign' or the 'different' were used in lieu of representation and analysis or in strategies of cultural mimesis. And finally, we wish to unravel the reasons and modalities through which 'modernity' and 'mode' (fashion) came to be associated especially in nineteenth-century movements of modernisation of non-European empires, economies and societies.

Antonia Finnane in her 'Fashions in late imperial China' questions if it is appropriate to look for the existence of fashion in Ming and Qing China, when the very definition of fashion is European at heart. She concludes that 'fashion is distinguishable from a fashion industry, which is a modern phenomenon'. While contemporary fashion is dominated by complex economic and productive interests, fashion in late imperial China belonged to the urban culture of thriving cities such as Suzhou and Guangzhou, but was not supported by a large-scale industrial apparatus. These types of questions have been recently raised by scholars in the field of global history and Finnane's conclusions – in her case backed by substantial and precise research – could be extended to other empires and states in Asia as well as the Americas (Belfanti 2008). Foreigners, in particular Europeans, saw no evidence attesting to the existence of fashion in China. Yet a 'culture of fashion' pervaded urban areas: 'nowadays', commented a contemporary, 'the very servant girls dress in silk gauze'. But this, Finnane warns us, was no simple extravagance. It was part of a process of urban life in which the power of different regional 'styles' (in a way not dissimilar to Paris or London fashions) increasingly guided the consumer choices of maids as well as mistresses. The fashion system of late imperial China was not a closed one. Finnane shows its versatility in absorbing foreign influences from as far away as Korea and Mongolia, and in its frequent references to antiquity, something that has been more widely studied by art historian Craig Clunas (Clunas 1991). Thus it looked temporally in several directions, complicating once again the relationship of fashion to time.

The following two essays by Emma Tarlo and Ken'ichiro Hirano consider instead the relationship between 'East' and 'West' in clothing and fashion. Today, Western European clothing is the everyday attire of people living in all continents. Historians of fashion, but also historians interested in the dynamics of global economic, social and cultural power, have considered such a phenomenon as a 'sartorial convergence' actively shaped by Europe and the United States (Zelinsky 2004). Starting with Russia in the early eighteenth century, as Christine Ruane tells us in her short text, the adoption of Western clothes has been seen as the embodiment of 'modernity' and associated with perceived forward-looking, and socially and economically progressive, attitudes of the West. This is the case – among the many – of Meiji Japan, Latin America (as considered by Rebecca Earle) and the Ottoman Empire (examined by Suraiya Faroqhi). Western dress was seen as a dynamic force of change and was favoured over the concept of national costume.

Emma Tarlo considers the problems faced by Indians in their relationship with European clothing. Since clothing had been an important way to express social and religious affiliations, few people in India were prepared to abandon their 'traditional' attire. The majority of the rural population and almost all women continued to dress in predominantly Indian styles throughout the period of British rule. Yet, for the small but significant minority of British-educated Indian men, European dress was an essential component of the notion of 'civilisation' that could not be ignored. The donning of European clothes by Indians was controversial as it fast became a political act of alignment with the ruling British power and by the twentieth century – following Gandhi's *kadhi* campaign asking Indians to wear homespun cotton cloth – a plain act of treason. Tarlo discusses also the difficult position of Europeans in negotiating differences between their attire and that of Indians. Some Britons appreciated differences in dress without assuming the superiority of European styles. Others actively sought to revive Indian dress in an attempt to protect a threatened culture and aesthetic. This mixed position left space for a more straighforward proclamation of European superiority in the nineteenth and twentieth centuries when those Europeans who did not uphold strict divisions between European and non-European dress were labelled as 'white baboos'.

The idea of 'appropriateness' and 'modernity' of Western dress is further explored in a essay by Ken'ichiro Hirano on 'The Westernisation of clothes and the state in Meiji Japan'. Hirano's essay starts with a position diametrically opposite to that expressed by British colonists in India. According to Korean philosophers, those who wore proper East Asian clothes were human beings, but those who wore Western garments were beasts. Yet this position was in the nineteenth century discarded by most Asian nations and empires in the conviction that the 'modernity of the West' could only be achieved by adopting its 'modern clothing'. Some contemporaries went so far as to suggest that the Westernisation of clothes *was* modernisation. Hirano takes us to one of the best-known examples of Westernisation of attire: that of Meiji Japan. In August 1871 the Meiji Emperor issued a mandate ordering all high officials to wear Western clothes. The following year the Meiji Emperor himself appeared for the first time in public in a Western uniform. Hirano's essay raises three issues: firstly, it asks what models Japanese officials could use. The uniform was seen as the best way to implement such reform. Once used as a way to be distinguished and stand out, the European uniform was applied throughout the entire civil system to ensure standardisation across levels and classes that no local dress could offer. Secondly, Hirano questions the degree of diffusion of such a reform across society. Only in the late 1880s did frock-coats start being used by local officials, and become the norm for the Japanese civil servant. It took even longer for civilian forms of European dress to become popular: schoolboys started wearing European uniforms in the mid-1880s, producing a new generation of Western-dressed Japanese at the turn of the century. Finally Hirano's essay reflects on the role of gender in this sartorial transformation. The Empress of Japan continued to appear alongside her Western-dressed husband in full Japanese dress. Only after a long delay and some calculated risks, the Empress too was forced to embrace Western dress, bestowing pieces of cloth on the wives of local officials of high rank beforehand, so that they, too, could wear Western clothes to greet her. Yet, gender remained a key factor in the preservation of local dress: while Europe praised itself in feminising fashion, European fashionable attire was the preserve of men in many empires and countries around the world.

In the essay 'Western modes and Asian clothing', Verity Wilson uses a comparative methodology in order to demonstrate the cultural meanings of the borrowing of 'other people's dress' both in Europe and Asia. While some Westerners in Asia were ambivalent about wearing local dress, conversely some Asian visitors to Europe and America went to great lengths to ensure their Western garb struck the appropriate note. Wilson investigates this semantic ambivalence for the cases of Japan, China, England and the United States in the late nineteenth and twentieth centuries, by drawing on examples that range from Prince Arthur, Queen Victoria's son, to the celebrated early twentieth-century English musician Violet Gordon

Woodhouse. Wilson suggests that we should not over-politicise our reading of transcultural sartorial choices. There is an aesthetic element in the choice (and by converse, also a refusal) of 'someone else's' attire that cannot be explained simply by invoking politics, modernisation or nationalist causes. She observes with reference to the 1930s' wearing of exotic garments: 'Clothes from elsewhere had the power to hold back the banality of everyday life; the "other" in this case was not necessarily a geographical colonised domain, rather a landscape of leisure and sensation'. In other examples, the wearing of attire belonging to another culture might be a necessity. This is the case, Wilson observes, with missionaries and explorers, from Matteo Ricci visiting China in the late sixteenth century onwards, who embraced local costume for the mimetic need to 'blend in'.

The participatory need of fashion is further explored in a short and deft text by Margaret Maynard on the matter of respectability and fashion in colonial Australia. Maynard argues that colonials had a keen sense of the necessity for fashion but that 'distance' allowed welcome relaxation of standards, especially for women in a new and hot climate in which even neighbours might live far away. Alice Taylor provides an acute analysis of how the materiality of fashion articulated complex discourses over slavery and abolitionism in early nineteenth-century Britain. That certain women's fashion accessories were a type of slogan in the anti-slavery campaigns will come as a surprise to those who think that fashion is necessarily morally bankrupt. This part concludes with some present-day reflections on problems and issues raised historically. Karen Tranberg Hansen shows the methodologies used in her research on African fashion and in particular the still powerful role of the West to dictate the 'rules' of fashion through concepts such as 'the catwalk' or the importance of imported garments from Europe and North America into the African market. Annika Rabo reveals instead the conceptual disharmony between post-9/11 notions of Islam and the creation of 'Islamic fashion' for the sophisticated cosmopolitan consumer. Finally, Hazel Clark brings us back to issues raised by Verity Wilson's analysis by considering through the case of Hong Kong the meanings of orientalism today. In a careful reading of the contemporary advertising of Shanghai Tan, Clark reveals the complex and politically charged issues that come to play when considering extra-European fashion. Eroticism, exoticism, gender ambiguity, nostalgia and the selling back to Asia of such imagery both reinforce and challenge the 'demands and desires of twenty-first-century lifestyle'.

Bibliography and further reading

Books and articles

Adshead, S. A. M. (1997) *Material Culture in Europe and China, 1400–1800: The Rise of Consumerism*, New York: Palgrave Macmillan.

Allerton, C. (2007) 'The Secret Life of Sarongs: Manggarai Textiles as Super-skins', *Journal of Material Culture*, 12, 1, pp. 22–46.

Allman, Jean (ed.) (2004) *Fashioning Africa: Power and the Politics of Dress*, Bloomington, IN: Indiana University Press.

Anderson, C. (2001) 'Fashioning Identities: Convict Dress in Colonial South and Southeast Asia', *History Workshop Journal*, 52, pp. 153–73.

Appadurai, A. (ed.) (1986) *The Social Life of Things: Commodities in Cultural Perspective*, Cambridge: Cambridge University Press.

Barnes, R., and Eicher, J. B. (eds) (1992) *Dress and Gender: Making and Meaning in Cultural Contexts*, Oxford: Berg.

Bean, S. S. (1989) 'Gandhi and Khadi, the Fabric of Indian Independence', in A. B. Weiner and J. Schneider (eds), *Cloth and Human Experience*, Washington and London: Smithsonian Institutions, pp. 355–76.

Belfanti, C. M. (2008) 'Was Fashion a European Invention?', *Journal of Global History*, 3, 3, pp. 419–43.

Bogatyrěv, Petr (1971) *The Functions of Folk Costume in Moravian Slovakia*, Paris and The Hague: Mouton. First published as Volume I of *Publications of the Ethnographic Section of Matica Slovenska*, 1937; trans. from Slovak by Richard G. Crum.

Brook, T. (1999) *The Confusions of Pleasure: Commerce and Culture in Ming China*, Berkeley: University of California Press, esp. pp. 218–38.

Buckridge, S. O. (2004) *The Language of Dress: Resistance and Accommodation in Jamaica, 1760–1890*, Jamaica: University of the West Indies Press.

Cheang, S. (2006) 'Women, Pets and Imperialism: The British Pekingese Dog and Nostalgia for "Old China"'*Journal of British Studies*, 45, 2, pp. 359–87.

Clunas, C. (1991) *Superfluous Things: Material Culture and Social Status in Early Modern China*, Hawaii: University of Hawaii Press, esp. ch. 6.

Clunas, C. (1999) 'Modernity Global and Local: Consumption and the Rise of the West', *American Historical Review*, 104, 5, pp. 1497–1511.

Colchester, C. (ed.) (2003) *Clothing the Pacific*, Oxford and New York: Berg.

Comaroff, J. (1996) 'The Empire's Old Clothes: Fashioning the Colonial Subject', in D. Hawes (ed.), *Cross-Cultural Consumption: Global Markets, Local Realities*, London: Routledge, pp. 19–38.

Crihfield Dalby, L. (1993) *Kimono: Fashioning Culture*, New Haven and London: Yale University Press, 1993.

Dauncey, S. (2003) 'Illusions of Grandeur: Perceptions of Status and Wealth in Late-Ming Female Clothing and Ornamentation', *East Asian History*, 25–6, pp. 43–68.

Earle, R. (2001) '"Two Pairs of Pink Satin Shoes!!" Race, Clothing and Identity in the Americas (17th–19th Centuries)', *History Workshop Journal*, 52, pp. 175–95.

Earle, R. (2003) 'Luxury, Clothing and Race in Colonial Spanish America', in M. Berg and E. Eger (eds), *Luxury in the Eighteenth Century: Debates, Desires and Delectable Goods*, Basingstoke: Palgrave Macmillan, pp. 219–27.

Faroqhi, S., and Neumann, C. K. (eds) (2004) *Ottoman Costumes: From Textile to Identity*, Istanbul: Eren.

Finnane, A. (1996) 'What Should Chinese Women Wear? A National Problem', *Modern China*, 22, 2, pp. 99–131.

Finnane, A. (2003) 'Yangshou's "Modernity": Fashion and Consumption in the Early Nineteenth Century', *Positions*, 11, 2, pp. 395–425.

Finnane, A. (2005) 'Looking for the Jiang Qing Dress: Some Preliminary Findings', *Fashion Theory*, 9, 1, pp. 3–22.

Finnane, A. (2007) *Changing Clothes in China: Fashion, History, Nation*, New York: Columbia University Press.

Foster, H. B. (1997) *"New Raiments of Self": African American Clothing in the Antebellum South*, Oxford and New York: Berg.

Guy, J. (1998) *Woven Cargo: Indian Textiles in the East*, London: V & A Publications.

Hau-Nung Chan, A. (2000) 'Fashioning Change: Nationalism, Colonialism, and Modernity in Hong Kong', *Postcolonial Studies*, 3, 3, pp. 293–309.

Hendrickson, H. (ed.) (1996) *Clothing and Difference: Embodied Identities in Colonial and Postcolonial Africa*, Durham, NC: Duke University Press.

Jirousek, C. (2000) 'The Transition to Mass Fashion System Dress in the Later Ottoman Empire', in D. Quataert (ed.), *Consumption Studies and the History of the Ottoman Empire, 1550–1922: An Introduction*, New York: CUNY Press, pp. 201–41.

Johnston Laing, E. (2003) 'Visual Evidence for the Evolution of "Politically Correct" Dress for Women in Early Twentieth Century Shanghai', *Nan Nu: Men, Women and Gender in Early Imperial China*, 5, 1, pp. 69–114.

Ko, D. (1997) 'Bondage in Time: Footbinding and Fashion Theory', *Fashion Theory*, 1, 1, pp. 3–27.

Ko, D. (2007) *Cinderella's Sisters: A Revisionist History of Footbinding*, Berkeley: University of California Press.

Kriger, C. E. (2006) *Cloth in West African History*, Lanham, MD: AltaMira Press.

Küchler, S., and Miller, D. (eds) (2005) *Clothing as Material Culture*, Oxford: Berg.

Lynch, A. (1999) *Dress, Gender and Cultural Change: Asian American and African American Rites of Passage*, Oxford and New York: Berg.

Lynn, H. G. (2005) 'Fashioning Modernity: Changing Meanings of Clothing in Colonial Korea', *Journal of International and Area Studies*, 11, 3, pp. 75–93.

Mai Chen, T. (2001) 'Dressing for the Party: Clothing, Citizenship, and Gender Formation in Mao's China', *Fashion Theory*, 5, 2, pp. 143–72.

Martin, P. (1994) 'Contesting Clothes in Colonial Brazzaville', *Journal of African History*, 35, 3, pp. 401–26.

Maskiell, M. (2002) 'Consuming Kashmir: Shawls and Empires, 1500–2000', *Journal of World History*, 13, 1, pp. 27–65.

Maynard, M. (1990) 'Civilian Clothing and Fabric Supplies: The Development of Fashionable Dressing in Sydney, 1790–1830', *Textile History*, 21, 1, pp. 87–100.

Maynard, M. (1994) *Fashioned from Penury: Dress as Cultural Practice in Colonial Australia*, Cambridge: Cambridge University Press.

Meléndez, M. (2006) 'Visualizing Difference: The Rhetoric of Clothing in Colonial Spanish America', in R. A. Root (ed.), *The Latin American Fashion Reader*, Oxford: Berg, pp. 17–30.

Noma, S. (1974) *Japanese Costume and Textile Arts*, trans. Armins Nikovskis, New York: Weatherill.

Perani, J., and Wolff, N. H. (1999) *Cloth, Dress and Art Patronage in Africa*, Oxford and New York: Berg.

Prestholdt, J. (2004) 'On the Global Repercussions of East African Consumerism', *American Historical Review*, 109, 3, pp. 755–81.

Quataert, D. (1997) 'Clothing Laws, State, and Society in the Ottoman Empire, 1720–1829', *International Journal of Middle East Studies*, 29, pp. 403–25.

Rabine, L. W. (2002) *The Global Circulation of African Fashion*, Oxford: Berg.

Root, R. A. (2002) 'Tailoring the Nation: Fashion Writing in Nineteenth-century Argentina', in W. Parkins (ed.), *Fashioning the Body Politic: Dress, Gender, Citizenship*, Oxford: Berg, pp. 71–96.

Root, R. A. (2006) *The Latin American Fashion Reader*, Oxford: Berg.

Ross, R. (2008) *Clothing: A Global History: Or, The Imperialists' New Clothes*, Cambridge: Polity.

Ruane, C. (1995) 'Clothes Shopping in Imperial Russia', *Journal of Social History*, 28, 4, pp. 765–82.

Ruane, C. (1996) 'Clothes Make the Comrade: A History of the Russian Fashion Industry', *Russian History*, 23, 1–4, pp. 311–43.

Ruane, C. (2002) 'Subjects into Citizens: The Politics of Clothing in Imperial Russia', in W. Parkins (ed.), *Fashioning the Body Politic: Dress, Gender, Citizenship*, Oxford: Berg, pp. 49–70.

Sekatcheva, O. (2004) 'The Formation of Russian Women's Costume at the Time before the Reforms of Peter the Great', in C. Richardson (ed.), *Clothing Culture, 1350–1650*, Aldershot: Ashgate, pp. 77–91.

Sharma, S., and Sharma, A. (2003) 'White Paranoia: Orientalism in the Age of Empire', *Fashion Theory*, 7, 3–4, pp. 301–18.

Shively, D. H. (1964–5) 'Regulation and Status in Early Tokugawa Japan', *Harvard Journal of Asiatic Studies*, 25, pp. 123–64.

Shrimpton, J. (1992) 'Dressing for a Tropical Climate: The Role of Native Fabrics in Fashionable Dress in Early Colonial India', *Textile History*, 23, 1, pp. 55–70.

Simmel, G. (1904) 'Fashion', *International Quarterly*, 10, pp. 130–55.

Slade, T. (2010) *Japanese Fashion: A Cultural History*, Oxford and New York: Berg.

Tarlo, E. (1996) *Clothing Matters: Dress and Identity in India*, London: Hurst.

Tarlo, E. (2007) 'The Hijab in London: Metamorphosis, Resonance and Effects', *Journal of Material Culture*, 12, 2, pp. 131–56.

Tranberg Hansen, K. (2000) 'Other People's Clothes? The International Second-hand Clothing Trade and Dress Practices in Zambia', *Fashion Theory*, 4, 3, pp. 245–74.

Tranberg Hansen, K. (2003) 'Fashioning: Zambian Moments', *Journal of Material Culture*, 8, 3, pp. 301–9.

Turnau, I. (1991) 'The Main Centres of National Fashion in Eastern Europe from the Sixteenth to the Eighteenth Centuries', *Textile History*, 22, 1, pp. 47–66.

Welters, L. (ed.) (1999) *Folk Dress in Europe and Anatolia: Beliefs about Protection and Fertility*, Oxford and New York: Berg.

Wilson, B. (2007) 'Foggie diverse di vestire de' turchi: Turkish Costume Illustration and Cultural Translation', *Journal of Medieval and Early Modern Studies*, 37, 1, pp. 97–139.

Wilson, V. (1999) 'Studio and Soirée: Chinese Textiles in Europe and America, 1850 to the Present', in R. B. Phillips and C. B. Steiner (eds), *Unpacking Culture: Art and Commodity in Colonial and Postcolonial Worlds*, Berkeley: University of California Press, pp. 229–42.

Zelinsky, W. (2004) 'Globalization Reconsidered: The Historical Geography of Modern Western Male Attire', *Journal of Cultural Geography*, 22, 1, pp. 83–134.

Zilfi, M. C. (2004) 'Whose Laws? Gendering the Ottoman Sumptuary Laws', in S. Faroqhi and C. K. Neumann (eds), *Ottoman Costumes: From Textile to Identity*, Istanbul: Eren, pp. 125–42.

Printed resources

National Geographic contains anthropological images of great importance for non-European dress and fashion.

Online resources

Clothing the Pacific project, University College London: www.ucl.ac.uk/clothing-pacific/

Commodities of Empire project, Open University, UK: www.open.ac.uk/Arts/ferguson-centre/commodities-of-empire/index.html

Global Economic History Network cotton project, London School of Economics: www.lse.ac.uk/collections/economicHistory/GEHN/GEHNCottonResearchProjectNEW.htm

Great Lakes Research Alliance for the Study of Aboriginal Arts and Cultures: icslac.carleton.ca/grasac/

Chapter 16

Fashions in late imperial China

Antonia Finnane

W HAT DOES IT MEAN TO SPEAK OF FASHION in a Chinese historical context? Fashion, surely, can be identified in many periods of history, and in many places. It is related to taste, consumption and urbanisation. It entails short-term vicissitudes in vestimentary choices, and indicates the presence in particular societies of dynamic relationships between producers and consumers. In other words, fashion is distinguishable from a fashion industry, which is a modern phenomenon grounded in the industrial revolution. China did not have a fashion industry before the twentieth century, but it did have a lively trade in textiles – interregional and international – that was accompanied by an attention in Chinese cities to what was *à la mode*. Greater exposure to Chinese domestic life and closer familiarity with non-canonical Chinese texts would have alerted Western observers to this fact.

Fashion in China is historically associated most closely with Shanghai, which became the major centre of foreign investment and residence in the late nineteenth century. In the first half of the twentieth century, Shanghai was a voracious centre of consumption of everything from opium to clothes,[1] but before the Opium War in the nineteenth century, and the creation of the Treaty Port system which allowed foreign settlement in Shanghai among other places, it was a relatively modest place. Suzho, Hangzhou, Yangzhou and the Ming dynasty's 'Southern Capital', Nanjing, well exceeded it in economic and cultural productivity, and also in historical importance as sites of social and cultural change [. . .].[2]

Clothing is among the indices to the dynamism of these centres of southern culture. In the early seventeenth century, Gu Qiyuan (1565–1628) wrote of women's fashions in Nanjing that 'thirty years before, they changed only once in ten years', while now 'not three or four years' passed before some new style was apparent.[3] Suzhou at this time was performing something of the role played in Europe by Paris, setting the tone for new and extravagant styles of clothing.[4] In Hangzhou, one Xu Dunqin recalled around 1614 that half a century earlier his school friends all 'wore hats of [black] gauze and clothes of white cotton. Among them, only one or two well-born youths wore coloured clothing. Now everyone wears coloured clothing and white cloth is nowhere to be seen'.[5]

As for Yangzhou:

> The women [here] have nothing to do but sit around making up their faces, competing with each other in artful adornment. Their hair ornaments are of worked gold and jade, with pearls and kingfisher feathers added here and there. Their bedding is finely embroidered, their underclothing bright and gay. They are extravagant to the last degree.[6]

Extravagance and fashions are not the same thing. It is the commentary on change as expressed through consumption, not on expenditure per se, that permits us to talk about fashions in this period. This commentary is quite explicit. The clothing made and worn in Tongzhou (in Yangzhou prefecture) included 'long skirts, generous collars, wide belts [and] fine linings'. These garments were all subject to 'rapid changes, known as "contemporary styles" (shiyang). This is what is called outrageous dress (fuyao)'.[7] In the late Ming, there was much talk of 'outrageous dress'. The chatter accompanied a proliferation of disturbing new fashions in the prosperous cities of the lower Yangzi valley.[8]

Signs and symptoms of Ming fashions

When Zhu Yuanzhang (1328–98) established the Ming dynasty in the late fourteenth century, he was determined to rid the empire of the barbarian ways of Yuan era, including barbarian clothes. This meant abandoning the closefitting tunics favoured by the Mongols and a return, ideally, to the styles of the Tang dynasty.[9] Garments retrieved from tombs show that this restoration project was at least partially realised, but also provide evidence of the sustained influence of the far north on Chinese clothing.[10] To eradicate all traces of Yuan culture was of course impossible, especially given the continued residence in China of descendants of the original Mongol invaders and to this heritage were added new currents of influence arising from trade and other movements between China and neighbouring lands.

Wu Jen-shu points to three different manifestations of fashion in the Ming. One was fascination with the exotic: horse-hair skirts (maweiqun) from Korea, and a military-style tunic (kuzhe) apparently inspired by nomad warriors from the north. Both these (male) fashions developed first in the capital, perhaps due to the tribute trade missions that regularly made their way to Beijing, paying obeisance to the Son of Heaven before making their way to the markets. Weaving horse-hair was a rare skill in China when the Korean horse-hair garments first appeared, but by the late fifteenth century local weavers had mastered the art and were stealing the tails of horses owned by metropolitan officials to supply themselves with the materials necessary for the manufacture of the cloth.[11]

As for the military-style tunic, this evolved into the very commonly worn *yesa*, a garment with gathered or pleated skirt that became popular among well-to-do men in the sixteenth century. Wang Shizhen (1526–90) interestingly documents the *yesa*'s rise in social status. In the course of the sixteenth century it gradually displaced two other styles of tunic to the point that 'when grandees are attending a banquet, they must needs wear the *yesa*'. In his view, this was a case of military dress triumphing over refined clothing, and probably of barbarian triumphing over Chinese.[12] The *yesa* appears to have shared some formal features with the Qing dynasty court robe [. . .]. This suggests that the flared or gathered skirt – whether or not integrated with an upper garment – was a common look in male clothing across the far north, and had different points of entry into China.[13]

In a wide-ranging study of social life in Ming China, Chen Baoliang has documented further evidence of 'barbarian' influence on clothing, especially with reference to the persistence of Yuan terminology and styles. In the north, men wore a Mongol style of hat that they called 'barbarian hat' (*humao*), while a sort of hooded cloak worn by women was also of Mongol origin. The *bigia*, or long vest, was of Mongol origin, and so was the *zhisun*, a single colour garment which in the Ming was worn as regular dress by military officials. The words, no doubt like the garments, were Chinese approximations of the Mongol terms. Chen notes the lasting use of some Mongol words for clothing in places even as far from the north as Hainan Island.[14]

A second manifestation of Ming fashion lay in a return to the styles of antiquity – a retro trend quite separate from the sanctioned restorationism of the late fourteenth century. In the words of Gu Qiyuan, 'costume in the Southern Capital before the Jiajing and Wanli reigns [i.e. before 1522] was rather simple. Officials wore the biretta, scholars the square hat, and that was all. In recent years everyday there is a difference, every month something new. So what gentlemen wear now goes by all sorts of names: the Han cap, the Jin cap, the Tang cap . . .' and so on.[15] This observation incidentally points to the importance of the hat in the male wardrobe in China (Figure 16.1): it was an important signifier of social status, as well as, apparently, a convenient site of fashion experiment. But not only hats were involved in this retro movement: Tang-style satins and Song-style brocades were all the rage, accompanying a revival in the popularity of the fourth-century calligrapher Wang Xizhi (c. 302–c. 368) and the Yuan dynasty painter Zhao Mengfu (1254–1322): 'at present, a partiality for antiquity prevails throughout the empire'.[16]

The third manifestation lay in obvious novelty. Wu Jen-shu explains this in terms of retro fatigue: the recourse to antiquity ran its course and invention replaced renaissance. An example he offers is the Chunyang hat (named after a Daoist immortal): this combined Han and Tang styles but was also a departure from both. The Chunyang hat was emblematic of the 'new and strange' (*xinqi*) clothing that so frequently receives mention in late Ming texts. In the second quarter of the seventeenth century it was said to be extremely popular among youth, all of whom looked with contempt upon the ancient styles.[17]

These 'new and strange' styles flourished in a period otherwise known for the phenomenon of social climbing.[18] The tendency to social emulation, famously identified by both Thorstein Veblen and Georg Simmel as a driving force behind fashion,[19] was a significant factor in the vestimentary environment of the late Ming. Sumptuary regulations restricting the use of certain fabrics and types of adornment to people of certain

Figure 16.1 Two common hat styles of the Ming dynasty. *Left*, Xu Guangqi (1562–1633) in an anonymous portrait wearing the *wusha* (black gauze) hat that in historical dramas is often used to represent a Ming figure; *right*, Gu Mengyou (1599–1660) portrayed by Zeng Jing (1568–1650) (detail), wearing a *piaopiao* (fluttering) hat, with flaps before and behind, of the sort frequently portrayed in Ming illustrations.

status were flouted with impunity by commoner or merchant families that had profited from the commercialisation of the economy in the sixteenth and seventeenth centuries.[20] Nor were these solid citizens alone in breaching former dress codes. 'Nowadays', complained one writer, 'the very servant girls dress in silk gauze, and the singsong girls look down on brocaded silks and embroidered gowns'.[21]

It is difficult to squeeze all fashions into the social emulation category without qualification. When Chinese were taking their fashions from 'barbarians', clearly more than social status was at issue. The same can be said of respectable women looking to the demi-monde for inspiration. According to Yu Huai (1616–96): 'The clothes and adornment associated with southern entertainment were taken as the model everywhere . . . The length of gowns and the size of sleeves changed with the times. Witnesses referred to this as *à la mode* (*shishizhuang*)'.[22] To put Yu Huai's statement simply, the courtesans of the south established (women's) fashions for the empire. This may even have been through street fashion, for in the early seventeenth century prostitutes were on the streets in increasing numbers. 'In the big cities they run to the tens of thousands', wrote Xie Zhaozhe (1567–1624), 'but they can be found in every poor district and remote place as well, leaning by doorways all day long, bestowing their smiles, selling sex for living . . .'[23]

Considered in tandem, 'barbarian' styles and courtesan styles seem to indicate marked gender differentiation in sources of influence on Ming fashions. They broadly accord with the established dichotomies of north/south and outside/inside (*wai, nei*), and their influence was manifested, generally speaking, along gender lines. But they probably owed much of their appeal to the same factor: a certain ambiguity associated with the appropriation of exotic, exogenous, or in general 'outside' practices that gave the ensuing fashions a provocative charm. This ambiguity is well illustrated in an episode in the sixteenth-century erotic novel *Jin Ping Mei* [Plum in a golden vase] when Ximen Qing comments admiringly of his fetchingly dressed third and fifth consorts that they look like a pair of sing-song girls.[24] He gets snapped at for his pains, but that is not because his concubines do not want to look like courtesans. On the contrary, they closely scrutinise the clothes and adornment of the sing-song girls who visit their household, and with whom they must compete for the favours of their lord and master.[25]

Changing styles of women's dress

Prostitutes, whether high-class courtesans or common street girls, very probably served as the models for the painters whose depictions of women have left us with a visual impression of various sorts of clothing worn by women in the Ming and Qing dynasties. These paintings, in combination with book illustrations, artefacts from tombs, and textual references, point to a number of major stylistic variations in late Ming women's dress: the classic short jacket (*ru*) worn with skirt and short overskirt (*yaoqun*); the skirt worn with long jacket (*ao*); the open-sided gown or long vest (*bijia*); the long over-jacket (*pifeng*), and the 'paddy-field' or patchwork gown (*shuitianyi*).[26] Of these the paddy-field gown is overtly the most eccentric and would appear to fit into the category of 'outrageous dress' excoriated by commentators. Constructed of small, varicoloured squares of cloth, it may have been inspired by Buddhist robes, since Buddhist monks liked to make use of small off-cuts of fabric, discarded or donated, in accordance with the Buddha's own preference.[27] As a fashionable garment, a paddy-field gown would surely have been regarded as irreverent.

Historically, the most interesting development in Ming women's dress is the increasing prevalence of long upper garments at the expense of the high-waisted style of the *ru* or short jacket worn with skirt. This amounted to a major change in the architecture of Chinese women's dress, and presaged the long reign of the *ao* or long jacket during the Qing. The short jacket and skirt (*ruqun*) is the most commonly depicted women's fashion in figure paintings of the Ming and continued to be portrayed by artists right up until the nineteenth century, although late depictions are almost certainly based on earlier paintings or drawings rather than on life (Figure 16.2).[28] The ensemble has a passing resemblance to the *hanbok* or *kimono*, in sharp contrast to the *aoqun* (long jacket and skirt), which is the most familiar women's ensemble from the Qing.[29]

A prominent feature of women's dress in the late Ming was the over-gown (*pifeng, pi'ao*), which had virtually disappeared from China by the nineteenth century but appears to have been widely worn as everyday dress in the sixteenth and seventeenth centuries.[30] Chen Bao-liang traces the *pifeng* back to the late Tang, but as her own illustrations make clear, the generic garment underwent major shifts in style. An early

depiction of the garment in its most frequently represented style is to be found in a painting by Tang Yin (1470–1524).[31] A native of Suzhou, and commercially one of the most successful artists of hiss time, Tang Yin executed numerous paintings that portrayed beautiful Suzhou women dressed in fashionable clothing.[32] *The Palace Ladies of Meng of Shu*, perhaps his most famous work, purports to be of courtesans in the court of the Meng Chang (919–65), in Sichuan, during the interdynastic wars of the tenth century (Figure 16.3). In the colophon, the painter refers to the 'Daoist garb' allegedly worn by the women at Meng's behest. This might explain why they are portrayed wearing over-gowns rather than the short jacket and skirt common in other paintings of 'beauties' in the Ming, including by Tang Yin.

It was no doubt changes in the dimensions of the *pifeng* that occasioned some of the carping about women's clothing in the late Ming. Hems were descending and sleeves growing larger in the sixteenth century. With sleeves trailing well below the finger tips and descending hems threatening to cover skirts completely, the *pifeng* came perilously close to looking like a man's tunic (Figure 16.4). Hence the anxieties expressed by the distinguished official Huo Tao, who as Minister of Rites in Nanjing attempted in 1537 to reverse the trend:

> Men's and women's styles differ in length. A woman's upper garment is level with her waist, her lower garments: heaven embraces earth. When a woman's [upper] garment covers her lower garments, there is confusion between male and female.[33]

Portraits and other representational works of the early Qing suggest that the *pifeng* and *ruqun* were styles that lasted into the early eighteenth century (Figure 16.5),[34] while the photographic record shows that they were not evident in the nineteenth. This prompts questions about the common supposition that under the Manchus, Han Chinese women clung to the fashions of their predecessors. Clearly, the long, figure-concealing *pifeng* had much in common not only with the man's gown but also with the Manchu women's gown. Perhaps this helped dislodge the short jacket in favour of a longer one – the *ao* – which finally rendered the *pifeng* redundant. In any event, a garment which is rarely discussed and of which there are few surviving examples apparently had a critical role to play in the costume drama of Ming and Qing China. Its disappearance from the Han wardrobe and effective replacement by the *ao* contributed to the emergence of the distinctively Qing look in Han women's dress.

Figure 16.2 The short-waisted style common in Ming paintings of women is here portrayed by Ren Xiong (1798–1856), in a work not too different to one painted by Chen Hongshou (1598–1652) two centuries earlier. This charmingly stylised depiction shows a skirt (*changqun*), and over-skirt (*yaoqun* or *weishang*) with sash, and a cape or shawl (*pijian*) worn over short upper garment with long, close-fitting sleeves (*duanru* or *yaoru*). Ren Xiong *Yaqonq quishan tu* [Jade palace, autumn fan], nineteenth century.

Figure 16.3 The long coat depicted here is probably a garment referred to in Ming texts as the *pifeng*, also known as the *beizi*, which in the late Ming appears with great frequency in graphic representations of women. The outer garment in each case is of plain cloth, the skirt is printed. The women's faces are powdered to accent the brow, the nose, and the chin. Tang Yin (1470–1524), *Meng shu gongji tu* [Palace ladies of Meng of Shu].

Figure 16.4 A ball game in the grounds of a sixteenth-century bawdy house, as illustrated in an early edition of the novel *Jin Ping Mei* [Plum in a golden vase]. The men are members of a ball club, entertaining themselves and the onlookers by playing kickball with one of the ladies of the house, Cassia. She is described in the text as wearing a crimson skirt under a white silk front-fastening jacket (*ao*) coat, with her hair done in 'the Hangzhou style'. The illustration shows her wearing a full-length front-fastening over-garment with overlong sleeves, the latter a common feature in illustrations and paintings of women's dress in this period.

Figure 16.5 Both the *ruqun* (short jacket and long skirt) and *pifeng* (over-garment or coat) make an appearance in this early Qing painting. The artist was an astronomer and court painter in the Kangxi era (1661–1722). *Jiao Bingzhen Shinü tu* [Pictures of ladies], album leaf.

Qing fashions: the example of Yangzhou

The Qing dynasty is imagined as a much less exciting, less inventive period than the late Ming, except perhaps in terms of empire-building, and overall less is known about its material culture even though so many more material remains from that time are preserved in museums around the world. Not surprisingly, it is viewed also as a regime under which fashion experienced a decline.[35]

Before too quickly dismissing this era as uninteresting for fashion history, it is worth looking at what people wore in those times. Evidence from Yangzhou, for example, suggests a steady consumption of fashion from the late sixteenth to the nineteenth centuries and beyond. The materials are not abundant, but what they have to say permits a more nuanced vestimentary history than one written simply in terms of the dragon robes which dominate museum holdings. Local fashion trends here hint at the richer history that might result from a more broadly based study of textiles and clothing production in the Qing.

Situated north of the Yangzi River well upstream from Shanghai, Yangzhou lay far from the coast and was out of immediate each of foreign trade, which made it something of a backwater in the early twentieth century. In earlier centuries, however, it had been a large and prosperous city with a lively leisure economy.[36] The salt merchants who dominated local society were among the wealthiest men in China, renowned for their gardens and patronage of theatre and painting, as well as for more vulgar sorts of consumption.[37] In some respects a peculiar place, Yangzhou was also a participant in broader movements of social change involving commerce, social mobility, and changing gender configurations in urban China in the sixteenth to nineteenth centuries.[38]

In the late Ming, Yangzhou began to challenge Suzhou's position as the premier centre of wealth and consumption in the lower Yangzi valley. Suzhou was much the larger city, with a much sturdier economy,[39] but the expansion of the salt merchant presence in Yangzhou during the sixteenth century resulted in an extraordinary concentration of liquid capital there, and a growth in luxury consumption that was favourable to fashion. 'Suzhou style' and 'Yangzhou style' (*Su shi*, *Yang shi*) emerged as parallel, notionally contrasting but probably mutually influential modes of dress.[40] The city was sacked and its residents massacred in 1645, but in the early decades of the Qing it regained and even improved on its name for the good life. The poet and dramatist Kong Shangren (1648–1718), resident in Yangzhou in the 1680s, complained about the 'accountants, clerks, slaves and servants' of wealthy households in the city, because they were inclined to 'dress up in flashy clothes, putting on airs in order to snub others'.[41] His contemporary Li Gan complained: 'In all the empire, it is only in the prefectural city and suburbs of Yangzhou that clothes have to follow the times'.[42] Li Dou, the great chronicler of eighteenth-century Yangzhou, had much the same to say: 'Clothes worn in Yangzhou are always in the newest style (*xin yang*)'.[43]

From a morphological point of view, stylistic changes over this century and a half might seem slight compared to those in contemporary Europe, but much is probably hidden from the eye. That Manchu women were influenced by Han fashions is well known. In 1839, during the imperial marriage draft, the emperor ordered punishments to be meted out to the fathers of girls who were wearing wide sleeves in emulation of Han fashion.[44] The impact of Manchu styles on Chinese dress is less well documented, but clearly extended beyond the expectation that literati wear the Manchu long gown. A good example of its influence is the popularisation of the so-called *pipa* cut for the front of a jacket or vest. The *pipa* vest is familiar in Chinese costume history as a common item of dress among Manchu women in the late Qing. Numerous photos and surviving garments attest to its popularity.[45] The origins of the style appear to lie in the Manchu informal riding coat, which for ease of mounting the horse was cut short on the front left side.[46] In eighteenth-century Yangzhou, this style was affected by the likely lads who hawked food around the time of the Qing Ming (Grave-sweeping) festival in spring. According to Li Dou, they vied with each other to make an impression in their *pipa* jackets of indigo or lilac.[47] Han women rarely wore the *pipa* vest, but they could deploy the *pipa* cut on their jackets, a style depicted in the late nineteenth century by Wu Youru (Figure 16.6).

To look only at the shape of a garment and not at the material from which it was constructed is to overlook an important aspect of clothing culture in China, and indeed more broadly in the early modern world. The sites of Chinese fashion in the late imperial era were not quite the same as in modern Europe: cut and fit were less significant than the quality and colour of the fabric. Li Dou itemised the different sorts of cloth

Figure 16.6 Left Young girl depicted by Wu Youru (d. 1893) in a *pipa*-cut jacket and pleated skirt in the fish-scale style. Her hair is cut with a fringe in the 'number one' style, so-named for forming a straight line across the forehead, like the character for *yi* (one). The little boy's hair is in the 'potty lid' (*mazi*) cut, one of a number of styles for small boys that involved shaving part of the head. *Right* A much shorter version of the *pipa*-cut jacket is worn by this well-dressed military mandarin, photographed by John Thomson in the nineteenth century.

that went in and out of fashion in Yangzhou: silks and satins in different colours rapidly succeeded each other in popularity.[48] Hairstyles were also subject to fashionable changes – much like hats for men. This meant a thriving market in false hairpieces and hair adornments. According to Li Dou, Yangzhou women dressed their hair differently from women in other places – the apricot style, the double swallow style, and so on, but the fashion here seems to have spread to other places.[49] Both textiles and hairstyles continued to be a focus of fashion interest in the early twentieth century.

Notes

1   See Leo Ou-fan Lee, *Shanghai Modern: The Flowering of a New Urban Culture in China, 1930–1945* (Cambridge, MA: Harvard University Press, 1999); Sherman Cochran, ed., *Investing Nanjing Road: Commercial Culture in Shanghai, 1900–1945* (Ithaca: East Asia Program, Cornell University, 1999).

2   The idea of 'Shanghai as fishing village' before the Opium War has been challenged by Linda Cooke Johnston in *Shanghai: From Market Town to Treaty Port 1074–1858* (Stanford: Stanford University Press, 1995), but Michael Marmé has shown that miscalculations of the city's engagement in trade led her to overestimate its historical significance by a wide margin. See Marmé, *Suzhou: Where the Goods of All the Provinces Converge* (Stanford: Stanford University Press, 2005), pp. 245, 323–4, n. 70.

3   Wu Renshu, 'Mingdai pingmin fushi de liuxing fengshang yu shidafu de fenying', p. 74.

4   Craig Clunas, 'The Art of Social Climbing in Sixteenth-century China', *The Burlington Magazine*, 1333 (1059) (June 1991), p. 370; Timothy Brooks, *The Confusions of Pleasure: Commerce and Culture in Ming China* (Berkeley: University of Calfornia Press, 1998), pp. 220–2.

5   Lin Liyue, 'Yishang yu fengjiao: wan Ming de fushi fengshang yu 'fuyao' yilun', p. 124.

6   Jiangdu xianzhi [Gazetteer of Jiangdu country], Wanli edition (1597), 7, pp. 28b–29a.

7   Lin Liyue, 'Yishang yu fengjiao: wan Ming de fushi fengshang yu 'fuyao' yilun', p. 124.

8   Ibid. See also Wu Renshu, 'Mingdai pingmin fushi de liuxing fengshang yu shidafu de fanying', pp. 96–100.

9   Zhou Shaoquan, 'Mingdai fushi tanlun' [An essay on Ming costume], *Shixue yuekan*, 6 (1990), p. 34.

10 Shelagh Vainker, *Chinese Silk: A Cultural History* (London: The British Museum Press, and New Brunswick: Rutgers University Press, 2004), p. 156.

11 Wu Renshu, 'Mingdai pingmin fushi de liuxing fengshang yu shidafu de fanying', pp. 66–7.

12 Wang Shizhen describes three different garments evolving from the *kuzbe*: one was the *yesa*; another was the 'tangerine robe' (*chengzi yi*), worn with a cord around the waist; and the third was the 'Daoist gown' (*Daopao*), worn without the cord. Ibid., p. 67. See also entry on *yesa* in Zhou Xun and Gao Chunming, eds, *Zhongguo yiguan fushi da sidian* [Dictionary of Chinese costume] (Shanghai: Shanghai cishu chubanshe, 1996), p. 205. On Wang Shizen, see Barbara Yoshida-Kraft, 'Wang Shih-chen', in *DMB*, vol. II, pp. 1399–405.

13 On the disputed origins of the court robe, see Wilson, *Chinese Dress*, p. 35; Vollmer, *Ruling from the Dragon Throne*, pp. 63–9.

14 Chen Baoliang, *Mingdai shebui shenghuo shi* [A history of social life in the Ming dynasty] (Beijing: Zhongguo shehui kexue chubanshe, 2004), pp. 206–7.

15 Wu Renshu, 'Mingdai pingmin fushi de liuxing fengshang yu shidafu de fanying', p. 68.

16 Ibid., p. 70.

17 Ibid., pp. 70–1.

18 Clunas, 'The Art of Social Climbing'.

19 Thorstein Veblen, *The Theory of the Leisure Class: An Economic Study of Institutions* (New York: B. W. Huebsch, 1912); Georg Simmel, 'The Philosophy of Fashion' [1904], *American Journal of Sociology*, 62, 6 (1957), pp. 541–58.

20 Clunas, 'The Art of Social Climbing', pp. 370–1. See also Sarah Dauncey, 'Illusions of Grandeur: Perceptions of Status and Wealth in the Late-Ming Female Clothing and Ornamentation', *East Asian History* 25–6 (December 2003), pp. 61–2.

21 Clunas, 'The Art of Social Climbing', p. 370.

22   Lin Liyue, 'Yishang yu fengjiao', p. 128.

23   Xie Zhaozhe, *Wuzazu* [Five miscellanies] (Taipei: Weiwen, 1977), p. 196. On Xie, see Leon Zolbrod and L. Carrington Goodrich, 'Hsieh Chao-che', *DMB*, vol. I, pp. 546–50.

24   Hsiao-hisiao-sheng, *The Golden Lotus: A Translation from the Original of Chin Ping Mei*, trans. Clement Egerton (New York: Paragon Books, 1959), vol. I, p. 145.

25   See further, Dauncey, 'Illusions of Grandeur', pp. 58–9.

26   Zhou Xun and Gao Chunming, *Zhongguo lidai fushi* [Chinese costume through history] (Shanghai: Xuclin chubanshe, 1994), pp. 244–54.

27   Wong Hwei Lian and Szan Tan, eds, *Powerdressing: Textiles for Rulers and Priests from the Chris Hall Collection*, ex. cat. (Singapore: Asian Civilisations Museums, 2006), p. 395. There seems to be no extant example of a paddy-field gown, but the Chris Hall collection does include several fine examples of patchwork.

28   Ren Xiong's depiction of a woman with fan (see Figure 16.2) echoes a painting by Chen Hongshou, *Dui jing shi nū* [Lady looking in a mirror], which shows a woman in identical dress and comparable pose. See Liu Rendao, ed., *Zhongguo chuanshi minghua quanji* [Collected figure paintings of the Chinese heritage] (Beijing: Zhongguo xiju chubanshe, 2001), vol. 2, p. 322.

29   The terminology for Ming dress, both in the original texts and in the secondary literature, is relatively unstable. Different regional terms were used for the same item of clothing, and different items of clothing were worn in different places, so that there is some variation between north and south, and also over time. The term *ru* can serve as a synonym for *shan* or *ao*, themselves interchangeable terms, and while it generally refers to a short garment, the term '*changru*' (long *ru*) also exists. Zhou and Gao describe this as the precursor to the *ao*. Zhou Xun and Gao Chunming, *Zhongguo yiguan fushi da cidian*, p. 221. The term *ru* is used in *ruqun* in Hua Mei, *Zhongguo fuzhuang shi* [History of Chinese dress] (Tianjin: Renmin meishu chubanshe, 1989), p. 73, but is not employed in Zhou Xibao, *Zhongguo gudai fushi shi*, pp. 413–14.

30   Meng Hui, 'Pifeng xiaoshi' [A little knowledge about the *pifeng*], in Meng Hui, *Pan Jinlian de faxing* [Pan Jinlian's hairdo] (Nanjing: Jiangsu renmin chubanshe, 2005), pp. 81–103. Meng Hui provides an example of a short *pi'ao*, but the majority of her references and illustrations are to long garments. It is possible that the term *pi'ao* does refer to the shorter version.

31   Li Chu-tsing, 'T'ang Yin', in *DMB*, vol. 1, pp. 1256–9.

32   Ibid. On Suzhou in the Ming, see Marmé, *Suzhou*.

33   Huo Tao, *Wei'ai wenji* [Wei'ai's collected prose], quoted in Lin Liyue, 'Yishang yu fengjiao', p. 137.

34   See Shen Yizheng, comp., *Lidai meirn huaxuan* [Selected paintings of beauties through the ages] (Taipei: Yishu tushu gongsi, 1999), pp. 102–39.

35   Kenneth Pomeranz, *The Great Divergence: China, Europe, and the Making of the Modern World Economy* (Princeton: Princeton University Press, 2000), p. 155.

36   The classic, oft-cited essay on this city is Ping-ti Ho, 'The Salt Merchants of Yang-chou: A Study of Commercial Capitalism in Eighteenth-Century China', *Harvard Journal of Asiatic Studies*, 17 (1954), pp. 130–64. Specialist studies of the city include Tobie Meyer-Fong, *Building Culture in Early Qing Yangzhou* (Stanford: Stanford University Press, 2003) and Antonia Finnane, *Speaking of Yangzhou: A Chinese City, 1550–1850* (Cambridge, MA: Harvard University Asia Center, 2004).

37   See Ho, 'The Salt Merchants of Yang-chou'. On opera in Yangzhou, see Colin P. Mackerras, *The Rise of Peking Opera: Social Aspects of the Theatre in Manchu China* (Oxford: Clarendon Press, 1972), chapter 3. On gardens, see Zhu Jiang, *Yangzhou Yuanlin Pinshang lu* [An appreciation of the gardens of Yangzhou] (Shanghai: Shanghai wenwu chubanshe, 1984); on art patronage, see Ginger Cheng-chi Hsü, *A Bushel of Pearls: Painting for Sale in Eighteenth-century Yangchow* (Stanford: Stanford University Press, 2001).

38 For a review of this historiographical shift, see Harriet Zurndorfer, 'From Local His-
    tory to Cultural History: Reflections on Some Recent Publications', *Toung Pao*, LXXXIII
    (1997), pp. 387–96.
39 See Marmé, *Suzhou*.
40 Wei Minghua, *Yangzhou shouma* [Thin horses of Yangzhou] (Fuzhou: Fujian renmin chuban-
    she, 1998), pp. 153 ff.
41 Richard Strassberg, *The World of Kung Shang-jen: A Ma of Letters in Early Ch'ing China* (New
    York: Columbia University Press, 1983), p. 144.
42 Jonathan S. Hay, *Shitao: Painting and Modernity in Early Qing China* (New York: Cambridge
    University Press, 2001), p. 12. Translation adapted.
43 Wei Minghua, *Yangzhou shouma*, p. 143.
44 See e.g. Evelyn S. Rawski, *The Last Emperors: A Social Hierarchy of Qing Imperial Institutions*
    (Berkeley: University of California Press, 1998), p. 41.
45 Photographs taken by Stephane Passet in Beijing and Mukden for Albert Kahn in the
    period 1909–12, preserved in the Musée Albert Kahn at Boulogne-Billancourt, include a
    number of Manchu women wearing this style of vest.
46 See Vollmer, *Ruling from the Dragon Throne*, p. 60. Figure 16.2.
47 Zhou Xun and Gao Chunming, *Zhongguo yiguan fushi da cidian*, p. 243.
48 Wei Minghua, *Yangzhou shouma*, p. 143.
49 Ibid., p. 153.

Reforming dress in Peter the Great's Russia

Christine Ruane

Peter the Great was one of Russia's greatest rulers. During his reign (1682–1725) the tsar initiated a series of reforms that transformed Russia into a major European power. One of the earliest of these reforms commanded all Moscow residents to abandon their traditional dress in favour of European fashions. What began as a dress code for city residents quickly became the new uniform for public life throughout the Russian Empire. To modern eyes, Peter's dress reform appears to be an impetuous act on the part of an authoritarian ruler. In reality, prior to the eighteenth century European rulers had often issued laws controlling dress, but the Russian tsar's reform extended sumptuary laws even further. Peter became one of the first rulers (other examples: Emperor Meiji in the late 1860s and Kemal Atatürk of Turkey in the 1920s) to include dress reform as a fundamental part of his effort to modernise and 'Westernise' his empire.

So, how did clothing come to represent Westernisation? In Russia centuries of relative isolation from Western Europe meant that Russians dressed and behaved differently from the English, the French, and the Germans. Meanwhile, Western European elites began to use the French court as their cultural model, eliminating regional or national differences. Because the Russians were outside this courtly milieu, the Western Europeans imagined them, dressed in their caftans and long robes, as semi-Asiatic, uncouth barbarians. To overcome this prejudice Peter the Great quickly realised that his subjects must dress and behave like their European counterparts.

The tsar's command created much consternation for many Russians. After centuries of covering everything but their hands and their faces, elite women were expected to bare their bosoms and exchange their headdresses for elaborate wigs. The contours of men's bodies were also revealed in the tight-fitting breeches and waistcoats. While all members of the nobility were forced to wear European fashions at court functions, many preferred to wear Muscovite dress in the privacy of their own homes.

While it is difficult to know with any certainty how quickly Russians adopted European fashions as their exclusive form of dress, Peter and his successors made one thing perfectly clear: European dress was going to remain the standard for public life in Russia. The Russian adoption of European dress created a serious problem for Peter's government. How were Russians going to find out what the latest fashions were and where were they going to purchase these clothes? The only practical way for Russians to acquire their new clothes was to create a domestic fashion industry. With that in mind, Peter invited artisans from all over Europe to set up shop in Russia. Once there, they were to supply Russians with fashionable dress and train native artisans in the art of European tailoring and dressmaking. Entrepreneurs from the German states, France, and England established workshops, married, and raised their children in their new

Snapshot 21.1 A young St Petersburg family on the eve of the First World War. Each individual is wearing tasteful, well-made garments. There is nothing in their dress that identifies them as Russians. This cosmopolitanism – the ability of Russians to look like Western Europeans – was the goal of Peter the Great's dress reform. Private collection.

homeland. Over time, this influx of foreign talent and business practices allowed Russian entrepreneurs to become contributors to the increasingly cosmopolitan fashion industry.

If Peter the Great's dress reform was a commercial success, it helped to create a fissure in Russian cultural life. Those who adopted European dress and manners looked down upon those who remain wedded to the old ways and styles of dress. These debates about the role of dress in defining 'Russianness' attracted some of that country's leading intellectuals and artists. The result of that creative tension was the flowering of an entire generation of Russian artists in the early years of twentieth century (Lev Bakst, Sonia Delauney, Alexandra Exter, and Erté among others) who helped to create fashionable clothing for the new modern age. Consequently, the experimental dress designs of the Russian avant-garde have to be understood against the backdrop of Peter the Great's eighteenth-century dress reform.

Bibliography and further reading

Ruane, C. (1998) 'Caftan to Business Suit: The Semiotics of Russian Merchant Dress', in J. L. West and I. A. Petrov (eds), *Merchant Moscow: Images of Russia's Vanished Bourgeoisie*, Princeton: Princeton University Press, pp. 53–60.

Ruane, C. (2002) 'Subjects into Citizens: The Politics of Clothing in Imperial Russia', in W. Parkins (ed.), *Fashioning the Body Politic: Dress, Gender, Citizenship*, Oxford: Berg, pp. 49–70.

Ruane, C. (2009) *The Empire's New Clothes: A History of the Russian Fashion Industry, 1700–1917*, London and New Haven: Yale University Press.

Clothing and ethnicity in colonial Spanish America

Rebecca Earle

The 1763 painting (Snapshot 22.1, next page) by the Mexican artist Miguel Cabrera shows an elegantly dressed couple with their daughter, standing in a market. The image, an example of the distinctive eighteenth-century Spanish American genre known as *casta painting*, depicts the outcome of racial mixing. This work presents a Spanish man, an Amerindian woman, and their mestiza daughter. Although the purpose of such paintings is to offer a taxonomy of mixing – they were often produced in series that showed the results of every conceivable type of inter-ethnic coupling – one of their striking features is that the caste identity of the subjects is conveyed as much through their dress, behaviour and context as through their bodies. In this image, the indigenous identity of the mother is neatly expressed by her folded head-cloth and shawl, or *rebozo*, while her husband's European origins are proclaimed as clearly by his velvet frock coat, stylish tri-cornered hat, and powdered wig as by his smooth white cheek and hand. Their daughter, although ostensibly occupying a liminal ethnic position between the European and the indigenous, is dressed in impeccably European fashion, which hints at her successful incorporation into the world of the white elite, her partial indigenous origins notwithstanding.

In colonial Spanish America the use of clothing to delineate ethnic identity is not confined to paintings. In Spain's colonial universe racial identity did not reside solely, or sometimes even at all, in physical appearance. Instead, racial identities were profoundly social and performative, and for both elites and plebeians, clothing played an important role in this process. We can sense the significance of clothing to the performance of racial identity through its appearance in colonial law-suits. Individuals seeking to establish their racial status often appealed, not to the genealogies of their ancestors, but rather to the clothing that they typically wore. When in 1686 Quito Blas de Horta tried to demonstrate that he was not an Amerindian, he did not summon his parents. Rather, he produced a witness to affirm that he always wore 'Spanish dress' (Minchom 1994: 158, 190). Such racial self-reclassification through clothing was by the eighteenth century complemented by a complex legal system which allowed individuals to permanently change their official race through the acquisition of legal documents confirming a new racial identity. At the same time, sumptuary laws attempted to regulate unauthorised sartorial reclassification through stipulations of the clothing appropriate to people of different races and 'qualities'. Such legislation makes very clear that clothing was classified along racial lines. Decrees from sixteenth-century Mexico, for example, stipulate that that 'mestiza, mulata and black woman may not wear indigenous clothing, but only that of Spanish women' (Carrillo y Gariel 1959: 73). Clothing, in other words, was closely linked to caste identity in Spanish American daily life.

Casta paintings thus reflect this ability of clothing to display, or even determine, racial identity. They also capture the intricate nature of all such performances, for the

Snapshot 22.1   De Español, y d'India; mestisa, by Miguel Cabrera, 1763. Private collection, Mexico.

elements that comprised Spanish or indigenous identity were themselves embedded in the complex historical trajectories unleashed by colonialism and European economic expansion. Most profoundly, the category of Amerindian itself is of wholly colonial origin; the inhabitants of pre-Columbian América in no sense considered themselves members of a common group. It is thus fitting that in Cabrera's painting, the design of the fabric used in the 'indigenous' shawl worn by the mother, like the designs on some of the rolls of locally produced fabric in the market stall behind her, may be of southeast Asian origin, based on patterns imported by the Manila galleons that sailed regularly from the Philippines to Acapulco. Her indigenous identity, in other words, is in part confirmed by her indigenous dress, but that dress is itself a consequence of colonialism.

Bibliography and further reading

Carrera, M. (2003) *Imagining Identity in New Spain: Race, Lineage, and the Colonial Body in Portraiture and Casta Paintings*, Austin: University of Texas Press.

Carrillo y Gariel, A. (1959) *El traje en la Nueva España*, Mexico: Instituto Nacional de Antropología e Historia, p. 73.

Earle, R. (2001) '"Two Pairs of Pink Satin Shoes!!": Clothing, Race and Identity in the Americas, 17th–19th Centuries', *History Workshop Journal*, 52, pp. 175–95.

Minchom, M. (1994) *The People of Quito: 1690–1810: Change and Unrest in the Underclass*, Boulder: Westview Press, pp. 158, 190.

Chapter 17

British attitudes to Indian and European dress

Emma Tarlo

B. COHN HAS POINTED OUT HOW EUROPEANS, arriving in India for the first time, were invariably shocked by the 'nakedness' of the loinclothed Indian boatmen (Cohn 1990: 331). Figure 17.1 portrays two stereotyped British reactions to Indian dress. The notion of the 'graceful' (or picturesque) and the 'disgraceful' (or indecent) was frequently applied to both male and female attire. Where men's dress was concerned, the 'graceful' referred to the stitched robes worn by the Indian élite and the 'disgraceful' to the draped clothing popular among vast sections of the Indian population. In other words, subsumed within these two categories was a European assessment of most of the types of clothing worn by Indian men. We should therefore look briefly at what such assessments implied.

The 'disgraceful' sight of the loinclothed boatmen was not merely shocking to Europeans. It also confirmed their notion of the evolutionary inferiority of the Indian race – of its backwardness and barbarism. Furthermore, it revealed the blackness of the skin which was in itself regarded as a biological sign of racial inferiority. The effects of such a sight have been graphically described by Lieut.-Col. John Briggs in a letter to a young British man. Briggs's intention was to warn the novice about the strangeness of Indian customs which he defended on the grounds of cultural relativism and 'ignorance'. Describing the Madras boatmen, he wrote:

> To the European the sight is hardly human, to see a black animal kneeling on three bits of wood, connected only with the fibres of a coconut, paddling away alone several miles from land . . .
>
> What then must be the feelings of a person, landing fresh from London, without having witnessed any intermediate state of society between the

NEW ARRIVALS.

Mr. Griffin.—" Well. Miss Green, what are your impressions of the manners and customs of the Natives?"
Miss Green.—" I have not been sufficiently long in the country to judge, but the costume is really charming, somewhat scanty perhaps; but so *picturesque, so graceful, don't you think?*"
Mr. Griffin.—Hem! It strikes me at times as being rather *dis-graceful!*"
N. B.—Miss Green is looking *one* way, and Mr. Griffin the *other !!!*

Figure 17.1 NEW ARRIVALS. Mr Griffin: 'Well Miss Green, what are your impressions of the manners and customs of the natives?' Miss Green: 'I have not been sufficiently long in the country to judge, but the costume is really charming, somewhat scanty perhaps: but so picturesque, so graceful, don't you think?' Mr Griffin: 'Hem! It strikes me at times as being rather dis-graceful!' N.B. Miss Green is looking one way, and Mr Griffin the other!!! Reproduced from *The Indian Charivari*, 19 September 1873. Courtesy of OIOC.

height of European civilization in the finest city in the universe, and that to which he is so suddenly brought! (Briggs 1828: 26–8).

The notion of the 'gracefulness' of Indian men's dress held more ambiguous connotations. On the one hand, the term 'graceful' was clearly a sign of appreciation and many British men and women were impressed by the flowing nature of Indian robes (cf. Crooke 1906: 163, E. F. Elwin 1907: 44). On the other hand, it implied unmanliness. As Briggs put it, the male Indian elite 'are habited in long flowing linen robes, giving them in our eyes, an air of effeminacy' (Briggs 1828: 28). The terms 'effeminate' and 'childlike' were frequently used by the British to describe the clothes of the Indian élite, particularly the elaborate and colourful combinations worn by the maharajahs (for an example see Steevens 1899: 121–3). Such designations were part of a more general process

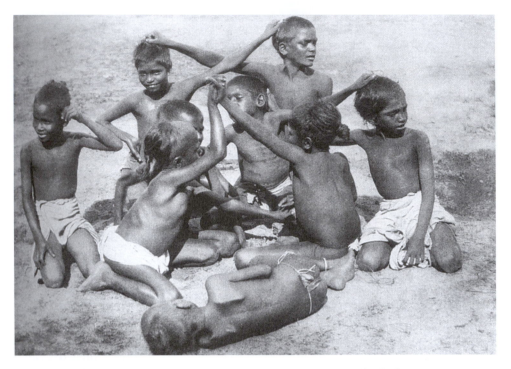

Figure 17.2 Hindu children playing, revealing the nakedness that so shocked Europeans in India. Reproduced from H. V. Glassesnapp's *Indien*, 1925. Courtesy of SOAS.

by which the politically dominant group tried to define the Indian male as powerless and subordinate in his own country. Ashis Nandy has highlighted the homology between political and sexual dominance which became increasingly important to the British as their power in India increased (cf. Nandy 1983: 4–11). When the British described Indian men's clothes as 'pretty' (Stuart 1809: 152), 'graceful' (Crooke 1906: 163, Elwin 1907: 44) and 'effeminate' (Briggs, *loc. cit.*) they simultaneously denigrated Indian men to the unenviable status of their own women, whom they perceived as attractive, pretty, dignified even, but largely irrelevant to serious political concerns. British attitudes to Indian dress therefore revealed their attitudes towards Indians in general.

Since my intention is to demonstrate the heterogeneity of Indian responses to European dress, it is perhaps unfair that I should speak of British attitudes as though they formed a homogeneous view. Clearly, if I were to examine the full gamut of British responses to Indian dress in the nineteenth century, I would find some variety. There were some Britons who appreciated differences in dress without assuming the superiority of European styles (cf. Shore 1837, Billington 1973 [1895]). Others actively sought to revive Indian dress in an attempt to protect a threatened culture and aesthetic (cf. Birdwood 1880; repr. 1988: 244, Havell 1912: 21–4). But the aim here is to expose the characteristics of the dominant racist stereotype rather than the views of the sympathetic minority. Furthermore this stereotype was so widely expressed in British diaries, novels, newspapers and political cartoons that it came to represent something akin to a shared imperialist view. This was increasingly the case in the nineteenth century. Whereas in earlier times British travellers mingled to some extent with Indians, the men often settling with Indian women and adopting at least some Indian customs (Bayly 1990: 73), by the nineteenth century British civil servants were increasingly expected to conform to a well-defined set of social values and codes of conduct. What had been a scattered and heterogeneous group of European merchants and entrepreneurs leading individualistic lives gradually became a more structured body of British political author-ity, the credibility of which rested to some extent on its ability to present a cohesive offi-cial view. According to this view, the British were superior beings and Indians inferiors. Furthermore the British, through improving 'native' behaviour and customs, felt that they could enable Indians to better themselves. The 'graceful' and, more particularly, the 'disgraceful' nature of Indian clothes acted for the British not only as proof of Indian effeminacy and barbarism but also as a justification for their civilising presence in India.[1]

Like British attitudes and policies, British clothes became, over time, increasingly homogeneous. Early European travellers in India were, it seems, comparatively free to choose their own clothing styles, and often adapted or discarded their heavy European attire in quest of clothes more suitable to Indian customs and climate (Bayly 1990: 73, Dar 1969: 73). Woodruff for example describes seventeenth-century British traders in Surat as wearing 'fine white linen coats', girdles, scarves, turbans and 'moorman's trousers' (cited in Dar 1969: 73). From paintings and descriptions it seems that most British men who chose to adopt Indian styles favoured loose stitched garments of cotton and silk to which they sometimes added European touches such as buttons and shoes.

As the British consolidated their political dominance in India in the early nine-teenth century, the wearing of Indian styles became increasingly unacceptable. It was seen as a 'sign of eccentricity' and even a 'cause of discredit' (Bayly 1990: 110). In 1830 legislation was introduced banning employees of the East India Company from wearing Indian dress at public functions (Cohn 1989: 310). Even in private, the Brit-ish adhered increasingly to the sartorial standards of Europe. Those who became 'de-Europeanised' through 'long residence among undomesticated natives' were referred to disparagingly by Lord Lytton as 'white baboos'[2] (Yule and Burnell 1903: 44).

The Europeanisation of British public and domestic life was part of the wider process through which the British came to distance themselves increasingly from their Indian sub-jects (cf. Cohn 1989, Nandy 1983). Maintenance of differences through dress and other social customs was important both for British self-esteem and as a means of demonstrat-ing British superiority to an Indian audience. Briggs described its importance as follows:

> . . . yet we should always preserve the European; for to adopt their [Indian] manners is a departure from the very principle on which every impression of our superiority, that rests upon good foundation, is founded . . . The European officer who assumes native manners and usages may please a few individuals, who are flattered or profited by his departure from the habits of his country; but even with these, familiarity will not be found to increase respect, and the adoption of such a course will be sure to sink him in the estimation of the mass of the community, both European and native, among whom he resides (Briggs 1828: 201).

Thus, along with the positive – the sense of security gained by maintaining sartorial standards – went the negative: fear that failure to maintain those standards could result in a British man sinking or being morally weakened.

It was essentially a fear that members of this small white minority might somehow be absorbed or at least tainted by the mass of Indians around them. Maintaining British standards of dress was a means of avoiding such deterioration. It became important for the Englishman in India to prove that he was as English as his fellows at home. If foreign influences were detected in his dress when he returned to England, they would be viewed critically. Woodruff tells how Hickey's 'gay coats caused so much talk when he first went home that he had to discard them' (cited in Dar 1969: 74).

This need to preserve impeccable British standards frequently featured in Anglo-Indian literature and journals. In 1873 the satirical journal *The Indian Charivari* published a column entitled 'Hints on Modern Etiquette'. In it, the fictional Lord Lushingslop warned his son of the sartorial perils of serving in India, 'a land so deplorably far from the centre of civilization'. He urged:

> Nothing can be worse taste than to adopt unhesitatingly the manners and customs of a strange country. An English gentleman should always be dressed, so that, were he suddenly dropped into Bond Street, he would pass unnoticed in the crowd (*The Indian Charivari*, 27 June 1873).

While such extracts betray a certain humour concerning dress, other accounts reveal the essential seriousness with which the British in India regarded their clothes. Aldous Huxley, for example, noticed the British civil servant's obsession with sartorial rituals even as late as the 1930s when such customs were no longer considered so important in England. He observed:

> From the Viceroy to the young clerk who, at home, consumes high tea at sunset, every Englishman in India solemnly dresses. It is as though the integrity of the British Empire depended in some directly magical way upon the donning of black jackets and hard-boiled shirts (cited in Alexander 1987: 268).

Huxley astutely recognised the British psychological dependence on such rituals.[3] One civil servant, Kenneth Warren, posted to an isolated out-post in Upper Assam, has left a revealing account of just what they meant for him:

> If you lost your self-respect you were not looked upon in a respectful manner. So in order to maintain my self-respect I put on a dinner jacket and dressed for dinner and I said to my servants, who were quite likely to get a bit slack just looking after a man by himself in the middle of the jungle, 'Now this is a dinner party and every night is a dinner party and you will serve dinner as though there are other people at the dinner table' (cited in Allen 1985: 62).

Naturally, retaining such levels of Britishness was a physical strain at times. In remote areas European clothes and the facilities for maintaining them were not easily available. Added to this was the inconvenience caused by their extreme unsuitability to the Indian climate. Not even children were exempt from wearing excessive layers of elaborate clothing in the afternoons (Allen 1985: 13). Women too complained of suffocating customs such as wearing kid or suede gloves at public functions in the heat of the mid-day sun (Barwell 1960: 109). Failure to abide by such rules could incur the risk of being asked to leave.

British obsession over dress related not only to social and psychological factors but also to their perceptions of the physical environment. The combination of alien customs and climate induced a fear of the unknown, and clothes provided an important means of physical as well as psychological protection. Cohn has written at some length about the development of British theories on the relationship between clothing and the pre-vention of tropical diseases (Cohn 1983a: 88–111). In particular Britons of both sexes were recommended to wear flannel underwear rather than linen since flannel, being a slow conductor of heat, was thought to guard the body against sudden changes in the atmosphere (ibid.: 1983a: 94). By the mid to late nineteenth century they were also rec-ommended to wear their *sola topis* whenever they went out of doors.[4] The *topi* not only protected them from the much-feared sun, but it also provided a distinctive type of head-wear, which made them – men, women and children alike – immediately recog-nisable as European.

To understand the political dimension of British clothing habits, it is necessary to examine not only British clothes but also British policy more generally. Why should the British have chosen to emphasise their social distance from Indians at precisely the time when they were apparently lessening the gap between British and Indian customs through advocating European education in India? In order to appreciate the British need to develop sartorial distance, developments in Indian men's dress in the same period also need to be examined. Throughout the nineteenth century, while the British were intensifying their Britishness, members of the Indian élite were beginning to adopt var-ious articles of European dress, and a few adopted an entirely European image. The sar-torial fastidiousness that developed among the British therefore coincided with, and was by no means unrelated to, the adoption of European dress by Indians (Figure 17.3). The fact that some Indian men were coming to look increasingly like Europeans actually had the effect of encouraging the British to make their own sense of sartorial correctness more rigid. In so doing they continually made their clothes and their accompanying rit-uals less accessible to the Indian élite. They were trying to escape 'imitation'.

The British desire to differentiate themselves from Indians was thus the opposite side of the coin from the Indian desire to integrate with the British. Similarly, the Brit-ish fear of 'sinking' was inextricably linked to their fear of Indians 'rising'.

Indian dress posed not merely a clothing dilemma but also an ethical dilemma for the British. On the one hand they felt it their duty to civilise barbaric natives and rescue them from their own primitiveness. It was with such notions of 'improvement' in mind that Captain Johnstone clothed the 'naked savages' of the Juang hills. But on the other hand the British did not want these natives to become *too* civilised. Captain Johnstone, for example, clothed them in Manchester saris, not European styles. If the British wanted to offer India the raiment of civilisation, it was civilisation with a cut-off point above which Indians were not supposed to climb.

The problem of how to clothe the Indian was further linked to the problem of the British economy. Although the British did not want Indians to adopt European styles, they did want them to buy and wear British manufactured textiles. By the late eight-eenth century, Britain had developed sufficient technology in machine-spinning and weaving to produce large quantities of cheap cotton textiles for home use and for

Figure 17.3 Goanese Christians who have clearly experienced the 'civilising' influence of Europeans. Note that the men wear full European dress while the women have retained Indian styles. European missionaries were mixed in their opinions as to whether or not Indian Christians should adopt European dress, an ambivalence reflected in the sarcastic saying that the spread of Christianity had become 'a matter of trousers' (Elwin 1907:43). Reproduced from W. Johnson's *The Oriental Races and Tribes, Residents and Visitors of Bombay*, vol. 2 (1866). Courtesy of Chris Pinney.

export. Previously, cotton textiles had been imported from India but from this time onwards Britain's need for Indian hand-woven textiles diminished. Its interests now lay in importing raw cotton which it could then export back to India in the form of cloth, spun and woven by machine in Britain.[5] But in order to produce textiles for the Indian market the British had to decide on the type of textiles they wished the Indian to wear.

The choice was not entirely theirs, since the majority of rural Indians were conservative in their tastes.

British interests and intentions were carefully codified in John Forbes Watson's famous work *The Textile Manufacturers and Costumes of the People of India* (1866). It was accompanied by eighteen volumes containing 700 'working specimens' of Indian textiles. These were to be regarded as 'Industrial museums' that would enable British manufacturers to study Indian tastes and imitate indigenous designs. Watson wrote: 'India is in a position to become a magnificent customer . . . *What is wanted and what to be copied to meet that want*, is thus accessible for study in these museums' (Watson 1866: 2–3, his emphasis). He pointed out that most of the clothes worn by the poorer sections of Indian society consisted of unstitched pieces of cloth. It was these 'plainer cheaper stuffs' worn by the 'hundreds and millions of lower grades' that the British should imitate (ibid.: 7). The more complex and elaborate garments worn by wealthy Indians were not, however, worth imitating since they could not be produced cheaply in England.

The British were successful in capturing a large proportion of the Indian demand for cotton textiles.[6] Aided by Indian conservatism, they could supply clothes for the Indian 'lower grades', and in doing so they could simultaneously keep the Indian masses looking suitably Indian. But it was more difficult to control the clothes of the Indian élite. Furthermore it was this small educated minority, not the Indian masses, that posed a threat to the British since it consisted of the most anglicised Indians who came dangerously close to integrating themselves with the ruling British élite.

The British had of course invented their own problem. It was succinctly expressed in Macaulay's famous 'Minute on Education' (1835). Macaulay, who favoured the introduction of European education in India, argued the need for 'a class who may be interpreters between us and the millions whom we govern; a class of persons, Indian in blood and colour, but English in taste, in opinions, in morals and in intellect' (cited in Vittachi 1987: 36). The inevitable consequence of such a policy was the narrowing of the cultural divide between the British and the educated Indian élite. The British attempted to subdue this uncomfortable closeness not only by increasing the rigidity of their own dress codes, but also by trying to limit the Indian adoption of Western styles (Chaudhuri 1976: 58, Cohn 1989). The idea was to keep differences apparent. An incident in the life of Madhusudan Datta reveals this process of racial differentiation at work. Datta had been sent to Bishop's College in Calcutta, where he was given a Western education and developed the Western tastes that Macaulay so recommended. Yet he was discouraged from sharing the college uniform of his fellows. Krishnamohan Bandyopadhay recalls:

> The ecclesiastical authorities had an idea at the time that natives in India should not be encouraged to imitate the English dress – the tail coat and the beaver hat. It would have been infinitely better if they had not interfered with questions beyond their province – for it was this interference that goaded a fiery spirit like Datta's into an obstinate resistance. The collegiate costume was a black cassock and band and the square cap . . . The authorities wished him to put on a white cassock instead of black. Dana said, *either collegiate costume or his own national dress* (cited in Radice 1986: 202).

OUR "WALLAHS."

1st *Wallah.*—"Who's that old bloke?"

2nd *Wallah.*—"Oh, he's only the fellow that educated me. He's devilish low, but I'm obliged to notice him. Though between ourselves, if it wasn't for his daughter, I'd be inclined to snub the old fool."

Figure 17.4 OUR 'WALLAHS'. 1st Wallah: 'Who's that old bloke?' 2nd Wallah: 'Oh, he's only the fellow that educated me. He's devilish low, but I'm obliged to notice him. Though between ourselves, if it wasn't for his daughter, I'd be inclined to snub the old fool'. Reproduced from *The Indian Charivari*, 18 August 1876. Courtesy of OIOC.

Datta, playing the British at their own game, appeared in college dressed in an elaborate Indian outfit of white silk with a highly colourful turban and shawl. The authorities, who felt this was embarrassingly like 'fancy dress', were finally forced to allow him to wear the ordinary uniform (ibid.). But the fact that he had to fight for such a basic right highlights the peculiarly self-centred aspect of British policies for 'improving' the Indian. As Macaulay's speech made clear, the British needed educated anglicised Indians as 'interpreters'. They were therefore willing to share their education system, but not their physical identity, with the Indian. As Chaudhuri put it:

> The Englishman in India . . . considered his way of life superior to every other . . . but was wholly opposed to sharing its higher or more respectable features with anybody who was not to the manner born . . . They were violently repelled by English in our mouths, and even more violently by English clothes on our backs (Chaudhuri 1976: 57–8).

Underlying this control of dress was a fear that the Indian male might be a little too successful in his 'imitation', and even rise above the very people who had enabled him to rise in the first place (Figure 17.4).

British attempts to control Indian dress were by no means limited to the sphere of education. Cohn has illustrated how the British chose to orientalise the uniform of the

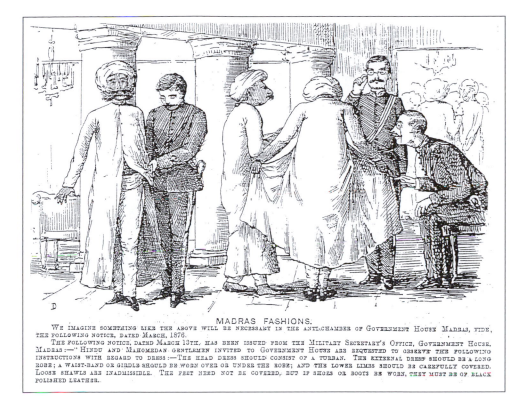

MADRAS FASHIONS.

WE IMAGINE SOMETHING LIKE THE ABOVE WILL BE NECESSARY IN THE ANTI-CHAMBER OF GOVERNMENT HOUSE MADRAS, VIDE, THE FOLLOWING NOTICE, DATED MARCH, 1876.

THE FOLLOWING NOTICE, DATED MARCH 13TH, HAS BEEN ISSUED FROM THE MILITARY SECRETARY'S OFFICE, GOVERNMENT HOUSE, MADRAS:—"HINDU AND MAHOMEDAN GENTLEMEN INVITED TO GOVERNMENT HOUSE ARE REQUESTED TO OBSERVE THE FOLLOWING INSTRUCTIONS WITH REGARD TO DRESS:—THE HEAD DRESS SHOULD CONSIST OF A TURBAN. THE EXTERNAL DRESS SHOULD BE A LONG ROBE; A WAIST-BAND OR GIRDLE SHOULD BE WORN OVER OR UNDER THE ROBE; AND THE LOWER LIMBS SHOULD BE CAREFULLY COVERED. LOOSE SHAWLS ARE INADMISSIBLE. THE FEET NEED NOT BE COVERED, BUT IF SHOES OR BOOTS BE WORN, THEY MUST BE OF BLACK POLISHED LEATHER.

Figure 17.5 MADRAS FASHIONS. 'We imagine something like the above will be necessary in the anti-chamber of Government House Madras, vide, the following notice, dated March 1876. . . . 'Hindu and Mahomedan gentlemen . . . are requested to observe the following instructions with regard to dress: The head dress should consist of a turban. The external dress should be a long robe; a waist-band or girdle should be worn over or under the robe; and the lower limbs should be carefully covered . . .' Reproduced from *The Indian Charivari*, 14 April 1876. Courtesy of OIOC.

army and the official dress of the Maharajas (cf. Cohn 1989). They also laid down regulations concerning what Indians should wear for official and ceremonial occasions (see Figure 17.5, also Chaudhuri 1976: 58). Such legislative demands caused considerable tensions which often became manifest over the controversial issues of headwear and footwear (cf. Cohn 1989).

To summarise, the British authorities disliked Indian men wearing European dress, but regarded Indian dress as primitive. They wanted Indians to progress from barbarism, but not to the full heights of European civilisation. These preoccupations are perhaps best summarised in Figure 17.6. Not even the improved and educated Indian male is portrayed in full European dress. It is a blatantly racist portrait of how far the British were prepared to let the Indian 'advance'. But there were some Indians who were not prepared to accept the somewhat grudging offer of partial civilisation. [. . .]

THE INDIAN CHARIVARI.—January 9, 1874.

" Origin of Species "
or
Improvement by "Natural Selection."
After Darwin.

1st *Geological Period.*

First Protoplasm, shapeless thing,
From which all Human kind did spring;
A spirit, jealous at the sight,
Gave it a kick, just out of spite, . *

* Note.—See introduction to Moore's "Lalla Rookh."

2nd *Period.*

Now Protoplasm lives on dry land,
" Baboon" he's called, with club in hand;
Baboons, however, talking shirk,
For fear they might be made to work!

3rd *Period.*

Immense improvement now he shows,
He takes on human shape, and woes;
He drops the " n," and tail at once,
And calls himself " Baboo the dunce."

4th, or *Modern Period.*

The scanty dress he used to use,
He now casts off for pants and shoes;
From "dunce" to scholar, man of parts,
He's changed, and " Master " is of " Arts."
This, and more titles all combined,
In Baboos of our day you'll find.

Figure 17.6 '"Origin of Species" or Improvement by "Natural Selection" after Darwin.'
Reproduced from *The Indian Charivari*, 9 January 1874. Courtesy of OIOC.

Notes

1   The desire to 'civilise' the native's dress was particularly apparent in missionary activi-
    ties where the naked were often quite literally clothed (cf. Cohn 1983a: 78–87). Elwin, a
    Poona missionary, aware of the problems of imposing European dress, wrote that 'people
    have sometimes sarcastically spoken of the spread of Christianity amongst the heathen as
    being made a matter of trousers' (E. F. Elwin 1907: 43). Elwin himself felt that 'advanc-
    ing refinement and civilization' was producing in Indians 'an instinctive desire to be more
    fully clothed' (ibid.: 43). Ultimately, however, he favoured the idea that Christian con-
    verts should be clearly distinguishable from Hindus. It was therefore 'advisable for them to
    adopt trousers' (ibid.: 44).
2   The Bengali term 'baboo' was originally used as a term of respect attached to a person's
    name. It was reserved for men of distinction, but by the late nineteenth century the Brit-
    ish frequently used it on its own. Used thus, it took on a negative connotation with insult-
    ing implications. It referred to what the British described as the 'superficially cultivated',
    ambitious, semi-anglicised, educated and 'effeminate' Bengali man, and was often used to
    refer to those native clerks who wrote English (Yule and Burnell 1903: 44). When Lytton
    accused Indianised Europeans of being 'white baboos' he was referring to their hybrid
    nature, an unsatisfactory mixture of the negative aspects of both races.
3   I have recently come across Helen Callaway's article 'Dressing for Dinner in the Bush',
    which gives some excellent Indian and African examples of how the British depended on
    such rituals, and a fuller analysis than I have space for here (cf. Barnes and Eicher 1993).
4   If caught outside without their *topis*, BORs ('British Other Ranks') were confined to bar-
    racks for fourteen days (Allen 1985: 37).
5   For a concise account of the history of Indian and British textile relations, see Swallow
    1982 and Bean 1989. For detailed historical accounts see Irwin and Schwartz 1966 and
    B. Chandra 1966.
6   Between 1849 and 1889 the value of British cotton cloth exports to India increased from
    just over £2m a year to just under £27m a year (Bean 1989: 362).

Bibliography

Alexander, A. (ed.) (1988) *The Penguin Book of Indian Cartoons*, Delhi: Penguin (India).
Allen, C. (1985 [1975]) *Plain Tales of the Raj*, London: Century Publishing.
Barwell, M. (1960) *India Without Sentiment*, Calcutta: New Age Publishers.
Bayly, C. (ed.) (1990) *The Raj: India and the British, 1600–1947*, London: National Portrait Gallery.
Bean, S. (1989) 'Gandhi and Khadi: The Fabric of Independence' in A. B. Weiner and
    J. Schneider (eds), *Cloth and the Human Experience*, Washington: Smithsonian Institute
    Press, pp. 355–76.
Billington, M. F. (1973 [1895]) *Woman in India*, Delhi: Amarko Book Agency.
Birdwood, G. (1880) *The Industrial Arts of India*, repr. 1988 as *The Arts of Indian*, Calcutta: Rupa.
Briggs, J. (1828) *Letters Addressed to a Young Person in India; Calculated to Afford Instruction for his Con-
    duct in General, and More Especially in his Intercourse with the Natives*, London: John Murray.
Chandra, B. (1966) *The Rise of Growth of Economic Nationalism in India: Economic Policies of Indian
    Nationalism Leadership, 1880–1905*, Delhi: People's Publishing House.
Chaudhuri, N. (1976) *Culture in the Vanity Bag*, Bombay: Jaico.
Cohn, B. (1989) 'Cloth, Clothes and Colonialism: India in the Nineteenth Century' in A. Weiner
    and J. Schneider (eds), *Cloth and Human Experience*, Washington: Smithsonian Institute
    Press.

Cohn, N. (1983) 'Cloth, Clothes and Colonialism', extended unpublished version of 1989 publication below, delivered at symposium at Troutbeck, New York.

Crooke, W. (1906) *Things Indian: Being Discursive Notes on Various Subjects Connected with India*: London: John Murray.

Dar, S. N. (1969) *Costumes of India and Pakistan: Historical and Cultural Study*, Bombay: D. P. Taraporevela.

Elwin, E. F. (1907, *Indian Jottings: From Ten Years' Experience in and around Poona City*, London: John Murray.

Havell, E. B. (1912) *The Basis for Artistic and Industrial Revival in India*, Madras: Theosophist Office.

The Indian Charivari (27 June 1873).

Irwin, J., and Schwartz, P. (1966) *Indo-European Textile History*, Ahmedebad: Calico Museum of Textiles.

Macaulay, T. B. (1835) *Minute on Education*.

Nandy, A. (1983) *The Intimate Enemy: Loss and Recovery of Self under Colonialism*, Delhi: Oxford University Press.

Radice, C. W. (1986) 'Tremendous Literary Rebel: The Life and Works of Madhusudan Datta (1824–73)', unpubl. PhD thesis, Faculty of Oriental Studies, Oxford University.

Shore, F. J. (1837) *Notes on Indian Affairs*, vol. 1, London: J. W. Parker.

Steevens, G. W. (1899) *In India*, London: Thos. Nelson.

Stuart, C. (1809) *The Ladies Moniter: Being a Series f Letters Published in Bengal on the Subject of Female Apparel*, London.

Swallow, D. (1982) 'Production and Control in the Indian Garment Export in Industry' in E. Goody (ed.), *From Cafe to Industry*, Cambridge University Press.

The Textile Manufacturers and Costumes of the People of India (1866).

Vittachi, T. (1987) *The Brown Sahib Revisited*, Delhi: Penguin Books.

Watson, J. F. (1866) *The Textile Manufacturers and the Costumes of the People of India* (with 18 vols of textile samples), London: G. E. Eyre and W. Spottiswood.

Yule, H. and Burnell, A. C. (1903 [1886]) *Hobson-Jobson*, London: John Murray.

Distance and respectability in colonial Australia

Margaret Maynard

Snapshot 23.1 Group, Yandilla, 16 November 1884. The Hume Collection, image no. 116, Fryer Library, the University of Queensland.

This photo of the Gore family taken in 1884 at Yandilla Station near Warwick, well inland from coastal Brisbane, Queensland's capital, comes from the rich collection of Hume family photographs (Snapshot 23.1). Katie Hume lived on the Darling Downs, part of a solid bourgeois family, her husband Walter a government surveyor. Her remarks about the Gores in a letter written some years earlier are worth noting. They show the complexity of social perceptions of respectability in colonial Australia at the time, even if the dress seems unremarkable to a modern viewer. Katie did not regard the Gores as vulgar but says even in this out of way spot they are 'considered very peculiar'. The wife does not have things 'as nice as she might' and unnecessary 'hugger mugger' is present in the household. The Miss Gores are decidedly 'fast': not called the 'Warwick Flashers' for nothing. Gracey, lounging in the wicker chair at 5 feet 9 inches was tall and, with her sister Jane, fond of riding and shooting. They talked mostly slang, their manners off hand. Miles from a major town, one family regarded itself as respectable, the other deemed to be not quite so. Yet Katie herself confesses in her letters to sometimes letting things slide. In mid-summer she could not cope with mourning dress indoors, resorting simply to white 'washing bodies' and a black skirt.

This example allows us to see how relativities of 'distance' and 'respectability' were played out in colonial dress. With Australia's geographical position far from Europe, the two factors had profound effects and were subjective, intertwined, gendered and class inflected. Yet sometimes their visual impact is hard to detect.

From the early nineteenth century, growing numbers of bourgeois colonial settlers had taken up residence in principal towns like Sydney, Melbourne and Brisbane, but also on pastoral holdings far from these centres. Some moved inland as administrators, surveyors or farmers. Settlers brought to Australia familiar habits of dressing and social mores. As if to ignore their distant location, they endeavoured to maintain prior standards, were in regular correspondence with friends and families left behind, and up to date with the latest styles worn at 'home'.

For upper echelon white settlers, especially women, 'distance' from Europe, or away from towns, caused worrying needs to demonstrate that what they wore (even if home stitched) kept pace with fashionable changes overseas. Women in the bush would even make their own replacement crinolines. They certainly made efforts to dress stylishly for public occasions or a studio portrait. But meshed with respectability, 'distance' could also mean 'ladies' kept slightly apart from 'colonials', those born in Australia with supposedly 'rough' manners.

Nevertheless, in the 'new' country, where the small elite class was based more on wealth than lineage, aberrations of dress did occur. Those who could afford it took vacations in 'the hills' like the Blue Mountains west of Sydney and Toowoomba west of Brisbane, escaping the long, hot and supposedly unhealthy summers. Out of the public eye, on pastoral leases and on vacation in hill stations, elite men and women's clothing was often unconventional, even careless. 'Distance' allowed welcome relaxation of standards.

Alternatively, 'respectability' could mean over-investing in propriety of dress in town and country as a form of social self-assurance. Maintaining it also meant encouraging, even requiring, 'uncivilised' indigenous people to put on 'white man's clothes' when entering European settlements or missions. For a middle-class woman, respectability might mean dressing with noticeable discretion in order to look different from gaudy goldfields women. For men, a stylish appearance was less pressing, especially if undertaking pastoral or other rural duties in riding gear, singlets and rough trousers. As the colony had few bespoke tailors, most men's suits were ready-made, often ill fitting. Visitors remarked how difficult it was to determine from dress the social status of an Australian man.

Bibliography and further reading

Bonnin, N. (ed.) (1985) *Katie Hume on the Darling Downs: A Colonial Marriage*, Toowoomba: Darling Downs Institute Press.

Inglis, A. S. (2007) *Summer in the Hills: The Nineteenth Century Mountain Resort in Australia*, North Melbourne: Australian Scholarly Publishing.

Maynard, M. (1994) *Fashioned From Penury: Dress as Cultural Practice in Colonial Australia*, Cambridge: Cambridge University Press.

Fashion and abolitionism

Alice Taylor

In the autumn of 2008, London hosted the RE: Fashion Awards, the world's first award show dedicated to 'ethical fashion'. A-list models, celebrities and designers attended the event, which championed the concept of 'style without compromise'. 'Ethical fashion' is the latest commercial campaign to tap into public interest in purchasing goods that are free of human, animal and environmental exploitation. The Body Shop and Product Red are additional examples of high profile companies and campaigns that pair social justice and environmentalism with fashion and consumerism – selling ethically sourced products and channelling consumer desire for fashionable goods into supporting a 'good cause'.

There is a tendency to think of consumer activism as a twentieth-century phenomenon. In actuality, moral consumerism and ethical fashion can be traced back more than two hundred years to the Anglo-American abolitionist movement. Beginning in 1780s in the United Kingdom and continuing unabated until 1865, when chattel slavery was abolished in the United States, British and American abolitionists mounted abstention campaigns (boycotting slave-grown products like sugar) and urged the public to shop ethically, to 'Buy for the sake of the slave'. Abolitionists wedded antislavery images and slogans with attractive goods to make their controversial cause more appealing and accessible to the wider public – in short they made antislavery fashionable.

It was the potter and abolitionist Josiah Wedgwood who in 1787 designed what would become the iconic emblem of the Anglo-American antislavery movement: an enchained, almost nude male slave kneeling beneath the declaration, 'Am I not a man and a brother?' Wedgwood's image was endlessly reproduced by abolitionists on both sides of the Atlantic. The kneeling slave (male, female and child) appeared on a diverse array of products including ceramics, jewellery, accessories, furniture, artwork, needlework, stationery, household objects and even on children's sweets and toys. Fashionable men had Wedgwood's cameo inlayed in gold on their snuffboxes and ladies wore it in hairpins, brooches, necklaces and bracelets. Such trends prompted abolitionist Thomas Clarkson to remark that, 'fashion which usually confined itself to worthless things, was seen for once in the honourable office of promoting the cause of justice, humanity and freedom'.

Women and girls were the driving force in the Anglo-American campaign to make antislavery fashionable. Female abolitionists – black and white, young and old, rich and poor – produced, marketed, sold and consumed antislavery merchandise; they organised boycotts, formed sewing circles and held antislavery fundraising fairs. Like Wedgwood, female abolitionists recognised the power of linking their cause to fashionable society and they solicited aristocrats, politicians (and their wives) and celebrities to sign antislavery petitions, attend social events (fairs, concerts, picnics) and to own and display abolitionist merchandise. Abolitionists hoped that endorsements by elite and

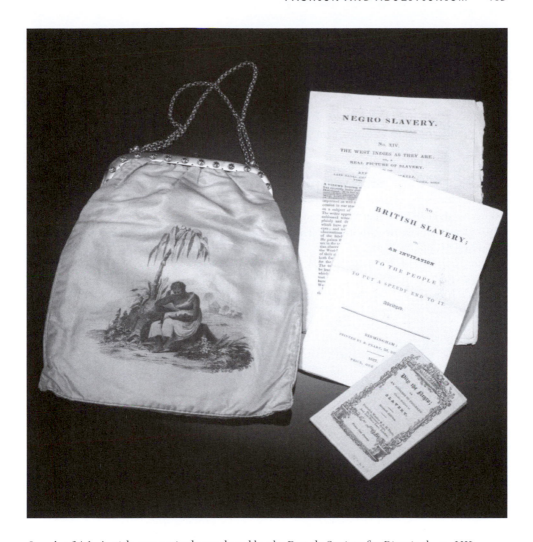

Snapshot 24.1 Antislavery reticule produced by the Female Society for Birmingham, UK, *c.* 1827. The materials are printed silk (design attributed to Samuel Lines, 1778–1863) with steel chain and frame. The bag measures 23.5 cm × 20cm. Bags using the same pattern were produced by female antislavery societies in the United States in the 1830s and can be found in several American museum collections. Victoria and Albert Museum, T.20-1951.

celebrated figures in Anglo-American and European society would legitimate the anti-slavery cause and make it more palatable to the ordinary public.

The silk antislavery reticule (Snapshot 24.1) from the collections of the Victoria and Albert Museum is a wonderful example of the intersection of abolitionism, fashion and celebrity. The bag was created by the Female Society for Birmingham and it dates from around 1827. Reticules were tremendously popular in the Regency period and women used them to carry such items as handkerchiefs, smelling salts and visiting cards. The Birmingham women gifted these bags to aristocracy, including King George IV and Princess (later Queen) Victoria, as well as to other prominent Britons and Americans. Female abolitionists in Britain and America traded designs and patterns and therefore fashionable bags were produced on both sides of the Atlantic. The bags featured a variety of images and verses and, like the V & A bag, oftentimes contained abolitionist literature. Antislavery reticules were intended to serve as objects of fashion and objects of propaganda. The inspiration behind such objects was to 'wrap the truth in gilt edges'; to use the power of shopping and the allure of beautiful things to broaden the audience for the abolitionist message.

Bibliography and further reading

Atkin, A. M. (1997) 'When Pincushions Are Periodicals: Women's Work, Race and Material Objects in Female Abolitionism', *ATQ: A Journal of American 19th-century Literature and Culture*, 11, pp. 93–114.

Midgley, C. (2007) *Feminism and Empire: Women Activists in Imperial Britain, 1790–1865*, London: Routledge.

Oldfield. J. R. (1995) *Popular Politics and British Anti-slavery: The Mobilisation of Public Opinion against the Slave Trade, 1787–1807*, Manchester: Manchester University Press.

Chapter 18

The Westernisation of clothes and the state in Meiji Japan

Ken'ichiro Hirano

T HE FAMOUS CAT IN NATSUME SOSEKI'S NOVEL, *I Am a Cat*, says, 'Man without clothes is not man'.[1] As he also says, the history of the human being is the history of clothes, not that of flesh and bones. In East Asia, traditional clothes have long been regarded as a symbol of *li*, proper human rites. A tenaciously anti-Western Korean philosopher[2] went further, saying that those who wore proper East Asian clothes were human beings, but those who wore Western clothes were beasts. Since the opening of Japan to Western civilisation, the clothes worn by the Japanese people have changed rapidly and drastically, so that people have become very conscious of the style of clothes they are wearing. Whether one wears modern Western clothes (*yōfuku* in Japanese) or traditional Japanese clothes (*kimono*) is not a simple question of style, but a broader, graver question of cultural choice, of identity, and of national independence. For clothes have the function, among others, of symbolising the world-view of the group of people who wear them.

In this chapter, in order to understand how a modern state exerted its influence over the transformation of a culture, we consider clothes as a cultural element that experienced a great deal of change in Japan during the Meiji period.

Characteristics of clothes as a cultural element

One of the characteristics of clothes as a cultural element is that they are multi-functional. The basic function of clothes is, of course, to cover and protect the human body. Another basic function is to facilitate man's carrying objects like weapons. Some scholars even say that this function is the origin of human clothing. This feature has much to do with the military uniform. Sometimes certain clothes are believed to be magical, possessing healing power. These can be said to be instrumental functions. On the other hand, clothes have various expressive functions, denoting sex, age, class and status, occupation, region, ethnic or national group, etc. People also express their aesthetic taste by the clothes they wear. For rituals certain types of clothes must be worn; in this case clothes are both instrumental and expressive.

Clothes are not only practical things but signs, as the Russian semiologist P. G. Bogatyrěv said.[3] They express, among other signs, the aesthetic, moral, and national outlook – in short, the will of the people wearing them. Thus, people are made quite conscious of what is expressed and symbolised by the clothes they wear. Because of this, it may become compulsory for a group of people to wear certain common clothes, which point up the commonality of those wearing them and differentiate them from other peoples. This can be seen most clearly in uniforms. In this chapter I am concerned with the national differences expressed by clothes, and particularly with the uniform's function of differentiating and integrating a nation.

Like many cultural elements, clothes change through time and under the influence of other cultures. Changes occur in style, in material and in colour, but also in dominant function and meaning. Multi-functional and multi-meaning as the clothes may be, it is not the case that all their functions are equally important; at a certain time one function may dominate others. The same is true of the signs expressed by clothes; a certain sign is regarded as most important during a certain period.

In comparison with some other cultural elements like housing, clothes cannot be easily combined with others of a different style. While the modern Japanese house is a rather grotesque mosaic of traditional and Western parts, the dress worn by the modern Japanese is either totally traditional or almost completely Westernised. This is because functional links are especially strong in the case of clothes. This has a significant consequence: once even a part of the clothing is changed by adopting an imported foreign element, a change in the clothing as a whole is inevitable. When this happens, the sign conveyed by the clothing also changes completely. The symbolic change is so complete that the people are sharply divided into two groups, one group totally accepting the new clothes and the other rejecting them completely.

Changes in clothing in early Meiji Japan

It is a well-known historical fact that Japan started adopting Western clothes during the last days of the Tokugawa period and the early Meiji era as part of the drive for modernisation of the country. It is also commonly held that the modernisation process of Japan was initiated at the top. In the case of clothes, indeed, Westernisation was ordered by the Tokugawa shogunate, by many clan governments, and by the Meiji government after the Restoration. As we shall see later, the Tokugawa shogunate and the clan governments initiated the modernisation of clothes by changing military uniforms to Western styles. And in August 1871 the Meiji Emperor issued a mandate ordering his high officials to wear Western clothes, after the government had instituted a new military uniform system in November the previous year.

In the 1871 imperial mandate, the Emperor reasoned that the adoption of Western clothes was necessary in order to keep the fundamental character of the Japanese polity unchanged and to imbue the state with the martial spirit inherited from the ancestors. In other words, the modernisation was imperative in order to maintain the independence of the state, and the Westernisation of culture was necessary for the modernisation – hence the adoption of Western clothes. As Kon Wajiro, a famous critic of contemporary Japanese living designs, said, the sole cause of the thoroughgoing change in Japanese culture was the arrival of the American *kurofune* (black ships): 'The *kurofune* frightened the Japanese into thinking that Japan might be occupied unless she completely renewed her military defence and shocked them into thinking that they had to change their clothes too'.[4] The historian Ienaga Saburo, who is well known for his struggle against the state censorship of Japanese school textbooks, has written a long article on the changes in the Japanese view of Western clothes. He maintains that the Westernisation of modern Japanese clothes was necessitated by the modernisation policy of the state,[5] and is even close to saying that the Westernisation of clothes as such *was* modernisation.

We can tentatively accept Ienaga's thesis. Generally, any cultural change is motivated by cultural necessity. In the period after the 1840s, it was necessary to change Japanese culture, to modernise and Westernise it, in order to secure Japanese freedom from foreign invasion. It is worth noting, however, that Japanese independence, even though it called for cultural changes, meant the preservation of traditional Japanese culture as well. In this sense, the Meiji Emperor's 1871 mandate was an expression of the grave dilemma of modern Japan. There was a great contradiction in Japan's adopting Western culture to fight against the West.[6] Therefore, in spite of the decrees mentioned above, there remained strong resistance to the adoption of Western clothes. The Tokugawa shogunate issued several orders prohibiting people from wearing 'strange clothes', permitting a restricted use of Westernised dress for military training only.[7] The fact that the Western clothes were adopted in spite of these prohibitions can only be taken as another indication of how strong the necessity was for cultural change in Japan at that time. In any case, there was a profound dilemma, which was later vividly manifested in two diametrically opposed attitudes taken by the Japanese people towards the new clothes.

The mainstream of the Meiji government was determined to Westernise Japanese clothes. In 1872, the Meiji Emperor himself started appearing in public in a Western grand ceremonial dress (Figure 18.1).[8] Officials in the central government offices quickly changed to the Western clothes, which were certainly much more suited to work in an office with desks and chairs.[9] Around 1870–5, there was the first wave of *bunmei kaika* [Civilisation and enlightenment], and not only clothes but many other elements were more or less Westernised. Following the military officers, soldiers, and officials, policemen and mailmen started wearing new Westernised uniforms. The officials at that time wore frock-coats; the business suits (*sebiro*), which are so uniformly worn by Japanese males nowadays as to be considered the uniform of the Japanese businessman, were not yet on the scene. By around 1887 the frock-coats had penetrated down to local officials and it became the norm for the Japanese official, when at work, to be seen in Western clothes.[10]

The second big wave of Westernisation came in 1884 with the opening of the famous Rokumeikan. Thinking that, in order to have the unequal treaties with the Western powers revoked, it was necessary to show to the Westerners that the Japanese could afford a 'civilised life', the then Foreign Minister Inoue Kaoru ordered the construction of a Westernised pavilion, called the Rokumeikan, where high officials and their wives gathered every evening for Western-style dancing and music. They were of course clad in Western dress. This was the first occasion on which Japanese women wore Western

Figure 18.1 Portrait of the Emperor of Japan, print by Hashimoto Chikanobu (橋本周延), late nineteenth century (colour woodblock-printed). BM Asia Department 1906, 1220,0.1596. © The Trustees of the British Museum.

Figure 18.2 HIM The Empress of Japan, photograph, late nineteenth century. George Grantham Bain Collection, Library of Congress, LC-B2-1409-3. Courtesy Library of Congress.

clothes, but it failed to become the springboard for the wholesale adoption of such clothes by Japanese women. For the dress that the ladies who gathered at the Rokumeikan were required to wear was an anachronistic *décolleté*, a form of dress that was already regarded as outdated in the West itself.[11] The Empress began to appear in public in Western clothes (Figure 18.2). When the imperial couple made a tour of inspection of a local area, the Empress bestowed pieces of cloth on the wives of local officials of high rank before-hand, so that they too could wear Western clothes to greet her.[12]

These endeavours by the Meiji government to reform the clothing of Japanese women failed, however. Even though it was becoming popular for Japanese males to wear Western clothes, Japanese women retained their traditional wear. This contrasting picture was to remain throughout the Meiji and Taisho periods (1868–1926) and into the early part of the Showa period (1926–89). Ienaga seems to suggest that Japanese women were backward in modernising their clothes.[13] However, it may well be that women could not find new clothes that met their everyday needs, or simply that they found their traditional wear satisfactory. To that extent they were not liberated. But precisely because of the Rokumeikan episode, which was synonymous with the Meiji government's rabid Westernisation, a movement calling for the preservation of national characteristics was building at that time. In this atmosphere, any attempt to Westernise the clothes of Japanese women would have failed. In other words, the problem of cultural dilemma should be stressed as much as the logic of necessity. But before examining this problem, let us look at the process of the adoption of Western uniforms in Meiji Japan.

The process of standardisation of modern Japanese clothes

The logic of necessity works most powerfully with military clothing. Like all other non-Western countries, Japan had to Westernise its military forces in order to resist the Western powers, and by the logic of cultural linkage had to Westernise its military uniforms too. However, it is not true to say that Japan adopted all-out Western uniforms from the beginning.

The first modern military exercise in Japan took place in a field called Tokumaru-gahara (in today's Itabashi-ku, Tokyo) on the initiative of Takashima Shuhan, Japan's first modern military scientist, who had been imprisoned by the Tokugawa shogunate because of his advocacy of military modernisation. Shooters who participated in this exercise wore an original uniform which Takashima created from traditional Japanese working suits.[14] Another famous proto-modern scientist named Egawa Tarozaemon, who was a petty local governor in Izu, volunteered to organise a platoon of musketeers from peasant soldiers recruited under his jurisdiction. To train them, Egawa invented shirts, trousers and hats which resembled traditional Japanese wear. Utilising local materials and even waste paper from his office, Egawa consciously created Japanese uniforms, changing them step by step for reasons of utility. For instance, he created a new hat by cutting the brim of the traditional broad-brimmed hat to facilitate the handling and carrying of the gun. He made the hat in the shape of Mount Fuji.[15] These are examples of the conscious rejection of outright imitation and the pursuit of indigenous rationality. We must take note of the fact that these moves were taken as a result of direct necessity – the rationale behind them was the danger of a Western invasion.

In 1858, a translation of a Dutch book of the uniforms of the Dutch royal army, with colour illustrations, was published by the Fukui clan.[16] This is one example of the strong interest shown by the Japanese in Western military uniforms. But they were more interested in how to differentiate ranks by uniforms, colours and ornaments than in direct imitation. Military uniforms became more and more varied in order to differentiate ranks, platoons, arms, clans and so forth.[17] There were cases of more frivolous and flattering imitation: individual officers bought Western uniforms in Yokohama or even ordered them overseas, simply to make themselves stand out.[18] After these various attempts at differentiation, Japanese military uniforms were finally made really uniform by the Meiji government. One should emphasise again that the Japanese did not borrow directly from the Western model. When the Tokugawa government sought France's military assistance in its final days, Napoleon III was responsive enough to send a whole set of French military uniforms, along with a group of military teachers, but the Tokugawa uniforms never looked like the French ones.[19]

The first army uniforms adopted by the Meiji government in 1870 were modelled on the French uniform only to a limited extent, while the navy uniforms followed the English model. In 1887, around the time when nationalism was on the rise, the army uniforms were changed to the Prussian style. In 1905, the year of Japan's victory in the Russo-Japanese war, the Japanese army adopted the notorious khaki uniform,[20] which was to be forever remembered as the symbol of that army. Study is required into how this uniform acted as an integrating force for the Japanese people, while being repugnant to all other peoples in Asia and in the world. It goes without saying that the khaki uniform standardised the thought and behaviour not only of the soldiers who wore it but also of the Japanese people as a whole.

Japanese schoolchildren are well known for wearing school uniforms. Until a decade or so ago, uniforms were even worn by college students. There are many countries where schoolchildren wear uniforms, but Japan is a special case in that the custom is almost universal.

The Japanese schoolboy started wearing a Westernised uniform around 1884, again shortly before the upsurge in nationalism.[21] The uniform was characterised by a jacket with a tight collar and brass buttons. Its colour was always black, except in summer, when it was pepper-and-salt. It is said to have been in the Prussian style. The basic function of the uniform is to symbolise a sense of belonging to a certain school, identifying the wearer with his schoolmates and differentiating his school from other schools. What is unique about it is that its basic form has always been the same throughout the country, with only such small symbols as the badge, the style of the buttons, and the number of white lines on the cap differentiating schools. It is also singular in that it started in state-run schools and then spread to private schools.[22]

On the other hand, the Japanese schoolgirl was far behind the boy in wearing a Westernised uniform. In fact, the first national women's teachers' college adopted a proto-Westernised uniform even before the Rokumeikan period, but this was soon abandoned and a more traditional style readopted.[23] It was well into the Taisho period (1910s and 1920s) before some private girls' high schools started having their students wear Westernised uniforms.[24] In contrast to the case of boys' uniforms, private schools took the lead here. More detailed research is needed into the role of the state, and in particular the Education Ministry, in institutionalising the school uniform in pre-war Japan.

Resistance to the Westernisation of clothes

There is much evidence to show that the Meiji oligarchy seriously wanted the people, both men and women, to wear Western clothes. It was deemed imperative for the modernisation of the country and the building of an independent nation.[25] Japanese men changed their clothes quickly, but, as we have seen, women did not. Why was there this difference? The probable reason is that, just as women's clothes were about to change, there was an upsurge in nationalism. It is not simply because Japanese women were backward. The people, or at least a proportion of them, wanted to preserve and revive their culture as a reaction to the excessive Westernisation sponsored by the state. And, indeed, men too began to return to the traditional *kimono* at around that time.

Also, the Western clothes were tight, formal, and uncomfortable. For example, the frock-coat had to be worn with a white shirt that had a very high collar. Around the time of the Sino-Japanese war, this led to the coining of a new word, *haikara*, which meant stylish or modern, though in most cases it was used to ridicule those who wore Westernised clothes and who were thus considered to be excessively Westernised. Another coinage, derived from the word *haikara*, was *bankara*. Since *ban* meant 'barbarian', this word was a more straightforward attack on Westernisation. The *bankara* style involved intentionally dressing like a rustic, wearing a ragged and dirty *kimono*. Both *haikara* and *bankara* indicate both how conscious the Japanese were forced to become regarding their clothes, and the fact that they could not go along with Westernisation to the end.[26]

In simplistic terms, *haikara* was seen to be appropriate to better-off, urban people, and *bankara* to the poor from the countryside. But often the same person dressed in *haikara* style at one time and *bankara* at another: there was a dualistic attitude which approved the Westernisation of clothes at one time and at another wanted to deny it. Many of those who pretended to be *bankara* knew that the Westernised clothes were necessary for the building of a strong Japan. Kenneth Pyle summarised the conflict felt by Japanese youth of the Meiji period:

> For many Japanese in this period of intense national consciousness, aliena-
> tion from their own cultural heritage posed perplexing dilemmas. Building
> a powerful industrial nation required supplanting much of Japanese tradi-
> tion with techniques and practices borrowed from the West. Young Jap-
> anese were troubled by the implications of this process, for the very
> modernity they sought had in some sense to be regarded as alien in origin.
> They were in fact painfully sensitive to the self-effacement that cultural
> borrowing implied. They saw in Westernisation the destruction of Japanese
> identity. Youth is typically attracted to the new; but was not the joy of inno-
> vation greatly lessened if the 'new' was not really new, but merely borrowed
> or imitated?
>
> But what was the alternative? Japanese uniqueness could be defined
> only in terms of the old and the traditional. Yet was it not the old and the
> traditional that would have to be discarded if the nation was to modernise
> and survive? And were not the old and the traditional bitterly symbolic of
> national impotence? Our concern here is with the attempts that young Japa-
> nese made to resolve these dilemmas – to reconcile the conflicting needs of
> cultural borrowing and national pride, to be both modern and Japanese.[27]

Two dualities in Japanese culture

As we have seen, the schoolboy's uniform started at state-run schools. The military uniform was of course instituted by the public authorities. And the frock-coat, and later the business suit, was above all the uniform of the public servant. We can conclude from this that, for the Japanese, Western clothes were clothes to be worn only in public. In private, when they were out of the public eye, they would change to the traditional *kimono*, the informal wear. The Japanese have lived with this sartorial dualism for a century. However, as the Westernised clothes worn in public were more or less standardised, and as the schoolboy's uniform spread from the state-run to the private school, the standardisation of clothes began to penetrate people's private lives.

When they wore Westernised clothes, the Japanese did not always feel physically and psychologically at ease. Yet they put up with wearing them, because they believed that by so doing they were supporting the state's policy of strengthening the country. In other words, wearing Western clothes was in harmony with the 'getting out of Asia and entering Europe' (*datsu-A nyū-Ō*) policy.[28] It is not necessary to dwell on the role of this policy in Japan's aggression against other Asian countries. The *haikara* style had much to do with the country's public policy toward Asia. However, this does not mean that the *bankara* style could be exonerated, simply because it represented resistance to the Westernisation of Japanese clothes. On the contrary, the *bankara* side of the modern Japanese mentality led Japan into the war against Asia and the world. Ultra-nationalistic pan-Asianists and so-called *tairiku ronin* (adventurers on the Asian continent) were full of *bankara* spirit. Because they were irritated by the Westernisation of Japanese culture led by the state, they at first wanted Japan to forge alliances with other Asian countries against the West; however, they soon abandoned such efforts in favour of Japan alone. In conclusion, both aspects of this Japanese duality had much to do with the course of history of modern Japan.

Conclusion

Many in the West, and also in developing countries, often praise or envy Japan, saying that she succeeded in modernising herself and yet kept much of her traditional culture as well. When they say this, however, they forget that Japan's modernisation ended in a fateful war. It is also clear that this state-led modernisation was not simply economic and political, but involved many painful cultural transformations, such as the one in clothing, and a process of profound contradiction and conflict.

On the other hand, the people were not simply passive, the victims of the cultural transformations engineered by the state. Some of them volunteered to participate in the process and many others, perhaps unwittingly, resisted it. But they did so within the broad framework dictated by historical conditions under which the non-West had to take the West as its model in order to resist it. All the cultural transformations were directed toward the building of a nation-state, and because of this both the people and state were blinded to the implications of the changes. It was inevitable that this would result in the kind of dualism mentioned above. The Japanese contradiction erupted before long, taking the form of military expansion in Asia and the Pacific.

Notes

1   Natsume Soseki, *Wagahai wa neko de aru*, chap. 7. Originally in *Asahi shimbun*, January 1906; *Complete Works (Soseki zenshu)*, vol. 2 (Iwanami Shoten, Tokyo, 1956), pp. 20–3;

quoted in Koike Mitsue, 'Ifuku no imi', in Yabe Akihiko, ed., *Seikatsu no naka no ifuku* (Ōbunsha, Tokyo, 1983), p. 19.

2   Lee Hang-ro, an entry to *Seoung-jung-won il-ji*, 11 September 1866; quoted in Kang Jae un, *Chōsen no jōi to kaika* (Heibonsha, Tokyo, 1977), p. 40.

3   P. G. Bogatyrěv, *The Functions of Folk Costume in Moravian Slovakia* (Paris/The Hague, 1971); this is an English translation of a book originally published in Slovak in 1937. Also see Kuwano Takashi, *Minshū bunka no kigōgaku: Senkakusha Bogatyrev no shigoto* (Tōkai Daigaku Shuppankai, Tokyo, 1981).

4   Kon Wajirō, *Nihon fukushoku shōshi*, in his Complete Works (*Kon Wajirō shū*), 7 (Domesu Shuppan, Tokyo, 1972), p. 324.

5   Ienaga Saburō, *Nihonjin no yōfuku kan no hensen* (Domesu Shuppan, Tokyo, 1976), p. 27.

6   Meiji Japan's was a typical case of antagonistic acculturation. The historian Arnold Toynbee characterised Meiji Japan's attitude toward Western civilisation as 'Herodian' as opposed to the 'zealot' attitude toward other civilisations; see A. J. Toynbee. *Rekishi, no kyōkun*, trans. by Matsumoto Shigeharu (Iwanami Shoten, Tokyo, 1957), pp. 86–9.

7   One of those orders is found as the entry of 1 July 1861 to *Zoku Tokugawa jikki*. See also Ienaga (note 5 above), p. 22.

8   *Nihon seikatsu bunka-shi*, vol. 7 (Kawade Shobō Shinsha, Tokyo, 1980), p. 206.

9   In one of his conversations with Li Hung-chang in 1876, Mori Arinori, then the Japanese Minister to China, justified the Japanese adoption of Western clothes by saying that Japanese old clothes were loose and comfortable, fitting for those people who wanted to live peaceful and uneventful lives, but they were totally unsuitable for those who worked hard. See *Mori Arinori zenshū*, vol. 1 (Senbundō Shoten, Tokyo, 1972), p. 162.

10   Shōwa Joshi Daigaku Hifukugaku Kenkyūshitsu, *Kindai Nihon fukusō-shi* (Kindai Bunka Kenkyujo, 1971), pp. 56–7.

11   This was brought to my attention by Professor Koike Mitsue of Ochanomizu Women's University, Tokyo. Also see Tanida Etsuji and Koike Mitsue, *Nihon fukushoku-shi* (Kōseikan, Tokyo, 1989), p. 159.

12   Ienaga (note 5 above), pp. 27–9.

13   Ienaga (note 5 above), pp. 11–13, 32–3.

14   Ōta Rinichiro, *Nihon kindai gunpuku shi* (Yūzankaku Shuppan, Tokyo 1972), pp. 7–10.

15   Ōta (note 14 above), pp. 13–14.

16   Ōta (note 14 above), p. 12.

17   Ōta (note 14 above), p. 16.

18   Ōta (note 14 above), pp. 24, 27–8.

19   Tanno Iku, ed., *Sōgō fukushoku-shi jiten* (Yūzankaku, Tokyo, 1980), p. 134

20   Ōta Rinichiro, 'Kindai Nihon gunpuku shi', *Hifuku bunka* (Bunka Fukusō Gakuin, Tokyo), no. 68 (October 1961), p. 17.

21   Tanno (note 19 above), pp. 240–3.

22   Shōwa Joshi Daigaku Hifukugaku Kenkyūshitsu (note 10 above), p. 53.

23   Shōwa Joshi Daigaku Hifukugaku Kenkyūshitsu (note 10 above), pp. 326–7.

24   Tanno (note 19 above), pp. 240–3.

25   For example, Mutsu Munemitsu, later to become Foreign Minister, who conducted Meiji Japan's long struggle for the revision of the unequal treaties, in 1886 urged the Japanese to start using Western-style food, housing and clothes in order that they might adopt Western civilisation in other fields like economics, politics and railroads. See Watanabe Shūjiro, *Hyōden Mutsu Munemitsu* (Dōbunkan, Tokyo, 1897), pp. 45–57.

26   For a brief discussion of the contrast between *haikara* and *bankara*, see Koike Mitsue, 'Kindai no danmen', in Tanida Etsuji, ed., *Fukushoku no biishiki* (Ōbunsha, Tokyo, 1980), pp. 98–9. The word *ban* ('barbarian') was used by the Chinese, the Koreans, and, to a lesser extent, the Japanese to refer to the Westerners after the East Asian encounter with

the modern West. When Japanese modernisation was well under way, however, the Japanese expression underwent a curious twist; people no longer referred to the Westerners by that word, and instead adopted a new expression, *ijin* ('aliens'). Since by then things Western were considered sophisticated, the Japanese expressed their anti-Western feeling by sardonically referring to their traditional styles by the word *ban*.

27 Kenneth B. Pyle, *The New Generation in Meiji Japan: Problems of Cultural Identity, 1885–1895* (Stanford University Press, Stanford, CA, 1969), p. 4.

28 Originally this was the title of a famous short article published by Fukuzawa Yukichi in 1885.

Ottoman clothing rules
Changes in the nineteenth and twentieth centuries

Suraiya Faroqhi

From the 1500s at the very least, servitors of the sultan had worn distinctive clothing demonstrating their rank and status; the Ottoman state apparatus also supplied military uniforms to its elite troops, the janissaries, including highly-decorated felt headdresses. Ranking officers and scribes all wore long loose-fitting robes, along with turbans that might be very large and elaborate for those of elevated status. Working men, on the other hand, were often depicted in knee-length robes. Certain colours and shades were reserved for certain categories of people; thus green turbans were the outward sign of the privileged status of the descendants of the Prophet Muhammad and off-limits to other people. Differences in the colours of clothing and shoes, enforced with more or less energy according to time and place, also served to mark off the non-Muslims; foreign visitors, normally expected to wear the clothing of their respective homelands, often adopted Muslim dress while travelling in the sultans' domains.

In the case of women, the colours of their skirts and shoes sometimes served to distinguish Muslims from non-Muslims; but as veiling was often customary among non-Muslims as well, religious distinctions were less apparent than among males. However, from the eighteenth century onwards, when Muslim women of some means began to follow fashion in their street clothing and not merely in the garb worn at home, females who adopted the new styles often became the butt of intense vituperation and official surveillance. Ottoman sultans and officials seem to have taken much less of an interest in the clothes of non-Muslim females. This attitude continued even at a time when the ruler drastically intervened to change the clothes of his male servitors.

After having abolished the janissaries with a good deal of bloodshed (1826), Sultan Mahmud II (r. 1808–39) decreed that military men and state officials would dress in close-fitting jackets and trousers, while only religious scholars and judges continued to wear loose-fitting robes and turbans as part of their official garb. In the mid-nineteenth century a coat known as the *stambouline* served as the formal garb of civilian officialdom; later on the frock-coat took its place. As the standard headdress the military men and officials were henceforth obliged to adopt the fez, originally an import from Tunis that in the 1700s had served as a support for the turban. But the shape of the fez, now exposed to view, in the later 1800s changed markedly from one decade to the next and thus became a 'fashion article'.

Female clothing only began to mutate in the second half of the nineteenth century when some women of the elite first included features such as the distinctive sleeves of Victorian fashion in garments that otherwise conformed to the Ottoman style. By the late 1800s, these elite women wore more or less conventional European fashions at home often inspired by Parisian models; outdoors they concealed these accoutrements by cloaks and veils. Bridal dresses were often cut out of embroidered Ottoman silks but by 1890 or 1900, featured the ruffles, puffed sleeves and trails of contemporary European fashion. By the early 1900s even some better-off Anatolian village women had adopted the ruffled dress at least for special occasions. At the same time, 'Ottoman-style' festive clothes continued to evolve. Thus the *bindallı*, a caftan frequently made of violet-coloured velvet with elaborate embroidery in gold and silver thread, also often worn by brides, seems to have become popular in the course of the nineteenth century.

By the early 1900s, as a certain number of upper-class women started to wear transparent face veils or even abandoned this item altogether, changing female fashions became a subject of intense debate in the press and particularly in caricature. Some commentators castigated women wearing European fashions for lack of patriotism and conspicuous waste, calling for a 'national' fashion. But this discourse was full of ambiguity as the same journals in which it was promoted also carried advertisements for those fashions that the editors claimed to abhor. 'National' fashion was also to facilitate replacing the non-Muslim seamstresses who sewed most of the fashionable dresses worn by Muslim women, who mostly had not yet made a place for themselves in this trade. Other commentators, by contrast, ridiculed the prurient excitement of men who now could see unveiled women walking about the streets or using – now desegregated – public transportation.

After the institution of the Republic in 1923, sea-bathing became fashionable. In the vicinity of Istanbul by the 1930s a few young women began to appear on the beach in bathing suits. Moreover in this period the fez, now considered a symbol of the defunct empire, was officially forbidden and quite a few people lost their lives in public protests against the hat which the government now attempted to impose on the male population. However, there was no attempt to forbid the veiling of women, although official disapproval was much in evidence. As a result of these measures, by the 1930s there was a clear division between the European clothing worn by the elite and state employees on the one hand and on the other, the brimless caps, baggy trousers (*şalvar*) and all-concealing coats (*manto*) cum headscarves typical of the non-elite in both town and country.

Bibliography and further reading

Brummett, P. (2000) *Image and Imperialism in the Ottoman Revolutionary Press*, Albany, NY: SUNY Press.

Faroqhi, S., and Neumann, C. (eds) (2004) *Ottoman Costumes: From Textile to Identity*, Istanbul: Eren.

Köksal, D., and Falierou, A. (eds) (forthcoming) *Women in the Late Ottoman Empire and the Turkish Republic*, Leiden: E. J. Brill.

Quataert, D. (2000) *Consumption Studies and the History of the Ottoman Empire, 1550–1922: An Introduction*, Albany, NY: SUNY Press.

Chapter 19

Western modes and Asian clothing

Reflections on borrowing other people's dress[1]

Verity Wilson

DIFFERENT CLOTHES HAVE CAUGHT THE IMAGINATION of men and women for a very long time. European engravers of the latter half of the sixteenth century became especially fascinated by the differences in national costumes. From 1562 to 1600 twelve costume books were published in Europe, perhaps the most comprehensive being Cesare Vecellio's 1590 book, *Habiti antichi et moderni di tutte il mondo*, where one Asian is clearly distinguished from another and there is an attempt to depict different social levels for India and China.[2] Asian artists, too, were looking and commenting on European styles of dress. A *namban* screen from early seventeenth-century Japan illustrates this (Figure 19.1). The name *namban* means 'southern barbarian' and the painting across the six-fold lacquer surface depicts the arrival of the Portuguese at the Japanese port of Nagasaki. There is a sense of caricature about the portrayal of these men from Europe with their Goanese servants, as if the Japanese artist was poking fun at such outlandish trousers. It is unlikely that the trousers, in reality, were so very ample but, filtered through the eyes of people who had never seen such a style, they appeared so. The Japanese also noted the dark skin, from months at sea, the beards and curly hair, the ruffed collars of the elite and the buttoned up doublets worn by these 'men of Inde' as the Japanese first called them. The transformation that these 'men of Inde' wrought upon the Japanese can be gauged from a depiction of the initial celebration of what became an annual festival at the newly rededicated Hachiman Shrine in 1635 in the provincial castle town of Tsu. The Japanese revellers are parading in Portuguese garb.[3] They are dressing up in others' clothes for the novelty of it.

In this essay I wish to unpack something of that sense of novelty while demonstrating the serious intent which racial and cultural cross-dressing has historically held for the wearers and viewers of clothes. I make no claims for the comprehensive nature of

Figure 19.1 Detail of six-fold lacquer screen made in Japan around 1600 showing the arrival of the Portuguese in Nagasaki. © Victoria and Albert Museum, London 803-1892.

this essay, but trust that my perhaps idiosyncratic choice of examples will serve to stimulate debate about the ways in which modes of dressing, which at first sight seem merely frivolous or shallow, are, in fact, central to the issues of identity and difference.

Nearly three hundred years after the townsfolk of Tsu delighted in imitating the capacious trousers of the Portuguese, the Japanese delegation sent to oversee the Japan–British Exhibition of 1910 posed with confidence and aplomb in what are perceived as 'western' suits (Figure 19.2). Hurriedly re-thinking the Aryan thesis on race to accommodate their 'civilised' Asian visitors, their British hosts were no doubt relieved that some channel of communication had been opened up via similarity of dress. Japan's newly minted status as a coloniser herself meant a change of approach for the British. The suit with collar and tie marks out the Japanese men, in their western counterparts' eyes, as 'one of us'. They wear Western suits; they can be empire builders. It is an example of clothing's remarkable, and remarkably simple, propensity to signify inclusion in, or exclusion from, a group.

The appropriation of Western garments by some segments of Japanese society in the late nineteenth century, and by others in different times and places, is not, of course, a straightforward clash between 'modernity' and 'tradition'. Visual images tend to simplify the distinction. In China, at celebrations to mark the beginning of the new republic in 1912, a picture delineated on a festive lantern showed a man wearing a 'half-and-half' hat. One half was in Western-style while the other half was shaped like an

Figure 19.2 The Japan–British Exhibition at the White City, London, 1910 (postcard).
Author's collection.

official's hat from the overthrown imperial regime. Across the hat was written: 'The
transition between old and new'.[4] In reality, these conceptual categories have fluid
boundaries and are entangled and interrelated.

I am aware that designating clothes as 'Western' for people who wear them in other
areas of the world may be inaccurate and cause some unease. I concede that the term
'cosmopolitan' or 'world' dress is preferable, but I would make a plea for using the
more contested terminology in certain historic circumstances.[5] 'Western' was how
people from countries outside Europe perceived them when they first encountered
them and 'Western' is often the word used in other languages.

The Japan–British Exhibition of 1910 is just one example of many such international exhibitions held in Europe and the Americas in the second half of the nineteenth century and the first part of twentieth, and they have many resonances for the
study of dress. They provided particularly intense and ideologically charged theatres
of national display and competition in which the dressed (and occasionally undressed)
bodies of other people materialised cultural and racial difference in particularly stark
forms. This was done through the presentation of human beings brought from all over
the world and displayed in native villages, apparently going about what was thought to
be their daily business. The difference between this and the freak show might seem
rather tenuous from the perspective of the present day and, indeed, may well have been

blurred in the minds of visitors, but it should be noted that the early proponents of the inclusion of such spectacles of native peoples included at least some who saw them as serious contributions to the nascent science of anthropology. It was of no concern at the time, and indeed mostly unknown to the visitor, that the exhibited people in what we now perceive as these unpalatable shows were wearing ceremonial clothes to do menial chores. The costumed presence of these peoples, the theatricality of what they wore, and their actual clothes, were the defining attributes which visitors to the exhibitions remembered. Flamboyant headdresses, flowing sleeves, elaborately knotted sashes enclosing living, moving bodies surely sustained the imagination in a way that native houses and accoutrements, the other hallmark of these constructed expressions of difference, did not. These hugely popular spectacles, begun at the Paris Exposition Universelle of 1889, were by no means the first opportunities that people had for gazing at others. Native people had been present, along with their country's exhibits, and some had worked as chefs and waiters, for example, at recreated cafés and teahouses at earlier exhibitions.[6] What one might class as freak shows both predated and ran alongside the very first Great Exhibition in Hyde Park, London, of 1851. *The Times* of London for Sunday 24 August 1851 advertised 'Golden Water Lilies – The Small-Footed Chinese Lady and family' who could be seen for one shilling, as well as 'Syrian Ladies and Musicians', recently arrived from Aleppo, illustrating their manners, customs, costumes and music at the Egyptian Hall in Piccadilly.

One of the main physical residues of these exhibitions took the form of museums. Curators are therefore the legatees of the human and other displays at these international fairs, for much of what was shown temporarily then came to reside permanently in museums. For example, a Paraguayan shirt, a white flannel *burnous* from Tunisia and a red Chinese dragon robe – pointedly, not European clothes – were some of the first dress items to enter the Victoria and Albert Museum in London early in its history. In trying to 'fill out' such clothes with human life, it is remarkable how many images show Europeans wearing them; such images have a valency for the understanding of transnational and shifting identities.

The photograph of two of Queen Victoria's sons (Figure 19.3), Prince Alfred on the right and Prince Arthur on the left, hangs in Osborne House, the much-loved royal home on the Isle of Wight in the south of England. These bedizened princes were fortunate indeed to have such a bountiful dressing-up chest but there is more of a spin than that to be put on this image. The two boys, dressed as Sikh princes, signified colonial appropriation and imperial possession in a very tangible way. There is no mistaking the echoes of empire with which the picture is imbued: the web of imperial rhetoric is woven too tightly round the offspring of the Empress of India.

In the same way that the Victorian princes engage with the other by dressing as their Sikh opposite numbers, so white military men do the same by dressing as the 'Noble Warrior'.[7] Clothing is the connective tissue that designates them as such. The fantasy of what an 'Oriental' warrior should look like became reality in the design of dress uniforms for officers and men of the Indian army (Figure 19.4). The cavalry units got the most colourful and dramatic outfits – a knee-length tunic in a bright colour, a striped or patterned cummerbund in the style of a princely Mughal sash and a full-wrapped turban. Although the Sikh state was annexed by Britain in 1849, British officers were impressed by the Sikh army's fighting skills. Their bravery and determination in defeat were noted and soon they were being recruited to serve for Britain. The

Figure 19.3 Prince Alfred (*right*) and Prince Arthur in Sikh dress photographed by Dr Ernst Becker, Osborne House, Isle of Wight, September 1854. The Royal Archives © HM Queen Elizabeth II.

Figure 19.4 Lt K. B. Joynson of the 15th Lancers, 1909. Courtesy of the Council of the National Army Museum, London.

turban and beard were retained as part of Indian army uniform for Sikh units until 1947 and their British officers sought to appropriate the soldiers' martial qualities by using their clothes.[8]

If we only looked at two pictures, Queen Victoria's small sons and Lt K. B. Joynson, the story would end there but, as my subsequent images and examples show, the narrative of dressing up is infinitely more ambivalent and nuanced.[9] It is a truism that we all draw on our own cultural assumptions and resources when we are trying to formulate a theory or make a judgement, and the 'Western modes' in the title of this essay refers not so much to styles of clothing but to ways of thinking and perceiving. The broad range of examples of people dressing up in others' clothes that I have selected here may be provocatively juxtaposed, but the one thing that they have in common is their subjects' own awareness of the clothes they inhabit; this is not my construction.

Violet Gordon Woodhouse (1870–1951) is very far from being a warrior despite donning an approximation of a Sikh turban (Figure 19.5). She was one of the twentieth

Figure 19.5 Violet Gordon Woodhouse in the late 1920s or 1930s. Courtesy of Jessica Douglas-Home and the Harvill Press.

century's most gifted musicians, the first person ever to be recorded on the harpsichord, and an early advocate for the revival of music by Scarlatti, Purcell and Bach on that instrument. She was the inspirer of devoted passion from both sexes and her evident physical allure – she lived in a *ménage à trois* at one point – was heightened by her choice of clothes. Her extensive wardrobe, under the influence of the great ballet impresario, Diaghilev, turned away from Europe and she bedecked herself in dazzling ensembles which she co-ordinated from disparate items, some of which were genuinely Asian, like the Chinese sleeveless dragon coat she is seen wearing here, and some of which were creations of her own. Violet Woodhouse's salon at her house in Gloucestershire became metropolitan Bloomsbury's rural twin.[10] As has been noted, the aristocratic bohemian hostesses who presided over such gatherings expressed their creativity in large part through their appearance. Dressing up and pleasure went triumphantly hand in hand and lavish, sparkling clothes refuted any hint of material deprivation.[11]

There is clearly some consternation about the contents of a will in George Smith's melodramatic painting, *The Rightful Heir*, exhibited at London's Royal Academy in 1874 (Figure 19.6). The dark-suited gentlemen studying the will are in sharp contrast to the robed usurper who seems to be mounting a spirited challenge to the small boy in a velvet suit. For the Victorian viewers of this narrative picture, the angry impostor's dress – a Chinese dragon robe – marked him out as unsavoury, linking 'Oriental' with 'untrustworthy'.

In Violet Woodhouse's case, she picks and chooses, mixes and matches from a variety of make-believe and real countries. The gesticulating Victorian in *The Rightful Heir* bears no resemblance to the meritorious Chinese bureaucrat for whom the robe was originally designed, and furthermore he dons it as a dressing gown, transforming what was a formal garment of status into something louche.

Figure 19.6 George Smith's oil painting, *The Rightful Heir*, exhibited in 1874. Reproduced courtesy the estate of Christopher Wood.

So, garments are appropriated and altered. We shape them in order to shape our appearance. No other artefacts are as malleable as clothes. The wisteria-clad garment, a gift to Edith Wilson (1872–1961), does not 'look like' traditional Asian dress (Figure 19.7). We modify the dress of others to parallel that of our own culture. Edith Wilson's dress was given to her by the Japanese Silk Growers' Association in 1920. As the wife of Woodrow Wilson (1856–1924), then President of the United States, she travelled extensively in an ambassadorial capacity on goodwill missions and several times visited Japan. The garment is appropriately emblazoned at the centre top with the crossed flags of the two nations, pointing up the diplomatic nature of the gift. When the presentation

Figure 19.7 Japanese *kimono* altered for Mrs Woodrow (Edith) Wilson, c. 1920. © The National Trust for Historic Preservation in Washington, DC.

was made to Edith Wilson in what must have been an act of ritualised gift-giving, the garment did not look like this. It was originally a *kimono*, that unmistakable visible signature of Japan. On her return to America, Mrs Wilson had the *kimono* re-tailored and we can speculate that she did so in order to make it wearable. It is known that she wore it on several occasions after it had been altered. The re-styling, while undeniably negating much that was 'Japanese' about it, nevertheless, set in motion a creative interaction. The alteration can be viewed as one woman's response to a sartorial dilemma. Edith Wilson would have been unable to wear the *kimono* in its original form. The entire ensemble of sash, wooden shoes and piled coiffure would have transformed the First Lady into a ridiculous spectacle, but failing to wear these correct accessories would perhaps have been seen as trivialising Japan's national dress. Mrs Wilson, as the consort of the man who presided over one of the world's most powerful nations, was not in the same position as many of her moneyed contemporaries who were still floating about their Frank Lloyd Wright homes in a miasma of *Japonisme* wearing *kimono* as artistic fashion garments.[12]

Before denouncing the violation of a traditional garment such at this, we should reflect on its fate had it remained intact. Edith Wilson, by adapting it to a form with which she felt comfortable, gave it a life over and above that for which it was intended. It was envisaged as a symbol of diplomatic amity but Edith Wilson saw other possibilities in a garment that otherwise would have remained a presentation piece.

Near the end of the twentieth century, when Edith Wilson's gesture might be differently inflected as post-modern, another wife in the public eye, Cherie Booth, the partner of the then Prime Minister of Great Britain, wore a sari to celebrate fifty years of Indian independence at the Indian High Commission in London, in 1997. The next day, on Friday, 14 November, the London *Evening Standard* trumpeted the triumph of Mrs Blair's clothing over that of her opposite number, the wife of the then Opposition leader, Ffion Hague, who merely wore Chanel. Cherie Booth had not borrowed the garment from a friend as the newspaper, presumably copying a neatly worded press release from Number 10 Downing Street, proclaimed. In fact, she had carefully orchestrated her appearance by consulting the British-born Punjabi designer, Babi Mahil, who runs the successful London shop Chiffons, whose clients include British Asians and Asians as well as Westerners.[13]

Mrs Stanley Charles Nott – for that is how she is addressed even though she has a name of her own, Lucille – was photographed in 1944 at Palm Beach in Florida for the frontispiece of the catalogue entitled *Chinese Art of World Renown* (Figure 19.8). The collection pictured and described in that catalogue belonged to her husband, Stanley Charles, and the treasures were displayed in their mansion aptly named 'Jadeholm'. Mrs Pierre Loeb – also addressed by her husband's name – in her Paris apartment in 1929 is photographed surrounded by tribal works of art and there is a Picasso paintings hanging there too.[14] Both these women have chosen to wear Chinese garments to chime with the aesthetics of their respective husbands' collection, as if wearing Western clothes would somehow diminish the appeal of the objects and intrude upon a carefully controlled and contrived mood. Their Chinese clothes serve as cues to social perception. In the same way that these rich women take on their partner's name, losing some part of their own identity in the process, so the foreign robes reconfigure them as part of their husband's collection. Although a totally female enterprise, a breeder of championship Pekinese dogs, Mrs Lilburne MacEwan from Staines, also exploits dress in a

Figure 19.8 Mrs Stanley Charles (Lucille) Nott in Florida, 1944.

similar vein. The 'Chinese-ness' of her trio of award-winning pedigrees – Palace Shi, Manchu Shansi and Chi Li – photographed for the 'Animal gossip' column of *The Ladies' Field* of 5 December 1901, is accentuated by their breeder's daughter, Miss MacEwan, standing beside these little champions in a Han Chinese woman's wraparound skirt and three-quarter-length gown and wearing a Manchu headdress.[15] Miss McEwan's clothes go unremarked both in the article and in the caption to the illustration for, while on the one hand, we are dealing here with an instance of 'the exotic', on the other hand, we should bear in mind the very commonplace nature of this particular manifestation of 'the exotic' for middle- and upper-class women in Victorian and Edwardian Britain. Quite simply, there were a lot of robes about and opportunities to dress up in them were by no means rare.

The clothes themselves were nearly always the 'real thing' and, despite the fact that they were favoured above other native items as easily transportable souvenirs for those who personally travelled in Asia, their authenticity was played up by performing artists who wanted to imbue them with a strong dose of orientalist mysticism.[16] It was also the case that such performers, who were very often women, wished to present themselves as professionals and these genuine garments perhaps lent some form of endorsement to their stage acts. Historically, the meeting place between East and West has been a place of illusions and for someone like Mademoiselle Maria Leontine who presented a programme of 'Ceremonial dances of China' in America in the 1930s, the Chinese dresses she chose to wear kept this illusion alive (Figure 19.9). Clothes from elsewhere had the power to hold back the banality of everyday life; the 'other' in this case was not

Figure 19.9 Front cover of Maria Leontine's performance publicity leaflet, *c.* 1935.

necessarily a geographical colonised domain, rather a landscape of leisure and sensa-tion.[17] Maria Leontine, Mrs Nott and Mrs Loeb, all in their separate ways hedged in by the prejudices of patriarchy, remind us that gender is another category of analysis pro-viding a mesh in which these images might be held.

The Takarazuka Revue was founded in 1913 by Kobayaschi Ichizo, a Japanese busi-nessman and Japan's Minister of Commerce and Industry between 1940 and 1941. Run by a patriarchal management, all Takarazuka's performers were, and are today, women, a contrast to the all-male Kabuki theatre. Today 700 people, ranked in a strict hierarchy, ensure the smooth running of Takarazuka's complex routines. The Taka-rasiennes, as the revue's actresses are nicknamed, specialise either in men's roles or those of women and they play these parts exclusively throughout their careers. Like the Kabuki actors, the cross-dressed performers appeal to a broad section of the public. The revue's audience spans both the generation and sex divides. In addition to portray-ing a range of men and women, the Takarazuka actresses play non-Japanese charac-ters from a variety of ethnic backgrounds. During the Second World War, the troupe's performances had a contemporary flavour, and places which had come under Japan's sway as a result of conquest provided the settings for some of the shows. The revue called *Peking*, for example, performed by Takarazuka in March 1942, saw the Japanese actresses appearing in renditions of Han Chinese and Mongolian dress. The revue was a musical representation of that city, extolling the benefits of Japanese colonial rule. The foreign characters impersonated by the Takarasiennes are based on stereotypical images, with costume and gesture providing easily recognised signatures of place and time.[18] All the following have appeared in Takarazuka's repertoire in recent years – white tie and tails in Fred Astaire-esque routines, spangled jackets and tight trousers for flamenco-like numbers as well as renderings, revue-style, of all-American classics such as *Gone with the Wind* and *Kiss Me Kate*.

The motto of Takarazuka, 'Modesty, fairness and grace', would, I feel sure, provide material for the stand-up British comedian, Eddie Izzard, an absurdist thinker and pur-veyor of what he terms 'carefully-crafted rubbish'. Like the actors from Takarazuka, he is a devastatingly charming performer, a cross-dresser like them, and one of the shows he toured was called *Dress to Kill*. Unlike the Japanese ladies, he takes the stage alone and makes no costume changes throughout his performance. There are no musicians, no sound effects, few props. He makes his impact by delivering a carefully timed monologue of eloquent nonsense and, of course, by his singular clothes. The outfit he wore for *Dress to Kill* was a skilfully organised mélange consisting of Chinese-style top, leather trousers and high heels. One definition of cross-dressing is wearing the clothing of a group one does not belong to, and, in that sense, all the pictures here fall into that category. How-ever, we would be hard pressed to put Eddie Izzard into any category and that, of course, is the whole point of his sartorial gesture. He does not accept the gendered nature of clothing and has understood its ambiguity as an indicator of gender. By dressing in this engaging fashion he is dismantling the rigid system of man versus woman. His choice of top, whether we view it as masculine or feminine, as something neutral or in-between, does have Chinese resonances. Embedded in Izzard's stage performance is a plea for Brit-ain to cleanse itself of its imperial past and to embrace a different type of global future. The garment he wears reinforces that message and makes the boundary between East and West more elastic, more open, less of a barrier. Eddie Izzard's clothing style moves us away from the inviolable and closed categories of 'gender' and 'race'.

In contrast to the complex negotiations of sexual and cultural identities presented by Izzard, the deployment by Madonna, a hugely successful popular music icon, of explicitly orientalist imagery may seem to some to be a throwback to earlier modes of appropriation which depended on an essentialised binary opposition between East and West. In the twentieth and twenty-first centuries, clothes themselves are no longer the only site of identity. Identity is written on the body. When Madonna received a Grammy award in Los Angeles on 24 February 1999, her muscular appearance caused gasps of surprise from the audience and the explosion of flashbulbs that followed resulted in all the next day's papers carrying photographs of her defined torso. The press were not so interested in the crimson satin *kimono* the singer wore to make her entrance. They therefore missed the power invested in bodily contrasts, for Madonna, by disrobing, had capitalised on the formulaic 'soft' body of the East versus the 'hard' Western body.

That contemporary performers play with costume and identity and reach across boundaries of all sorts serves to remind us that, in the past, this was not always acceptable. Living abroad very often involved a strict allegiance to the dress codes and mores of home for fear of being labelled as one who had 'gone native'. The Scottish community, to cite one example of many, is recorded as celebrating St Andrew's Day in Hankou, part of present-day Wuhan, in the 1930s with all the Gaelic pageantry that an expatriate community in China could muster. For the annual Caledonian Ball the hall was decorated with blue and white banners, thistle motifs and heather, clan shields and flags. The men donned kilts and sporrans, and ladies' frocks sported tartan sashes and ribbons.[19] Dressing up in other people's clothes was often best done when you were safely back in your own country. While local textiles might be utilised for fashioning Western-style dresses, as the novelist M. M. Kaye recalls being done in India under the Raj, there were real anxieties to do with loss of identity in a foreign land.[20] While foreigners donned indigenous clothes in portrait photographers' studios within Asia itself, this act of dressing up for the camera in borrowed dress maintained a respectable distance from the realities of native life. The Misukoshi Studios in Tokyo from the early twentieth century, for example, recorded European and American travellers' sojourns in Japan by producing postcard portraits of them in Japanese *kimono*.[21] The clothes here partake of the nature of 'props', the kind of studio costume which has a pedigree in a Western regime of visuality right back to the 'Oriental' turbans and robes to be found in the seventeenth-century Amsterdam studio of Rembrandt.

Edward Brenan, an official of the European-staffed Imperial Chinese Maritime Customs, played the part of a Chinese bureaucrat and dressed up in dragon robes for the camera too. He certainly owned a dragon robe ensemble, having been granted the right to wear the regalia by the Chinese in 1908. The dragon robe's original intended use was as a hierarchical garment and it was worn by male bearers of rank in the Chinese civil service. As such it was a uniform of office although Edward Brenan, as a foreigner, likely never wore it this way publicly and may never have put the robes on again after he had been photographed in them. The Scottish doctor, Dugald Christie, who carried out a successful plague eradication programme in Manchuria in 1912, was also presented with Chinese robes of the Imperial Order of the Double Dragon in 1897. He is reported to have enjoyed wearing them, and the photograph showing him in them, surrounded by his staff, is evidence of this. It is also evidence of the mismatch between such an impractical garb and the supremely practical job of running a hospital.[22]

The visual potency of a photograph of yourself in garments that you do not wear habitually has been a constant strand running through the images. All these people are deliberately posing and their appearance demanded an audience. They all had the sensation of wearing unfamiliar clothes. They had to adjust their stance to accommodate their bodies to clothing shapes that fasten, drape or hang differently from those they were used to. This accommodation, in turn, offered a mode of escape, but an escape that was safe.[23] With the exception of the Indian Army officer who, in any case, wears a hybrid style, the Asian clothes of these Westerners do not represent a full engagement with the countries from which the garments originated. There were Westerners, however, for whom the transformative attributes of native dress were both necessary and desirable. The Italian Jesuit, Matteo Ricci (1552–1610), at first adopted Chinese Buddhist robes and, as was the Jesuit way, sought support from the highest echelon in the land, namely the imperial throne. While this might have had obvious advantages, the obverse was also true, with Jesuit policies open to the scrutiny of meddlesome Chinese civil servants. To play down the religious aspect of his mission's work, Ricci swapped his Buddhist vestments for a Confucian scholar's dress.[24] City-dwelling foreign diplomats, administrators and merchants not only had access to both luxury and textiles and to tailors of Western-style clothing, they were also in touch with colonial suppliers in European countries. Missionaries of a later era than the Jesuits and plant-hunters, because their work had a different emphasis and was often conducted in remote regions, were much more reliant on local commodities. The plant-hunter George Forrest (1873–1932), who made seven expeditions to south-west China between 1904 and 1932 and who introduced a variety of rhododendron as well as other alpine flora to British gardens, perhaps first dressed in ordinary Chinese clothes as a disguise when fleeing from Tibetan attackers. In any case, he seems to have adopted the same manner of dressing whenever he was plant collecting.[25] Mildred Cable and the sisters Francesca and Evangeline French worked together as missionaries for the China Inland Mission and were resident in that country for over twenty years of their lives. Like Forrest, they wore modest, plain Chinese dress for their work in Shanxi province and Central Asia in the years between 1902 and 1923 (Figure 19.10). They were known as 'The Blue Lady', 'The Great Lady' and 'The Brown Lady' respectively by their converts after the colour of their clothes. Presumably these never varied.[26] In adopting such styles these doughty ladies were not only signalling their intent to accept, and be accepted by, the Chinese, they were also constructing images of 'Chinese-ness' that differed from the picturesque embodiment emanating from some of their fellow countrymen; each personified 'the Chinese' selectively.

That the journey between cultures could be traversed via clothes is a compelling idea. Clothing, as worn by all those presented in this essay, contributes to a conceptualisation of far-away countries. For many, these 'far-away countries' were seen as embodying beliefs, and so wearing clothes from those countries was an outward sign of your commitment to a cause. This was taken to extremes by such people as Maximiani Portas (1905–82), a French national with an English mother and a part-Greek father, who adopted both an Indian name, Savitri Devi, and the dress of India, a sari, in the service of a disturbing credo of Aryan supremacy. She spent the greater part of her adult life living in India and, despite the defeat of the Axis countries in the Second World War, Savitri Devi, nonetheless, looked forward to a new Nazi world order. Her eccentric and misguided philosophy as expressed in her publications has been taken up by neo-Nazi sects today. Near the end of her life, she was flattered to be invited to address racist right-wing groups in America but she died in England before she was able

Figure 19.10 The missionaries, Mildred Cable and Francesca French, in China between 1902 and 1923.

to fulfil her speaking engagements. At the time of her death at a friend's cottage in an Essex village in England, Savitri Devi was wearing a thin white sari.[27] Another lady who comes to mind at the mention of a sari is Mother Teresa, the Nobel prize-winning Albanian nun, whose life's work was also rooted in India. Her dedication took quite a different direction, that of alleviating poverty. Despite similar outward appearances in the form of a sari, and despite a deeply personal devotion to the place of India in the cosmic order, the work of Savitri Devi and Mother Teresa could not be further apart. Here clothes alone tell us nothing, reminding us of their semiotic limitations.

While some Westerners in Asia might be ambivalent about wearing native dress there in public, conversely some Asian visitors to Europe and America went to great lengths to ensure their Western garb struck the appropriate note. Gandhi is the supreme example of this and his many changes have been well documented and critiqued.[28] The transferences and translocations of the body were never to be in a single direction. One photograph (Figure 19.11), selected almost at random from the thousands of carefully-posed self images that survive from the period, can say little about politics, even the cultural politics, of its subjects. These young men in Shanghai, the

Figure 19.11 Young men in Shanghai, China, 1905. Author's collection.

Figure 19.12 Yeu Yung Ling, former lady-in-waiting to the Empress Dowager Cixi, photographed in the Thompson Studio, Hong Kong, 1910. Author's collection.

metropolis par excellence of Chinese modernity, present themselves to the lens of the camera in 1905 as 'modern Chinese', neither Westernised nor traditional. Taken in the Thompson Studio in Hong Kong in 1910, Yeu Yung Ling (Figure 19.12), a former lady-in-waiting to the Empress Dowager, has not only adopted European fashionable dress of the day but, like the group of Chinese young men, she has taken on a wholly novel pose and body language. Are these people Europeanised? Homi Bhabba has drawn attention to the way in which to be Westernised in the colonial context is to be emphatically *not* 'Western'.[29] These people are not fashion victims. They are players in the game of identities, a game which is not yet played out.

Notes

1   Keynote address presented at the Costume Society Symposium, Oxford, July 2001.

2   Donald F. Lach, *Asia in the Making Of Europe*, vol. II, *A Century of Wonder*, Book I *The Visual Arts* (Chicago: University of Chicago Press, 1970), pp. 78–104 (paperback edition, 1994).

3   Ronald P. Toby, 'The 'Indianess' of Iberia and Changing Japanese Iconographies of Other', in *Implicit Understandings: Observing, Reporting, and Reflecting on Encounters between Europeans and Other Peoples in the Early Modern Era*, ed. Stuart B. Schwartz (Cambridge: Cambridge University Press, 1994), pp. 323–51 (p. 337).

4   Henrietta Harrison, *The Making of a Republican Citizen: Political Ceremonies and Symbolism in China, 1911–1929* (Oxford: Oxford University Press, 2000), p. 30.

5   Suzanne Baizermann, Joanne B. Eicher and Catherine Cerny, 'Eurocentrism in the Study of Ethnic Dress', *Dress*, vol. 20 (1993), pp. 19–32; Joanne B. Eicher and Barbara Sumberg, 'World Fashion, Ethnic and National Dress', in *Dress and Ethnicity: Change across Space and Time*, ed. Joanne B. Eicher (Oxford: Berg, 1995), pp. 295–306.

6   Curtis M. Hinsley, 'The World as a Marketplace: Commodification of the Exotic at the World's Columbian Exposition, Chicago, 1893', in *Exhibiting Cultures: The Poetics and Politics of Museum Display*, ed. Ivan Karp and Stephen D. Levine (Washington: Smithson Institution Press, 1991), pp. 344–65.

7   Thomas S. Abler, *Hinterland Warriors and Military Dress: European Empires and Exotic Uniform* (Oxford: Berg, 1999).

8   Bernard S. Cohn, 'Cloth, Clothes and Colonialism: India in the Nineteenth Century', in *Cloth and Human Experience*, ed. Annette B. Weiner and Jane Schneider (Washington: Smithsonian Institute Press, 1989), pp. 303–53.

9   For an exemplary case study see Christine M. E. Guth, 'Charles Longfellow and Okakura Kakuzo: Cultural Cross-Dressing in the Colonial Context', *Positions*, vol. 8 (winter 2000), pp. 605–36.

10 Jessica Douglas-Home, *Violet: The Life and Loves of Violet Gordon Woodhouse* (London: The Harvill Press, 1996).

11 Elizabeth Wilson, 'Bohemian Dress and the Heroism of Everyday Life' in *Fashion Theory*, vol. 2, issue 3 (September 1998), pp. 225–44 (pp. 232–3).

12 *The Kimono Inspiration: Art and Art-to-Wear in America*, ed. Rebecca A. T. Stevens and Yoshiko Iwamoto Wada, exhibition catalogue (Washington: The Textile Museum and Pomegranate Artbooks, 1996), pp. 38–9.

13 Thanks to Dr Parminder Bhachu, Clark University, for the information about Babi Mahil.

14 James Clifford, *The Predicament of Culture: Twentieth-Century Ethnography, Literature, and Art* (Cambridge, MA: Harvard University Press, 1988), p. 210, Figure 3(a).

15 Thanks to Sarah Cheang, doctoral candidate at the University of Sussex, for sharing 'Animal gossip' with me. See also Sarah Cheang, 'The Dogs of Fo: Gender, Identity and Collecting', in *Collectors: Expressions of Self and Other*, ed. Anthony Shelton (London and Coimbra: The Horniman Museum and the Museu Antropológico da Universidade de Coimbra, 2001), pp. 55–72.

16 Costumes from the Monte Carlo Opera House, sold by order of the Societé des Bains de Mer, sales catalogue, Sotheby's, Sunday, 16 November 1980 includes authentic Asian dress as 'eastern' costume.

17 Verity Wilson, 'Studio and Soirée: Chinese Textiles in Europe and America, 1850 to the Present', in *Unpacking Culture: Art and Commodity in Colonial and Postcolonial Worlds*, ed. Ruth B. Phillips and Christopher B. Steiner (Berkeley: University of California Press, 1999), pp. 229–42.

18 Jennifer Robertson, 'Staging Ethnography: Theatre and Japanese Colonialism', in *Anthropology and Colonialism in Asia and Oceania*, ed. Jan van Bremen and Akitoshi Shimizu

(Richmond, Surrey: Curzon Press, 1999), pp. 266–84, Figure 10.2, p. 277; Dr Victoria Steele, in her address to the Costume Society symposium at Oxford in July 2001 referred to Lucile, Lady Duff Gordon (1863–1935) as designing cross-cultural costumes for the showgirls of the Ziegfeld Follies (1907–31) in New York. As with Takarazuka, there were no minority women represented in the troupe.

19   Susan Leiper, *Precious Cargo: Scots and the China Trade* (Edinburgh: National Museums of Scotland, 1997), pp. 83–4.

20   M. M. Kaye, *Golden Afternoon* (London: Penguin Books, 1998), pp. 207–8.

21   *The Kimono Inspiration*, ed. Stevens and Wada, p. 34, Figure 9 and p. 35, Figure 10.

22   Verity Wilson, *Chinese Dress* (London: Victoria & Albert Museum, 1986), pp. 12–17, Figure 3, p. 13; Leiper, *Precious Cargo*, p. 67.

23   Nancy J. Parezo, 'The Indian Fashion Show', in *Unpacking Culture*, ed. Phillips and Steiner, pp. 243–63.

24   Susan Naquin, *Peking: Temples and City Life, 1400–1900* (Berkeley: University of California Press, 2000), p. 209.

25   Leiper, *Precious Cargo*, pp. 64–5; E. H. M. Cox, *Plant-Hunting in China: A History of Botanical Exploration in China and the Tibetan Marches* (London: Collins, 1945), plates opposite pp. 126 and 158.

26   Mildred Cable and Francesca French, *The Story of Topsy* (London: Hodder and Stoughton, 1937).

27   Nicholas Goodrick-Clarke, *Hitler's Priestess: Savitri Devi, the Hindu-Aryan Myth, and Neo-Nazism* (New York: New York University Press, 1998), plate opposite p. 80.

28   Emma Tarlo, *Clothing Matters: Dress and Identity in India* (London: Hurst, 1996), pp. 62–9.

29   Homi K. Bhabha, *The Location of Culture* (London: Routledge, 1994).

Snapshot 26

Fashion and anthropology
The case of Africa

Karen Tranberg Hansen

Snapshot 26.1 Having a good time in a second-hand market in Lusaka, Zambia, 1992. Photo by Karen Tranberg Hansen.

The hallmark of anthropology is a contextual approach to the cross-cultural study of dress and its meanings. Most dress and fashion research in anthropology shares this general orientation while incorporating theoretical angles that are influenced by the specific topics under investigation. Because much of their work falls outside the West's conventional fashion canon, anthropologists have played an important role in demonstrating that fashion is not an exclusive property of the West. In recent years, much research on dress has explored the effects of globalisation. Rather than observing a homogenisation of Western-inspired fashion styles across the world, these new works reveal that stylistic choice is a complex and very diverse process. In effect, dress inspirations travel in all directions, across class lines, between urban and rural areas, and around the globe.

In their research, anthropologists pay attention to what people wear, the meanings attributed to dress, and how to interpret such meanings. I turn to my work on second-hand clothing consumption in Zambia as an example of the interaction of local and global influences in dress. My main concern has been to qualify conventional notions of second-hand clothing as cast-offs from the West's used clothing and of local people's dress practices merely as emulation of Western fashion. To do so, I explored what people in Zambia had made with these clothes, investing them with and divesting them of meanings in a variety of contexts.

Many observers view the growing import of second-hand clothing in a developing country like Zambia as a response to economic decline. What such an account misses is the opportunities this vast import offers consumers to construct visions of themselves through dress. Tracing the flow of second-hand clothing from the point of donation in the West, through its sorting and export, to its local distribution and consumption in Zambia, I explained how second-hand clothing was incorporated as desirable apparel into a gendered dress universe informed by a local cultural economy of judgement and style. A well-dressed adult in Zambia wears clothes that are well taken care of, with matched accessories to extend the good look of the clothes, carefully groomed hair and make-up to enhance the natural features, and poised manners and comportment. In this ideal scenario, women's clothing should not be tight and short, and men's never loose nor scruffy. This clothing ideal produces elegance and dignity within an overall 'look' that is neat and polished, neither too casual, flamboyant nor extravagant.

In my research I used several methods to examine both the supply and demand side of the second-hand clothing market and to explore how wearers and viewers attributed meanings to dress in Zambia. For one, participant observation in tailors' workshops enabled me to study how tailors and customers reached decisions about design and style, to discuss how tailors created and developed style, and to ask customers about their decision to go to the tailor rather than formal shops or the second-hand clothing markets. Some tailors display photo albums of their styles, old pattern books, and European and South African fashion magazines while others use simple drawings. Many customers bring garments or photos of a dress they want copied or they describe what they want the tailor to sew. 'Going to the tailor' offered rich insights into one phase in the 'meaning-making' of clothing.

Widespread repair and material alteration of second-hand clothing in tailors' workshops remake anonymous garments to fit their new owners. But the cultural ideas that help refashion second-hand clothing into local ensembles achieve the effect of 'the latest' through ongoing interaction. This is evident on the street and in social gatherings, in what people wear and how, and in their commentaries about ensembles and the scrutiny with which they examine design and styling. Depending on location in class and regional terms and on gender and age, people in Zambia attribute meanings about freedom from wants and normative constraints into second-hand clothing consumption and in so doing, they also comment on their own position in a global world.

Bibliography and further reading

Hansen, K. T. (2000) *Salaula: The World of Secondhand Clothing and Zambia*, Chicago: University of Chicago Press.

Kuechler, K., and Miller, D. (eds) (2005) *Clothing as Material Culture*, New York and Oxford: Berg.

Niessen, S., Leshkowich, A. M., and Jones, C. (eds) (2003) *Re-orienting Fashion: The Globalization of Asian Dress*, New York and Oxford: Berg.

Islamic fashion

Annika Rabo

Snapshot 27.1 Catwalk in the Nordic Museum, Stockholm, 1 October 2008, organised and sponsored by the research project Islamic Fashion in Europe. Photo © Orasis foto.

Is the term 'Islamic fashion' an oxymoron? Scores of non-Muslims find it difficult to link Islam with fashion and numerous Muslims believers insist that their way of dressing should not be associated with fickle sartorial trends. Others find the term contradictory since we do not talk about Christian, Hindu or Buddhist fashion. Nevertheless, Islamic fashion is undeniably a phenomenon of social, cultural and economic importance in the contemporary world. From Indonesia to Morocco and the USA, and from Europe to Africa, designers, stylists, garment producers and retailers are making a great deal of money from Islamic fashion. This large and growing market is mainly catering to Muslim women who are, or want to be, *hijab chic*. They signal modesty by means of covering their hair, arms and legs, yet underline that such dress can be beautiful and stylish. Islamic fashion is obviously not a uniform phenomenon. While well-known Parisian designers create showpieces for very rich Muslim clients, large 'Islamic' department stores in, for example, Turkey, cater to middle- and lower-class professional women. They want to wear strict but attractive clothes to signal their particular way of being modern consumers.

But there is also a flourishing street fashion in which the creativity of the individual wearer is highlighted. Young Islamic street fashion inspired the outfit shown in the Snapshot 27.1. The headgear is an exaggerated version of a style which has travelled from Turkey to north and west Europe. In that move it has become less Turkish and more generically European Islamic. This headgear plays with ideas of femininity by pretending to cover an enormous bun of hair. The bun may in fact be a rag, a stocking or cardboard. In this picture the scarf is combined with other clothes that young women in many parts of the world buy and put together in eclectic ways. The picture is taken at a catwalk in Stockholm in 2008 which was part of a research project on Islamic fashion in Europe. This project had an interest in how Islamic fashion travels across the globe. 'High fashion' is inspired by street wear, which in turn is influenced by elements from 'traditional' dress.

Today many non-Muslims in the West may associate Islamic dress with closure, rigidity and control of the female body. But this has not been the case historically. In the early eighteenth century Lady Mary Wortley Montagu lived in Istanbul for a year as the wife of the British ambassador. She wrote letters which, in great detail, depicted the clothes and the fashion among noble and rich women in the Ottoman Empire. These women were shocked by the uncomfortable clothes Lady Mary initially wore. They thought Lady Mary's husband had forced her into wearing a corset to protect her chastity. In the eighteenth century the loose fitting and comfortable 'Turkish dress' travelled and became fashionable for wealthy women and men in north and west Europe. 'Islamic fashion' has thus, for a long time been part of, and influenced, the development of 'Western' sartorial tastes.

Bibliography and further reading

Moors, A., and Tarlo, E. (2007) 'Introduction', *Fashion Theory*, 11, 2/3, pp. 133–41.

Navaro-Yashin, Y. (2002) 'The Market for Identities: Secularism, Islamism, Commodities', in D. Kandiyoti and A. Saktanber (eds), *Fragments of Culture: The Everyday of Modern Turkey*, New Brunswick, NJ: Rutgers University Press, 2002, pp. 221–54.

Scarce, J. (1987) *Women's Costume of the Near and Middle East*, London: Unwin Hyman.

Orientalism today

Hazel Clark

Taken from the Shanghai Tang 2006 autumn/winter collection, this image (Snapshot 28.1) appears to be a clear example of 'Sinity', the neologism coined by Roland Barthes to describe a French petit-bourgeois idea of China as a 'peculiar mixture of bells, rickshaws and opium dens'. The scene is both exotic and eroticised. The relationship of the two women is ambiguous. The seated Chinese woman and her outfit are androgynous, but her pose is masculine. The recumbent Causcasian woman is relaxed, open, and inviting. The colours of their garments and the staged interior are moody, dark reds and black. Where are they supposed to be – perhaps in an opium den or a brothel in 1930s' Shanghai?

Image has been a particular issue for Shanghai Tang since its inception in Hong Kong in 1994, with the ambition of being the first Chinese luxury brand. Having an initial intention of reviving hand-tailoring skills associated with Shanghai, the brand adopted a nostalgic and orientalised design imaginary based on the city in the 1930s, at the height of its internationalism, modernism and fashionability. But how and why could a colonised Chinese city in the 1930s impact globally the fashion in the late twentieth and twenty-first centuries?

Since the 1970s the global fashion system had looked to China for design 'inspiration', spurred by the gradual opening up of the country, but also continuing a tradition of orientalism evident in Western fashion and design since the sixteenth century. In its early days Shanghai Tang's orientalist strategy was commercially successful, especially when global fashion and design was referencing Hong Kong's cultural heritage prior to its 1997 'handover' to China. Tourists and local expatriates frequented the 1930s flagship store in central Hong Kong, as they did when its first New York store opened in 1997. The company's ambition 'to revitalize Chinese innovation and to interweave it with the dynamism of the 21st century' (see www.shangahaitang.com), appeared likely to be fulfilled. But the brand could not sustain itself on an orientalist imaginary alone, as its subsequent design and business history proved. In 1998 it was sold to Richemont, the Swiss luxury goods company, which embarked on an ambitious global expansion plan, underpinned by a revised design strategy.

The image we are looking at represents the latter of three diversified ready-to-wear ranges which the brand now retails: seasonal, classic, and authentic. Each features Chinese signifiers which are recognisable to outsiders, such as the Mandarin collar, loop and knot fastenings, or the use of silk. In 2007 the company inaugurated the Mandarin Collar Society 'to abolish the necktie'. This gimmicky initiative is also revealing. Neckties have ceased to be the sartorial norm for Western men as, world wide, dressing has become more casual, while retaining the option to dress up and display sexuality. This scenario has introduced the possibility of Chinese traditions in dress being applicable to

Snapshot 28.1 Shanghai Tang autumn/winter collection 2006. Reproduced with permission of Shanghai Tang.

the demands and desires of twenty-first-century lifestyle. While our image is styled to represent the brand's original nostalgic design, the clothes themselves are wearable in the twenty-first century. They represent how the image and reality of fashionable dress can provide us with challenges, which in this case leads us to more subtle definitions of the term 'orientalism' today.

Bibliography and further reading

Barthes, Roland (1993, original edition 1973) *Mythologies*, London: Vintage.

Clark, Hazel (2000) 'Fashion, Identity and the City: Hong Kong', *Form/Work: An Interdisciplinary Journal of Design and the Built Environment*, 4 ('The Fashion Issue' edited by Mark Stiles and Michael Carter), pp. 81–92.

Clark, Hazel (2009) 'Fashioning "China style" in the Twenty-first Century', in Eugenia Paulicelli and Hazel Clark (eds), *The Fabric of Cultures: Fashion, Identity, and Globalization*, London and New York: Routledge, pp. 177–91.

PART 6

Modern to hyper/ultra-modern
The twentieth century

Peter McNeil and Giorgio Riello

When we write about the recent decades – and indeed much of the twentieth century – scholars *do not* 'reconstruct a past that they can never know' as observed by Fritz Stern in his *Varieties of History* (1970). Depending on our age, we either remember or were a part of the Grunge style of the 1990s, the New Romantics of the 1980s, the Punks of the 1970s, the boutiques of the 1960s, the prohibitions of post-war rationing, or through our parents', grandparents', aunts' and uncles' memories, tales of short pongee silk dresses imported from China in the 1920s and the shock of seeing men walk around for the first time without neckties and hats. Of course our memories and recollections are also partial and influenced by our relationship to society. Our closeness and our personal relationships to dress in the recent past colour our interests and inflect our positions; sometimes it leads to books being written and preconceptions being challenged. It is impossible to remain neutral, detached and uninvolved: the fashion history of the recent past has, more than any previous fashion and perhaps more than most other types of histories, collective memories and personal stories, a strong 'presence in the present'.

The closeness to us of much of twentieth-century history makes it difficult to classify it as history at all. Needless to say that much of the study of fashion in the twentieth and the first decade of the twenty-first century is not done through the use of historical methodologies. It is the social sciences – anthropology, ethnography and sociology in particular – and the arts and humanities – from cultural studies to the creative and performing arts – that structure our understanding of fashion in the century since the end of the First World War. Yet, historians feel uncomfortable in considering twentieth-century fashion as an appropriate manifestation of what we have defined in the Introduction as 'the eternal present'. Much of this century is now becoming 'historicised': this does not mean that it is relegated to the resting home of memory, but that it can no longer be seen as belonging to one unified 'cultural project', in particular that of the catch-all of 'modernity'. The simple escamotage of introducing time in the analysis of twentieth-century fashion through stylistic 'time-lines' is redundant and insufficient, now confined to the worst depths of modern social science analysis or the most conservative types of histories of costume for the middle classes.

In what ways, then, is history present in the analysis of twentieth-century fashion? One should first notice how certain methods used in contemporary history have been fruitfully used in the study of fashion. This includes the recovery of personal memory through oral history or the use of collective documentation such as surveys and reports, and the recovery of material memory, in particular through the preservation, archiving and interpretation of artefacts. As noted in our Introduction, the latter is a particularly important area for the history of fashion, with museum collections acquiring large numbers of garments, accessories and textiles on a daily basis. These 'costume and dress' collections are important for researchers for two reasons beyond the simple artefactual preservation of a 1920s' Poiret dress rather than a 1990s Gucci bag. They firstly create a connection in time with other artefacts in the same collection and also similar holdings belonging to different times, thus providing a useful tool to critique notions of linearity and the progression of history. Secondly, costume collections of the twentieth century are the result of the capacity to 'sift' through time: they teach us that not everything should or will be preserved; a museum is not a clothes-bag, as Valerie Steele so cogently put it (Steele 1998). The twentieth century appears so near to us because of the enormous rate of survival of memory, documents and artefacts (enhanced by digital forms such as videos, televisions, recordings and new techniques of preservation). Yet, the analysis of the twentieth century is as much based on our *discarding* or disregarding most of the materials so readily available and in circulation.

A second way in which twentieth-century fashion is being drawn into history derives from the fact that the unity of what Hobsbawm calls the 'short century' (1918–89) or the 'long century' (from 1918 to the continuing present) can be sharply criticised. From the 1960s, academics and journalists claimed the incipient arrival of a new era, something following 'modernity' and opposing the modernist project. This was inappropriately named 'postmodernism', as the modernist project had not finished (despite complaints about high-rise low-income housing). Llewellyn Negrin in this *Reader* considers the intellectual premises of postmodernism and their consequences for the way in which fashion was created, conceptualised and experienced by people. She, and many scholars like her, have raised questions regarding the ways in which postmodernism can really be seen in opposition to everything that came before. This *Reader* is unable to engage extensively with this intellectual problem but nonetheless observes how postmodernism is no longer 'the condition of the present': it does not explain the wiki and Facebook society of much youth around the world, the worries of a globalised economy and many other features of today's society. This is why the *Reader* prefers to present the transition in time 'from-to' by drawing on a classic label such as 'modernity' and perhaps a much more open one of 'hyper-modernity' and 'ultra-modernity'. We have consciously chosen these less charged labels to characterise the twentieth century in the belief that many of the features of modernity are still present, yet they have mutated into phenomena whose scale, complexity and structure could not easily fit within a modernist conception of time, space and humanity.

We do not wish to imply that history is fast becoming the favourite tool of analysis of twentieth-century fashion. A major difference between the past one hundred years and the earlier periods that we have covered in this *Reader* is the role of ideology. The Fashion Studies of the recent past is ideological, and rightly so. It must speculate upon issues of a personal or subjective nature as we debate the difference between fashion and dress. It has to address socialism, feminism, black power, gay rights and sustainability. It also has to debate questions of access. Everyone wears dress but not everyone wears fashion, although some voices in this section argue very forcefully that the dress–fashion nexus needs to be reconsidered. The relationship of the general population to the fashion system is quite different since the 1970s: new modes of communication – MTV, cable TV, the web and diversified journalism – have given faster and easier access to fashion ideas, as did the growth of international tourism and cheap air travel.

Designers also work from new concepts of fashionability. It is the case that in the 1960s youth culture and counter-culture, as well as ideological critiques of fashion from feminism changed the role of the designer. Designers could no longer be quasi-aristocratic dictators who directed the hem length and colour palette for a season for women's clothes. As street fashions were adopted even by the older generation and society gave increasing premiums to youthfulness, it was suggested that the fashion system of couture (exclusive artisanal fashion produced in fashion 'capitals' such as Paris since the 1860s) was about to become extinct. In the club clothes from the 1970s to the late 1980s, so artfully explored by Sally Gray in this *Reader*, designers found a new arsenal of fashion energy and 'authenticity'. By the 1990s, a designer such as Walter van Beirendonck (Wild and Lethal Trash, spring/summer 1997) included a battery-operated panel attached to the waist, merging memories of disco with the alien and supernatural power and strangeness popular in visual fictions of the 1990s.

We highlight the role of design and designers as the twentieth century – the century of the consumer and consumer excess – provides us with a unique set of information on fashion creation and fashion's creators: it is also the century of the couturier, the designer, the branding expert and the fashion 'industry' at large. By virtue of this quality, the twentieth century lays bare the complexity of variables that influence and at the same time constitute 'fashion'. Fashion in the twentieth century cannot be understood without looking at hidden cultures like S & M and sexual undergrounds, at the gay and lesbian clubbing communities, at black urban American culture, at non-Western indigenous clothing traditions. The bourgeois must slum it a little more than they were willing to do in the nineteenth century and maybe even dress like a working-class person of colour. The student of fashion is also asked to master numerous aspects of visual culture – architecture, industrial design and art practice – that have been key in the philosophical questioning of traditions and practices in fashion. Otherwise it would be impossible to understand why some designers turned to deconstruction – which does not mean tearing clothes but rather rethinking the 'ground' on which clothes and their construction are figured. Designers like Maison Martin Margiela questioned the notion of dress as commodity and made clothes from old socks and other debris. Japanese designers like Rei Kawakubo questioned and synthesised deeply held cultural systems about what a garment should look like, what a sleeve or a cape should be. Issey Miyake suggested that clothes might be a type of industrial product like cling wrap that could be customised at will by the owner.

Fashion history enables us to re-imagine how both famed and anonymous designs developed, what ideas and forces shaped design within a social setting. It enables an understanding of the place of both the famed designer and the anonymous maker in contemporary society and how the design profession developed at different rates in different fields. This *Reader* permits connections to be made between certain key episodes. Design and fashion history enables us to assess the increasing status of the designer in industrial and post-industrial societies (i.e. from the eighteenth century onwards).

The modern conception of the celebrity designer as somewhat dictatorial, from whom one can 'buy' taste, is a model which emerged within nineteenth-century French couture. Paul

Poiret (1879–1944), the famous couturier of the early twentieth century, used a different notion of pre-empting what clients already wanted – 'I respond to your hidden intentions by anticipating them'. He established a fashion 'house' in 1904, which also had perfume and what amounted to a home-ware line, including textile ranges produced at the École Martine by untutored girls valued for their 'natural' drawing skills. Nancy Troy, in her 'Poiret's modernism and the logic of fashion' distils her important research on couture culture and modernist aesthetics, drawing also on modernist ideas of production and industry that played out simultaneously with the 'art' of fashion. Orientalism in fashion is difficult to assess; as Troy argues of the work of Paul Poiret in the early twentieth century, it can be a symbol of conventional luxury or transgressive liberation at the same time. Troy sees both Poiret and Coco Chanel (1883–1971) as embracing modern ideas of the ready-made, which sat somewhere between the original and the mechanical reproduction. Thus Poiret licensed 'genuine copies' of his clothes in the USA and *Vogue* compared Chanel's little black dress to the Model T Ford. Poiret, the master marketing expert, promoted his minaret fashion line through a range of devices from plays to department store promotions, then faced the diffusion, copying and piracy of his self-construction as artist and innovator. Troy notes the irony that in his North American tours, Poiret embraced a model of vulgar theatre – the fashion show – that attempted to stave off the vulgarised copying of his own already theatrical designs. Going beyond the language of fine art, Poiret turned to the law, threatening to prosecute all but the 'genuine copies' of his clothes. His trademark might be protected, but copyright law did not protect clothing and textile designs, which had to resort to design patents, much more difficult to obtain and to pursue. American copyright law failed to recognise his garments as works of art; patent law failed to identify the originality in his designs. In North America, Troy concludes, Poiret was neither artist nor inventor, simply the owner of a trademark and an entrepreneur, the very label he had struggled to flee.

Reconsider the case of the French designer Charles Frederick Worth (1826–95), mentioned in part 4 of this *Reader*. He famously refused to admit some comers to his dress salon, who clamoured to gain access to his amazing confections in which fabric was woven *à la disposition* – to shape without cutting – and garnished with incredible trimmings. Worth promoted extreme new fashion such as the crinoline and, as a male designer modifying the appearance of women, he is an early example of the notion of the 'dictator-designer'. The matter of consumer agency and power is central to competing and different understandings of fashion: is it a vast conspiracy of price-fixing and duplicity, or is it a source of identity-formation and consumer play? The design historian Gregory Votolato provides a refreshing view of mid-twentieth-century fashion in the context of his wider study of the democratisation of design amidst the greatest consumer society in the world, the United States of America. Rather than condemning or judging this consumption, a trend which is very marked in parts of the sustainability lobby, Votolato asks what this consumption enabled. His conclusion is that in home-sewing, customisation, and the purchase of cheap mass-produced garments, many newly created for a segmented market in which youth and leisure were now forces, people tried to create a better world for themselves. They modified their own environments, in every way from painting kitchens to buying *Vogue* patterns, and in so doing both participated in and remade their own, the pre-packaged items that business and social pressures suggested they pursue. Thus in this important revisionist view, the 1950s is not characterised as a frightful period of difficult corsets and absurd Tampax commercials in which women become princesses for a period. Rather, it can be thought of differently as a precursor of the customisation and subcultural fashion play that we think of as emerging from the unemployment of

Thatcher's Britain and the free-market drift of Reaganomics. Fashion to Votolato is not a homogenising force, but 'a part of the American consciousness, and the freedom that it offers its wearers to look and do as they please'.

A number of snapshots by significant scholars of fashion are introduced at this point in order to sketch historical shifts but, more importantly, to indicate methodological positions essential for the study of fashion. Caroline Evans, in 'The origins of the modern fashion show' draws on art history and cultural theory in order to re-imagine the strange power of the fashion model and fashion show at the time of the development of the audience for photography and cinema. Rebecca Arnold, in 'Women designing modernity', considers the aesthetic choices in cut and structure that informed women designers interested in creating a new vision of 'woman' for the modern world. Alexandra Palmer, in 'Haute couture', unpacks the myths surrounding the couture, explaining that it is a concept premised in a perfection of skill that was also predicated upon a new relationship between the maker and the customer. Patricia Mears, in her summary of the career of Madame Grès, uses her deep understanding of artefacts to consider a design ethic that was sometimes 'outside' fashion. Sanda Miller, in a difficult and probing brief, goes beyond the clichés of the art–fashion debate to consider the philosophical grounds on which art and craft are assigned social and aesthetic value. Louise Wallenberg explains the close connections between early twentieth-century fashion and film, in which a film house might appear like a richly appointed department store where the models and new styles that people watched on the screen were then available for them to replicate in their other leisure time. Stella Bruzzi continues the filmic theme, exploring the historical challenge in assessing films for which designs are lost, designers anonymous and in which clothes had to be produced to propel characterisation and also not appear too new, too ahead, for the audiences. Hers is a useful corrective to the cliché that contemporary fashion on screen is always avant-garde or so stylised as to be beyond the immediate grasp of the spectator-consumer.

The snapshots forementioned operate from methods and techniques of scholarship that developed after the 1960s in conjunction with the 'new art history', design history and studies of popular culture. Llewellyn Negrin's important study of fashion and postmodernism is not just a topic but also a critique of how the whole concept of fashion is being understood and interpreted by both academics and the marketplace. Her summary of the functionalist critique of women's fashion by the suffrage movement and later by modernist proselytisers permits many useful connections to be made with Parts 4 and 5 of this *Reader*. Indeed her essay seems to be one of the few carefully argued critiques of the position advocated by feminist scholars such as Elizabeth Wilson and Kaja Silverman that emphasise the constructed rather than the essentialising aspects of dressing. Wilson's stance is always more nuanced, a fact recognised by Negrin, and most of her writing contains within it a distrust of the free market and the second-class place that still-patriarchal societies assign to women. Nonetheless, a scholar such as Wilson refuses the type of caricatured position offered in bestselling books by Naomi Klein, who in her attack on the cosmetics industry addressed at both men and women refuses in the end the possibility that pleasure or experimentation might be positive forces in lived experience (Klein 2000). Negrin takes a strong position that we must also consider the general tenor of contemporary society, in which 'the cult of appearances' is valued over all other characteristics. Here we could expand that notion to consider the recent pornography or what we might call the 'smut' of food (Gordon Ramsay; and mean-spirited American cooking competitions) and nouveau-riche interior and garden design (*Grand Designs, Ground Force, Property Ladder*) which were fuelled by a speculative bubble of wealth and aspiration which burst in a most unseemly manner while this book was being concluded. Negrin prompts readers to consider whether the 'uncritical embracing of the notion of self as appearance' as crafted by Jean Baudrillard is really a 'liberatory' position. In the desire to rebut the 'utilitarian rationality of modernism, postmodern theorists of fashion have tended to lose sight of the equally limiting reduction of self-identity to appearance'. This is, Negrin concludes, a 'reduction which has been particularly damaging to women'.

Our use of the expressions 'hyper-modern' and 'ultra-modern' signals our conviction that the period post-1980 has no 'unity' like say 1940s fashion, where there were distinct regional differences and attitudes towards respectability and fashion, but clothes silhouettes looked fairly similar around the First World and gloves had to match the bag. From the 1970s, designers debated the relationship between high-style elite modes and popular and occupational dressing from 'below'. The notion that there is a straightforward correlation between fashion, class, politics, leisure and music-taste allegiance has been challenged by recent theorists who argue that we have entered the age of the 'post-subculturalist' (Muggleton 2000). This concluding part of the *Reader* also engages with the contemporary overlapping the 'global'. We have not chosen to work with a notion of the global that is the story of world fashion, i.e. the existence of fashion in different parts of the world. Rather, we commissioned an essay from the Italian intellectual Simona Segre Reinach in which she considers the ways in which nation states and fashion producers use the locality and history of a region to create 'advantages' in the arena of global production. In a piece of writing founded in her ethnographic research in the fashion industry, Segre points to the irony that when Italian fashion goods are marketed in China, the enormous mass-production connections and complex web of making and outsourcing are obscured. Instead, near-redundant notions of the sole artisan and entrepreneur working in their dim and monastic workshop are mobilised as well as the same scenarios of the craft and material advantages of artistic city-states that were used so effectively to create for mainly American markets the notion of 'Made-in-Italy' in the 1950s. Segre Reinach points to the racism involved in aspects of the fashion scene, in which Chinese consumers are considered to not 'get' fashion and to be involved instead in a type of scramble lacking any discrimination. Connections could be proposed with earlier critiques of fashion, from the 'butcher's wife' of eighteenth-century London who wore clothes too fine for her, or the 'literary dustman' of nineteenth-century England. Segre Reinach suggests a huge fashion world that is still poorly understood, little researched, and yet about to transform the world fashion stage.

A range of special snapshots have been commissioned for this part of the *Reader*. Toby Slade considers the culturally specific notion of 'play' that informs young Japanese consumption of fashion, in which threats to cultural order are contained and compartmentalised in ways different from the West. D. J. Huppatz describes the branding strategy developed by Ralph Lauren in which a type of *gesamtkunstwerk* was applied to retailing. Marc de Ferrière le Vayer examines the development of fashion brands from the notion of the expanded commercial space of the boutique to wider marketing strategies that he artfully terms 'porno chic'. Elizabeth Wilson, in a challenging brief, comments on 'ethics and the future of fashion'. In raising other consumer sectors such as the production of toys, Wilson proposes that fashion should not continue to be denigrated as the malevolent force that it is made out to be: 'No more than any other productive enterprise can fashion escape the economic system. Yet there is a possible ethical future for fashion – as for other areas of visual culture – if it confronts those areas in which it is open to criticism and if consumers confront the way in which we have come to expect to access our clothes'.

Finally this part wishes to highlight the limits of 'presentist' notions of intellectual understanding: it is not simply a matter that all things become possible in fashion in recent years. The late Richard Martin, a curator and perhaps the greatest twentieth-century essayist on fashion, has written on Lagerfeld's coat-dress for Chanel autumn/winter 1996, a garment which 'inverts' Gabrielle Chanel's modernity and encases his model in a lavishly embroidered extended cardigan or coat dress, a version of the Coromandel screen which decorated Chanel's apartment at the Ritz. The piece relates as well to aspects of orientalism and the creation of a hybrid garment, the *cheongsam*, aspects of which are so well explored in this *Reader* by Antonia Finnane, Hazel Clark and Simona Segre Reinach. As Martin writes of this piece of fashion, Lagerfeld, like his younger contemporary Jean Paul Gaultier, has an 'acute and buoyant knowledge of history, demanding that the past be assimilated into the present, but that the present can only tolerate and integrate a past that is specifically germane to modern living' (Martin 1997: 95). Lagerfeld wraps the piece in 'an aura of art and power', and in adopting the elements of venerated decorative arts it elevates fashion, which so often is marginalised as trivial. 'The consumer . . . buys conspicuous value, an indurated sense of treasure' (Martin 1997: 97). Through such manoeuvres Lagerfeld proclaims his succession in the House of Chanel. And of course, the dress was shown in Chanel's apartment at the Ritz. Fashion is not just about the strategies of the wearers, but of the designers, stylists and purveyors, who are part of the *habitus* of the field. As Martin argued in his musing on Gaultier, Lagerfeld and Versace, 'much of the enmity engendered by fashion is because the art is too socially-implicated, too socially ambitious, and even given to social-climbing' (Martin 1997: 91).

Fashion history reveals the role of dress as a vehicle of self-fashioning and identity in post-industrial society. Fashion will concern all students of humanities, as fashion is a potent crucible for understanding the power and status of design in the post-Enlightenment 'world of appearances'. Through a process of analogy, evaluation and differentiation we understand our own modernity and the characteristics of our age. A fascination with the past is a means of understanding ourselves. History shows that not all introduced fashions will succeed, that consumers have more say than both markets and moralists might think, and that within the space of just decades, visions of beauty and the human form can be radically transformed. This *Reader* wishes you to be critical about the notion of homogeneous fashion. Many readers will be aware that the minute they arrive in an airport in a foreign country, the way their clothes are worn and their bodies move in their garments, articulate and indicate cultural difference. Fashion is one of the visible proofs that the world has not collapsed into one great blancmange of commercialised sameness. Traditions persist, people make choices, and dress is about a relationship between a body, garments and also urban and social space that is highly specific.

Bibliography and further reading

Owing to the vast number of publications on twentieth-century fashion, we decided to give preference to books. We understand that this list, perhaps more than other parts' further readings aids, is partial and incomplete.

Arnold, R. (2001) *Fashion, Desire and Anxiety: Image and Morality in the 20th Century*, London: I. B. Tauris.

Arnold, R. (2008) *The American Look: Sportswear, Fashion and the Image of Women in 1930s and 1940s New York*, London: I. B. Tauris.

Barthes, R. (1990 [original English edition 1983; French edition 1967]) *The Fashion System*, trans. M. Ward and R. Howard, Berkeley: University of California Press.

Berry, S. (2000) *Fashion and Femininity: Screen Style in 1930s Hollywood*, Minneapolis and London: University of Minnesota Press.

Blaszczyk, R. L. (ed.) (2007) *Producing Fashion: Commerce, Culture, and Consumers*, Philadelphia: University of Pennsylvania Press.

Blau, H. (1999) *Nothing in Itself: Complexions of Fashion*, Bloomington: Indiana University Press.

Breward, C. (2004) *Fashioning London: Clothing and the Modern Metropolis*, Oxford and New York: Berg.

Breward, C., and Evans, C. (eds) (2005) *Fashion and Modernity*, Oxford: Berg.

Breward, C., and Gilbert, D. (eds) (2006) *Fashion's World Cities*, Oxford: Berg.

Breward, C., Ehrman, E., and Evans, C. (2004) *The London Look: Fashions from Street to Catwalk*, London and New Haven: Yale University Press.

Bruzzi, S. (1997) *Undressing Cinema: Clothing and Identity in the Movies*, London and New York: Routledge.

Bruzzi, S., and Church Gibson, P. (eds) (2000) *Fashion Cultures: Theories, Explorations, and Analysis*, London: Routledge.

Brydon, A., and Niessen, S. (eds) (1998) *Consuming Fashion: Adorning the Transnational Body*, Oxford and New York: Berg.

Buckley, C., and Fawcett, H. (2002) *Fashioning the Feminine: Representation and Women's Fashion from the Fin de Siècle to the Present*, London: I. B. Tauris.

Charles-Roux, E. (1975) *Chanel*, trans. N. Amphoux, New York: Alfred A. Knopf.

Clark, J. (2004) *Spectres: When Fashion Turns Back*, London: V & A Publications.

Cole, S. (2000) *Don We Now Our Gay Apparel: Gay Men's Dress in the Twentieth Century*, Oxford: Berg.

Constantino, M. (1997) *Men's Fashion in the Twentieth Century: From Frock Coats to Intelligent Fibres*, New York: Costume and Fashion Press.

Cunningham, P. A. (2003) *Reforming Women's Fashion, 1850–1920: Politics, Health, and Art*, Kent, OH: Kent State University Press.

Dior (2007) *Dior – 60 Years of Style: From Christian Dior to John Galliano*, London: Thames & Hudson.

Dior, C. (2007) *Dior by Dior: The Autobiography of Christian Dior*, London: V & A Publications.

Dufreigne, J.-P. (2004) *Hitchcock Style*, New York: Assouline.

Ehrenkranz, A. (1994) *A Singular Elegance: The Photographs of Baron Adolph de Meyer*, San Francisco: Chronicle Books.

English, B. (2007) *A Cultural History of Fashion in the Twentieth Century: From the Catwalk to the Sidewalk*, Oxford and New York: Berg.

Evans, C. (2003) *Fashion at the Edge: Spectacle, Modernity and Deathliness*, London and New Haven: Yale University Press.

Evans, C., and Thornton, M. (1989) *Women and Fashion: A New Look*, London: Quartet.

Fillin-Yeh, S. (2001) *Dandies: Fashion and Finesse, Art and Culture*, New York: New York University Press.

Gaines, J., and Herzog, C. (eds) (1990) *Fabrications: Costume and the Female Body*, London and New York: Routledge.

Ganeva, M. (2008) *Women in Weimar Fashion: Discourses and Displays in German Culture, 1918–1933*, Columbia, SC, and Woodbridge: Camden House.

Glynn, P. (1982) *Skin to Skin: Eroticism in Dress*, London: Allen & Unwin.

Green, N. (1997) *Ready-to-Wear and Ready-to-Work: A Century of Industry and Immigrants in Paris and New York*, Durham, NC: Duke University Press.

Guenther, I. (2004) *Nazi Chic? Fashioning Women in the Third Reich*, Oxford and New York: Berg.

Hall, S., and Jefferson, T. (eds) (1976) *Resistance through Rituals: Youth Subcultures in Post-war Britain*, London: Hutchinson.

Hebdige, D. (1979) *Subculture: The Meaning of Style*, London: Methuen & Co.

Hodkinson, P. (2002) *Goth: Identity, Style, and Subculture*, Oxford: Berg.

hooks, b. (1992) *Black Looks: Race and Representation*, Boston: South End Press.

Horwood, C. (2005) *Keeping up Appearances: Fashion and Class between the Wars*, Stroud: Sutton.

Jobling, P. (2005) *Man Appeal: Advertising, Modernism and Men's Wear*, Oxford: Berg.

Johnson, K. K. P., and Lennon, S. J. (eds) *Appearance and Power*, Oxford: Berg.

Kalman, T., and Kalman, M. (2000) *(Un)Fashion*, New York: Harry N. Abrams.

Keenan, W. J. F. (ed.) *Dressed to Impress: Looking the Part*, Oxford: Berg.

Klein, N. (2000) *No Logo: No Space, No Choice, No Jobs*, London: Flamingo.

Koda, H., and Bolton, M. (2007) *Poiret*, New York: Yale University Press.

Lipovetsky, G. (1994) *The Empire of Fashion: Dressing Modern Democracy*, trans. C. Porter, Princeton: Princeton University Press.

Mackrell, A. (2005) *Art and Fashion: The Impact of Art on Fashion and Fashion on Art*, London: Batsford.

Martin, R. (1988) *Fashion and Surrealism*, London: Thames & Hudson.

Martin, R. (1997) 'A Note. A Charismatic Art: The Balance of Ingratiation and Outrage in Contemporary Fashion', *Fashion Theory*, 1, 1, pp. 91–104.

McRobbie, A. (1999) *The Culture Society: Art Fashion and Popular Music*, London and New York: Routledge.

Moseley, R. (ed.) (2005) *Fashioning Film Stars: Dress, Culture, Identity*, London: BFI.

Muggleton, D. (2000) *Inside Subculture: The Postmodern Meaning of Style*, Oxford: Berg.

Müller, F. (2000) *Art and Fashion*, trans. A. Rubin, London: Thames & Hudson.

Müller, F., and Bowles, H. (2008) *Yves Saint Laurent: Style*, Paris: Éditions de la Martinière.

Niessen, S., Leshkowich, A. M., and Jones, C. (eds) (2003) *Re-orienting Fashion: The Globalization of Asian Dress*, Oxford and New York: Berg.

Palmer, A., and Clark, H. (eds) (2005) *Old Clothes, New Looks: Second Hand Fashion*, Oxford and New York: Berg.

Paulicelli, E. (2004) *Fashion under Fascism: Beyond the Black Shirt*, Oxford and New York: Berg.

Peiss, K. (1998) *Hope in a Jar: The Making of America's Beauty Culture*, New York: Henry Holt.

Pochna, M. F. (1992) *Nina Ricci*, Paris: Editions du Regard.

Polhemus, T. (1978) *Fashion and Anti-fashion: An Anthropology of Clothing and Adornment*, London: Thames and Hudson.

Polhemus, T. (1994) *Streetstyle: From Sidewalk to Catwalk*, London: Thames & Hudson.

Polhemus, T., and Proctor, L. (1978) *Fashion and Anti-Fashion: Anthropology of Clothing and Adornment*, London: Thames and Hudson.

Polhemus, T., and Proctor, L. (1984) *Pop Styles*, London: Vermilion.

Pringle, C. (1999) *Roger Vivier*, London: Thames & Hudson.

Ross, A. (ed.) (1997) *No Sweat: Fashion, Free Trade and the Rights of Garment Workers*, London and New York: Verso.

Salazar, L. (2008) *Fashion v. Sport*, London: V & A Publications.

Schiaparelli, E. (2007) *Shocking Life: The Autobiography of Elsa Schiaparelli*, London: V & A Publications.

Schreier, B. A. (1984) *Mystique and Identity: Women's Fashions of the 1950s*, Norfolk, VA: Chrysler Museum.

Smith, B. C., and Peiss, K. (1989) *Men and Women: A History of Costume, Gender, and Power*, Washington, DC: Smithsonian Institution.

Steele, V. (1988 [2nd edition Berg 1998]) *Paris Fashion: A Cultural History*, New York and Oxford: Oxford University Press.

Steele, V. (1996) *Fetish: Fashion, Sex and Power*, Oxford: Oxford University Press.

Steele, V. (1998) 'A Museum of Fashion Is More Than a Clothes-bag', *Fashion Theory*, 2, 4, pp. 327–35.

Steele, V., and Park, J. (2008) *Gothic: Dark Glamour*, New Haven: Yale University Press.

Stern, F. (ed.) (1970) *The Varieties of History: From Voltaire to the Present*, New York: Macmillan.

Stewart, M. L. (2008) *Dressing Modern Frenchwomen: Marketing Haute Couture, 1919–1939*, Baltimore: Johns Hopkins University Press.

Tranberg Hansen, K. (2000) *Salaula: the World of Secondhand Clothing in Zambia*, Chicago: Chicago University Press.

Trede, R., and Polan, B. (2009) *The Great Fashion Designers*, Oxford and New York: Berg.

Troy, N. J. (2003) *Couture Culture: A Study in Modern Art and Fashion*, Cambridge, MA: MIT Press.

Vinken, B. (2005) *Fashion Zeitgeist: Trends and Cycles in the Fashion System*, Oxford and New York: Berg.

Vogue (2006) '*Vogue*: Special Double Issue', *Fashion Theory*, 10, 1/2.

Votolato, G. (1998) *American Design in the Twentieth Century*, Manchester: Manchester University Press.

Welters, L., and Cunningham, P. A. (eds) (2005) *Twentieth-century American Fashion*, Oxford and New York: Berg.

White, P. (1994) *Haute Couture Embroidery: The Art of Lesage*, Berkeley: LACIS.

Wilcox, C. (ed.) (2007) *The Golden Age of Couture: Paris and London, 1947–57*, London: V & A Publications.

Wilson, E. (1991) *The Sphinx in the City: Urban Life, the Control of Disorder, and Women*, London: Virago Press.

Chapter 20

Poiret's modernism and the logic of fashion

Nancy J. Troy

PAUL POIRET DOMINATED THE WORLD OF FASHION in the early twentieth century. Not only did he introduce a radically simplified female silhouette, but he also pioneered the sale of women's clothes together with lifestyle accessories such as perfume and decorative objects for the home. His meteoric rise to prominence as a couturier in the years just before the outbreak of the First World War depended not simply on the distinctive character of his clothing and other designs but also, and perhaps more crucially, on his ability to project an aura of originality in the face of mass production. In the 1920s, when that balancing act could no longer be sustained, Poiret's star status went into a gradual but inexorable decline.

Alongside his striking innovations in costume style and construction, Poiret developed a sharply honed marketing strategy that called for promoting his dresses and other fashionable products as works of art, while presenting himself as an inspired artist and patron of the arts. Although he embraced modernism in the range of contemporary artists whose work he supported, his attitude was marked by elitist individualism tinged with nostalgia for a vanishing era of authenticity and integrity, a time when artists could effortlessly sustain a myth of purity and independence from the constraints of commodity culture. Paradoxically, Poiret's modernity and his notoriety were achieved through his inspired deployment of art discourse, which distanced him from the vulgar crowd and appealed to a wealthy, discreet clientele; at the same time, however, by marshalling the visual and performing arts, architecture, interior decoration, and graphic design, he attracted constant attention from the press, became visible to a vast public audience, and created a seemingly unquenchable demand for his dresses.

Just as his deployment of the arts as promotional vehicles to advance his signature style enabled Poiret to position his clothes (and himself along with them) at the pinnacle of fashion, so, too, the popularity he achieved by this means assured the vulnerability of

Figure 20.1 Paul Poiret (1879–1944), *c.* 1913. Library of Congress Prints and Photographs Division, Washington, DC, LC-USZ62-100840.

his dresses to copying and pastiche. The very strategies he used to portray his clothes as unique, even avant-garde creations – indeed, as works of modern art – encouraged the production of a profusion of copies destined for mass consumption. The resulting wide-spread availability of his designs amounted to a popularisation that simultaneously validated his singular pre-eminence in fashion and destroyed his aspirations to status as an artist among the cultural elite.

Given the nature of haute couture as an artisan-based enterprise, Poiret's business was capable of creating only a limited quantity of high-quality, work-intensive products; once demand exceeded that limit, standardised methods of quantity production, to which his couture house was ill-adapted, were inevitably set into motion. When manufacturers better equipped to satisfy a mass market began to exploit the enormous consumer demand Poiret's own designs elicited, he found himself in an impossible bind. Faced with uncontrolled and often illegal or unauthorised copying of his own unique models, he tried to restrain such mass production in order to protect his elite business; at the same time, he was compelled to enter the mass market not only to support his high-end trade but also to protect his financial interest in the exploitation of his designs. Both of these options were likely to be losing propositions because, in the first instance, it was impossible to prevent illegal or unauthorised copying; and, in the second, once he offered less expensive garments to a mass market, exclusive, high-end clients would refuse to pay the top prices required for him to break even on his made-to-order merchandise. This conundrum highlights the inherently contradictory nature of what might be described as the logic of fashion – the insurmountable problem faced by the couturier when unique creations saturated with artistic aura are subjected to the conditions of mass production for widespread consumption in an industrialised economy.

Poiret's desire to resolve this predicament, which is characteristic of modernist art as well as fashion, led him in 1916–17 to adopt a different but no less contradictory marketing strategy, offering his own reduced-price copies of his dresses, models that in 1916 he would advertise in *Vogue*, oxymoronically, as 'genuine reproductions'. In doing so, Poiret effectively erased the distinction between originality and reproduction, much as Marcel Duchamp did in choosing his readymades during these same years. Where Duchamp embraced the commodity as part of his effort to expose the precarious status of high art in a rapidly changing economic and social environment, Poiret tried to make mass-produced clothing palatable in the couture context by introducing clothes that were described in the *Vogue* advertisement as giving women 'the opportunity to own a Paul Poiret creation without paying the usual excessive price'. Like the readymade, the 'genuine reproduction' dress was a hybrid, devised to reconcile the contradiction between art and industry. It also exposed the inherent instability of the logic of fashion, poised on the point where distinctions between the high-art original and the supposedly debased reproduction collide and dissolve.

Poiret was not the first dressmaker to grapple with the relationship between originality and reproduction, or to use the arts to facilitate his access to high culture and the elite society of those with enough money to purchase couture clothing. Both Charles Frederick Worth and Jacques Doucet, the two couturiers for whom Poiret worked before establishing his own business in 1903, had formed significant collections. Yet Poiret proved to be especially adept at exploiting modern art for the benefit of his many commercial enterprises. Soon after embarking on his independent career, he recalled in his memoirs, 'I began to receive artists, and to create around me a movement'. Among the many contemporary artists with whom he associated and whose work he collected were Jean-Paul Boussingault, Constantin Brancusi, Robert Delaunay, André Derain, Kees van Dongen, Raoul Dufy, André Dunoyer de Segonzac, Paul Iribe, Roger de La Fresnaye, Marie Laurencin, Georges Lepape, Henri Matisse, Jean Metzinger, Amedeo Modigliani, Luc-Albert Moreau, Francis Picabia, and Pablo Picasso. Today, this would doubtless be regarded as an eclectic assemblage and mixed in value, but before the First World War, when Poiret purchased the great majority of works of art he owned, these figures could be counted among the most advanced painters, sculptors, and graphic artists of the period. Yet Poiret was careful not to transgress the bounds of good taste as he assembled his collection, which was composed, he recalled in 1934 in *Art et phynance*, 'of sure values, because I was always a prudent pioneer'. This approach mirrored his understanding of the need for restraint in fashionable dress, where, as Poiret noted in *Harper's Bazaar* in 1913, he was 'never so far ahead as to be out of reach'. Dresses, he believed, should be characterised by simple lines and architectural construction rather than fancy drapery or added ornament; the woman should draw attention, not her gown. In order to emphasise this point, he told a story, quoted in *Women's Wear Daily* in 1912, about a famous actor who appeared in public with a small boutonniere in his lapel: 'Someone asked him why he did not wear a larger one and he replied: "Were I to wear a large ribbon everyone would see it. As it is now, some will notice it"'. Poiret's attitude as a couturier, like his approach to art collecting, seems to capture perfectly the dialectical workings of the logic of fashion, which require a carefully calibrated oscillation not only between novelty and tradition but also between distinction and conformity, correlating the quest for visibility with the determination not to be seen.

As a young man, Poiret had dabbled in painting, a pastime he continued to pursue with varying intensity throughout his life, and early on he seems to have sought the company of artists. Francis Picabia was a childhood friend, and Poiret met the Fauve painters André Derain and Maurice de Vlaminck before his marriage in the autumn of 1905. A devotee of the illustrated and satirical press, he encountered there the work of several of his closest artist friends and colleagues, including Paul Iribe, a graphic artist and designer of jewellery and furniture. In 1908, Poiret invited Iribe to create a deluxe album illustrating his couture clothing and to design the label that Poiret would use for the next twenty years. In 1909, Poiret commissioned Dufy to create vignettes for his new couture-house stationery (a different image for each day of the week), and later the vignette for his design outlet, as well as the invitations and decorations for one of Poiret's most notorious parties. After seeing Dufy's woodcuts inspired by *images d'Épinal* (popular prints, often of military subjects), produced between 1909 and 1911 to illustrate a book of poems by Guillaume Apollinaire, Poiret launched Dufy's career as a textile designer, commissioning him to make woodcuts for fabrics in a similarly powerful graphic style that exploited the stark contrast between black and white, or light and dark colours. While Poiret's contacts with these and other artists resulted in commissions related to his professional activities, he was also building his art collection during these years, and the two spheres overlapped and enriched one another. Virtually all of the graphic artists who worked for Poiret's businesses were represented in his collection, but the connections between Poiret's professional life and his art patronage were more complex than this relatively familiar relationship would suggest. For example, in 1909, after Boussingault was introduced to Poiret as the artist chosen to illustrate an article he was writing for *La grande revue*, Poiret became Boussingault's most supportive patron by inviting him to create a large decorative painting for his new *maison de couture*. Boussingault, in turn, was closely associated with two other young painters, Luc-Albert Moreau and André Dunoyer de Segonzac, whom Poiret also supported, not only by purchasing works of art but also, more importantly, by arranging for all three to exhibit together in 1910 at the Galerie Barbazanges, a commercial gallery on the premises of his couture house. (Poiret rented it to a dealer but retained the right to organise one or two shows each year.) In March 1911, the gallery held an exhibition featuring graphic designers in Poiret's orbit, including Georges Lepape, who created a second deluxe album of Poiret couture clothing that year. Then, in late February and early March 1912, Poiret invited Robert Delaunay and Marie Laurencin to share the gallery in a two-person exhibition, the first significant showing by either artist. At this point, Poiret could legitimately claim to be an important patron and promoter of advanced tendencies in contemporary art. He owned an early landscape, *View of Collioure*, by Matisse as well as at least two works by Picasso. In 1912, not only did Poiret purchase Brancusi's *Maiastra* (a polished-bronze sculpture acquired from the artist), but he also bought La Fresnaye's *The Card Players* and four smaller decorative paintings by Laurencin from the Maison Cubiste, a controversial ensemble of furnishings that was prominently displayed at the Salon d'Automne that year.

In addition to his principal business as a dress designer, beginning in 1911, Poiret manufactured a luxuriously packaged line of perfumes named after his eldest daughter, Rosine, and he ran a small, loosely organised arts school that furnished designs for his decorative arts atelier and marketing outlets, named after his second daughter, Martine. The interlocking and mutually reinforcing character of his collecting and other artistic pursuits, on the one hand, and his various entrepreneurial activities, on the other, struck contemporary observers as a brilliant marketing strategy that would benefit all of his products. In a 1912 article describing the interior of the newly inaugurated Martine boutique, a correspondent for *Vogue* remarked that, while it was common practice to combine the sale of hats, caps, bags, belts, and other apparel accessories, 'certainly couturiers have never before insisted that chairs, curtains, rugs and wall-coverings should be considered in the choosing of a dress, or rather that the style of a dress should influence the interior decorations of a home'. Like Josef Hoffmann and other members of the Wiener Werkstätte, Poiret embraced the notion of the total work of art that encouraged him to position his clothing within a larger (interior) design context. But while Hoffmann and other vanguard architects tended to regard design as a means of social engineering and often imposed their own aesthetic preferences on their clients, for Poiret the total work of art was less a utopian ideal than the physical expression of a personal business empire applied to the feminine spheres of haute couture, perfumes, and the decorative arts. His mutually reinforcing activities functioned as elements of an overarching entrepreneurial strategy that effectively obfuscated its own commercial nature.

In order to sell clothes, perfume, and furnishings to his aristocratic and wealthy bourgeois clients, Poiret had to avoid practices associated with establishments appealing to lower- and middle-class markets. If European and American dry-goods and department stores initially created their mass audiences by extensive advertising of cut-rate merchandise on billboards and in cheap magazines and newspapers, and by displaying their wares in enormous quantities, Poiret protected the allure of his products by not advertising, at least not to large audiences, and by appropriating the fine arts to promote the originality, uniqueness, and aesthetic quality of his designs. 'I am not commercial', Poiret told the *New York Times* in 1913. 'Ladies come to me for a gown as they go to a distinguished painter to get their portraits put on canvas. I am an artist, not a dressmaker.'

Poiret maintained this rhetorical posture even in advertisements for Rosine perfumes, which were described in the introduction to an illustrated brochure, *Les parfums de Rosine*, by the writer Fernand Nozière as 'the knowing, meticulous, refined creations of an artist'. For the same brochure, Poiret commissioned Roger Boutet de Monvel to write evocative texts that accompanied the colour photographs of each of the bottled perfumes. The scents were presented in carefully crafted boxes designed by Martine to hold the hand-painted bottles, individual works of art that were specially created to harmonise with the perfumes they contained. Excerpts from poems by Baudelaire and Verlaine, as well as endorsements by famous contemporary actresses, reinforced the message that Rosine perfumes were unusual, aestheticised, and glamorous commodities, 'the most expensive because [they were] the best', as the text proclaimed of Rosine's 'True Eau de Cologne'.

If it was Poiret's goal in all his diverse enterprises to blur the distinction between fashion, decorative arts, and fine art, he set about doing so by self-consciously staging his performances as couturier, designer, art collector, party giver, and entrepreneur. Poiret has been described as a highly theatrical figure, and the theatre, in turn, featured prominently in many of his activities, encompassing not only the costumes he created for public performances but also the fashion shows and the parties he staged in his couture house, a stately eighteenth-century *hôtel* renovated for him in 1909 by Louis Süe, a young painter turned architect and decorator. There, in addition to installing a small proscenium and stage for the presentation of fashion shows indoors, Poiret also used the garden as a backdrop, where on occasion he would film his mannequins in motion, which allowed him to take his fashion show on the road. The garden also functioned as a venue for at least one of several highly theatrical and wildly extravagant costume parties that Poiret staged, and in which he performed the starring role. These fêtes, widely reported in the Parisian press and enthusiastically copied in the highest social circles, provided yet another, extremely effective kind of unconventional publicity for Poiret's businesses. Although he repeatedly denied that his parties had anything to do with advertising or self-promotion, he was forced to acknowledge that widely circulating critique: 'Naturally there have been people who have said that I gave these fêtes as an item of advertisement', he acknowledged in his memoirs, 'but I want to destroy this insinuation, which can only have originated in stupidity'. Whatever their creator's intention, these affairs contributed significantly to Poiret's renown. Upon closer scrutiny, their many links to his commercial interests become readily apparent.

The most extravagant of Poiret's parties, which he called 'The Thousand and Second Night', was a fantasy, based on the tales of *One Thousand and One Nights*, that came to life on the evening of 24 June 1911. For this occasion, Poiret and his wife required their 300 guests (mostly artists and patrons of the arts) to dress up in 'oriental' costumes. Those who failed to do so were refused entry, unless they were willing to outfit themselves on the spot in Persian-style clothes that Poiret said in his memoirs he had designed 'according to authentic documents'. He thus used the occasion of a sumptuous party to demand that everyone in his circle accept the controversial features of his latest creations, including the so-called *jupe culotte* and 'harem' trousers, which dominated his spring 1911 collection. These innovations were introduced early that year, probably in response to the impact of Léon Bakst's designs for the Ballets Russes' *Schéhérazade*, which Poiret had seen when it premiered in Paris in June 1910.

The 'Thousand and Second Night' enabled Poiret and his art-world guests to act out a fantastic evocation of the Orient, staged as a cross between an extravagant fashion show and an elaborate theatrical performance on the grounds of his *maison de couture*. When in 1913 he was invited by several department-store magnates to tour major cities in North America, Poiret leaped at the opportunity to capitalise on the notoriety of his oriental styles in elite Parisian circles by introducing them directly to much broader audiences in the United States. During the three weeks of his American visit, he addressed thousands of women in public lectures, closed several significant business deals, including one with *Harper's Bazaar* to supply that magazine with a series of exclusive, illustrated articles, and he made numerous appearances at major department stores, including, in New York alone, J. M. Gidding, Gimbels, Macy's, and Wanamaker's. Along the way he developed a spectacular marketing strategy that proved to be enormously effective, although it differed markedly from his customary practice, which was characterised by the privacy and elitism of his couture house in Paris. The high visibility of Poiret's tour was a result of the particular conditions governing the merchandising of French fashions in America, which took place in the public arena dominated by leading department stores, rather than the carefully controlled environment of Poiret's *hôtel*, the site of his business headquarters as well as his private home.

Figure 20.2 Poiret model – Gimbels, March 1914. Photo by Bain News Service. Library of Congress Prints and Photographs Division, Washington, DC LC-USZ62-85524.

In order to lure ever more customers, by the end of the nineteenth century American department stores, like their French counterparts, had developed what the *Dry Goods Economist* described in 1903 as 'spectacular methods of bringing people within their doors': including such entertainments as 'cooking lessons, automobile shows, stereopticon displays, moving pictures, or the presentation of some novel and interesting exhibit . . . Very often these openings are held in the evening and partake of the nature of a reception, no goods being sold and visitors being treated as the guests of the concern'. It was, the author noted, a very effective, though also very expensive, form of advertising. William Leach (1984) has described the theatrical dimension of these practices, which he dates to the 1890s, 'when merchants started to build their own auditoriums, [and] department stores literally became theatres, putting on plays, musicals, concerts, and, in some instances, spectacular extravaganzas'. Thus the department stores shared with Poiret some of the same strategies of covering their marketing with a veneer of culture. In general, department stores sought the largest possible client base, using art and theatre to make prosaic goods appeal to a wide spectrum of potential buyers. Poiret, on the other hand, stressed the high-end, luxury aspects of art and spectacle in order to build a relatively small, elite clientele through individual sales in his couture house in Paris. By coming to America, however, he entered the domain of the department store, where art and especially theatre operated more explicitly and with much wider appeal. Here, as Leach has pointed out (1993), '[t]he upper-class French trade . . . became an American mass market'.

The effectiveness of American merchandising methods had a direct impact on sales of Poiret's so-called lampshade tunics and harem trousers, two especially popular orientalising designs that clothed fashionable women in trousers and appeared to challenge traditional gender identities. Notwithstanding their controversial implications, in April, within six months of Poiret's visit, *Vogue* declared it 'a safe wager that every woman in the land possessed at least one of [his lampshade] tunics during the past season'. This claim may be dubious, but it is nevertheless instructive insofar as it illuminates the context in which Poiret discovered that his exclusive dress designs were being copied for mass production and sale at cut-rate prices in the United States. Not only was Poiret confronted with pirated garments, but he also recognised 'the labels which were sewed in them as nothing but counterfeits of his original label'. According to *Vogue* in 1915: 'He immediately placed the matter in the hands of his attorney, who started an investigation which revealed the fact that not only were Poiret labels being imitated and sold throughout the country by a number of manufacturers, but the labels of other prominent couturiers were also being duplicated. In fact, it was discovered that quite a flourishing trade in these false labels had become well established in America'. Just as Poiret's entrepreneurial dream became reality, at the moment when, as *Vogue* put it, 'every woman in the land possessed at least one of his tunics', the dream was turning into a nightmare of uncontrollable proliferation. Poiret was neither effectively overseeing the new developments in manufacturing and marketing, nor was he benefiting financially from them.

Of course Poiret was not alone in facing this dilemma. All the major French couturiers of the period recognised the double-edged sword of the American marketplace, where traditionally they made their most lucrative sales but where they were now also losing increasingly high sums to largely unregulated imitators. As the tension between the original and the industrially produced copy was emerging as a principal concern for Poiret and other purveyors of high-end fashion, it was no less a growing concern for avant-garde artists during the teens and twenties. No figure of the period explored this terrain more compellingly than Marcel Duchamp, for whom the marriage of the object of industrial production with the original work of art was consummated by affixing the signature of the artist to an indifferently chosen, machine-made article, resulting in what Duchamp called the 'readymade', a term he appropriated from the realm of mass-produced, ready-to-wear clothing.

Duchamp's first readymade took the form of a bottle rack purchased in 1914 at a Parisian department store, the Bazar de l'Hôtel de Ville. By having this common, mass-produced object inscribed with a word or phrase (exactly what this was is not known) and with his name, Duchamp stripped it of functional purpose, treating it instead like a work of art. In an interview with Pierre Cabanne that was published in 1987, Duchamp recalled: 'It was in 1915, especially, in the United States, that I did other objects with inscriptions, like the snow shovel, on which I wrote something in English. The word "readymade" thrust itself on me then. It seemed perfect for these things that weren't works of art, that weren't sketches, and to which no art terms applied. That's why I was tempted to make them'. Characteristically, he sought to dispel any possible misconception that the readymades might be singular or unique. As he told Cabanne: 'Another aspect of the "readymade" is its lack of uniqueness . . . the replica of a "readymade" delivering the same message; in fact nearly every one of the "readymades" existing today is not an original in the conventional sense.' Duchamp did not simply alienate objects from their functional contexts in order to move them to the sphere of fine art, he placed them in an ambiguous, seemingly contradictory conceptual zone that corresponded neither to conventional expectations for art nor to commonly held notions of the industrially produced commodity. Belonging equally yet nevertheless problematically to both or neither realms, the readymades testified to what Duchamp regarded as the crisis of traditional art making brought on by industrialisation.

Duchamp's notion of the readymade as limited in production yet neither original nor unique corresponds surprisingly closely to the inherently contradictory terms in which Poiret described the 'genuine reproduction' dresses he designed for the American market in 1916–17, at the same time that Duchamp, a Frenchman in America, was designating his readymades. As physical objects the readymades retained the form of the multiple, yet their titles, signatures, and inscriptions functioned like Poiret's often-forged label or the titles he assigned to his own 'genuine reproductions' to charge with aura things that would otherwise be unexceptional, widely available, industrially produced commodities. The result in each case was an object that articulated a contradiction, an oxymoron, an instability, a constant oscillation between opposite poles. Like the readymade, the 'genuine reproduction' occupied an alternative position that both exposed and reconciled (but never denied) the dualities of art and industry, original and reproduction.

Poiret introduced his 'genuine reproductions' to American patrons in early 1917, when he circulated a sober brochure printed on ordinary, semigloss paper, the cheapness of which was only partially disguised by an upscale wrapper designed by Eduardo García Benito. Fourteen costumes on mannequins were presented in straightforward, black-and-white photographs accompanied by descriptions and prices of the outfits, as well as by illustrations of Poiret labels specially designed to identify the garments as authorised reproductions. A caption noted, 'Every genuine reproduction must have one of these labels'. As a whole, the brochure represented a telling departure from the deluxe, limited edition albums by Iribe and Lepape that had helped to establish Poiret's artistic identity before the war. That compound of elitist self-representations had undoubtedly been undermined by wartime conditions, and it would in any case have been at odds with the character of the merchandise Poiret was now seeking to promote: clothing aimed at 'the American woman at large' and offered in 1917 in *Vanity Fair* at prices comparable to those of 'ordinary garments manufactured in the ordinary way'. Unfortunately for Poiret, who was still in the army in 1917, the French War Ministry refused him permission to pursue his grandiose scheme for expansion in the United States, which in addition to dresses also envisioned the sale of perfumes, furniture, fabrics, and glassware. A planned New York office was short-lived at best, and the dreams of Poiret's American backers of a substantial return on their investment were presumably dashed when the United States entered the war on 6 April 1917.

Poiret appears to have been devastated by this turn of events; although his career in the world of fashion was far from over, he never recovered the dominant position he occupied in the industry before the war, nor did he develop the potential benefits of the ready made that he had explored in the form of his 'genuine reproductions'. The reasons were financial as well as organisational, but they also involved Poiret's vision of fashion, which veered away from the moderate pricing, licensed mass production, and sporty styles that he had designed for American women during the war. Having been frustrated in that experiment, he reverted to the ways in which he had always privileged originality, individuality, and art – as he had done even in grappling with the challenges posed by American models of marketing in an environment increasingly characterised by large capital investments that underwrote mass production and encouraged consumption on an unprecedented scale.

In order to support himself and his family during the war, Poiret had been forced to give up such markers of elite status as his chauffeur-driven limousine, as well as a property near Paris where he had staged several costume parties. When he returned to Paris after the armistice, he reassembled his employees and reopened his couture house but found that most of his assets were still tied up in real estate, while his couture, interior decoration, and perfume businesses desperately needed infusions of fresh capital. In 1918, he sold the building he owned on the rue du Colisée, adjoining his other couture-house properties, and the following year he parted with one of his most treasured sculptures, a Tang Dynasty bodhisattva, which was supposedly acquired by the Metropolitan Museum of Art in New York.

Poiret obviously knew that the fashion business was being transformed by new production and marketing paradigms, some of which – the licensing of models for reproduction by wholesale manufacturers, for example – he had pioneered himself, but after the war he lacked the financial resources and apparently also the will to make the changes required to profit from that knowledge. Anyone who lived through the war would have been aware that the lives of European and American women had been changed by the necessity of assuming responsibilities and positions outside the home that had previously been reserved for men. Nevertheless, Poiret resisted the practicality, stylistic simplification, and rationalisation to which other couturiers – most notably Coco Chanel – more readily adapted their styles and, eventually, also their own methods of production and distribution. In 1917, the marketing brochure for his own line of 'genuine reproductions' had emphasised the supposedly typical American qualities of comfort and adaptability by stressing the youthful character of his clothes and their appropriateness either for 'the business girl' or 'the athletic girl'. But in the early 1920s Poiret rejected this same rhetorical and stylistic discourse when it came to dominate the couture profile of his increasingly successful rival, Chanel.

While Chanel embraced the trend toward youthful, simple, and functional clothes, Poiret rejected the sporty style he himself had pioneered in 1916–17, and railed against the boyish fashion silhouette, nicknamed 'la garçonne', inspired by the heroine of a 1922 novel by Victor Margueritte who personified the so-called New Woman by challenging traditional norms of female comportment. In remarks published in *Forum* that same year, Poiret declared his disdain for such 'cardboard women, with hollow silhouettes, angular shoulders and flat breasts. Cages lacking birds. Hives lacking bees'. Instead of the modern, impersonal simplicity of what would become Chanel's signature 'little black dress', in the early 1920s Poiret often turned for inspiration to historical, regional, and folkloric styles. Although some of his designs were relatively simple and straightforward, too many others were eccentric or richly spectacular. Thus, although Chanel had not actually gone to America or appealed directly to American women, she succeeded where Poiret failed in creating a style that responded to the desires of these women for practical, comfortable clothes.

The simplicity of a Chanel dress assured not only that it could be adapted to suit virtually any woman – in 1926 *Vogue* described it as a uniform for all women of taste – but also that it would be easy to copy and distribute in the burgeoning postwar ready-to-wear market. In fact, unlike Poiret, Chanel apparently did nothing to resist the wholesale copying of her couture clothes, the style of which gave aesthetic expression to the industrial character of the readymade. In 1926, *Vogue* described the little black dress as 'The Chanel "Ford"', and suggested that the quality of Chanel's clothing was assured by its brand name, just as the Ford name guaranteed the quality of the company's cars. This conjunction exposes a contradiction embedded not only in the little black dress but also in Poiret's 'genuine reproductions' (as well as in Duchamp's readymades) between the mass-produced object and the signed work of an individual artist. There, in the play between originality and reproduction, the logic of fashion emerges as a mechanism for understanding the cultural impact of the transformation from an artisanal to an industrial economy. Caught in the grip of that logic, Poiret's artful self-construction as a couturier and as a modernist ultimately succumbed to the pressures of commodity culture.

Haute couture

Alexandra Palmer

The rise of named and celebrated dressmakers, couturiers and their establishments paralleled the development of small shops or boutiques, department stores and shopping itself as a public, social and cultural activity. Historically, dressmaking and dress design were a private arrangement undertaken in a domestic setting. Tradespeople delivered textiles, trims and accessories to the homes of upper-class clients in order for them to make a selection, and the middle and lower classes purchased goods at established stalls in towns, fairs or from pedlars. The actual design and making up of garments was a negotiation between the client and her female dressmaker, with the exception of riding habits and corsets that were traditionally made and fitted by male tailors. By the mid-eighteenth century, luxury shopping was 'like attending art salons, frequenting cafes, and promenading . . . one did not go shopping merely to purchase clothing, but to buy, or at least be, where all the rest of fashionable society was currently buying' (Jones 2004: 154). The new role of the *marchande de modes* located in boutiques selling ribbons, feathers and accessories and offering advice on selections and styles were precursors to modern day celebrity designers. Daniel Roche notes that in Paris these striking shops animated and changed the 'humdrum face of the city' (Roche 1994: 327).

By the mid-nineteenth century clients visited an individual dressmaker in their shop, thereby inverting the earlier domestic model. Customers still selected textiles and composed their ensembles in collaboration with the dressmaker, but the new setting required the customer to undress, be fitted and dress again in a situation far removed from the home. Thus the haute couture salon evolved into a hybrid space that combined the setting of an artist's studio with a domestic salon and boudoir. Dressmakers and couturiers sought the most beautiful and luxurious materials from the leading manufacturers of silks, velvets, laces and trims, that could be purchased as an exclusive by an individual couturier. They began to mark their names and locations on the designs. Labels were usually placed on the petersham waistband sewn into the bodice, thereby legitimising their clients' visits. It was evidence of the identity of the couturier with the design, and validated the clients' time and financial investment at the haute couture salon. Thus the client and couturier were intertwined in the haute couture system.

The custom dressmaking business known as haute couture, was formally established as the Chambre syndicale de la confection et de la couture pour dames et fillettes in 1868; an organisation that combined custom and ready-to-wear. In 1910 couture completely separated from the ready-to-wear industry and was rechristened the Chambre syndicale de la couture Parisienne. Strictly speaking, 'haute couture' only refers to made-to-order and made-to-measure fashion produced in Paris by accredited haute couture houses. The rules for membership were revised several times, most importantly in 1945 and again in 1992. However, the aim remained substantially unaltered:

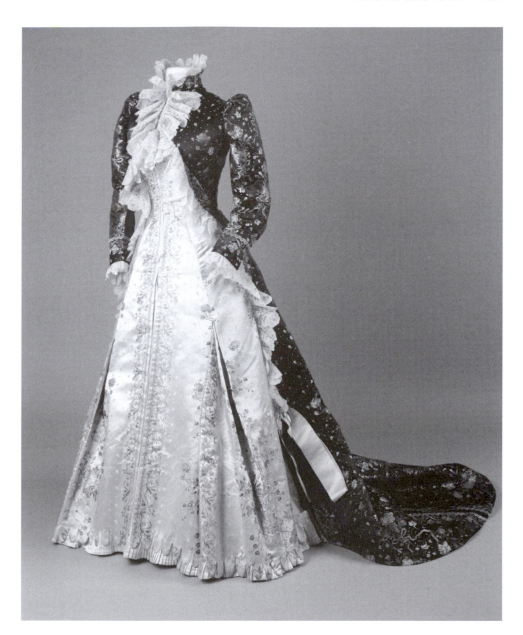

Snapshot 29.1 Directoire revival tea gown by Worth, *c.* 1895. ROM 969.223, with permission of the Royal Ontario Museum © ROM.

to maintain the highest standards of French design and fabrication, a nationalist agenda stemming from Jean Baptiste Colbert's mercantile legislation in 1665.

There are three basic principles. The house must be situated in Paris, and contain a deluxe showroom, a salon, and ateliers that employ a minimum number of qualified workers full time. Twice a year, spring and autumn, the house must show a minimum number of original designs on live mannequins. The designs must be made-to-measure in-house and can be custom ordered by private clients. Thus private clients visit and

Snapshot 29.2 The woven waist tape sewn into the tea gown is stamped with the name and address of the couturier 'Worth, 7 Rue de la Paix, Paris'. ROM 969.223, with permission of the Royal Ontario Museum © ROM.

select from pre-existing designs that are modified for individual taste. Haute couture lines cater to the social season, and many also offer smaller *demi-saison* collections. The Paris collections attracted the attention of the international fashion press that disseminate reports on the latest styles through articles, sketches, photographs and film.

From the late nineteenth century until the First World War, haute couturiers relied upon an international private clientele that travelled to Paris, in part to visit the *maisons* and up-date their high fashion wardrobes. After the war, as the numbers of private clients dwindled, haute couture increasingly had to rely upon professional commercial buyers, prestige department stores and small exclusive shops that sold the Paris clothes directly to local customers as well as offering in store, made-to-measure reproductions. England and the United States were the most important commercial clients. The 1929 stock market crash resulted in the US imposing high import duties on foreign goods, making imported Paris haute couture exorbitantly expensive as it was taxed according to materials, embroidery, furs, fittings and embellishment. In response, Paris catered directly to the American market, not only in terms of designs that they hoped would suit foreign taste, but also by offering new legal and commercial forms of couture called a *toile* (the design made up in muslin) and a paper pattern. Both avoided the heavy import duties and gave the commercial buyer all the design information needed to reproduce the original design or to manufacture a cheaper version by changing the textile and reducing the details and level of workmanship. Thus haute couture was the principal design source for mass-market ready-to-wear from the 1920s until the 1960s.

Bibliography and further reading

Jones, Jennifer M. (2004) *Sexing La Mode: Gender, Fashion and Commercial Culture in Old Regime France*, Oxford and New York: Berg.

Palmer, A. (2001) *Couture and Commerce: The Transatlantic Fashion Trade in the 1950s*, Vancouver: UBC Press; Toronto: Royal Ontario Museum.

Parmer, A. (2009) *Dior: A New Look, a New Enterprise (1947–57)*, London: V & A Publications.

Parmel, P., and Grumbach, D. (2006) *Fashion Show: Paris Style*, Boston: MFA Publications.

Roche, Daniel (1994) *The Culture of Clothing; Dress and Fashion in the 'Ancien Régime'*, Cambridge: Cambridge University Press.

Steele, V. (1998) *Paris Fashion: A Cultural History*, 2nd edition, Oxford and New York: Berg.

Troy, N. J. (2003) *Couture Culture: A Study in Modern Art and Fashion*, Cambridge, MA: MIT Press.

The origins of the modern fashion show

Caroline Evans

The fashion show, being barely a hundred years old, is a relatively modern phenomenon in the long history of Western fashion. Its origins lie in the development of the French haute couture system in the late nineteenth century, with its global trade networks across Europe and the Americas. As well as making top-end clothing for individual clients, haute couture houses sold model garments, and the rights to reproduce them, to manufacturers and wholesalers at all levels of the market. Fashion shows were part of this process, and evolved as much for the convenience of the overseas buyers coming to Paris as for the individual clients, for the latter could also see fashion in motion at the theatre, in extravagant stage costumes designed by the couturiers.

The cultural capital of French fashion was high and the *défilé*, known in English as the mannequin parade or, simply, the spring or autumn openings, became a key way to disseminate and promote the French ideal. Charles Frederick Worth's wife Marie modelled from the 1850s, and mannequins, commonplace in French couture houses from the 1880s, were also sent to model in the Bois de Boulogne and at the Paris races where they attracted the attention of both amateur and professional photographers.

In London, in the late 1890s, Lucile theatricalised the show, building a little stage with filmy curtains: she turned it into a society event, with invitation cards and refreshments, and she promoted the extraordinarily modern glamour of her London mannequins who she used to open her branches in New York and Paris in 1910 and 1911 respectively. From the late 1890s, the fashion show developed simultaneously in Europe and the USA, in department stores and couture houses alike. While French shows were often predicated on exclusivity, the Americans were frequently ahead of them in popularising the show as a form of mass spectacle.

All the early proponents of the fashion show were astute at self-promotion, marketing and international sales. While Worth, Lucile and Poiret alone have tended to be credited with its invention, and they themselves contributed to this myth, many other designers were important too, including Pinguat, Redfern, Paquin, Doucet and Patou.

All these designers recognised how to promote their designs by showing them in motion. Walter Benjamin (1892–1940) described the advent of 'new velocities' that gave modern life an altered rhythm. Among these, the fashion show and the cinema emerged almost simultaneously. Both had the capacity to convey speed, immediacy and movement. From 1900, the desire to see clothing in motion raged: mannequins tangoed, slithered, swaggered and undulated before private clients and trade buyers alike. Poiret toured Europe with his exotic French mannequins in 1911, while Patou recruited sporty North Americans to his Paris catwalk in 1925 where they modelled in chorus-line formations. Vionnet and Chéruit grouped their mannequins by the colour of their dresses, turning individual bodies into abstract patterns on stage. In New York, the

Snapshot 30.1 'Evening gown in all its splendor': woman modelling evening gown by Lucile at the spring fashion show of the National Retail Garment Association held at the Commodore Hotel, New York, *c.* 1921. © Lucile, from Underwood & Underwood, New York Library of Congress, LC-USZ62-100835.

department store Lord & Taylor's specially constructed sets for the mannequin parades pre-dated the angular, Expressionist sets of European avant-garde cinema.

The mannequin parade was a phenomenon of early twentieth-century modernity and, more specifically, of modernism. Its emergence coincided with the rationalisation and standardisation of the body in other fields of work, leisure and art. These included early time and motions studies, the streamlined syncopation of the chorus line, and the modernist body of art and architecture. In this way, the 'modernism' of the early fashion show was not so much an aesthetic as part of a rationalising programme. It drew on the artistic language of modernism, the better to translate business and management methods into visual seduction. Approximately a hundred years later, the modern fashion show is still doing something remarkably similar, turning hard business into a unique form of stagecraft and theatricality.

Bibliography and further reading

Evans, C. (2001) 'The Enchanted Spectacle', *Fashion Theory*, special issue on 'Fashion and Performance', ed. G. Gregg Duggan, 5, 3, pp. 271–310.

Kaplan, J. H., and Stowell, S. (1994) *Theatre and Fashion: From Oscar Wilde to the Suffragettes*, Cambridge: Cambridge University Press.

(2006) *Showtime: Le Défilé de mode*, Paris: Musée Galliéra de la Mode de Paris; also published as (2007) *Fashion Show: Les desfilades di moda*, Barcelona: Museu Tèxtil i d'Indumentària.

Madame Grès
Master couturier

Patricia Mears

Alix Grès (1903–93) created gowns of exquisite beauty and dressed many of the most stylish women of the twentieth century. Although Grès was minute – she stood no more than five feet tall – countless magazine images and museum collections around the world attest that the venerated couturier was a giant in the world of fashion and was one of the most brilliant dressmakers of the twentieth century. Her work is noted for its use of innovative construction techniques that allowed her clothing to transcend the fickleness of fashion.

Despite the high regard in which Madame Grès is held, her working methodology remains mysterious. When journalists describe her work in glowing but cursory terms, it is often because her innovations in construction are beyond the scope of their knowledge. Furthermore, the complexity of her very particular approach to the *métier* made analysis difficult for the casual viewer.

My analysis of her work extant in American and French museum collections as well as numerous objects in private hands leads to the assessment that there are three predominant stylistic and structural elements of her work: her classically inspired pleated gowns usually made of matte silk jersey; her simple and geometric designs based on ethnic costume; and the three-dimensional, sculptural quality that was a hallmark of much of her work. Her classically-inspired gowns were first crafted at the onset of her career and were made until her retirement. The sculptural pieces were first made starting in the mid-1930s, became very prevalent in the 1940s and 1950s – many of which with their corseted bodices and full, crinolated skirts were anathema to her overall body of work – evolved and became ever lighter and more buoyant during the last twenty years of her career. Grès's last major stylistic and technical development was the creation of garments inspired by the construction of non-Western dress, such as saris and serapes.

Grès was a *couturière* in the traditional sense of the word. She did not sketch or leave the technical process to assistants. Every garment from her atelier was crafted by hand, by her, using either inexpensive muslin to create a prototype or the actual ground fabric itself. She rose early in the morning and worked well into the evening nearly every weekday of her life, draping and manipulating fabric with great speed, dexterity, and alacrity.

Grès was a master technician whose work has often been compared to other great dressmaking innovators of the twentieth century, such as Madeleine Vionnet (1876–1975) and Cristóbal Balenciaga (1895–1972). In the early part of her career, Grès created garments clearly based on Vionnet's philosophy of draping to produce supple, body-revealing fashions with a minimum of cutting and sewing, but used a more

Snapshot 31.1   Pale pink matte silk jersey evening dress (label: Grès / 1 Rue de la Paix / Paris, 1955). The Museum at FIT, 77.187.1. Gift of Mrs E. L. Cournand.

intuitive, self-taught approach that eschewed Vionnet's mathematical balance and precision. Grès entered the last phase of her working life, from 1960 to 1988, while Cristobal Balenciaga was the most influential force in French fashion design. Instead of designing Balenciaga-style collections, which gave the appearance of being rigid and architectonic, Grès continued to produce soft, sculptural garments. She was able to hold onto the techniques learned in the early phase of her career and amplify them to make her unique fashions in the decades after Balenciaga closed his house in 1968. During the last twenty years of her career, Grès was the last working *couturière* from the golden age of French fashion design.

An important point to note is that Grès was not a fashion trendsetter in the obvious sense and did not create novel, thematic collections, so her work is often considered to exist outside the realm of changing fashion. Yet, as the stylistic and technical changes in her work prove, Grès did follow general design trends, responding to changes in fashion with a belief that the craft of dressmaking was the crucial element inherent in all her designs.

Bibliography and further reading

Benaim, L. (2003) *Grès*, Paris and New York: Assouline.
Horyn, C. (1996) 'The Mystery of Madame Grès', *Vanity Fair*, February, pp. 128–41.
Mears, P. (2007) *Madame Grès: Sphinx of Fashion*, New Haven and London: Yale University Press.

Fashion as 'art' versus fashion as 'craft' revisited

Sanda Miller

The iconic French designer Gabrielle 'Coco' Chanel (1883–1971) defined fashion thus: 'a style'. In her first interview for television given to Jacques Chaseur in January 1959, Chanel refused certain stereotypes of fashion as high-status cultural practice. The seventy-five-year-old sacred monster made the retort: 'it is a craft that must be carried out with the greatest rigour. That is what is called a style. That is not fashion. Fashions change too often. Why should fashion in spring be different from winter? Style and fashion are not the same thing' (documentary, 1994).

The Greek thinker Plato (427–347 BC) defined craft (*techne*) as the skill in the making of which required a specialised ability: knowing how to achieve a certain end. In the *Sophist* (*c.* 360 BC) he analysed the notion of 'productive craft', that is the bringing into being of something that did not previously exist: the carpenter makes a chair; the sculptor makes a sculpture and both require both skill and *episteme* (knowledge). Thus, production of all things is imitation; making a chair requires the knowledge of what a chair 'is' (its *chairness* or Ideal Form thereof).

Art as society defines it today is a much more recent and Romantic conceit grounded in what Walter Benjamin called its 'aura', but for the Classical Greeks making a wooden chair, a marble statue of Zeus or writing the *Iliad* were all democratically defined as *technai*. *Art* and *craft* have been regarded as 'binary oppositions' by the late twentieth-century French philosopher Jacques Derrida (1930–2004) whose respective definitions hinge on 'functionality' squarely placed centre stage in the debate and can be summarised as follows: 'X' is not functional, therefore 'X' is 'art' and versus 'X' is functional, therefore 'Y' is 'craft'.

One might pause and ask why is this question being posed in the first place? Is fashion a form of 'art' or is fashion a 'craft'? Let's reverse the question: instead of asking 'is fashion art?', we might ask 'can art be craft?' and the unequivocal answer is, 'yes'. In 1926 the Romanian born Parisian avant-garde sculptor Constantin Brancusi (1876–1957) sailed to New York to attend the opening of his exhibition at the Brummer Gallery. Upon arrival, the customs authorities deemed a bronze version of *The Bird in Space* as a technological implement and Brancusi had to pay tax. He promptly sued the Customs Office and a law suit followed. Jacob Epstein (1880–1959) acted for the defence, and when asked why is *The Bird in Space* art, he replied: 'because it pleases my sense of beauty. I find it to be a beautiful object', thus prioritising 'aesthetic pleasure' and returning us to the Romantic principle.

At the same time that Brancusi was working, the fashion designer Paul Poiret (1879–1944) was redefining conceptions of beauty and form for fashionable women. To what extent can we divorce a garment by this designer from its functional dimension and look at it instead as purely an arrangement of shapes and colours, as Epstein had done with Brancusi's *Bird in Space*? Three hypotheses could be presented for consideration. *Intentionality* has always played an important role in art criticism to the extent that we even have the *Intentional Fallacy* – that is, arguing from the object to the artist's intentional meaning – is deemed logically faulty. We cannot therefore argue that Alberto Giacometti's (1901–66) *Four Women on a Tall Base* (1950) is an expression of his criticism of capitalism, because we are Marxist critics, or a criticism of the position of women in French society, because we are feminist critics. The work of art may indeed *contain* but would not necessarily *reveal* the artist's intention. As a consequence, 'intentionality' was replaced by two new theoretical frameworks within the academic discipline of art history from the 1970s: *the institutional theory of art* and *the historical definition of art*, as proposed by George Dickie (1974) and Jerrold Levinson (1979) respectively. The status of the work of art is conferred either by the museum context or the academic discipline of art history, with the art market playing a connected role as well. Thus Andy Warhol's (1928–87) *Brillo Box* (1963) poses the question 'what is art?' within an historical context and narrative posing questions of status and practices.

Can we conclude that even if we allow that the primacy of intention regarding the final cause (*telos*) of an object is altered either inadvertently (Brancusi) or deliberately through a number of external agencies (Warhol), it would be possible to argue that a dress by Paul Poiret (functional and therefore defined as 'craft') can only in certain contexts (displayed for aesthetic pleasure in a museum) be art? Paradoxically too, a 'great' sculpture by Brancusi or a 'work' by Warhol (both not functional and therefore defined as art) can only in certain contexts (*Bird in Space* being a case in point, seen by the customs official as a utilitarian implement) but not in others, be 'art'. Is it simply a matter of viewing context that decides whether fashion becomes art? There cannot be a simple answer and this matter requires ongoing re-evaluation and analysis rather than simple posturing.

Bibliography and further reading

Alperson, P. (ed.) (1991) *The Philosophy of Visual Arts*, Oxford: Oxford University Press.

Beardsley, M. C. (1966) *Aesthetics from Classical Greece to Present: A Short History*, New York: Macmillan.

Carroll, N. (1999) *The Philosophy of Art: A Contemporary Introduction*, London: Routledge.

Dickie, G. (1974) *Art and the Aesthetic: An Institutional Analysis*, Ithaca and London: Cornell University Press.

Interview reproduced in the documentary on Gabrielle Chanel entitled *Private Lives* for the BBC television series 'Arena', 1994.

Levinson, J. (1979) 'Defining Art Historically', *British Journal of Aesthetics*, 19, pp. 232–50.

Chapter 21

Nice threads: identity and utility in American fashion

Gregory Votolato

Gatsby's butler was suddenly standing beside us, 'Miss Baker?' he inquired. 'I beg your pardon, but Mr Gatsby would like to speak to you alone? . . .

She got up slowly, raising her eyebrows at me in astonishment, and followed the butler toward the house. I noticed that she wore her evening-dress, all her dresses, like sports clothes – there was a jauntiness about her movements as if she had first learned to walk upon golf courses on clean, crisp mornings.[1]

As F. SCOTT FITZGERALD SUGGESTED IN THIS PASSAGE from *The Great Gatsby*, the role of fashion in American life became intimately bound up with leisure and sport. When the Dutch historian J. H. Huizinga wrote of play as a leading influence in the development of modern culture, he acknowledged the importance of the leisure movement which, more than any other social trend, would define American life in the twentieth century.[2] But the image of sport and recreational play which came to dominate American fashion in the second half of the century was only made possible by the liberation of the garment industry from the model of Parisian couture – this was accomplished when the German army occupied Paris in 1940.

Up until that time, American culture as a whole was deferential, whether from necessity or simply from habit, to the model of European culture. The fine arts clung to the traditions of Raphael and Michelangelo and to the modernism of Picasso. French, Italian and English styles prevailed over conservative architecture and furnishing, while modern decoration was linked to the 1925 Decorative Arts Exposition in Paris or to the Bauhaus.

when Paris started a fashion . . . the whole world followed. In 1939 Balenciaga designed a dress with a flounce . . . Early in 1940 Schiaparelli,

following the trend, was showing them too, and the flounce was launched
. . . so *Vogue* says flounces . . . and flounces says Fifth Avenue and West
Forty-second Street and Seventh Avenue this fall, all the way from approximately $350 to $11 . . . Thus does a French designer's whimsey become a
'fashion Ford', worn in Paris, France and Paris, Arkansas.[3]

So wrote H. Stanley Marcus, Vice-President of the Neiman Marcus store, shortly
after the fall of Paris. He pointed to painting and architecture as two fields in which
the emulation of European models by Americans had led only to second-rate copies.
But, he declared that when Grant Wood and Thomas Hart Benton 'painted what they
saw and knew' and Frank Lloyd Wright 'tried to meet the requirements of American living', they achieved a standard equal to any work being produced in the capitals
of Europe. Marcus went on to argue that only through enforced emancipation from
Europe would real creativity flower in American culture. His point was that with the
coming of war in Europe the three-billion-dollar American garment industry needed,
for the first time, to depend on its own design talent to contribute fresh ideas on which
the prosperity of the industry relied.[4] Marcus observed that a global market existed
which the huge, mechanised American industry was perfectly suited to service, if
its designers could come up with the inspiration which the world's fashion audience
expected.[5]

But where would they get their inspiration? Like Wright, Benton and Wood, fashion designers had the American scene as a source – the lives of ordinary people living
in a variety of particular landscapes and climates. The culture of the street, its politics, dangers and opportunities offered innovations in dress expressing new identities
devised by individuals and groups. They had the nature of work in America, from the
factory floor to the cattle ranch. But perhaps the richest source was leisure, for it occupied the greatest amount of time and interest in most Americans' lives. Mass-tourism
provided contacts with a staggering variety of cultures which captured the imagination of fashion-conscious Americans. Both Hollywood and the publishing industry were
central to modern leisure and provided an endless flow of fantasy based on popular narratives which fuelled fashion trends throughout the century.

At the turn of the century, the massive popularity of Charles Dana Gibson's magazine illustrations of the physically active American woman contributed to the popularity of the shirtwaist, a form of dress borrowed from men's clothing, which was both
proper and comfortable and which, as a universal, mass-produced garment, crossed
class lines and ethnic barriers. More than any other garment, the shirtwaist ensured
that ready-made clothing, as opposed to couture, became the mainstay of the fashionable American's wardrobe. Subsequently, the economic success of the mass-market
United States garment industry, centred in New York's Seventh Avenue, depended on
the universal acceptance of the casual model of dressing, not only for sport and relaxation, but for all occasions.[6] Like the Gibson Girl, the Arrow Collar Man of the early
1920s was an illustrator's abstraction which embodied the attributes of the ideal young
American. Advertising illustrations by J. C. Leyendecker portrayed athletic young
men, like those described in the novels of F. Scott Fitzgerald, thoroughly at ease in the
casual clothing associated with the relaxed and gentlemanly sports of golf, tennis and
sailing (Figure 21.1). The Arrow Collar man was not only a great corporate emblem,
but became a symbol of the all-American hero.[7]

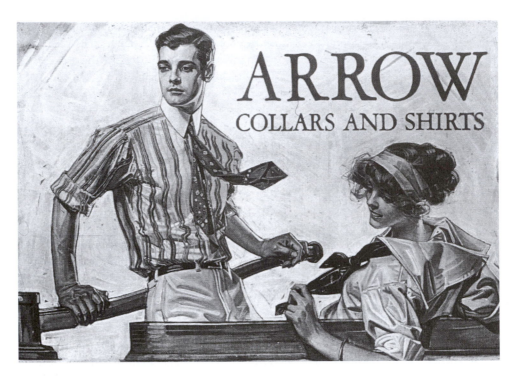

Figure 21.1 The sporty Arrow Collar man represented the ideal American man. His clothing combined fitness for purpose with casual elegance. Painting by J. C. Leyendecker, c. 1920.

Marcus identified the particular strength of American designers in their ability to respond to the developing opportunities of mass leisure and to conceive sportswear with a home-grown, regional accent. The California designers and manufacturers, he wrote, 'succeeded in striking a new note in play clothes. They had a freer range of color, and they have derived inspiration from native sources'.[8] A perfect climate for year-round outdoor activities contributed to the laid-back life of fun in the sun which came to be associated with the south-west. The rootlessness and diverse experiences of its new population of immigrants from older parts of the country and from abroad combined with exotic local traditions to create a rich and fluid culture receptive to design innovation. Denim, long associated with western work clothes, Indian hand-made silver buttons, and cowboys' bandanas all made appearances during the late 1930s in suits and dresses by the Santa Fe designer Alice Evans. At the same time, Hollywood stars such as Marlene Dietrich and Katharine Hepburn were among the first women to wear trousers and trench coats. And it was in California that semi-nudity on the beach first found acceptance.

The importance of sport went beyond its stylistic influence to provide a new model for culture as a whole. It involved the democratisation of leisure time and new attitudes toward health, gender and sexuality. It related to manufacturing methods and to the development of new materials. And it required appropriate responses by designers to physical activities originating mainly among young people who were inventing new forms of play and modifying older ones. The development of tennis, golf, water sports, winter sports, cycling, running, as well as spectator sports, such as baseball and basketball, called for continuously creative responses from the fashion world. The real need for comfortable and functional clothing by sportspeople was followed by the creation of sporty clothing for spectators or fans.

In earlier times and in older cultures, when leisure was thought to be exclusive to the rich, the luxury of free time was signified by styles which inhibited mobility: bustles, corsets and bound feet. These fashion devices were badges of class. But in the American century, design was increasingly devoted to freeing up the human body for movement; and movement was for anyone, regardless of their income or birth. Sports apparel and uniforms were soft and lightweight, with comfort and ease their primary design criteria. Stretch ski pants and loose, down-filled parkas were typical of the practical sports clothing which became ubiquitous fashion items. Sport was one of the great democratising forces of modern times. Baseball made national heroes out of poor boys who had learned to play the game in vacant city lots. Boxing and athletics gave international prominence to Black athletes in a time when segregated schools and lunch counters were legal expressions of Southern apartheid. Tennis and competitive swimming brought women under the spotlight of publicity during the 1920s and 1930s.[9]

Sportswear also had a profound affect on the role of the wearer in the fashion system. Whereas couturiers exercised full authority over the way their customers looked through the design of complete ensembles, the sportswear industry of America relied on the production of 'separates' which allowed the purchaser to decide how they should be worn and with what. In the 1930s, the men's sports jacket evolved from the earlier sporting 'blazer'. Unlike the conventional suit jacket, which it resembled closely, it could be worn with dress trousers, casual slacks, khakis, jeans, shirt and tie, turtleneck sweater, polo shirt or T-shirt.

Although garments had been sold individually for decades, the importance given them by designers, such as Bonnie Cashin in the 1930s and later Calvin Klein, significantly altered the position of the designer, who became the supplier of a kit of parts which offered the buyer considerable choice in constructing a personal look. While the much-vaunted 'death of the designer' has been undermined by the status of Calvin Klein or Ralph Lauren in the 1990s, their role has become less authoritarian and more enabling. The new wearer has been encouraged to be more involved in the creation of fashion by the selection of elements and the composition of an outfit. As a result, the old joke of two horrified women appearing at a party wearing complete, identical outfits was far less likely to occur at the end of the century than it was in 1950.

Sportswear, in its purest form, is the carefully devised response to the needs of modesty under conditions of the most strenuous physical activity. As a result of its connotations of health and its functionalism, sportswear earned a reputation for 'rightness', establishing around it an aura of moral superiority. Nike jogging shoes told us that the wearer valued exercise for physical and mental well-being and knew how to enhance his or her performance by wearing the correct apparel. Like the short tunic worn by Olympic athletes in ancient Greece, modern sportswear attained a classical status through its economy of material and expression of purpose.[10]

In this spirit, Claire McCardell's use of natural materials and free construction produced swimwear and casual dresses which were interpreted as exemplars of functionalism, earning her an exhibition at the Museum of Modern Art in the mid-1940s.

The bathing chemise:
the new beach figure

Taking the plunge now,
at the resorts:
the newest bathing-suit
fashion in a month
of November—
covered to the collarbone,
the shape built inside
instead of outside,
the look long-bodied
and high-bosomed and easy-waisted,
definitely in line with the silhouette-news
made in Paris this autumn.
By contours, Vogue predicts,
a bathing suit to reckon with,
as well as to swim in.
Facing page: Honey-beige cotton,
crinkled to stay that way, rimmed with white.
By Carolyn Schnurer, in Crown cotton.
About $18. Bonwit Teller; Julius Garfinckel;
Jenss'; I. Magnin. Kleinert as in cap
at Bonwit Teller. Lingerie sunglasses,
This page: Red and white checks
on elasticized Chromspun acetate and cotton
nothing to it but fashion, seams of it.
By Claire McCardell, about $20.
Lord & Taylor; Halliday's; L. S. Ayres.
"Tangerin Pink" lipstick
and nail polish, Helena Rubinstein.

Figure 21.2 Athletic chic – a 1954 chemise-cut bathing suit by Claire McCardell in elasticised Chromspun acetate and cotton. McCardell's designs embodied the relaxed and unpretentious aspects of post-war American life.

McCardell's innovative adaptation of the ease and naturalness of sportswear to clothes for all occasions became known as 'The American Look' (Figure 21.2). Her simple, elegant and unpretentious designs combined the durability of work clothes with the comfort of sportswear; their affordability and classlessness were pure expressions of the democratic principle in modern design. While, in the late 1940s, Dior was reasserting the dominance of Paris as the world's fashion capital with his stiffly constructed New Look dresses, McCardell offered the American woman an equally refreshing change from wartime styles with her range of casual, mid-calf, full circle skirts in soft cotton. Her dresses featured natural shoulders with lithe, close-fitting bodices which gave the wearer the animated look 'of a Martha Graham dancer'.[11]

Perhaps the most distinctive American look to emerge since the 1970s resulted from professional women combining sportswear with business clothing. Typical ensembles would include tailored suits and nylons worn with sport socks, trainers and full-length down-filled parkas. Among the most innovative high-fashion designers of the 1990s, Donna Karan, through 'her invention of the "body", adapted the American tradition of easy, sporty clothes into the environment of *Wall Street* (the movie)'.[12] Karan promoted her products through a post-feminist manifesto which encompassed a range of issues from sex and glamour to body type and gender. She presented her clothing as a kit of parts, enabling 'women of character' to create their own personal style. And she exploited her own image, smart, chic and well connected, 'as if she is just her customers, and vice versa'.[13] Karan's monumental DKNY advertisements were an outstanding addition to the commercial mural art of Manhattan and quickly became as familiar around the world as McDonald's Golden Arches or the red and yellow Kodak logo.

Sports clothing also claimed the moral high ground as a rational response to the health and hygiene movement initiated in the later nineteenth century. As the benefits of sun, water, fresh air and exercise became commonly accepted, the clothing which enabled individuals to partake in them became associated with both good sense and a new religion of the body. The new health deities were also sex gods and goddesses, and the bathing suit was the most effective vehicle for putting their bodies on public display. More than any other form of dress, the bathing suit undermined the virtue of modesty. Exposure on the beach became a symbol of modernity and emancipation for both sexes and a powerful protest against Victorian values.

The modern bathing suit began with the work of Carl Jantzen and his partners John and Roy Zehntbauer who, together, invented the 'elastic stitch' in 1917. Using two sets of mechanical knitting needles in place of the single pair used for ordinary jersey, they created a fabric which could stretch like a 'second skin'. They also introduced a new method of assembling the suit which produced a snug, wrinkle-free fit and streamlined shape which became known as the 'California look'. The healthy, erotic image made possible by Jantzen's innovations was popularised by slick magazine and billboard advertising which massively increased sales (Figure 21.3). By 1930 Jantzen was the world's largest manufacturer of swimsuits with over one and a half million sold that year.[14]

The development of synthetic Lastex fabric in the 1930s helped to perfect the form-fitting suit, producing a convincing facsimile of nudity. Meanwhile, the bare-chested man had become a respectable sight on American beaches. By the mid-1950s, his loose-fitting 'boxer trunks' had shrunk to tight, minuscule 'briefs'. For women, the two-piece bikini of 1946 was touted to be 'the most explosive fashion event of the forties'.[15] It set a marker on the road to near nudity surpassed only by Rudi Gernreich's 'topless' suit of 1964. The trend toward revealing previously hidden parts of the anatomy persisted into the 1980s, conveying the increased sexual freedom of the period, but also imposing new restrictions, such as the tyranny of slenderness. The modern bathing suit was 'a form of undress which functioned as a symbol of dress' and it combined the eroticism of simultaneous disclosure and concealment. It was said that 'If clothing is a language, then a bathing suit is a telegram'.[16] But in the 1990s, like the newly invented fax or e-mail, the bathing suit was made to carry much more complex and subtle messages than a telegram could. Changing sexual politics, fear of skin cancer from over-exposure to the sun, and a fashion for historical costume brought with them a postmodern cover-up. This first reversal of the modern trend toward nudity was reflected in the modest, neo-1960s, two-piece suits and 1930s revival, one-piece streamliners by Norma Kamali and Anne Cole. Men joined in the cover-up with a fashion for surfers'

Figure 21.3 Jantzen pioneered the nude look achieved through the use of new synthetic fabrics from the early 1930s. The sleek shapes of their swimwear complemented the streamlining of industrial design products and commercial architecture.

all enveloping wetsuits and the arrival of loose-fitting, knee-length 'bags' in the 1980s (Figure 21.4).

Conventions of dress and the design of clothing seldom changed as rapidly as they did after the Second World War, when Americans were migrating to the new suburbs and adopting a pattern of life which centred on DIY and gardening. Leisure pastimes such as fishing and golf and very casual, unplanned socialising with neighbours around the barbecue or the breakfast bar encouraged a relaxed manner of dress which called for new purpose-designed clothing. The men's wash and wear polyester leisure suit, with matching shirt-tailored jacket and trousers, was designed specifically to distinguish home dressing from office dressing. Alternatively, ad hoc combinations of existing clothing types became popular. These included traditional work clothes, such as jeans

Figure 21.4 Casual clothing accentuates the graceful, fluid movements and gestures of modern sports. Like loose-fitting baseball uniforms and generously cut basketball shorts, the baggy 'jams' and loose tops of the 1980s and 1990s reveal the body through drapery.

and khakis, worn with sportswear, such as short-sleeved polo shirts and tennis shoes. By the 1960s, both were being worn with sports jackets, signalling a new respectability and a relentless rise up-market.

Lévi Strauss of San Francisco, the largest apparel manufacturer in the world, has made its blue denim work pants to the same pattern since 1850. Since then, over 800 million pairs of their sturdy, cheap, standard garments have been made and worn. Style-conscious men and women began to wear them in the 1930s; but it was not until the 1960s that jeans became a staple of fashionable dress. Their associations with rebellious youth, established in the early 1950s by movie stars such as Marlon Brando and James Dean, and famous motorcycle gangs including the Hells Angels and Amboy Dukes, led them to be adopted as the basis of an ad hoc uniform by the counter-culture generation of the Vietnam period. Worn skin tight, low-cut and flared, they popularised the sexiness previously connected with sailors' trousers. Yet their proletarian origins and associations with America's historical development established them as a form of national costume. The natural cotton and traditional dyes, from which they gained their durability and good ageing qualities, connected them to the growing ecological consciousness of the 1960s and after. Their unisex appeal also reflected the new gender awareness inspired by the women's movement. Transformation of jeans from mass utility wear, associated with cowboys and construction workers, to a universal garment appropriate in almost any context, made them the single most prominent item of American apparel.[17]

Designers manipulated the form of jeans to bring them in line with changing fashion trends such as the flared leg of the 1960s and the loose fit of the 1980s (Figure 21.5); they embroidered them and studded them and added their labels to give them class. But individual wearers went further, changing their form, cutting them off short, patching them, slashing them and decorating them by hand to express an infinite variety of meanings, all aimed at personalising a standard product, mass produced by the millions.

Other articles of functional clothing also found their niches in popular taste. The engineer's boot took its place alongside Indian moccasins, running shoes, sneakers and ballet slippers as everyday footwear. Waxed jackets, riding boots, and denim bib-fronted overalls, the clothing of farmers and other rural types, were worn with unlikely separates by fashionable men and women to achieve a country looks for domestic leisure. Basic cotton knit T-shirts became popular with both sexes and all ages for everyday activities and acquired tone to be worn with high fashion suits. They were also adapted by top designers, such as Lilly Pulitzer and Kasper, as full-length dresses. But most commonly, T-shirts were printed with messages using both words and pictures to identify their wearers with places, products, issues and ideas. And like blue jeans, they were subjected by their wearers to all manner of manipulation, from slashing and tearing, to tie-dyeing, in pursuit of the unique example of a standard product.

The century has seen many styles which reflect individual interests and tastes emerging from outside the fashion industry. 'Street-fashion' has reflected a belief that creativity was just as likely to bubble up from the native originality of individuals in the lower reaches of society – in other words, those untainted by professional training, commercial motives or educated taste – as to trickle down from high-fashion design houses. In 1969, Rudi Gernreich declared that 'fashion starts in the streets. What I do is watch what the kids are putting together for themselves. I formalize it, give it

Figure 21.5 Jeans, flared or straight-legged in 1976. Like the shirtwaist at the turn of the century, jeans became a staple garment adaptable to changes in prevailing taste. Similarly, the Adirondak chair was made in many variations on a standard form providing the comfort of the living room outdoors.

something of my own, perhaps, and then it is fashion.'[18] But whether or not Gernreich's 'something' was necessary as a seal of fashion approval is debatable.

From the early 1960s the process of creating fashion often began in the thrift shops

Figure 21.6 Thrift shop chic. Combinations of old and new, up-market and down, formal and casual, all contributed to the inventive collage of style since the 1970s. Originality and wit were the hallmarks of this approach to fashion.

which flourished in cities and towns all over the country (Figure 21.6). Like the 'synthetic' assemblage technique of Picasso, later known in America as 'junk sculpture' or as bricolage, combining cast-off clothing and accessories in new and unexpected ways became attractive to many young people reacting against the standardised materialism of bourgeois culture and against the authority of the art or fashion establishment. The influence of the thrift shop look was aped in Ralph Lauren's casually layered and seemingly improvised costumes designed for Woody Allen's 1978 film, *Annie Hall*. The costumes worn by Diane Keaton in the film layered oversized men's clothes with oddly selected women's separates. They accurately conveyed the character's uncertain but try-anything brand of creativity. While real Annies had been out in the street since the early 1960s, Lauren eventually marketed the look as mainstream fashion in the late 1970s. Thus the traditional model–series relationship was inverted for fashion, as it was when Detroit car makers picked up styling details and colours from grass-roots customisers.

Street style, inspired by the favoured tastes of ethnic groups or of self-conscious subcultures, such as beatniks, urban gays and New Wave punks, also served as a means of promoting new political and social agendas. Anti-war students of both genders demonstrated their political views in the 1960s by wearing military jackets, boldly decorated with anti-military symbols, in combination with other distinctly civilian garments, such as psychedelic or flower-printed shirts, ethnic accessories and the controversial long hair of the period (Figure 21.7).

Figure 21.7 Political protest and social outrage found expression in customised garments such as this flak-jacket worn by a marcher at the Anti-Vietnam War Moratorium, Washington DC, November 1969. The raised fist, symbol of the Black Power Movement, became a familiar image on college campuses during the late 1960s.

Stage and film costumes also reflected the political and subcultural issues bubbling up from popular discontent in the second half of the century. In 1953, when Marlon Brando wore Levis, T-shirt, black leather jacket and motorcycle boots in *The Wild One*, the combination was given an erotic charge which helped to established it as a lasting image of sexy alienation. *The Wild One* became both a straight and gay model, inspiring later underground films such as Kenneth Anger's *Scorpio Rising*, in which the customisation of apparel, bikes and interior settings all related to themes of malevolence, sex, death and the individual within a cult. In the spirit of sexual liberation which had been represented by the bikini and the miniskirt for women, the 1970s disco group Village People costumed themselves in caricatured uniforms based on gay icons of the period. Their eroticised stereotyping of the work clothes and uniforms worn by hard-hat construction workers and highway patrolmen elevated commonplace appearances to the status of fetishes. Meanwhile, in the bars and bath houses of San Francisco, Key West and New York, similar outfits were being worn as statements of a new, aggressively masculine image for gay men. In contrast, shaved heads, army fatigues and work boots became the austere uniform of both men and women in the darker atmosphere of queer culture following the appearance of AIDS.

From the love of old clothes central to thrift shop style, the fashion industry was reminded of the value of history. But like mainstream furniture and interior design, automotive and fashion design had often responded to earlier styles. The first automobile bodies took their designs from earlier conveyances such as chariots and carriages. And in the 1960s, Detroit looked to its own past for inspiration, offering new takes on pre-war vertical radiator grills, landau roof irons and continental spare wheels, all adapted to the latest projectile body shapes. Similarly, postmodern fashion began to combine the modernism of designers such as Bill Blass and the futuristic styles of Rudi Gernreich with historical references, treating history as a dressing-up trunk in which unrelated references could be combined in challenging and witty ways. Lew Magram's Acrilan turtleneck bodysuit (1974) could be worn with a ruffled tuxedo shirt, unbuttoned, and flared Levis over cowboy boots – and the look was unrestricted by gender or race!

In the 1980s and 1990s, American fashion designers evoked periods ranging from Early Christian to New Frontier.[19] Innovations were based on 'self-conscious and learned archaism and renewals more fundamental than merely nostalgic'. Like postmodern architects, fashion designers employed 'a hybrid historicism . . . arising from a mingling of models and surpassing discrete traditions'.[20] Film fashions played a role in popularising historical styles, such as the archaeological, late 1940s California casuals featured in Roman Polanski's period thriller *The Two Jakes* (1990) and revived as late-century club wear in the 1997 comedy *Swingers*. The return to traditional lines was also promoted heavily by Ralph Lauren in his interpretations of classic American work clothes and sportswear for men and women. Inspiration for his collections included pre-war casual country wear, Native American costume and western pioneer's garb.

The work of Norma Kamali developed from contemporary casual to rigorously archaeological, with some of her designs verging on reproduction. In a similar historical mode, Calvin Klein's 1995 line abandoned the relaxed look of sportswear in favour of highly constructed, minimalist contours refering back to early 1960s designs by Cassini and Givenchy for Jacqueline Kennedy and Audrey Hepburn. Klein featured formality and controlled tailoring intended to re-establish the high standards of an earlier period. But despite such a historicist retreat from casual clothes, the love of sportswear is so deeply a part of the American consciousness, and the freedom it offers its wearers to look and do as they please is so precious, that they will not be sacrificed easily.

Notes

1 F. Scott Fitzgerald, *The Great Gatsby* (first published 1926; repr. London, 1973), p. 57.
2 Richard Martin, *All American: A Sportswear Tradition* (New York, 1985), p. 8.
3 H. Stanley Marcus, 'America is in Fashion', *Fortune* (August 1940), p. 81.
4 The garment industry was the third largest industry in the United States by 1975 according to William Lippincott, President of FIT: Sarah Tornerlin Lee, *American Fashion* (New York, 1975), p. vii.
5 Martin, *All American*: 'Sportswear is a unique American language of style expressing our casual and leisure requirements as well as our informality and truth to mass production' (Marvin Feldman, Introduction).
6 Figures gathered in the 1980s described the garment district of New York as housing over 6,000 clothing manufacturers, producing two-thirds of American-made women's clothes and half of all American menswear, Gini Frings, *Fashion from Concept to Consumer* (Englewood Cliffs, 1982; repr. Englewood Cliffs, 1987), p. 119.
7 Martin, *All American*, p. 16.
8 Marcus, 'America is in Fashion', p. 141.
9 Fitzgerald's fictitious character, Jordan Baker, was a tennis champion, see note 1.
10 Martin, *All American*, p. 12.
11 Ibid., p. 39.
12 Correspondence with Helen Rees, 1 September 1996.
13 Ibid.
14 Lena Lencek and Gideon Bosker, *Making Waves, Swimsuits and the Undressing of America* (San Francisco, 1989), p. 11.
15 Ibid., p. 90.
16 Ibid., p. 19.
17 Martin, *All American*, p. 16.
18 Gernreich quoted in Amy de la Haye, *Fashion Source Book* (London and Sydney, 1988), p. 125.
19 New Frontier was the name given to the policies of the Kennedy presidency (1961–3).
20 Richard Martin and Harold Koda, *The Historical Mode, Fashion and Art in the 1980s* (New York, 1989), p. 7.

Women designing modernity

Rebecca Arnold

In the late nineteenth century women's lives began to change: they entered the work-place, shopped in the new department stores, and began to make decisive moves into the public realm. New patterns of leisure and travel were equally influential. Women's greater visibility meant they needed garments that enabled them to negotiate these spaces. This was a gradual process, which continued well into the twentieth century and, although it was mainly middle- and upper-class women who experienced these changes initially, city life spread opportunities and ideas of fashionability to a growing number of women.

Some of the most significant designers of modern clothes for modern women were female. In the early twentieth century this included couturiers such as Jeanne Paquin (1869–1936) and Callot Soeurs, and perhaps most dramatically, Lucile, whose designs suggested fashion's prominent role in the construction of a new visual and material language to create clothing suitable for contemporary life. However, it was not until Chanel's style fully evolved, first in her own dress, and later in her couture collections that a recognisably new aesthetic emerged to clothe women in modernity. While she was not the only designer to produce this minimal, sportswear-influenced image of active femininity based on smart separates, menswear style tailoring and strong accessories, she came to embody the style. She simultaneously crystallised an important idea of what a fashion designer can be, by becoming the ultimate incarnation of her fashion house's style. Indeed, Chanel had designed herself before she began to design and market this ideal to other women.

Female designers, the most significant of whom used fashion as a means to construct new modern identities, dominated the interwar period. Their work expressed the ambiguities of modernity: it was feminine, yet frequently drew upon masculine templates, it was luxurious yet simple, and it often drew upon ideas from the avant-garde, but was quickly copied and mass-produced for a wider market. Madeleine Vionnet's creations were an important example of this. She drew upon many of the same influences used by modern architects to explore space, geometric form and three-dimensionality. She was also inspired by modern art, in particular futurism, and worked with the Italian designer Thayaht (1893–1959) to experiment with representation of the body and movement.

Vionnet, Chanel and other women including Elsa Schiaparelli (1890–1973), and less well-known names such as Louiseboulanger and Maggy Rouff, drew upon their own experience of modern femininity, to create clothes that worked with the body and women's lives. However, their work principally addressed the elite, despite various less expensive ready-made lines, and licensing deals that brought their clothes to a wider audience in Europe, North and South America and Australia.

In the 1930s, ready-to-wear designers were emerging in America who produced

Snapshot 33.1 Dress designed by Claire McCardell (1905–58) and manufactured by Townley Frocks, New York, *c.* 1949. This dress is shaped by seven darts on each shoulder and is extensively gathered at the waist. McCardell, in working with a manufacturer, Townley Frocks, made her vision of the new mobile woman available through reasonable department store pricing. © National Gallery of Victoria, Melbourne, Australia.

clothes for the mass market based upon these same tenets of lifestyle, simplicity and active femininity. Women such as Clare Potter, Vera Maxwell, and most famously, Claire McCardell, rose to prominence, designing the kind of clothes they wanted to wear themselves. Born out of a strong sportswear aesthetic, their designs focused on interchangeable separates and adaptable dresses that took women from home, to work-place, to social event with minimal effort. Marketing campaigns created an empathetic link between designer and wearer, and suggested the ease with which American ready-to-wear could be bought, worn and cared for. In New York, McCardell embodied this 'American Look', which was to be consolidated during the Second World War, in the absence of news concerning the Parisian influence on fashion. California, too, evolved a similarly easy-to-wear style, in the hands of women including Pat Premo.

Their designs made apparent women's role in the modern world. They expressed the shifting environments, spaces and activities that women had to undertake, often in the course of one day. Between the 1920s and 1950s a way of designing and wearing simple but stylish fashions was created by women, for women. It was to remain a domi-nant fashion aesthetic, to be taken up later in the twentieth century by designers includ-ing Donna Karan, Miuccia Prada and Jil Sander.

Bibliography and further reading

Arnold, R. (2009) *The American Look: Fashion, Sportswear and the Image of Women in 1930s and 1940s New York*, London and New York: I. B. Tauris/Palgrave Macmillan.

Steele, V. (1992) *Women of Fashion: Twentieth Century Designers*, New York: Rizzoli.

Yohannan, K., and Nolf, N. (1998) *Claire McCardell: Redefining Modernism*, New York: Harry N. Abrams.

Fashion and the moving image

Louise Wallenberg

Snapshot 34.1 Rudolph Valentino (glass negative). Early 1920s. George Grantham Bain Collection. © Library of Congress, LC-DIG-ggbain-38803.

With very few exceptions, the intimate relations between fashion and film have escaped the attention of film scholars and fashion scholars alike. Given their many common characteristics, and the fact that they arose as important modern phenomena almost simultaneously, this is surprising. Both fashion and cinema are commercial industries as well as artistic forms of cultural expression. As such, they are dependent on one another – and have always been. As culturally vital and economically central components of an expanding visual and consumer culture in the late nineteenth century these two industries started connecting symbiotically with each other. Their linked relationship would continue within the late modernity of the twentieth century.

The first decade of cinema following its 'birth' in 1895, was one of *attraction*, referred to by film scholars as 'cinema of attraction'. The public fascination and appeal lay in the technical innovation of representing 'reality' via moving images. Cinema at first consisted of various kinds of documentary footage shot with a stationary camera. Soon, as the technique developed (with continuity editing as a leading principle) and as audiences started to demand feature films, cinema developed into a fictive and narrative medium. As a storytelling entertainment, for which the *mise-en-scène* (which includes costumes) is crucial in the make-believe and for which the *milieu* of the upper class prevailed, the screen started to function as a *shopping window*. The screen/window positioned its spectators not only as possible but also desiring consumers as they peeped into the luxurious world of the rich.

The department stores, which by the late nineteenth century had emerged as the most important retailers of fashion, offered and made available the fashions that were exhibited in the movies. The connection between the space of the cinema itself and the department store's early architectural incarnation with their excessive ornamentation and lighting further emphasised the relationship. American film scholar Jane Gaines, who has written one of the first works on film and fashion, notes: 'At the turn of the century, the French *grand magasin*, the US emporium, and the motion picture palace were all designed as exquisite containers for opulence and excess – the fruits of mass production displayed in their magnitude and multiplicity' (Gaines 2000: 101). The department store and the cinema – both as theatres (the actual place) and as representations (as image) – offer goods and dreams to consumers looking in. Cinema may be seen as a seductive shopping window, displaying fashion and fashionable goods to its spectators and would-be consumers, *and* as a fashion show or fashion spread in which its stars are involved in displaying fashionable costumes.

Fashion goals were also connected to cinema through overt marketing 'tie-ins'. The fashion industry used cinema to promote its latest trends by incorporating its products into the idealised world presented in cinema (a world which is, apart from being upper class, generally white and heteronormative). Likewise, cinema uses fashion to enhance the desirability of the idealised world it presents. In Charles Eckert's words (1978), film functions, or was made to function, 'as a merchandiser of goods', imposing a *desire* in the spectator to buy that which the film frame, as a shopping window, offered her or him. And as some of the most famous fashion designers, from the 1930s and onwards, were invited to create costumes for the screen, the symbiotic relationship between these two industries became even more tangible.

The bridge between film and fashion, as well as between the cinema and the department store, has always been the film star. Already in the early 1920s, the athletic, young, and slender bodies of certain actors came to constitute the perfect mannequins of fashion, there for everyone to see. Consequently, the silver screen worked, and still works, as a perfect billboard for the fashion industry from product to imagery.

Bibliography and further reading

Bruzzi, S. (1997) *Undressing Cinema, Clothing and Identity in the Cinema*, London: Routledge.

Eckert, C. (1978) 'The Carole Lombard in Macy's Window', *Quarterly Review of Film Studies*, 3, pp. 1–21.

Fischer, L. (2003) *Designing Women: Cinema, Art Deco and the Female Form*, New York: Columbia University Press.

Friedberg, A. (1993) *Window Shopping: Cinema and the Postmodern*, Berkeley: University of California Press.

Gaines, J. (2000) 'Dream/Factory', in L. Williams and C. Gledhill (eds), *Reinventing Film Studies*, London: Arnold.

Gaines, J., and Herzog, C. (1990) *Fabrications: Costume and the Female Body*, London: Routledge.

Totalitarian dress

Djurdja Bartlett

Totalitarian dress is a type of clothing opposed to fashionable dress. While fashion is a fast-changing phenomenon that thrives in commercial surroundings and takes into account individual desires, totalitarian dress depends on officially promoted ideologies, and is imposed on its wearers rather than being freely chosen by them. In medieval Europe, sumptuary laws ordered that social distinctions between higher and lower classes should be visually expressed through dress. By dividing people according to their social status these laws constrained the majority of the population, but gradually disappeared with the advance of the industrial society. The mass production of clothes, the new lifestyles brought about by the development of large cities, as well as the emancipation of women, made fashion available to the masses.

In contrast to fashion, totalitarian dress did not result from the rise of the mass market and the democratisation of consumer choices. Instead, its appearance was indebted to the political events that defined the period from the 1870s when the formation of modern nation states and sets of ideologies, from the utopian and the socialist to the nationalist and the fascist, arose on the European world stage. Shaped by these ideologies, and always conscious of the bourgeois values to which it was opposed, totalitarian dress appeared in various guises from the beginning of the twentieth century.

While it was not versatile like quixotic and ever-changing fashion, totalitarian dress cannot be identified simply with drab uniform. The utopian dress, for instance, proposed by the Russian constructivists in the early 1920s, was informed by an attempt to abolish social distinctions and make men and women equal. While the radical ambition of constructivist dress was never actually produced owing to the poverty of post-1917 Russia, its puritanical and proletarian asceticism returned in later historical contexts. In contrast to the Western fashions of the pre-Second World War era, the austere work uniform became the officially preferred type of dress in East European socialist countries in the late 1940s. In the 1930s and 1940s, the Italian fascists' black shirts and the blue shirts worn by the Spanish Falange members sartorially regimented the political body, while simultaneously giving it symbolic precedence over any individual body. At the same time, in a significant turn from the traditional, tightly fitted dress called *qipao*, communist Chinese women started to wear the Lenin suit – a jacket-and-trouser combination featuring a large turned-down collar and a double row of buttons. From the 1950s, the Chinese communist government imposed on the whole nation a plain uniform worn by its leader Mao Zedong, which symbolically abolished class differences.

The totalitarian regimes did not always envision their favourite dress as an ascetic or monastic uniform. In the 1930s in Stalinist Russia, smart dresses decorated with domestic ethnic motifs announced the birth of socialist fashion. Their archaic and timeless aesthetics demonstrated that they did not succumb to Western fashion trends that were considered frivolous by the state. As historical accounts of the socialist times demonstrate, these dresses could not be bought in the shops. Their role – to visualise the progress that the socialist totalitarian regimes conjured up in their self-imposed cultural isolation – was strictly ideological. Other ideologies incorporated ethnic motifs in their totalitarian dresses. In the 1930s and 1940s, Italian fascism tried to impose a new national conscience through its attempts to create an 'authentic' Italian fashion, while German national socialism relied on the dissemination of the *dirndl* (a traditional

Snapshot 35.1 Uniform for women tram conductors, *Žena a móda*, Prague, 1952.

Snapshot 35.2 Soviet collection at the Budapest Socialist Dress Contest, *Zhurnal Mod*, Moscow, 1955.

dress worn especially in southern Germany and Austria) to 'create' the perfect Aryan German woman.

In general, totalitarian dress thrives in situations of political, economic and cultural isolation imposed by regimes that hold power over their citizens. This is in contrast to fashion, which presupposes a free flow of ideas, well-developed international networks of trade, and the concept of an individual who is not subject to any authority without her or his consent.

Bibliography and further reading

Bartlett, D. (2004) 'Let Them Wear Beige: The Petit-bourgeois World of Official Socialist Dress', *Fashion Theory*, 2, pp. 127–64.

Finnane, A. (2007) *Changing Clothes in China: Fashion, History, Nation*, London: Hurst & Company.

Paulicelli, E. (2004) *Fashion under Fascism: Beyond the Black Shirt*, Oxford: Berg.

Fashion and film

Stella Bruzzi

Courturier Elsa Schiaparelli once said, what Hollywood did today, fashion would do tomorrow. Film influences fashion but at times the reverse has also been true. Hollywood, for example, dropped its hemlines following the vogue for longer fashions set by Jean Patou in 1929. Conversely, cinema's fashionability has always been part of its appeal: Adrian's robes for Joan Crawford in *Letty Lynton* (1932 – the year Crawford was first named 'The most imitated woman of the year') were widely copied, as was Edith Head's party dress for Elizabeth Taylor in *A Place in the Sun* (1951). Later, films such as *Bonnie and Clyde* (1967) and *Annie Hall* (1977) had a notable impact on contemporary fashions.

Recently, one can see this pattern of mimicry in both clothes and accessories. Retro aviator shades made a comeback after Tom Cruise wore them in *Top Gun* (1986); after the success of Quentin Tarantino's second movie, *Pulp Fiction* (1994), the black suits and monochrome outfits of French designer Agnès b. (along with Uma Thurman's Chanel 'Rouge Noir' nail varnish) became synonymous with cool. In this millennium, one could point to the innate fashionability of *The Matrix* trilogy (1999 onwards). But on the whole long production times have historically made it impossible for cinema to slavishly imitate fashion; mainstream cinema especially has proved conservative and unadventurous. Edith Head, Hollywood's most renowned costume designer, once remarked that she did not want to be 'caught out' by fashion trends dating her designs by changing so fast; costumes should thus be 'middle of the road'.

Fashion's relationship to film extends beyond the domain of film's fashionability. In the 1920s, 1930s and 1940s, few fashion designers did much work for films, with the exception of Chanel, who in 1931 went to MGM. Her Hollywood film work was not deemed a success, and she soon returned to Paris, later designing costumes for such films as *L'année dernière à Marienbad* (1961). The most important fashion designers have not always been those who have become involved in film. Christian Dior, despite the universal influence of the New Look, only lent his designs to a small and eclectic series of films including *Les enfants terribles* (1949) and *Stage Fright* (1950). In rare instances, individuals have had dual careers as fashion and costume designers, the most notable example being Jean Louis who was simultaneously head designer at Columbia then Universal and a working couturier, supplying clothes to stars such as Doris Day.

Hubert de Givenchy's collaboration with Audrey Hepburn fundamentally changed the relationship between film and fashion. In *Sabrina* (1954), as in the later *Funny Face* (1957), the distinction between the costume designer and the couturier is signalled ironically within the films' Cinderella narratives as in both Edith Head produced the drab, ordinary clothes that Hepburn wore as the lowly chauffeur's daughter or bookshop assistant, while Givenchy designed the show-stopping, post-transformation evening gowns.

In the wake of Givenchy's collaboration with Hepburn it became more common-place to use couturiers alongside costume designers: Hardy Amies (Queen Elizabeth II's favourite fashion designer) designed the wardrobe for *2001: A Space Odyssey* (1968); Yves Saint Laurent designed the costumes for Catherine Deneuve's character Séverine in *Belle de Jour* (1967); Ralph Lauren produced the costumes for *The Great Gatsby* (1974); Giorgio Armani clothed *The Untouchables* (1987). Other designers who have worked in films include Nino Cerruti, Ralph Lauren, Donna Karan and Calvin Klein. Fashion is more often considered a craft than an art, and selfconsciously artistic, spectacular fashions have been reserved for selfconsciously spectacular, art-house movies, the quintessential example being Jean Paul Gaultier, who costumed *The Cook, The Thief, His Wife, and Her Lover* (1989), *Kika* (1993), *La cité des enfants perdus* (1995) and *The Fifth Element* (1997). Against this, the accessibility of fashion in film has become hugely significant and audiences respond positively to being able to buy and emulate what they see on screen. The thrift shop black suits of *Reservoir Dogs* (1992), for instance, inspired London department store windows and Nicole Kidman's teddy in *Eyes Wide Shut* (1999) sold out immediately.

What has emerged is a fluid, flexible interaction between fashion and film – sometimes fashion borrows from film, often the exchange is reversed.

Bibliography and further reading

Berry, S. (2000) *Fashion and Femininity: Screen Style in 1930s Hollywood*, Minneapolis and London: University of Minnesota Press.

Bruzzi, S. (1997) *Undressing Cinema: Clothing and Identity in the Movies*, London and New York: Routledge.

Bruzzi, S., and Church Gibson, P. (eds) (2000) *Fashion Cultures: Theories, Explorations, and Analysis*, London: Routledge.

Chapter 22

The self as image
A critical appraisal of postmodern theories of fashion

Llewellyn Negrin

U NTIL RECENTLY, MOST FEMINIST CRITIQUES of women's fashion have been underpinned by a functionist paradigm in which fashion has been criticised for failing to obey the principle of practical utility. Thus for instance, the suffragist movement in the mid-nineteenth century criticised female dress insofar as it hindered the physical mobility of women and was detrimental to their health. Theorists such as Veblen and Loos in the early twentieth century also criticised the highly ornate and impractical dress of women as an unnecessary and wasteful indulgence, symptomatic of the economic dependence of women on men. Somewhat later, in the 1940s, theorists such as de Beauvoir developed these arguments further[1] and these formed the basis for the criticism of female fashion in the 1970s and 1980s by feminist theorists such as Brownmiller, Baker and Oakley.

In opposition to such forms of apparel, these critics advocated more functional modes of dress which eschewed adornment designed to enhance the sexual allure of the wearer. They argued that women should adopt a more 'natural' form of dress which revealed the body for what it was rather than seeking to transform it by artificial means in conformity with some externally imposed ideal of beauty. Implicit in this mode of critique was a principle which was central to modernist design – namely, the idea of 'form follows function' in which the 'rationality' of manufactured artefacts was assessed in terms of their practicality. In this paradigm, good design was that which resulted in the production of objects which could fulfil their function in the most efficient way possible. The aesthetic form of the object was derivative of its practical function. Thus, anything considered superfluous to the functioning of the object was deemed 'unaesthetic'.

Increasingly however, this functionalist paradigm has come under criticism by postmodern designers[2] and theorists such as Wilson, Sawchuck and Hollander who have argued that the assumption that there is a 'natural' or 'functional' mode of dress which serves certain universal, biologically determined needs such as warmth and protection, is untenable, since what is considered 'natural' or 'functional' is itself culturally determined. As they point out, to assume that there is a mode of dress which reflects the body 'as it really is' wrongly presupposes that the body pre-exists culture when in fact it is always inescapably encoded by cultural norms. In place of an appeal for clothing which is 'functional' or 'natural', recent theorists of fashion such as Wilson and Silverman argue instead for forms of dress which highlight the constructed nature of the body and of self-identity. In these theories, dress becomes a parodic play in which the body of the wearer is denaturalised.

However, as I shall argue in this essay, this conception of dress is also problematic insofar as it leaves unchallenged the reduction of self-identity to image which the advertising and fashion industries now endorse and promote. While postmodern theorists of fashion have revealed the untenability of the notion of the 'natural' body as a criterion by which to assess the rationality of particular modes of dress, their alternative definition of liberatory dress is equally limiting insofar as it fails to question the privileging of the cult of appearance over all other sources of identity formation which has become a hallmark of postmodern culture. Nowhere is this clearer than in the later writings of Baudrillard where fashion is uncritically embraced precisely insofar as it epitomises the society of the spectacle and the cult of the artificial. While other postmodern theorists of fashion such as Wilson, Young and Silverman maintain a more critical perspective on fashion than does the later Baudrillard, nevertheless, they share in common an acceptance of the notion of the self as image.[3]

It is from this perspective that I shall examine the postmodern challenge to the functionalism of earlier critiques of fashion. In order to set the context for my analysis of postmodern theories of fashion, it is necessary first to outline the paradigm against which they have reacted.

Functionalist critiques of fashion

During the nineteenth century, when the first feminist critiques of fashion were developed, female dress was criticised for reinforcing the subservience of women to men because of its impractical and excessively ornate nature (Tickner 1984). Amelia Bloomer, an American feminist in the 1850s, for instance, criticised the female dress of the day insofar as it hindered the physical mobility of women, reinforcing the confinement of women (at least those of the middle class) to a sedentary form of existence in the domestic sphere. Female dress, particularly the corset, was also criticised for being detrimental to the physical health of women. Bloomer proposed a new form of dress for women which she saw as being more functional, comfortable and hygienic – namely pantaloons – to replace the many layers of heavy under-petticoats which were the fashion of the day.

Theorists in the late nineteenth and early twentieth centuries such as Veblen and Loos, also criticised women's fashion from a similar perspective. In his book, *The Theory of the Leisure Class* (1970), Veblen criticised the highly decorative and impractical dress of women of his day whose primary function was to symbolise the wealth and status of their husbands. Whereas prior to the nineteenth century, the dress of both men and women of the upper classes had been extremely ornate, symbolising the fact that they did not have to work for a living, in the nineteenth century, ornate dress became the sole preserve of middle-class women, their male counterparts adopting much more aus-tere forms of dress. The reason for this lay in the fact that, whereas previously women had participated actively in the economic life of the household, once the place of work became physically separated from the place of domicile, they were no longer required to engage in any form of labour, including domestic labour, which was generally carried out by servants. The fact that middle-class women did not have to work for a living was seen as indicative of the wealth and status of their husbands and was made visible by the extravagant clothes which they wore. As Veblen (1970: 126) wrote:

> It has in the course of economic development become the office of the woman to consume vicariously for the head of the household; and her apparel is contrived with this object in view. It has come about that obvi-ously productive labour is in a peculiar degree derogatory to respectable women, and therefore special pains should be taken in the construction of women's dress, to impress upon the beholder the fact . . . that the wearer does not and cannot habitually engage in useful work. Propriety requires respectable women to abstain more consistently from useful effort and to make more of a show of leisure than men of the same social classes . . . [A woman's] sphere is within the household, which she should 'beautify' and of which she should be the 'chief ornament' . . . By virtue of its descent from a patriarchal past, our social system makes it the woman's function in an especial degree to put in evidence her husband's ability to pay . . .

Furthermore, the fact that women consented to wearing these clothes was symp-tomatic of their subservience to their husbands or fathers since they were far more uncomfortable and incapacitating than the dress for men. As Veblen (1970: 127) wrote:

> Wherever wasteful expenditure and the show of abstention from effort is . . . carried to the extent of showing obvious discomfort or voluntarily induced physical disability, there the immediate inference is that the indi-vidual in question does not perform this wasteful expenditure and undergo this disability for her own personal gain in pecuniary repute, but in behalf of someone else to whom she stands in a relation of economic depend-ence; a relation which in the last analysis must . . . reduce itself to a rela-tion of servitude . . . The high heel, the skirt, the impracticable bonnet, the corset, and the general disregard of the wearer's comfort which is an obvi-ous feature of all civilized women's apparel, are so many items of evidence to the effect that in the modern civilized scheme of life the woman is still, in theory, the economic dependent of the man – that, perhaps in a highly idealized sense, she still is the man's chattel.

The Austrian architect, Adolf Loos was another who criticised women's fashion for its ostentation and lack of practicality. His critique of women's fashion was influenced by the idea that 'form should follow function' which became the guiding principle of the modernist movement in design. According to this doctrine, a well-designed object was

one whose aesthetic form was determined by its practical function. Utilitarian considerations were primary while those aspects which did not contribute to the more efficient functioning of the object were deemed unaesthetic, i.e. beauty became equated
with or reduced to utility, the two being indistinguishable. In his view, the elaborate
nature of women's dress was an unnecessary and wasteful indulgence, requiring a huge
expenditure of labour to produce and affordable only by the wealthy. Furthermore, it
was objectionable insofar as it was indicative of an unrestrained sensuality. In his essay
'Ornament and Crime' (1966), he argued that the progressive taming of those base
instincts which threatened the stability of civilisation manifested itself in the removal of
ornament, i.e. in the removal of all that which was superfluous to the rational functioning of society. Male dress, in its emphasis on practicality and its avoidance of ostentatious ornamentation, was much more rational and democratic than that of females.[4] To
quote Loos (1982: 102):

> The clothing of the woman is distinguished externally from that of the
> man by the preference for the ornamental and colourful effects and by the
> long skirt that covers the legs completely. These two factors demonstrate
> to us that woman has fallen behind sharply in her development in recent
> centuries. No period of culture has known as great differences as our own
> between the clothing of the free man and the free woman. In earlier eras,
> men also wore clothing that was colourful and richly adorned and whose
> hem reached the floor. Happily, the grandiose development in which our
> culture has taken part this century has overcome ornament. The lower the
> culture, the more apparent the ornament.

The reason for the lack of progress towards a more rational form of dress for women lay
in the fact that they remained economically subservient to men and so still depended
on their appearance to attract and they keep a husband. Whereas men gained a sense of
their own identity through their activities in the public arena, women were defined primarily by their appearance. As Loos (1982: 103) wrote in his article 'Ladies' Fashion':

> That which is noble in a woman knows only one desire: that she hold on to
> her place by the side of the big, strong man. At present this desire can only
> be fulfilled if the woman wins the love of the man . . . Thus the woman
> is forced to appeal to the man's sensuality through her clothing, to appeal
> unconsciously to his sickly sensuality for which only the culture of the times
> can be blamed. The vicissitudes of women's fashion are dictated only by
> changes in sensuality.

Many of the elements of these early critiques of female fashion continued to inform
the writings of theorists later in the twentieth century such as de Beauvoir who, in *The
Second Sex* (1975: 543) argued that:

> The purpose of the fashion to which [woman] is enslaved is not to reveal her
> as an independent individual, but rather to offer her as prey to male desires;
> thus society is not seeking to further her projects but to thwart them. The
> skirt is less convenient than trousers, high heeled shoes impede walking; the

least practical of gowns and dress shoes, the most fragile of hats and stockings are the most elegant; the costume may disguise the body, deform it or
follow its curves; in any case it puts it on display. Costumes and styles are
often devoted to cutting off the feminine body from any activity . . . Para-
lysed by inconvenient clothing and by the rules of propriety – then woman's
body seems to man to be his property, his thing. Make-up and jewellery also
further this petrification of face and body. The function of ornamental attire
is to metamorphise woman into idol.

She also pointed out that elegance was bondage for women in that being well dressed
required a great deal of money, time and care, deflecting their energies away from
more worthy pursuits. Unable to exercise their creativity in other ways, they resorted
to converting themselves into works of art. Admired for how they looked rather than
for what they were, women became mere objects for the male gaze.

In the 1970s and 1980s, feminists such as Oakley (1981: 82–5), Brownmiller
(1984), Baker (1984) and Coward (1984: 29–36) reiterated the oppressive nature of
feminine ideals of beauty which generated in women a permanent sense of dissatisfac-
tion with their appearance, undermining their self-esteem. Concurring with the view
of earlier critics, they argued that female dress, in contrast to male dress, was much
more subject to the vagaries of fashion, each change signalling the eroticisation of yet
another part of the female body. Not only did these frequent changes in fashion construct the female body as a site of constantly shifting erogenous zones, but they also
encouraged the female consumer to spend more and more on clothes in an effort to
keep up to date. In this respect, women became yoked to the imperatives of the capitalist economy which used the mechanism of built-in obsolescence as a way of increasing
expenditure on consumer goods.

Feminists such as Orbach (1978), Chernin (1983), Baker (1984) and Coward
(1984: 21–5, 39–46, 74–82), also drew attention to the new pressures brought to bear
on women by the advent of body-shaping techniques such as plastic surgery, diet and
exercise. While female dress became less restrictive, this did not indicate that it had
become more liberated since there were now more effective ways of moulding the body
in accordance with the ideals of feminine beauty. These new techniques for fashioning
the female body operated in an insidious way. For, though women were now encouraged to participate in exercise and to eat wisely, ostensibly to improve their health and
fitness, the real *raison d'être* for these activities was to attain the body shape deemed
desirable by a patriarchal society – a body shape which was becoming increasingly thin-
ner. This new ideal, as Coward pointed out (1984: 39–46), was really that of the pre-
pubescent female. What made such a figure attractive was that it symbolised a sexuality
which was not yet aware of itself. The adolescent girl was someone who possessed
erotic allure without however being in command of her sexual desires.

Decrying the oppressive nature of feminine norms of beauty then, feminists such
as Brownmiller, Chernin and Orbach argued for a return to the 'natural' body, i.e.
for an acceptance of the way one was rather than seeking to mould one's body artificially, in accordance with unrealistic aspirations.[5] More functional modes of dress
which enhanced ease of movement and comfort and deliberately eschewed those forms
of adornment designed to promote the erotic appeal of the wearer such as high heeled
shoes and cosmetics were also advocated by members of the Women's Movement. In

their place, feminists often adopted forms of dress considered 'mannish' such as dungarees and boots.[6] The idea of 'burning one's bra' became emblematic of the feminist attempt to dispense with the restricting yoke of female dress which deformed the body into 'unnatural' shapes in order to conform to the prevailing ideals of female beauty.

The postmodernist challenge to functionalist critiques of fashion

In recent times however, a number of theorists such as Wilson (1987, 1990a, 1990b), Sawchuck (1987), Silverman (1986), Hollander (1993) and Gaines (1990) have challenged some of the basic assumptions underlying this functionist critique of fashion. First, they have questioned the assumption that there is such a thing as a 'natural' body which pre-exists culture, arguing that the body is always-already encoded by culture. Indeed, the very concept of a 'natural' body is specific to Western society. As Mascia-Lees and Sharpe (1992: 3) write for example:

> [Often it is assumed] that the unadorned, unmodified body is an unspoiled, pure surface on which culture works . . . This dehistoricizes and decontexualizes the body. It ignores the particular meaning that both the body and the specific modifications to which it is subjected have for the people being represented. It resolves all bodies into the Western notion of the body as prior to culture and thus, as natural. Contemporary theorizing . . . has contributed recently to exposing 'the natural' as a Western cultural construct, calling into question the often taken for granted dichotomy between nature and culture . . . Understanding the body not as simple materiality but rather as constituted within language is . . . intended to question traditional notions of the body as prior to or outside of culture.

Hollander's argument in her book *Seeing through Clothes* is salutary in this regard. She points to the impossibility of regarding the body as unmediated by culture as indicated by the fact that the way the nude has been portrayed in art has been shaped by the prevailing notions of fashionable dress. Rather than depicting the naked body 'as it really is', artists have been unconsciously influenced by the ideals of beauty which were manifest in the dress of the time. As Hollander (1993: xii–xiii) writes:

> It is tempting to . . . subscribe to the notion of a universal, unadorned mankind that is universally naturally behaved when naked. But art proves that nakedness is not universally experienced and perceived any more than clothes are. At any time, the unadorned self has more kinship with its own usual *dressed* aspect than it has with any undressed human selves in other times and places, who have learned a different visual sense of the clothed body. It can be shown that the rendering of the nude in art usually derives from the current form in which the clothed figure is conceived. This correlation in turn demonstrates that both the perception and the self-perception of nudity are dependent on a sense of clothing – and of clothing understood through the medium of a visual convention.

Once the social constitution of the body is acknowledged, then it is no longer tenable to uphold the naked body as being more 'genuine' or 'authentic' than the adorned body and to see fashion as the repression of the 'natural' body as earlier feminists tended to do since both the naked and the clothed body are equally products of culture. Both are 'artificial' in that they have been constituted by social conventions. A corollary of this is that the notion that certain modes of dress are more 'natural' than others and therefore to be preferred can no longer be sustained. This is made quite clear by Wilson (1987: 213) who argues that:

> . . . the search for the 'natural' in dress must . . . be a wild goose chase, for such a project tries to deny, or at least does not recognize that dress is no mere accommodation to the body as a biological entity, nor to geography or climate; nor does it merely link the two. It is a complex cultural form, as is the human conception of the body itself.

The same sort of criticism also applies to the notion of 'functional' dress upheld by the early critics of fashion, particularly Veblen and Loos. In arguing for a more 'rational' form of dress in which all that was superfluous to its practical function was removed, both Loos and Veblen assumed, at least implicitly, that there were certain biologically determined needs that pre-existed culture – such as the need for warmth and protection – and that the most rational form of dress was that which served these needs.

The problem with the concept of needs as biologically given was that this placed them beyond the reach of critical discussion. No longer was it possible to debate what constituted a basic need. The task simply became one of finding the most efficient means to achieve a pre-given end. What the modernist critics of fashion failed to re-alise is that 'function' itself is culturally defined and that what is considered a basic need in one culture may not be so in another. Thus, for example, while some cultures deem clothes to be an absolute necessity, other peoples living in the same climatic conditions have no need of clothes. The natives of Tierra del Fuego, for instance, did not wear clothes even though the climate was damp and chilly (Wilson, 1987: 55). One cannot assume, then, that there is some universal, objectively given set of physiological needs in terms of which the rationality of particular forms of clothing can be assessed. It is too simplistic to assume, as Veblen and Loos did, that there are certain universal criteria of comfort and practicability in dress, for what may be considered 'functional' dress in one epoch or culture may not be so in another.

Another aspect of functionalist critiques of fashion which has come under attack has been their puritanical asceticism in which anything which was deemed superflu-ous to the practicality of dress was discarded. It was on this basis, as we have seen, that Veblen and Loos railed against ornamentation in women's dress, preferring the more austere, restrained nature of male dress. However, as a number of critics have pointed out, in privileging the utilitarian over the merely aesthetic, what Veblen and Loos failed to realise was that they were in a certain sense being complicitous with the technocratic rationality of the capitalism of their day which valued only that which had a practical utility. As Adorno (1984: 83) argued in his critique of Veblen:

> . . . he confronts society with its own principle of utility and proves to it that according to this principle, culture [and one could add, the aesthetic

realm] is both a waste and a swindle . . . Veblen has something of the bourgeois who takes the admonition to be thrifty with grim seriousness. Thus
all of culture becomes for him the meaningless ostentatious display typical
of the bankrupt.[7]

In their one-sided emphasis on practical utility, Veblen and Loos failed to acknowledge
that as well as pragmatic needs, humans also have non-material needs such as the need
for meaning, for understanding one's identity and relation to others, for beauty, etc.
Such needs derive from the fact that unlike other animals, humans are self-conscious
beings who have the capacity to posit goals and ideals not determined by natural
instincts and impulses. To quote Adorno (1984: 86) once again:

> Luxury has a dual character. Veblen concentrates his spotlight on one side
> of it: that part of the social product which does not benefit human needs
> and contribute to human happiness but instead is squandered in order to
> preserve an obsolete system. The other side of luxury is the use of parts of
> the social product which serve not the reproduction of expended labour,
> directly or indirectly, but of man in so far as he is not entirely under the
> sway of the utility principle.

It is these ideas which have informed a number of recent theorists of fashion. As Wilson
(1987: ch. 11) has argued, previous feminist critiques of fashion have denied the legitimacy of the aesthetic pleasures derived from dress. In her view, to understand all
'uncomfortable' dress as merely one aspect of the oppression of women is fatally to over-
simplify, since dress is not and never has been primarily functional and is certainly not
natural. As anthropologists are only too well aware, the reasons why people wear clothing and other forms of bodily adornment often have little to do with the functions of
warmth and protection. The importance of the non-functional needs served by clothing
is indicated by the fact that even those feminists who sought to adopt a practical mode
of dress never entirely eliminated purely decorative elements. For example, while they
wore masculine boots, they were sometimes painted in rainbow colours; they also often
adorned themselves with rings and long, bright earrings made of feathers, beads or metal
and coloured their hair. Fashion, banished from clothing, reappeared surreptitiously in
forms of adornment that were less obviously feminine or sexualised. Wilson also questions just how functional the feminist 'uniform' of dungarees was, arguing that it was
more for symbolic reasons – i.e. the fact that they were traditionally regarded as male
attire rather than for their practicality – that they were worn. In her view, the pointless-
ness of fashion, which is what Veblen abhorred, is precisely what makes it valuable. As
she writes (1987: 245), 'it is in this marginalized area of the contingent, the decorative,
the futile, that not simply a new aesthetic but a new cultural order may seed itself'.

Wilson also argues that the early feminist rejection of the purely decorative in dress
betrays an unwitting alliance with puritanical, Christian denunciations of fashion. As
she points out (1987: 209), many of the movements for dress reform in the nineteenth
and early twentieth centuries were inspired by Victorian and Christian ideas of propriety. These movements abhorred women's fashion insofar as it was seen to be too
overtly erotic. In their view, the ornateness of women's fashion threatened to drag
them into the stagnant waters of immorality. The similarity between the Christian

critique of fashion and that of Loos is particularly striking in this regard. As we have seen, Loos quite explicitly decried ornament as symptomatic of an unbridled eroticism which threatened the rational order of civilisation. Equating moral purity with simplicity, Christian dress reformers advocated a plainer form of dress which was regarded as being more 'natural' and hence 'truer' than the elaborate artifice of the women's fashion of the day. In the process, they failed to realise that the 'natural' was just as artificial as the form of dress they were criticising.

Likewise, Sawchuck has argued that critiques of fashion have often been tied to a Christian discourse which is intent on repressing women's potentially subversive sexuality and returning them to the confines of the domestic sphere. As she writes (1987: 68):

> . . . the dress reform movements of the early twentieth century were often less concerned with making women more comfortable than with returning them to the proper sphere of the home; they were part of the movement for social purity. Just as improper dress indicated a woman's lack of reason and her immorality, a proper form of dress was said to enhance her 'natural' beauty, emphasising her health and freshness and promising her fecundity.

She concludes that the argument for austerity in dress and the return to more neutral forms valourises what is seen as characteristic of men – namely, their rationality – and reinforces the stereotypical conception of women as superficial, duplicitous and in possession of a sexuality which, if not kept under control, poses a threat to men.

This view is shared by Schor who, in her book *Reading in Detail* (1987), contends that the denigration of the decorative by critics of fashion betrays a contempt for the feminine since, traditionally, the decorative has been associated with women. Repeatedly, as she points out, the ornamental has been associated with feminine duplicity and decadence. Ornament has often been dismissed as being trivial, superficial, lacking in substance, irrational – all features which have been attributed to the feminine. This is evident in neo-classical aesthetics for example which, as she argues (1987: 45), has been:

> . . . imbued with the residues of . . . a sexist imaginary where the ornamental is inevitably bound up with the feminine . . . This imaginary femininity weighs heavily on the fate of the detail as well as of the ornament in aesthetics, burdening them with the negative connotations of the feminine: the decorative, the natural, the impure and the monstrous.

In her view then, the feminist critique of the decorative in dress continues to partake in the denigration of that which has traditionally been associated with the feminine.

Hanson adumbrates further on this theme in her article 'Dressing Down Dressing Up: The Philosophic Fear of Fashion' (1993). She argues that underlying the hostility to fashion is a fear of, or discomfort with, the body. Western thought, and philosophy in particular, have privileged the mind over the body and have therefore been dismissive of anything associated with the body. While the realm of the mind represents all that is rational, the realm of the body is equated with the irrational and thereby devalued. Underlying this hatred of the body is a wish to evade the acceptance of our mortality. As disembodied minds, we can avoid having to recognise the necessarily contingent nature of our existence. Since fashion is intimately connected with the body, philosophers have thus been largely hostile to it. As she points out, philosophers can only appreciate the aesthetic when it is dissociated from the body. As a realm of disinterested pleasure, the aesthetic is granted a superior status to the merely physical pleasures of the senses. Fashion however, calls attention to the physicality of the body and to its ephemeral nature. While it may seek to disguise the changing, always ageing human body, in its very transitoriness, it actually ends up by underscoring the fact of mortality. Fashions are born and die; they may sometimes be revived but the revivals are never quite the same as the originals. Thus, whereas philosophers can appreciate the beauty of a work of art, attention to dress is scorned since it is inseparable from attention to the body. She argues that insofar as feminists share with philosophers their hostility towards fashion, they are unwittingly perpetuating this denigration of the body. And this is particularly problematic for feminists since the body has traditionally been associated with the feminine while the mind has been equated with the masculine. So, in being dismissive of the body and all that is associated with it, feminists are acquiescing in a patriarchal ideology which devalues all that which falls outside the sphere of the mind. As she (1993: 235) writes:

> Philosophy's drive to get past what it takes to be the inessential has usually been linked with a denial or devaluation of what it has typically associated with the woman. Thus, even when traditional philosophy turns to aesthetics and, for once, interest can focus unashamedly on appearances, an opportunity is still sought to disparage the body. A tradition that displays this sort of embarrassment about carnality . . . may not be the most agreeable companion on the quest to reassert and revaluate women's lives and feminine experience.

Critical appraisal of postmodern theories of fashion

Having rejected the notion of 'natural' or 'functional' dress as a yardstick by which to assess the rationality of particular modes of dress, recent theorists of fashion such as Silverman, Wilson and Young have proposed that the most liberatory form of dress is that which highlights the fact that the body is a cultural construction. Silverman, for instance (1986: 148), argues, contrary to earlier feminist critiques of fashion, that the constant transmutations of female dress, far from being oppressive of women, are potentially more disruptive both of gender and of the symbolic order than is the relatively static nature of male dress which defines identity as fixed and stable rather than as fluid and mutable. In particular, she champions 'op shop' dressing, which involves the self-reflexive adoption of previous styles. What is salutary about this mode of dress for her is not simply that it acknowledges the 'fake' nature of all styles, but that it highlights the fact that there is no true self behind the various guises that one adopts. One's identity is equated with the guises which one adopts. It is not the case that the self exists independently of the clothes that one wears. Rather, one is defined through one's mode of dress. As Silverman writes (1986: 149), 'clothing not only draws the body so that it can be seen, but also maps out the shape of the ego'.

Likewise, Wilson argues for a mode of dress as masquerade – not in the sense of putting an ironic distance between the costume/uniform/camouflage and the wearer who sports it as a mask or disguise but, rather, as the form in which the body actually manifests itself. As she writes (1990a: 233):

So far as women are concerned – and fashion is still primarily associated with women – contemporary fashions arguably have liberatory potential . . . For in 'denaturalising the wearer's specular identity' contemporary fashion refuses the dichotomy, nature/culture. Fashion in our epoch denaturalises the body and thus divests itself of all essentialism. This must be good news for women, since essentialist ideologies have been oppressive to them. Fashion often plays with, and playfully transgresses, gender boundaries, inverting stereotypes and making us aware of the masquerade of femininity.

In a similar vein, she writes (1990a: 216) that 'with punk, women transgress norms of feminine beauty; when a young woman shaves her head and draws red lines round her eyes, the very notion of make up and hairstyles as an enhancement of what 'nature' has provided is gone and the body is treated more radically than ever before as an aspect of performance'.

Young also praises fashion insofar as it offers women the invitation to play with identities. As she writes (1994: 208–9):

One of the privileges of femininity in rationalized instrumental culture is an aesthetic freedom, the freedeom to play with shape and colour on the body, to don various styles and looks, and through them exhibit and imagine unreal possibilities . . . Such female imagination has liberating possibilities because it subverts, unsettles the order of respectable, functional rationality in a world where that rationality supports domination.

The problem, however, is that a mode of dress which declares the constructed nature of identity is not sufficient to define it as liberatory. Indeed, in the present age when self-identity has increasingly been defined in terms of one's physical appearance by the advertising industry, one could argue that modes of dress which promote the view of the self as a series of changing guises are conservative insofar as they leave unchallenged the reduction of self-identity to an image which is constructed by the commodities one buys. As Kellner points out in his analysis of Madonna, for instance, while her radical transmutations of appearance highlight the social constructedness of identity, fashion and sexuality, at the same time (1994: 178):

. . . by constructing identity largely in terms of fashion and image, [she] plays into precisely the imperatives of the fashion and consumer industries that offer a 'new you' and a solution to all of your problems by the purchase of products and services. By emphasizing image, she plays into the dynamics of the contemporary image culture that reduces art, politics, and the theatrics of everyday life to the play of image, downplaying the role of communication, commitment, solidarity and concern for others in the constitution of one's identity and personality.

While Young promotes women's play with various guises as subversive of the instrumental rationality of capitalism, this form of rationality is no longer dominant. Now, it is precisely the hedonistic experimentation with different styles of appearance which is the main legitimising ideology of our age as the consumption of commodities has come to assume an ever greater importance in the capitalist economy.[8] Whereas in the past, individuals were seen to have an identity apart from the goods they possessed, in the present era, one's identity is defined in terms of the image that one creates through one's consumption of goods, including the clothes one wears. As Featherstone points out (1991: 187–93), in our modern consumer culture, a new conception of the self has emerged – namely, the self as performer – which places great emphasis upon appearance, display and the management of impressions. This replaces the nineteenth-century concern with character in which primacy was given to such qualities as citizenship, democracy, duty, work, honour, reputation and morals. Likewise, Finkelstein writes in *The Fashioned Self* (1991: 5): '[in the modern era] we have fused together the capacity for conspicuous consumption with the presentation of personality'. She goes on to argue (1991: 190) that:

> . . . the emphasis given to the presentation of the self in our daily social life,
> and the proliferation of goods, services and techniques aimed at allowing us
> to produce a distinctive identity have the effect of deflecting attention away
> from a more valuable source of identity, namely, the historical precedents
> and the immediate politics of our circumstances.

While experimentation with various modes of dress can contribute to the subversion of traditional notions of gender identity, for instance, there is the very real danger in our present era, where appearance has become the central means of defining one's identity, of losing sight of the fact that rebellion through fashion is not in itself sufficient to bring about social change. As Wilson herself acknowledges (1990b: 35–6):

> . . . however we might want to get away from the Puritanism of the left in
> order to celebrate fashion as a legitimate and highly aesthetic pleasure, there
> are still problems about defending it . . . This call to hedonism can repre
> sent a flight from more threatening problems; and the recognition of pleas
> ure and beauty as important forces in our lives – which emphatically they
> are . . . can easily degenerate into . . . an abdication of discrimination that is
> merely decadent.

In the postmodern era, rebellion has primarily taken the form of adopting a certain style – i.e. of projecting a certain image – through the clothes one wears, rather than engaging with the economic and political structures which produce social inequality as evidenced by the various youth subcultures which first made their appearance in the postwar period. As Clarke et al. write (1977: 47–8):

> [Subcultures] 'solve', but in an imaginary way, problems which at the con
> crete material level remain unresolved. Thus the 'Teddy Boy' expropria
> tion of an upper class style of dress 'covers' the gap between largely manual,
> unskilled, near-lumpen real careers and life-chances, and the 'all-dressed-
> up-and-nowhere-to-go' experience of Saturday evening.

One must be careful, then, not to become so preoccupied with the ironic play with various guises that one loses sight of the fact that there is more to forging one's identity than changing appearances. While clothes are potent symbols, it is not sufficient to simply adopt a different appearance as a way of redefining oneself. To quote Finkelstein once again (1991: 190):

> . . . when a heightened or developed consciousness is sought through the cultivation of the body, then an era dawns in which only a partial under-standing of collective social life can exist. In such a society, the continu-ity between the body politic and the private body has not been understood thoroughly enough to engender a sense of interest in those communal actions which are necessary for the progressive liberalization of a society.

The task today, then, is not so much that of 'de-naturalising' the body, since the fash-ion industry already does this, but, rather, of challenging the reduction of self-identity to the image one constructs through the clothes one wears. Arguing in a similar vein, Foster contends (1985: 10) that it is now more important to struggle against the notion of woman as 'artifice' than that of 'woman as nature'. Instead of upholding the notion of artifice in dress as subversive and seeking to extend it to encompass not only female but male dress as Wilson proposes (1990a: 233), it is the very notion of self as image which needs to be interrogated. It is one thing to recognise that, in the postmodern era, self-identity has become equated with one's style of presentation and another to accept this uncritically.

The inadequacy of the notion of 'artifice' as a criterion for defining dress which is subversive is particularly clear in the later writings of Baudrillard where he abandons his earlier critical stance on fashion to embrace it wholeheartedly. Baudrillard (1981) characterises present-day society as a post-industrial one in which the world of produc-tion has given way to the world of consumption and of the spectacle. Whereas the early phases of capitalism were governed by an instrumental rationality in which technical efficiency was the primary consideration, now the main concern is with the styling of the appearance of commodities to seduce the consumer. Commodities are now con-sumed not because they ostensibly satisfy some practical need but because they serve as ways of differentiating individuals within the social hierarchy. In the context of capi-talist society where one's social position is no longer fixed at birth, commodities do not so much reflect but rather create status distinctions. For Baudrillard, these 'objects of consumption' function as signs whose meaning is not derived with reference to any-thing external to them but rather from their relation to other signs. Whereas in the past, objects were defined either in terms of their use value, their exchange value or their symbolic value (i.e. as symbolic of the relation between people as in gift exchange) now their meaning resides solely in their relation to other signs. As Baudrillard writes (1981: 67):

> . . . an object is not an object of consumption unless it is released from its psychic determinations as *symbol*; from its functional determinations as *instrument*; from its commercial determinations as *product*; and is thus *liber-ated as a sign* to be recaptured by the formal logic of fashion.

The phenomenon of fashion for Baudrillard epitomises the present age, which is char-acterised by the growing independence and importance of the sign, for it is a system of freely circulating signs which commute and permutate without limits, colonising ever more areas of social life from clothing to politics, economics, morality, sexuality, etc. Signs, including the clothes we wear, no longer represent something which exists independently of them, but rather are taken as the only reality. We live in a world constituted solely of images which are no longer seen to refer to anything beyond themselves but are themselves constitutive of what is taken to be real. The modern individual is fashioned and is more interested in the authority of the sign than in the elements it represents. Once clothing becomes dominated by the logic of fashion, its meaning transmutes in a completely random manner according to Baudrillard. Thus, for instance (Baudrillard, 1981: 79):

> . . . neither the long skirt nor the mini-skirt has an absolute value in itself – only their differential relation acts as a criterion of meaning. The mini-skirt . . . has no [fashion] value except in opposition to the long skirt. This value is, of course, reversible: the voyage from the mini – to the maxi – skirt will have the same distinctive and selective fashion value as the reverse . . .

In his early writings, Baudrillard criticised the constant permutations in fashion as giving the appearance of the new while in fact everything remained the same. As he argued in *For a Critique of the Political Economy of the Sign* (1981: 51, fn 30):

> Fashion embodies a compromise between the need to innovate and the other need to change nothing in the fundamental order. It is this that characterizes 'modern' societies. Thus it results in a game of change.

In his view, the accelerated renewal of objects often serves as a substitute for real cultural and social progress. To quote him once again (1981: 50):

> . . . fashion . . . masks a profound social inertia. It itself is a *factor* of social inertia, insofar as the demand for real social mobility frolics and loses itself in fashion, in the sudden and often cyclical changes of objects, clothes and ideas.

Furthermore, fashion masks social inequalities by claiming to be accessible to everyone. 'It is one of those institutions that best restores cultural inequality and social discrimination, establishing it under the pretense of abolishing it' (1981: 51). Likewise, in his other early writings on fashion in *Symbolic Exchange and Death* (1993: 87–95), Baudrillard argues that fashion simulates the new, the latest, the most up to date, as it recycles past forms and models. Thus, 'fashion is paradoxically out of date, the non-contemporary'. Simulating 'joy in appearances' and 'the innocence of becoming', fashion represents the triumph of the artificial, 'the seizure of the living by the dead'. Fashion is thus 'the frivolity of the *déjà-vu*' in its incessant replacement of one series of recycled forms by another.

However, in his later writings, particularly his work *Seduction* (1990b), he upholds the society of the spectacle as superior to the earlier phases of capitalism which were dominated by the logic of production. In his view, the society of the spectacle represents a liberation from the tyranny of technocratic reason which subjected the free play of the senses to the iron rule of practical necessity. Consequently, he now celebrates the phenomenon of fashion which, for him, epitomises the society of the spectacle where the cult of appearances is all important.[9] Fashion revels in the creation of images, making no pretence about their fabricated nature. In his work *Seduction*, fashion and cosmetics become part of 'that radical metaphysics of appearance' which is part of the game of seduction. He valorises appearances per se against depth models and presents positively Baudelaire's celebration of fashion and make-up. Fashion becomes part of a celebration of artifice, appearance and sign games. While philosophers have traditionally condemned seduction insofar as it operates within the realm of artifice and appearance, for Baudrillard it is precisely this fact which constitutes its strength. His valorisation of seduction lies in the fact that it openly acknowledges that there is nothing beyond the realm of appearances and thus, rather than searching in vain for some 'truth' which transcends the world of artifice, it concerns itself with mastering the symbolic universe. He argues further that, generally, women have been more adept than men at the game of appearances and that rather than criticising as artificial women who wear make-up etc. as feminists have done, they should recognise that women's real strength lies in their mastery of the realm of the symbolic. As Baudrillard (1990a: 133) writes:

> For woman is but appearance. And it is the feminine as appearance that defeats the masculine as depth. Instead of protesting against this 'offensive' formula, women would do well to let themselves be seduced by the fact that here lies the secret of their strength, which they are beginning to lose by setting up feminine depth against masculine depth.

What Baudrillard fails to realise however, is that in celebrating the notion of woman as artifice, he loses sight of the fact that such a view acquiesces to the advertising industry which promotes the judgement of people, particularly women, by their appearances rather than by their deeds. In doing so, he overlooks the way in which the emphasis on appearance has been oppressive for women insofar as it has come to substitute for other forms of self-realisation. Since women's self-esteem and success have been seen to depend more on their looks than on their achievements, many women have tended to become obsessed with the fashioning of their appearance to the detriment of the development of other aspects of their self-identity.[10]

In conclusion, then, Baudrillard's uncritical embracing of the notion of self as appearance in his later writings highlights the limitations of postmodern theories of fashion which seek to define liberatory dress in terms of that which de-naturalises the body. While postmodern theorists such as Wilson, Young and Silverman do not completely forsake a critical perspective on fashion in the way that the later Baudrillard does,[11] nevertheless, their upholding of the notion of the self as defined by the various guises which it assumes, can be seen to be complicit with our contemporary culture of the spectacle which privileges the cult of appearance over all other sources of identity formation. In their desire to rehabilitate the legitimacy of the aesthetic pleasures of dress and to expose the one-sidedness of the utilitarian rationality of modernism, postmodern theorists of fashion have tended to lose sight of the equally limiting reduction of self-identity to appearance – a reduction which has been particularly damaging to women.

Acknowledgements

Thanks to the referees who made many useful comments and suggestions on an earlier version of this essay.

Notes

1   Bell also developed his critique of dress at this time. Like Veblen, he was critical of the way in which the sumptuous nature of women's dress had been used to symbolise the wealth and status of their husbands though, in contrast with Veblen, he did not wish to set up functional dress as a universal ideal (1978: 184).

2   Radice (1984) provides a useful outline of the critique of the modernist doctrine of 'form follows function' by postmodern designers.

3   Wilson criticises the early Baudrillard for his negative view of fashion (1990a: 220–1), but in his later work he actually takes an even more positive view of fashion than Wilson, as I shall argue later in this essay.

4   As Finkelstein (1991: ch. 4) points out, such an assumption is highly questionable. While male dress may have been less ornate than female dress, it was still very much subject to the vagaries of fashion as witnessed, for example, in the many changes undergone by the necktie.

5   Shilling (1994: 63–7) provides a useful discussion of Orbach and Chernin in this regard.

6   See Oakley (1981: 83) for a description of feminist garb in the 1970s.

7   See Adorno (1979: 31–41) for a further elaboration of his critique of functionalism as expounded by theorists such as Loos. Wellmer (1983) also provides a critique of the vulgar functionalism of modernism drawing on the arguments of Adorno.

8   See Giroux (1993–4) for a development of this argument. See also Bordo (1993), who points out the similarity between postmodern notions of the body and self-identity and those promoted by the fashion and advertising industries.

9   Kellner (1989: section 4.1) presents a useful discussion of Baudrillard's views on fashion. See also Barnard (1996: 150–5) and Tseelon (1995: 128–35).

10   See Freedman (1988) for a further elaboration of this point.

11   See Young (1994: 201–3, 209) and Silverman (1986: 148), for instance, where they indicate their reservations about fashion.

Bibliography

Adorno, T. W. (1979) 'Functionalism Today', *Oppositions*, 17, pp. 31–41.

Adorno, T. W. (1984) 'Veblen's Attack on Culture', in Thomas McCarthy (ed.) *Prisms*. Cambridge, MA: MIT Press, pp. 73–94.

Baker, N. C. (1984) *The Beauty Trap*, New York/Toronto: Franklin Watts.

Barnard, M. (1996) *Fashion as Communication*, London and New York: Routledge.

Baudrillard, J. (1981) *For a Critique of the Political Economy of the Sign*, St Louis: Telos Press (orig. 1972).

Baudrillard, J. (1990a) 'The Ecliptic of Sex', in P. Foss and J. Pefanis (eds) *Revenge of the Crystal*, Sydney: Pluto Press, pp. 129–62.

Baudrillard, J. (1990b) *Seduction*, London: Macmillan Education Ltd (orig. 1979).

Baudrillard, J. (1993) *Symbolic Exchange and Death*, London: Sage Publications (orig. 1976).

Bell, Q. (1978) *Of Human Finery*, London: Hogarth Press (orig. 1947).

Bordo, S. (1993) '"Material Girl": The Effacements of Postmodern Culture', in *Unbearable Weight: Feminism, Western Culture and the Body*, Berkeley and Los Angeles: University of California Press, pp. 245–76.

Brownmiller, S. (1984) *Femininity*, New York: Linden Press, Simon and Schuster.

Cherin, K. (1983) *Womansize: The Tyranny of Slenderness*, London: The Women's Press.

Clarke, J., S. Hall, T. Jefferson and B. Roberts (1977) 'Subcultures, Cultures and Class', in S. Hall and T. Jefferson (eds) *Resistance through Rituals: Youth Subcultures in Post-War Britain*, London: Hutchinson.

Coward, R. (1984) *Female Desire: Women's Sexuality Today*, London: Paladin.

de Beauvoir, S. (1975) *The Second Sex*, Harmondsworth: Penguin (orig. 1949).

Featherstone, M. (1991) 'The Body in Consumer Culture', in M. Featherstone, M. Hepworth and B. S. Turner (eds) *The Body: Social Process and Cultural Theory*, London: Sage Publications (orig. 1982), pp. 170–96.

Finkelstein, J. (1991) *The Fashioned Self*, Oxford: Polity Press.

Foster, H. (1985) *Recodings*, Port Townsend, WA: Bay Press.

Freedman, R. (1988) *Beauty Bound: Why Women Strive for Physical Perfection*, London: Columbus Books.

Gaines, J. (1990) 'Introduction: Fabricating the Female Body', in J. Gaines and C. Herzog (eds) *Fabrications: Costume and the Female Body*, London and New York: Routledge, pp. 1–27.

Giroux, H. A. (1993–4) 'Costuming Social Change: The "United Colours of Benetton"', *Cultural Critique*, Winter, pp. 5–31.

Hanson, K. (1993) 'Dressing Down Dressing Up: The Philosophic Fear of Fashion', in H. Hein and C. Korsmeyer (eds) *Aesthetics in Feminist Perspective*, Bloomington: Indiana University Press, pp. 229–42.

Hollander, A. (1993) *Seeing through Clothes*, Berkeley: University of California Press.

Kellner, D. (1989) *Jean Baudrillard: From Marxism to Postmodernism and Beyond*, Cambridge: Polity Press.

Kellner, D. (1994) 'Madonna, Fashion, and Identity', in S. Benstock and S. Ferriss (eds) *On Fashion*, New Brunswick, NJ: Rutgers University Press, pp. 159–82.

Loos, A. (1966) 'Ornament and Crime', in L. Munz and G. Kunstler (eds) *Adolf Loos, Pioneer of Modern Architecture*, New York: Praeger (orig. 1908).

Loos, A. (1982) 'Ladies' Fashion', in *Spoken into the Void: Collected Essays 1897–1900*, Cambridge, MA: MIT Press (orig. 1902).

Mascia-Lees, F. E. and Sharpe, P. (1992) 'Introduction', in *Tattoo, Torture, Mutilation and Adornment: The De-Naturalization of the Body in Culture and Text*, Albany: State University of New York Press, pp. 1–9.

Oakley, A. (1981) *Subject Women*, New York: Pantheon Books.

Orbach, S. (1978) *Fat Is a Feminist Issue*, London: Arrow Books.

Radice, B. (1984) *Memphis*, New York: Rizzoli.

Sawchuck, K. (1987) 'A Tale of Inscription/Fashion Statements', in A. Kroker and M. Kroker (eds) *Body Invaders: Panic Sex in America*, New York: St Martin's Press.

Schor, N. (1987) *Reading in Detail: Aesthetics and the Feminine*, New York and London: Methuen.

Shilling, C. (1994) *The Body and Social Theory*, London: Sage Publications.

Silverman, K. (1986) 'Fragments of a Fashionable Discourse', in T. Modleski (ed.) *Studies in Entertainment*, Bloomington and Indianapolis: Indiana University Press, pp. 139–54.

Tickner, L. (1984) 'Why not Slip into Something a Little More Comfortable?', in M. Rowe (ed.) *Spare Rib Reader*, London: Penguin.

Tseelon, E. (1995) *The Masque of Femininity*, London: Sage Publications.

Veblen, T. (1970) *The Theory of the Leisure Class*, London: Unwin Books (orig. 1899).

Wellmer, A. (1983) 'Art and Industrial Production', *Telos*, 57, pp. 53–62.

Wilson. E. (1987) *Adorned in Dreams: Fashion and Modernity*, London: Virago.

Wilson, E. (1990a) 'These New Components of the Spectacle: Fashion and Postmodernism', in R. Boyne and A Rattansi (eds) *Postmodernism and Society*, London: Macmillan Education, pp. 209–36.

Wilson, E. (1990b) 'All the Rage', in J. Gaines and C. Herzog (eds) *Fabrications: Costume and the Female Body*, New York and London: Routledge, pp. 28–38.

Young, I. M. (1994) 'Women Recovering our Clothes', in S. Benstock and S. Ferriss (eds) *On Fashion*, New Brunswick, NJ: Rutgers University Press, pp. 197–210.

Fashion and club culture, 1970–90

Sally Gray

Encountering the dimly lit bodies of strangers on the dance floor created the essential visuality and sensuality of clubbing, enhanced by lighting effects, oceanic pulsing of music and party drugs like MDA and MDMA (Ecstasy). Dance clubbing, from the early 1970s 'disco' to the hugely popular dance clubs in the late 1980s, revolved around two cultural axes: 'mainstream' clubs and 'underground' clubs which retained their roots in African-American music and gay male urban culture. Partly because of these roots, clubbing fostered links between identity politics, dancing and dress. Seminal dance music DJs Larry Levan and Frankie Knuckles, for example, were involved as teenagers in the Manhattan drag scene and Levan hung out with students from New York's Fashion Institute of Technology for whom sewing, dressing and dancing were of equal importance. Artist David McDiarmid designed and made, in the 1980s, lamb-suede dance floor outfits, to be worn by gay men at New York's Paradise Garage (1977–87). With loose tops, elastic-waisted baggy pants, they were easy to dance in and established a 'tribal' group identity among those who wore them.

Practicality and ease of movement were important in dressing for 'hard core' dancing: garments with pockets (for keys, money, drugs); fabrics that would breathe and still work when wet; outfits which could be discarded in layers as the dancer got hot (tied around the body or stuffed into a back pocket and replaced as the dancer returned to the street). A variety of garments met this need: cotton T-shirts (especially white to pick up UV lighting), Levis, construction boots, Converse sneakers, sweatshirts (including zippered and hooded ones), sweatpants and other forms of baggy elastic-waisted pants, bandanas and hand towels (for sweaty heads and necks). Outdoor venues – gay male Fire Island New York in the 1970s or sexually eclectic Ibiza, Spain, in the 1980s – allowed the extreme utility of tiny swimsuits on near-naked bodies. Clubs and raves in Europe in 1987–8 saw the Ibiza-look, of rainbow-hued shorts, T-shirts and bandanas, with Smiley badges, denoting being 'on-one' (Ecstasy) worn by both men and women.

Less practical but popular mainstream disco dress in the 1970s included tight-fitting printed polyester shirts, flared polyester pants, high-heeled platform boots or Gucci-style loafers for men – accurately portrayed in the 1977 film *Saturday Night Fever* – and for women; flowing fabrics, Spandex, Lurex, sequins, colourful lamés and high heels. Door policies at some clubs (Studio 54 in New York; Le Beat Route and Blitz, in London, among others) established 'look' as a condition of entry for patrons.

London clubs in the 1980s such as Blitz, Camden Palace and Kinky Gerlinky saw an inventive sartorial play with gender and sexual identity, including in the early 1980s 'new romantic' dress; combining the coloured hair and extreme make-up of punk with glitter, lace, tulle, leather and skirts for both men and women. Gender-bending experimentation achieved an artistic peak in the queer costuming of Leigh Bowery at the

Snapshot 37.1 Paradise Garage devotee, artist and DJ, David McDiarmid wears a self-designed dance floor outfit of Lurex and lamé, with after-party Aviator shades, New York, 1981. His 1980 art work *Disco Kwilt* is in the background. Reproduced with permission of the David McDiarmid Estate. Photograph (attrib.) Robert Cromwell.

London club Taboo in the mid-1980s. The ubiquitous 1980s' London 'hard times' club-bing look consisted of battered (often black) Levis, flying jackets, T-shirts (often white, sometimes with slogans), Doc Martens and Converse All-stars worn by both black and white males. The establishment of the Ministry of Sound as a music, clothing and mer-chandising brand in 1991 signalled the fact that clubbing had become a global business and was less concerned with dress and identity experimentation.

Bibliography and further reading

Evans, C., and Thornton, M. (1987) *Women and Fashion: A New Look*, London and New York: Quartet.

Lawrence, T. (2003) *Love Saves the Day: A History of American Dance Music Culture, 1970–1979*, Durham, NC, and London: Duke University Press.

Osborne, B. (1999) *Twenty Years of Losing It: The A–Z of Club Culture*, London: Hodder and Stoughton.

Fashion in the 1980s
A time of revival

Alistair O'Neill

The referencing of history in British fashion, utilising past styles of dress seemingly drawn at will from varying periods, was established as a practice-based form of enquiry in the early 1980s. Vivienne Westwood turned to a copy of Norah Waugh's *The Cut of Men's Clothes 1600–1900* in the National Art Library at the Victoria and Albert Museum for the cut of her Pirates collection (A/W 1981/2), while fashion students at St Martin's School of Art turned to the illustrations of their dress history textbooks, as journalist Iain R. Webb recalls:

> You spent your day at St. Martin's making an outfit to wear that evening, and if you decided to be a historical character, then that's what you were. And then another time it might be that you dress up as some kind of diagonally-cut, future robotic person; and it was fabulous from that point of view.
>
> (*The Rebel Look*)

This reached its apotheosis in the graduate collection of John Galliano in 1984, inspired by the sartorial verve of *Les Incroyables*, in post-Revolution, eighteenth-century France. These experiments developed into a way of thinking about and using history that has come to define late twentieth-century British fashion design. As Caroline Evans confirms:

> Fashion designers call up these ghosts of modernity and offer us a paradigm that is different from the historian's paradigm, remixing fragments of the past into something new and contemporary that will continue to resonate into the future.
>
> (Evans 2003)

Yet this was not the only form of historicism at play in the design culture of 1980s' Britain. The opening of Scott Crolla's shop on Dover Street, Mayfair, in 1985 offered suits and shirting made from chintz furnishing fabric, offering a postmodern commentary on a fabric that time-travelled the wearer back through the decorative schemes of home counties domestic interiors, the commercial trade of a colonial past, and the exotic nurseries of eighteenth-century London, to a representation of England as a civilised and tamed garden.

The blossoming of floral fabrics initiated another revival of Liberty Tana cotton prints, this time promoted by an advertising campaign in 1988 that asked 'Why take Liberty's?' doctoring a vintage black and white stage photograph of Elvis Presley to look

like his blue suede shoes were covered with a printed fabric of Alpine flowers. This was another kind of historicism, but one where the conventions of representing femininity in the consumer culture of the 1950s, was translated into the self-conscious styling of male appearance in the 1980s, typified by the Levi's 501 advertising campaign featuring male model Nick Kamen. The advertisement signalled a return to the look of the post-war era, but as creative director John Hegarty underlines, the imprecise nature of the references betray the creative historicism at its heart:

> I thought it would be more interesting to do the ad with a period look. The 1950s idea wasn't in the brief. It just happened, and out of that we estab-lished a mythical period for Levi's. Grapevine, the music that backed the ad, was a 60s not a 50s song – it came to me simultaneously and there was no real logic to it.

> (*Campaign* 1996)

The advertisement prompted the return of jeans with antiquated details such as a button fly, and shrink-to-fit fabric adjustment; while the sale of boxer shorts, first spearheaded by Paul Smith who sold them alongside the Filofax (another outmoded personal item), brought the feel of historicism closer then ever.

Bibliography and further reading

Campaign, 20 September 1996.
Evans, C. (2003) *Fashion at the Edge*, New Haven: Yale University Press.
'The Rebel Look' (2008) Programme 3, *British Style Genius*, BBC Television.

Snapshot 38.1 Cardigan and leggings by Jean Paul Gaultier, *c.* 1989 (cotton, acetate, viscose, Lycra and elastane). Gaultier, like many other European designers including John Galliano, was both a part of and influenced by the club culture and the music of the 1980s and early 1990s. This complex garment has numerous cultural references. Its cardigan is embroidered in the manner of Chinese imperial robes, set off by a 'frieze' or border in Greek-key style. The eclecticism of the garment is thus deliberate. The leggings are stretch black Lycra and refer to both gay male culture and the exercise cult of the 1980s. National Gallery of Victoria, Melbourne, Australia, 1995.12.a–b.

Fashion and adornment

Michael Carter

Snapshot 39.1 *A French invasion —on the fashionable dress of 1798* by Isaac Cruikshank, Lewis Walpole Library 798.0.4. Courtesy of the Lewis Walpole Library, Yale University.

Adorn and *adornment* are part of a family of words such as *dress*, *decorate*, and *ornament*, that refer to a set of actions which transform and enhance a body by the addition of some kind of physical material. Each word is a way of designating different forms that can be taken up by the dressed body. *Dress(ing)* produces a body in a 'proper' condition, ready and able to appear in public. *Decorate* refers to the addition of beautifying materials that may be easily removed. *Ornament*, on the other hand, suggests the shifting of the object into a coherent register of materials and motifs for a prolonged, or even, permanent length of time. At first sight there appears to be little that allows adorn and adornment to be distinguished from decorate and ornament. But a closer examination of the two words reveals a cluster of meanings not caught by conventional dictionary entries. There are differences both in the relation of the body to its supplement (adorn) as well as the kinds of materials and objects that are used as adornments.

Unlike its three companions, adorn and adornment lack a sharply defined set of meanings that would allow us to readily identify adorning activities. Nor is there a specific set of objects that may be identified as adornments. One reason for this is that adornment has received little in the way of critical analysis in contrast to, say, the dense and sophisticated discourse on the ornamental. The great exception is Simmel's essay 'Adornment'. At the heart of the essay is his observation that adornment 'intensifies the wearer's being' and it is this 'intensification', not only of the being of the wearer, but also of the emotions that are engendered in the beholder, that enables *adornment* and *adorn* to be separated from their apparent synonyms *decorate* and *ornament*.

Being in a state of adornment means being removed from, and elevated above, the realm of the everyday and its inhabitants. Although there are no objects or materials that are inherently adornments, what gets used and how creates something very different from daily dress, be it fashionable or non-fashionable. The adorned state is a temporary one, an intermittent condition that lasts only for the duration of the 'special occasion' to which adornments are thought appropriate. To be adorned can mean the use of expensive materials and objects (jewellery) in such a way as to almost overwhelm, or substantially alter, the body shape of the wearer. Adornment is very often associated with marking out of status and hierarchical distinctions (ceremonial wear). But in each case the adornments are removed when the event, or period, comes to an end.

Simmel's notion that adornment was accompanied by intensification in the being of the wearer stretched to include all forms of dress. No matter how inconsequential and mundane was an element of one's appearance, its wearer radiated a modicum of social feeling. As one's dress gained in sumptuousness and complexity, and moved towards the pinnacle that was adornment, so too did the emotions of the beholders match the increasing intensity of these changing ensembles. Being adorned moves the wearer into their most 'elevated' position where the 'radiation' of their personality is at its strongest. The beholders, the recipients of this powerful 'radiation', experience a sliding sequence of emotions that passes through envy, admiration, emulation and awe. Surely somewhere nearby sits the statue of the god or goddess, adorned with a garland of flowers.

Adorn and *adornment* did not fare well with the rise of mass democracies and the onset of a modernist aesthetic. The former alighted on male dress and changed it into an ensemble devoid of any *overt* caste distinctions. The latter dreamt of a 'pure' beauty where objects would be cleansed of all their extraneous elements. *Adorn* and *adornment*, and the world they referred to, came to be seen as archaic remnants from an old order. It could only be properly applied to things that had died out or things that, as yet, had not been modernised. H. G. Wells's 1905 comment on the political significance of women's adornments captures perfectly this waning in the importance of 'trimmings' and the need for women's dress to be modernised. 'Women, disarmed of their distinctive barbaric adornments, the feathers, beads, lace and trimmings . . . would mingle . . . In the counsels and intellectual development of men'.

As ever more areas of our daily life have been modernised, adornment and adorn have retreated until now they are words whose home lies in the poetic or literary rather than as a means of negotiating everyday life.

Bibliography and further reading

Loos, A. (2000) 'Ornament and Crime' in I. Frank (ed.), *The Theory of Decorative Art 1750–1940*, New Haven: Yale University Press, 2000, pp. 288–94.

Semper, G. (2000) *Concerning the Formal Principles of Ornament and Its Significance as Artistic Symbol*, trans. D. Britt, in I. Frank (ed.), *The Theory of Decorative Art 1750–1940*, New Haven: Yale University Press, 2000.

Simmel, G. (1997) 'Adornment' in D. Frisby and M. Featherstone (eds), *Simmel on Culture*, London: Sage, pp. 206–11.

Ethics and the future of fashion

Elizabeth Wilson

Serious analysts of fashion have always had to contend with a view of their subject as both trivial and immoral. In the early modern period clerics denounced fashion for its vanity, worldliness and incitement to sexual sin. These religious grounds were displaced in the nineteenth century by objections to its crippling effects on women's bodies, the unhygienic nature of yards of dusty skirts and to the appalling conditions of the workers in the increasingly industrialised mass production of fashionable garments. To these objections were added those of feminists, both in the nineteenth century and in the 1970s and 1980s. Fashion, it seemed, was wholly *unethical* from every point of view.

Today, exploited workers still provide us with the cheap fashion we crave. Women are still objectified by the over-sexualisation of Western fashion – although it could be argued that the Islamic veil, whether fashion or anti-fashion, also draws attention to and thus sexualises women (even if that is the opposite of what is intended). To these perennial concerns have been added the problems that fashion, especially cheap, throwaway 'fast' fashion, poses for the environment. Cotton requires excessive amounts of water; synthetics are in some cases made from oil; fashion is so cheap and so much of it is produced that second-hand clothes have lost much of their resale value and simply go straight to landfill. Fashion, in other words, contributes to the destruction of the planet.

These objections, however, are misplaced. It is not *fashion* that causes drought, anorexia, drug addiction, female self-hatred, dreadful working conditions and environmental degradation. The desire to alter and adorn the body has existed, does and will exist in all human societies. It is an inescapable part of human culture and human communication. Few, moreover, apart from hardcore puritans, object to the human wish to beautify one's appearance, cut a dash or play a role in the social panorama. Insofar as body fascism and the policing and denigration of women are concerned, fashion is simply the messenger from a sexist, celebrity-mad mass culture, channelled through popular journalism, the internet and Hollywood. Equally, the fashion industry is merely like many others (for example, the toy industry) in pushing down wages to raise profits at reckless cost to the environment. No more than any other productive enterprise can fashion escape the economic system. Yet there is a possible ethical future for fashion – as for other areas of visual culture – if it confronts those areas in which it is open to criticism and if consumers confront the way in which we have come to expect to access our clothes.

The resources of the planet are not infinite, therefore, sustainable fashion is important as never before. Sustainability would mean an end to throwaway fashion. We do see the beginnings of a new attitude in that vintage and second-hand fashion has become not only acceptable, but fashionable and desirable. The belief that well-made garments are objects of beauty and artistry to be valued over time (as used to be the case) must replace the thought of a garment as rather like a packet of cigarettes, to be rapidly consumed, or a newspaper to be read and tossed aside. Once we understand that fashion is a cycle rather than an arrow pointing through time in one direction, we may more readily be able to spend more money on 'investment' fashions that may be at some point temporarily retired and then at a later date brought out again. Current trends in clothes swapping provide an example of the new attitude that is beginning to develop.

Finally, in a global economy and with global media, fashion may in the future be less Western centred. The enigma here is the influence of Islam. The veil, where compulsory, ensures that women do not enter public space on the same terms as men; ultimately its symbolism represents the separation of the sexes and the rejection of that bodily display, which not only Western fashion but much of Western art promotes and depends on (for example in modern dance and classical painting). This real difference of views concerning bodily display is unlikely to be resolved any time soon and is seldom discussed. Yet if fruitful dialogue could replace the denunciations from both sides, perhaps a convergence might be possible, in which the faux-sexual and vulgar aspects of Western fashion might be moderated, while the validity of personal display per se was still upheld.

Bibliography and further reading

Ribeiro, A. (1986) *Fashion and Morality*, London: Batsford, 1986; revised edition, Oxford and New York: Berg, 2003.

Chapter 23

Italian and Chinese agendas in the global fashion industry[1]

Simona Segre Reinach

IT IS DIFFICULT TO APPLY THE CONCEPT OF 'AUTHENTICITY' to the case of fashion, which has always been the outcome of hybridising and cross-overs. Today, the idea of a historical and geographical 'origin' of fashion, identified with Europe and long cultivated by fashion scholars, is questioned, if not wholly rejected. Capitalism and fashion are very closely related, especially within large-scale industrial systems of production, but the exclusion of fashion from the history of non-European cultures and economies is no longer acceptable. Similarly, the idea that costume and dress in other countries and cultures may not be comparable to fashion as experienced in the West is subject to criticism.[2]

To some extent the opposition between fashion (as quintessentially European and Western) and costume (for all the others) is also no longer valid. The contrast between the unchangeable nature of costume (of generic *others*) and the mutability of *our* fashion is something that often does not correspond to reality, as it rests on the ethnocentric idea that there are people 'without fashion' and people 'with fashion'.[3] Recent scholarship argues instead that 'traditional' garments evolve in different ways, according to their cultural context. New definitions are sought for terms like 'traditional', 'ethnic' and 'folk' dress (Skov 2003, 2004a, 2004b; Eicher, Evenson, Lee 2000; Hansen 2004). Similar considerations are emerging from practice: designers in countries with either the presence of strong ethnic minorities or long-established sartorial traditions are now developing 'fashions' (Franci 2008) and 'dress systems' distinct from the Western ones. They acquire autonomy in fashion design, production and consumption, as in the case of Islamic fashion (Tarlo 1996).

Conversely, fashion in the West is no longer the result of the consultation of a 'catalogue of taste', as it was in the 1980s and 1990s with the 'discovery' of ethnic. For a long time fashion in the West drew on a history of 'inspirations' from faraway places reinterpreted in a context composed of key cities such as Paris, London, Milan and New

York (Gilbert and Breward 2004). Fashion today appears polycentric and studded with the presence of active and creative fashion designers coming from many parts of the world.

Fashion no longer is the exclusive property of the West. Contemporary fashion is created rapidly and in great volume in Latin America, Africa and Asia, redefining both consumption and fashion itself in the process, and propelling multi-directional style shifts across the globe (Hansen 2004: 370). This does not lead to an 'aesthetic multi-culturalism', sign of an unproblematic acceptance of the most varied fabrics, forms, colours and brands. On the contrary, it is a precise 'power field', as defined by Pierre Bourdieu, in which the relationship between ideation, production and consumption plays a determinant role. Emerging economies and societies pose new questions and propose new scenarios for fashion. It is not just a matter for 'new' countries, like India, China, Russia or the Arab Emirates to be interested in adopting 'our fashion'; there is a convergence between their interest in the culture of fashion and our interest in theirs. Both sides sell and acquire new aesthetics within a global market.

Creativity is a key criterion in the hierarchical order of economies, cultures and cities within a global system. India and China, for instance, are often coupled together when referring to the emerging economies of Asia. However, when referring to hier-archies of fashion they are substantially different. India developed fashion design that is linked to a long-standing textile tradition, although the latter is not free from orient-alising interpretations (Dwyer 2006, Colaiacomo and Caratozzolo 2010). India, although a 'competitor' on the level of production for the Western fashion system, is associated with the most typical ethnocentric prejudice in the history of fashion, an Orientalism presented within the customary approaches of colonialism.

In the case of China we deal with something different. China, unlike India, does not belong to the Olympus of fashion. China is often described as a *débutante* in fash-ion and the expression 'Chinese fashion designer' appears almost as a contradiction in terms. The country with one of the oldest historical traditions (five millennia of civi-lisation; a hierarchy of most complex and sophisticated aesthetic codes; the production and diffusion of precious silks, etc.), is inexplicably seen as lacking any tradition, as if everything had been happening just in the last few years under the condescending and controlling eye of the West. 'Fashion' and 'China' can seem incongruent, particularly when used in a historical context. The vast, solemn, unchanging Chinese empire of the popular imagination is difficult to reconcile with how we think of whimsical fashion, whilst its recent 'history' is indelibly stamped with the homogeneity of the Cultural Revolution and the Mao suit. What remains of Chinese fashion are scattered references to the use of the *cheongsam* in the inter-war years by Shanghai girls. This *reductio ad absur-dum* explains why journalists insist that China has only recently 'discovered' fashion (Finnane 2008: 291).

The case of China shows how fashion is asked to define itself by providing a sense of identity. Yet, this exercise in differentiation and distinctiveness is accompanied by an increasing difficulty in identifying where and when the ideation, design, production and consumption of most industrial products occur. The relocation and international outsourcing of production that has characterised industrial manufacturing since the 1980s has created many complex paths in the material creation of a garment.

One can argue that fashion – the capacity to produce aesthetics and therefore to start up a sort of 'mimetic desire' as philosopher René Girard calls it – is at the very heart of national identity (Girard 1999). Having or not having a 'national fashion' on

Figure 23.1 Shanghai Fashion Week poster at Donghua University, 2008. Photo by Simona Segre Reinach.

which to rely is fundamental for the success of brands operating in the contemporary market, even if production may be carried out at a transnational level. One might say that the importance of national fashion is actually due to the very fact that production *is* transnational. In the interactions between Italians and Chinese who together make and sell fashion, the theme of national identity clearly emerges. The existence of shared aesthetics informing the capacity to produce fashion is in this case a negotiation between the positive idea that 'Italy has fashion' and the negative one that 'China does not have fashion'. This characterises the communication choices of the 'Made in Italy', and the nature of collaboration between Italians and Chinese in the designing, production and distribution of brands and products.

The 'globalisation' of fashion over the last generation has not necessarily challenged a Euro-centred vision of fashion. Since the 'Japanese revolution' in fashion in the early 1980s, cities other than the traditional Milan, Paris, New York and London have established themselves in the increasingly packed calendar of fashion weeks. Asian megalopolises like Shanghai, Singapore, Hong Kong, Dubai and Shanghai confer prestige to European and Western brands and, vice versa, base part of their own prestige on the presence of foreigners and their ability to host them in their region (Figure 23.1). The possibility of creating fashion, of being recognised as 'author countries', is however part of a process in which hierarchies and roles are being constantly renegotiated according to the contexts and players concerned.

In 2007–8 China became the privileged theatre in which many Italian and other European companies chose to be on show. The celebrated Pirelli calendar for 2008 was set in Shanghai with garments designed by John Galliano for Dior. Erminegildo Zegna set its corporate catalogue in Beijing, printing it on paper recalling the rice paper used for Chinese ideograms, and locating its *mise-en-scène* in sophisticated and rarefied settings, a mixture of exoticism and the Orientalist magnificence of Chinese culture. Ferragamo celebrated the eightieth anniversary of the fashion house with a travelling exhibition entitled 'Salvatore Ferragamo: The Evolving Legend', inaugurated at the MoCa Museum in Shanghai, followed by a select party at which the emerging Italian dancer Roberto Bolle performed (Figures 23.2 and 23.3). In the words of Wanda Ferragamo, the shoe-designer Salvatore's widow, whose children and grandchildren were there to ensure everything was fittingly luxurious: 'My family and I chose China, and specifically Shanghai, to celebrate the company's eightieth anniversary given the city's rich history and traditions'.[4]

The example of Ferragamo should not be considered merely a tribute to one of the most important markets for their brand. The Ferragamo press release focused on the celebration of Italian identity and used the setting of China to reinforce the message of the presumed cultural roots of fashion. Indeed, it was in China that Italianness was aptly conveyed through ideas that included the Renaissance, artisanal skills and the *bel paese* entrepreneurship, all represented in the faux-Florentine palazzo reconstructed for the party and the *tableau vivant* or pageant of the 'shoemaker's workshop'. Two shoemakers made shoes by hand 'as they once did', wearing immaculate aprons and glasses perched on their noses, in an artisanal shop reconstructed as part of the exhibition's itinerary. Similarly, the advertising and communication of other 'Italian' firms (some of which were invented for the Chinese market), like Sharmoon, an Italo-Chinese joint venture, the Piombo brand and Maurizio Baldassari, mixed Renaissance architecture, holidays in Tuscany, *savoir vivre*, good taste and *dolce vita*.

Needless to say, these examples do not emphasise Italian production in China: this tends to be concealed, because China is still synonymous in people's minds with the notion of poor-quality goods. Rather, they signal the presence of prestigious Italian brands – made in China, or in Italy, or in both countries, according to the trajectories of transnational capitalism – in the equally prestigious Chinese market. Rather than one country producing fashion for others – the 'factory of the world' – China is presented here in a range of images as a fashion-consuming country, a fast-developing market characterised by the presence of the best of customers: the *nouveaux riches*.

Between production and consumption, however, the question of Chinese 'authorship' or as mentioned above, its capacity to offer a shared aesthetic, remains unsolved. The association of China and fashion still seems to constitute a sort of oxymoron. There are historical, cultural and structural reasons for the lack of recognition of 'Chinese' fashion; yet China boasts a wide-ranging production of fashion, at all levels. We may only briefly mention the factors that make it difficult to 'see' or to recognise Chinese fashion, restricting it to the role it plays once the producers connect in business partnerships with Italian firms.

Although China is today the main world producer of apparel, clothing production alone does not mean creating 'fashion'. In the period of the Cultural Revolution (1967–76), the West's anti-bourgeois ideology sparked off young people's 'anti-fashions', initially intended to coincide with the emergence of a new 'post-bourgeois fashion' life and

Figure 23.2 A sculpture of a famous Ferragamo sandal (1938) is placed in front of the Shanghai shopping mall Plaza 66 to promote the Salvatore Ferragamo Evolving Legend exhibition (29 March–7 May 2008). The exhibition took place at the Shanghai Museum of Contemporary Art to celebrate the eighty-year anniversary of the company. Photo by Simona Segre Reinach, 2008.

appearance. In China it led to the utopia of the abolition of fashion *completely*, in favour of totalitarian uniformity. Chinese fashion has therefore been constructed from the different ideas of 'Chineseness' provided by Chinese tailors in Hong Kong, often in flight from the Cultural Revolution, as well as Chinese designers based in Taiwan and in the United States. Their creations were forms of exoticism aimed especially at Western consumers, as for example with Vivienne Tam, a Chinese-born fashion designer who moved first to Hong Kong and later to New York. The most fitting example of this fictional 'Chineseness' is the Shanghai Tang brand (currently merged in the Richemont luxury group) created by a Hong Kong entrepreneur (before reunification) and distributed in chain stores in Europe and the US, and now also in mainland China.

The first mainland Chinese 'fashion designers' started from fashion ground zero after 1978. Their backgrounds require some elucidation as their motives and training are very telling. They came from the disciplines of dance, such as the choreography of propaganda, theatre or from the state-run art schools. For this reason, and because of the artistic tradition of clothing culture in avant-garde Western aesthetics, they consider fashion as an artistic not a commercial phenomenon. The marketing of clothes is instead the prerogative of the powerful brands managed by the state, aimed at attracting investment from abroad to acquire know-how, sometimes by placing Western fashion designers at the head of local production.

Today a new generation of Chinese fashion designers is torn between the criticism

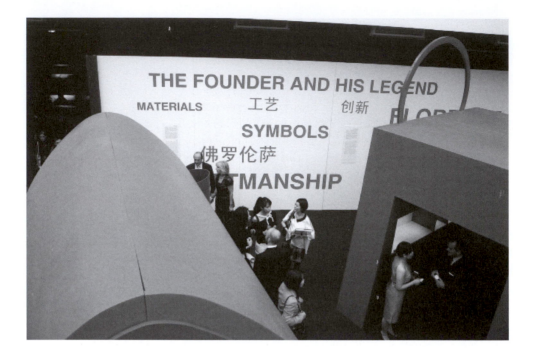

Figure 23.3 The opening of Salvatore Ferragamo Evolving Legend exhibition at the Shanghai Museum of Contemporary Art, 29 March 2008. Four concepts in English and in Chinese illustrate the 'legend' of the founder Salvatore Ferragamo: materials, symbols, Florence, craftsmanship. Photo by Simona Segre Reinach, 2008.

of facile exoticisms, fictional identities and Orientalism (to which they often yield). To this weight of an orientalism sold back to their own people, others search for an 'authentic Chineseness', whilst they simultaneously negotiate their slight familiarity with the industrial production run by the state, and the powerful competition of European brands. They are placed under pressures quite different from a student designer in Sydney or Seattle. As Antonia Finnane writes in a more general sense:

> One impediment to the more creative deployment of historical aesthetics in fashion, and in the arts more broadly in China, is the tight grip maintained by the ruling Communist Party on interpretations of history and culture (Finnane 2008: 281–2).

The resulting fragmented reality of Chinese fashion (the different idea of Chineseness of mainland Chinese and those of the diaspora, the lack of collaboration between artists/designers/creators and the clothing and textile industry, the interference of the state) makes it difficult to synthetically perceive what Chinese fashion really is today. It becomes easier to define it in negative terms, that is what *it is not*.

So the Chinese designers are not 'totally Italian with high drama and nor are they Japanese with understatement over strong basic structure. The Chinese deconstructionists are unique. There is a pragmatism, experimentalism and a visual impact. This is why I see Chinese fashion becoming another great icon for the fashion world. There is an energy' (Seno 2008).

In these disjunctures, Italo-Chinese partnerships take place and 'Italian superiority regarding style' takes shape. Every single Italian working in the fashion sector in China – from the technician to the entrepreneur, whether or not he/she has or lacks design skills, but plays a business, technical or even managerial role – tends to support a *natural* disposition for beauty, in the name of his/her 'Italianness', to offset the naivety of Chinese taste, its lack of style and discernment. An extract from an interview with an Italian manager clearly expresses this concept: 'When you look at what people are wearing you can see the difference; the Italians are used to wearing fashionable clothing so they have a feeling for style and fashion; the Chinese don't have that feeling yet'. Altagamma (the association of top-quality Italian brands) similarly makes its own statement: 'Our mission is to affirm the Excellence of Altagamma member companies and promote, together, the primacy of the Italian lifestyle and culture in the world' (Altagamma website).

As we have seen, this is a partial view. The perspective is in fact overturned when we speak of the Chinese as consumers. Unlike the production partner, the Chinese consumer is extolled as demanding and expert: the Chinese consumer must be able to show good taste by choosing Italian style, but not by expressing their own. Two great cultures, the Italian and the Chinese, face each other as equals, as in the Ermenegildo Zegna claim *Great Minds Think Alike*, but only in the expected direction, that of consumption. The 'glorious Chinese past' is evoked in marketing communication but turns into the opposite stereotype – that of the poor-quality Chinese imitator – when the issue is running a business together. What the inauguration ceremony of the Beijing Olympics in 2008 'One world one dream' sought to do was exactly this, to link the glorious past, detaching it from the colonial and Orientalist interpretation, instead connecting it to the technological present (Figure 23.4).

Italian actors operating in the Chinese setting also resort to notions of inherent ability. 'Creativity is something you are born with, you can't be taught it', or 'Italians have fashion in their DNA', are the types of statements gathered during fieldwork. They might be explained by the need to preserve precise power relations within many of these partnerships. If style cannot be learned or taught, then those deciding and commanding can only be Italian. The superiority in style is not the starting point for a sort of naturalisation of taste, but it is the final goal in complex, conflicting negotiations to maintain control not only of production, but increasingly of distribution and retail, right down to the most remote provinces where the partnerships in Italo-Chinese joint ventures take shape every day. For Italians, the low esteem and the playing down of Chinese authorship are ways to handle relations with the Chinese to their own advantage: the Chinese are no longer production partners for exports alone, but production and sales partners in their own country, in competition therefore with a specific Chinese fashion. They are present at all levels from the top (with designers such as ZucZuz, Ma Ke, He Yan, etc.), to the middle level (with the leading state, semi-private and private clothing companies such as Cathaia, Youngor, Metersbonwe, etc.), and right down to the low level of the market with fast fashion brands.

The 'workshop of the Italian shoemaker' is therefore not a romanticisation or exoticism for export, in a play of reciprocal charms, of red lanterns versus Renaissance workshops, but a necessary marketing tool in a period of global fashion, to be

Figure 23.4 Poster at Donghua University, Shanghai, 2008. The connection between Olympic games and fashion shows the increasing importance of a national aesthetics. Photo by Simona Segre Reinach.

strengthened and conveyed also at home. After Shanghai, the Salvatore Ferragamo Evolving Legend exhibition reached Milan, and it will move on to New York in a circular movement aimed at increasing credibility and meaning. A journalist from *Repubblica*, one of Italy's major newspapers, wrote: 'In his collection the fashion designer (Giambattista Valli) is inspired by the art of the Italian Renaissance also in the case of colours, like red Pontormo, a great deal of black and Bronzino green' (*La Repubblica*, 16 January 2009).[5]

The Chinese must be able to show good taste by choosing Italian style, but not by expressing their own mode and aesthetic. The two great cultures, Italian and Chinese, face each other as equals, as in the claim *Great Minds Think Alike*, but only in the expected direction, that of increased consumption. The 'glorious Chinese past' evoked in communication strategies concerns only one part of China and melts into the opposite stereotype of the poor-quality Chinese imitator when it is a question of running a business together.

Notes

1   The following observations are part of a broader project centred on the work relation-ships between Italians and Chinese and on the approaches to the training of a transnational class of workers. The research was conducted in Italy and China, between 2002 and 2008 jointly with Sylvia Yanagisako (Stanford University) and Lisa Rofel (University of Califor-nia at Santa Cruz).
2   This has also led to a revision of the issue of the relationship between fashion, anti-fashion, counter-fashion, political utopias and fashion.
3   Like the opposition between 'peoples with writing and peoples without writing' elabo-rated by Structuralism in the 1970s.
4   From 'Ferragamo Celebrations, Shanghai', *Wallpaper* http://www.wallpaper.com/ fashion/ferragamo-celebrations-shanghai/2183.
5   Pontormo was the art name of the Renaissance artist Jacopo Carucci (1494–1557), famous for his shade of red. Bronzino was the art name for the artist Agnolo di Cosimo (1503–72), well known for his use of green.

Bibliography

Bao Ming Xin (2008) 'A Brief History of Chinese Fashion Design', in *China Design Now*, ed. Zhang Hongxing and Lauren Parker, London: V & A Publications.

Belfanti, C. M. (2008) *Civiltà della Moda*, Bologna: Il Mulino.

Colaiacomo, P. and Caratozzolo, V. (2010) 'The Impact of Traditional Indian Clothing on Italian Fashion from Germana Marucelli to Gianni Versace', *Fashion Theory*, 14, forthcoming.

Crane, D. (2000) *Fashion and Its Social Agendas: Class, Gender, and Identity in Clothing*, Chicago: University of Chicago Press.

Finnane, A. (2008) *Changing Clothing in China: Fashion, History, Nation*, New York: Columbia University Press.

Gilbert, D. and Breward, C. (2006) *Fashion's Worlds Cities*, Oxford: Berg.

Girard, R. (1999) *Mensonge romantique et vérité romanesque*, Paris: Hachette Littérature.

Kawamura, Y. (2004) *The Japanese Revolution in Paris Fashion*, Oxford: Berg.

Merlo, E. and Polese, F. (2006) 'Turning Fashion into Business: The Emergence of Milan as an International Hub', *Business History Review*, 80, pp. 415–47.

Ong, A. (2007) 'Per favore rimanete! Soggetti pied à terre nella megacittà, www.posseweb.net (November).

Redini, V. (2008) *Frontiere del 'Made in Italy': Delocalizzazione produttiva e identità delle merci*, Verona: Ombre Corte.

Rofel, L. (2007) *Desiring China. Experiments in Neoliberalism, Sexuality and Public Culture*, Durham, NC, and London: Duke University Press.

Segre Reinach, S. (2005) 'China and Italy: Fast Fashion versus Pret à Porter. Towards a New Culture of Fashion', *Fashion Theory*, 9, 1, pp. 1–12.

Segre Reinach, S. (2006) *Manuale di Sociologia, Comunicazione, Cultura della moda, vol. IV, Oriental-ismi*, Rome: Meltemi.

Segre Reinach, S. (2009) 'La moda nella cultura italiana', in *La cultura italiana*, gen. ed. L. L. Cavalli, Sforza, Turin: Utet.

Seno, Alexandra A. (2008) 'Shanghai: The Allure of Individualism', *International Herald Trib-une*, 22 February.

Skov, L. (2003) 'Fashion-nation: A Japanese Globalization Experience and a Hong Kong Dilemma', in *Re-Orienting Fashion. The Globalization of Asian Dress*, ed. S. Niessen, A. M. Leshkowich and C. Jones, Oxford: Berg.

Skov, L. (2004a) 'Seeing Is Believing: World Fashion and the Hong Kong Young Designers Contest', *Fashion Theory*, 8, 2, pp. 165–94.

Skov, L. (2004b) 'Ethnic Style in Fashion' in V. Steele (ed.) *Encyclopedia of Clothing and Fashion*, New York: Scribner, pp. 417–18.

Steele, V. and Major, J. (1999) *China Chic: East Meets West*, New Haven and London: Yale University Press.

Tranberg Hansen, K. (2004) 'The World in Dress: Anthropological Perspectives on Clothing, Fashion and Culture', *Annual Review of Anthropology*, 33, pp. 369–92.

Volonté P. (2008) *Vita da stilista*, Milan: Bruno Mondadori.

Wilson, E. (2003; first edition 1985) *Adorned in Dreams*, London: I. B. Tauris.

Yanagisako, S. (2005) 'Made in Translation: Transnational Capitalism and the New Silk Road', unpublished paper presented at the conference 'Europe in Motion, Europe at the Crossroads: A Conference on the Politics of Circulation in Europe', University of Chicago, Modern European History and Anthropology of Europe Workshop.

Made-in-Italy

Between past and future

Giovanni Luigi Fontana

Snapshot 41.1 Catwalk in the Sala Bianca of Palazzo Pitti, Florence, 1951.

The catwalk organised by Giovanni Battista Giorgini at Palazzo Pitti in Florence in February 1951 is normally considered to be the beginning of the global ascendancy of Made-in-Italy. In reality the 1951 catwalk was the result of a long-standing process based on creativity, technical skills and knowledge of Italian producers that had matured during the second half of the nineteenth and the first half of the twentieth centuries. Some have argued that the high level of craftsmanship and good taste was the legacy of the Renaissance and that Italian products continued to enjoy international appreciation during the centuries that followed. As for many industrialising nations, at the turn of the twentieth century it was the heavy industrial sectors that exploited the opportunities of growing international consumer markets. Yet, manufacturing (from manus – hand and *facere* – to make, therefore 'hand made') and high-quality artisan production remained an important asset for Italy.

Craftsmanship remained high especially in places like Florence where artisan production had a long tradition. Florence had been capital of the newly formed Italian state from 1864 to 1870 and its economy developed by exploiting the idea of the 'great Florentine arts' and the attractions that these had especially for foreigners. The idea of Florence as the 'Athens of Italy' was based not just on high art but also on artisan products of a more standardised nature such as jewellery, silversmithing, leather goods, furniture and furnishing, mirrors, mosaics, and of course fashionable clothing. In Rome too one could see the emergence of a local *alta moda* (high fashion) already at the end of the nineteenth century when the city became the capital of Italy (in 1870) and, thanks to the presence of the Italian royal family, fast became the national centre for luxury production and consumption. By the early twentieth century some of the Roman *sartorie* (tailors), such as Pieragostini, and *modisterie* (seamstresses), such as the Sorelle Caramelli, had international reputations. The tailor Domenico Caraceni dressed both King George V of England and his son, the Duke of Windsor. A third centre for fashion was Milan, the city becoming in the period between 1860 and 1920 the most important centre for the fashion press. It was in this period that Milan created the so-called *maniere milanesi* (Milanese manners), a form of elegance specifically styled around this new 'city of fashion'.

One can say that it was in the interwar period that some of the most important firms of the Made-in-Italy came to the fore, such as Guccio Gucci in leather manufacturing, Salvatore Ferragamo in shoemaking, and several *case di moda* (maisons de couture or fashion houses) such as Adele Aiazzi Fanteschi, Virginia Calabri, and Giuseppina Del Bono, that increasingly looked at how to differentiate themselves from Parisian style. Milan and Florence were the key centres for the diffusion of a 'fashion culture' that was indispensable for boosting internal demand and creating at the same time consciousness regarding the value of creativity and originality.

Central, however, to the different experiences of Florence, Rome and Milan was the idea that the comparative advantage of Italian fashion was not material, but immaterial: the 'good taste' that for centuries had put the country at the pinnacle of artistic achievement and was now pervading the applied arts and the production of high-class consumer goods, clothing included. The immaterial aspect of Italian fashion and the Made-in-Italy has been profoundly linked to Italian taste, culture, art and lifestyle. After the Second World War the imaginary realm of Italian fashion has been internationalised through concepts such as *la dolce vita* (literally 'the sweet life' from Fellini's eponymous film of 1960) and Hollywood sul Tevere (Hollywood on the river Tiber), the Italo-American film studios where films such as *Cleopatra* and *Ben Hur* were shot.

Carlo Marco Belfanti has suggested that Italian fashion is and has been since its early beginnings a 'cultural industry' that combined 'tourism and shopping, modernity and tradition, artisan skills and cultural embeddedness' (Belfanti 2008: 13). Partially this explains the association between Made-in-Italy and fashion (from Gucci to Ferragamo, the Sorelle Fontana and a younger generation that includes Armani, Versace, Fendi, Dolce & Gabbana, as well as accessories' producers such as Tod's and Safilo). However this association hides the complexity of a phenomenon that includes sectors such as marble surfacing, decorative ceramics, wood furniture, design appliances, and, not to forget, food, especially the classic products of the Mediterranean diet, including olive oil, cheese and pasta. What connects these different sectors with the best known fashion firms is not just their shared belonging to a wide notion of Made-in-Italy. Most of the brands renowned for their Italian style and quality are small and medium-sized firms often belonging to industrial districts, groups of firms operating in the same sub-sectors at relative close geographical proximity to one another.

One can conclude that the Made-in-Italy is something systemic. On the face of global competition, Italian products are not just something produced in Italy, but are the materialisation of long-standing processes of learning, testing and positioning those products and concepts to them related into a story (or history) that is situated within Italian tradition. Yet this is something that cannot be easily planned and whose many features become delineated only after they occurred. The Made-in-Italy is not a product or an attribute of Italian producers but is firstly a characteristic of the Italian productive system, a quality that, as Quadrio Curzio and Fortis remind us, 'only those who live in it are able to appreciate and value' (Quadrio Curzio and Fortis 2000: 15).

Bibliography and further reading

Belfanti, Carlo Marco (2008) 'Introduzione', *Annali di storia dell'impresa*, 19 (issue on 'Prima del' [made in Italy]), pp. 9–13.

Belfanti, Carlo Marco, and Giovanni Luigi Fontana (2005) 'Rinascimento e Made in Italy', in M. Fantoni (ed.), *Il Rinascimento italiano e l'Europa, vol. 1: Storia e storiografia*, Vicenza: Angelo Colla Editore, pp. 618–36.

Gundle, Stephen (2007) *Bellissima: Feminine Beauty and the Idea of Italy*, New Haven and London: Yale University Press.

Quadrio Curzio, Alberto, and Marco Fortis (eds) (2000) *Il Made in Italy oltre il 2000: Innovazione e comunità locali*, Bologna: Il Mulino.

The contemporary Japanese consumer

Toby Slade

Japan has a long and unique history of self-imposed cultural isolation that continues to influence how sartorial fashions are received and used as props in many areas of Japanese social life. It is impossible to assess contemporary Japanese fashion life without reference to Japan's unique history. In the Meiji period (1868–1912), Japan developed a complicated double life of outwardly embracing modern fashions while at home maintaining Japanese modes of dress that were also not 'traditional' but subject to change and reform. Foreign influences were always kept at bay and thus also controlled, and the degree to which foreignness was allowed to co-mingle with what was conceived as a Japanese central core was restricted. Even the casino-like space of the nineteenth-century Rokumeikan was constructed and furnished with European activities such as dining at table and playing cards in mind, such that the Western clothes worn there matched the Western leisure activities these clothes suited and demanded. Once away from the Rokumeikan, the evening suit or bustle dress would be removed. Such a space and such a clothing policy were a deliberate piece of statecraft to confront the racist notion that the average Japanese was either sub-human or effeminate in his clothing and therefore inferior to a European.

Even at a linguistic level the use of a different set of characters, *katakana*, for foreign words, provides a most basic separation of things Japanese and not Japanese in origin. The consequence is that today many fashions, while seemingly enthusiastically embraced, are adopted only within the category of a passing and limited fad. The Japanese exhibit a tendency to reduce threats to established order to the notion of 'play'. Sado-masochistic references in contemporary fashion are not seen to refer to a sex act but rather a surface style or interest. This is called in Japanese '*S/M play*', the *play* part being a means of neutralising any deeper implications of challenge to middle-class values in the Marquis de Sade's provocations to marriage, sex and transgression. In this way, foreign concepts that could be a challenge to Japanese culture and norms are linguistically put into an experimental and non-serious category, where their threat is reduced. In this way the enthusiasm for new fashions keeps them within sets of regulated categories. Punk, gothic or hippy fashions are taken on with a stylistic perfection but without any of the accompanying social challenges. They are not expressions or acts of social provocation; rather they are used for entirely different purposes from that of their foreign originals. The Japanese consumer is therefore not speaking a homogeneous global or international fashion language when she or he ardently adopts foreign trends: a marijuana leaf on a backpack is not an indication that the wearer has ever tried the drug; a swastika on a cap is not an indication of the wearer's politics, and foreign words on a T-shirt, however offensive, are often not understood by the wearer.

The inclination can be seen across fashion institutions and structures. The fashion press has from the early period of the reopening of Japan until today, been far more

Snapshot 42.1 Couple in Harajuku, Tokyo, 2009. This couple play with different sartorial elements safe in the knowledge that they will be interpreted purely for their aesthetic value without any of the associated social challenges that more radical or idiosyncratic fashion might have in other countries. Photograph: Alastair Slade.

Snapshot 42.2 Girl in Harajuku, Tokyo, 2009. The phenomenon of *cosplay* (costume play) has been interpreted as a kind of performance art with wearers adopting fashions based on fantasy and approaching the ridiculous. It is a minority mode but it does characterise an extreme form of the entire Japanese approach to fashion where foreign clothing forms are only *played* at because notions of the 'Japanese' and the 'foreign' are so firmly partitioned. Photograph: Alastair Slade.

didactic than its Euro-American equivalents. While Western fashion magazines always used envy and class as means to create the desire for new forms, presenting many images as unattainable ideals, the Japanese fashion magazines have always presented foreign fashion in very instructional terms, filling pages with information on how to precisely and affordably imitate any particular style. Codes of 'formal' and 'casual', 'masculine' and 'feminine', 'provocative' and 'conservative' are all slightly, or sometimes entirely, different from the Western forms from which they developed. Such categories can be seen in the construction of contemporary Japanese fashion magazines, which rely on the notions of looks or categories with much more instructional text than their European counterparts. Fashion in Japan is about categories and conventions, and aesthetics are not necessarily seen to influence social norms. Even the purchasing of luxury goods such as branded handbags is viewed differently owing to history. The Japanese were introduced to Western fashion virtually overnight with no long period of nouveau-riche aspiration and uptake, and the middle-class Western horror of *parvenus* does not carry the same charge in Japan. The wider implication of this essential difference in how fashion is represented and modelled is that fashion can be used in a more playful and disposable way as it is kept separate from any essential identity as such. It is, to a far greater degree than elsewhere, a form of play and to a lesser degree a tool of creating and expressing a permanent selfhood.

Ever greater 'social liquidity' within contemporary capitalism has led to the instability of knowledge and canons of taste. This is the driving compulsion of modern fashion. The example of the historical and contemporary Japanese consumer shows that the seemingly radical embrace of newness in fashion can sometimes be a mask of deep conservatism. This can be true when fashion is regarded only as an aesthetic activity and its other social meanings or functions as provocations are disregarded because of its categorisation within the realm of play. In Japan, the enthusiasm for fashions and the speed of their overturning keep them firmly regulated. They are not being used to express the 'essence' of a Japanese person but are more like an artistic pursuit which can be put away at another time. The example of Japan, as with many cases across Asia and the world, shows that the ideas of 'self-fashioning', so popular in fashion studies today, are often inapplicable. Fashion's forms, uses and motivations do not simply radiate out from Paris and New York, they are often unique to the history and culture in which they exist.

Bibliography and further reading

Barthes, R. (1982) *Empire of Signs*, trans. Richard Howard, London: Jonathan Cape.
Brown, Kendall H., Minichiello, Sharon A., et al. (2001) *Taisho Chic: Japanese Modernity, Nostalgia and Deco*, Honolulu: Honolulu Academy of Arts.
Slade, T. (2009) *Japanese Fashion: A Cultural History*, Berg: Oxford.

Luxury brands and fashion

An un-natural marriage?

Marc de Ferrière le Vayer

Snapshot 43.1 'Saddle bag' by John Galliano for Dior, 2000 (cotton, leather, metal, Velcro). This bag was a part of a customised series in which none were quite the same. It is witty in its combination of the WASP glamour of Hermès and Gucci equestrian-themed leather goods, with the vulgarity of street graffiti and trailer trash logos. Such a bag could not be machine-made – its 'quality' is too high; yet it tends to play with and obscure that process of making. Most consumers have no idea how such goods are produced today, quite different from the couture customer of the 1950s. © National Gallery of Victoria, Melbourne, Australia, 2002.185.+

Since the 1960s, the great French luxury brands, part of couture and perfume production, have become interested in the fashion world. This was initially done with caution and only more recently in a more direct way, as it was understood that this new engagement with fashion could produce a certain confusion for couturiers' marketing strategies, business communication and the perception of their brand by the general public.

The pioneer of this new relationship between fashion and luxury was Yves Saint

Laurent (1936–2008), who popularised his brand 'Saint Laurent Rive Gauche'. The concentration of capital and the creation of large corporations in the luxury sector, along the lines of LVMH (Louis Vuitton Moët Hennessy), has since the 1980s contributed to the success of this new business model that is now widely adopted in the sector. Industrialists are now the owners of famous haute couture brands that they often purchased at high prices. Their return on investment is created through a strategy of 'declination of the brand', that is to say the capacity to extend the value of the brand across products of different values and belonging to different consumer markets. The best known manifestation of this idea is the omnipresence of ready-to-wear lines of the 'great brands'. The 'declination of the brand' is not confined to the world of fashion, but includes perfumes and accessories.

This commercial and marketing strategy is a historical break from several points of view. It has produced a certain degree of confusion as it no longer distinguishes between production of exceptional pieces or high luxury and those of mass or serial production. What follows is a communication or public relations difficulty, which the companies attempt to solve by engaging in forms of so-called 'porno chic', the use of pornographic aesthetics combined with pop culture, notable in their photography and advertising.

This confusion between 'high' and 'low', and between serial and unique, has also profound economic consequences as it has reconfigured the geography and boundaries of fashion. Haute couture, which is sometimes a loss-making activity, has played a great part in rebranding and communication. This has become evident since the 1980s when, in restricting this role to the haute couture, the traditional position of the important French brands has weakened, thus allowing the emergence of fierce Italian, but also American competition. This can now be seen in the success of new brands such as Dolce & Gabbana, or of more established ones such as Gucci and Calvin Klein.

These are among the most important changes around luxury branding in the last decade. Marcel Rochas, for instance, left haute couture in order to dedicate himself to perfumes, but he maintained his legitimacy in the arena of high-quality production. Since the 1980s, entry into the circle of luxury brands has changed dramatically with the creator or the industrialist being offered several possible routes. The first is through 'collections', still linked to fashion, examples of which are the Americans Hilfiger and Calvin Klein, or the French designer Jean Paul Gaultier, who progressively shaped their brand's image by organising events and fashion parades. The second route into the luxury business is instead for a fashion or read-to-wear brand to launch out into perfumes – considered by default to be a luxury product – and thus to acquire commercial or marketing legitimacy, and to become a luxury brand in the mind of consumers.

These practices seem to have produced several consequences. French haute couture has not benefited from these changes. The number of *maisons* active in the haute couture sector is fast declining. Although the rules to become a member of the Chambre syndicale de la haute couture have been relaxed, the reality is that this type of business activity has lost its economic importance. More significantly, the centre of fashion has moved, with the Milan Fashion Week becoming more important than the week of Paris fashion parades. In so doing, the mythic centre of fashion, Paris itself, finds a threat not from creation or production, but from marketing.

Bibliography and further reading

Berry, C. J. (1994) *The Idea of Luxury: A Conceptual and Historical Investigation*, Cambridge: Cambridge University Press.

Danziger, P. N. (2005) *Let Them Eat Cake: Marketing Luxury to the Masses – As Well as the Classes*, Chicago: Kaplan Business.

Thomas, D. (2007) *Deluxe: How Luxury Lost Its Luster*, London: Penguin.

Fashion branding
Ralph Lauren's stage

D. J. Huppatz

In the last two decades of the twentieth century, mass marketing brought about significant changes in fashion's production and consumption. American designers such as Ralph Lauren and Calvin Klein circumvented the Parisian haute couture system by developing innovative brand strategies aimed at a broad clientele. For them, design originality was not as important as creating recognisable conscious (or unconscious) associations with existing mythologies. Drawing from popular traditions, cinema or media culture, fashion branding became the art of staging identities, constructing a complete artifice comprising themed collections, advertising campaigns, graphic styles and retail spaces (particularly the flagship store). Once considered the essence of fashion, material products such as clothing and accessories were reconceived as props within carefully orchestrated narratives of lifestyle and identity.

Developed in the late 1960s, Lauren's 'Polo' brand evoked a certain European style: masculine and sporty but simultaneously aristocratic and elite. Over the next decade Lauren based his collections on a set of mythical figures – sportswear for gentleman athletes, ties and monogrammed blazers for Ivy League college graduates, and the understated elegant casualwear of his English aristocratic collections. Lauren soon branched out into women's wear and coherent 'themed' collections such as his 1978 'cowboy' collection, and in the early 1980s, an 'American folk' and a 'safari' collection. The themes themselves were particularly nostalgic – historical references imbued his collections with an authentic aura – and particularly American, with the emphasis on individuals, non-conformists and outsiders (the cowboy, the aristocrat, and the adventurer on safari). But if Lauren's lifestyle narratives were nostalgic and patriotic, they were not derived from any shared remembering of real historical events or figures, but rather from a cinematic remembering originating in sources such as *Brideshead Revisited*, *The Great Gatsby*, *High Noon* or the Merchant Ivory films.

Lauren's thematic visions were fully realised in the early 1980s when he and photographer Bruce Weber developed an innovative style of fashion advertising. Rather than single-model shoots in studio settings, Weber created long spreads for magazines, up to twenty pages, with little or no text, shooting non-models or non-actors in appropriate locations. Lauren and Weber's cinematic narratives of an 'authentic' life – lived as an individual with wealth enough to enjoy leisure time – appealed to American aspirations. By purchasing a shirt or a sweater, a consumer attained social status by becoming an actor in a fantasy lifestyle, escaping from the banal drudgery of work or suburban life. Lauren's 1986 flagship store in Manhattan, Rhinelander Mansion (Snapshot 44.1), became the ultimate stage for acting out such aspirations, with clothing displayed like props in stately aristocratic 'sets' furnished in dark wood panelling, and finished with gilt-framed portraits and antique furniture.

Snapshot 44.1 Rhinelander Mansion, Madison Avenue, New York. Originally the Gertrude Rhinelander Waldo House, 1898, Rhinelander Mansion was renovated and redesigned by Naomi Leff as the Polo/Ralph Lauren flagship store in 1986. Photo by D. J. Huppatz.

Utilising fashion, graphic, photographic and interior design, Lauren constructed a cultivated lifestyle, appealing to a nostalgic yearning for traditional values, authenticity and stability in a rapidly changing society. Not coincidentally, Calvin's Klein's brand was also constructed with the aid of Weber, but differentiated from Lauren's by referencing another set of fantasies, largely drawn from pornography. While Klein's contemporary minimalist style (echoed in his Madison Avenue flagship store by John Pawson) seemed opposed to Lauren's nostalgic one, their methods for constructing lifestyle narratives were remarkably similar. In the late twentieth century, mass-market fashion brands were no longer differentiated via materials, forms, production values or even style, but via their constructed identities: their 'total design'.

Bibliography and further reading

Agins, T. (1999) *The End of Fashion: The Mass Marketing of the Clothing Business*, New York: William Morrow and Company.

McDowell, C. (2002) *Ralph Lauren: The Man, The Vision, the Style*, London: Cassell Illustrated.

Tungate, M. (2008) *Fashion Brands: Branding Style from Armani to Zara*, 2nd edition, London and Philadelphia: Kogan Page.

Index